PSYCHOLOGY
AND THE
PARANORMAL

Sara Miller McCune founded SAGE Publishing in 1965 to support the dissemination of usable knowledge and educate a global community. SAGE publishes more than 1000 journals and over 800 new books each year, spanning a wide range of subject areas. Our growing selection of library products includes archives, data, case studies and video. SAGE remains majority owned by our founder and after her lifetime will become owned by a charitable trust that secures the company's continued independence.

Los Angeles | London | New Delhi | Singapore | Washington DC | Melbourne

PSYCHOLOGY AND THE PARANORMAL

EXPLORING ANOMALOUS EXPERIENCE

DAVID F. MARKS

$SAGE

Los Angeles | London | New Delhi
Singapore | Washington DC | Melbourne

Los Angeles | London | New Delhi
Singapore | Washington DC | Melbourne

SAGE Publications Ltd
1 Oliver's Yard
55 City Road
London EC1Y 1SP

SAGE Publications Inc.
2455 Teller Road
Thousand Oaks, California 91320

SAGE Publications India Pvt Ltd
B 1/I 1 Mohan Cooperative Industrial Area
Mathura Road
New Delhi 110 044

SAGE Publications Asia-Pacific Pte Ltd
3 Church Street
#10-04 Samsung Hub
Singapore 049483

Editor: Donna Goddard
Editorial assistant: Marc Barnard
Production editor: Imogen Roome
Copyeditor: Diana Chambers
Proofreader: Leigh C. Smithson
Indexer: Adam Pozner
Marketing manager: Camille Richmond
Cover design: Wendy Scott
Typeset by: C&M Digitals (P) Ltd, Chennai, India
Printed in the UK

© David F. Marks 2020

First published 2020

Apart from any fair dealing for the purposes of research or private study, or criticism or review, as permitted under the Copyright, Designs and Patents Act, 1988, this publication may be reproduced, stored or transmitted in any form, or by any means, only with the prior permission in writing of the publishers, or in the case of reprographic reproduction, in accordance with the terms of licences issued by the Copyright Licensing Agency. Enquiries concerning reproduction outside those terms should be sent to the publishers.

Library of Congress Control Number: 2019953062

British Library Cataloguing in Publication data

A catalogue record for this book is available from the British Library

ISBN 978-1-5264-9106-0
ISBN 978-1-5264-9105-3 (pbk)

At SAGE we take sustainability seriously. Most of our products are printed in the UK using responsibly sourced papers and boards. When we print overseas we ensure sustainable papers are used as measured by the PREPS grading system. We undertake an annual audit to monitor our sustainability.

To the stranger in Cuba who saved me from the ocean:
Para un héroe desconocido: me salvaste la vida con un acto de valentía desinteresada. ¡Gracias!

RIP, Peter McKellar, mentor, friend, collaborator:
your *Imagination and Thinking* always an inspiration.

RIP, Marcello Truzzi, sociologist from afar:
your *zetetic legacy* lives on; long may it thrive.

CONTENTS

About the author ix
Preface x
Acknowledgements xix

PART I: BASIC PRINCIPLES AND PROCESSES 1

1 Science and Anomalous Experience 3
2 The Origins of Subjective Anomalous Experience 15
3 Psychological Processes and Anomalous Experience 37

PART II: SUBJECTIVE ANOMALOUS EXPERIENCE CLAIMED TO BE PARANORMAL 57

4 Synchronicity 59
5 Remote Viewing and Psychic Staring 89
   With contributions from Harold E Puthoff, PhD and Rupert Sheldrake, PhD
6 The Ganzfeld, Subjective Validation and the Newly Discovered Sixth Sense 119
   With contributions from Daryl Bem, PhD, Susan Blackmore, PhD and Adrian Parker, PhD
7 Precognition Effect and Dream-ESP: Methodological Lessons in the Search for Deep Truth: Arrival of the Super-Powers 154
   With contributions from Daryl Bem, PhD and Stanley Krippner, PhD
8 Psychokinesis, Dice and Random Number Generators: 'Mind Over Matter' en Route to Neverland 181
   With a contribution by Dean Radin, PhD

PART III: SUBJECTIVE ANOMALOUS EXPERIENCE USUALLY NOT – BUT OCCASIONALLY – CLAIMED TO BE PARANORMAL — 201

  9 The Hypnotic Trance as an Altered State of Consciousness — 203

10 Out-of-Body and Near-Death Experiences — 228

11 Homeostasis: Letting the Genie Out of The Bottle — 262

PART IV: CONCLUSIONS — 289

12 Take-Home Message: Psi is a Spontaneous Process that Cannot be Summoned at Will in a Laboratory Experiment — 291

Appendix: Concepts, Measures and Methods — 314
Bibliography — 338
Index — 395

ABOUT THE AUTHOR

David F. Marks was raised in southern England in the city of Portsmouth, with its large harbour and historical connections with the Royal Navy. The city was the birthplace of Charles Dickens and Isambard Brunel, both having fathers with connections to the dockyard. Watching ships arriving and leaving port was one of the author's childhood hobbies. Not fancying a life at sea, however, he took to bookish activities, studying psychology at Reading and Sheffield universities. With a PhD under his belt, he immigrated to Dunedin, New Zealand, another city with a large harbour in the beautiful South Island. After working in New Zealand, Australia, Japan and the USA, David returned to London.

The author has published 25 books including *A General Theory of Behaviour* (2018), the first general theory for psychology as a natural science. David's daughter, Jessica, owns a restaurant in Dunedin, New Zealand; his son, Michael, is a teacher in Ware, Hertfordshire. David lives in Arles, Provence, France with his wife, Alice. His connection to Portsmouth remains strong, making regular visits to his father Victor who lives close to the harbour entrance.

> We are tied to the ocean. And when we go back to the sea, whether it is to sail or to watch – we are going back from whence we came. (John F. Kennedy)

PREFACE

[An ESP experiment] immediately appeals to his [or her] unconscious readiness to witness a miracle, and to the hope, latent in all [people], that such a thing may yet be possible. Primitive superstition lies just below the surface of even the most tough-minded individuals, and it is precisely those who most fight ... (Jung, 1960)

It is of natural science to investigate nature, impartially and without prejudice. (Smythies, 1967)

One ingredient of an interesting life is anomaly.

An anomaly defies immediate explanation and adds spice. Beyond spice, anomalies offer hope that something – whatever it may be – exists beyond the everyday. We humans live in hope eternally. But what does one mean when labelling something as an 'anomaly'? I do not mean the kind of oddness or peculiarity in human behaviour that is everywhere to be seen. I am referring to things that really should not be so, the weird, the spooky, when looking in the mirror, the face that isn't you. Anomalistic experiences are strange, peculiar or surreal. As one engages with the experience, an instinctive thirst to understand it springs forth, the desire to discover something new. Our goal here is to do precisely that, to dig beneath the surface of anomalistic experience, to take a close look at psychology and the paranormal, to put psi 'under the microscope'.

One should not be surprised if all is not as it seems, and we can expect anomalies aplenty here.

APPROACH

I approach this book with anticipation, wondering where the adventure might lead. I hoped it would lead towards new insights, explanatory theory and nuggets of new knowledge. How, you may well ask, can that be? Surely, an 'expert' about psychology and the paranormal should already have reached an opinion one way or the other, a strong point of view?

Not so. I genuinely have no idea where this new investigation will lead. I write as a zetetic.[1] I have a map and a set of place names,[2] but what exists at each place is uncertain. I last visited this field 20 years ago. Now, with 'new eyes' and new evidence, one's understanding could be significantly different compared to 20 years ago. Unlike previous visits, I am giving the psi hypothesis an initial probability of being a real, authentic and valid experience of 50%.

Please take a minute to consider your own current degree of belief in ESP. Indicate your current belief with an arrow on the Belief Barometer below.[3]

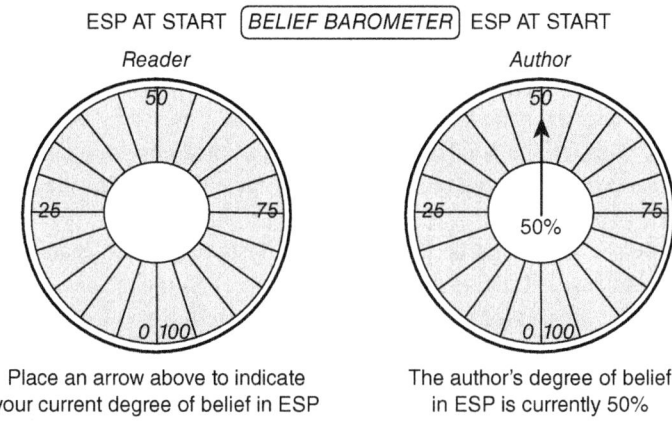

Figure P1 Belief barometer readings at the start of this book

My objective is to cut a path through the vast, tangled jungle of publications about psi with a machete that is sharp and decisive. With each new claim, one reads, reflects, questions, reflects some more and, at one particular moment, ultimately decides the degree of plausibility that a specific claim possesses. 'Belief Barometers' are available throughout to monitor your and my particular degree of belief for each individual claim. The variation in degrees of belief indicate one's sensitivity to evidence. One needs to be flexible. If somebody says '0%' or '100%' to absolutely everything, that surely indicates intransigence and intolerance of ambiguity.

One cannot profess definite explanations in advance because that would be blinkered. If one already *knew* the answers, one would cease to investigate. I would not be writing this at all and you would not be reading. The truth would already be out and about and we would be picking at the flesh of dead learning like vultures at a dead elephant.

No true zetetic starts from a fixed position. One suspends judgement while seeking and exploring with an open mind. In any science, ideas are provisional,

---

[1]Zetetic from the Greek, *zētētikós*, from *zētéō*, 'to seek to proceed by inquiry'.
[2]*Tópos*, the Greek name for 'place' (τόπος); 'topic' in English.
[3]Belief Barometers appear throughout this book. Please give your own unique, personal degree of belief independently of anybody else – especially the author.

pending further investigation. Those who assert a fixed point of view before looking at the evidence break the 'golden rule of science', which is to let conclusions follow the evidence.

Anomalistic psychology includes the entire spectrum of conscious experience in all of its glorious splendour. By examining in-depth the evidence for and against any particular claim, one earns the right to offer conclusions. All conclusions are tentative, however, pending further investigation by independent researchers. I am minded to recall Heraclitus' dictum, 'You cannot step into the same river twice, for other waters are continually flowing on'. Having stepped into the 'paranormal river' on a few occasions, it has been a different river each and every time.

It is impossible here to include everything that anomalistic psychology has to offer. The selected topics are phenomena that have received significant attention from researchers over the last 50 years. Fun though they may be, Big Foot, the Loch Ness Monster, the Tooth Fairy, Clever Hans, mediums, ouija boards and the wonders concocted by stage mentalists didn't make the cut. See them in the 'red tops' and on YouTube.

This book is in four parts. Part I is about basic principles, theories and processes. In Chapter 1, I define the field of this survey as the 'science of anomaly'. In Chapter 2, I present a new integrative review and theory of paranormal experience. In Chapter 3, I discuss some of the key psychological processes that increase our understanding of anomalous experiences and beliefs.

Part II is concerned with empirical and theoretical perspectives on some of the best known 'classic' subjective anomalous phenomena that are claimed to be paranormal. For three of these, Coincidences, Remote Viewing and Psychic Staring, I report original studies carried out with my collaborators. In Chapter 4 on 'Synchronicity', we enter a mysterious zone of subjective meaning and objective improbability. The chapters on the Ganzfeld, Precognition, Dreams and Psychokinesis summarise the evidence collected by the world's most distinguished investigators who add their personal perspectives to the mix.

Part III concerns three subjectively anomalous experiences that are usually not given paranormal interpretations: the Hypnotic Trance State, Out-Of-Body Experience (OBE) and Near Death Experience (NDE). For the Hypnotic Trance chapter, I describe unique and original laboratory research. For the OBE section I rely on research by others. For the NDE section, a lucky personal escape offers intriguing insights into independent systematic investigations. Chapter 11 proposes a new scientific theory to explain the spectrum of conscious experiences and states, some of which are associated with psi.

Part IV provides a conclusion and 'take-home message'. Finally, an Appendix provides concepts, methods and measures which should be helpful to readers wishing to embark upon studies of their own.

It is helpful to look at the general terrain of 'anomalistic psychology' both subjective paranormal experiences (SPEs) that are claimed by some authorities to be paranormal and other SPEs not generally claimed to be paranormal, with intriguing differences between the two. To over-simplify the situation, the paranormal world is a metaphorical 'war zone' with 'believers' (so-called 'sheep') and 'skeptics' ('goats').[4] The two sides battle against each other with no holds barred. The stakes are high, and all too often the battle becomes personal. They fight not only about the rights and wrongs of empirical studies, but about the very nature of science, the meaning of life and the substance of reality. Unfortunately, the debate sometimes descends into acrimony, from which neither party returns unscathed.

Returning to the world of psi after a 20-year respite, I am curious to see what has changed. Anomalistic psychology has become the new ontological battle-ground about all things paranormal (Luke, 2011). A growing stockpile of methods and findings can be considered supportive of a paranormal interpretation. My position has changed and I no longer believe that strongly partisan views are helpful. Progress requires dialogue and I wish to put down a marker that says: 'Peace. Nobody won. Stop fighting.' That's not to say there won't be criticism; there must be, otherwise there can never be progress.

DIFFERENCES IN BELIEF

To establish dialogue, six leading psi advocates and one ex-advocate contribute their expert viewpoints: Drs Daryl Bem, Susan Blackmore, Stanley Krippner, Adrian Parker, Hal Puthoff, Dean Radin and Rupert Sheldrake. I warmly thank them all.

I present the best evidence that I can find, critique it and also offer psychological theories. Whenever possible I use verbatim quotations to represent the views of advocates concerning specific claims. Nobody can ever legitimately say that a

---

[4]The majority of 'skeptics' are disbelievers or deniers who have adopted the label 'skeptic' for its more temperate connotations. The late Marcello Truzzi was one of two co-founding chairs of the leading US skeptical organisation CSICOP (the Committee for the Scientific Investigation of Claims of the Paranormal, now called CSI). Truzzi became disillusioned with the organisation, saying they 'tend to block honest inquiry, in my opinion ... Most of them are not agnostic toward claims of the paranormal; they are out to knock them'. Using the title of 'skeptic', Truzzi claimed that this association of debunkers could claim an authority to which they were not entitled: 'critics who take the negative rather than an agnostic position but still call themselves "skeptics" are actually pseudo-skeptics and have, I believe, gained a false advantage by usurping that label'. Genuine or 'classical' skepticism is the zetetic view to suspend judgement and enter into a genuine inquiry that assumes that any claim requires justification. Maintaining a zetetic position of open inquiry requires a steady hand and a critical mind. There is no room for naivety, but a touch of Socratic irony may at times be helpful. A protracted correspondence between Martin Gardner and Marcello Truzzi, indicating their two contrasting viewpoints, has been published by Richards (2017).

paranormal claim has been 'disproved' and, if the truth of a claim is undecided, it is only possible to say that it is neither confirmed nor disconfirmed.

'Belief Barometers' are printed at the end of sections and chapters. I accept full responsibility for the views, opinions and beliefs that I assert in this book. They represent nobody's views but my own. Whatever one thinks, the world is always independent of how we might wish it to be. There is nothing *wrong* about believing in psi if one chooses to, and skeptics and scientists have no place disparaging such beliefs. Belief in the paranormal is normal. As sociologist Andrew Greeley put it:

> The paranormal is normal. Psychic and mystic experiences are frequent even in modern urban industrial society. The majority of the population has had some such experience, a substantial minority has had more than just an occasional experience, and a respectable proportion of the population has such experiences frequently. Any phenomenon with incidence as widespread as the paranormal deserves more careful and intensive research than it has received up to now ... People who have paranormal experiences, even frequent such experiences, are not kooks. They are not sick, they are not deviants, they are not social misfits, they are not schizophrenics. In fact, they may be more emotionally healthy than those who do not have such experiences. (Greeley, 1975: 7)

Scientists should be agnostic about the ontological status of paranormal experience and examine the circumstances that constrain or facilitate exceptional experiences. In approaching each claim, I maintain a zetetic viewpoint, neither believing nor disbelieving, attending to the evidence. Only after completing a thorough survey of evidence is one entitled to an informed opinion. A zetetic must not be naive, however.

I follow Marcello Truzzi:

> The ground rules of science are conservative, and in so far as these place the burden of proof on the claimants and require stronger evidence the more extraordinary the claim, they are not neutral. But, we also need to remember, evidence always varies by degree, and inadequate evidence requires a tolerant reply which requests better evidence, not a dogmatic denial that behaves as though inadequate evidence were no evidence. (1987: 73)

Carl Sagan also offers wise advice:

> It seems to me what is called for is an exquisite balance between two conflicting needs: the most skeptical scrutiny of all hypotheses that are served up to us and at the same time a great openness to new ideas. Obviously those two modes of thought are in some tension. But if you are able to exercise only one of these modes, whichever one it is, you're in deep trouble.
>
> If you are only skeptical, then no new ideas make it through to you. You never learn anything new. You become a crotchety old person convinced that

nonsense is ruling the world. (There is, of course, much data to support you.) But every now and then, maybe once in a hundred cases, a new idea turns out to be on the mark, valid and wonderful. If you are too much in the habit of being skeptical about everything, you are going to miss or resent it, and either way you will be standing in the way of understanding and progress.

On the other hand, if you are open to the point of gullibility and have not an ounce of skeptical sense in you, then you cannot distinguish the useful as from the worthless ones. (Sagan, 1995: 25)

PROGRESS IN SCIENCE

The first 20 years of the 21st century brought many astonishing scientific discoveries: the first draft of the human genome, graphene, grid cells in the brain, the first self-replicating, synthetic bacterial cells, the Higgs boson, liquid water on Mars and gravitational waves. Not bad going in such a short time! During this same period, anomalistic psychology has grown at an enormous pace with increased numbers of investigators and publications (Figure P2). Disappointingly, however, new discoveries or theories are few and far between. If there has been one discovery, it might be stated thus: the science of anomalistic experience is more complex and obscure than most psychologists ever imagined. When we are at the beginning of new venture like this, we must not be deterred by having no real answer to two of the hardest questions in science: What is consciousness and what is it for? [5]

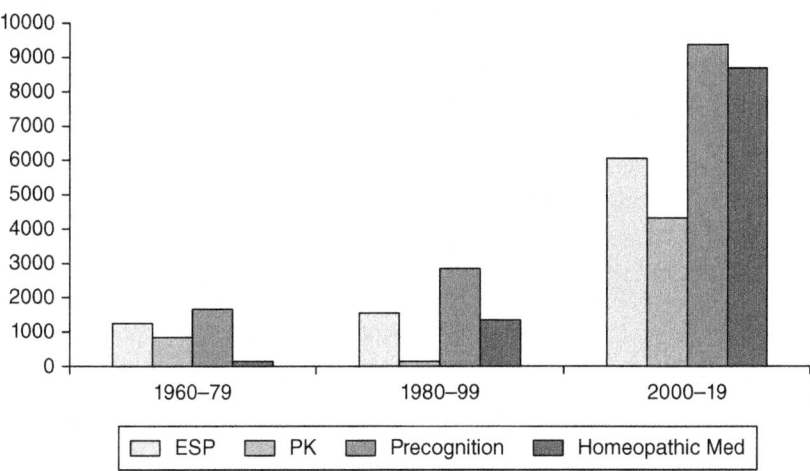

Figure P2 Growth in research publications about paranormal topics in 20-year periods, 1960–2019

---

[5]Nagel (2012) and Strawson (2006), among others, argue for the ancient philosophy of pan-psychism, in which all physical objects from atoms to the cosmos have conscious experience. Elsewhere, I have described consciousness as 'a direct emergent property of cerebral activity' (Marks, 2019).

One of the greatest scientific minds, Stephen Hawking, said that: 'Science is beautiful when it makes simple explanations of phenomena or connections between different observations' (Sample, 2011). It has been said that advances in science come not from empiricism but from new theories. Parapsychology, following its 'big sister' psychology, has always been heavily empirical. Its rapid growth is indexed by multitudes of empirical studies in the absence of notable theoretical developments. By becoming more theory-driven, the field of 'psychology/parapsychology' as an integrated whole is likely to make faster progress.

It seems counterproductive to treat parapsychology and psychology as separate fields. Bringing the 'para' part back into mainstream Psychology helps to integrate the discipline. This book takes a step in that direction. Psychology/parapsychology contain myriad variables, A, B, C ... N ... X, Y, Z. An established strategy for developing new research is for the investigator to identity 'gaps' in the field and to set about filling those gaps with correlational and experimental studies with almost every possible permutation and combination of variables. The gap-filling approach is one strategy for keeping productivity high but, often, it is at the expense of developing new theories. As already noted, the academic world is based on quantitative measures of performance[6] and the number of publications a researcher can claim matters. This drive towards publications leads to what I call 'Polyfilla Science'. For every 'hole' investigators can fill, they are almost guaranteed a peer-reviewed publication. 'Polyfilla Science' exists on an industrial scale, keeping hundreds of thousands of scientists busily occupied in hot competition. The 'winners' of the Polyfilla competition are the ones who tick the highest number of boxes and harvest the most citations.[7]

'Polyfilla Science' can be represented as a multidimensional matrix of cells where the task of science is viewed as filling every last cell in the matrix (Figure P3). This method of doing science is more akin to a fairground shooting gallery than to theory-driven science. Popular though it is, 'Polyfilla Science' isn't the only game in town and a theory-driven approach is also available. Theory is used to identify the principles behind questions that need answering in a process of confirmation and disconfirmation of predictions. When one considers the fact that there are 100,000 psychology majors in the US alone, all needing a research project, it is no wonder that the Polyfilla approach is so popular.[8]

In comparison to the scientific discoveries in other fields, psychology and parapsychology have made no world-changing discoveries in the last 50 years. By this, I mean discoveries that are worth telling to your grandchildren (if or when you

---

[6]Numbers of publications, citations, grant monies, prizes, promotions and awards.
[7]One of the world's most published and ambitious 'Polyfilla' psychologists told me a self-effacing story about the occasion he went for an interview for a post at the University of Oxford. A member of the panel asked: 'Dr X, you have a huge number of publications. But what does it all mean?' He didn't know how to answer and was rejected for the post.
[8]Polycell Multi-Purpose Polyfilla Ready Mixed, 1 Kg, #1 best-seller on Amazon.co.uk, 16 May 2019.

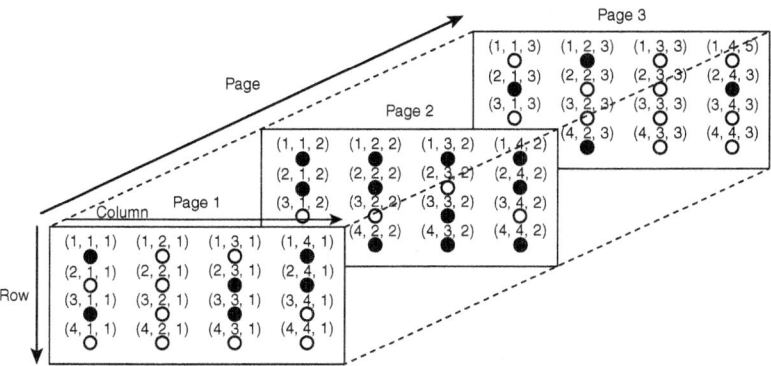

Figure P3 A representation of science as a three-dimensional space of rows, columns and pages. The space can be extended indefinitely in all directions. The cells are filled or unfilled. In this example, page 1 has 6 filled and 10 unfilled cells, page 2 has 10 filled and 6 unfilled cells, and page 3 has 4 filled and 12 unfilled cells.

have any). In my opinion, the lack of significant theoretical developments and the Polyfilla Approach are two of the main reasons for this lack of progress. All this needs to change. We need to change the industrial-academic culture.

This book is geared towards the needs of teachers, researchers and students of anomalistic psychology, general psychology, parapsychology and consciousness, all exciting, fun areas where nothing can be taken for granted. The book covers topics that many students want to learn, but traditional course structures and stuffy, 'old-school' professors resist putting them in the curriculum. Slowly, that is all changing. I review here the best and most recently available evidence across a wide range of areas. My focus is post-2000 up-to-and-including 2019.[9] I use a theory-driven approach to integrate vast swathes of disparate empirical literature into theories and hypotheses about cause and effect. This book is no easy read, but it goes to the boundaries and challenges current assumptions.

One must beware of – and avoid – the 'streetlight effect', otherwise known as the 'drunkard's search' principle. This is the ingrained bias of searching only where it is easiest to look. You probably already know the parable:

> A police officer sees a drunk person searching for something under a streetlight and asks what the drunk has lost. They say they have lost their keys and they both look under the streetlight together. After a few minutes the police officer asks if the loser is sure they lost them here, and the drunk replies, no, and that they lost them in the park. The police officer asks why they are searching here, and the drunk replies, 'this is where the light is'.

---

[9] The history of the field is adequately reviewed by others – e.g. John Beloff (1993) or Caroline Watt (2017).

We must look wherever the 'keys' may actually be found, not where it is easiest to look. The search for psi is a complex, winding trail of traps and pitfalls. When we observe evidence, we must not, a priori, rule it out as subjective validation or confirmation bias. An openness to being wrong may cause uncomfortable feelings, but knowledge and truth are never givens. When we are lucky enough to discover something new, this is a piece of hard-won treasure.

I present here new theories in the spirit of open inquiry. Possibly these theories are wrong. So be it: If possible, falsify my theories, throw them out and develop better ones. By testing and falsifying theories, newer, better theories can be developed and the process can continue indefinitely in the never-ending search for truth. When I share thoughts and conclusions, readers will wish to contest and challenge them with arguments and evidence. All good!

Humans have walked on the Moon and are heading to Mars, yet we still do not understand consciousness. One starting point is to separate fact from fiction in the field of anomalistic psychology. In aiming to do precisely that, we are clearing a path through a thick undergrowth of confusion hopefully towards a more informed understanding of that which makes all of this possible: consciousness.

ACKNOWLEDGEMENTS

I warmly acknowledge the invaluable help, support and advice from my family, friends, associates, past colleagues and students, especially the late Peter McKellar, Jack Clarkson, Richard Kammann, Jack Hilgard, Martin Gardner and Robert Morris (RIP). I thank a group of world-leading investigators for their significant contributions to this book: Daryl Bem, Susan Blackmore, Stanley Krippner, Adrian Parker, Hal Puthoff, Dean Radin and Rupert Sheldrake. I thank Luis Portela, Founder and Chair of the BIAL Foundation, which funded multiple elements of research that receive coverage in this book, including my attendance at the BIAL Symposia 'Behind and Beyond the Brain' which facilitated discussions with many parapsychologists whose work I acknowledge with herein. I owe a debt of appreciation to Ray Hyman who was my sabbatical host at the University of Oregon and for introducing me to Marcello Truzzi and other members of his circle, and to Bob Audley and the late Aimable Robert Jonckheere (Jonck) at University College London. My friends David Maclean in Oamaru and Max Lowrey in Dunedin, New Zealand, offered multiple inspirational conversations and, in the latter case, photographs over several decades.

The publishing team at SAGE Publications provided encouragement at every stage. In particular Robert Patterson (commissioning editor), Donna Goddard and Katie Rabot were instrumental in helping this book happen. I thank Neil Dagnall of Manchester Metropolitan University who kindly reviewed and commented on 10 chapters. I acknowledge a debt of gratitude for critique, information or assistance to multiple experts with whom I have had the good fortune of interacting, collaborating and, in many instances, becoming friends. Thanks must go to hundreds of researchers all over the world whose works are listed in the Bibliography. Responsibility for error rests entirely with the author.

While writing this Preface, BBC news announced that on this day (8 August) 50 years ago, the Beatles had recorded their final album, *Abbey Road*. That day they strolled over the nearby pedestrian crossing to create one of the most famous album covers of all time. Meanwhile, this inveterate swot had his head down writing his PhD dissertation. Checking other headline events that year, London is described as 'Rather dry and cool. A very dry early autumn'. The Who, Pink

Floyd and Jimi Hendrix took over the airwaves. Charles de Gaulle stepped down as President of France to be replaced by Georges Pompidou, Willy Brandt became Chancellor of West Germany and Neil Armstrong became the first man to walk on the Moon. The Woodstock Festival took place in New York State and the Archies topped the British charts for eight weeks with 'Sugar, Sugar', explaining why the Beatles and the Stones took over the charts on both sides of the Atlantic.

My PhD at Sheffield University (where Joe Cocker's 'Grease Band' played most Saturdays) contained a study from October 1968 that produced a median probability of .70 that a man would be landed on the Moon by November 1970. In fact, the first man arrived on the Moon 16 months earlier, on 16 July 1969. Also, that year Richard Nixon was sworn in as US President, the 'Stonewall Riots' occurred in Greenwich Village, and *Ummagumma*, Pink Floyd's fourth album, was released on 7 November 1969. Interesting times!

In the 50 years since 1969, huge changes have happened. The world average temperature has increased by 1.0 degree Centigrade and the population has more than doubled from 3.6 to 7.7 billion. In a world where hunger is endemic, it may seem anomalous that 2 billion people are overweight or obese. However, throw in poverty and the low quality of cheap food, and the phenomenon is more easily explained.

Another contributor, so I believe, is psychological homeostasis, a founding principle in the General Theory of Behaviour (Marks, 2018). The General Theory makes an appearance here to account for anomalous experience. If it succeeds, that would be pleasing.

David F. Marks
Arles, Bouches-du-Rhône, Provence-Alpes-Côte d'Azur, France
8 August 2019

PART I
BASIC PRINCIPLES AND PROCESSES

1
SCIENCE AND ANOMALOUS EXPERIENCE

The science of parapsychology began with the interest aroused by the reports of spontaneous human experiences and events that are familiarly known as 'psychic.' These puzzling phenomena have never been claimed by any of the conventional branches of science, and until comparatively recent decades they had been ignored by all but a few scientists. Yet records of such occurrences have come from peoples of all cultures and periods and, simply as reported human experiences, they would manifestly have some proper claim on the attention of Science. (Rhine & Pratt, 1962: 5)

Outline: Anomalous experience must be one of the most fascinating challenges in contemporary science. Anomalistic psychology is dedicated to the investigation of anomalous experience – with the paranormal playing a central role. It is the one field that many students would love to study if only their professors would include it in the curriculum. Among the 'public' there is increasingly widespread interest and acceptance of paranormal claims. In this book, I take a zetetic approach of open inquiry in and an unbiased search for evidence. This approach willingly examines new discoveries and theories as challenges to one's worldview. It requires a systematic consideration of the evidence for and against each individual claim without prejudice or any a priori assumptions. Believe anything, full steam ahead, as long as one is prepared to back up belief with evidence and reason. This chapter begins by steering a course through a patch of the traditional chaos and confusion that is the lair of the supernatural explorer.

ANOMALIES

Anomalies may be rare, but they happen. The tiger is ready to leap. She is well hidden and you cannot see her. Anomalies – data patterns that do not fit one's expectations – are always there ready to surprise. When an anomaly leaps out, one instinctively adopts a defensive manoeuvre: what, why, when and how? If one can find no physical or psychological cause, then, after sustained inquiry, one may tentatively hypothesise something weird or paranormal may have happened. On a rare occasion, one may even be forced to think again, to revise one's 'worldview'. That lurking tiger is waiting to surprise us. Preoccupied with the 'stresses of life', one may choose to stroll on but only at one's peril. Then, pow! – the tiger pounces with claws and teeth glinting. If one wishes to become more 'anomaly-literate', this book is a good place to start.

Anomalies of many kinds feature in literature, movies and games. A person can't remember their identity. A person sees a doppelganger, a freaky, identical version of themselves. A person leaves their body and they see themselves from way above. After taking a drink, pill or potion, they find themselves in a tunnel running towards the centre of the earth. After a frightening cardiac arrest, one enters a tunnel of light, sees brightly shining lights, hears a choir of singing angels and the voice of God. In observing street magic, a cigarette is changed into a live, white mouse. In volcanology, a magnetic effect in volcanic eruptions is found to be a normal feature of volcanic activity (Johnston & Stacey, 1969). In banking, anomalous credit card transactions indicate identity theft (West & Bhattacharya, 2016). In space exploration, anomalous space craft readings signify a faulty component (Hundman et al., 2018). An anomaly indexes something of interest to attend to. Not only do anomalies of every kind surprise, puzzle, entertain and educate, they also can have significant scientific and personal meaning.

Some anomalies occur on an everyday basis as remarkable occurrences we call 'coincidences'. One thinks of a person one hasn't seen in a while and that person telephones a few minutes later (precognition or good luck?). One thinks of a delicious fish-and-chip meal and, a few minutes later, one's partner arrives with a newspaper parcel from the local chippie (telepathy or good luck?). Feeling stressed about a deadline, one develops a headache and views a 'mind-control' guru on *YouTube* and the headache goes (placebo effects, paranormal healing or good luck?). These events could be everyday examples of psi beyond science as we know it. But are they, and how can we possibly know? This is the starting point for a study of anomalistic psychology.

Science follows a hypothetico-deductive process that progresses in an ever-widening spiral. This spiral can continue indefinitely until, one fine day, an anomaly occurs.

Any anomaly is a challenge: either the anomaly must be reconciled with existing theory, or the spiral can be exited and a new spiral begun, so the hypothesis–study–data–test–analysis cycle can start all over again. In practice, it is rare for a scientific spiral to be exited. The exit door is always available, but there is resistance to using it. Anomalies are 'explained away' or simply ignored.[1]

---

[1] As one example, consider the trance logic experiment described in Chapter 10. The study presented clear-cut evidence of an anomalous conscious state that was inconvenient to the majority of researchers in the field who were pursuing another theoretical path. In spite of its publication in the leading hypnosis journal, the study was totally ignored by the hypnosis research community.

Science and Anomalous Experience

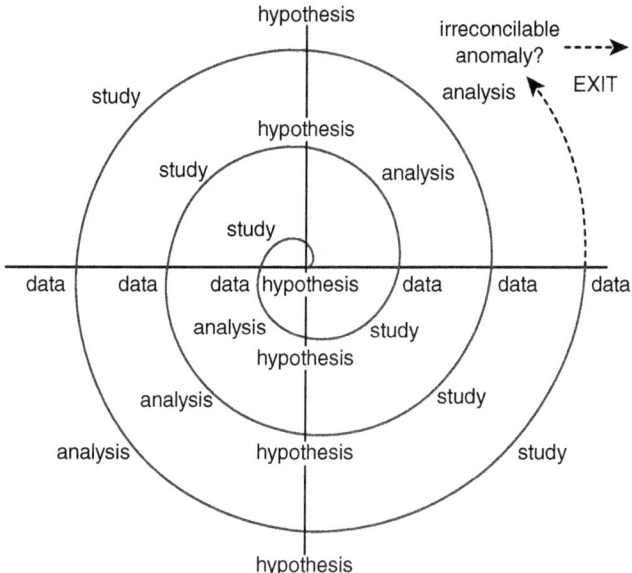

Figure 1.1 The Spiral of Science. A hypothesis is tested by running a study followed by data collection and data analysis. This leads to a further hypothesis and the start of the next cycle. The hypothesis-study-data-test-analysis cycle can continue until an anomaly occurs that cannot be incorporated into existing theory. At this point the spiral should be exited to enter a new spiral of hypotheses and studies.

Anomalies that cannot be explained or ignored because they are too puzzling, may require revolutionary change to scientific theory. Consider the 'Aether Theory' of 18th-century physics. The Aether Theory attempted to answer the question: What is light? According to Robert Boyle, light is transmitted by a substance called 'luminiferous aether'. In an empirical test of the theory in 1887, Albert Michelson and Edward Morley found no significant difference between the speed of light in the direction of movement through the presumed aether and its speed at right angles. This result was considered crucial evidence against the existence of the aether, the physical medium necessary for the propagation of light, so Aether Theory had to be dropped and today is considered nothing more than a weird historical curiosity. This turning point in physics encouraged Albert Einstein to develop his theory of special relativity. Similarly, if psi[2] could be shown to be real, then the psi anomaly would have to be accommodated by existing scientific theories[3] or a revolutionary change to psychology, biology, and maybe also physics, would be called for.

---

[2] Psi refers collectively to telepathy, clairvoyance, precognition and psychokinesis.
[3] Attempts are already being made to integrate anomalous cognition within theoretical physics – e.g. Bierman (2010); Carr (2008); Dobyns (2009); Radin et al. (2012); Shoup (2009).

Anomalies are divided into different categories according to the scientific arena where they are observed. In psychology and parapsychology, the two terms 'anomalous experience' and 'anomalous cognition' are commonly used. One definition states: 'The acquisition, by mental means alone, of information that is blocked from the ordinary senses by shielding, distance, or time' (May, 2010). Psi-advocate Edwin May is convinced that psi has moved beyond reliable and repeated demonstration: 'Except for instructional purposes, there simply is no reason to conduct exclusively evidentiary experiments again with the ganzfeld, remote viewing, or with random number generators. Rather we must conduct process-oriented studies to figure out how psi works' (May, 2010: 213–14). Not everybody is as convinced as May and, as we shall see, many investigators continue to search for what appears to be an elusive process. For many researchers, the ontological question remains unanswered: does psi exist? Or, with continually improving methodology, is psi destined to disappear like the aether? We return to this question throughout the book. The issue can really only be decided by addressing each particular scientific claim in turn based on its merits.

Scientific traditions – or what Thomas Kuhn (1962/2012) refers to as 'paradigms' – are challenged by anomalies, which, as noted, may trigger scientific revolutions. For Thomas Kuhn, scientific revolutions come about in two ways: either (1) an anomaly is discovered – a new fact that cannot be explained by the existing paradigm; or (2) out of dissatisfaction with pre-existing theories, scientists invent new theories. For Thomas Kuhn, the discovery of a new anomaly may require a new theory to go along with it. However, theorising about the nature of an anomaly takes time.

Let's explore next what is meant by the term 'paranormal'.

PARANORMAL PHENOMENA

The term 'paranormal' is applied to phenomena that are assumed to exist *beside* or *beyond* natural science (Greek: παρά, para, from beside, by the side of, by, beside). Paranormal phenomena are anomalous experiences that are impossible to explain within the established principles of science. As a matter of definition, paranormal phenomena lie outside the realm of human capabilities as conceived by science, violating natural scientific laws.[4]

Systematic laboratory research was started by Joseph Banks Rhine (1885–1980). Rhine was an American botanist who came to Duke University in North Carolina in 1927 to work with his mentor William McDougall. He was famous for his application of the scientific method to the study of mediums and his exposé

---

[4]In earlier eras, the paranormal was referred to as the 'supernatural' – e.g. see Inglis (1977). The term 'supernatural' remains popular, with 195 million hits on Google, while the term 'paranormal' produces a mere 95 million hits (13 December 2018). Lindeman and Svedholm (2012) suggest that 'paranormal, supernatural, magical, and supernatural beliefs are not fundamentally different'.

of a Boston medium named 'Margery'. At Duke, he developed experimental methodology for parapsychology, concentrating on telepathy, psychokinesis, clairvoyance and precognition. Publication of his book in 1934 on extrasensory perception made Rhine very famous (Rhine, 1934/2012). He founded the *Journal of Parapsychology*, the Foundation for Research on the Nature of Man, and the Parapsychological Association.

Figure 1.2 Joseph Banks Rhine (on the right) with Hubert Pearce experimenting with Zener cards in 1934.

Source: J. B. Rhine (1934). *Extra-Sensory Perception*. Boston Society for Psychical Research, 1934. (Image in the public domain.)

Claims of the paranormal are contradicted by existing scientific principles. Paranormal phenomena were defined by one of the earliest British investigators, John Beloff (1974) as:

> ... phenomena which in one or more respects conflict with accepted scientific opinion as to what is physically possible .... Such phenomena are variously referred to as 'parapsychological', 'parapsychical', 'psychical' or 'psychic' but ... the convention now widely current in the technical literature [is to use] the abbreviation 'psi'. Psi phenomena fall into two main categories: psi cognition, better known as ESP (Extrasensory Perception), and psi action, better known as PK (Psychokinesis). (p. 1)

It is necessary to differentiate beliefs in the paranormal (PB) from actual subjective paranormal experience (SPE). There are measures for each of these.

Tobacyk's (2004) revised paranormal belief scale is one example. Thalbourne's (1995) Sheep–Goat Scale includes items on both paranormal belief and paranormal experience. Scales specifically designed to assess paranormal experience are the Anomalous Experiences Inventory (AEI; Gallagher, Kumar, & Pekala, 1994) and the Subjective Paranormal Experience Scale (SPES; Dagnall, Drinkwater, Parker, & Clough, 2016).

There is no reason why phenomena that appear anomalous today, and so lie outside the fuzzy boundaries of science, should not, at some future time, be included within science. If confirmed by solid and sound investigations, 'scientifically unaccepted beliefs' ('SUBs') should be part and parcel of science textbooks in 50 or 100 years from now. Those textbooks would likely be unintelligible to scientists living today, and today's books will likely appear laughably naive and just plain wrong to future generations. However, no scientific revolution has yet been triggered by any paranormal anomaly. Yet nobody can say that it will never happen. Scientists always start by attempting to explain any anomalies within existing theories, especially theories about psychological processes, human biases in decision making, methodological errors, technological limitations and faulty statistics. There will be plenty of this here in this book, which is not a happy home for astrologists or star-gazers. The main problem for the Paranormal Hypothesis is the long-term inability over a century to produce a single repeatable experimental finding that is not contested on methodological or statistical grounds. Finding a replicable, uncontroversial demonstration of psi is the 'holy grail' of parapsychology. Everybody, except perhaps Dr May, continues the search, including this author.

The Australian parapsychologist Harvey Irwin (2009) proposes two components of 'SUBs': parapsychological beliefs and 'belief in black magic' (spells, incantations, devil worship and hell). Here I discuss the former in some detail but, apart from data on beliefs and a brief discussion of survival, mostly not the latter.[5] I also leave aside misperceptions and factual beliefs that contradict the best available evidence in the public domain (Flynn, Nyhan, & Reifler, 2017). However fascinating religious and political (mis)perceptions and beliefs may be, I deal here only with phenomena relevant to science.

Finally, in my list of omissions, I do not include entertainers, mentalists or self-proclaimed psychics – all of whom are charlatans with one thing in mind: to sucker one – and make a fortune doing so.

Paranormal phenomena violate what the philosopher C. D. Broad called the 'basic limiting principles of science' (Broad, 1953). The term 'paranormal' refers to hypothesised processes that are believed to be 'physically impossible', lying outside the realm of human capabilities as presently conceived by mainstream

---

[5] Supernatural beliefs and claims are major elements of many cults and religions. However, an appropriate review would require several additional volumes, which I am happy to leave to people more qualified.

science. An enormous diversity of paranormal phenomena and beliefs have been claimed through human history. For example, it was once a popular belief that the earth is flat (flat-earthers still exist) and the moon is made of cheese – green cheese even – was popular among children (Slaughter, 1902).

However, one must draw limits around the field or we will never know where it ends. Thalbourne and Delin (1994) suggest that 'paranormal' should refer to alleged experience of 'psi', alleged experience of psychokinesis, belief in an afterlife and the possibility of contact with spirits of the dead. These three categories together with a few other abilities and anomalous phenomena are listed in Table 1.1.

Table 1.1 Phenomena and abilities commonly labelled 'anomalous'

	Anomalous phenomena	Description	Illustrative study
1	Extrasensory abilities, including telepathy, clairvoyance, remote viewing, clairaudience, and psychic staring (ESP).	The ability to transmit information using other than the known sensory modalities.	Wahbeh et al. (2018)
2	Precognition and prophetic dreams (PC).	The above-chance level ability to know something before it happens.	Mossbridge & Radin (2018)
3	Telekinesis or psychokinesis (PK).	The ability to move objects with no apparent physical contact or energy transfer.	Dullin & Jamet (2018)
4	Dissociative experience.[1]	Splitting of consciousness into two or more discrete states that may be unaware of the existence of the other(s).	Lemche et al. (2016)
5	Out of-the-body experiences (OBEs).	The ability to experience one's centre of awareness as outside the physical body and the sensation of seeing the environment from an elevated or displaced viewpoint.	Lopez & Elzière (2018)
6	Near-death experiences (NDEs).	The ability to reach the threshold of death, survive, and describe the experience of death or dying.	Moore & Greyson (2017)
7	Paranormal and psychic healing.	The ability to heal illness using a procedure beyond established biomedicine.	Sawa et al. (2018)
8	Spiritualism, ghosts, poltergeists and witchcraft.	Communicating directly with spirits and/or the dead through a medium; seeing ghosts; using rituals, spells or charms.	Paxton (2017); Emmons (2017); Jahoda (2018)

(Continued)

Table 1.1 (Continued)

	Anomalous phenomena	Description	Illustrative study
9	Monsters.	Creatures outside biological science – e.g. Bigfoot, Yeti, the Loch Ness monster.[2]	Bougie (2017)
10	Aliens.	Intelligent beings yet to be identified from other planets or solar systems.	Geppert (2018)

[1]As we shall see in the next chapter, dissociation may play a key role in the genesis of paranormal experience.
[2]The search for 'Nessy' continues. University of Otago geneticist, Professor Neil Gemmell, is conducting a DNA study which, to date, has detected DNA from about 3,000 species in water samples collected from Loch Ness. Professor Gemmell believes that the monster may be a 'giant eel' or another large species of fish (*The Guardian*, 5 September 2019).

Spirit mediumship and seances were of central interest to parapsychological researchers in the 19th and 20th centuries. Today, these performances have been thoroughly discredited and the words 'spirit' and 'soul' rarely find their way into science, but they still find a limited place in parapsychology. According to Gary E. Schwartz (2012):

> If (a) materialism is an incomplete description of nature and the universe, and if (b) 'nonmaterial' concepts like energy (including fields) and information are necessary for a more complete and accurate portrayal of nature and the universe, then (c) it is useful to consider how the spiritual terms spirit and soul may be related to the scientific concepts of energy and information.

Given the limited and tentative knowledge that we possess about nature and the universe, it is appropriate to hold some measure of humility. What we think we know now may be wrong. What we assume today to be beyond science may be comfortably explained by it one day in the future. In this venture into the world of anomaly and the paranormal, one's watch-words must be 'humility' and 'caution'. It seems prudent and wise to keep one's options open. There are truths far beyond our capacity to comprehend at this time. As scientific knowledge grows, so our potential for understanding scientific anomalies increases along with the capacity to create new paradigms. However, one reserves the right to be critical of evidence that falls short of the requirements of a fully scientific approach to laboratory and statistical methodology. I turn to consider the increasing prevalence of paranormal beliefs and experiences.

INCREASING PREVALENCE OF PARANORMAL BELIEFS IN THE US

When talking about beliefs, one refers to a conviction that an object, property or ability actually exists. Beliefs have cognitive, emotional and behavioural features.

One feels one's beliefs as much as one thinks them. Beliefs project the self. When a person's beliefs are challenged, the person feels like they are being attacked personally. This is why the 'Battle of the Paranormal' rages between believers and skeptics with such a passion. People take it personally when anyone disagrees with them.

Beliefs are acquired from many sources, mainly family, friends and associates, along with stories, myths and legends, social media, video games, the printed word and education. Being ready, willing and able to defend one's beliefs using rational argument is one of the values of education. With widening access to scientific education one might have expected to see reduced levels of superstition and paranormal beliefs. Not so – the reality is far from this. Intense interest in the paranormal in all media is having a sustained impact. One might wonder where J. K. Rowling might be today with Harry Potter without all the magic, wands and wizardry – still in a café with a heap of unpublished manuscripts?

Beliefs in the paranormal have been universally popular since time immemorial and they are still popular everywhere today. In some places, the incidence of such beliefs is increasing.[6] According to Lindeman and Aarnio (2006), more than a third of US adults believe in psychic powers and ESP. That figure hasn't changed. The Chapman University Survey of American Fears Wave 5 (16 October 2018) involved a US random sample of 1,190 adults. The sample showed high and increasing rates of paranormal beliefs, ranging from belief in aliens and psychic powers to Bigfoot and haunted houses, compared to previous years (Figure 1.3).

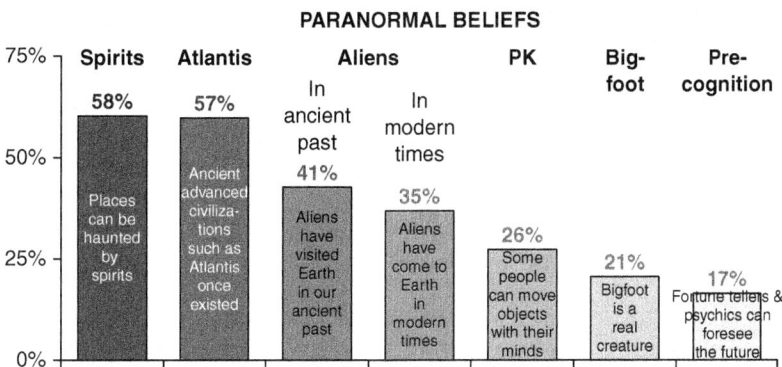

Figure 1.3 Prevalence of paranormal beliefs in a US sample in 2018. The margin for error was +/– 3%. Data from Chapman University (2018).

---

[6] I do not include 'new age' beliefs in healing and religion, receiving growing acceptance – e.g. Hanegraaff (2018).

The most popular paranormal belief among US adults was haunting by spirits (57.7%), followed by the belief that ancient, advanced civilisations, such as Atlantis, once existed (56.9%).[7] More than two out of five (41.4%) believe that aliens visited Earth in our ancient past and more than a third believe aliens are visiting now (35.1%).[8] US Americans are quite skeptical about fortune tellers, with only approximately 17.2% believing that others can see the future.[9]

In 2018, paranormal beliefs were the norm in the US. Only around one-quarter of US adults (24.1%) did not hold any of seven beliefs. More than 75% of US adults stated they believed in at least one paranormal phenomenon (see Figure 1.3).

The Chapman University Survey included the same questions in three consecutive years. It is striking how rapidly the incidence of paranormal beliefs increased between 2017 and 2018, when prevalence of 6 out of 7 beliefs increased, the only exception being the belief that fortune tellers and psychics can foresee the future. In 2018, US citizens were 14% more likely to believe that aliens had visited the earth than in 2016. US people had also become 7% more likely to believe in Bigfoot in two years. It is impossible to say what caused these changes.

UK PREVALENCE OF PARANORMAL BELIEFS

Paranormal beliefs are every bit as popular in the UK, where there are also high reporting rates of SPEs. Castro, Burrow, and Wooffitt (2014) surveyed a nationally representative sample of 4,096 adults aged 16-plus across Great Britain in 2009. Among British adults, 37% reported at least one SPE; women, the middle-aged or individuals in the south-west[10] are more likely to report such experiences. A study in a northern English metropolitan university by Neil Dagnall and colleagues (2016) included 1,215 adults, 75.7% (920) female and 24.3% (295) male. The most frequently reported subjective paranormal experiences (SPEs) were ESP (23%), astrology (15%), haunting (14%) and contact with the dead (13%). The majority who reported experiences related to ESP (73%), haunting (69%) and witchcraft (67%) recalled actually having more than one experience. Incidence of PK (46% vs. 54%), contact with the dead (46% vs. 54%), and astrology (44% vs. 56%) contained roughly equal proportions reporting single versus multiple experiences.

---

[7] The most common paranormal belief (57.9%) was: 'I have been protected by a guardian angel.'
[8] Alien visitation, if it happened, would not necessarily be paranormal.
[9] The US population appears to be relatively skeptical about fortune tellers.
[10] If you are English, you will know that the south-west, especially Somerset, is rich in history, myths and legends. Glastonbury, a centre for a New Age community, boasts of an abbey that dates back to the 7th century, claimed to be King Arthur's final resting ground.

Of the respondents claiming an SPE, 43% reported one experience type, while 57% reported different types of SPEs. Within multiple experiencers, 94% identified between 2 and 5 experience types and 6% more than 5 experience types. Many psychologists consider the case for the paranormal 'unproven' and write off paranormal research as a waste of time. Countering such dismissers, Caroline Watt and Richard Wiseman (2009) suggest that they are missing a trick, because 'Regardless of whether these beliefs and experiences are "correct", they are clearly an important part of what it is to be human' (in Irwin, 2009, location 63). The ontological issue – whether paranormal abilities exist – is irrelevant to the fact that large numbers of people believe in the paranormal and report paranormal experiences.

BELIEFS AND EXPERIENCES: A CHICKEN-AND-EGG PROBLEM

Philosophers use the term 'belief' to refer to the 'attitude' we have whenever we take something to be the case or regard it as true. Thus, a belief is a degree of conviction that an idea is true (e. g. swans are white), or that a capability exists, or that an event is likely to happen (e.g. that Australia would retain the Ashes in 2019). Beliefs are not fixed, concrete entities that forever remain the same. Belief is socially constituted and coloured by feelings. Holding a belief and having a direct experience of the thing, idea or event are not one and the same. I may never see a swan, nor go, or listen on the radio, to the Ashes Test Series, but I can still accept that both propositions are true. However, there is plainly a relationship between beliefs and the witnessing of objects or events that are the subject of those beliefs. So, actually having a paranormal experience is strongly supportive of paranormal belief.

A person can believe something to be the case, e.g. that there are Yetis in the Himalayas, yet never see, hear or otherwise experience a Yeti. However, if a person visits the Himalayas and thinks that they observe a Yeti, then, logically, their belief in Yetis should ordinarily become significantly stronger. Beliefs are always fallible, but direct experience strengthens belief. Let's consider these two propositions, a and b.

a) Having a subjective paranormal experience produces stronger paranormal belief

If a person really does see a Yeti, their belief in Yetis normally is expected to become stronger. But what if one has never seen a Yeti but, in the light of stories told by others, believes that Yetis exist high up in the Himalaya mountains? In this case, the connection can run in the opposite direction to that of a) above. If one believes that something may be the case – e.g. that Yetis exist – and goes looking for the very thing, one is more likely to find it, or something that looks rather like it. A person looking for a Yeti sees a footprint from a large bear might well think they've discovered a Yeti.

b) Having a strong paranormal belief increases the likelihood of a subjective paranormal experience

The two statements a and b indicate a circularity between beliefs and experiences that can be difficult to unravel. If we measure only the *correlation* between experience and belief, which is the preferred statistical route for the majority of studies, there is no way of knowing the causal direction of the association or even whether there is one at all. It's the chicken and egg problem all over again, with no logical way of deciding which comes first.[11]

One way to break the circularity between belief and experience is to take a lifespan perspective by looking at the issue developmentally and prospectively, using cohorts of people and controlling for known characteristics such as childhood events, poverty and education. Whichever comes first in a person's lifetime, belief or experience, can then be unravelled in a more controlled fashion. Using this approach, it is possible to explore the factors in early life experience that predispose some individuals to have subjective paranormal experience. We do not yet know which factors are likely to predispose people to have SPEs, so how do we explain the wide individual differences in the tendency to have paranormal experiences? In the next chapter, there is a theory that aims to answer this question.

QUESTIONS

1. What is an 'anomaly'?
2. What does 'paranormal' mean?
3. How many kinds of paranormal phenomena are you aware of? Write a list.
4. Which, if any, of the different paranormal phenomena do you believe in? Write a list.
5. Choose one and describe the evidence in favour of this belief. Alternatively, if you do not hold any such beliefs, state what it would take to convince you.
6. Can you think of any anomalous experiences not included in Table 1.1?
7. Describe an anomaly in your own life that you couldn't explain.

---

[11]The results of an analysis by Houran and Lange (2004) indicate that more intense belief increases experience, rather than vice versa. However, both options remain possible.

THE ORIGINS OF SUBJECTIVE ANOMALOUS EXPERIENCE

In any developed science, there is, of necessity, a wide gap between the diverse facts of observation and those few types of observed fact which form the basis of important generalizations and from which a body of theory is then derived. For the very act of reducing observation to order involves the neglect of many pertinent facts; a theory which attempted to take account of everything would be smothered by its own complexity. Thus all generalizations and theories necessarily refer to artificially simplified situations. (Whitehead, 1938: 271)

Outline: The process of theory construction is like solving a scientific jigsaw puzzle: from the multiple pieces one is looking for one coherent picture. The puzzle here is why one large group of individuals have subjective paranormal experiences (SPEs) and an almost equal number do not? The jigsaw becomes a theory of SPE, which highlights factors in childhood, notably trauma. The Homeostasis Theory links childhood trauma with dissociation, fantasy, coping and SPE into one causal chain. The theory holds that childhood trauma causes depersonalisation, compartmentalisation and defensive fantasy in a homeostatic striving to regain feelings of safety and control. The Homeostasis Theory fits a large body of findings from multiple studies that are reviewed in this chapter.

EXISTING THEORIES OF SPE

Why do so many people have anomalous paranormal experiences while others do not? Like all natural phenomena, variation in SPE follows a normal distribution. Genetic and epigenetic variations are almost certainly part of the answer, as all human traits are heritable to a certain extent. Yet an environmental theory is necessary to explain the non-genetic part of the variation. What differentiates people with paranormal experience from the others? To date, in addition to the theory that paranormal experiences are cognitive aberrations (see Chapter 3), there have been five main theories:

1. *Socialisation to a Cultural Source*, absorbing paranormal beliefs and experiences through exposure to family members and close friends with a shared culture of paranormal belief – e.g. joining religious, cultist groups, reading astrology columns or New Age literature, watching paranormal-themed entertainment on television (Sparks & Miller, 2001), YouTube, games and social media that promote paranormal content. The Cultural Source Theory points to the relevance of the cultural context of paranormal experience, but this theory does not adequately explain the huge variations that exist between people in the number and intensity of their paranormal beliefs and experiences.
2. The *Social Marginality Theory* suggests that paranormal experiences are more likely in socially marginal people with limited education, low income, low social status, ethnic minorities, unstable sexual relationships and few friendships (Bainbridge, 1978). The world of the paranormal is said to provide compensation for the pressures arising from 'structured social marginality'. However, this theory is inconsistent with the observation that a widely diverse population reports paranormal experiences, not only people who can be categorised as socially marginal (Castro et al., 2014; Emmons & Sobal, 1981).
3. The *Experiential Source Theory* of McClenon (1994a, b) suggests that anomalous experiences have a universal physiological basis, which acts as a source of recurring beliefs in spirits, souls, life after death, and magical abilities. McClenon's (2000) content analysis of a collection of 1,215 accounts of anomalous experiences indicated that experiences of apparitions, paranormal dreams and waking extrasensory perceptions have uniform structures, and that these experiences coincide with recurring ideas within folk traditions. However, McClenon's Source Theory is speculative and, to date, it has not received the attention it deserves; the theoretical predictions require testing by independent researchers. At this point, it is impossible to say whether the theory is correct or incorrect, or correct for some people and incorrect for others.
4. The *Motivational Theory* of Marks and Kammann (1980) holds that paranormal beliefs satisfy fundamental needs for meaning and release: 'We seem to have a profound yearning for a magic formula that will free us from our ponderous and fragile human bodies, from realities that will not obey our wishes, from loneliness and unhappiness, and from death itself' (Marks and Kammann, 1980, p. 156; see also Singer and Benassi, 1981, p. 50; and Zusne and Jones, 1982, p. 210). According to the motivational theory, paranormal beliefs serve a basic human need to escape the harsh realities of life experience. While one accepts the need for release from from despondency, isolation and despair, the reason why such a large proportion of people affirm paranormal experiences and beliefs while another almost equally large proportion show no such inclination remains unexplained by the motivational theory.

5. The *Illusion of Control Theory* of Irwin (1993) suggests that order, control and meaning in the physical and social world are essential for emotional security and psychological adjustment: 'paranormal belief constitutes a cognitive bias through which reality may be filtered without threatening the individual's sense of emotional security. In essence the way in which paranormal beliefs achieve this effect is by creating a transient "illusion of control" (Langer, 1975) over events that are anomalous or are in reality not controllable by the individual' (Irwin, 1993; Irwin & Watt, 2007, p. 234). Thus, the theory holds that paranormal believers are people having a greater need for an illusion of control. Irwin's model was given some empirical support by Lawrence, Edwards, Barraclough, Church and Hetherington (1995) and by Rogers and Lowrie (2016). However, Watt, Watson and Wilson (2007) found a relatively small (−.18) correlation between perceived childhood control and paranormal belief. What is also missing from Irwin's model is the process causing both increased proneness to fantasy and paranormal experience. It is also necessary to understand the place of SPE in a child's development and the crucial role played by the brain's ability to preserve homeostasis.

In outlining the case I am presenting here, it is necessary to review the complex literature about a topic of great social relevance and sensitivity: the incidence of childhood trauma and abuse, and the associated processes of dissociation, fantasy proneness and SPE. Thousands of relevant studies have been conducted and it is necessary to pinpoint the ones that provide key pieces in the puzzle. One by one, the jiggled-up pieces of a large theoretical jigsaw are unscrambled and fitted into a single picture of the origin of SPEs.

CHILD ABUSE[1], DISSOCIATION AND SPE

Over the past decade, 'celebrity' child abuse cases have brought the issue into a spotlight of public attention: in 2012, the Jimmy Savile scandal hit the headlines in the UK; in 2019, the Michael Jackson scandal created a storm of controversy in the US. Also in 2019, the conviction in Australia of the Pope's closest adviser, Cardinal George Pell, for sexual abuse, led Pope Benedict XVI to apologise for many cases of proven child sexual abuse involving priests. This issue is far larger than the metaphorical 'elephant in the room' – it is a blue whale.

David Finkelhor (1994, 2008; Finkelhor, Shattuck, Turner, & Hamby, 2014) at the University of New Hampshire suggests that 20% of girls and 5% of boys in the US fall victim to child sexual abuse. Furthermore, during a one-year period, 16% of youth ages 14–17 had been sexually victimised and, over the course of their lifetime, 28% of youth aged 14–17 had been sexually victimised. The late 1980s and early 1990s saw an increase in the reporting of childhood sexual abuse in the US. The US Department of Health and Human Services' Children's Bureau (2010)

---

[1]Here, a child is any individual aged 0–17 years inclusive. For a more detailed description of the theory, please see Marks (2020).

reported that the vast majority of victimised children – 78.3% – suffer neglect, 17.6% suffer physical abuse and 9.2% are sexually assaulted, yet the impact can be equally profound across all categories. The National Institute of Justice (2003) suggested that 3 out of 4 sexually assaulted adolescents were victimised by someone they knew well. More than 25% of children and adolescents in the US are exposed to a traumatic event by the age of 16, and many are exposed to repeated events (Costello, Erkanli, Fairbank, & Angold, 2002).

Since the late 1980s, the detrimental effects of child sexual abuse (CSA) on the well-being of victims has been systematically researched. A child victim of prolonged sexual abuse usually develops low self-esteem, a feeling of worthlessness and an abnormal or distorted view of sex and becomes withdrawn and mistrustful of adults, or even suicidal (Cohen, Deblinger, Mannarino, & Steer, 2004; Davis & Petretic-Jackson, 2000; Finkelhor, 1987; Marshall, Marshall, Serran, & O'Brien, 2009; Münzer, Fegert, & Goldbeck, 2016; Paolucci, Genuis, & Violato, 2001; Putnam & Trickett, 1993; Romano & De Luca, 2001). The psychological understanding of childhood trauma draws on the clinical theorising of the French psychologist Pierre Janet (1859–1947; Ellenberger, 1970; Van der Hart & Horst, 1989). Pierre Janet is credited as being one of three 'founding fathers' of psychology along with Wilhelm Wundt and William James, both of whom also make appearances in this book. Janet was interested in the integration of experiences associated with trauma, which he found associated with 'vehement emotion and a destruction of the psychological system', a process that he called 'dissociation' (Van der Kolk & van der Hart, 1989: 1532). Dissociation is a process that may be crucial to our understanding of anomalous experience and is a core construct of this field. Dissociation occurs when mental functions are alleged to split into different systems or 'compartments'. The splitting is uncontrolled and unpredictable, and can create multiple difficulties and complexities for the individual's stream of consciousness. 'Compartmentalised' or automatic parts can exist outside of conscious awareness or memory recall (Ellenberger, 1970; Ludwig, 1983: 93; Van der Kolk & van der Hart, 1989). Janet's dissociation theory focused on the role of dissociation, and especially compartmentalisation, in conditions induced by trauma, and is relevant for research into traumatic stress and post-traumatic 'hysteria' (Van der Hart & Horst, 1989).

Dissociation has been defined as 'an experienced loss of information or control over mental processes that, under normal circumstances, are available to conscious awareness, self-attribution or control, in relation to the individual's age and cognitive development' (Cardeña & Carlson, 2011: 246). The most extreme form of dissociation occurs in dissociative identity disorder (DID), a psychiatric condition with two or more distinct personality states, including memory gaps and discontinuity in sense of agency and selfhood. The evidence suggests that DID is most prevalent in emergency psychiatric settings in approximately 1% of the general population (Dorahy et al., 2014). Hence, the vast majority of people experiencing dissociation do not suffer from the extreme symptoms of DID. Typically, sufferers of DID display alterations known as 'alters' whereby their mental functions are changed unpredictably (American Psychiatric Association, 2013). DID was popularised in the books *The Three Faces of Eve* (Thigpen & Cleckley, 1957) and *Sybil* (Schreiber, 1973), and also adapted into films. Alters are often depicted with disturbed or violent behaviours such as occurs in Stevenson's (1886/1924) *The Strange Case of Dr. Jekyll and Mr. Hyde*. Santoro, Costanzo and Schimmenti (2019) review the prominence and misrepresentation of DID in popular culture, films, games and videos. Research indicates that DID frequently originates in repeated episodes of abuse and neglect in a child's relationship with attachment figures (Dorahy et al., 2014; Schimmenti, 2017, 2018).

Meta-analysis of research on dissociation in psychiatric disorders using the Dissociative Experiences Scale (Lyssenko et al., 2017) finds that the largest dissociation scores occur in DID, followed by post-traumatic stress disorder (PTSD), borderline personality disorder and conversion disorder. Patients with somatic symptom disorder, substance-related and addictive disorders, feeding and eating disorders, schizophrenia, anxiety disorder, obsessive compulsive disorder (OCD) and most affective disorders also show raised dissociation scores. Dissociation can also be benign, without ill effects or disturbances to everyday behaviour or conscious experience, beyond perhaps some limited impact on dreaming (Giesbrecht & Merckelbach, 2006).

In dissociation there is a difference between two qualitatively different phenomena, 'detachment' and 'compartmentalisation' (Holmes et al., 2005). Detachment incorporates depersonalisation, derealisation and similar phenomena such as out-of-body experiences, all of which can occur in combination (Sierra & Berrios, 1998). Detachment involves feelings of being 'spaced out', 'unreal' or 'in a dream'. Patients may have SPEs in which events seem as though they are not really happening, with the external world seeming pallid and two-dimensional. 'Peri-traumatic dissociation' involves a sense of detachment at the moment a traumatic event occurs and can be evaluated with 'The Peritraumatic Dissociative Experiences Questionnaire' (Marmar, Weiss, & Metzler, 1997). It is thought that in peri-traumatic detachment, the encoding of information is disrupted so that memories of the traumatic event may be incomplete. Such fragmented memories can trigger intrusive images and flashbacks (Brewin, Dalgleish, & Joseph, 1996). Peri-traumatically encoded feelings of detachment may be a part of the intrusive memory that is re-experienced, or perhaps the process of re-experiencing itself generates feelings of detachment. Becoming totally immersed in a traumatic memory to the point of believing that the event is actually happening again ('flashbacks') seems to be relatively rare.

Compartmentalisation is the inability to deliberately control processes or actions or information in memory that would normally be amenable to self-control (Brown, 2006; Cardeña, 1994; Holmes et al., 2005). Compartmentalisation incorporates an inability to bring normally accessible information into conscious awareness (e.g. dissociative amnesia). The functions that are no longer amenable to deliberate control, and the information associated with them, are said to be 'compartmentalised'. One of the defining features of this phenomenon is that the compartmentalised processes continue to operate (Brown, 2004; Hilgard, 1977; Janet, 1907; Kihlstrom, 1992; Oakley, 1999). Dissociation is viewed as an adaptive strategy to intense stress or trauma that leads to conditioned dissociative reactions, which can prevent adequate processing and integration of information (Eisen, Goodman, & Davis, 2002; Koopman, Classen, & Spiegel, 1994; Lynn & Rue, 1994; Putnam, 1997). Repeated trauma can sensitise a child to hyperarousal, leading to dissociative responding under stress (Perry, Pollard, Blakley, Baker, & Vigilante, 1995). It must be acknowledged that many abused people do not evidence having dissociative experiences (Hall, 2003). However, the theory to be presented applies to the sizeable proportion of cases where trauma triggers dissociation. Dissociation is an adaptive mechanism that aids survival in the following situations: 1) direct and close encounter with a dangerous perpetrator using force or having malevolent intent – e.g. when skin contact occurs; 2) in the presence of body fluids with danger of contamination – e.g. blood or sperm; 3) when bodily integrity is already injured – e.g. invasion, penetration, sharp objects (e.g. teeth and knife) at the skin (Schauer & Elbert, 2015).

The Homeostasis Theory holds that SPEs are among the more frequent consequences of childhood trauma. There is a large literature of supportive evidence. Ellason and Ross (1997) found that ESP experiences correlated .45 and .44 respectively with the level of childhood physical and sexual abuse. Ross and Joshi (1992) obtained similar findings with a random sample of 502 Canadian adults. Reports of paranormal or extrasensory experiences were common and linked to a history of childhood trauma and dissociation. Ross and Joshi conceptualised SPE as one aspect of dissociation triggered by child abuse. SPEs discriminated between individuals with childhood trauma histories, and those without trauma histories. Perkins and Allen (2006) compared paranormal belief systems in individuals with and without childhood physical abuse histories, using the Tobacyk Revised Paranormal Belief Scale and an SPE questionnaire with 107 students. They found that psi and spiritualism beliefs were among the most strongly held among abused students, and these were at a significantly higher level in abused versus non-abused participants (Ps). Perkins and Allen concluded: 'by providing a sense of control, certain paranormal beliefs may offer a powerful emotional refuge to individuals who endured the stress of physical abuse in childhood' (2006: 349).

In the context of both detachment and compartmentalisation, it has been proposed that ideas and fantasies of the paranormal serve a *restorative function* aimed at resetting the psychological system. In an earlier book, we stated a general hypothesis that humans 'have a profound yearning for a magic formula that will free us from our ponderous and fragile human bodies, from realities that will not obey our wishes, from loneliness or unhappiness, and from death itself' (Marks & Kammann, 1980: 156). It is suggested that individuals are able to use paranormal ideation as a coping strategy for past traumas in a search for stability, restorative justice, compensation or even revenge (Wuthnow, 1976). If emotional security and psychological adjustment depend upon the conviction that the physical and social worlds are orderly and meaningful, then a paranormal worldview provides an adaptive framework for structuring otherwise chaotic, unpredictable or unfair experiences that can make them more comprehensible and controlled (Irwin, 1993a, b).

RATIONALE FOR AN INTEGRATIVE THEORY

Trauma in childhood evokes an instinctual survival need to regain a sense of control, which increases the appeal of paranormal abilities to provide mastery over threats to safety and other incomprehensible events. When children experience persistent terror without escape, as in neglect, attachment disruptions, incest or other sexual trauma, dissociation is protective against emotional distress (Bailey & Brand, 2017). Repetitive childhood physical or sexual abuse, or other forms of trauma such as neglect, are all found to be associated with the development of dissociative states and disorders (Putnam, 1985). Dissociation, detachment and compartmentalisation can be considered adaptive to childhood trauma because they can reduce the degree to which the distress is overwhelming. However, if detachment and compartmentalisation continue in adulthood, they tend to be maladaptive. The dissociative adult may automatically disconnect from any situations that are perceived to be unsafe or threatening, without taking time to determine whether there is any real danger. This tends to leave the person 'spaced out' or 'dreamy' and unable to protect themselves in conditions of real danger, making them vulnerable. In the following sections, different strands of research about childhood trauma, dissociation, fantasy and paranormal ideation are integrated into a single, coherent theory.

This Homeostasis Theory of SPE hypothesises a need for power and control in the face of adversity (Bandura, 1989; Prilleltensky, Nelson & Peirson, 2001; Taylor & Armor, 1996). It incorporates neurobiological evidence from the Polyvagal Theory (Porges, 2017) and the principles of homeostasis from the General Theory of Behaviour (Marks, 2018) to explain one origin of paranormal ideation. The central plank of the theory is the neurobiological evidence concerning the changes that accompany repeated childhood neglect and abuse, which are thought to permanently alter developmental processes of adaptation in producing a 'use-dependent' brain:

> Childhood trauma has profound impact on the emotional, behavioural, cognitive, social, and physical functioning of children. Developmental experiences determine the organizational and functional status of the mature brain ... There are various adaptive mental and physical responses to trauma, including physiological hyperarousal and dissociation. Because the developing brain organizes and internalizes new information in a use-dependent fashion, the more a child is in a state of hyperarousal or dissociation, the more likely they are to have neuropsychiatric symptoms following trauma. The acute adaptive states, when they persist, can become maladaptive traits. (Perry et al., 1995: 271)

In addition to the neurobiological changes, child abuse and neglect are associated with increased risk for psychiatric disorders, including depression, bipolar disorder, PTSD, substance and alcohol abuse, and also medical disorders such as cardiovascular disease, diabetes, irritable bowel syndrome, asthma and others (Nemeroff, 2016). Persistent biological alterations associated with childhood maltreatment include changes in neuroendocrine and neurotransmitter systems and pro-inflammatory cytokines, in addition to alterations in brain areas associated with mood regulation. A systematic review found that individuals with at least four abusive childhood experiences (ACEs) are at increased risk of multiple health outcomes compared with individuals with no ACEs (Hughes et al., 2017). Associations were found to be weak or modest for physical inactivity, overweight or obesity, and diabetes (odds ratios (ORs) of less than two); moderate for smoking, heavy alcohol use, poor self-rated health, cancer, heart disease and respiratory disease (ORs of two to three), strong for sexual risk taking, mental ill health and problematic alcohol use (ORs of more than three to six), and strongest for problematic drug use and interpersonal and self-directed violence (ORs of more than seven).

Exposure to violence is thought to activate a set of threat responses in a child's developing brain. Excessive activation and arousal of the neural systems involved in threat responses alter the developing brain which, in turn, produces functional changes in emotional, behavioural and cognitive functioning. The existence of a graded relationship of ACE scores to outcomes in multiple domains parallels the cumulative exposure of the developing brain to the stress response with resulting impairment in multiple brain structures and functions (Anda et al., 2006).

One implication of trauma-dependent neurobiological changes is that paranormal ideation is able to become an adaptive coping strategy for victims of child abuse. I describe next a series of linkages, beginning with fantasy proneness, mental imagery and dissociation.

FANTASY-PRONENESS, MENTAL IMAGERY AND DISSOCIATION

Everybody daydreams. Fantasy, daydreams and imagination are integral processes within healthy functioning, playing an adaptational role in daily life (Klinger, 1990; Marks, 2019b; Singer, 1983). Fantasy and daydreams reflect our current concerns, regulate mood, organise experience, provide self-relevant information, facilitate learning, and stimulate decision making (Rauschenberger & Lynn, 1995). But, like everything else, there are widespread variations in fantasy proneness across the population. Fantasy proneness (FP) refers to an enduring personality trait of individuals who are thought to spend a large part of their life daydreaming in fantasy. Daydreaming is ubiquitous (Singer & McCraven, 1961), taking up 30–50% of our daily thinking time (Kane, Brown, McVay, Silvia, Myin-Germeys, & Kwapil, 2007).

From the very beginning of research on FP, Wilson and Barber (1983: 359–64) suggested that people with FP have psychic experiences, realistic out-of-the-body experiences, and experiences of apparitional entities. Wilson and Barber also proposed that extreme fantasy is a coping strategy for dealing with loneliness and isolation by providing a means to escape from aversive environments. FP requires the generation of mental imagery, those quasi-perceptual experiences that occur in the absence of an objective stimulus. Large individual differences exist along a continuum of reported vividness and controllability of images (Marks, 2019b).

Individuals at the fantasy-prone end of the normal distribution (1–5%) experience vivid, uncontrollable images of hallucinatory quality which seem *as real as actual events* (Marks & McKellar, 1982; Wilson & Barber, 1983). Another small percentage (2–3%) of people at the opposite end of the distribution are unaware of any mental imagery at all (Zeman, Dewar, & Della Sala, 2015).

The brain has a special 'default network' that participates in internal modes of cognition such as autobiographical memory retrieval, envisioning the future, conceiving the perspectives of others and daydreaming. The default network appears to be a specific, anatomically defined brain system (Buckner, Andrews-Hanna, & Schacter, 2008) that would be activated on a frequent basis among people with FP. The default network also has a key role in the brain's representation of the self (see Chapter 10). From the 1980s and 90s, it had been hypothesised that FP is a process that is exacerbated by child abuse and that it may be a trait, like absorption, a variable that is related to FP (Kunzendorf, Hulihan, Simpson, Pritykina, & Williams, 1997–1998) and which is genetically mediated (Tellegen, Lykken, Bouchard, Wilcox, Negal, & Rich (1988). Lynn and Rhue elaborated the FP construct to include 'a unique constellation of personality traits and experiences coalesced around a deep, profound and long-standing involvement in fantasy and imagination' (1988: 35). Fantasy-prone individuals are believed to share a unique set of characteristics, including the experience of vivid memories, the ability to voluntarily hallucinate and superior hypnotic abilities (Wilson & Barber, 1983). Many phenomena associated with FP also include absorption (Green & Lynn, 2010; Levin & Young, 2002; Lynn & Rhue, 1988; Merckelbach, Horselenberg, & Muris, 2001), aversive childhood experiences (Geraerts et al., 2006; Pekala, Kumar, Ainslie, Elliot, Mullen, Salinger, & Masten, 1999; Rauschenberger & Lynn, 1995; Rhue & Lynn, 1987; Sánchez-Bernardos & Avia, 2004; Somer & Herscu, 2018), hypnotic abilities (Green & Lynn, 2008; Terhune, Cardena, & Lindgren, 2010), hallucinatory abilities (Giambra, 2000; Larøi, DeFruyt, van Os, Aleman, & Van der Linden, 2005), mental imagery (Levin & Young, 2002), and paranormal beliefs and experiences (Bartholomew, Basterfield, & Howard 1991; Berkowski & Macdonald, 2014; French, Santomauro, Hamilton, Fox, & Thalbourne, 2008; Gow, Lang, & Chant, 2004; Hough & Rogers, 2007; Irwin, 1990; Lawrence, Edwards, Barraclough, Church, & Hetherington, 1995; Merckelbach et al., 2001; Parra, 2006; Perkins, 2001; Rogers, Qualter, & Phelps, 2007; Spanos, Cross, Dickson, & DuBreuil, 1993).

There are two connections with FP that are particularly salient: (i) *among individuals reporting a history of childhood abuse, the incidence of FP is especially high* (Lynn & Rhue, 1988; Rhue, Lynn, Henry, Buhk & Boyd, 1990); (ii) *dissociation is linked to both child abuse and FP* (Pekala et al., 1999; Rauschenberger & Lynn, 1995). These two findings have led to a renaissance of Janet's trauma theory (TT).

As noted, dissociation is considered a psychological defence mechanism for victims of traumatising events such as sexual molestation, natural disaster or combat (Putnam, 1991). The TT holds that victims are able to compartmentalise their perceptions and memories and detach themselves from the full impact of the trauma, and that these dissociative processes possibly continue throughout their entire lives. Vonderlin, Kleindienst, Alpers, Bohus, Lyssenko, and Schmal (2018) investigated the relationship between childhood interpersonal maltreatment and dissociation in 65 studies with 7,352 abused or neglected individuals, using the Dissociative Experience Scale (DES). The results revealed higher dissociation in victims of childhood abuse and neglect compared with non-abused or neglected subsamples sharing relevant population features, with highest scores for sexual and physical abuse. Earlier age of onset, longer duration of abuse, and parental abuse significantly predicted higher dissociation scores.

As they would, skeptics doubt the correctness of the TT and propose a fantasy theory (FT) instead.[2] In this theory fantasies of trauma among naturally fantasy-prone are produced in suggestible patients who are vulnerable to the 'planting' of false memories by overly zealous psychotherapists. The FT is associated with the 'False Memory Syndrome' movement, an organisation of people accused of childhood sexual abuse,[3] with multiple court cases brought by alleged perpetrators, usually parents claiming innocence of abuse (Belli & Loftus, 1994; French, 2009; Giesbrecht, Lynn, Lilienfeld, & Merckelbach, 2008; Lynn et al., 2014; Porter, Yuille, & Lehman, 1999). The possibility that therapeutic techniques could create illusory memories of abuse became a major debating point that has divided psychotherapists and researchers into opposite camps. The vehemence of the opposing camps is reminiscent of the 'Battle over Psi'.

In a systematic review of memory implantation, Brewin and Andrews (2017) found that recollection of suggested events can be induced in 47% of Ps, but only in 15% of cases are these experiences likely to be rated as full memories. Brewin and Andrews concluded that susceptibility to false memories of childhood events seem to be quite restricted. The jury is still out, but there is little doubt that a significant proportion of recovered memories of child abuse is veridical – i.e. they are based on actual events.

Dalenberg et al. (2012, 2014) also reviewed numerous studies in a meta-analysis to determine whether the TT or FT received the majority of empirical support. They concluded that the TT was most consistent with the evidence, which included several supportive longitudinal studies. Dalenberg and colleagues found the trauma–dissociation relationship to be modest for childhood sexual abuse (CSA; $r = 0.31$) and physical abuse ($r = 0.27$), but stronger among individuals with DID (0.54 for CSA and 0.52 for physical abuse). However, dissociation scores predicted only 1–3% of the variance in suggestibility. Other studies have found that individuals with DID are no more suggestible or prone to creating false memories than individuals with PTSD, actors simulating DID

---

[2] Also called the 'sociocognitive' or 'iatrogenic' model. Any effect resulting from healthcare professionals, products or services that unintentionally lead to illness or adverse effects is termed 'iatrogenic'.

[3] The False Memory Syndrome Foundation (FMSF) is a non-profit organisation founded in 1992 by Pamela and Peter Freyd after their adult daughter Professor Jennifer Freyd accused Peter Freyd of sexually abusing her as a child (Dallam, 2001).

or healthy controls (Vissia et al., 2016). A continuum of trauma-related symptom severity was found across the groups, which supports the hypothesis of association between the severity, intensity and age at onset of traumatisation, and the severity of trauma-related psychopathology. The evidence from Vissia et al. (2016) supported the TT of DID and challenged the core hypothesis of the FT. However, the issue is not yet fully resolved (Brand et al., 2018; Merckelbach & Patihis, 2018). A further issue to complicate this already complex picture is that unusual sleep experiences can also precipitate episodes of trait dissociation (van Heugten-van der Kloet, Merckelbach, Giesbrecht, & Broers, 2014).

The closeness of victims to perpetrators has also been one focus of studies. The impact of abuse is more intense and longer lasting when linked to betrayal. The betrayal version of the TT proposes that one response to betrayal is keeping knowledge of the trauma out of conscious awareness (Freyd, 1996, 1997). Although this 'betrayal blindness' may benefit survival for ongoing abuse by helping to maintain significant relationships, this compartmentalisation of reality can lead later to psychological and behavioural problems. Gómez, Kaehler, and Freyd (2014) ran three exploratory studies to examine the associations between exposure to betrayal trauma, dissociation and hallucinations, which found that betrayal trauma increases the likelihood of dissociation and hallucinations.

How might high proneness to fantasy, then, lead to SPEs? The Vividness Hypothesis claims that fantasy-prone people are more likely to experience visions, voices and apparitions of extreme vividness, leading them to conclude that such events have a psychic origin (Blackmore, 1984; Marks, 1988). Hallucinogens and psychedelic substances tend to increase a state of FP in people who might otherwise be less fantasy prone. The discoverer of LSD, Albert Hofmann (in Hofmann & Ott, 1980), wrote:

> in the LSD state the boundaries between the experiencing self and the outer world more or less disappear .... Feedback between receiver and sender takes place. A portion of the self overflows into the outer world, into objects, which begin to live, to have another, a deeper meaning. In an auspicious case, the new extended ego feels blissfully united with the objects of the outer world and consequently also with its fellow beings. This experience of deep oneness with the exterior world can even intensify to a feeling of the self being one with the universe.

A sense of awe and oneness with nature does not require LSD, but is likely to be magnified by LSD and may also trigger 'paranormal' experiences (Luke & Kittenis, 2005; see also Chapter 11).

As noted, multiple studies have examined the relationship between FP, imagery vividness and SPE. Merckelbach, Horselenberg, and Muris (2001) found that the Creative Experiences Questionnaire (CEQ), a brief self-report measure of FP, correlated with dissociativity in the range of .47–.63 and also with paranormal experiences. Wiseman and Watt (2006) felt that the evidence should be treated with caution given that the measures employed are intercorrelated and may reflect the operation of a single underlying concept. They refer to Kirsch and Council (1992) and cite Thalbourne's (2000) concept of 'transliminality', which is claimed to underpin a range of imagery factors, including frequency of dream interpretation, FP, absorption, magical ideation and mystical experiences. Other studies, however, suggest that the Vividness Hypothesis may indeed be correct, especially when combined with high absorption (Glicksohn & Barrett, 2003). In Brazil, Alejandro Parra and Juan Carlos Argibay (2012) compared people who claimed psychic abilities with a non-psychic control group and found that the 'psychic' group (n = 40) had significantly higher scores on dissociation, absorption and FP than did the 'non-psychic' group (N = 40). In Australia, Gow, Hutchinson, and Chant (2009) tested 114 females and 59 males who were classified as 'anomalous experiencers' (n = 125), 'anomalous believers' (n = 39) and 'non-believers' (n = 9), according to their responses on a 'Measure of Anomalous Experiences and Beliefs'. In the experiencer group, significant correlations occurred between FP and five subscales of paranormal belief and significant moderate to low correlations with both the 'intuition' and 'feeling' dimensions of the Myers–Briggs Type Indicator. Dissociation was also found to be related to global paranormal belief and to the subscales of psi, superstition and extraordinary life forms.

Parra (2015) assessed 348 educated believers for their paranormal or anomalous experiences, and capacity for visual imagery under eyes-open and eyes-closed conditions using the Vividness of Visual Imagery Questionnaire Revised (VVIQ-R; Marks, 1995) and a 10-item self-report inventory designed to collect information on spontaneous paranormal/anomalous experiences. The results showed that VVIQ scores and paranormal/anomalous experiences correlated significantly, especially for Aura, Remote Healing and Apparitions, but only in the open-eyes condition. Parra (2015) noted:

> These results also highlight the fact that mental imagery ability may be psi-conducive, and it is interesting to note that the VVIQ may be helpful in identifying and selecting better psi-scorers in psi experiments, and may even be of use in psychomanteum (sic) and aura-seeing research. The other advantage of the VVIQ is its ease of administration and speed of data analysis.

In another study, Parra (2018) found that psychic/high-psi-scorers scored significantly higher than nonpsychic/low-psi-scorers on both subscales of the VVIQ.

Lawrence and colleagues (1995) proposed a model of paranormal experience (SPE) and belief (PB), which included fantasy (but not dissociation) as a predictor. In Lawrence's model, trauma was found to have two causal routes in influencing SPE – one direct, the other indirect (Figure 2.1). However, the omission of dissociation appears to have been a significant limitation of the Lawrence et al. model. My current proposal is to assume that dissociation is the most significant sequela of extreme forms of ACE and that fantasy, paranormal experience and paranormal belief are among the consequences of the process of dissociation. Figure 2.1 shows the supervenient role of dissociation in the fantasy that is generated following childhood trauma.

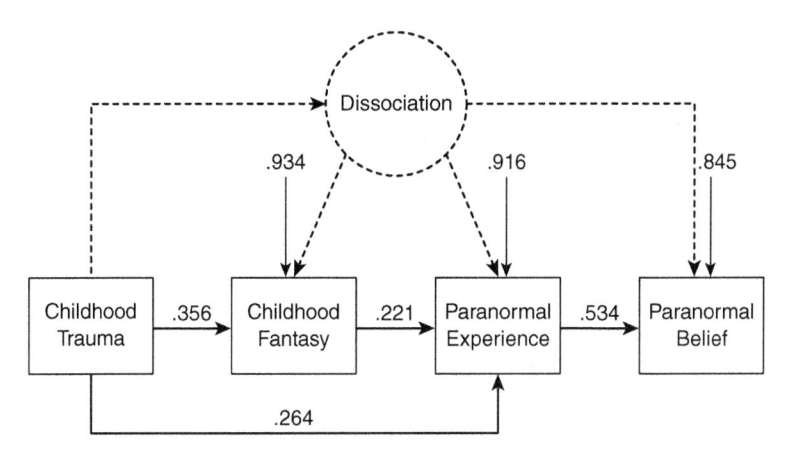

Figure 2.1 A theory of childhood trauma, dissociation, paranormal experience and belief as an extension of the model originally suggested by Lawrence et al. (1995) shown with continuous lines. The model is extended to include dissociation as the main sequela of childhood trauma with causal connections to childhood fantasy, paranormal experience and paranormal beliefs (broken lines).

The Homeostasis Theory suggests that the psychological system strives to restore safety, security and equilibrium by dissociating into compartments to inhibit action and generate compensatory fantasy. Homeostasis performs a restorative function with its ability to deploy the entire resources of the psychological system, including affect, fantasy, and the approach-avoidance-inhibition system, to reset the imbalances created by dissociation. The reset restores feelings of safety and control (Marks, 2018, 2019c). The hypothesised stabilising role of homeostasis is consistent with the theory of Silvan Tomkins, who proposed that the 'primary motivational system is the affective system and biological drives have impact only when amplified by the affective system' (Tomkins, 1962). Clinical studies have established that involuntary images and difficult-to-control memories are associated with dissociation, trauma, stress, anxiety and depression. Sufferers often report repeated visual intrusions concerning real or imaginary events that are 'usually extremely vivid, detailed, and with highly distressing content' (Brewin, Gregory, Lipton, & Burgess, 2010). These elements are precisely the sequelae of a dissociative response to ACE.

PSYCHOSIS, HALLUCINATIONS, CHILDHOOD ADVERSITIES AND DISSOCIATION

The association between childhood adversities (CAs) and the onset of psychotic episodes (PEs) is receiving the attention of clinical researchers who widely agree that childhood trauma is a risk factor for the development of psychosis. Since Janet, the relationship between childhood trauma and symptoms of psychosis has been explained as one consequence of dissociation. For example, Varese, Barkus, and Bentall (2012) explored the hypothesis that the effect of childhood trauma on hallucination-proneness is mediated by dissociative tendencies. Patients with schizophrenia spectrum disorders (n = 45) and healthy controls (with no history of hallucinations; n = 20) completed measures of hallucination-proneness, dissociative tendencies and childhood trauma. Compared to healthy and non-hallucinating clinical-control Ps, hallucinating patients reported both significantly higher dissociative tendencies and childhood sexual abuse. Dissociation was found to positively mediate the effect of childhood trauma on hallucination-proneness, a mediational role that was 'particularly robust for sexual abuse over other types of trauma' (Varese et al., 2012: 1025). They concluded that the results are consistent with dissociative accounts of the trauma–hallucinations link.

Meta-analyses of the association between childhood trauma and the severity of hallucinations, delusions and negative psychotic symptoms in clinical populations have confirmed the association. In a meta-analysis of 29 studies (4,680 Ps) Bailey et al. (2018) found that, in individuals with psychosis, childhood trauma was significantly correlated with the severity of hallucinations ($r = .199$, $P < .001$) and delusions ($r = .172$, $P < .001$) but not with the severity of negative symptoms. These results lend support to theories that childhood traumas may lead to hallucinations and delusions. McGrath et al. (2017) assessed CAs, PEs and DSM-IV (*Diagnostic and Statistical Manual of Mental Disorders*, 4th edition) mental disorders in 23,998 adults in the World Health Organization (WHO) World Mental Health Surveys. People who had experienced any CAs were found to have an increased odds of later PEs (odds ratio (OR) 2.3, 95% confidence interval (CI) 1.9–2.6). CAs reflecting maladaptive family functioning, including abuse, neglect and parent maladjustment, were found to exhibit the strongest associations with PE onset at all life-course stages. Sexual abuse was observed to produce a strong association with PE onset during childhood (OR 8.5, 95% CI 3.6–20.2), while other CA types were associated with PE onset in adolescence. McGrath et al. (2017) concluded that exposure to CAs is associated with PE onset throughout the life-course, with sexual abuse being most strongly associated with childhood-onset PEs.

Muenzenmaier et al. (2015) tested the dose–response relationship between CA and delusions and hallucinations, including the effects of dissociation on the relationship. The prevalence of CA in individuals with psychotic disorders was high, with each additional CA being associated with a 1.20 increase in the incidence rate ratio (95% confidence interval (CI) 1.09, 1.32) for hallucinations and a 1.19 increase (CI 1.09, 1.29) for delusions, supporting a dose–response association. After controlling for the mediating effects of dissociative symptoms at follow-up, CA remained independently associated with delusions. Muenzenmaier et al. (2015) proposed that cumulative CAs can result in complex reactions, including dissociative, post-traumatic stress disorder and psychotic symptoms.

A review of 19 quantitative studies investigated the relationship between voice-hearing and dissociation between 1986 and 2014 (Pilton, Varese, Berry, & Bucci, 2015). The authors concluded that dissociation may be implicated in voice-hearing as a mediating factor. In a clinical study with 71 patients diagnosed with psychosis, Perona-Garcelán et al. (2012) found that childhood trauma was positively associated with the dissociation scale scores (r = .40) and the hallucination (r = .36) and delusions scale scores (r = .32). Depersonalisation was found to be a potential mediator between childhood trauma and hallucinations, but not between childhood trauma and delusions. In another study of depersonalisation mediation in the relationship between childhood maltreatment and both hallucination-proneness and delusional ideation, Cole, Newman-Taylor, and Kennedy (2016) used a cross-sectional design in a non-clinical group. They found that dissociation mediated the relationship between early maltreatment and hallucination-proneness and delusional ideation.

It has been suggested that the content of hallucinations may be formed out of dissociative memories of traumatic events (Mauritz, Goossens, Draijer, & van Achterberg, 2013) and that it could reflect the experiencer's perceived lower social self-appraisal as a consequence of childhood abuse (Birchwood, Meaden, Trower, Gilbert, & Plaistow, 2000).

In the next section, I examine another piece in the jigsaw, the Polyvagal Theory, which concerns the organism's defences when safety is challenged by an imminent threat.

THE POLYVAGAL THEORY OF SAFETY

The Polyvagal Theory is a neurobiological theory of safety. The Polyvagal Theory describes an inbuilt system within the nervous system for evaluating threat, which enables a shift in the body's physiological defences. Think of the drawbridge going up at the main gates of a castle when enemy soldiers are detected at the edges of the estate. The goal of the psychological system is to continuously monitor the environment for threats by searching for unique cues. When a threat or lack of safety is perceived, the system actively inhibits outward responses to promote safety and well-being with feelings of love, security and trust. Safety is associated with specific environmental features and unconscious bodily responses as well as making conscious cognitive evaluations. Adaptive survival resides in the evolutionary wisdom of the body and nervous system that function outside the realm of awareness. These neural processes that evaluate risk in the environment without awareness are called 'neuroception'.[4] Evaluations of risk and lack of safety in potentially dangerous relationships play a secondary role to our visceral reactions to people and places (Porges, 2017: 43; Figure 2.2).

The Polyvagal Theory concerns the vagus, the tenth cranial nerve and the primary nerve in the parasympathetic nervous system (PNS). The vagus connects brainstem areas with structures in the body, including the neck, thorax and abdomen. Polyvagal Theory involves the changes in the autonomic nervous system (ANS) and a unique

---

[4]We will return to consider neuroception in Chapter 6 when discussing the theory of human magnetosensitivity.

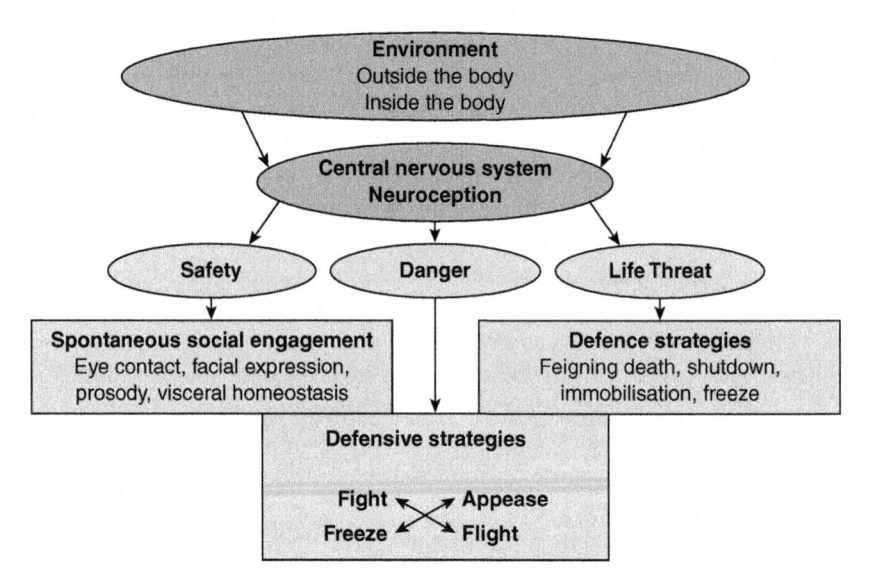

Figure 2.2 The Polyvagal Theory of Safety (adapted from Porges, 2017)

change in the vagal motor pathways that first occurred with the emergence of mammals in evolution. When the ventral vagus and the associated social engagement system are optimally functioning, the ANS supports health, growth and restoration. According to the Polyvagal Theory, defence reactions are manifested as either an increase in SNS activity, which inhibits the function of the dorsal vagus to promote fight and flight behaviours, or as a shutdown manifested as depressed SNS activity and a surge of dorsal vagal influences that results in fainting, defecation and an inhibition of motor behaviour, as seen in mammals feigning death (Porges, 2017).

Neuroception is the neural process that evaluates environmental risk from cues that trigger shifts in autonomic state prior to conscious awareness. We constantly monitor the environment for safety both with and without awareness. One example is the sense of danger we may experience immediately prior to a mugging. If somebody suddenly runs up from behind and rips a person's bag off their shoulder, it would be a perfectly natural reaction to freeze. Other victims may switch into 'fight' mode, others into 'flight'. These responses occur prior to any conscious decision. Neuroception shifts the ANS response to cues of safety, danger or threat by activating the social engagement system and shutting down the fight/flight and the body's defence systems. This includes the face, heart and myelinated vagus (Porges, 2017). Finally, Figure 2.3 shows how the pieces of the jigsaw fit together.

THE HOMEOSTASIS THEORY OF SPE

Here we take a look at the complete picture of the theory.

If we are to make sense of the connections between childhood trauma, dissociation and SPE, we need to consider the options for an infant or child who

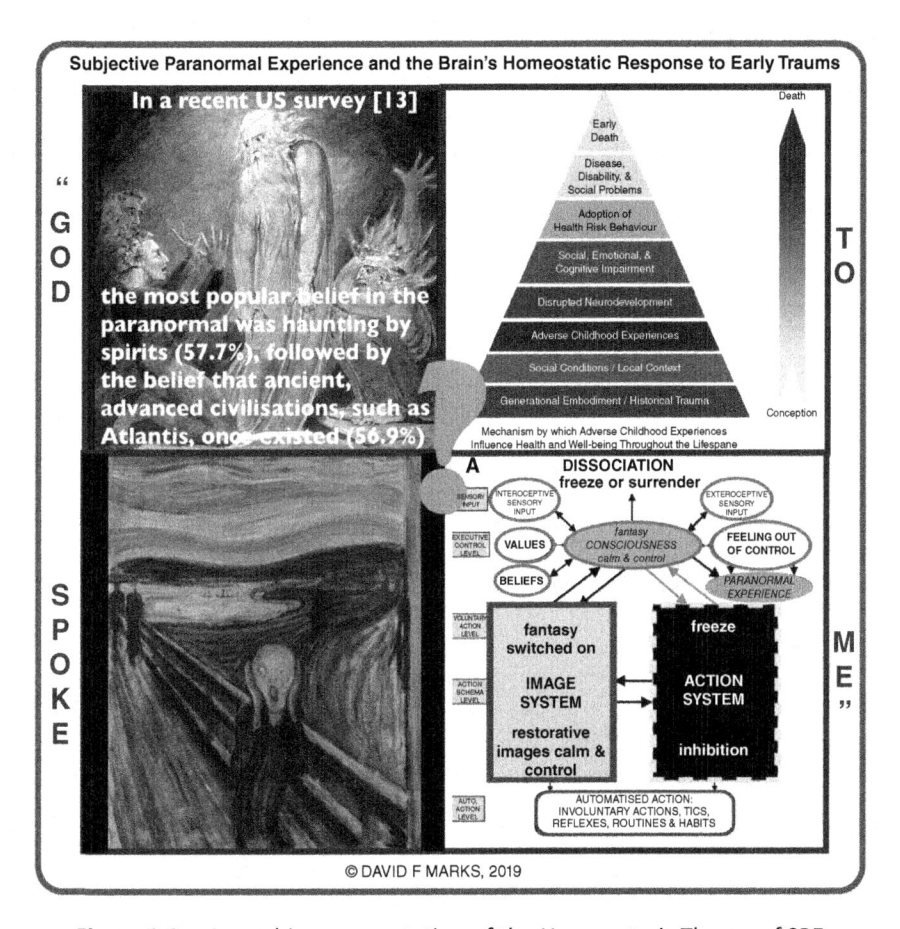

Figure 2.3 A graphic representation of the Homeostasis Theory of SPE (Marks, 2019c)

is confronted by a significant threat of harm from a person who may be a close family member, another known person or even a complete stranger. Being able to cope with such a threat has profound evolutionary significance, and how the organism responds is likely to be a life-and-death issue. Every living organism is endowed with a powerful mechanism that has been especially designed to deal with threats to life called the 'Approach–Avoidance–Inhibition (AAI)' system. This system controls the individual's fight, flight or freeze response. A well-established principle is the universal striving towards pleasure and away from pain that underlies all approach and avoidance behaviour. Organisms approach sources of potential pleasure and satisfaction, and studiously avoid potentially aversive stimuli and confrontations with danger. Essential similarities in the neural systems underlying painful and pleasant sensations are based on the opioid and dopamine systems respectively (Leknes & Tracey, 2008). This 'do or die' neural circuitry evolved to ensure survival. This survival circuitry is activated either by stimuli that are life-sustaining or by stimuli that threaten survival. Activation of the pain and pleasure circuits alert the sensory systems to pay attention and prompt motor action (Lang & Bradley, 2010). The approach–avoidance concept is pivotal to the organisms' systems of self-defence (Elliot, 1999). However, the AAI system also includes a mechanism for behavioural inhibition, which is activated in the approach–avoidance conflict. It has been proposed that an 'Action Schemata' (AS) system coordinates and controls action with the AAI system (Marks, 2018). Further details of these systems are given in Chapter 10.

The innate species-specific defence reactions of the AAI system – fleeing, freezing or fighting – are rapidly acquired when organisms are still young and relatively immature (Bolles, 1970; Wichers et al., 2015). In infants and young children, the first reaction to continuing threat is to cry and then to freeze. The ability to fight or flee is not usually available. Freezing allows better sound localisation and visual observation of the environment for potential threat. Cessation of movement is also a form of camouflage that reduces the risk of attracting attention by predators. Traumatised children often develop a 'sensitised' hyperarousal or 'sensitised' dissociative pattern in association with freezing when they feel anxious. Freezing can escalate to complete dissociation (Perry et al., 1995).

An adaptive homeostatic mental and physical response to childhood trauma consists of a dissociative response of freezing and/or surrender involving fantasy and imagery. Figures 2.4 and 2.5 show a representation of a general behavioural control system with two co-active subsystems for the control and timing of action, the 'Action System', and for the control and timing of imagery, the 'Image System' (Marks, 2018, 2019b, 2019c).

The Dissociative Setting is activated in the child's response to trauma. The Image System is fully switched on and the Action System is switched off, giving a Freeze or Surrender response. The child under threat withdraws into an inner world of detachment and derealisation in which stabilising fantasy of calm and self-control are utilised to restore homeostasis. Post-traumatic fantasy is a normal homeostatic balancing process to produce equilibrium in a system experiencing unjustified life threat, loss or harm. There is every reason to expect trauma-based fantasy to be restorative of missing love objects in the form of voices, hallucinatory images or the felt presence of missing persons, or in fantasies of personal survival beyond death. The genesis of fantasy- and affect-laden paranormal experience in dissociative self-defence causes paranormal ideation of coping and survival. Fantasy and daydreaming increase the likelihood that a person will experience altered states of consciousness, striking coincidences and beliefs in the paranormal, which help to restore a sense of balance and control.

The theory views dissociation as the system's innate response to threat with defensive immobilisation, involuntary freezing and the feigning response of playing dead. As in all behaviours, there are gradations in reactions to life threats,

Origins of Subjective Anomalous Experience

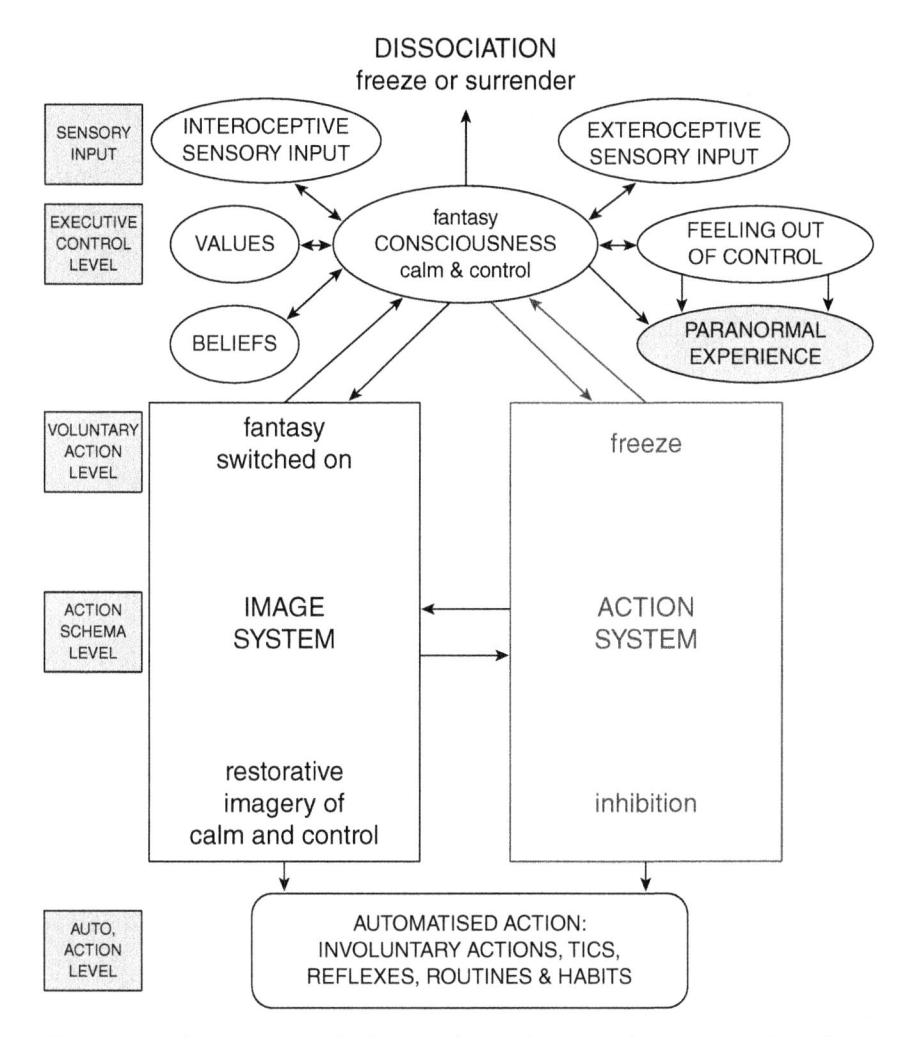

Figure 2.4 The Homeostasis Theory of SPE. The control system consists of two co-active, parallel systems, an 'Action System' and an 'Image System'. In any response to danger, one system can switch down its activity, allowing the other system a greater share of control. In this diagram, the Image System is dominant with a setting for freeze or surrender while, in reciprocal fashion, the Action System is inhibited. The Image System is fully activated to produce fantasy, calmness, stillness and self-control.

ranging from total shutdown and collapse to immobilisation when muscles lose tension and the mind dissociates from the traumatic event, similar to the REM state during sleep. I turn to consider 12 hypotheses that follow from the theory, with a brief statement of the support from the research literature.

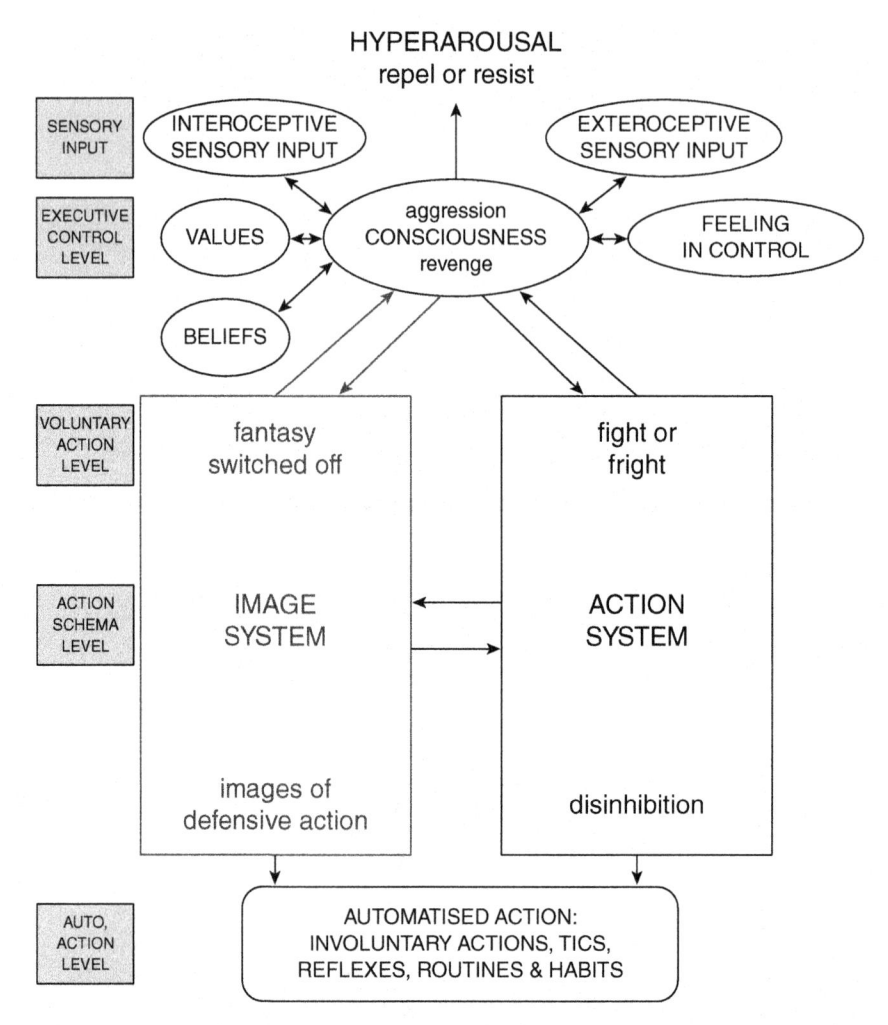

Figure 2.5 The Homeostasis Theory of SPE showing the system set for fight or flight with actions of aggression or revenge. This setting is available to older adolescents and adults but not to infants and young children who would normally respond with the system shown in Figure 2.4.

HYPOTHESES

The following 12 hypotheses result from the theory and I cite illustrative studies relevant to these hypotheses:

H1: SPEs should be more common in people reporting childhood abuse (supported: Lawrence et al., 1995; Parra, 2019; Rabeyron & Watt, 2010; Sar, Alioğlu & Akyüz, 2014; Scimeca, Bruno, Cava, Pandolfo, Muscatello, & Zoccali, 2014).

H2: SPEs should be more common among people with dissociative symptoms (supported: Wahbeh, McDermott, & Sagher, 2018).

H3: SPEs should be more common among people with high fantasy proneness scores (supported: Council & Huff, 1990; Dasse, Elkins, & Weaver, 2015).

H4: SPEs should be more commonly reported by females than by males and paranormal beliefs should be stronger in females than in males (supported: Blackmore, 1997; Castro, Burrows, & Wooffitt, 2014).

H5: One common response of children to extreme negative affect (trauma, fear and anxiety) is dissociation, detachment, derealisation and restorative fantasies of control and calm (supported: Cook et al., 2017).

H6: Dissociation in adulthood is more common in people reporting childhood abuse (supported: Chu & Dill, 1990; Vonderlin et al., 2018).

H7: FP is more common in people reporting childhood abuse (supported: Rhue & Lynn, 1987; Somer & Herscu, 2018).

H8: Paranormal beliefs are more prevalent in people reporting high levels of FP than in others (supported: Ellason & Ross, 1997; Irwin, 1990).

H9: Individuals who claim paranormal abilities score higher on dissociation and fantasy than individuals who do not claim paranormal experiences (supported: Parra & Argibay, 2012).

H10: FP and coping style fully mediate the relationship between trauma and paranormal beliefs (supported: Berkowski & MacDonald, 2014).

H11: Belief in ESP and PK is a vehicle for exercising a need for power and control at a fantasy level (supported: Roe & Morgan, 2002).

H12: Among victims of childhood abuse, a dissociative response such as PTSD is more likely to be released when trauma occurs in adulthood (supported: Brewin, Andrews, & Valentine, 2000).

SUMMARY

The overall excellent fit between the theory and empirical findings provides one solution for the puzzle that I have identified. However, there may be missing pieces to be filled into a bigger picture that is not yet clearly visible. It is unlikely that the theory can explain the origins of *all* SPEs, which really would be too good to be true. All theories are eventually replaced by better theories but, at least, this theory makes a start. It has been well documented that dissociative states are much more common among individuals who have been traumatised in childhood and that the defensive use of fantasy provides a beneficial coping strategy. However, there must be other causal pathways to SPE, one of which is the possibility that some of the experiences are veridical, let us not forget.

The Homeostasis Theory holds that childhood trauma and dissociation act together to produce SPE in a significant number of people. Childhood trauma is a prevalent social scourge requiring victims to put up a robust system of self-defence against potential perpetrators. One instinctual defensive strategy is dissociation and the associated fantasies and feelings of calm and control. The theory provides a comprehensive account for a large number of findings in the published literature. New prospectively controlled research is required to test theoretical hypotheses on a large sample of children together with alternative hypotheses about the origins of SPE.

QUESTIONS

1. In what ways can dissociation be described as adaptive?
2. Describe 'detachment' and 'compartmentalisation'.
3. What are the characteristics of the fantasy-prone person?
4. What is the 'false-memory syndrome'?
5. How does the Polyvagal Theory relate to trauma?
6. Compare and contrast the Action and Image Systems.
7. What limitations do you see in the Homeostasis Theory?

3

PSYCHOLOGICAL PROCESSES AND ANOMALOUS EXPERIENCE

An individual who commits a fallacy is being deceived into accepting a conclusion which merely looks correct. (Wason, 1964: 30)

Outline: Psychological processes can provide some helpful insights into the nature and function of anomalous and paranormal experience. Nobody is perfect and people frequently erroneously attribute paranormal characteristics to experiences or events that have normal explanations. Interpretations of anomalous experiences are open to a host of psychological influences, including fast and slow thinking, memory and cognitive factors, worldview, confirmation bias, subjective validation and the 'Forer Effect'. It seems useful to separate anomalous beliefs such as urban legends from paranormal beliefs. In one's appreciation of anomalistic experience, the search for the meaning is reinforced by the reward of surprise.

The range of subjective anomalous experiences that can be encountered is vast. Few limitations exist on when, where and how they may occur. Our culture is filled with religious and historical myths and legends, instilling a mindset that is steeped in superstitious myths and beliefs of the supernatural. Sleep, dreams and daydreams kindle charming fantasies that challenge one's daytime reality testing. Apart from dreams – if we can only remember them – the visions of artistic works capture the magic of dream-world fantasy (Figure 3.1).

In our two-million-year evolutionary history, the scientific worldview papers over the deep reserve of partly conscious magical thought and feeling. Multiple psychological analyses reveal a deep, archaic pool of paranormal ideation that undergirds thinking, feeling and behaviour. This ancient treasure chest of mythology, fear and mystery bequeaths the world of psi with an heirloom of anti-scientific

Figure 3.1 Grandville, *Un Autre Monde* (Juggler of Universes), 1844

fantasy that opposes rationality and reduction. In dealing with this groundswell of scorn, scientists are inadequately prepared to provide information and advice as a counterweight to the shadowy occult world lying beneath the thin veneer of human rationality. The fearful defensiveness of many practitioners makes science seem unattractive and irrelevant.

I review here psychological processes that influence and structure supernatural beliefs and experiences. I indicate how people are deceived into accepting fiction as fact simply because it feels right to do so. There are no surprises here, except the realisation that human reasoning – held up to be the pinnacle of intelligence – is such an imperfect instrument when it is compared to logical thinking in its most ideal form. Accordingly, SPE is viewed as one huge cognitive aberration.

REASONING ABILITY

Based on a huge body of research, Daniel Kahneman (2011) suggested that people think in two different ways: fast, intuitive and automatic versus slow, reflective and deliberate. You, me and everybody are influenced by cognitive biases and heuristics. These are practical approaches to problem solving, learning or discovery that are sufficient for immediate goals but are never optimal or perfect. Research on decision making (Kahneman, 2011), reasoning (Evans, 2008) and moral judgement (Greene, 2013) converge towards the 'Two Systems' Theory: a hypothetical fast route and a slow route that can override the fast route if we need to let it (Stanovich & West, 2000). The study of biases and heuristics compares actual human performance with the 'normative' standards of logic and rationality. Guess what? People don't do very well.

One of the first studies to compare human reasoning with logic was Wason's (1964, 1968) 'selection task': The 'subject' or participant (P) is shown four cards showing two letters (A and D) and two numbers (3 and 7). They are told that each card has a number on one side and a letter on the other. The experimenter says they have the following rule in mind: 'If there is an A on one side, then there is a 3 on the other.' The unsuspecting P is invited to turn over *only* the card(s) that are necessary to determine whether the experimenter's rule is true or false. Before reading on, which cards must be turned over? Please take a guess.

Only a small minority makes the correct selection: 'the A card and the 7 card'. The vast majority of people get this puzzle totally wrong. Peter Wason (1964) explained the situation thus:

> In deductive reasoning a valid inference follows necessarily from its premises, i.e. it would be inconsistent to assert the premises and deny the inference. A fallacious inference is an invalid inference which has the appearance of validity. An individual who commits a fallacy is being deceived into accepting a conclusion which merely looks correct. For example, an individual presented with the statement, 'all A are B' might suppose that 'all B are A' follows from it. On the other hand, this mistake would not be made if a statement of the same form had been used to express a known fact, e.g. 'all monkeys are animals'. (Wason, 1964: 30)

We will return to research on reasoning later in the chapter. This research occurred in parallel with studies of fallacies, heuristics and biases in judgement and decision making. Krueger and Funder (2004) listed no less that 42 cognitive biases, many of which can play a role in paranormal belief formation and interpretation anomalies. The majority of studies in anomalistic psychology are cross-sectional and correlational, using a 'Polyfilla' approach. A few representative studies are reviewed before discussing a laboratory study.

EXPLAINING INDIVIDUAL DIFFERENCES IN PARANORMAL BELIEF

One hypothesis to explain the widely differing paranormal belief levels is that there is a cognitive 'deficit' related to *misrepresentation of randomness*. We know that people are not generally all that accurate when it comes to estimating probabilities. They might often use incorrect assumptions, ignore relevant facts or base their decisions on misleading heuristic devices (Marks & Clarkson, 1973; Tversky & Kahneman, 1974). People demonstrate fast and intuitive thinking that can often get things badly wrong. There is also a common bias to seek a subjective form of validation rather than an objective form of proof (Marks, 2000).

A series of studies by a team of investigators at Manchester Metropolitan University led by Neil Dagnall has been testing these ideas by examining the association between probabilistic biases – misperception of chance and the conjunction fallacy – and paranormal beliefs. Their first study investigated whether paranormal belief is associated with a general weakness in probabilistic reasoning or with the misrepresentation of chance (Dagnall, Parker, & Munley, 2007). Dagnall, Parker, and Munley (2007) used a range of probabilistic reasoning tasks (perception of randomness, use of base rate information, the conjunction fallacy and the derivation of expected value). Only perception of randomness and not general reasoning weaknesses correlated with paranormal beliefs. In a second study, Dagnall, Drinkwater, Parker, and Rowley (2014) again found that perceptions of randomness were associated with the Ps' degree of paranormal belief, supporting the hypothesis that believers are more prone to misrepresent chance.

At the University of Chicago, Stephen Gray and David Gallo (2016; GG) used a broad array of tasks to examine cognitive and thinking styles across three independent samples. GG measured memory accuracy and distortion using the following:

1. A version of the Deese–Roediger–McDermott task (DRM; Roediger & McDermott, 1995) to test participants' memory for studied words as well as false memory for non-studied but associated words.
2. A criterial recollection task (CRT) requiring Ps to accurately recollect different kinds of information (e.g. font colour or pictures) associated with studied words (Gallo, 2013).
3. An imagination inflation task (IIT) using guided imagery to bias estimates of the occurrence of childhood events from autobiographical memory (Garry, Manning, Loftus, & Sherman, 1996).

They tested short-term memory using:

4. The reading-span (RSPAN) and operation-span (OSPAN) tasks (Daneman & Carpenter, 1980; Turner & Engle, 1989).

In addition, GG included measures tapping analytical or critical thinking:

5. The Shipley Institute of Living Scale (Zachary, 1986), which contains a logical reasoning component in which Ps are required to look at a pattern of letters, numbers or words and indicate the next item in the pattern. The Shipley also includes a vocabulary test.
6. An argument evaluation task (AET; Stanovich & West, 1997), which requires Ps to evaluate the quality of the positions and arguments that other people make when debating various public issues.
7. The remote associations test (Mednick, 1962), in which Ps are given three words (e.g. 'stalk', 'trainer', 'king') and required to solve the puzzle by identifying the fourth word that connects all three (e.g. 'lion').
8. A conspiracy theories questionnaire, based on items from Oliver and Wood (2014), which assessed the likelihood that Ps would endorse conspiracy theory statements about current and historical events relative to matched-control items as a baseline.

Several personality and self-report measures previously linked to propensity for memory distortion included the following:

9. The Dissociative Experiences Questionnaire–Comparative (DES-C; Wright & Loftus, 1999).
10. The Tellegen Absorption Scale (TAS; Tellegen & Atkinson, 1974).
11. The Need for Cognition Questionnaire (Cacioppo, Petty, & Kao, 2004).
12. GG also asked Ps questions to assess their worldview – e.g. beliefs about Darwin's theory of biological evolution – to determine whether paranormal beliefs generalised to rejection of all scientific beliefs, or instead whether they were specific to paranormal phenomena.
13. Finally, a question about overall life satisfaction.

Three groups of 700–1,000 Ps were screened online using the Sheep–Goat Scale and demographic variables before entering either a lab session (Study 1) or two further online sessions (Studies 2 and 3). From these large groups, groups of 40+ believers and 40+ skeptics were selected for each study, with an approximately 50:50 male/female split and an average age of around 26–27. Eleven coefficients were at $p < .05$ and eleven were at $p < .01$. This 'Polyfilla' study created uncertainties for conclusions about statistical significance. The main limitation is that GG could not draw causal conclusions because this was a cross-sectional study. However, they found that around 70% of the believers had beliefs in line with their close friends and family, and that psychic beliefs were correlated with higher life satisfaction. However:

> there were no consistent group differences on tasks of episodic memory distortion, autobiographical memory distortion, or working memory capacity, but skeptics consistently outperformed believers on several tasks tapping

analytical or logical thinking as well as vocabulary ... psychic belief was associated with greater life satisfaction ... highlighting the role of both cognitive and noncognitive factors in understanding these individual differences. (GG, 2016: 242)

I turn to evidence about the connections between a more wholistic concept, a person's worldview, and their perceptions of anomalous experience.

WORLDVIEW

Approximately 2,500 years ago a person who we call 'Buddha' is alleged to have surmised: 'We are what we think. All that we are arises with our thoughts. With our thoughts we make the world' (Koltko-Rivera, 2006: 3).

Buddha defines a 'worldview' as the way we make the world with our thoughts. Once again, we enter a 'World of Twos' where there are said to be two kinds of people.[1] One of the founders of anomalistic psychology, William James, believed that humans are either 'tender-minded' or 'tough-minded' (James, 1890). Tender-minded people interpret events as intangible metaphysical processes, while tough-minded types prefer observable and physical factors. Leonard Zusne and Warren Jones (1989) held that paranormal beliefs are one aspect of 'worldview', a philosophical outlook that is a 'subjective and esoteric perspective on humanity, life, and the world at large'. To give it a name, I suggest the 'Metaphysical Worldview', is a worldview that makes sense of the world in a subjective, emotional and intuitive way (Zusne & Jones, 2014). The Metaphysical Worldview exists in contrast to a material, objective, scientific approach which is marked by empiricism: an 'Empiricist Worldview'. Thus, the 'Worldview Hypothesis' can be examined by looking for evidence of a 'Worldview Trait', a continuum with 'Metaphysical' at one end and 'Empiricist' at the other (Figure 3.2). Where do you place yourself along this scale?[2]

If we assume that people's worldviews fall along a 'worldview continuum', then it is possible to explore the degree to which the intensity of people's paranormal beliefs is associated with their score along the metaphysical–empiricist dimension. Is there any evidence for such an association?

Emilio Lobato and colleagues (2014) investigated the association between three categories of epistemically unwarranted beliefs:[3] paranormal, conspiracy and pseudoscientific claims. For this, they needed another scale. A person's core knowledge confusion (CORE) was measured using the CORE scale (Lindeman & Aarnio, 2007). This 30-item scale examines core ontological confusions (e.g.

---

[1] This idea itself is a worldview.
[2] Pencils only please.
[3] These are beliefs lacking reliable supportive scientific evidence.

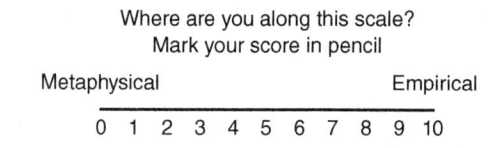

```
            Where are you along this scale?
               Mark your score in pencil
    Metaphysical                        Empirical
    ────────────────────────────────────────────
    0   1   2   3   4   5   6   7   8   9   10
```

Figure 3.2 The 'Metaphysical–Empirical 10-Point Scale'

lifeless objects are living; artificial objects are animate). Ps were asked whether the statement was literally true or not literally true. Moderate to strong positive correlations were evident between the three categories of beliefs, suggesting that believers in one type tended to also endorse other types. The CORE measure was predictive of both paranormal and conspiracist beliefs, suggesting that intuitive/metaphysical thinking may be common to both paranormal and conspiracy believers.

Harvey Irwin, Neil Dagnall, and Kenneth Drinkwater (2016) investigated the association between paranormal beliefs and scientific attitudes using two hypotheses:

H1: The intensity of paranormal beliefs is negatively related to a general appreciation of the values of science.

H2: The intensity of paranormal beliefs is negatively related to an intrinsic disposition for skepticism.

As expected, paranormal believers had a relatively low regard for the values of science and were weakly skeptical, as Lobato et al. (2014) had found. The effect sizes were modest, but the findings fitted the theory that worldview types have differing views on the paranormal.

Conspiracy theories are an interesting category of anomalous beliefs in which hidden groups are imagined to be working in secret to achieve sinister objectives (Goertzel, 1994). According to a 2015 poll, 37% of US adults believe that global warming is a hoax, 20% think that there is a relationship between vaccines and autism, and 15% believe that the medical and pharmaceutical industry create new diseases to sell the cure (Van der Linden, 2015). The same poll found that 71% of US adults believe in miracles, 42% believe in ghosts, 41% believe in ESP and 29% believe in astrology. A specific worldview contains meta-level beliefs in the mistrust of authority, the conviction that nothing is quite as it seems, and a more or less general condition of deception (Swami et al., 2011; Wood et al., 2012). The endorsement of any specific conspiracy theory may depend on whether an individual accepts a conspiratorial worldview (Imhoff & Bruder, 2014), which inclines people away from analytical–rational processing towards intuitive–experiential processing.

A Polish study explored whether conspiracy beliefs are weaker in association with increased reasoning ability (RA) (Jastrzębski & Chuderski, 2017). Contrary to expectations, the results showed that RA explained less than 2% of variance in conspiratorial beliefs. However, RA predicted almost 9% of variance in paranormal and pseudoscientific beliefs in line with another study (Rindermann, Falkenhayn, & Baumeister, 2014). The strongest association (r = .72) was between irrational and conspiratorial beliefs. The association between conspiratorial, paranormal and pseudoscientific beliefs supports the hypothesis of a common metaphysical worldview. A consistent finding was obtained by Ståhl and Van Prooijen (2018), who showed that analytic thinking is associated with a lower inclination to believe in conspiracy theories and paranormal phenomena, but only among empiricist individuals who strongly value epistemic rationality.

Drinkwater, Dagnall, and Parker (2012) found that reality testing and paranormal belief are associated with General Conspiracist Beliefs (GCB) and also specific conspiracies. The tendency to use intuitive–experiential thinking could help to explain the finding that belief in conspiracy theories is associated with a rejection of science (Lewandowsky, Gignac, & Oberauer, 2013). Ted Goertzel (1994) holds that conspiracies are a 'monological' belief system, which is said to provide easy, automatised explanations for new phenomena, which could otherwise challenge the comfort of existing beliefs. Goetzel's hypothesis was supported by Dagnall and colleagues (2015), who assessed 223 volunteer undergraduates, postgraduates, university employees and alumni on measures of cognitive–perceptual factors (schizotypy, delusional ideation and hallucination proneness) and conspiratorial beliefs (general attitudes towards conspiracist thinking and endorsement of individual conspiracies). They found that 'Positive symptoms of schizotypy, particularly the cognitive–perceptual factor, correlated positively with conspiracist beliefs. The best predictor of belief in conspiracies was delusional ideation' (Dagnall, Drinkwater, Parker, Denovan, & Parton, 2015: 1). However, delusional ideation was most strongly associated with conspiracism, but in total, cognitive–perceptual factors accounted for only 32% of the variance. Dagnall et al. (2015) concluded that the conspiracy worldview can often be adaptive in seeking truth and social advancement. Their sanguine view of conspiratorial thinking contrasts with the more common pejorative interpretation of conspiracist thinking.

The international rise in populist political views provides another arena to evaluate the associations between worldview and conspiracist thinking. One study explored the relationship between populist attitudes and conspiracist beliefs on the individual level with American samples (Castanho, Vegetti, & Littvay, 2017). Belief in conspiracies with greedy elites was associated with populist attitudes. Another domain is climate science. The conspiracist rejection of science includes the assertion that inconvenient scientific findings constitute a 'hoax'. Lewandowsky et al. (2013), in an internet survey of the US population, found that a conservative/free-market worldview predicted rejection of climate science. Conspiracist ideation was associated with wholesale rejection of scientific propositions. Given the vehemence of people's worldviews, how tenacious are they and do they ever change?

IS ONE'S WORLDVIEW FIXED FOR ALL TIME?

The answer to this question is 'No'. Rarely, perhaps once or twice in a lifetime, a person's worldview may change; not for everybody, but for some, although the exact proportion is unknown. On a rare occasion even scientists change their minds. Thomas Kuhn talked about 'paradigm shifts' in science. Paradigm shifts also sometimes occur in individuals as they encounter new experiences. I quote from one P, 'Michael', around 16 years old, from a study by François Mathijsen:

> And then, wow! In that moment, it sent shivers down my spine (voice falters). It really terrified me! Because I couldn't believe it and then, boom! I mean, I actually went from 'I don't believe it' to 'I do believe it'. I believe in spiritualism. I believe there must be something in the afterlife. (Mathijsen, 2011)

Mathijsen suggests that 'sudden, sometimes brutal' changes typically occur in four stages: cognition–emotion–cognition–emotion, which he calls the 'hermit crab' phenomenon. These four stages occur when a person has an experience that radically calls into question their fundamental beliefs and knowledge:

> The person is confronted, out of the blue or without prior expectation of how the situation will unfold, by an event that categorically renders the experience inconsistent with what the person was anticipating or assuming. A powerful event, an accident, some grave personal news, the perception of an unusual or paranormal phenomenon ...
>
> It is primarily young people with an experiential intelligence, that is to say, the more creative and emotional, who tend to believe in and desire paranormal experiences, seeking among other things to fulfil a need for a relationship or deal with their fears. However, some of these experiences are in turn a source of anxiety and destabilisation due to the risk of paradigm disruption. A disruption which, if mishandled, if it does not result in a new stable internal structure, could be one of the keys to understanding the emergence of a schizotypal personality. (Mathijsen, 2011)

The worldview hypothesis receives strong confirmation from research on – of all things – *confirmation bias*.

CONFIRMATION BIAS

Confirmation bias is the tendency to seek out evidence consistent with one's worldview, while ignoring, dismissing or selectively reinterpreting evidence that contradicts that view (Nickerson, 1998). Raymond Nickerson defined the term in this way: 'Confirmation bias ... connotes the seeking or interpreting of evidence in ways that are partial to existing beliefs, expectations, or a hypothesis in hand' (p. 175). Nickerson quotes philosopher Francis Bacon (1620/1900), who explained paranormal beliefs by what he termed 'pernicious predetermination'. The 'pernicious predetermination' of confirmation bias involves selective perception of evidence and predisposes us to cling to views even after they have been unambiguously discredited. Lilienfeld, Ammirati, and Landfield describe some of the consequences of confirmation bias as follows:

> Like most large-scale cult movements … virtually all violent regimes fan the flames of extreme confirmation bias in their citizens, especially their youth, by presenting them with only one point of view and assiduously insulating them from all others. Under Hitler, the Nazi government effectively hijacked the educational system by mandating a uniform curriculum emphasizing Aryan superiority, Jewish depravity, and the necessity of racial purity and by subjecting teachers to a month of systematic training in Nazi principles …. Educational materials that 'contradict[ed] German feelings' were expunged, and teachers who deviated from the party line were fired. (2009: 391)

In a classic experiment, psychologists Hastorf and Cantril (1954) took advantage of a rivalry football game between Dartmouth and Princeton in 1951. The game had been a tough one, with escalating rough play, rule violations and penalties. Among the several injuries, the star Princeton quarterback was put out of action. Surveys of students after the game show that each side was convinced the other side was guilty of foul play. Since the entire game had been filmed, Hastorf and Cantril had 50 students from each college watch the movie soon after to detect as many violations by both sides as they could. Even though the students were in a lab experiment, which required accurate perception, they saw more infractions being committed by the team that was not their own.[4]

Confirmation bias leads one to seek out evidence supporting only one side – our own side – of a polarised issue. In the context of politics, this process is referred to as 'partisan selective exposure' (Stroud, 2010). A YouTube TED lecture about ecology attracts an audience consisting mainly of ecologists. A lecture on the 'End of Capitalism' attracts an audience of left-wing socialists and anarchists. A lecture on the 'Dangers of World Religions' attracts atheists. Much of the time authors, teachers, preachers, priests and prophets are 'preaching to the converted'. People have mindsets that foster 'positive illusions' (Taylor & Gollwitzer, 1995) and provide frameworks for organising new experience (Rosenthal, 1994). Snapchat, Instagram, Facebook and Twitter serve as echo chambers where people confirm and reinforce their pre-existing views (Flaxman, Goel, & Rao, 2016). One singer/band/team/film/supermarket/brand/whatever is the one and only 'hot' favourite of the day and the rest appear unprintably bad. Not only do people adhere like glue

---

[4]Chapters 5 and 6 give examples of subjective validation in remote viewing and ganzfeld ESP experiments.

to their beliefs, values and preferences, people use sticking plaster to cover over embarrassing cracks or blemishes.

It has been well documented for almost a century that an idea, thought or memory is never a copy but a construction based on an 'effort after meaning' (Bartlett, 1932; Neisser, 1967). What we experience as a solid foundation of 'truth' or 'fact' is actually a self-made creation. One's mental world is built on foundations that are not quite as robust as one may wish them to be. As noted, humans are rarely paragons of reason and rationality. Beliefs are not automatically updated by the best available evidence, but they have an active life of their own, as if fighting tenaciously for survival. One's basic beliefs guide our reading, our listening, our feelings, our trust in others and how to rationalise contrary information. There is an unavoidable striving for stability and equilibrium which resets thoughts and feelings to a fixed point (Marks, 2018).

Selective exposure protects one's beliefs from more dramatic forms of contradiction (Hart, Albarracín, Eagly, Brechan, Lindberg, & Merrill, 2009). When a famous illusionist/self-proclaimed psychic X visited the city of Dunedin, New Zealand, I identified seven different opportunities to obtain information about X's alleged psychic abilities: four media interviews, two newspaper stories and one stage performance. Of 17 Ps who, before X's visit, were already 'believers', 15 selected 3 or more of the available exposures. Of 20 'non-believers', only 10 selected as many as 3 exposures ($X2(1) = 6.13$; $P < 0.02$) (Marks, 1986).

Another type of confirmation bias occurs when we see a close correspondence between a specific piece of information and one's choices and preferences. Subjective validation involves seeing what we expect and wish to see. For example, in the context of a personality description of oneself, this phenomenon has been called 'personal validation' or the 'Forer Effect' (Forer, 1949). The phenomenon reveals a bias wherein one tends to consider a statement or another piece of information to be correct if it has any personal meaning or significance. The Forer Effect is discussed below.

People cannot always predict what they will read or hear and inevitably they end up facing information that does not support their views. In this case, one falls back on a second line of defence: one actually misperceives or misunderstands the data.

Whenever a person misreads unfavourable or neutral evidence as giving positive support to their beliefs, they are displaying confirmation bias. Self-deception – the worst kind!

THE FORER OR BARNUM EFFECT

Just for fun, I print here a 'personality reading'. Please try to read this paragraph with an open mind, putting aside your prejudices. (If you have seen this before, just skip to the next section.)

> You have a need for other people to like and admire you, and yet you tend to be critical of yourself. While you have some personality weaknesses you are generally able to compensate for them. You have considerable

unused capacity that you have not turned to your advantage. Disciplined and self-controlled on the outside, you tend to be worrisome and insecure on the inside. At times, you have serious doubts as to whether you have made the right decision or done the right thing. You prefer a certain amount of change and variety and become dissatisfied when hemmed in by restrictions and limitations. You also pride yourself as an independent thinker and do not accept others' statements without satisfactory proof. But you have found it unwise to be too frank in revealing yourself to others. At times you are extroverted, affable, and sociable, while at other times you are introverted, wary and reserved. Some of your aspirations tend to be rather unrealistic.

Now judge how well this description fits you. Is it:

- excellent;
- good;
- fair;
- poor;
- wrong?

Try to imagine how you would feel if you had answered a personality test three days ago and the above text was an 'official' report by a psychologist. Unless you are very skeptical, the chances are you would at least say 'fair' and more likely you would say 'good' or 'excellent'. That is what the majority of college students do. Here is an example of what one group of 66 students felt:

Table 3.1 Student responses to the Forer Effect (Marks & Kammann, 1980)

Rating of personality report	Number of students	%
Excellent	29	44
Good	30	45
Fair	6	9
Poor	1	2
Wrong	0	0
	66	

This result has been found repeatedly by psychologists all over the world for the past 70 years. It is an entertaining classroom demonstration of the power of 'cold reading' in the propagation of pseudo-scientific beliefs (Dunn & Chew, 2006). After giving each student the same personality report, we reveal the hoax immediately by asking if any student will volunteer to read aloud their personality report to the class. As the reader gets into the sketch there is a restless titter, then some groans, then laughter, then reading in chorus and finally applause. When the exercise is well handled, students strongly approve of the 10-minute deception as an excellent lesson in fallacious thinking.

This all began in Los Angeles in 1948 when psychologist Bertram Forer accused a night club graphologist of peddling the same statements that were true of practically everybody – the handwriting expert replied that their art must be valid because their clients said their readings were correct. This made Forer wonder: do people really believe such general statements as being uniquely true for them? To find out, they bought an astrology book and wrote the personality sketch above and, sure enough, the students were completely taken in (Forer, 1949).

Forer's result is a special case of subjective validation in which a person can always find ways to match themselves up with the description given. Our personalities are not as fixed and constant as we usually like to imagine. Everybody is shy in one situation, bold in another, clever at one task, bumbling at another, generous one day, selfish the next, independent in one group of people, but conforming in another group. Thus, we can usually find aspects of ourselves that will match up with a vague statement, although the specific examples of self will be different from one person to the next.

If you are told 'You have a great need for other people to like and admire you', you can recall your own particular thoughts of wanting to make friends or be more popular. If you are told nearly the opposite – for example, 'You don't need other people to be your true self' – you can recall personal times when you spoke your mind without regard for popular opinion or, alternatively, times when you just enjoyed being alone. When we examine Forer's sketch more closely, it actually contains several near opposites. Forer's Effect, which he called the 'fallacy of personal validation', casts a new light on occult effects that tell people who they are, such as astrology horoscopes, biorhythms, palmistry, graphology, tarot and fortune telling. In each case, a person is told (ambiguously) what kind of day to expect, what kind of a person they are, or what the future will bring (usually a 'tall, dark stranger'). Life itself is a fluctuating stream of diverse moments, and there is a good chance that we can remember or seize upon events that agree with the diagnosis. Like students who get the Forer Effect, we end up saying that it was so specific that it was right 'on the nose'. Meanwhile, the evidence against the validity of these occult prophecies keeps accumulating.

Every time a 'victim' receives a personal validation, they not only fool themselves, but they give the personality reader false confidence in their powers of diagnosis. The validity of fortune telling, horoscopes, palm reading, psychological testing and other diagnoses is in no way supported by the fact that people feel the readings are true. Classic!

ANOMALISTIC EXPERIENCES IN THE LABORATORY

As noted, people may develop paranormal beliefs by misinterpreting perfectly normal experiences as paranormal. It has not proved easy to identify the characteristics of people who tend to make these false positives. What if these kinds of misattributions could be captured and studied close up under laboratory conditions? This is exactly what two investigators at the University of Toulouse managed to achieve. Romain Bouvet and Jean-François Bonnefon (2015) used a laboratory setting to investigate how thinking styles can influence supernatural beliefs. They hypothesised that reflective or non-reflective thinkers would operate differently in interpreting a single uncanny event that invited a supernatural explanation. Bouvet and Bonnefon based their hypotheses on the 'Two Systems Theory' (outlined above). They used the 'Cognitive Reflection Test' (CRT) to evaluate the thinking style of different individuals (Table 3.2).

Table 3.2 The Cognitive Reflection Test (CRT; Frederick, 2005)

Below are several problems that vary in difficulty. Try to answer as many as you can.

(1) A bat and a ball cost $1.10 in total. The bat costs $1.00 more than the ball. How much does the ball cost? _____ cents

(2) If it takes 5 machines 5 minutes to make 5 widgets, how long would it take 100 machines to make 100 widgets? _____ minutes

(3) In a lake, there is a patch of lily pads. Every day, the patch doubles in size. If it takes 48 days for the patch to cover the entire lake, how long would it take for the patch to cover half of the lake? _____ days

These three questions tend to produce a compelling but incorrect intuitive response. Non-reflective thinkers tend to give a greater number of incorrect responses (trusting their initial intuitions), whereas reflective thinkers tend to give a greater number of correct responses (using analytic reasoning to override their initial intuitions). Like many of the more intriguing laboratory studies in psychology, there was a layer of deception. Bouvet and Bonnefon told their Ps that they were investigating astrological signs as a predictor of personality. Ps completed the CRT and the Paranormal Belief Scale (Tobacyk, 2004). After 8 minutes, the experimenter showed them 'their' personality profile, which always consisted of 10 classic Barnum statements. After studying the profile for 2 minutes, the Ps were asked to rate the accuracy of this description on a 7-point scale ranging from 'nothing like how I am' and 'exactly how I am'. This 'Barnum index' was used as a proxy measure of the Ps' acceptance of the efficacy of astrology for the personality profiling.

Ps' prior belief in the paranormal was found to have no significant effect on the Barnum index, but CRT scores were negatively associated with the Barnum index ($\beta = -.33$, $p < .004$, 95% CI = $[-.55, -.11]$). Both reflective and non-reflective thinkers were likely to acquiesce to the Barnum statements, but only reflective thinkers appeared to suppress that belief by deliberating on the dubious source of the Barnum description. One limitation of the study is that the Ps' longer term interpretations were not recorded. However, the result is consistent with the hypothesis that reflective thinkers can override the temporary intuition that astrology might result in an accurate personality profile. Non-reflective thinkers tended to remain convinced that the uncanny experience supported the accuracy of astrology. Bouvet and Bonnefon's findings support the hypothesis that 'metaphysical' thinkers are more reliant on spontaneous intuition in interpreting an anomalous experience as supernatural. Neat study!

DIFFERENTIATING ANOMALISTIC BELIEFS

Are beliefs in anomalous events all of a kind? Or do different beliefs have different properties and implications? Do conspiracy beliefs, such as the urban legend (UL) that the 1969 moon landings were staged, and paranormal beliefs, such as the belief that dreams prophesise the future, have similar causal mechanisms? Brotherton and French (2014) claim that conspiracy theories are associated with reasoning and heuristic biases just like paranormal beliefs. On the other hand, Dagnall et al. (2017) (ND's team) found significant divergence between UL and paranormal beliefs in their interactions with cognitive–perceptual factors. ND's team argue that validation of ULs mainly derives from acceptance of unreliable information as authentic and so they hypothesise a stronger relationship between endorsement of ULs and a lack of reality monitoring than for paranormal beliefs that are broader and more diffuse. ND's team invited a sample of 222 volunteers to complete an Urban Legends Questionnaire, the Reality Testing subscale of the Inventory of Personality Organisation, the Revised Paranormal Belief Scale and the Schizotypal Personality Questionnaire Brief. The cognitive–perceptual factor within the schizotypal scale was most strongly associated with anomalistic beliefs. However, complex relationships existed between reality testing, the cognitive–perceptual factor and anomalistic beliefs. Specifically, poor reality testing explained more variance in ULs, while the cognitive–perceptual factor of schizotypy accounted for more variance in belief in the paranormal. Thus ND's team suggested that anomalistic beliefs vary in nature and composition. Conspiracy beliefs are more strongly associated with conjunction, a specific bias of overstating the likelihood of multiple intersecting events, whereas paranormal beliefs are more closely associated with misperception of chance, the general bias to see casual relationships within random data. Cool!

CONSCIOUSNESS

It is essential to examine the extensive functions of consciousness as a predictive system, as the hub for action, perception, attention, affect regulation, cognition and information processing (Marks, 2018, 2019b). In a nutshell, consciousness is what enables the person to be an effective and intelligent decision maker. It constructs a personal and a public identity for the 'self' – it is the 'I' in 'I am thinking, therefore I am'. Consciousness is a centre for constructing and changing values and beliefs. It sets both altruistic and selfish goals, and anything in between. It serves as a coordinating centre for beliefs and values. Consciousness has 'layers' and 'levels' and is capable of dissociation, splitting and confusion. It can represent information, beliefs and values in an honest way or it can simulate, pretend and be deceitful. It can be subject to hearing of voices and other hallucinations. Consciousness is not in control of its contents at all times. It is subject to unbidden images, illusions and delusions. It fantasises, daydreams and dreams. Above all else, consciousness maintains psychological homeostasis for the whole organism, but it remains imperfect.

It is impossible to discuss the psychology of anomalistic beliefs and experiences in the absence of the hugely significant asset of consciousness. In describing *A General Theory of Behaviour*, I suggest:

> Organisms are adapted to each other and the environment because there is an inbuilt striving toward security, stability, and equilibrium … the primary motivation of all of consciousness and intentional behaviour is psychological homeostasis. Psychological homeostasis is as important to the organization of mind and behaviour as physiological homeostasis is to the organization of bodily systems. Consciousness is the 'I am' control centre for integration and regulation of (my) thoughts, (my) feelings, and (my) actions with (my) conscious mental imagery as foundation stones.
> (Marks, 2018)

The General Theory proposes a hierarchical control system with an executive level, a schema level and an automatised level. The executive level of consciousness controls and monitors the schema level, which in turn controls and monitors the automatised level. This system of levels enables moment-by-moment adjustments to goal-seeking behaviour. Goals are set at the executive level of consciousness, guided by values and beliefs that inform actions, inhibit actions, or reflect on what action to take, as the situation requires. Consciousness of any freely operating human would be 'tied up in knots' if the miniscule details of every elementary task needed volitional control. Mechanisms for automatic control are on a different level than volitional control. Volitional control with meta-level consciousness is only required when a new purpose for a new project is formulated. The key point is that a new project has a personal meaning and coherence within the life-space of a unique individual. Feeling, meaning, intention, and a sense of timing and flow are important influences on the quality and energy of actions. Feeling is integrated with the meaning and purpose of an action through the meta-system of consciousness.

The primary role of consciousness, therefore, according to the General Theory, is to make predictions, and here's the rub – *predictions are based on beliefs*. Consciousness has purpose, desire and intentionality, is social in nature, and the centre for integrating feelings, beliefs and actions. Consciousness has an inbuilt motivation to drive the organism towards pleasure and away from pain. It is a centre for perceptions, interoceptive and exteroceptive. Consciousness is a 'storehouse' of memories, based on schemas from the past, including autobiographical memories from which information and images can be retrieved. Following Frederic Bartlett (1932), it has been widely documented that human cognition is never a simple copying process, but entails a constructive striving or 'effort after meaning'. He proposed that remembering, imagining, thinking, reasoning and understanding are efforts to establish coherence. Using our beliefs, we try to forge connections, consistency and coherence between what we sense, feel and 'know'. If we encounter an obstacle to coherence – a misfit or an anomaly – then we strive mightily to overcome it, which leads directly to the feeling of surprise.

THE REWARD OF SURPRISE

Consciousness is hugely beneficial when taking decisions and making predictions. Optimal decisions and accurate predictions are essential for successful adaptation to the changing world. Accurate prediction is a hallmark of intelligence as it operates in evolution and individual development. An event that is unpredicted is salient to consciousness. A surprising event can take two main forms: a reward (positive valence) or a punishment (negative valence). A large chocolate birthday cake is, for most children, a reward. Being sent early to bed with no supper and all devices removed is a punishment. Rembrandt's little self-portrait is ambiguous – reward or punishment? – because the expression, in either case, looks much the same (Figure 3.3).

Figure 3.3   Rembrandt van Rijn, 1630. Reward or punishment?

Coincidences, prophetic dreams or OBEs are almost always unpredicted experiences that are remarkable, striking and strange. By their very nature, anomalous events are nearly always surprising. The surprisingness of anomalous experience, more often than not, functions as a reward. This reward of surprise reinforces a continuously updated sense of mastery and control within an increasingly uncertain environment. The intensity of surprise is in direct proportion to the impact of an experience. The question is, can any of these assumptions be quantified?

Measuring the difference between posterior and prior beliefs provides one helpful procedure to quantify surprisingness using a Bayesian framework. Itti and Baldi (2006) found that surprise is an attractor of human attention. Itti and Baldi measured the extent that humans look at surprising items in TV programmes and video games. Their findings showed that people are 'strongly attracted towards surprising locations, with 72% of all human gaze shifts directed towards locations more surprising than the average, a figure that rises to 84% when considering only gaze targets simultaneously selected by all subjects'. Itti and Baldi concluded that their definition of surprisingness – as the distance between the posterior and prior distributions of beliefs – would be applicable to sensory data in general. Cool conclusion!

Research in neuroscience also finds that surprisingness is attended to and acts as a reward for learning. In research with macaques, Hayden, Heilbronner, Pearson, and Platt (2011) found that surprisingness is explicitly calculated by the brain and is represented by modulations of the firing rates of single neurons in the dorsal anterior cingulate cortex in a probabilistically rewarded choice task. Preuschoff, 'tHart, and Eisenhauser (2011) found that surprise is signalled by pupil dilation. The surprise response was dissociated from the effect of the expected reward, which had little effect on the pupillary response. Claudio Lavin, René San Martin and Eduardo Rosales Jubal (2014) replicated the pupil dilatory effect of surprise in a learning gambling task.

Traditionally, the ancients interpreted anomalous events as signs or 'auguries' presaging events of significance. Auguries consisted of naturally occurring events such as thunder and lightning, chickens crossing the road, or anomalous events more generally. Today, we cannot escape – nor should we want to – the surprise that is hard-wired into our system. We go on high alert the moment anything unusual happens. It is in our very nature to give anomalies our undivided attention. Yet scientists fully aware of the significance of an inconvenient anomaly may choose to ignore it, wishing to remain undisturbed in their comfortable bubbles.

SUMMARY

It is logical to explore anomalistic experience in two stages. First, what happened? The experience must be considered in the light of established principles and processes of perception and cognition. Fast and slow thinking, worldview, cognitive factors, confirmation bias, subjective validation and the Forer Effect can all exert some influence on how an experience is perceived and interpreted. The search for the meaning is reinforcing and doubly so with the additional reward of surprise. After all of the 'dross' of bias, error and distortion have been eliminated, the second stage of interpretation is entered – what does it mean? Like gold dust in the prospector's pan, is an anomaly still there once all of the 'ballast' has been shaken out? Or have we found 'fool's gold'? Answering these questions is the focus for the remainder of this book.

QUESTIONS

1. Describe fast and slow thinking.
2. What is meant by a 'worldview'?
3. What is a 'confirmation bias'?
4. What is 'subjective validation'?
5. What is the Forer Effect?
6. Name five different functions that are proposed for consciousness.
7. What is meant by the 'reward of surprise'?

PART II
SUBJECTIVE ANOMALOUS EXPERIENCE CLAIMED TO BE PARANORMAL

4
SYNCHRONICITY

In antiquity, everything is symbol or emblem … the whole of nature is represented and disguised. (Voltaire, 1764/2019)

[F]or the 'one chance in a million' will undoubtedly occur, with no less and no more than its appropriate frequency, however surprised we may be that it should occur to us. (Fisher, 1937)

(Coincidences) are invariably fascinating: they suggest that everyday life can be surprising, or indeed uncanny, apparently guided by mysterious or even spiritual forces. They can be meaningful for the people who experience them, sometimes profoundly so, and can inform decisions about significant life events, such as careers or relationships. It is important to be clear that when we use the term, 'meaningful coincidence', we are not referring to confluences of thought and events that, though pleasing, are no more than happenstance. Rather, we refer to moments that can be taken to suggest the universe has a vested interest in our affairs and intervenes to bring about specific consequences. (Stockbridge & Wooffitt, 2019).

Outline: In exploring 'Synchronicity' we enter a netherworld, a 'noetic zone' between the outer world of concrete objects and the inner world of subjective meaning. The crucial importance of the subjective meaning of coincidences to the experiencer is ignored by the leading psychological theories. The in-depth analysis of any truly remarkable coincidence opens a realm that normally remains unconscious. An analysis of a single striking experience is presented. I choose a personal example rather than an already published coincidence, because this exposed the all-important subjective meaning. The coincidence is analysed from two contrasting points of view, the statistical and the psychological. The statistical odds of the event are estimated to be one-quintillion-to-one (10^{-18}). For psychological science, these odds are astronomical. The traditional scientific account holds that even this most unlikely of coincidences is inevitable within the laws of chance. An alternative hypothesis suggests an acausal, synchronistic mechanism. Indications from the chronology, context and consequences of the experience make this account plausible. However, no objective procedure exists for choosing between the two accounts and which one prefers is entirely subjective.

Everybody experiences coincidences. They are a statistical inevitability. They may also be more than a statistical artefact. Coincidences have been defined as the 'conjunction between inner and outer states: between thoughts, feelings, and images in one's mind and features of events in one's environment' (Beitman, Celebi & Coleman, 2009).

Few can match from their own supply of strange events that most famous of coincidences, the case of the two US Presidents, Abraham Lincoln and John F. Kennedy. A compendium of this curiosity was published in *TIME* magazine in 1964 with the following points:

Lincoln was elected in 1860, Kennedy in 1960.

Both were deeply involved in the civil rights struggle.

The names of each contain seven letters.

The wife of each President lost a son when she was First Lady.

Both Presidents were shot.

Both were shot on a Friday.

Both were shot in the head, from behind, and in the presence of their wives.

Both presidential assassins were shot to death before they could be brought to trial.

The names John Wilkes Booth and Lee Harvey Oswald each contain 15 letters.

Lincoln and Kennedy were succeeded by Southerners named Johnson.

Tennessee's Andrew Johnson, who followed Lincoln, was born in 1808; Texan Lyndon Johnson, who followed Kennedy, was born in 1908.

Etc., etc., etc. The complete list is much longer. I will not try the reader's patience by continuing it, as the whole of it is online.

One can hear the familiar toll bell of subjective validation (SV) and a chorus of skeptical derision. One of many troubles with synchronicity-type anomalies is that SV and confirmation bias apply almost endlessly. I confess that I am as big a sucker for SV as anybody else. In addition, there is often no objective way of computing the statistical probability of the event's occurrence by the random workings of chance. I describe a personal coincidence in detail: what happened, the estimated odds of its occurrence, and possible explanations, both statistical and psychological, and most importantly, its personal meaning. It is useful first to consider factors that might tip the balance over to interpret a coincidence as paranormal.

WHY INTERPRET A COINCIDENCE AS PARANORMAL?

There is a distinction to be made between an anomalous experience (AE) itself – i.e. the 'raw', immediate experience as it happens versus the interpretation of the experience (AEI). One way of thinking about the process is to consider two stages: 1) the fast, raw, sensory stage of the AE itself; 2) the more processed, slower stage of the AEI. Imagine this scenario: walking in a moonlit forest at night and one sees (Stage 1) a shimmering, translucent shape flickering under the moonlight (the AE). Stage 2, a few moments later, one makes the determination that the sensory data is a ghost, or that it is actually nothing more than a shimmering, translucent shape flickering under the moonlight (AEI). These two interpretations provide contrasting theories of the AE: on one hand, 'P-Theory' uses paranormal ideas of the Metaphysical Worldview, versus, on the other hand, the standard scientific description drawn from the Empiricist Worldview, 'N-Theory'. These two contrasting interpretations are always available for any anomalous experience. People vary in which of these two, P or N Theory, they usually prefer.

It is noticeable that these two theories are not symmetrical: N Theory always supersedes P Theory. The Law of Parsimony[1] dictates that N Theory is normative, mainstream and primary, while P Theory is exceptional, side-stream and secondary. If one can explain an experience using N Theory, then P Theory must be automatically ruled out because 'entities' such as ESP should not be invented needlessly. Thus, a P Theory interpretation is always contingent upon the failure of all the N Theory ones one can think of. An event can only be interpreted as evidence of the 'paranormal' after all of the so-called 'rational' and 'scientific' explanations have been systematically and mercilessly eliminated. If this lop-sided situation did not exist, there would be no need for this book. Thus, any analysis of the meaning and nature of experience is weighted permanently towards a conservative preference for N Theory. Sounds unfair – right? That's the main reason why the writer Arthur Koestler got so hot under his collar about mechanistic science, as we shall learn later.

The same logic applies to scientific studies. The necessary condition to exhaustively disconfirm every possible N Theory interpretation of any anomaly puts P Theory to disadvantage. The bottomless bucket of N Theory never empties. P Theory is always vulnerable to criticism by N theorists who never run out of N Theory explanations. If no other N hypothesis can be verified, then the default position for any N Theorist is to shout 'fraud' (or to whisper in case there's a lawyer nearby). Almost every skeptic I have known, except the late Mark Hansel, admit to believing that fraud occurs much more generally then they can afford to say publicly, owing to the libel laws.[2]

---

[1] The Law of Parsimony, or Occam's razor, states that the most simple of two competing theories should be the preferred one, and that entities should not be multiplied needlessly.
[2] With the possible exception of Randi, Mark Hansel was the only one who had the 'balls' to come out and say it.

Next, we turn to look at studies of the varying levels of acceptance of AE and AEI that exist across people. Most of these studies are carried out by died-in-the-wool skeptics.

The distinction between AE and AEI is nicely implemented in the 'Survey of Anomalous Experiences', a questionnaire of 20 items that separates reports of anomalous or inexplicable events from the interpretations of the events as paranormal (Irwin, Dagnall, & Drinkwater, 2013). The P is asked to click on the option that most closely represents their own position; if they have had an experience more than once, they choose the option that is most often the case. The instructions state:

> Surveys suggest that anomalous, uncanny or seemingly inexplicable experiences are very common in our society. This questionnaire asks if you personally have had some of these experiences, and asks also what you make of them. For each item simply click on the option that most closely represents your own position; if you have had the experience more than once, choose the option that is most often the case.
>
> Q1. I have had a dream about something of which I was previously unaware, and subsequently the dream turned out to be accurate.

The response options are as follows:

> 'Yes, and it must have been an instance of telepathy or ESP.
> Yes, but it was probably just a coincidence or unwitting insight.
> No.' (Irwin et al., 2013)

In the previous chapter we looked at processes that are thought to influence why somebody might be drawn towards, or away from, an AEI. Here, I consider other factors that are relevant to striking coincidences. Typically in such studies, there is predilection for crude binary categories ('sheep' vs 'goats', etc). Some of these factors are drawn from the 'Survey of Anomalous Experiences' by Irwin et al., (2013).

Cognitive deficits

This topic risks raising the hackles of even the most calm and collected reader, especially psi believers. I apologise in advance for any upset, but it would be remiss of me to leave it out, much as one might wish to do so. To my way of thinking, this particular hypothesis sinks to the very bottom of the pig bucket labelled 'Egality'. The 'cognitive deficits hypothesis' holds that *believers in the paranormal are cognitively 'inferior' to disbelievers* (Alcock, 1981; Alcock & Otis, 1980; Gray & Mill, 1990; Irwin, 1993) – i.e. in common language, psi believers are 'a bit thick'.[3] I strongly disagree with this opinion because the evidence to support this view simply is not out there.

---

[3] The cognitive deficits hypothesis is reminiscent of the eugenicists' racial hypothesis of intelligence for which the evidence is artefactual (Marks, 2010). The deficits approach is countered by the evidence that coincidences are functional as a means of causal discovery (Griffiths & Tenenbaum, 2007; Johansen & Osman, 2015). Yet cognitivists neglect the personal meaning of coincidences that makes them so striking.

Chris Roe (1999) suggested that any of the deficits reported by researchers could simply be experimental artefacts. Roe controlled for the perceived methodological shortcomings of previous studies by dividing 117 Ps into groups of believers, neutrals and disbelievers. Each P evaluated an abbreviated experimental report that was either sympathetic or unsympathetic to parapsychology. Roe found no differences in assessment ratings and so failed to replicate the deficit effect, supporting the artefact interpretation. Overall, findings on cognitive deficit have been inconsistent and unimpressive. For example, Wiseman and Watt (2006) concluded a review with the conclusion that: 'with the possible exception of the relationship between belief in psychic ability and performance on syllogistic reasoning tasks, *the existing literature does not support the notion that believers and disbelievers in psychic ability differ in their levels of general cognitive functioning*' (p. 5). Well said!

More recent studies, however, claim to find evidence of deficits, but the level of control of the sheep–goat effect is unknown. For example, Matute, Yarritu, and Vadillo (2011) proposed that illusions of causality produce paranormal beliefs so that the prevalence of paranormal beliefs in society is associated with a 'general bias towards perceiving a causal link where no evidence exists' – i.e. an illusion of causality. Blanco, Barberia, and Matute (2015) found that paranormal believers 'expose themselves to biased information and develop more causal illusions than nonbelievers in the laboratory', but only when the information is ambiguous. Rogers, Fisk, and Lowrie (2016) found that paranormal belief was associated with more conjunction errors (CEs), especially for confirmatory over disconfirmatory conjunctions. Along similar lines, Rogers, Fisk, and Lowrie (2017) found that belief in psychokinesis predicted more CEs, that belief in extrasensory perception and life after death did not predict CEs, and that less-qualified individuals made more CEs, a somewhat mixed bag of findings. The data from Dagnall et al. (2014) supported the notion that paranormal belief arises from a bias associated with misperceived randomness and did not replicate the findings of Rogers, Davis, and Fisk (2009) and Rogers, Fisk, and Wiltshire (2011) in finding no consistent relationship between the level of paranormal belief and conventional conjunction problems.

Emotion-based reasoning

Emotion-based reasoning (EBR) is the tendency to use inferences that are emotionally appealing rather than logically derived. EBR has been found to predict the intensity of paranormal belief. Irwin et al. (2013) and Dagnall, Irwin and Drinkwater (2017) found associations between proneness to AEs and emotion-based reasoning and suspension of reality testing. They also found an association between proneness to paranormal attributions of AEs and emotion-based reasoning.

One of the strongest advocates of the emotional thinking/cognitive deficits viewpoint of AE is Professor Marjaana Lindeman (2017) of the University of Helsinki. In the *Encyclopedia of Personality and Individual Differences*, Lindeman states – and, for the sake of accuracy, I quote verbatim:

> These studies demonstrate clearly that people who believe in paranormal phenomena do not enjoy intellectual challenges .... When compared with nonbelievers, believers prefer more simple to complex problems, and they have lower cognitive motivation to analyze one's thinking and the available information. They also score lower on the Actively Open-Minded Thinking Scale, which measures openness to new ideas, spending time on problems before giving up, and willingness to change one's beliefs, and finally, to switch perspectives (Sá et al. 1999). Instead of thinking analytically, believers prefer to rely on their intuitions, go by their instincts, and use their heart as a guide for action. Moreover, if the effect of intuitive thinking style is separated out, the relationship between gender and paranormal beliefs decreases. Women's higher intuitive thinking style may thus partly explain the recurrent finding that women endorse paranormal beliefs more than men do. (Lindeman, 2017: 2)

Or could it be, à la Lindeman, that women do not 'enjoy intellectual challenges' as much as men do? That idea must go down like a lead balloon in a progressive country like Finland. There is a lot to unpack here, but the message is clear: *'people who believe in paranormal phenomena do not enjoy intellectual challenges'*. One could perhaps rephrase the message as follows: *'scientists who do not believe in paranormal phenomena do not enjoy intellectual challenges'*.

Suspension of reality testing

One popular theory suggests that psychological processes underlying the formation of coincidences and other AEs may have a common cause with delusional ideation. Suspension of reality testing, failing to test inferences with rational assessment and re-evaluation, correlates with paranormal belief (Dagnall et al., 2010; Irwin, 2003, 2004). Irwin, Dagnall, and Drinkwater (2012) investigated the relationship between paranormal beliefs and distortions in reasoning associated with psychotic delusions. A sample of 250 people completed questionnaires measuring the intensity of paranormal beliefs, schizotypal biases in reasoning and the need for closure. Dimensions of paranormal belief were found to be associated with reasoning biases. Pechey and Halligan (2012) found that paranormal beliefs were associated with delusion-like beliefs, but non-significantly with scientific, political and social beliefs. Irwin et al. (2013) also found an association between proneness to paranormal attributions and suspension of reality testing. Whose idea of 'reality', one might wonder?

Another predictor of proneness to AE is schizotypy, a degree of subclinical psychotic-like thinking and behaviour that is distributed across the population (Claridge & Beech, 1995). It must be noted that a high schizotypy score does not imply any actual pathology (Goulding, 2004). One component of schizotypy is unusual perceptual experience (Mason, Claridge, & Jackson, 1995), and there is evidence that the association between schizotypy and unusual experiences may extend beyond perceptual experiences to include a range of AEs (Alvarez López, Teixeira do Carmo, & Pueyo, 2000; Byrom, 2009; Clancy, McNally, Schacter, Lenzenweger, & Pitman, 2002; Farias, Claridge, & Lalljee, 2005; Fleck et al., 2008; Koffel & Watson, 2009; Maltby & Day, 2002; Mason & Claridge, 1999; McCreery & Claridge, 2002; Parra, 2006; Wolfradt, Oubaid, Straube, Bischoff, & Mischo, 1999). In a study by Irwin et al. (2013), proneness to AEs was positively related to schizotypal tendencies. In my own studies, I reached a similar conclusion (Marks, 2006).

Executive dysfunction

Believers in the paranormal are also claimed to exhibit 'defects in central executive functioning'. Wain and Spinella (2007) argued that, like moral and religious beliefs, paranormal beliefs play a role in guiding people's behaviour. From this conjunction, they suggest that the same central organising neurobiological components in the prefrontal cortical system represent all three types of behavioural control. They examined whether the three areas of belief were associated with executive functions as measured by the Executive Function Inventory in a community sample. While religious beliefs related positively to both moral attitudes and paranormal beliefs, moral attitudes were unrelated to paranormal beliefs that related inversely to impulse control and organisation. However, the results did not fully replicate. Irwin et al. (2013) found that the claimed association between proneness to AEs and executive dysfunction was only partially confirmed. They also found no significant association between proneness to paranormal attributions and executive dysfunction; and the association between proneness to paranormal attributions and executive dysfunction schizotypal tendencies was only partially supported. There is a lot of food for thought here, but also some methodological problems that leave matters undecided.

Problems with cognitive and personality research

The majority of the research on cognitive and personality factors has used cross-sectional designs, prohibiting conclusions about causation. In addition, it is notable how few of the correlation coefficients between the variables reach even the modest figure of .50, meaning that a large majority of the variability is unaccounted for (more than 75% of variance). Another common methodological problem with AE studies is the 'sheep–goat' effect. Research led by skeptics may tend to reproduce the investigators' own skeptical attitudes by inhibiting the honest expression of paranormal beliefs (Irwin, 1991; Roe, 1999). This is the widely documented problem of 'demand characteristics' (Orne, 1962): the professor knows what she believes, expects and wants, and credit-point-accumulating 'subjects' fall into line. When researchers who are neutral or positive towards parapsychology attempt to replicate the findings of skeptical investigators, the findings are often inconsistent. However, neutral or believer-led studies are equally vulnerable by containing the opposite kind of bias. Solutions to the sheep–goat issue include employing neutral data-collectors, double-masking controls, or, at the very least, keeping the investigators' beliefs masked from the Ps. Deliberate control for the sheep–goat effect is possible using sheep and goat investigators, and comparing their findings (e.g. Wiseman & Schlitz, 1997). For all these different reasons, it is always possible, after reviewing the entire collection of factors, one may still end up with an 'AEI' that remains obscure and uncertain. Such is the case in the example to follow, an uncanny event I call the 'Chiswick Coincidence'.[4]

Coincidence, what Jung called synchronicity, can be highly puzzling, a contiguity[5] of events that appear to have no causal connection between one another. From this first-hand experience, and a number of others, I am aware that a coincidence that seems to go way beyond the laws of chance can elicit a strong sense of the paranormal. I describe and analyse here without embellishment the 'Chiswick Coincidence' (CC) for the light it may shed on anomalistic experience.[6]

THE CHISWICK COINCIDENCE

23 August 2018: At 35,000 feet on the midday flight from Marseille to Heathrow, wondering how to spend the afternoon. Unable to go straight home because an estate agent has arranged a viewing with a tenant, so how would I fill this time? I decide to go for lunch at one of my regular haunts, a pub by the Thames called the 'City Barge'.

A few seconds after this decision, I open my kindle and select to continue reading *The Man Who Was Thursday: A Nightmare* by Gilbert K. Chesterton (GKC; 1908 [2004]), that I had started a few days earlier. I flip the first page

---

[4] Chiswick is a district in West London.
[5] Contiguity refers to sequential occurrence or proximity of stimulus and response, causing their association in the mind.
[6] Any rational reader may well view my 'Chiswick Coincidence' with a healthy degree of skepticism. However, please use as much empathy as you can muster and it may begin to make sense. Ask what you would believe under similar circumstances.

where I see in stark black-and-white a description of that very place which, moments previously, I had decided to visit:

> 'I think,' said Gregory, with placid irrelevancy, 'that we will call a cab.' He gave two long whistles, and a hansom came rattling down the road. The two got into it in silence. Gregory gave through the trap the address of an obscure public-house on the Chiswick bank of the river. The cab whisked itself away again, and in it these two fantastics quitted their fantastic town.

The match between a free and voluntary thought to visit this very specific location and Gregory's choice to do exactly the same thing, seemed remarkable. The immediate impact was profound. It was as if I had been hit on the head with a hammer. A door had opened to a numinous world of strangeness that usually lies below the threshold of one's consciousness. One encounters this noetic zone only in unique, special circumstances. I have previously glimpsed the noetic world during other wondrous events, listed here in no particular order:

- A near-death experience (see Chapter 10).
- Hypnotically suggested past-life regression.
- Lucid dreams – e.g. dreams of flying.
- Dreams of events never experienced – e.g. a dream of a powerful earthquake.
- Seeing the aurora borealis and the aurora Australis.
- Seeing fish and coral when snorkelling in the Indian Ocean.
- Seeing the Egyptian pyramids through a plane window.
- Seeing icebergs breaking away from the Greenland ice-shelf through a plane window.

For me, the Chiswick Coincidence is in the same league. The 'noetic zone' is a realm one enters on rare occasions. The encounter is always surprising. Like other coincidences that I have experienced, the Chiswick anomaly is complex and multi-layered; an experience I will never forget. This case study begins with a description of the experience. I will follow the recommended procedures described in the Appendix:

> There is always a need to authenticate such cases by carefully checking the circumstances and the reliability of reporting together with any evidence that may be available from other sources. However even elaborate efforts made towards substantiating spontaneous experiences may fail to reveal definite evidence that can be relied upon to draw definite conclusions. The case study is an exploratory method which is difficult if not impossible

to convert into reliable scientific data. However, the case method is an important source of ideas concerning the properties of psi as it functions spontaneously even if it is impossible to reach any definite conclusions.

With these provisos, I turn to analyse this experience from the perspective of seven overlapping layers.[7]

SEVEN LAYERS OF SYNCHRONICITY

First layer

The CC consisted of two elements:

> **Element 1:** A firm called 'Chestertons' would be showing my apartment to a potential tenant.

A few seconds later:

> **Element 2:** I open my kindle and read a novel by G. K. Chesterton.

The first layer of coincidence is that the original firm of estate agents called Chestertons[8] is the ancestral family of the author GKC.[9]

Second layer

The second layer is the fact that the decision to go to the Chiswick riverside pub was followed a few seconds later by reading about a 'public-house on the Chiswick bank of the river'. We need to know a little more about a) the pub, and b) the kindle.

Historical records indicate that the City Barge has existed since 1484 when it was known as 'The Navigator's Arms'. Its first appearance in the licensing lists was in 1787 when it was the 'City Navigation Barge'. As the 'City Barge' it was refurbished in 2014. Historical sources point to at least five or six pubs on the Chiswick side of the river at the time of GKC's story. The pub GKC had in mind could have been any or none of these; perhaps it was only a figment of his imagination. However, two clues make the City Barge a good candidate. Photographs of the City Barge from 1910, two years after the publication of *The Man Who Was*

---

[7]The reader might care to explore a personal coincidence using this method of 'layer analysis' which can reveal the fuller significance of synchronicity.

[8]In more than 200 years since being established in 1805, the firm has undergone many changes. Full details of the company are posted at: https://en.wikipedia.org/wiki/Chestertons

[9]The reader should bear in mind that, in London, there are hundreds of different estate agents.

Thursday, show Thames barges tied up directly outside the City Barge. Also, when the two characters in GKC's story, Gregory and Syme, leave the pub, they go out by the river-side door and 'close to the opening lay a dark dwarfish steam-launch'. This description fits the City Barge perfectly.[10]

A Kindle is a portable library. At that time, mine had 1.33 GB containing hundreds of books on my impossible wishlist of reading material, consisting of the complete works of Shakespeare, Chaucer, Dickens, Joyce, Austen, Pepys, Swift and Zola. On the date in question, there were 498 works containing 146,817 pages.[11] With 350 words per page, there were at least 50 million words on my Kindle. *The odds of reading the particular five words 'public-house on the Chiswick bank' on the very first page that I opened is around one-in-10 million (10^{-7}).* But the story does not end here.

Third layer

I checked my diary for the things I would be doing on the days immediately following the date of this event (23 August 2018). My diary says I had a meeting with my commissioning editor, Robert Patterson, to discuss this very book. Now that seems curious.

Fourth layer

The plan to write this book meant that I would need new material. Although I was at the earliest stages when the Chiswick incident happened, I can imagine no more suitable illustration for a book on anomalistic experience than this very incident. Reflecting back, I can also see the part played by the CC in resetting my paranormal 'Belief Barometer'.

Fifth layer

Enter – or, I should say, re-enter – Martin Gardner (MG), the mathematical wizard, prolific author, and brilliant friend. Martin had kindly written the Foreword to two of my previous 'psi' books, *The Psychology of the Psychic* (Marks & Kammann, 1980; Marks, 2000). Martin died in 2010, leaving a legacy of hundreds of literary and scholarly works and a readership of millions (e.g. *Fads and Fallacies in the Name of Science*, 1957; *Mathematics, Magic and Mystery*, 1956; *The Annotated Alice: The Definitive Edition. Lewis Carroll*, 2000).

---

[10] The City Barge is a 10-minute drive from Bedford Park, the 'queer artificial village' called 'Saffron Park' that features in GKC's novel.

[11] With the settings on the Kindle as they were at that time, there are 4–5 Kindle pages to every printed page.

But there was something that I hadn't previously known. In researching *The Man Who Was Thursday*, I discovered a Special Annotated Edition of the Chesterton book by none other than Martin Gardener (1999). Discovering this special annotated edition seemed enigmatic. The connection between Gilbert K. Chesterton, Martin Gardner and this very book does not end here.

Sixth layer

As Chesterton noted, 'hardly anybody who looked at the title ever seems to have looked at the sub-title; which was "A Nightmare," and the answer to a good many critical questions' (*Autobiography*, Kindle Locations, 1301–3). Two key themes of *The Man Who Was Thursday* are *free will* and *evil*. The CC helped to cement a change in my stance from skeptic/disbeliever to zetetic enquirer. My eyes were opened to the genius Gilbert K. Chesterton, a very special writer, and to his amazing metaphysical novel. *The Man Who Was Thursday* has been rated as one of the greatest works of 20th-century literature. I quote from the American Chesterton Society website (www.chesterton.org/who-is-this-guy/):

> Gilbert Keith Chesterton (1874–1936) cannot be summed up in one sentence. Nor in one paragraph .... But rather than waiting to separate the goats from the sheep, let's just come right out and say it: G.K. Chesterton was the best writer of the 20th century .... The reason he was the greatest writer of the 20th century was because he was also the greatest thinker of the 20th century .... What was it he defended? He defended 'the common man' and common sense. He defended the poor. He defended the family. He defended beauty. And he defended Christianity and the Catholic Faith.

It was a pleasant surprise to read that GFK defended the 'common man', common sense and the poor. Gilbert Chesterton made no secret of the fact that he believed in God, prayer and the afterlife.

Seventh layer

Like GKC, MG believed in God, prayer and the afterlife. In his autobiography, MG stated that he loved reading:

> anything by G. K. because of his never-ceasing emotions of wonder and gratitude to God, not only for such complicated things as himself, his wife, and the universe, but for such 'tremendous trifles' (as he once called them) as rain, sunlight, flowers, trees, colours, stars, even stones that 'shine along the road/That are and cannot be.' (Gardner, 2013: 205)

GKC and the philosopher-poet Miguel de Unamuno were Martin's two mentors. Martin's autobiography mentions God no less than 128 times.[12] He wrote:

> Just as knowing how a magic trick is done spoils all its wonder, so let us be grateful that wherever science and reason turn they plunge finally into stygian darkness. I am not in the least annoyed because I do not understand time and space, or consciousness, or free will, or evil, or why the universe is made the way it is. I am relieved beyond measure that I do not need to comprehend more than dimly the nature of God or an afterlife. I do not want to be blinded by truths beyond the capacity of my eyes and brain and heart. I am as contented as a Carnap with the absence of rational methods for penetrating ultimate mysteries. (2013: 341)

For a lot of different reasons, and in completely unexpected ways, the Chiswick Coincidence 'opened my eyes' to a clearer understanding of somebody I thought I knew. It added meaning to other life experiences. At a seventh layer, I find that the coincidence revealed yet another synchronicity: the shared values and beliefs of Martin Gardner, and a man I could never have met, Gilbert K. Chesterton, author of a great metaphysical novel. These events exerted a strong influence on the content of this chapter. In that sense, the whole incident was an exercise in one kind of 'precognition': inspiring future action.

THE COMBINED PROBABILITY OF THE SEVEN LAYERS

Hume (1902/1748) stated: 'That no testimony is sufficient to establish a miracle, unless the testimony be of such a kind, that its falsehood would be more miraculous, than the fact, which it endeavours to establish'. Bearing Hume's maxim in mind, I estimate here the probabilities for the synchronicity at each layer followed by a combined probability estimate.[13]

> **Layer 1:** The probability that the estate agent and GKC were from a single family is estimated to be 10^{-3}. This estimate takes into account the number of West London estate agencies (500+) and the chance that the agent I had previously selected would have a familial connection with GKC, the central character in this episode.

---

[12] By comparison, Chesterton's autobiography mentions 'God' 62 times.
[13] The skeptics may argue that calculating a probability of an event after it has happened is problematic because, after the fact, the probability of the event is 100%. However, this argument is a red herring. We know the chance of obtaining a six from the roll of a die is one-sixth both before and after the die is rolled. The same point applies here because the number of alternative outcomes can be directly computed.

Layer 2: The probability that thinking of, and planning to visit, the Chiswick riverside pub would be followed a few seconds later by seeing the words 'public-house on the Chiswick bank' is estimated to be 10^{-7}. This estimate takes into account the huge quantity of Kindle text (in excess of 50 million words) that I could have selected to read on this occasion.[14]

Layer 3: The probability that on the same visit to London I would meet my publisher to discuss this very book is estimated to be 10^{-1}, which aligns with the frequency of such meetings, approximately once a year.

Layer 4: The probability that the CC would be a useful experience to put into this book is estimated to be 10^{-1}.

Layer 5: Taking into account the fact that, before this incident, I knew nothing about GKC, the probability that somebody who had written Foretwords to two of my previous books, Martin Gardner, would also have written a Special Annotated Edition of *The Man Who Was Thursday* is estimated to be 10^{-4}.

Layer 6: The probability that lifelong personal values, to defend the 'common man', common sense and the poor, would correspond to GFK's values is estimated to be 10^{-1}.

Layer 7: The synchronicity in values and beliefs between Martin Gardner and Gilbert K. Chesterton, author of *The Man Who Was Thursday*, is estimated to be almost a certainty. Martin loved GKC's writing. I doubt that he would have done so without shared values and beliefs.

In addition, it is necessary to consider the boundary conditions. An aircraft on a short-haul flight offers a variety of activities: doing nothing, doing a puzzle, watching a film, listening to music, snoozing, chatting, looking out of the window, drinking a tea or coffee, reading a newspaper, magazine, book or Kindle. I estimate the probability that I chose to read my Kindle to be 10^{-1} (one in ten).

The combined probability **P** of the seven synchronicities and the boundary condition is:

$$\mathbf{P} = 10^{-3} \times 10^{-7} \times 10^{-1} \times 10^{-1} \times 10^{-4} \times 10^{-1} \times 1 \times 10^{-1}$$
$$= 10^{-18}$$

i.e. one in one quintillion (a million, million, million).[15]

---

[14] An alternative computation of the odds is as follows. Consider, X, the area defined by 'public house on the Chiswick bank' as a 1 km by 25 m wide stretch of the river bank = 1/40th sq km. If Y is the UK with an area of 242,495 sq km, the odds of selecting X from Y are X/Y = 1/9,699,800 or 1 in 10 million. These odds are a massive underestimate. I could have thought of any place in the world I had ever visited, meaning that Y would be many orders of magnitude larger.

[15] A quintillion is 1 followed by 18 zeros: 1,000,000,000,000,000,000. Big!

BOX 4.1 HOW LARGE IS ONE QUINTILLION?

One quintillion is so huge, it is difficult to comprehend without a concrete illustration. Imagine that we convert this number into rice grains – one quintillion rice grains. The rice grains are all husked and light brown in colour. Completely at random, imagine that I replace one of the rice grains with a grain-sized gold nugget.

There are 15,432 grains in each kilogram. The total weight of the one quintillion rice grains would be 64,800,414,722,654 kilograms. With a density of 753 kg per cubic metre, the rice would take up a volume of 86,056,327,653 cubic metres. Comparing this volume to the world's largest mountain, **this amount is one-and-a-half Mount Everests**!

For the last 20 years, global rice consumption has averaged close to 54 kilograms per person (see: www.statista.com/statistics/256002/global-per-capita-rice-use-since-2000/). **The enormous mountain created by one quintillian rice grains could feed the entire world population of 7.7 billion for 156 years. The odds of finding a single grain of gold inside this enormous rice mountain are identical to the odds of the Chiswick Coincidence.**

Figure 4.1 Mount Everest

Image © Pavel Novak, reproduced under a Creative Commons Attribution-Share Alike 2.5 Generic license (https://creativecommons.org/licenses/by-sa/2.5/). No changes made.

These odds are so astronomical that one must consider the possibility of a paranormal explanation. Not to do so would be irrational and contrary to open inquiry.

EXPLAINING THE COINCIDENCE

How might this seven-layered, one-in-one-quintillion coincidence be scientifically explained? One can consider the following as viable candidates.

Hypothesis 1 – N Theory: Coincidences are bound to occur every once in a while, purely by chance

The nugget of the coincidence lies in Layer 2:

> **Event A:** choosing by free will to go to a particular place for lunch. (GPS: 51.486747,–0.282573 DD).
>
> **Event B:** choosing by free will to read moments later a story that contains an exact reference to the same place: a 'public-house on the Chiswick bank of the river'.

Considered independently, neither event is extraordinary. Only their near simultaneity appears extraordinary. If I had read the passage a few months, weeks or even days previously or at some time in the future, I simply would have noticed that I knew just such a place, but I would not have blinked an eyelid. Any Londoner is familiar with the experience of seeing references to familiar places in novels or movies, and the reference to the Chiswick pub would not have seemed remarkable at all.[16]

It is necessary to consider the possibility of a hidden cause, something that might create the illusion of synchronicity when it isn't really there. One possibility is that GKC may have frequently mentioned places in and around Chiswick, in which case the coincidence might not be quite so odd after all. It is possible to test this hypothesis. It is said that Chesterton was one of the most prolific writers of all time. He wrote around 80 books, several hundred poems, 200 short stories, 4,000 essays and several plays. I downloaded the *Delphi Collected Works of GK Chesterton* onto my Kindle. Using the Kindle search function, I found only seven occurrences of the word 'Chiswick' in GKC's Collected Works and only one reference to a pub on the river. *This makes the coincidence seem even odder.*

---

[16]Diaconis and Mosteller (1989: 859–60) suggest that 'multiple endpoints' can be as personally significant as the one that actually occurred – i.e. the reference to the 'obscure public house on the Chiswick side of the river' could have been a reference to many other personally significant places, reducing the odds. However, in this case, only one specific reference to a pub on the Chiswick bank of the Thames could have matched my specific plan to visit the City Barge immediately after arriving at Heathrow airport. There could have been references to more generic categories such as 'going for lunch by the river' that would also have matched the plan, albeit less specifically, but there weren't any.

Another possibility is that I may have already seen the passage on a previous occasion. This possibility can be safely eliminated for two reasons. First, if I had already seen this passage, I would already have noticed the connection between one of my favourite riverside haunts and GKC mentioning it. In this case, seeing it for a second time would not have seemed so very remarkable. Second, a Kindle automatically remembers the point reached at a previous reading and obligingly opens the selected book at that page. In my previous reading of the book, I had left the story at the page immediately prior to the page where the crucial passage is located.

The ultimate skeptical explanation is possibly the most accurate and the one most difficult to discount. It says that coincidences are just that – coincidences; that a coincidence is a coincidence is a coincidence – a random, chance kind of thing. Something similar to the CC is happening with someone somewhere every second of the day. When a striking coincidence happens, it is bound to attract attention, but it is purely the wheels of chance that are turning and nothing else.

Hypothesis 2 – P Theory: Reverse causality by an unconscious reading of the text triggered my decision to visit the pub on the Chiswick side of the river

What about this paranormal interpretation? It is essential to allow P Theory a fair hearing. Just to recap, the two key elements were:

> **Event A:** deciding by free will to go for lunch at the City Barge. (GPS: 51.486747,-0.282573 DD).
>
> **Event B:** deciding by free will to read, only moments later, a story, which contains an incident about a 'public-house on the Chiswick bank of the river'.

What if Event B occurred before Event A? This P Theory explanation would run as follows: before I switch on the Kindle, I 'see' the story about the Chiswick pub inside my Kindle using an unconscious process of clairvoyance. Seeing this text at an unconscious level triggers my decision to go to the City Barge. After I switch on the Kindle and read the text, this time at a conscious level, I feel wonderment and surprise: 'How could this happen?' In reality, this is not a coincidence at all – *it was my unconscious reading about the Chiswick pub that caused me to make the decision to visit it*. There are other P Theory explanations that are consistent with the event. One involves precognition: I knew I was going to read about a pub on the Chiswick side of the river and this foreknowledge triggered my plan to go there. This P Theory account is available in the explanation of synchronicity by C. G. Jung (1960) but it is rarely considered seriously in psychological science.

If one remains open to the possibility of psi, there can be no problem in considering (without necessarily accepting) P Theory explanations.[17] If skeptics object that there is no evidence for clairvoyance, unconscious perception, or precognition, that it just cannot be so, the P Theorist might confidently retort: 'Normally, yes, you are correct, but on this occasion all three happened.'

The stubborn fact remains that there is no rational way of resolving this matter. Unless one is willing to rule out one form of explanation by fiat, then which interpretation one accepts rests purely upon subjective judgement and taste based on one's willingness or not to entertain a paranormal interpretation. A skeptic must refuse a paranormal interpretation and always choose the statistical account, however long the odds against it. A believer may choose the paranormal account if they so wish, or they can choose to discount it. What should the zetetic do? I believe the zetetic should aim to consider with care every possible explanation before reaching a provisional conclusion. It should always be remembered that the case for unconscious clairvoyance and precognition remains unconfirmed, but neither has it been disconfirmed.

Summary and conclusion

On a homeward journey, involving multiple free choices, a remarkable set of synchronicities happened (Figure 4.2). The laws of probability suggest that the odds against this coincidence set are one-quintillion-to-one. Both 'N Theory' and 'P Theory' interpretations are available and no definitive method exists for deciding between them. This incertitude requires a neutral stance and a degree of humility any definite interpretation of this particular AE.[18] My search for a scientific explanation was matched by an equally compelling realisation that there might not be one. Only personal preference – based purely on intuition – allows one to reach a conclusion. In either case, science seems incomplete.

---

[17] Physicist Gerald Feinberg (1975) sees no incompatibility between modern physics and precognition: 'Instead of forbidding precognition from happening, [accepted physical] theories typically have sufficient symmetry (between past and future) to suggest that phenomena akin to precognition should occur. ... Indeed, phenomena involving a reversed time order of cause and effect are generally excluded from consideration on the ground that they have not been observed, rather than because the theory forbids them. This exclusion itself introduces an element of asymmetry into the physical theories, which some physicists have felt was improper or required further explanation. ... Thus, if such phenomena indeed occur, no change in the fundamental equations of physics would be needed to describe them.'

[18] Michael Thalbourne (2006) dismisses skeptical explanations based on chance 'as a bottomless pit, able to swallow up each and every coincidence that does not already have a normal explanation'. The fact is, with regard to this coincidence, there is no fool-proof method to say whether the P Theory or the N Theory interpretation is correct. It comes down to making one's own subjective evaluation.

Figure 4.2

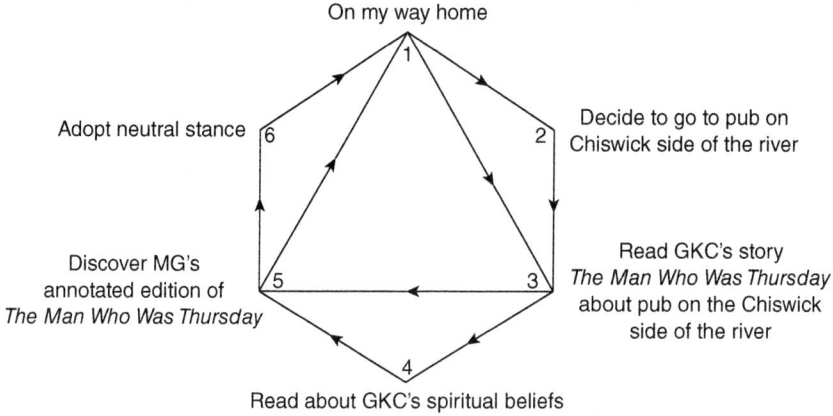

Nodes:
- 1: On my way home
- 2: Decide to go to pub on Chiswick side of the river
- 3: Read GKC's story *The Man Who Was Thursday* about pub on the Chiswick side of the river
- 4: Read about GKC's spiritual beliefs
- 5: Discover MG's annotated edition of *The Man Who Was Thursday*
- 6: Adopt neutral stance

TRIANGLE 1, 2, 3: DISCOVERY OF THE COINCIDENCE
TRIANGLE 3, 4, 5: RESEARCH LIFE & BELIEFS OF GKC
TRIANGLE 5, 6, 1: RE-VISIONING OF BOOK
TRIANGLE 1, 3, 5: CHANGING FROM SKEPTICAL TO ZETETIC APPROACH TO THE PARANORMAL

Figure 4.2 The chronology, meaning and impact of the Chiswick Coincidence

THE ROOTS OF COINCIDENCE[19]

In several notable books, Arthur Koestler offered the opinion that mainstream science is mechanistic, straitjacketed and narrow. Through his penetrating writings and legacy to science, the Koestler Chair at the University of Edinburgh, Koestler makes a lasting contribution to research on the paranormal.[20]

In *The Roots of Coincidence*, Koestler (1972) discusses the paranormal speculations of scientists, especially physicist Wolfgang Pauli, biologist Paul Kammerer and psychoanalyst Carl G. Jung. Koestler developed the suspicion that Darwin's theory of evolution must be wrong. Koestler's conclusion that there are 'more things under the stars than are dreamt in our philosophies' is something one can readily agree with. The question is, what are those things?

---

[19]This section draws on ideas in my earlier books on the paranormal (Marks, 2000; Marks & Kammann, 1980).
[20]The Koestler Chair in Parapsychology was founded with a bequest from Koestler's will. The declared intention of Arthur and Cynthia Koestler was to further scientific research into 'the capacity attributed to some individuals to interact with their environment by means other than the recognised sensory and motor channels'. Koestler himself wished to establish a parapsychology chair at University College London, but the then Head of the Psychology Department, Professor Bob Audley, informed me that he was not enthusiastic about the idea. Following discussions with Dr John Beloff, the chair was installed at the University of Edinburgh in 1985. The first Koestler Chair in Parapsychology was occupied by the late Professor Robert Morris from 1985 until his death in 2004. The chair is currently occupied by Professor Caroline Watt.

We can easily detect Koestler's acceptance of P Theory, which shines out like a beacon. Koestler's hypothesis about the roots of coincidence can justifiably be summarised by the statement that 'coincidences do not arise by chance from any normal progression of natural events'. There is an analogy from the field of astronomy. Think of a solar eclipse, which on average occurs in any particular location only once every 375 years. If we think about the movement of the moon around the earth and of the earth around the sun, it does seem unlikely that the three spheres will be found lying along a single straight line. However, on rare occasions, it is inevitable that such alignments will happen. Coincidences follow a similar principle: in the long run, independent events do 'line up' to create striking, once-in-a-million personal coincidences.

THE PRINCIPLE OF THE LONG RUN

'Koestler's fallacy' is the assumption that coincidences cannot arise by chance – which, of course, they can.[21] With each new coincidence that he or his contacts encountered, Koestler automatically assumed that something paranormal had occurred. Yet in probability theory, an event that is very improbable in the short run becomes inevitable somewhere in a very long run of observations. In truth, this is a fallacy made by everybody who attributes coincidences to the paranormal.[22] Unless some remarkable coincidences can be shown to have an alternative source to the statistical one, the 'fallacy' would not be a fallacy after all.

Let's explore first how the statistical explanation of coincidences actually works in practice. To give a handy example, imagine that we flip five coins at once. The probability of five heads is 1/32, or about .03. However, if we repeat the flipping of the five coins ten different times, then the probability of getting five heads somewhere in the ten tests is about .27. In 100 coin flips, the probability of five heads rises to .96, almost a certainty. However, if we stop anywhere in these 100 tests and ask for the probability of five heads on the very next trial, we are back to the starting point with a probability of .03 because we have switched from a long-run question to a short-run question. It is incorrect to interpret the results of a long run as if they came from a short run. It is crucial to remember that we normally perceive and recall short runs, not the almost infinite run that occurs over one's entire lifetime. Human memory and attention are limited commodities.

A famous paper by George A. Miller (1956) entitled 'The Magical Number Seven, Plus or Minus Two' begins as follows:

---

[21] The question about whether *all* coincidences are chance events is undecided.

[22] Koestler fell under the spell of this fallacy in much of his writing about the *The Roots of Coincidence*. For this reason, a little unkindly, we, Marks and Kammann (1980), gave the fallacy his name. The fallacy, if indeed it is always a fallacy, certainly does not belong only to Koestler.

> My problem is that I have been persecuted by an integer. For seven years this number has followed me around, has intruded in my most private data, and has assaulted me from the pages of our most public journals. This number assumes a variety of disguises, being sometimes a little larger and sometimes a little smaller than usual, but never changing so much as to be unrecognizable. The persistence with which this number plagues me is far more than a random accident. There is, to quote a famous senator, a design behind it, some pattern governing its appearances. Either there really is something unusual about the number or else I am suffering from delusions of persecution. (Miller, 1956: 81)

The essential point about George Miller's persistent integer 7 (+/−2) is that 7 (+/−2) represents *the number of items, thoughts or events one can readily recall in the continuous stream of one's consciousness*. One is living in a continuous 'bubble' consisting, at any one moment, of a short run of only about seven things. When we are happily bobbing along in our bubbles attending to everyday wants and needs, everything just normally seems to bobble along swimmingly, and we are content to live with this short run of events. However, on rare occasions, when we encounter a remarkable coincidence, we may well perceive, on the spur of the moment, that something odd has occurred. Inside one's bubble world of 7 (+/−2) one cannot see the huge run of events gradually accumulating over one's lifetime. If we could see this astronomically long sequence of events all at once, we would more easily perceive the fact that anomalistic synchronicities must inevitably happen. In steps the statistician.

The Principle of the Long Run (PLR) holds that, in the long run of events, coincidences are inevitable.[23] The principle can be easily discerned in any basic coin, dice or card situation where the choices are fixed and well defined. It is much less obvious in the more complex world of everyday experience where many things are happening all of the time with no easily computable end-points. It is possible to illustrate the PLR with a simple thought experiment. If you can work through this example, you will quickly see why remarkable coincidences can so easily happen.

At the end of an ordinary day, imagine that a person can recall 100 distinct events[24] – e.g. wake up, have a pee, cup of tea, plate of muesli, cup of tea, shower, get dressed, go to the station, buy a paper and a packet of Polos, catch the train, read the paper, suck on a Polo, get off the train, etc., until, finally, it's get into bed, go to sleep and dream. A coincidence requires a matching similarity or correspondence between an event A and another event B, and so we need to calculate the

---

[23] The Principle of the Long Run reappears in another guise as the 'Law of Truly Large Numbers' in Diaconis and Mosteller (1989).
[24] 100 is an intuitive 'guestimate'.

total number of different *pairs* of events that are available in a set of 100 (n) single events. This is calculated by the formula:

$$_nC_r = \frac{n!}{(n-r)!r!}$$

where the number of events n =100 and r = 2.

The calculation can be performed most easily as follows. The first event can be paired with each of 99 others. The second event can be paired with each of 98 others (because it has already been paired with the first event). Proceeding in this way, one can see that the total pairs is: 99 + 98 + 97 + 96 + ... + 3 + 2 + 1 = 4,950 pairs of events for one person in one day. Bearing in mind that we tend to remember coincidences for years to come, let us assume that a person can remember all the important coincidences over the most recent 10 years (3,650 days).[25] Let us assume, in addition, that the person has access to 1,000 people throughout their life consisting of family, friends, acquaintances, neighbours, colleagues, fellow passengers on the commute to work, on social media, etc. We are therefore ready to multiply 4,950 × 3,650 × 1,000, which gives a total of 18,067,500,000 pairs. That Arthur Koestler (and his many correspondents who wrote specifically about coincidences) could identify 40 notable coincidences among a collection of 18 billion pairs of events does not seem surprising and does not provide a reason to invoke the paranormal. On the contrary, a good sample of coincidences is inevitable in a population of 18 billion pairs of events.[26]

Of course, when each coincidence individually occurs in a person's short-run bubble, it seems exceedingly odd. This is because our memory is not up to the task of paying attention to the entire collection of multiple billions of non-synchronous non-coincidences. These non-events are not perceived as paired and it does not much matter whether the match is between names in a magazine, telephone calls from thought-of people or plans to visit 'obscure' public houses on the

---

[25] We can compute the number of pairs over a single person's adult lifetime of 60 years: 4,950 × 60 × 365 = 1,084,050,000 pairs + 15 × 4,950 = 74,250 extra pairs for leap days, giving a total of 1,084,124,250 – i.e. slightly more than one billion pairs. If a coincidence is a one-in-ten-million event, then we can expect around 100 striking coincidences in one lifetime; at one-in-100-million, there would be only 10 per lifetime; at one-per-billion, only one. A one-in-one quintillion coincidence should not happen. The only way that it could happen would be if we were to increase the value of n to, say, 500, but is that a plausible assumption?

[26] In *Irrationality: The Enemy Within*, Stuart Sutherland (1992) misapplied the 18 billion figure as follows: 'Arthur Koestler sought to establish the truth of the paranormal by pointing to fifty coincidences *that had occurred in his life*, which he claimed could not be given any normal explanation, but Marks and *[Kammann]* point out that in a lifetime he would have been exposed to over 18 billion pairs of events: it would be most unlikely if some of the members of a pair did not match' (p. 227). As computed in footnote 28, there would be only about one billion event pairs in a single lifetime.

Chiswick side of the river – they are all equally good P Theory mysteries. This is the Principle of Equivalent Coincidences by which any coincidence is as good as any other. It is not the probability of any particular coincidence that matters, but the probability of *any* coincidence over the long run of natural events, which approaches 1.0.

First root of coincidence: Probability

The first root of coincidence is the inevitability that over the long run thoughts tend to match events before those events happen.[27] With billions of possible combinations of thoughts and events over one's lifetime, a select few are bound to produce synchronicities. If not, then one isn't paying attention. Several biases in perception and judgement contribute to this fallacy (discussed in more detail in the previous chapter). First, in one's 7 +/− 2 bubble world one notices and remembers coincidences whenever they occur. Second, we do not notice the vast population of non-coincidences – and why the heck should we? Third, one's failure to notice non-events creates the Short Run Illusion that makes coincidences seem not only improbable, but impossible. Fourth, we overlook the Principle of Equivalent Coincidences, that one coincidence is as good any other as far as P Theory is concerned.

As part of an innate tendency to harmonise goals with actions, feelings and beliefs, one tends to seek any indication that one's beliefs are correct or, at least not wrong, by looking for positive confirmation and neglecting disconfirmation (Nickerson, 1998). Confirmation bias and SV both have general relevance to paranormal beliefs and experiences, as will become apparent in later chapters.

The second root of coincidence: The unseen cause

The second root of coincidence is the Principle of the Unseen Cause. A variety of unseen causes tend to interfere with our subjective interpretation of anomalous phenomena, both as individual perceivers and as scientific investigators. Some well-known examples of unseen causes are, in no particular order:

- sensory cues;
- non-random sequences;
- deception or manipulation;
- sleight-of-hand;
- pranks or hoaxes;
- wishful thinking;
- expectancy effects;

---

[27]Luke (2012) suggests that attributing chance probability to apparently related phenomena is 'randomania', a label for believing that everything one cannot currently explain is just due to chance and coincidence.

- confirmation bias;
- subjective validation;
- population stereotypes;
- hidden knowledge;
- feelings;
- intoxication.

None of us is ever immune to the above processes. Practical methods to overcome these problems in laboratory research are available (see Appendix, and more detailed discussion in Chapter 3). In the case of the spontaneous occurrence of the Chiswick Coincidence, there is no capability to eliminate the influence of all these factors. I can state that I believe that none of these hidden causes are applicable. The one I fear the most is SV. I argue that SV can be ruled out because of the extremely well-matching details. However, as the author of the experience, I am an interested party and have a conflict of interest, so my personal judgement about SV in this account lies in jeopardy. This judgement rests with others.

THE PARADOX OF COINCIDENCE

According to the Principle of the Long Run, a coincidence is always a chance event, no matter how miniscule the probability. If the possibility of 'paranormal coincidences' is contemplated,[28] the mainstream scientific approach requires that the paranormal coincidences would be mixed in with the purely chance-based coincidences and therefore made invisible. From this assumption, it follows that science is ruling out of existence the very phenomenon that it is attempting to explain – e.g. the possibility that some coincidences are caused by an as yet undefined, non-chance process X.

The mainstream assumption that coincidences must always be chance phenomena means that the conventional criterion for evaluating the statistical significance of an observation does not operate in the case of coincidences. The standard criterion for rejecting a null hypothesis H_0 is $p < .05$. For coincidences, however, the probability could easily be as low as $p < .000000000001$ (10^{-12}) or even smaller, and the occurrence would still be assumed to fall within chance levels.

This double standard in evaluating the statistical significance of coincidences is intriguingly paradoxical. The more improbable an outcome, the more it is said to be consistent with the null hypothesis. How is one to escape this paradox? To avoid miscounting paranormal events as ordinary chance events and defining them out of existence, it is necessary to hypothesise two populations of coincidental events – those due purely to chance and those that have a putative paranormal source.

Consider another thought experiment: imagine a coincidence with odds of 10 to the minus 12. This is one chance in a million million. Consider the possibility

---

[28] A zetetic must allow this possibility.

that there is an alternative to the normal (null) hypothesis that we can call the 'paranormal hypothesis':

H0: The null hypothesis – what occurred was purely chance.

H1: The paranormal hypothesis – what occurred was too improbable to be caused by chance and so must have a paranormal explanation.

The hypothesis that there are two distributions of coincidences each having a mean and standard deviation is represented in Figure 4.3.

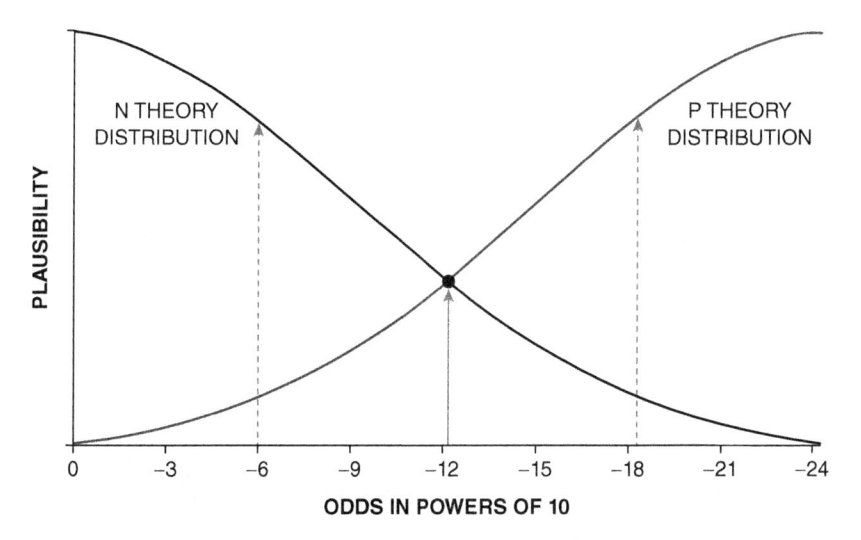

Figure 4.3 Plausibility of events with different odds derived from one of two distributions for chance (N Theory) and non-chance (P Theory) coincidences. The shape of the distributions is folded normal and, arbitrarily, the dispersions are set to provide a cross-over point where an odds of 10^{-12} has a Bayes factor of 1.0 (thin vertical line). Events with odds to the left of this line have Bayes factors < 1.0 and to the right of this line, Bayes Factors > 1.0. The vertical dotted lines indicate events with odds of 10^{-6} and 10^{-18} and Bayes factors of .20 and 5.0 respectively.

According to this hypothetical framework, there is a cross-over point with a Bayes factor of 1.0 at an odds value of 10^{-12}. The hypothesised existence of a separate population of paranormal events places N Theory and P Theory on an equal footing and avoids a double standard. It is impossible to say whether this theory correct.[29] The cross-over point could be anywhere, and the theory is pure speculation.

---

[29]Laurence Browne (2017) proposes four categories – a) random chance; b) natural causality; c) supernatural causality; d) synchronicity – to represent the four main ways in which coincidences are customarily explained. In the model of Figure 4.2, we include types a and c.

THE COMBINED PROBABILITY OF MULTIPLE COINCIDENCES

For whatever reason, I have experienced many remarkable coincidences. In addition to the CC, I describe in my blog four other coincidences in my lifetime and, in due course, I will add several others.[30] For now one can focus on these first five and ignore the others. It is possible to compute the odds that all five of these events could happen to a single individual. To determine the combined probability of five independent events, A–E, one is required to multiply the individual probabilities:

$$P(A \text{ and } B \text{ and } C \text{ and } D \text{ and } E) = P(A) \times P(B) \times P(C) \times P(D) \times P(E)$$

The five coincidences were as follows:

A. **An obscure public house on the Chiswick bank of the river:** $P = 10^{-18}$ = one chance in one quintillion (a million, million, million).
B. **Coincidence or luck?:** $P = 10^{-10}$ = one chance in 10 billion.
C. **Citizen 63 – Marion Knight:** $P = 4.5 \times 10^{-10}$ = 4.5 chances in 10 billion.
D. **The case of the flying horseshoe:** $P = 1.3 \times 10^{-12}$ = 1.3 chances in a million, million.
E. **Under the wallpaper:** $P = 5.08 \times 10^{-9}$ = 5 chances in a billion.

By multiplication, the combined probability of these five independent events is:

$$P = 10^{-18} \times 10^{-10} \times 4.5 \times 10^{-10} \times 1.3 \times 10^{-12} \times 5.08 \times 10^{-9}$$

$$\underline{P = 3 \times 10^{-58}}!$$

Without doubt, 3×10^{-58} is one of the lowest probabilities ever calculated for a set of observations in psychological science. *Yet, according to the Principle of the Long Run, there is nothing extraordinary here, move on.* As a scientific explanation of extraordinarily improbable anomalies, the long run principle is untenable. To make sense of such astronomically extreme odds, it appears necessary to hypothesise a second source of coincidence anomalies.

There is no a priori reason to accept that all coincidence events, however infinitesimally tiny the probability, must forever be shielded from alternative theories by the laws of probability that were devised for card players and casinos.

I turn to consider an aspect of the CC beyond consideration of probability and statistics. As several investigators have recommended, notably Carl Jung, it is necessary to examine meaning. Oddly, this is something psychologists rarely do, especially the Jungian kind of meaning.

---

[30] See: https://davidfmarks.com
Please feel free to leave comments, queries or feedback there if you wish to do so.

SYNCHRONICITY, MEANINGFULNESS AND EMERGENCE

'The numinosity[31] of a series of chance happenings grows in proportion to the number of its terms' (Jung, 1955: n. 11). An important feature of the synchronicity in every coincidence is its *meaning*. Striking coincidences often appear to the experiencer to offer evidential support to psi as an underlying mechanism, especially precognition. Carl Jung (1952) viewed synchronicity as an 'Acausal Connecting Principle' which he defined as: 'informative, emotionally charged, and transforming the observer's beliefs or point of view'. He defines synchronicity thus: 'Synchronicity therefore means the simultaneous occurrence of a certain psychic state with one or more external events which appear as meaningful parallels to the momentary subjective state – and, in certain cases, vice versa' (Jung, 1960: location 385). Synchronicity occurs in another way in music, song and dance; the artful use of rhythm, timing and flow between individual actors binds feelings, thoughts and behaviours (Marks, 2018). Behavioural entrainment and synchronisation in movement, song and rhythm enable people to match timing, rhythm and flow of action to produce enjoyable shared experience and bonding (Reddish, Fischer, & Bulbulia, 2013). The universality of synchronised action across species implies an evolutionary advantage (Marks, 2018: 32–3). It is not surprising that we imbue synchronicity with impact, importance and meaning if we are hard-wired to do so.

As an account of phenomena that exist beyond the material world of cause-and-effect, Carl Jung's theory of synchronicity represents an intellectual challenge to Cartesian mind–body dualism:

> It is impossible, with our present resources, to explain ESP, or the fact of meaningful coincidence, as a phenomenon of energy. This makes an end of the causal explanation as well, for 'effect' cannot be understood as anything except a phenomenon of energy. Therefore it cannot be a question of cause and effect, but of a falling together in time, a kind of simultaneity. Because of this quality of simultaneity, I have picked on the term 'synchronicity' to designate a hypothetical fact equal in rank to causality as a principle of explanation .... I consider synchronicity as a psychically conditioned relativity of space and time. (Jung, 1952: loc. 288)

In this light, in what ways can coincidences be explained besides the statistical PLR approach? One can begin by accepting that consciousness is an emergent property of the brain that produces meaningful images, feelings and synchronicities. Whether or not one is prepared to accept Jung's theory of archetypes, it is

---

[31]Numinosity is 'emotional resonance', psychologically associated with experiences of the self.

perfectly feasible that meta-level structures create images, symbols of the self. I quote Joseph Cambray:

> When these symbols are accessed by consciousness and experienced affectively, they often coincide with a sense of deeper purpose or function, though their fullness can barely be intuited, if perceived at all. This suggests that synchronicities can be explored as a form of emergence of the Self and have a central role in individuation or psychological maturation (taken as a homologue of biological evolution), providing a more scientific basis for this aspect of Jung's thought…. Meaningful coincidences are psychological analogues that spur the evolution of both the personal and the collective psyche, organizing images and experiences into previously unimagined forms. (Cambray, 2004: 417–19)

Thus, synchronistic experience is a form of psychological emergence. To Jung, *meaningful* coincidences must be distinguished from *meaningless* happenstance groupings because they rest on 'archetypal foundations'. Jung discusses Rhine's ESP experiments as giving the subject's unconscious 'a chance to manifest itself'. Regardless of the subject's own skepticism, an ESP experiment

> immediately appeals to his [or her] unconscious readiness to witness a miracle, and to the hope, latent in all [people], that such a thing may yet be possible. Primitive superstition lies just below the surface of even the most tough-minded individuals, and it is precisely those who most fight. (Jung, 1952: loc. 385)

In the case of coincidences, Jung argues that synchronicity serves as an augury or omen. Jung was convinced that:

> However incomprehensible it may appear, we are finally compelled to assume that there is in the unconscious something like an a priori knowledge or immediate presence of events which lacks any causal basis. At any rate our conception of causality is incapable of explaining the facts. (Jung, 1952: loc. 572)

In agreement with Jung and Cambray, synchronicity can be viewed as an emergent process of the self within consciousness. Consciousness evolved with the significant evolutionary advantage of an emergent, purposeful and integrative process of psychological homeostasis to direct holistic control (Marks, 2019). The case for consciousness as an emergent property was made by Roger Sperry in 1969:

> The long-standing assumption in the neurosciences that the subjective phenomena of conscious experiences do not exert any causal influence on the sequence of events in the physical brain process is directly challenged in this current view of the nature of mind and the mind–brain relationship. A theory of mind is suggested in which consciousness, interpreted to be a direct emergent property of cerebral activity, is conceived to be an integral component of the brain process that functions as an essential constituent of the action and exerts a directive holistic form of control over the flow pattern of cerebral excitation. (1969: 532)

Consciousness has an explanatory role in the behaviour of organisms through an equilibrium-creating process at a meta-level of control. An experience that is re-represented in the mind is always based on metacognition, as a homeostatic form of self-control. The intimate connection between the self, intentionality, and purposive goal-seeking behaviour has the pre-eminent advantage of ipseity.[32] Only a conscious being can have the quality of selfhood, the first-person quality of consciousness that all experience articulates from a first-person perspective as 'my' experience.

CODA

In the light of the above analysis, one can sense merit in Jung's acausal theory. Two key events in direct conscious experience were acausally connected with such an infinitesimally low probability that it stretches plausibility to accept the classical statistical explanation. Reflecting on the potential meaning, in addition to Figure 4.2, I could not stop speculating that what-if, in some unknown way, the event presaged a strange precognitive element in line with Jung's theory? Daft as it may sound, like the protagonists of Chesterton's novel, would I be offered membership into a secret society?[33] I wanted to dismiss this conjecture as too incredible for words, but it held a fascination that could not be easily resisted.

As I sat at the City Barge mulling over what had happened, a few feet from the riverside, a personable middle-aged man and his partner struck up conversation. We spent a pleasant hour in light, midsummer's day chit-chat about the place, music, travel, those kinds of things. Before going on our separate ways, we arranged to meet again and exchanged contact details.

A few days later, we met at The Horse and Groom, in Windsor, just across the road from the castle. My associate greeted me with nothing less than the unmistakable Masonic handshake. Cryptically he enquired: 'I was just wondering, are you one of us?' 'No', I said, 'I thought membership was strictly invitation only'. His reply was perfectly matter-of-fact: 'If you wish to join, just knock on the door of your nearest lodge'.

Who was it who said truth is stranger than fiction?[34]

SUMMARY

An anomaly involving multiple synchronicities occured on seven levels. The laws of probability suggest that the odds were one-quintillion-to-one. A speculative hypothesis proposes separate populations of normal and paranormal coincidences. This idea places N Theory and P Theory on an equal footing and avoids a double

---

[32]Individual identity, selfhood. We return to this concept in Chapters 10 and 11.
[33]In GKC's novel, the protagonists are undercover members of a secret society of anarchists.
[34]Freemasonry in England and Wales contributed more than £48m to charity in 2019 and annually gives 18 million hours of unpaid voluntary work in their communities. No offence to the Grand Order, but, in spite of its impressive charitable work, the symbology, rituals and robes deter me from seeking membership. However, while checking the proof copy on 23 March 2020, I received my first ever email from the United Grand Lodge inviting me (and the entire population!) to join a 'Nine O'Clock Toast' to the NHS busily fighting COVID-19.

standard. An alternative hypothesis that synchronicity involves acausal elements receives support from an unexpected precognitive element. There can be little doubt that synchronicity and meaning are existential processes having an ancient biological role. Whether any particular coincidence is finally considered to be a chance or a paranormal event is a subjective choice. This uncertainty is an intrinsic quality of the experience itself. In spite of everything, the entire episode could be nothing more than subjective validation.

QUESTIONS

1. List three factors that might influence a person to interpret an AE as paranormal.
2. List three methodological issues with research on AE.
3. What is Jung's theory of 'synchronicity'?
4. Which of the seven levels in the CC seem the most striking to you?
5. Describe a remarkable coincidence from your own life and try to explain it.
6. What questions would you want to ask the author about the CC?
7. Which interpretation of the CC do you favour and for what reasons?

Draw an arrow on the Belief Barometer in Figure 4.4 to represent your degree of belief that the Chiswick Coincidence is evidence of the paranormal.

CHISWICK COINCIDENCE: EVIDENCE OF THE PARANORMAL?

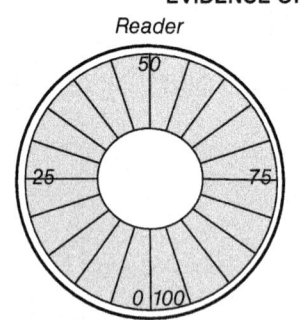

Reader — Please indicate your degree of belief that the Chiswick Coincidence was a paranormal event

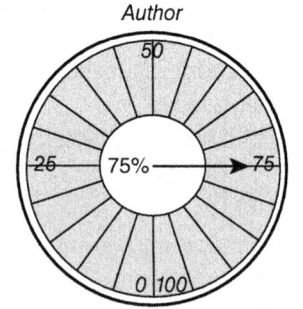

Author — The author's barometer reading is set at 75%

Figure 4.4 Belief barometer readings

5
REMOTE VIEWING AND PSYCHIC STARING

With contributions from Harold E. Puthoff, PhD and Rupert Sheldrake, PhD

> Albert Einstein once said, 'Failure is success in progress.' And on that account, we have made very good progress toward success. (Katz, Grgić, & Fendley, 2018)

Outline: In a spirit of open inquiry, a zetetic examination of evidence is necessary, suspending any judgement until the best evidence has been reviewed. In the case of remote viewing, there are well-known 'classic' studies and new evidence from 2000 to 2019. This review begins by exploring the 'classic' remote viewing (RV) studies and the claims made for RV in the light of that evidence, both pro and con. In addition, another protocol concerned with 'psychic staring' is explored. For both procedures the quality of the research is well below the standard for controlled scientific experiments. For both RV and psychic staring, there is objective evidence of incomplete randomisation and a failure to eliminate sensory cues. The leading investigators refuse to acknowledge these fundamental problems concerning the inadequate scientific controls and they continue to maintain that the psi effects are real when the evidence does not support this claim.

REMOTE VIEWING AS A WEAPON IN THE 'COLD WAR'

According to the Parapsychological Association,

> Several thousand [remote viewing] trials have been conducted by dozens of investigators over the past 25 years, involving hundreds of participants.

> The cumulative database strongly indicates that information about remote photos, actual scenes, and events can be perceived. Some of these experiments have also been used to successfully study precognition by having a participant describe a photo that would be randomly selected in the future. (Parapsychological Association, 2019)

A recent paper claims: 'Undoubtedly the most important project demonstrating the human mind's ability to locate and describe the characteristics of distant objects and people is Star Gate [remote viewing]' (Tressoldi & Pederzoli, 2018). Strong praise indeed! If laboratory psi can be found anywhere, the RV experiment must surely be one of the first places to look.

Rarely does parapsychology research become entwined with military operations. However, the possibility that gifted remote viewers may have the capability to describe foreign military targets attracted the attention of the US Department of Defence. One research effort called 'Star Gate' was part of the 44-year stand-off between the US and the USSR known as the 'Cold War' (1947–1991). The policy of deterrence was based on the possession of nuclear weapons by both sides. Like the classic stand-off in 'western' movies, whoever fires first is generally the winner. In the Cuba Missile Crisis, when Soviet missiles were thought to be installed a few hundred miles from the North American continent, nobody flinched and no nuclear bombs were dropped on New York, London or Moscow. The Cold War is fêted as a success. The input to this war from parapsychology was 'Star Gate', a programme that received total funding from 1972 to 1995 of $19.443 million (May & Marwaha, 2018).

In an RV experiment, the investigators determine whether information can be gained about a remote site or target. The information transfer is believed to occur without any special altered state of consciousness, equipment or technology. In a typical RV experiment, a pool of places is created within a defined geographical area or region. An independent third party randomly selects a remote 'target' location. The experimental remote viewer, without prior knowledge of the target, attempts to sketch or describe that remote target. The procedure is repeated on a number of occasions. Target photos, or a list of targets, and the set of responses are independently randomised. An independent person, called the 'judge', attempts to match the correct targets with the responses. If 'information transfer' has successfully occurred, the responses should correspond to the correct targets.

RV is the alleged psi-ability to describe a geographically distant target beyond the level that can be achieved by chance alone (i.e. by guesswork). It is a procedure that involves no special apparatus. The ability to video and livestream with Smart phones makes the RV procedure even more interesting. If you want to give it a try, you can easily experience the RV experiment first-hand. The originators of the RV protocols must be congratulated for developing a method for the scientific study of ESP which uses natural geographical targets instead of the tedious card-guessing tasks developed by Rhine. The simplicity of the procedure belies the hidden complexity involved. For example, there are five categories of personnel involved: the target pool selector, the remote viewer (receiver), the in-house experimenter or interviewer, the outbound investigator (the beacon, traveller or sender), and the independent judge. To keep the procedure tightly controlled, these five roles must be kept distinct. The remote viewer is given a particular detail about the target, such as its geographical coordinates, a descriptive location or an 'address' and, at a specified time either *before (precognition) or during (clairvoyance or telepathy)* the beacon's visit to the target, provides a description of it.

The RV experiment should be carried out 'double-blind', whereby neither the remote viewer nor the interviewer knows the identity of the target. Targets are selected at random from a prearranged set by a target pool selector. In each trial, an arranged interval of time is allowed for the outbound team to arrive at the target (e.g. 30 minutes), and then the remote viewer attempts to describe the target. They are taken to the target afterwards to provide detailed feedback. After a prearranged fixed number of trials, a randomised list of targets and transcripts of the remote viewers' descriptions are given to an independent judge who ranks each description at each target site in order of descriptive accuracy. Statistical analysis follows using a standard procedure (Morris, 1972).[1]

In some experiments, no travelling sender or beacon is involved. The remote viewer is simply given a set of coordinates and nothing more. Investigators claim that the size of the target (down to 1mm square) and its distance (up to 10,000 miles) do not impair the viewer's ability to perceive the target. The RV protocol has also been adapted to predict events with multiple discrete possible outcomes such as the rise and fall of the stock market. This technique was called 'associative remote viewing' (ARV). Imagine how wealthy the successful remote viewer could become. To the best of my knowledge, there are no RV millionaires.

The earliest research efforts on RV were led by physicists Harold Puthoff and Russell Targ based at Stanford Research International (SRI) in Palo Alto, California. Their RV research received worldwide attention when *Nature* published a landmark paper containing their initial findings: 'Information transmission under conditions of sensory shielding' (Targ & Puthoff, 1974). This was the first paper on psi in this prestigious journal and it gained enormous publicity. In part, this media cloudburst occurred because the paper contained a positive laboratory trial with self-proclaimed psychic Uri Geller (Figure 5.1).[2] Two judges each matched the responses to the targets without error, a result with an a priori probability of $(10!)^{-1} = 3 \times 10^{-7}$ (3 chances in 10 million).

---

[1] Documentary footage of the original SRI researchers and critics recorded by the BBC is available on YouTube: *The Case of ESP – Original, Uncut 1983 BBC Horizon Film* at: https://youtu.be/h2Gog3xMluA

[2] Uri Geller is the person who claimed he would stop Brexit using telepathy: www.theguardian.com/politics/2019/mar/22/uri-geller-promises-to-stop-brexit-using-telepathy

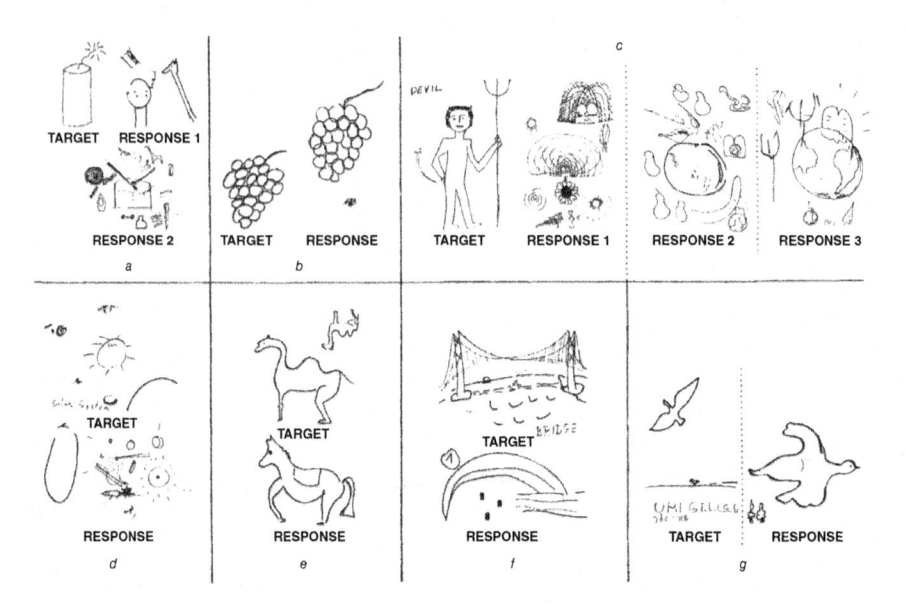

Figure 5.1 Target pictures and responses drawn by Uri Geller

Reproduced from Targ and Puthoff (1974) by permission.

In the mid-1970s, while working at the University of Otago in New Zealand, I carried out an in-depth study of the SRI research protocols. Genuinely excited by the SRI findings, I wanted to get to the bottom of what had actually happened. I visited Russell Targ and Harold Puthoff at SRI, visited their independent judge, Arthur Hastings, obtained the original datasets and materials given to the judge, and carried out replication attempts of the RV experiments. I also met Uri Geller on several occasions and tested his alleged psychic abilities. In a nutshell, what I discovered was not a revolution in science but a set of seriously sloppy methodological flaws.

Unfortunately, I discovered many factors that invalidate the Targ–Puthoff experiments. There is clear evidence of major sensory cues, lack of randomisation, and data-selection in which the experiments in an 'official' published series (with the remote viewer, H. Hammid) were selected from a longer series. In addition, I believe that there is evidence of statistical errors in evaluating the results from the series of experiments involving more than one P (the Elgin–Swann, Pease–Cole, visitor and technology series). A further undesirable feature of the Targ–Puthoff research is that the nominal targets were specified for the judge *post hoc* following the collection of the remote viewer's descriptions. Publishing photos of the targets – taken after the judging had been done – from angles that were designed to emphasise the similarities to drawings made by the remote viewers – can easily convince the naive reader who might fail to note that these photoqraphs were *not* part of the original protocol. These and many other troublesome problems are outlined in some detail in my earlier publications. With my associates Richard Kammann and Christopher Scott, these criticisms were published in *Nature* (Marks, 1986;

Marks & Kammann, 1978; Marks & Scott, 1986) and in *The Psychology of the Psychic* (Marks & Kammann, 1980; Marks, 2000). The RV technique helped the investigators to subjectively validate their perceptions of psi and to ignore the many flaws in their protocols. To this day, Targ and Puthoff cite their RV research in the most glowing terms as evidence of psi, acting all the while as if nothing was wrong with their procedures, or, if it was wrong, that it was specific to one experiment and was adequately fixed. Progress in science depends upon criticism, correction and replication. As a zetetic and critic, one cannot flinch from the fact that science needs rules for administering procedures and controls in experiments and, when those rules are broken, the problems need to be called out.

RV research has produced some highly divergent views about the quality of the methods and the reliability of the findings. In 1996, Jessica Utts stated:

> Using the standards applied to any other area of science, it is concluded that psychic functioning has been well established. The statistical results of the studies examined are far beyond what is expected by chance. Arguments that these results could be due to methodological flaws in the experiments are soundly refuted. Effects of similar magnitude to those found in government sponsored research at SRI and SAIC have been replicated at a number of laboratories across the world. Such consistency cannot be readily explained by claims of flaws or fraud. (p. 3)

Extensive researches of my own, on the other hand, led me to conclude:

> remote viewing had received no empirical support. Star Gate failed for the same reason the earlier SRI studies failed – inadequate experimental controls. This is becoming a recurring theme in the search for evidence of psychic powers. As we enter the new millennium, having looked high and low for ESP, and having chased it around many corners, we are no closer to a genuine discovery than ever before. Psi remains a tantalizing dream, an artifact of SV, lacking real substance in nature. Believers in psi could be forgiven for abandoning their search, never more to chase the rainbow of psi. However, it can safely be predicted that they will never do so. (Marks, 2000: 95)

Documentation from one of the leading RV advocates, Edwin May, director of the SRI/SAIC programme from late-1985 to 1995, is available in the first of his four-volume set of archives (May & Marwaha, 2018).[3] Bearing in mind that both

---

[3] 'The Archives are not a novel, not easy reading' (Tart, 2018). This 546-page volume containing 41 reports, 45 annexes and a 12-page Bibliography is available at Amazon for the princely sum of £110.78 (Volume 1 only). With obfuscating jargon, multiple acronyms and repetitive content, this is a turgid document. The archive is not a scientific document but a series of detailed technical reports designed for sponsors and oversight committee members. The archive contains no insightful criticism or acknowledgement of the major methodological failings in Star Gate.

Jessica Utts and I had access to the same evidence base, our points of view could not have been further apart. Twenty years later, is there any convergence towards a more neutral compromise? To answer this question, I review here the RV research published in peer-reviewed journals in the 20-year period 2000–2019.[4]

TRAPS AND PITFALLS

Along with the ganzfeld to be discussed in the next chapter, RV is the most perfect situation for subjective validation (SV). It sets the perfect set of traps for any investigator, however sophisticate. Unless the investigator is fully prepared to eliminate *all* the potential traps and pitfalls, an RV experiment is a fail-safe method of producing SV. Every single P can be fooled by this powerful cognitive illusion into believing that they are witnessing ESP. I know because I have been there. Anybody who experiences the full power of SV as a remote viewer or investigator has two options when the outcome is announced: their experience can be confirmed or shattered by the statistical results (Table 5.1). Cells A and D are congruent, while B and D are incongruent. An investigation that contains flaws is highly likely to produce an artefactual congruent matching when there isn't any genuine matching to be had. Fortunately, one develops some degree of immunity; there is a 'once-bitten, twice shy' aspect to the experience that both believers and skeptics can feel with equal force. A major goal for any RV investigator must be to strengthen their immunity to SV.

Table 5.1 Four outcomes associated with strong and weak subjective validation in an RV study.

Subjective validation	Statistically significant matching	Statistically non-significant matching
Strong	A Congruent: ELATION	B Incongruent: DISAPPOINTMENT
Weak	C Incongruent: SURPRISE	D Congruent: AFFIRMATION

A typical set of results from an RV experiment is shown in Figure 5.2. The remote viewer and independent judge were both strongly convinced that they had each made a correct matching of a target and drawing, B in the case of the remote viewer but D in the case of the judge. *Drawing D was produced by the remote viewer for a completely different target, the railway station.*

---

[4]Only peer-reviewed journal articles are included in this review. Articles about research prior to 2000 are excluded, as are books, book chapters, conference papers, magazine articles, internet sites and posts, YouTube videos and other sources that are not peer-reviewed are therefore, considered unreliable.

A. View of target from the road.

C. View from steps above house.

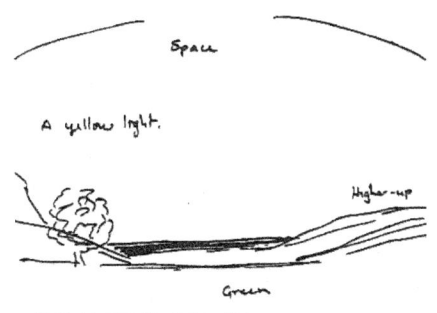

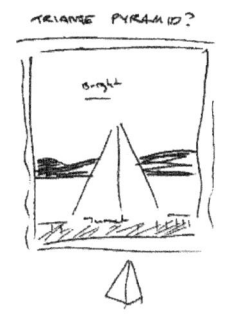

B. Subject's final drawing.

D. Judge's first choice.

Figure 5.2 An RV experiment with an A-frame house as target. Photographs A and C were taken at the target site immediately after the remote viewer produced his drawing (photo B). The remote viewer was happy that his drawing looked similar, so he thought, to the view from the steps above the house (photo C). In fact, the outbound investigator only observed from street level (photo A) and never went to view the scene from above the house. On the other hand, the independent judge chose the drawing shown in photo D as the best match to the target. He was convinced that this drawing was the correct match with the target, yet it had been produced for a completely different target.

Reproduced from Marks (2000).

SV creates a powerful trap inside every RV experiment. One needs to beware, or one will fall straight into it, you, me and everybody else. TV journalists seem to be particularly vulnerable. To ignore SV is naive; to deny it or pretend it doesn't exist is to risk being totally fooled. I learned from hard-won experience that RV opens the door to SV. At the early stages of running RV experiments, it can seem almost self-evident that ESP must be involved. The astonishment, elation and rush of adrenalin at the apparent correspondences between the remote viewer's description and the target are palpable and real. The SV is also strongly reinforcing to the remote viewer, who is likely to become 100% convinced that their RV ability is real. It doesn't much matter whether they start out as a skeptic or a believer, the experience is compelling. An apparent matching or 'hit' between a description and a target can almost always be found between any description or drawing and any target site. Bearing in mind that the formal statistical results are not actually

A. 'Triangular' grave.

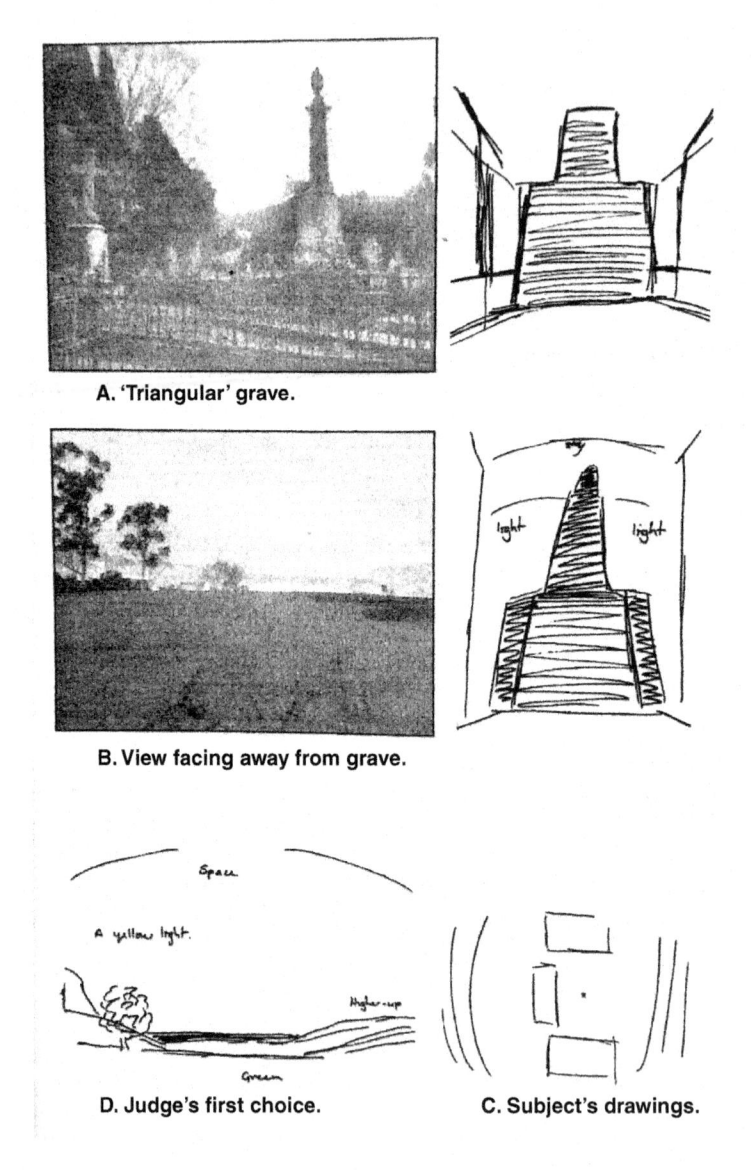

B. View facing away from grave.

D. Judge's first choice.

C. Subject's drawings.

Figure 5.3 The second target in the New Zealand RV series, a 'triangular' grave. The remote viewer's drawings were eerily accurate. However, the independent judge matched these drawings with another target (statue of Robert Burns). Both the remote viewer and the judge believed they had correctly matched the description with the target.

Reproduced from Marks (2000).

obtained until after the complete series of trials has been run, the pattern of subjectively validated successes can continue unabated for the entire sequence. The final let-down is when the statistical results are presented at the end of the series.

In my New Zealand experiment, trial 2 produced an even more convincing outcome than trial 1. The remote viewer, CT, drew shapes that looked like the target, and talked about a sombre feeling (Figure 5.3). On visiting the target site, CT was utterly convinced that he had described it almost 100% correctly. He actually went pale and started to shake a little. However, the judging produced a different outcome. The judge completely missed these apparent similarities and matched another target, an unusual 'triangular' grave, with CT's drawing for the previous experiment with the A-frame house. The judge was as surprised as the remote viewer when the results were finally obtained. Both expressed their doubts and were disillusioned about the science involved. The final outcome after seven trials was not statistically significant.

Investigators themselves are as vulnerable to SV as remote viewers and judges. SV is a universal process that has everybody fooled. When investigators have the remote viewer's description, it is easy to identify corresponding features post hoc between the description and the target. Targets consist of complex buildings, locations and environments. If investigators take photographs at the target site *after* having seen the remote viewer's description, there is every possibility that matching correspondences will be observed and reproduced in their publications. How much of the RV literature contains this form of post hoc SV is unclear. As a reviewer for *Nature*'s RV papers, it was necessary to recommend against publication of studies containing this most basic form of SV. A few investigators seem totally oblivious to SV and never even mentioned it in their publications.

If you want to experience RV/SV, all you have to do is run an RV experiment. Find two willing volunteers and off you go. Avoid the traps the best way that you can, but I can promise you, you will definitely experience seductive SV.

A FATAL FLAW IN THE SRI RV EXPERIMENTS

A fatal flaw with the original Targ–Puthoff RV series with Pat Price was that the transcripts contained multiple sensory cues providing the judge with the information necessary to place the transcripts in correct order (Marks & Kammann, 1978). The judge, Arthur Hastings, was given the listing of targets in the correct chronological order. In a follow-up study, the investigator team claimed to have 'edited the transcripts carefully, removing all phrases suggested as potential cues by Marks and Kammann, and removing any additional phrases for which even the most post hoc cue argument could be made'. When the newly edited transcripts were matched against a randomised list of targets, they claim that they obtained equally significant results (Tart, Puthoff, & Targ, 1980). However, Christopher Scott and I obtained copies of the transcripts edited by Dr Tart. To our utter amazement, we found many sensory cues that had been left unedited from the transcripts (Marks & Scott, 1986). How could such an obvious error have been possible?

This act of commission is way beyond sloppiness. It carries the hallmarks of wilful data manipulation, otherwise known as fraud. The deliberate inclusion of sensory cues in Targ and Puhoff's final dataset removes any credibility from their claim to have proved the existence of ESP. As a zetetic, I believe that this type of experimental flaw has to be called out. Adopting the zetetic approach is not a mandate to give blank cheques to researchers who flout the most basic rules and codes of practice. The continued use of flawed data is not a desirable procedure in any case. New experiments should be conducted with the flaws removed, and if the original findings are not replicated, then it is time to move on and do something else.

However, in spite of the many known flaws, Targ and Puthoff continue to cite their studies as experimental 'proof' of ESP. In accepting an Outstanding Career Award in 2009 from the Parapsychological Association, Russell Targ stated:

> In 1974, we at SRI worked with retired Burbank, CA, police commissioner Pat Price and carried out nine double-blind RV trials in which Price was asked to describe Hal Puthoff's randomly chosen locations. From a pool of 60 possible locations, Price had seven first place matches ($p = 3 \times 10-5$, effect size = 1.3). In 1975, we were asked by the CIA to find an inexperienced 'control' subject. I chose my good friend, photographer Hella Hammid. In nine doubleblind trials of outdoor locations, she obtained five first place matches, and four second place matches ($p = 2 \times 10-6$, effect size = 1.5). (Targ, 2010: 270–1)

No mention here of the sensory cues and non-randomisation of target lists. From this address, it is as if these fatal flaws had never existed. This misrepresentation of scientific findings by one who has had an 'Outstanding Career' leads one to question the standards and scholarship of the Parapsychological Association. Promotion of flawed science and wilful neglect of the multiple methodological flaws in what are promoted as perfect examples of psi research, are tantamount to fraud and detrimental to the credibility of the Association, its members and Parapsychology more generally.

This review of the pre-2000 RV literature has been a disappointing let-down. In the next section, RV studies from 2000 to 2019 are reviewed. Is there any reason to believe that these more recent studies provide a more positive picture of RV research?

REMOTE VIEWING RESEARCH, 2000–2019

Before turning to the studies themselves, it is helpful to clarify the scientific criteria that enable one to assess a paranormal claim. One of the most basic criteria, of course, is the elimination fraud. However, after fraud has been ruled out, the criteria for assessing claims need to be clarified. Schooler, Baumgart, and Franklin (2018) differentiate between 'entertaining' a paranormal claim and 'endorsing' a paranormal claim. Entertaining a paranormal claim is no great shakes. It is achieved simply by talking about a claim as if it might be correct. This is what I am doing in this part of the book. Endorsing a claim is a much larger step, one that cannot be taken lightly. Schooler et al. present criteria for endorsement of claims that are extraordinarily high but not insurmountable:

1. Careful evaluation of design by skeptics and supporters prior to the initiation of the protocol.
2. Preregistration of protocol, including data analysis using both standard and Bayesian procedures.
3. A computer-implemented procedure using locked code that cannot be tampered with.
4. A procedure that can be carried out by Ps without interaction with experimenters as it takes place.
5. Off-site logging of data.
6. Careful independent analysis of data by multiple statisticians blind to condition.
7. Analysis of data must reveal highly significant results when analysed using both standard and Bayesian procedures.
8. The resulting protocol must itself be replicated by numerous independent laboratories.
9. Ideally, the protocol should be transformed into a paradigm that can have demonstrable real-world outcomes – for example, predicting the stock market. (Franklin et al., 2014)

Holding these criteria in mind, I searched the peer-reviewed scientific literature on RV from 2000 to 2019. Only four studies could be identified, one being a meta-analysis of 21 other RV studies (Table 5.2).

Storm, Tressoldi, and Di Risio (2010) ran meta-analyses on three categories of experiment, which included a homogeneous set of 14 standard free-response RV studies. They defined this category of studies as 'standard free response (no ganzfeld or similar noise reduction techniques to alter the normal waking cognitive state through hypnosis, meditation, dreaming, or relaxation)'. The analysis covered the period from March 1997 to 2008. Storm et al. conducted Internet searches through EBSCOhost of the relevant databases, including PsycINFO, PsycARTICLES and CINAHL, as well as other relevant databases (i.e. Medline, Web of Science, Lexscien and InformIT) using the keywords and subject headings: extrasensory perception, ESP, ganzfeld, PK, telepathy, clairvoyance, precognition, anomalous cognition, parapsychology, paranormal and psi. The number of Ps had to exceed two (!) and target selection had to be randomised using a random number generator or a table of random numbers. However, the latter criterion was assumed in a number of cases, not actually confirmed in print. Studies also had to provide 'sufficient information (e.g. z scores or number of trials and outcomes) for the authors to calculate the direct hit rates and to apply appropriate statistical tests and calculate ES as $z/\sqrt{n}$. The studies included in the Storm et al. meta-analysis of RV studies are listed as follows (Table 5.3).

Table 5.2 Four peer-reviewed publications of RV studies from the period 2000–2019.[1]

	Authors	Title	Journal	Comments	Outcomes
A	Targ & Katra (2000)[2]	RV in a group setting	Journal of Scientific Exploration, 14, 107–114.	A poorly controlled classroom project; sensory cues available and subjective.	Statistically significant effect but unreliable.
B	Storm (2003)[3]	RV by committee: RV using a multiple agent/ multiple percipient design	Journal of Parapsychology, 67, 325–342.	A poorly controlled and naive study. For example, sometimes LS was in contact with the outbound team by cell telephone to adjust departure times. Also, LS accompanied the first independent judge (MT) to the targets. MT had to be replaced by a second judge (RP) who was unaccompanied (Stage 2, p. 333). There is no record of what information may or may not have passed back and forth between MS, RP and LS. LS writes: 'Sensory leakage, however, might still be a problem with this judging procedure', suggesting this paper should not have been accepted for publication.	Inconclusive findings based on a methodologically weak study.
C	Wiseman & Watt (2010)[4]	'Twitter' as a new research tool: a mass participation test of RV	European Journal of Parapsychology, 25, 89-100.	A mass participation RV study using Twitter with over 5,000 responses over five trials.	No statistically significant findings.

Authors	Title	Journal	Comments	Outcomes
D Storm, Tressoldi, & Di Risio (2010)	Meta-analysis of free-response studies, 1992–2008: assessing the noise reduction model in parapsychology	*Psychological Bulletin*, 136, 471–485.	See Table 5.3 below for further details.	Overall result from meta-analysis of free-response studies inconclusive.

[1]Three 'associative remote viewing' studies were focused on predicting stock market values and need to be considered as studies of precognition: Kolodziejzyk (2012), Smith, Laham, and Moddel (2014) and Katz, Grgić, and Fendley (2018).

[2]Targ and Katra (2000) claim: 'Blueprint accuracy sometimes can be achieved, and reliability in a series can be as high as 70%. With practice, people become increasingly able to separate out the psychic signal from the mental noise of memory, analysis, and imagination. Targets and target details as small as 1 mm can be perceived. Again and again, we have seen that accuracy and resolution of RV targets are insensitive to variations in distance' (p. 108). However, this was a classroom demonstration with uncontrolled methodology and the possibility of sensory cues and undoubtedly large amounts of subjective validation. The study fails to meet even the most basic criteria for publication in a scientific journal.

[3]Sensory cueing was a possibility in the judging process with the first of two judges. The investigator (LS) accompanied the first independent judge (MT) to the target in a car. LS claims that he never spoke to MT or communicated in any other way with him during the ranking procedure, nor could he from the distance at which he stood. Using the description provided in the publication, the procedures are unclear and would be almost impossible to independently replicate.

[4]In the largest RV study ever done, Wiseman and Watt (2010) used a non-blind judging procedure in Trial 1 to explore confirmation bias, which they found. With blind judging in Trials 2–5 the group failed to identify the correct target and no significant association was found between belief in psychic ability and choice of target in any of the four trials.

Table 5.3 Studies meta-analysis of RV research included in a collection of free-response studies (Category 3 of Storm, Tressoldi, & Di Risio, 2010).[1]

No.	Authors and date	Trials	Hits	Z ES	(z/√n)	Comment
1.	da Silva et al. (2003)	54	10	−0.94	−0.13	
2.	Holt (2007), artists	15	6	1.04	0.27	
3.	Holt (2007)	15	7	1.58	0.41	
4.	Holt & Roe (2006)	40	10	0.00	0.00	
5.	Lau (2004)	937	232	−0.12	−0.01	
6.	**May (2007)**	**50**	**32**	**4.57**	**0.65**	Conference proceedings; unreliable.
7.	Parra & Villanueva (2006)	138	38	0.59	0.05	
8.	Roe & Holt (2006)	120	28	−0.32	−0.03	
9.	Roney-Dougal et al. (2008) clairvoyance	24	5	−0.24	−0.05	
10.	Roney-Dougal et al. (2008) precognition	24	4	−0.71	−0.15	
11.	Simmonds & Fox (2004) walking controls	20	2	−1.29	−0.29	
12.	Simmonds-Moore & Holt (2007)	26	8	0.45	0.09	
13.	Steinkamp (2000) clairvoyance	74	17	−0.27	−0.03	
14.	Steinkamp (2000) precognition	75	16	−0.60	−0.03	
15.	Steinkamp (2001) Series 3, precognition	100	21	−0.81	−0.08	
16.	Steinkamp (2001) Series 3, clairvoyance	100	28	0.58	0.06	
17.	**Storm (2003)**	**10**	**5**	**1.84**	**0.58**	RV by committee; reviewed in Table 5.2 above.
18.	Storm et al. (2007)	76	16	−0.66	−0.08	
19.	Storm & Thalbourne (2001)	84	22	0.13	0.01	
20.	**Targ & Katra (2000)**	**24**	**14**	**3.54**	**0.72**	RV in a group setting; reviewed in Table 5.2 above.
21.	Watt & Wiseman (2002)	58	17	1.61	0.21	
	Overall median of the findings			0.00 (median)	0.029 (mean)	

[1] Storm et al. (2010) included a few RV studies in Category 3 but these were treated as free-response data. This meta-analysis therefore went beyond RV research.

The median effect size Z value of the sample of 21 scores in Table 5.2 falls exactly at 0.0 (Holt & Roe, 2006). Overall, the results show a weak negative mean effect size of 0.029 (Stouffer Z = 2.29, p = .989), which is a very long away from being statistically significant. With three high outliers, 0.58, 0.65 and 0.72, the distribution is skewed towards the high end and not normal. The evidence is highly equivocal. As a consequence of methodological concerns, the three studies producing the statistically significant effects are inconclusive. Taking into account the methodological problems listed in the table, the pattern of results suggests that the RV effect is unconfirmed, but not disconfirmed, by these studies.

I sent a copy of this chapter to the world's leading RV investigator, Dr Harold E. Puthoff,[5] who kindly contributed the following statement.

A PERSPECTIVE ON REMOTE VIEWING

Prof. Marks has provided a detailed overview of the field of investigation of information gathering by what is often labeled 'paranormal' means, specifically the field that typically goes under the rubric of 'remote viewing (RV).' Due to the nature of the product (descriptive material, including verbal narratives and sketches of target materials), Prof. Marks rightly points out that simple comparisons of subject responses to target materials invite potentially misleading elements of subjectivity that he labels subjective validation (SV). Recognition of this factor has in the field led to an analysis protocol wherein judges are asked to blind-match the RV-generated materials to the target materials on a blind basis wherein the judge does not know during judging which RV-generated response goes with which target. Unfortunately, even this attempt at objective analysis can introduce subjective factors of its own – e.g., have transcript materials presented to a blind judge been sufficiently scrubbed to remove tell-tale clues that provide information about, say, other targets in a series and thereby eliminate the possibility of completely unbiased matches. Unfortunately, post-hoc attempts to assess the significance of this possibility by skeptical investigators who are not blind to the outcomes can invite its own form of confirmation bias.

Given the above conundrums, it would appear that the best way to determine whether there is any evidence for RV as an additional attribute of human sense perception is to examine those cases where application leads to useful outcomes under conditions where problematical factors such as the above cannot in principle play a role in determining the outcome. As a researcher in the government-sponsored RV program at SRI (Stanford Research Institute) in the 70's and 80's, a plethora of examples come to mind, but I'll limit

(Continued)

---

[5]H. E. Puthoff, Ph.D., President and CEO EarthTech International, Austin, Texas. Dr Puthoff's willingness to provide his perspective is appreciated. While we do not agree about the evidence to date, we agree that progress can only occur when the methodological issues are fully addressed.

my remarks to just two case studies whose final RV-determined outcomes are independent of potentially-contaminating factors of the type often raised by critics.

'MULTIPLE PROTECTIVE SHELTER' SERIES

As a result of concern over the growing vulnerability of the U.S. ICBM force during the Carter Administration, the USAF's Space and Missile Systems Organization (SAMSO) proposed a multiple protective shelter (MPS) or 'shell game' dispersal system of missile deployment (Puthoff, 1996). In MPS basing a number of MX advanced mobile ICBMs would be shifted periodically among a substantially larger number of basing points (e.g., by underground railroad) to confuse the targeting of an attack against them. Typically, the ratio of ICBMs to silos was to be approximately one in 20–25.

As a simulation of whether the RV process could be used to defeat such a shell-game process, a microcomputer-automated study carried out by SRI consultant Charles Tart of the University of California, Davis, was used to evaluate this possibility (Tart, 1976). For this task ten test subjects who had scored at the $p = 0.05$ level or better on a previous RV screening procedure were asked to participate in a formal study of 500 trials each to determine for each trial which of ten possible positions on a circular display had been designated as the target by the microcomputer's random number generator. Such an experiment is totally automated, double-blind and lacking subjective judging factors. Out of the ten subjects, five were statistically significant at $p = 4 \times 10^{-5}$ or better, and the best subject averaged a 24.8% hit rate (only 10% expected) over the 500 trials. The latter's 24.8% hit rate over the 500-trial run is a result whose probability of occurrence by chance is only $p = 4 \times 10^{-28}$. Further analysis of the data, taking advantage of the redundancy power of a standard sequential-sampling averaging technique (Puthoff & Targ, 1976) revealed that such a hit rate would be sufficient to determine a simulated missile location with high accuracy. Based on this simulation we assessed that the MPS system was potentially vulnerable to RV information gathering.

STOCK MARKET SERIES

One often hears a skeptic of RV say, 'If they're so psychic, why ain't they rich?' As it happens, during the RV program at SRI an opportunity to address just such a challenge arose. A colleague who was a stock market investor offered that, knowing of the RV program at SRI, he would be willing to trade silver futures for 30 consecutive market days based strictly on daily RV-predicted outcomes, and to donate 10% of his winnings to a charitable cause of our choice. The offer/challenge was accepted as a one-off, definitive test.

The technique employed was an ARV (Associational Remote Viewing) procedure, well-known in the community of RV investigators. In this method a team of remote viewers is asked to each describe (free-response) a target object to be shown them at the close of the market on the following day, the selection of that object to be determined by the following day's market activity (e.g., if market up, a tape measure; if down, a wooden figurine – see Fig. 5.4 for an example).

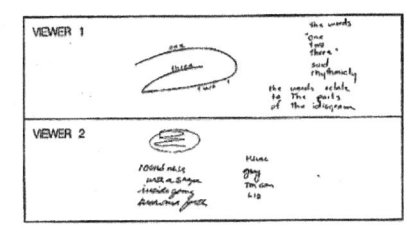

Figure 5.4 ARV targets, a wooden figurine and a tape measure, and the two best responses

By virtue of the daily market-determined feedback, a new pair of objects is chosen each day from a pool unknown to the remote viewers. The task of the RV judge is to determine from the viewers' transcripts and drawings the likely feedback object of the object pair, and hence (in advance) the associated market movement. For the tape measure/wooden figurine case, the two best responses shown in Fig. 5.4 led the judge to choose the tape measure as the following day's likely market-determined feedback object, which turned out to be correct.

The sequence in detail is:

- Remote viewers (RVers) generate transcripts, attempting to describe the object to be shown them the following day.
- Without reference to the transcripts two objects are selected by a colleague of the RV judge and secretly assigned (by use of a random number generator) as the market-up, market-down objects.
- By examination of the transcripts the RV judge determines a consensus vote as to which of the two objects is likely being described as the future feedback object, the code is broken, and the associated market-movement prediction is passed on to a trader.
- At the close of the following market day the actual 'ground-truth' market-movement object is shown the RVers for feedback, closing the loop.
- The process is then repeated for the following day's market investment.

Seven individuals interested in the challenge volunteered to be RVers for this experiment. The number of RV trials/person ranged from a maximum of 36 (six pilot, 30 market

(Continued)

trials) to a minimum of 12. Individual hit rates were 10/12 (83.3%), 26/36 (72.2%), 19/28 (67.9%), 23/36 (63.9%), 18/30 (60.0%), 19/32 (59.4%), and 12/28 (42.9%), for a total of 127/202 (62.9%), an overall result statistically significant at $p < 1.6 \times 10^{-4}$. The consensus judging carried out for each trial yielded a somewhat higher market result of 21/30 (70.0%), significant at $p < 2.2 \times 10^{-2}$ (Puthoff, 1984).

On the basis of the RV-determined market choices that ran 70/30 instead of the 50/50 expected by chance, the investor's winnings were a little over a quarter million dollars ($260,000), yielding for the charitable cause its 10%, $26,000.

SYNOPSIS

The zetetic examination of evidence approach for RV taken by Prof. Marks is in principle a worthwhile endeavor, and some of the traps and pitfalls that can lead to inflated claims of RV efficacy need to be heeded. Unfortunately, *confirmation bias* is a two-edged sword that can show up for both advocates and skeptics, with the latter dismissing some studies with simply-worded phrases like 'a strong possibility of sensory leakage' without data to support backed by double-blind analytical assessments as would be required for the advocates.

It is for these reasons that, from my perspective, an advocate for RV as a verified human sense perception best serves his case by choosing as exemplars those studies (as in the two examples above) wherein RV is used to yield unambiguous outcomes that for methodological reasons are in principle judged to be independent of subjective biased interpretation. Once established, exploration of the RV potential under a variety of protocols with attention to detail is then well worth the effort and can (and has, in this author's perspective) provide information of value (May & Marwaha, 2018).

Summary

In spite of the well-documented criticisms of RV studies from the 1970–99 period,[6] my review of the post-2000 literature reveals an identical set of problems. Well-controlled studies produced no evidence of RV (e.g. Wiseman & Watt, 2010). On the other hand, poorly controlled studies contain the strong possibility of sensory leakage and show statistically significant effects (Storm, 2003; Targ & Katra, 2000), but no convincing evidence of RV. In the 45-year period since the original study by Targ and Puthoff (1974), the overall quality of RV studies has not improved and the claimed 'proof' of RV ability, in the opinion of this author, is still not available.

---

[6]Marks (1968, 2000); Marks and Kammann (1978, 1980); Marks and Scott (1986).

The Parapsychological Association's official position that RV is proven provides one example of how incorrect and misleading information is conveyed to the public. In assuming that the PA's statement on its website must be correct, independent investigators can continue to cite the early Puthoff–Targ studies as if they were an unblemished version of the truth (e.g. Schooler, Baumgart, & Franklin, 2018). In spite of the methodological flaws diffused throughout their studies, RV advocates continue to hold up their findings as 'proof' of RV right up to the present day (e.g. Puthoff, 2019; this chapter). In addition, the PA is misleading generations of people into thinking that RV is a proven scientific fact when the situation is exactly the opposite. That needs to change. As an associate member of the PA, I advocate the removal of false propaganda from the PA website.

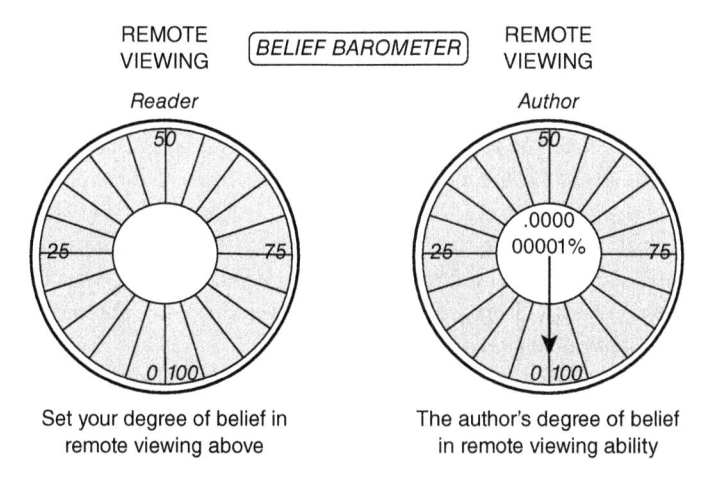

Figure 5.5 Belief barometer readings

PSYCHIC STARING

A popular experiment related to remote viewing involves 'Psychic Staring' (PS). The 'starer', or looker, gazes at the staree (P), directly or via closed circuit television (CCTV). As an optional extra, the P's biological activity can also be monitored during the staring. It is claimed that the starer's attention influences the staree so they can feel that they are being stared at. It is claimed that the staree's moods can even be controlled by this other person. Creepy or what?

The hypothesis of PS was first studied systematically by Titchener (1898). More recently, there has be one major 'celebrity' exponent of PS, the biochemist, plant physiologist and scientist of the paranormal, Rupert Sheldrake. When Sheldrake (1994) published the first evidence for PS, the inevitable controversy followed. *Nature, New Scientist* and the BBC all became involved in refuting or promoting Sheldrake's claims. In September 1981 *Nature* carried an editorial entitled 'A book for burning?' (Maddox, 1981). In another journal, Christof Koch (2005) wrote that: 'I'll not comment on Sheldrake's papers because I think it is a waste of time.' I also expressed doubts about the staring phenomenon because of new evidence obtained in my lab at Middlesex University (Colwell, Schröder, & Sladen, 2000; Marks & Colwell, 2000, 2001). The staring effect became a much vaunted phenomenon. Questionnaire surveys in Britain, Sweden and the US found that more women (81%) than men (74%) said they had felt they were being stared at. This experience occurred most commonly with strangers in public places, such as streets and bars. Also, more women (88%) than men (71%) found that they could stare at others and make them turn around (Sheldrake, 2003).

There are at least five explanations of PS. The first hypothesis (H1) is that PE is a paranormal ability in people and animals who can 'feel' or detect when they are being stared at by using an unknown communication channel. The second (H2) is that people tend to turn round spontaneously to check the environment, peep, and use peripheral vision, auditory or olfactory clues. By chance, if they notice someone looking at them they will remember it. If they do not notice, they simply forget it. The third hypothesis (H3) is that, by turning round to look, the movement attracts someone's attention behind them, so the two people catch each other's eyes (Titchener, 1898). The fourth explanation (H4) is that the PS effect is a special laboratory artefact produced by pseudo-randomisation in the experiments (see below). The fifth explanation (H5) is cheating, which can never be eliminated, is difficult to prove, and one never can know for sure whether it exists in any individual case.

PS tests were carried out with thousands of adults and children. The research was popularised through *New Scientist* magazine, BBC TV and the Discovery Channel with the procedures on their and Sheldrake's (www.sheldrake.org) web sites, so it is perfectly easy to organise replication experiments. There were tens of thousands of trials, which, according to Sheldrake, produced around 55% of correct guesses compared to the 50% mean chance expectation (MCE) (Sheldrake, 2003). Because of the huge sample size, this result has a statistical significance that is off the chart ($p = 1 \times 10^{-20}$). This tiny p value represents an odds of one in 100 million, million, million – at least 150 rice-grain Mount Everests.

The idea that 'unseen' staring can be detected is supported by incidence rates reportedly as high as 68–86% (Coover, 1913), 74% (Williams, 1983) and 92% (Braud, Shafer, & Andrews, 1993a). Staring in everyday life can, of course, be seen or unseen. I suspect a good majority of it is seen, but then avoided by averting the gaze. I remember one staring incident when my son, Mike, was about eight years old. One day as we were walking along a neighborhood street, Mike became perturbed when he felt that other people were staring at him. I asked Mike how he knew this unless he had been staring at them. I think Mike saw the point because his feeling of being stared at disappeared shortly after that. This observation confirms Titchener's explanation (H3), attributing the cause of the feeling of being stared at to the staree, not the starer, and the attribution of causality to the starer can often be a misinterpretation.

TRY IT AT HOME

If you want to give PS a try, why not get together a few friends or classmates and give it a whirl? It is a bit of harmless fun that provides an opportunity for a class exercise if you have a vacant slot in the timetable. There is no harm in doing a few informal tests first for practice. However, if you want to get serious, please try PS with your 'eyes open' to the following issues:[7]

1. How to properly randomise the sequence of stare and no-stare trials? PSs could learn to respond to any patterns in the trial randomisation.
2. How to prevent sensory cueing of the investigator and the PS – for example, peeping or peripheral vision, or auditory or olfactory clues?
3. How to ensure accurate recording of data?
4. How to stop somebody cheating? The starer might whisper or signal to the PS whether they are looking or not looking. Perhaps use windows or CCTV to block this type of cheating.
5. How to avoid experimenter effects? Whether experimenters or starers are believers or skeptics themselves might influence the results.
6. How to carry out the proper statistical procedures?

I turn to consider the evidence for and against PS published over the period 2000 to 2019.

META-ANALYSIS FINDS A LACK OF METHODOLOGICAL RIGOUR

The criterion for inclusion of research in this review is publication in a peer-reviewed journal.[8] In spite of a rush of enthusiasm for PS in the 1990s, with an initial spate of journal articles, a fairly broad-based search yielded only a few peer-reviewed articles post-2000:[9] Sheldrake (2005), Watt (2006)[10] and a meta-analysis by Schmidt, Schneider, Uyys, and Wallach (2004). With the widespread availability of CCTV, it seems odd that so few peer-reviewed studies of PS have been reported. One cannot help wondering whether a multitude of non-significant studies are stuck away in file drawers somewhere. There is no way of knowing.

---

[7] For full details on avoidance of artefacts, see Sheldrake (2001).
[8] For a host of different reasons, books, magazines and blogs are unreliable sources and cannot be included as scientific evidence.
[9] Sheldrake, Overby, and Beeharee (2008) report an automated internet PS study which the authors admit was unsupervised and therefore unreliable. Ferris and Rock (2009) reported a significant staring effect.
[10] Watt (2006) reported 96 undergraduate student projects supervised by Koestler Parapsychology Unit staff, including three staring studies with statistically non-significant effects, although 'all 3 found effects in the predicted direction and of a reasonable magnitude ($r = 0.15$)'.

However, if PS is real, meta-analysis of the best available studies should reveal it. Schmidt et al. (2004) examined 15 remote staring studies between 1989 and 1998, and 36 'Direct Mental Interaction in Living Systems' experiments. For PS they found a small or trivial overall average effect size for PS of d[11] of .13 ($p < .01$). The investigators stated:

> there is a lack of high-quality studies and such studies may reduce the overall effect size or even show that the effect does not exist .... The lack of methodological rigour in the existing database prohibits final conclusions and calls for further research, especially for independent replications on larger data sets. There is no specific theoretical conception we know of that can incorporate this phenomenon into the current body of scientific knowledge. Thus, theoretical research allowing for and describing plausible mechanisms for such effects is necessary. (Schmidt et al., 2004: 245).

INDEPENDENT REPLICATION OF PS FAILS

Schmidt et al. (2004) did not include one high-quality study carried out by Schlitz, Wiseman, Watt, and Radin (2006), which failed to replicate the PS effect. Two studies by Colwell, Schröder, and Sladen (2000) (CSS) also failed to replicate the PS effect[12] but yielded a possible explanation as to how the PS effect may have happened in the first place. In the first of two experiments by CSS, two main conditions in which Ps were given feedback or no feedback were compared under strictly controlled laboratory conditions. Twelve volunteers – seven men and five women – who believed in PS were tested individually in a situation where they sat near a one-way mirror with their back to the mirror. They were stared at or not stared at over a sequence of trials. Sheldrake's original sequences were downloaded from the *New Scientist* web site to guide the order of staring and non-staring trials. Each P received the first 12 sequences in the same order, with 20 trials in each sequence. The beginning and end of each trial was signalled to the PS on a monitor, after which they indicated whether or not they thought they were being stared at by pressing one of two response buttons. No feedback was given on the accuracy of each trial for the first three sessions (60 trials), but on the remaining nine sequences (180 trials) the word 'correct' or 'false' appeared after each response. The results are summarised in Table 5.4.

---

[11]d is a measure of effect size (see Chapter 2).
[12]These studies were published after the review period. I base this section on Marks and Colwell (2000, 2001) to provide more detail on PS methodology.

Table 5.4 Overall accuracy scores in experiment one (CSS)

	Non-feedback trials			Feedback trials		
	Stare	No stare	Accuracy	Stare	No stare	Accuracy
Average	16.4	13.5	29.9	53.7	45.0	98.7
Mean chance Expectation	15.0	15.0	30.0	45.0	45.0	90.0

Without feedback, the scores did not differ from the MCE (29.9 vs. 30.0). With feedback, however, there was statistically significant above-chance accuracy, with 98.7 correct trials compared to an MCE of 90.0 ($p < .001$).

Bingo! Proof positive of PS – Sheldrake's original findings are confirmed.

Not so fast ...

Before leaping to conclusions, one needs to look carefully at the different results obtained with and without feedback. The two sets of results suggest a rational explanation of these data. As a result of the feedback, could the starees perhaps have been learning something useful about the sequences? If the sequences that had been used to generate the trial sequences were not perfectly random, then there could have been a predictable patterning in their structure.

How could this be? Well-known lab lore indicates that experimenters sometimes (often?) use pseudo-random sequences rather than truly random ones (Brugger, Landis, & Regard, 1990). The pseudo-random procedure enables experimenters to equalise the number of trials in two different experimental conditions (e.g. stare versus non-stare), but this equalising tactic has consequences. Pseudo-random sequences with neatly equalised frequencies of stare and no-stare trials have the potential to enable the starees to learn the sequence structure. Learning this structure would partly result from the fact that there are no long runs of the same event. This absence of short runs corresponds to human expectations that long runs will not happen, and so, after a short run of the same event, the participant, who is basically guessing what is going to happen next, thinks it will be best to switch to the alternative event. This strategy is known as the 'gambler's fallacy'. Learning the sequence structure tends to improve with exposure and so, to test for this possibility, the 12 sessions were divided into four blocks of three sessions each. Accuracy scores were compared across the four blocks and the average accuracy level improved from block 1 (no feedback) through blocks 2–4 (with feedback). This result showed that Sheldrake's so-called 'random' number sequences were not random at all because they contain a definite, predictable structure. Therefore, an analysis of Sheldrake's sequences was undertaken.

The number of repetitions in a sequence of 20 binary events should be 9.5 (Wagenaar, 1970, 1972). The numbers of repetitions in Sheldrake's 12 sequences are: 6, 6, 6, 8, 8, 8, 8, 9, 9, 7, 7, 7, averaging 7.42, way below the chance level.

The average probability of a repetition is 0.39, well below what would be expected in a truly random sequence (0.50). Another way of analysing the patterning in the sequence trials is to divide the series of stare (S) and no stare (N) trials into the eight possible trios or 'three-tuples' – i.e. SNS, SNN, SSN, etc. (Rapoport & Budescu, 1997). In theory, a random sequence should contain an equal number of the eight kinds of three-tuples, each having a probability of 1/8 = .125. The frequency of each trio was analysed across the 12 sequences. There were huge deviations from a random distribution, with many more alternating sequences (SNS and NSN) than there should have been and far fewer sequences of SSS and NNN. The deviations from randomness were both highly significant and highly statistically significant ($p < .001$), a result that is fatal to Sheldrake's PS research project.

From the above analysis, it seems highly likely that the Ps in the Sheldrake/*New Scientist* PS project were able to score well above chance purely by *learning the non-random structure of the sequences using the feedback*. In other words, Sheldrake's highly hyped results were purely an artefact of patterning in the stimuli. This idea receives support from the literature on 'implicit learning', which suggests that the learning can take place incidentally without conscious awareness (Reber, 1989). There is also a huge literature on 'probability learning' that suggests that people are very good at learning the global and local probabilities in the patterning of events (e.g. Servan-Schreiber & Anderson, 1990). The tendency of the Ps to avoid multiple repetitions was well matched by Sheldrake's sequences that showed exactly the same property. The fact that starees can guess when staring is likely to occur at above-chance levels makes it highly possible that Sheldrake and his many *New Scientist* and website co-investigators had found nothing more than a well-known ability to notice patterns. This finding spells disaster for the whole PS project.

On the other hand, keeping one's options open in true zetetic fashion, it could be argued that improvement was not due to learning, but to *increased sensitivity* to unseen staring with repeated exposure, so that psi could still happen on top of the pattern learning effect. A critical test of the two explanations was arranged by conducting a rerun of the first experiment, but this time using genuinely random sequences. Improving performance would support the paranormal explanation, whereas an implicit learning explanation would predict failure to beat the mean chance expectation level.

MORE FAILURES TO REPLICATE

CSS repeated the first experiment using 10 properly randomised sequences taken from random number tables instead of the Sheldrake/*New Scientist* non-random sequences.[13] Tests of randomness were carried out and passed. Feedback was

---

[13]The starer in Experiment 2 was a different person. This leaves an opening for more controversy. Sheldrake claimed that the starer in Experiment 2 was a skeptic and the starer in Experiment 1 was a believer, citing Wiseman & Schlitz's (1997) finding of a 'sheep–goat' effect on PS. However, this was a red herring; the two starers in the two experiments were both open to the possibility of PS. They would not have participated otherwise.

given in all sessions, the first one of the 10 being purely for practice. In this case, no improvement in guessing rates occurred over the three blocks of trials. The results of this experiment support the hypothesis that the improvement in accuracy during staring episodes observed in experiment one was due to pattern learning. When no feedback was provided and pattern learning was blocked (experiment one, blocks 1–3), no ability to detect staring was observed and also no learning. These data suggest that there is no evidence of a general ability to detect unseen staring when the staring and non-staring trials are properly randomised or when no feedback is provided. The only positive results were in the context of feedback and the non-random sequences generated by Sheldrake.

Unfortunately, in his *New Scientist* citizen science series, Rupert Sheldrake could not control for sensory cueing or cheating, two other major limitations. One of the main reasons for carrying out experiments in the lab rather than in the pub, classroom or playground is to eliminate sensory cueing, non-randomisation and certain types of cheating. Some studies have attempted to eliminate these problems by increasing the physical separation and blocking sensory leakage. For example, Williams (1983) linked starer and staree, positioned in rooms 60 feet apart, by CCTV. Following a random number sequence, the monitor in the starer's room would come on for 12-second periods, enabling them to view the staree, and these constituted the staring periods. Presumably, 12-second non-staring periods were also provided. A positive detection effect was obtained. No feedback was given and so implicit learning would not be possible. However, as in Sheldrake's research, randomness of sequences was not controlled for, and the possibility of a matching in bias between experimental and response sequences exists, which could lead to increased accuracy (Gatlin, 1977).

Explanations in terms of sequence randomness would not account for the positive results obtained by Braud, Shafer, and Andrews (1993a, b) however. This research used a set-up similar to that of Williams (1983), except that the measure of detection was physiological-spontaneous phasic skin-resistance response (SSR), which measured sympathetic autonomic nervous system arousal. However, the robustness of Braud et al.'s findings is open to question, since some replications have found the effect (Schlitz & LaBerge, 1997), while others have failed (Wiseman & Smith, 1994; Wiseman, Smith, Freedman, Wasserman, & Hurst, 1995). Collaborative research by Wiseman and Schlitz (1997), using the same methodology, the same equipment, in the same location, at the same time, with participants from the same pool, resulted in evidence of a staring detection effect for Schlitz (a psi believer) but not for Wiseman (a skeptic). Possible reasons for these experimenter effects are discussed, though no firm conclusions are drawn, and further research on this experimenter effect seems warranted. However, CSS and Baker (2000) point out that the detection of staring at a subconscious level provides no support for conscious awareness of being stared at in the absence of normal sensory information. Baker's research, which included 'informal staring' at individuals in everyday situations before asking them if they had been aware of being stared at, and laboratory sessions in which Ps acted both as starers and starees, provided no empirical support for a conscious ability to detect unseen staring.

There are real methodological problems still to be resolved in the field of parapsychology. Lance Storm (2006) declared:

> It is a well-accepted fact that parapsychologists conduct extremely rigorous experiments with very much tighter controls compared to other disciplines (cf. Sheldrake, 1998) – not because psi is so elusive, but because of the controversial nature of psi that invariably compels non-parapsychologists to attack parapsychology at its core (i.e., the way parapsychologists design their experiments). It has reached the point where conventional explanations like sensory leakage, selective reporting, and outright fraud, are not only passé, but also insulting to the professionally minded parapsychologist.

The evidence of severe flaws in both RV and PS research suggest a very different picture. I disagree with Storm's conclusions. The problems in research on parapsychology are not passé but remain ever present – *sic passim*.[14]

Summary

Rupert Sheldrake makes the bold claim that people are able to consciously detect unseen staring at above-chance levels. Unfortunately, Sheldrake's sequences were patterned and unsuitable for this research. The sequences followed the same patterning that people who guess and gamble like to follow: relatively few long runs and many alternations. The biased nature of Sheldrake's sequences has several unfortunate implications for the PS hypothesis. First, implicit or explicit pattern learning occurs when feedback is provided. When the patterns being guessed mirror naturally occurring guessing patterns, the results can even go above or below chance levels without feedback. Thus, significant PS results might occur purely from non-random guessing. The *New Scientist* web site disseminated Sheldrake's non-random sequences and misled amateur scientists all over the world. This may well have influenced the scientific education and rigour of some of society's most motivated and enthusiastic young scientists. It also may have increased paranormal beliefs by suckering thousands of amateur investigators with spurious findings. The evidence from properly controlled studies provides no support for the claim that people can detect unseen staring using psi. Unfortunately for the PS hypothesis, the evidence is not there. All we have, yet again, is methodological flaws and investigator denial.

In the interest of fairness, the final comments on PS research were invited from the leading investigator, Dr Rupert Sheldrake. I sent a copy of this chapter to Dr Sheldrake seeking his comments, which are reproduced verbatim below.

---

[14]*Sic passim*: throughout.

RESPONSE BY RUPERT SHELDRAKE

I am grateful to David Marks for this opportunity to respond to his chapter.

This chapter is similar to an article he published in the *Skeptical Inquirer*, with John Colwell (Marks & Colwell, 2000) and to an article in *The Skeptic* (Marks, 2003) to both of which I replied. Marks does not refer to a comprehensive discussion of the sense of being stared at in a special issue of the *Journal of Consciousness Studies* (Volume 12, No 6, 2005), entirely devoted to this subject, with two target articles by me, fourteen articles by other researchers, including several sckeptics, and my response to these articles (Sheldrake, 2005). Readers interested in a detailed discussion of this phenomenon, technically known as scopaesthesia, should refer to this special issue of the *Journal of Consciousness Studies*.

The great majority of studies on the detection of unseen stares have shown positive, statistically significant effects. In my review in the *Journal of Consciousness Studies*, I summarise data from tens of thousands of trials, including 21 experiments of my own (excluding online tests), in 20 of which the outcome was positive, and also from 37 independent investigations in universities, colleges and schools of which 36 showed a positive effect (Sheldrake, 2005). I was notified of all these 37 investigations in advance and included all the data from them. I also summarize the data from a long-running experiment on the detection of staring from behind in Amsterdam at the NeMo Science Centre. More than 18,000 looker-subject pairs took part over several years, with positive results that were astronomically significant statistically, as analysed by Dutch statisticians and researchers.

In most of these experiments, including the Dutch test, the sequence of looking and non-looking trials was fully randomised. Only a small minority of these experiments used the randomized sequences that Marks discusses in his chapter. In any case, almost all the subjects were tested only once, leaving no scope for the implicit learning of any patterns in the randomization sequences. Also, many of these tests did not involve feedback, which would be essential for Marks' implicit learning hypothesis.

In addition to all these experiments, several committed skeptics have obtained positive results when investigating the detection of staring from behind, contrary to their expectations. They then tried to explain away their own data.

Robert Baker, a veteran Fellow of the Committee for Skeptical Inquiry, stared at people from behind while they were working in the library at the University of Kentucky. He then introduced himself and asked them to fill in a response sheet. Two people out of his 40 unwitting subjects reported that they had been aware they were 'being observed and stared at', and three reported they felt something was 'wrong'. Baker noted that while he was staring at these three subjects, they were restless, but he assumed that their restlessness was a chance coincidence. He also 'discarded' the results from the two people who said they knew they had been stared at. He dismissed their reports as 'suspect', because one of these people claimed he had extrasensory abilities, and the other thought she was being spied on (Baker, 2000). This is one of the 'failures to replicate' that Marks refers to.

(Continued)

Richard Wiseman, another Fellow of the Committee for Skeptical Inquiry, together with his graduate student Matthew Smith, carried out staring experiments using a CCTV method, and found a significant positive effect, with undergraduate students doing the staring (Wiseman and Smith, 1994). This positive effect did not agree with Wiseman's expectations, so he explained the results as a statistical artefact. I asked him if I could analyse his data to test his statistical hypothesis. At first he told me the files were 'inaccessible'. I persisted, and he finally managed to retrieve the data for some of the subjects, which he kindly sent to me. I found that these data did not support his explanation (Sheldrake, 2005). The sense of being stared at. Part I: Is it real or illusory? *Journal of Consciousness Studies* 12, 10–31. Wiseman then changed the procedure so that in subsequent experiments, he did the staring himself, or asked one of his colleagues to do so. He then obtained the chance-level results he expected.

Likewise in the CSS paper that Marks discusses in detail, in the first experiment, with a student doing the staring, the results were strikingly positive and the subjects improved with practice. In order to explain this effect, Marks suggests that there might have been an implicit learning of patterns in the counterbalanced sequence of trials that I used in some of my experiments, which CSS also adopted, following a suggestion by Richard Wiseman that such sequences should be used so that the number of looking and not-looking trials was similar, a randomization method that Wiseman used himself.

Marks and his colleague John Colwell did not actually examine the pattern of responses in these tests to see whether they agreed with the implicit learning hypothesis. In 2001, I asked Colwell for the data so that I could test this hypothesis, but he declined my request. He wrote, 'My feeling is that nothing conclusive would emerge.' (Email from John Colwell to Rupert Sheldrake, 29 March 2001).

In the second experiment carried out by CSS, there was a different starer, one of Marks' colleagues. The results were now at chance levels. Marks describes the fact that there was a different starer as 'a red herring'. But, as he points out himself, in experiments carried out by Richard Wiseman and Marilyn Schlitz using a CCTV method, Schlitz obtained positive, statistically significant results while Wiseman did not, showing a clear effect of the person staring. In a subsequent interview, Wiseman said he found staring 'an enormously boring experience' and that in most of the trials he was 'pretty passive about it' (Watt, Wiseman and Schlitz, 2002).

Marks concludes: 'Unfortunately for the PS hypothesis, the evidence is not there. All we have, yet again, is methodological flaws and investigator denial.' But in fact there is plenty of evidence for the sense of being stared at, despite the attempts of Marks and other committed skeptics to deny it.

Fortunately, experiments on staring detection are simple and inexpensive, as Marks points out. More sophisticated methods of instructing lookers and recording guesses by subjects will soon be possible using apps on mobile phones. Students could perform experiments on staring detection as part of their science education. They would learn much by taking part in controversial research at the frontiers of science.

SUMMARY

1. RV and PS are two kinds of anomalous experience that are claimed by the leading investigators to present strong evidence of the paranormal. However, both protocols are highly prone to SV, sensory cues, poor randomisation and other methodological issues.
2. Unfortunately, the quality of the research in both areas has been poor. In assessing RV and PS as examples of anomalous cognition, it is difficult to reach any judgement other than 'case unsupported but not disproved'. It also seems reasonable to expect straightforward answers to the following questions:
3. If 'Blueprint accuracy' of RV is achievable, with a reliability as high as 70%, if 'targets as small as 1 mm can be perceived' and if 'accuracy and resolution of RV targets are insensitive to variations in distance', as claimed, why did the US government cease funding such an invaluable project to national security?
4. If RV operates precognitively with the accuracy claimed by leading investigators, why are these investigators not in the Forbes' World's Billionaires list and banned from every casino in the world?
5. If people can perform PS with 55–60% accuracy as claimed by Rupert Sheldrake, why does the effect appear when experiments are poorly controlled and disappear when they are well controlled?
6. Why was it necessary for the authors of a peer-reviewed meta-analysis in a reputable journal to state: 'there is a lack of high-quality studies and such studies may reduce the overall effect size or even show that the effect does not exist'?
7. In the light of the objective failure of the leading investigators to answer any of these questions, even a zetetic must consider RV and PS effects to be unproven, yet neither are they disproven.

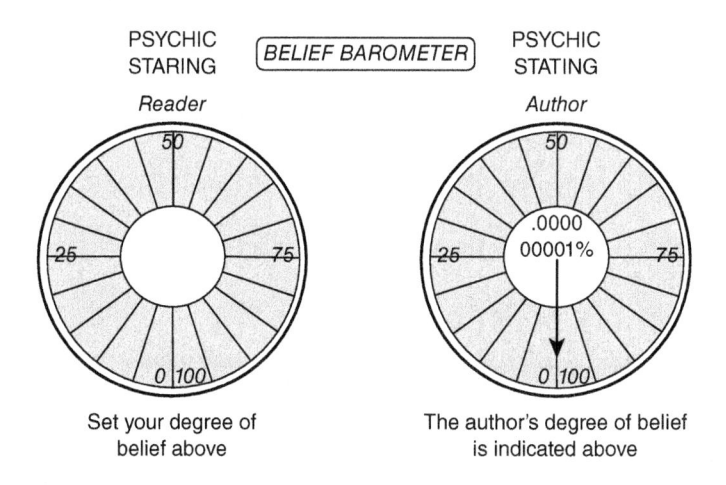

Figure 5.6 Belief barometer readings

QUESTIONS

1. In your own words, describe the procedure for testing RV ability.
2. Name three things to avoid in an RV experiment.
3. What is wrong with photographing a target site *after* an experiment is finished?
4. What is your personal opinion about RV, giving reasons?
5. Describe in your own words the procedure for testing PS ability.
6. Name three things to avoid in carrying out a PS experiment.
7. What is your personal opinion about PS, giving reasons?

6

THE GANZFELD, SUBJECTIVE VALIDATION AND THE NEWLY DISCOVERED SIXTH SENSE

With contributions from Daryl Bem, PhD, Susan Blackmore, PhD and Adrian Parker, PhD

[A] man who is running through a forest; it seems that he is being hunted – at the same time, the receiver says: 'Trees. People running. Fleeing.' Suddenly, the man falls down in a deep muddy pool – at the same time, the receiver says: 'Falling. Muddy.' The camera zooms in on the man's face – at the same time, the receiver says: 'Blond hair. 70s hairstyle. Curly-ish. White face.' All of these utterances appear to describe exactly what is being shown on the film. (Westerlund, Parker, Dalkvist, & Hadlaczky, 2006: 23)

Addition to the known roster of sensory systems, not merely of a new organ or example, but of a new class or major modality, is a rare event. (Bullock & Szabo, 1986)

Outline: Welcome to the detective story that is the ganzfeld (GF) research programme. The GF is based on the idea that when sensory stimulation is 'blanked out', ESP can 'get through' more easily. The GF is a homogeneous field designed to minimise visual and auditory noise that is claimed to be psi-conducive. Following multiple GF studies that showed initially promising results, and five meta-analyses, the results have been

(Continued)

> inconsistent. It is apparent that no individual study or retroactive meta-analysis can ever be decisive. The proposal to employ preregistered, prospective meta-analysis has the potential to break the impasse that exists in this and many other areas of parapsychology. In another new development, a recently proposed magneto-sensitivity theory hypothesises a hidden sensory channel that may be involved in some aspects of information transfer, including GF–ESP, between living organisms. The recent discovery of magnetite (magnetic cells) and cryptochrome (yellow enzymes that help cells to breathe) in the human brain supports this theory. The evidence pro and con, and the questions that remain to be answered, are summarised.

The ganzfeld has been one of the most popular settings for psi research for 50 years. An 'aura' of high confidence surrounds the GF – or it used to. In his book *The Conscious Universe*, Dean Radin writes: 'We are fully justified in having very high confidence that people sometimes get small amounts of specific information from a distance without the use of the ordinary senses. Psi effects do occur in the ganzfeld' (Radin, 1997: 88). In agreement, Jessica Utts suggests that it would be:

> wasteful of valuable resources to continue to look for proof. No one who has examined all of the data across laboratories, taken as a collective whole, has been able to suggest methodological or statistical problems to explain the ever increasing and consistent results to date. Resources should be directed to the pertinent questions about how this ability works. (1995: 311)

How can such awesome confidence be justified?

GF findings attracted the inevitable controversies that surround psi, especially methodological problems (Hyman, 1985), p hacking (Vyse, 2017) and accusations of experimenter cheating (Blackmore, 1987; this chapter). There are two ways of breaking the impasse. One is the preregistration of studies combined with prospective meta-analysis (Watt & Kennedy, 2017). Another is to consider new theories about sensory transmission that may help to explain why some studies find psi and others do not. Recent neurobiological studies indicate the presence of billions of magnetite cells in the brain and human magnetoreceptors. Human magneto-sensory capability to detect the geomagnetic poles unaided by light, maps or other established sensory cues now seems a possibility. This finding has led to the speculation that humans may possess a previously hidden sensory capability. The magneto-sensitivity theory is consistent with GF studies showing that geomagnetic activity tends to block or attenuate ESP scoring rates and that an inverse square law of distance has been observed in a few ESP studies. The hypothesis is unlikely to find favour among psi investigators as the new sense would rival and possibly even replace psi as a theory of information transfer. I review here recent research with the GF, where much of the fundamental research on ESP has been carried out over the last three decades. Then I review a recent hypothesis of a sixth sensory modality, which has relevance to anomalistic psychology and so deserves our consideration.

THE GANZFELD

The term 'ganzfeld' (German for 'entire field') was originally used by the Gestalt psychologists as a method to study perception (Wertheimer, 1923). It involves a homogeneous, sensory field encompassing the visual and auditory modalities, producing a mild form of perceptual deprivation.[1] In an audio-visual GF experiment, translucent hemispheres (e.g. halved ping-pong balls) are placed over the eyes of the P (Hochberg, Triebel, & Seaman, 1951) with diffused red light projected from an external source, together with a sound track of unstructured sounds ('white' or 'pink' noise) played via headphones while the person remains in relaxation. This GF set-up is said to be 'psi-conducive' to images and thoughts that are claimed to have an extrasensory origin (Braud, Wood, & Braud, 1975; Honorton & Harper, 1974; Hyman & Honorton, 1986, 2018; Milton, 1999; Parker, 2000; Terry & Honorton, 1976).[2] The GF procedure is summarised as follows.

At a distant location, a 'sender' or 'agent' attempts to 'send' information from a randomly selected target (e.g. postcards, art prints, film clips).[3] An impression period duration of 20–40 minutes is recommended. Several groups of four targets form the target 'pool', with a randomly selected target for each session from the larger pool. The selected target is placed in a non-adjacent room to minimise the possibility of sensory leakage of target information. The participant's (P's) mental impressions, or 'mentation', is recorded during or immediately after the impression period. A rating of the similarity between the mentation and the four possible targets is carried out by the P or by an independent judge (IJ) while they 'blind' to the actual target identity. No ties are permitted, and the target identity is revealed to those involved in judging only after the results have been recorded.

When the IJ correctly selects the target, this is called a 'hit'. Typically, each P contributes one data point, a 'hit' or a 'miss', to a study, which has a mean chance expectation (MCE) or hit rate (HR) of 25%. It is claimed that the average GF-ESP

---

[1] A video simulation of the GF is available on YouTube at: www.youtube.com/watch?v=o63ztZlpdoE. In a real GF, the total visual field is included.

[2] The ESP/psi concept entails a hypothetical form of energy transfer between individuals (telepathy), between objects and individuals (clairvoyance), or between future events and individuals (precognition) all occurring beyond the established five senses. The energy involved has been labelled 'psychic' or psi, but has never been measured physically, chemically or biologically.

[3] In common with all other tasks for the measurement of psi, no description is available about how the 'sending' process operates.

study reports an HR of around 31% rather than the expected 25% (Bierman, Spottiswoode, & Bijl, 2016). However, since the earliest GF ESP studies in the 1970s, there have been hundreds of studies producing a mixed bag of results, not always positive.

In an early GF study, Hochberg et al. (1951) confirmed that a GF loses its colour whether illuminated with red or green light. In most cases, complete disappearance of colour was obtained, but with individual differences in adaptation and phenomenal content. The spontaneous perceptual changes become more structured over time, changing from light spots, or 'phosphenes', and simple geometrical patterns to well-developed, vivid imagery. The imagery within the GF has been compared to hypnagogic imagery that occurs between waking and sleep.[4] However, that hypothesis remains unconfirmed and was not supported by a study that made a direct comparison. Wackermann, Pütz, Büchi, Strauch, and Lehmann (2002) explored the brain's EEG activity with 12 volunteers in varying conditions of sleep onset, GF, and eyes-closed relaxed waking. The Ps recalled momentary mentation in a predefined cycle and gave ratings of their experience along ordinal scales, producing a total of 241 mentation reports. The GF EEG spectrum showed similar trends to the EEG spectrum of waking states. Only an increase in 'absorption' differentiated the GF state from the other states, and the findings did not support the hypothesis that GF imagery is hypnagogic in nature.

Interest in the GF arises from its alleged psi-conducive nature (Honorton, 1977). W. G. Braud (2002) argued that the GF produces 'stillness of mind' and 'cognitive quietude' in accordance with the model of (mental) noise reduction. Theoretically, by increasing the signal-to-noise ratio (i.e. reducing the noise), any psi information should be more easily detected (Figure 6.1).

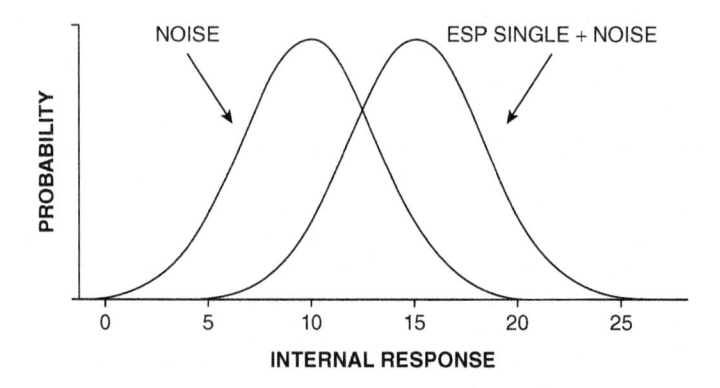

Figure 6.1 The signal detection model of ESP in the GF

---

[4] A description of GF-induced imagery is given by Wackermann, Pütz, and Allefeld (2008).

Relaxing in the presence of a field of homogeneous sensory stimulation, one's attention is directed towards thoughts, images and feelings, and these impressions are more salient when external stimulation from noise and other distractions is reduced. Thus, the GF is the method of choice for a psi-conducive procedure ideally suited to psi investigations in the laboratory. However, it is worth repeating the statement of caution made in Chapter 5 about RV research in the context of the GF:

> The GF is the perfect situation for subjective validation (SV) and it sets the perfect trap for any investigator, however sophisticated. Unless the investigator is fully prepared to eliminate all of the potential traps and pitfalls, a GF experiment is the perfect way to produce SV. Every participant can be fooled by this powerful cognitive illusion into believing that they are witnessing ESP.

With this in mind, I turn to impressive series of successful GF studies conducted by Professor Adrian Parker at Göteborg University in Sweden.

SUCCESSFUL SWEDISH GANZFELD STUDIES

Adrian Parker (2000) reported a three-year GF project entitled 'Psi and the ganzfeld: a replication extension study' at the Department of Psychology at Göteborg University, Sweden. The results of five standard GF studies and one multiple target GF (the serial GF) study are reported. The correspondences that are observed in any GF study may be due either to anomalous information transfer (e.g. telepathy) or to a cognitive illusion caused by subjective validation. An example of a purely chance matching of target and response is quoted as follows:

> [A] man who is running through a forest; it seems that he is being hunted – at the same time, the receiver says: 'Trees. People running. Fleeing.' Suddenly, the man falls down in a deep muddy pool – at the same time, the receiver says: 'Falling. Muddy.' The camera zooms in on the man's face – at the same time, the receiver says: 'Blond hair. 70s hairstyle. Curly-ish. White face.' All of these utterances appear to describe exactly what is being shown on the film. The next thing that happens in the clip is that the man can no longer keep his head above the surface, so he disappears into the mud – at the same time, the receiver says: 'Dead man in the water.' (Westerlund et al., 2006: 23).

Parker reports the findings of his GF studies as follows:

> The standard GF studies form a highly significant and consistent data base with an overall hit-rate of 36% (40% in the case of auditory monitored studies) and a mean effect size of .25 (.34 in the case of the monitored studies).

This database has been used to study psychological correlates of psi in terms of psychometric tests. The most successful of these tests are the Australian Sheep Goat Scale, the Magical Ideation Scale, and 'Feeling' scores on the Myers-Briggs Inventory. Other scales that were used as predictors of psi-scores with varying degrees of success included the Transliminality Scale, the Defence Mechanism Test, and the Tellegen Absorption Scale. (Parker, 2000: 1)

On the basis of some highly significant results, Parker made the following list of conclusions:[5]

- The results in terms of direct hits are statistically highly significant. For the monitored studies, the p-value is .0001 (one-tailed) and for all studies p is .0012 (one-tailed) ...
- The significant results were initially dependent on the success of the main experimenter (AP), but the analysis of subject recruitment showed that this could be explained by this experimenter's avoidance of testing psychology students who scored much lower than the two groups recruited from the public. (Parker, Frederiksen, & Johansson, 1997)
- Ps who were recruited from New Age centres and from a newspaper advertisement scored in the auditory monitored studies at about a 40% level of direct hit frequency (where mean chance expectancy is 25%), while the student group scored at a mere 9% direct hit frequency (Parker, Frederiksen, & Johansson, 1998).
- In the latest two studies, a second generation of experimenters have taken over the main role from those involved in the first three studies, with a result that the level of hitting has still persisted and is independently significant.
- The success rate of 37–47%, while only in one study coming in the region of our intended goal of 50%, appears nevertheless to be consistent when we recruit Ps from our recommended sources (members of the general population who report spontaneous ESP experiences).
- The results show a clear relationship to belief in and personal experience of psi phenomena. It would seem that success is not related to the kind of personal psi experience that can be described as just a one-off crisis event, but rather to psi-experiences that occur often and are integrated into the person's life or personal philosophy. The analysis of the scores on the Sheep-Goat and Magical Ideation Scales indicates that hitters are characterised by a factor beyond pure belief in psi, but it is as yet unclear what this factor is. After the items relating to psi belief were eliminated from the MAS, those making hits

---

[5]To ensure accuracy, the conclusions are quoted verbatim from Adrian Parker's (2000) report, by permission. For sake of brevity, a few of the less vital conclusions are omitted.

could still be distinguished from those making misses by their higher scores on this scale (Parker, Grams, & Pettersson, 1998). Although it is often thought to relate to a proneness towards psychosis, the MAS consists, in fact, of a heterogeneous series of questions, and further work is planned at identifying the items that are most closely related to psi performance.
- Defensiveness failed at least on the measures analysed here using the DMT, to discriminate between hitters and missers (Parker, Grams, & Pettersson, 1998).
- A 'feeling type' may also be more successful, especially with targets than have a strong change in emotional content (Parker, Grams, & Pettersson, 1998).
- Target films showing dramatic changes appear to do slightly better (Parker, Grams, & Pettersson, 1998).

There is no question, Adrian Parker's results are astonishing. The results are highly consistent and the high hit rates suggest that the GF psi effect is replicable. Most importantly, the GF psi effect is qualitatively close to spontaneous psi-experiences that appear in 'real-life'. The GF, therefore, appears to have produced the 'holy grail' of psi research – but has it?

What happens next in Adrian Parker's GF project is about as astounding as the original findings. Six years later, Parker's research team make a complete about-face and describe how remarkable GF results can be obtained by that perennial spoiler of psi studies – subjective validation.

REMARKABLE CORRESPONDENCES LINKED TO SUBJECTIVE VALIDATION

There can be little doubt that remarkable correspondences between GF mentation and target content are obtained in GF experiments. Nobody – not even the most extreme skeptics – deny that. So there is a crucial question: are the remarkable GF correspondences a psychical or psychological effect? Westerlund, Parker, Dalkvist, and Hadlaczky (2006) attempted to answer this.

To investigate the role of SV, Joakim Westerlund with Adrian Parker and colleagues designed four studies. In Study 1, 20 short segments showing the most remarkable correspondences between GF mentation and film-clip content were chosen while 'blinded' to whether the chosen film-clip had been a target or a decoy. Only six of the segments showed correspondences between the mentation and the target, which is close to chance expectation level. The investigators write:

> Apparently, the results give no support to the psi hypothesis. Remarkable correspondences between GF mentation and target content, which so often have been reported from other GF experiments, were also observed in the experiment under investigation in the present study. However, remarkable correspondences were also observed between GF mentation and the

content of the decoy clips, and the distribution of the correspondences on target and decoy clips was, in fact, very close to chance level. So perhaps the remarkable correspondences between GF mentation and target content observed in the present and previous studies are not that remarkable after all. Perhaps they are altogether or mostly the result of subjective validation (a concept used by Marks, 2000, in explaining similar coincidental 'hits' both in experimental work and real life).

In Study 2, 11 students rated the six correspondences that were 'hits' as being equally as impressive as the 14 that were 'misses'. Because the correspondences that were hits were not rated as significantly more impressive than the correspondences that were misses, the investigators concluded that 'the result is, thus, consistent with the notion that the remarkable correspondences so often reported in GF experiments are due to subjective validation'.

In Studies 3 and 4, the hypothesis that the 14 correspondences that were 'misses' could have been due to 'displacement clairvoyance' was tested and shown to be very unlikely. The authors concluded that 'it is possible to obtain what at least some people consider to be very remarkable correspondences between mentation and film content by chance alone' (p. 23). In more specific terms, the investigators also concluded that 'The correspondences that were hits were not rated as significantly more impressive than the correspondences that were misses. The result is, thus, consistent with the notion that the remarkable correspondences so often reported in GF experiments are due to subjective validation' (p. 39). This study provides a robust demonstration that the GF may be measuring nothing but SV. Worse than this, Parker's fabulous-looking results went into severe decline and could not be replicated in his later studies. Reflecting back on his successful GF studies and why the encouraging early results faded away, Parker writes:

> This was an exciting and inspiring time for us because it appeared that the 'real-time digital GF' was giving us the much-sought-after portal through which we could observe some of the psychological processes that mediate real-life psi functioning .... Regrettably, the ambience necessary for the good teamwork that seemed to be enabling the success did not last. The attitude towards university-based parapsychology in Sweden unexpectedly changed for the worse and became hostile. Tensions grew within the research team, culminating in a crisis over whether or not the primary analysis should be based on receivers' own evaluations of the GF mentation (advised by Parker) or on that of an external judge (preferred by another experimenter). Finally, a reluctant agreement was reached prior to running the experiment to use both sources of assessment (but for the purpose of the doctoral thesis, the overall results were primary). The outcome was that the judge's scores were at chance level and psi-missing occurred in the form of a statistically significant negative score for the receiver evaluations. (Goulding, Westerlund, Parker, & Wackermann, 2004)

Four years later, when the university prospects for parapsychology in Sweden had drastically worsened, we attempted to repeat the earlier GF results with a much more complicated procedure that enabled potential target film clips to be primed before being selected. We obtained only chance scores (Parker & Sjödén, 2010). Perhaps symptomatic of the prevailing pessimism, Parker did not first try the procedure out using himself as P. Whatever their nature, none of the earlier type of remarkable real-time correspondences reappeared in these new data. If they were mere subjective validations, as my psi-critic colleague Westerlund would have expected, then they should have. It was Westerlund who carried out the 'remarkable' reassignment of the mentation reports from the above psi-missing experiment, so that they were now matched to new randomised targets. The fact that the new dummy matches did not differ in quality from those of the original hits indicated to Westerlund that the real-time hits were all mere subjective validations. There was, however, a flaw in this argument – namely that these particular original hits were few in number and were from a series that had not given psi-hitting, but psi-missing (see comments by Parker in Westerlund, Parker, Dalkvist, & Hadlaczky, 2006). The story of the Gothenburg experiments reinforces the idea of the 'elusiveness of psi' or even 'the trickster effect' of psi. The expression 'morphing' is suggested here as an alternative term that emphasises how psi does not necessarily evade or hide but rather changes its form. The use of the term 'morphing' avoids the anthropomorphising of the trickster but still describes how psi is neither robust nor an ability that can manifest in the same form irrespective of the conditions. Instead, it would seem that psi arises as an expression of the conscious, and perhaps more so, the unconscious mind influencing random data. (Parker & Millar, 2014: 47)

In addition to the ever-present elusiveness of psi, risk of decline and SV – accepted by Parker's critical colleague Joakim Westerlund, but not by Parker himself – one must consider the methodological complications of the GF and how procedural error may produce the illusion of psi when psi itself is absent.

METHODOLOGICAL COMPLICATIONS

On the surface, the GF is a simple and direct method for the investigation of psi. The GF has the three essential components: a stimulus, a sender, a receiver and little else. The practical reality is rather different. The apparent simplicity is somewhat illusory because the essential procedural requirements for any investigation of ESP must be rigorously implemented.

1. Elimination of all sensory cues during the target selection, sending and judging. Any sensory cues from differential handling or viewing of the selected target – e.g. crimping, bending or smudging of photographs by using a duplicate set of targets for judging, must be removed. If the agent or investigator is present

during the judging, then they could potentially cue the person doing the judging to choose one picture (or video clip) rather than another.
2. Randomisation of target sequences is necessary to preclude the possibility of the subject or the judge guessing the type of target on any specific trial.
3. The data analysis should include all of the collected data rather than specific subsets that may bias the results in favour of psi hypothesis.

The short list of crucial experimental controls looks deceptively simple enough because in the everyday practice of the psychology laboratory all sorts of unexpected things can happen, not the least, human error. These 'unexpected things' are of two main kinds: accidental lapses in procedure (ALP) or deliberate manipulation, cheating and fraud (DMCF). If an independent observer sees something going wrong, it is extremely difficult to say which of these alternatives is causing the problem. This point can be illustrated by an investigation published by Susan Blackmore (SB; 2018). In 1979, SB had received a grant from the Society of Psychical Research to visit Carl Sargent's (CS) laboratory in Cambridge.[6] CS had published many GF studies that had suggested strongly positive evidence of psi (Sargent, 1981, 1982; Sargent & Harley, 1982). SB describes her visit as follows:

> [Sargent's GF] research was providing dramatically positive results for ESP in the GF and mine was not, so the idea was for me to learn from his methods in the hope of achieving similarly good results .... After watching several trials and studying the procedures carefully, I concluded that CS's experimental protocols were so well designed that the spectacular results I saw must either be evidence for ESP or for fraud. I then took various simple precautions and observed further trials during which it became clear that CS had deliberately violated his own protocols and in one trial had almost certainly cheated. I waited several years for him to respond to my claims and eventually they were published along with his denial. (Harley & Matthews, 1987; Sargent, 1987)

CS was invited to provide an account of the errors that SB had observed, but he declined to offer any explanation, even when requested to do so by the Parapsychological Association (PA). The PA President, Stanley Krippner, wrote to CS at no less than four different addresses, but still received no reply. The PA's 'Sargent Case Report' dated 10 December 1986 found that, in spite of strong reservations about CS's randomisation technique, there was insufficient evidence that CS had used unethical procedures.[7] CS was 'reproved' for failing to respond to the PA's request for information. However, CS had allowed his PA membership to lapse through non-payment of dues, but he was informed that,

---

[6] By all accounts, CS was a somewhat eccentric character who, contrary to university regulations, literally 'lived in' his laboratory for a period of time.
[7] The PA report was critical of SB's 'covert manoeuvres' to obtain information about CS's procedures, which they thought may or may not be considered unethical, depending on one's premises.

should he wish to renew his membership, his application would be considered with 'extreme prejudice'. CS left Cambridge University under a cloud. However, he co-authored three books on psi with Professor Eysenck up to 1993 (Eysenck & Sargent, 1982, 1984, 1993) before moving on to a new career.[8] SB's concerns about CS were to have more implications when she later discovered that all nine of his GF studies were included in Honorton's (1985) meta-analysis (see below).

I obtained an update from Susan Blackmore on her current thinking about the possibility of fraud by CS and on psi research more generally, which I reproduce below. Here are Susan Blackmore's answers to five specific questions:

1. **Do you think, in the light of everything that has come to light, CS committed fraud at Cambridge? (Ideally, a yes or a no).** Yes, at least on one specific trial.

2. **Do you think, in the light of everything that has come to light, that DB knew that CS had, or may have, committed fraud but used CS's findings in a meta-analysis anyway, regardless? (Ideally, a yes or a no).** Yes.

3. **On a scale of 0–100%, what was your degree of belief in the reality of psi immediately prior to, and immediately, after visiting CS at Cambridge? (I appreciate this is retrospective and based on memory, but I am interested in an informal appraisal of the impact of the visit).** I don't like to do this. My beliefs were in turmoil throughout this period. I certainly had a phase of significant belief after I saw how well-designed his studies appeared to be and before I spent further time in his lab. But I cannot put any meaningful numbers to this.

4. **Do you think CS knowingly deceived anybody (including possibly himself) or was he simply a victim of confirmation bias/subjective validation?** The former.

5. **Is there anything else you would like to say about research on psi?** In the light of my decades of research on psi, and especially because of my experiences with the GF, I now believe that the possibility of psi existing is vanishingly small, though not zero. I am glad other people continue to study the subject because it would be so important to science if psi did exist. But for myself, I think doing any further psi research would be a complete waste of time. I would not expect to find any phenomena to study, let alone any that could lead us to an explanatory theory. I may yet be proved wrong of course.

(Blackmore, personal communication, 1 August 2019)

---

[8] Two editions of the book by H. J. Eysenck and Sargent (1982, 1993) raise questions about how much Eysenck knew of the fraud accusations against Sargent following Blackmore's SPR report in 1979. In the 1982 edition, the procedural problems with Sargent's GF research are not even mentioned. In the 1993 edition, the authors refer to 'spirited exchanges on GF research' between Blackmore, and Sargent and Harley (p. 189). However, the GF evidence of psi is described by them as 'very, very powerful indeed'. They do not mention of the accusations of fraud, CS's departure from Cambridge University, and his repeated non-cooperation with the PA enquiry.

FIVE META-ANALYSES OF GANZFELD ESP

It is generally accepted that no individual study can ever be considered conclusive because there is always the possibility that methodological factors will create uncertainties about the findings. For this reason, many researchers tend to place their trust in meta-analyses, which integrate multiple findings into a single estimate of the effect being measured. To date, there have been five GF ESP meta-analyses:

1. Charles Honorton (1985).
2. Lance Storm and Suitbert Ertel (2001).
3. Daryl Bem and Charles Honorton (1994).
4. Julie Milton and Richard Wiseman (1999).
5. Lance Storm, Patrizio Tressoldi, and Lorenzo Di Risio (2010).

One cautionary note from the get-go: it seems a little lax procedurally that an investigator doing meta-analysis can *select or deselect a study using any reason they choose in full knowledge of the study findings*. This is the complete opposite to what is generally viewed as good research practice. A psi-skeptic might yield to a bias to exclude a study having a significant psi effect, while a psi-believer might yield to a bias to exclude a study having a non-significant psi effect. Four of the five meta-analyses above reported statistically significant above MCE results, which can be interpreted as positive and replicable evidence of psi (see Figure 6.2). However, the waters have been muddied, or poisoned even, by accusations of

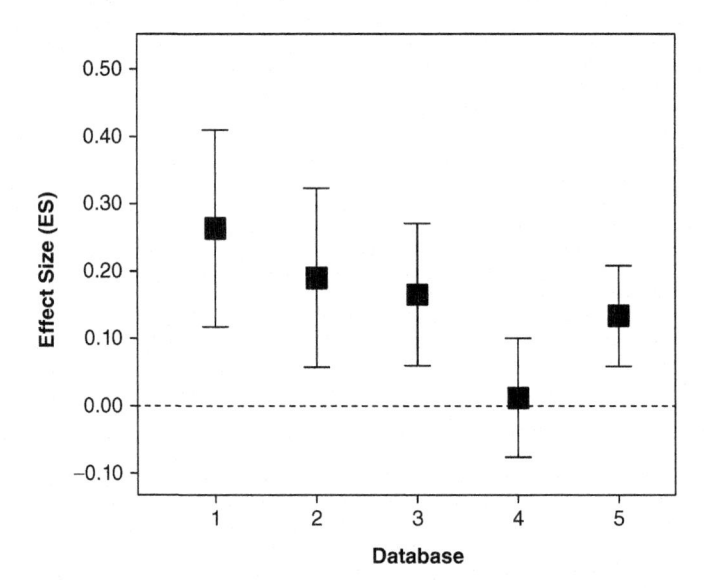

Figure 6.2 Comparison of five GF mean effect sizes (with 95% confidence interval): (1) Honorton (1985; N = 28); (2) Storm and Ertel (2001; N = 11); (3) Bem and Honorton (1994; N = 10); (4) Milton and Wiseman (1999; N = 30); and (5) Storm, Tressoldi, and Di Risio (2010; N = 29).

Reproduced from Storm, Tressoldi, and Di Risio (2010), with permission.

data manipulation and fraud. These same four meta-analyses yielding positive psi hit rates included the highly contentious studies conducted by Carl Sargent (1982; Sargent & Harley, 1982).

Investigators have debated at length how to interpret the five meta-analyses. All of them have been criticised on various grounds, including issues about the definition of what is the 'standard' version of the GF; statistical methods of how meta-analyses should be carried out; cut-off dates and inclusion criteria; how to deal with the heterogeneity, or variation, in the results; and how to handle the 'outliers', the exceptionally high- or low-scoring studies. One of the simplest ways of biasing a meta-analysis is by including supportive studies and excluding non-supportive studies. This biasing may be entirely innocent or it could be deliberate; in any particular case, it is almost impossible to determine which. The old saying about 'one bad apple spoils the barrel' is true of meta-analysis. This can be seen from the experiences recounted by Blackmore (1987, 2018). We have noted above SB's concerns about Carl Sargent's studies at the University of Cambridge and the possibility of cheating.

Susan Blackmore's concerns about CS's studies became all the more acute when she discovered that Charles Honorton (1995) had classified all nine of CS's studies as 'adequate for randomization'. This was in spite of the fact that seven of the studies had used the flawed method that she had observed in CS's lab at Cambridge University. Bear in mind that Blackmore (1987) had published her concerns about CS's curious 'errors' eight years before Honorton did the meta-analysis. To see what impact CS's studies may have had on the results, SB repeated Honorton's calculation but counted the seven CS studies as flawed. Lo and behold, a significant correlation ($r = -.32$, $t = 1.73$, $p < .05$, 1-tailed) existed between randomisation and z-score, as previously found by Hyman (1985), indicating that badly randomised studies tend to produce statistically significant outcomes. SB submitted a report on her finding to the *Journal of Parapsychology* in January 1987. In February, the editor accepted SB's paper for publication, but in May 1988, informed SB that 'they were behind schedule and unable to publish it after all'.[9] This example shows how the results of a meta-analysis could be distorted by 'bad apples' and yet the latter can remain hidden.

The story continues with the publication of Bem and Honorton's (1994) meta-analysis in the prestigious *Psychological Bulletin*. They presented the same meta-analysis and concluded that 'the psi GF effect is large enough to be of both theoretical interest and potential practical importance' (Bem & Honorton, 1994: 8). They admitted that 'One laboratory contributed nine of the studies. Honorton's own laboratory contributed five. ... Thus, half of the studies were conducted by only two laboratories' (p. 6). However, they failed to say *which* laboratory contributed those nine studies and did not even mention CS, giving no references to his papers and none to Blackmore's. To quote SB, 'No one reading

---

[9] I have never previously heard of an editor accepting a paper for publication and afterwards rejecting it because of lack of space.

their review would have a clue that serious doubt had been cast on more than a quarter of the studies involved'.

What SB says next is alarming:

> I have since met Bem more than once …. I told Bem how shocked I was that he had included the Sargent data without saying where it came from and without referencing either Sargent's own papers or the debate that followed my discoveries. He simply said it did not matter …. It matters that Sargent's experiments were seriously flawed. It matters that Bem included these data in his meta-analysis without referencing the doubt cast on them. It matters because Bem's continued claims mislead a willing public into believing that there is reputable scientific evidence for ESP in the GF when there is not. (Blackmore, 2018)

The third meta-analysis was published in the prestigious journal *Psychological Bulletin* by Bem and Honorton (1994). Their results showed an overall hit rate of 32%, compared to an MCE of 25%. Ray Hyman, who had published a joint paper with Honorton on experimental controls for the GF (Hyman & Honorton, 1986), critiqued Bem's statistical methods in the same issue of *Psychological Bulletin* (Hyman, 1994).

Rarely does an investigator admit to not caring about rigour. However, Daryl Bem's approach seems to be condemned by his very own words. Bem is quoted as saying:

> I'm all for rigor but I prefer other people do it. I see its importance – it's fun for some people – but I don't have the patience for it. … If you looked at all my past experiments, they were always rhetorical devices. I gathered data to show how my point would be made. I used data as a point of persuasion, and I never really worried about, 'Will this replicate or will this not?' (Engber, 2017, cited by Vyse, 2017)

To obtain a balanced picture of GF research, I invited Professors Daryl Bem and Adrian Parker to comment. Professor Daryl Bem kindly provided the following remarks:

I am an Emeritus Professor of Psychology at Cornell University. I have a BA degree in physics from Reed College and some additional pre-doctoral work in physics at MIT. I also have a PhD in psychology from the University of Michigan. I am known primarily for my theories of self-perception, sexual orientation, and the continuity of personality across time and situations. Like most psychologists, including author David Marks, I was skeptical about the existence of psi (ESP) during my first 34 years in the field. And, like Marks, I too was disturbed that magician Uri Geller was able to convince psi researchers at one laboratory that he possessed psychic abilities.

It is also relevant that I have been a stage magician for approximately 60 years, specializing in 'mentalism' (fake psi). Knowing this, parapsychologist Charles Honorton invited me to his laboratory in 1983 to inspect his ganzfeld procedure both as an experimental psychologist and a 'mentalist' to see if there were any flaws that would compromise the validity of his experimental procedures.

I judged Honorton's procedures to be free from both experimental artefacts and possible cheating by staff members or participants, so I offered to co-author an article we could submit to a mainstream psychology journal if he obtained instructive results. In 1994, we published the article 'Does Psi Exist? Replicable Evidence for an Anomalous Process of Information Transfer' in the widely read *Psychological Bulletin*.

One of the decisions we faced in the article was how to deal with Blackmore's charge that Sargent had cheated in his experiments. We did not want to endorse or deny her accusations, nor did we want to enter the debate itself. As noted in this chapter, half the studies were conducted by two laboratories, Sargent's and Honorton's own. So, we reported the results of the meta-analysis both with and without their experiments:

> It is possible for one or two investigators to be disproportionately responsible for a high replication rate, whereas other, independent investigators are unable to obtain the effect. The ganzfeld database is vulnerable to this possibility. As Blackmore notes, the 28 studies providing hit rate information were conducted by investigators in 10 different laboratories: One laboratory contributed 9 of the studies; Honorton's own laboratory contributed 5. ... Thus half the studies were conducted by only 2 laboratories, 1 of them Honorton's own.
>
> But even if all of the studies conducted by these 2 most prolific laboratories are removed from the analysis, the Stouffer z across the 8 other laboratories remain significant ($z = 3.67$, $p = 1.2 \times 10^{-4}$). Four of these studies are significant at the 1% level ($p = 9.2 \times 10^{-6}$) and each was contributed by a different laboratory. Thus ... the significance of the overall effect does not depend on just one or two of them (Bem & Honorton, 1994).

So I was being neither flip nor sarcastic when I told Blackmore that it did not matter whether Sargent cheated or not: The database shows a significant effect even if his studies are omitted. Contrary to Blackmore's statement, there *is* reputable scientific evidence for psi in Honorton's meta-analysis. (I have also conducted an independent ganzfeld experiment in my own Cornell laboratory that yielded strong and significant positive results.)

Professor Adrian Parker kindly provided the following remarks:

> David Marks and I share the same starting point. Science should function as 'a candle in the dark' but skeptics are not always the good guys and not always holding the candle. Nor are scientific laws written in stone: To paraphrase Immanuel Kant, scientific laws are merely our mind's ways of trying to understanding the world and not part of the world. Finally, we deplore the hostility in this field in making it more like religious confrontations than an expression of curiosity.
>
> Concerning my ganzfeld work, we agree on the precautions needed. These were fully incorporated and the soundness of our procedure was evaluated during a visit by an external expert (Robert Morris). External technicians tested the laboratory rooms for sensory leakage.
>
> What remains to be made crystal clear is that it is perfectly legitimate to analyse subjective experiences in experiments that are statistically significant. These experiences can generate hypotheses and predictions, which in turn can be tested. Accordingly, here is an example of a transcript from a real-time *hit* (when the text is recorded at the same time as the film-clip) for which I suggest the reader plays the role of scientist and compares this with David's example of a *false match*. The target clip was an animated version of *Wind in the Willows* and the responses to it are given without editing and in real-time with the synchronised film images described in the parentheses:
>
>> 'Spiky thing' (focus on a spiked shaped car mascot falling off the car hood), 'rocks' (roundish rock statues focused on, then fall), 'racing car driver' (image of the Toad as the racing car driver), 'midnight sky' (image of midnight sky), 'trains' (image of a steam train), 'something at two levels' (a car and a train travelling parallel at different levels), 'something slithering by' (a weasel's arm moves or slithers forth) 'geyser' (the car radiator explodes, water shoots up), 'something Y shaped' (out of the hay at the crash-site the Toad's legs point upwards in a Y shape).
>
> It should be emphasised that the P, as in all our sessions, had no prior knowledge of our library of film clips from which the target and the control clips were randomly selected (Parker, Persson, & Haller, 2000).
>
> What can be learned from this? David Marks might say this is a further example of 'subjective validation', but if so it was typical of one in six of our real-time hits and none of our misses. There is, moreover, a crucial distinguishing difference from Marks's quotation of the passage including 'Dead man in muddy water' taken from my work with Joakim Westerlund. That example is a highly connected sequence of events, whereas our most striking examples concern sequences of *sudden unpredictable changes of content* (one of our criteria that seems to correlate with success).
>
> However there is something else that can be learned from this particular hit. The participant in the example here was a ganzfeld research psychologist with a high success rate. She took part because I thought important in the setting up the Ganzfeld at Gothenburg to have the presence and involvement of a successful experimenter. Since then I have gone on to write a paper (Parker & Millar, 2014) revealing one of the best kept secrets

in parapsychology: Successful experimenters with their own psychic experiences make successful participants and vice versa.

What can then account for the Westerlund findings? The material used there was 'contaminated' in the sense that the recordings were taken from an experiment where participants were consistently avoiding choosing the correct target. The misnomer 'psi-missing' for this might suggest that Marks is right to dismiss this concept but rather than missing, a closer meaning would be 'psi-jinxed' – the uncanny ability to *consistently* make the wrong choice. This concept may well be an important discovery of psi-research. It fits with some real-life observations and similar negative effects have been discovered in subliminal perception and the psychotherapeutic relationship.

Nevertheless, I am glad that David Marks focuses on the replication problem. He writes that our studies 'went into severe decline and could not be replicated'. I have always been keen on replication. As a young psychology student, in my very first ESP experiment I discovered by testing 30 volunteers two who scored very significantly. After confirming their abilities, my first act was to pass them on to my supervisor John Beloff and my colleague Brian Millar. Independent of me, Beloff and Millar obtained significant results albeit under a short period. Remarkably neither had previously found gifted participants and nor were they to do so in the future. Likewise, the ganzfeld successes under discussion were immediately replicated by two graduate students. The subsequent 'failure' – or statistically significant 'psi-jinxing effect' – can also teach us something important: Relationships between experimenters and participants matter. In this case a major disagreement occurred between myself and the experimenter almost culminating in the termination of the project. Because psychology aspires to be like physics such details are seldom publicised. As for the earlier success, I learned the P that I passed on to Beloff had 'a crush' on me. Her scores declined when I left Edinburgh for Sweden to be with my girlfriend. Naturally I made no mention any of this in my report.

Marks has already put on record my comments on the effect on our morale of the sudden hostility towards and loss of funding for psi-research in Sweden occasioned by a new appointment. A similar example of how changes in university leadership can have a dire effect on morale seems to have occurred in the case of the group of young and enthusiastic doctoral students led by Carl Sargent at the University of Cambridge. Because of the allegations of Susan Blackmore against Sargent, Marks rightly brings up the issue of experimenter fraud. Yet it has to be said there was no smoking gun, Blackmore's ethical standards in this affair were less than desired, and crucially there are significant findings without Sargent's involvement.

Actually there should be no disagreement between David Marks and myself over the importance of the experimenter. His own attempts to replicate the Sheldrake work were initially successful using an experimenter who was positively inclined towards psi until he changed the experimenter. Recently psychology's own best kept secrets was revealed: only about one third of major findings were found to be replicable.

Finally Marks and I agree that many skeptics like their New Age counterparts have a low tolerance for ambiguity. This just might explain the extreme values of the Disbelief

(Continued)

> Barometer. We share one further expertise: the area of hypnosis and suggestibility. I guess David is aware of the power of suggestibility in presenting readers with his own barometer reading and then pressurising them to permanently record their own – but then there are those who are counter-suggestible! As for finding a theory, much speaks for psi not being an anomaly but an attribute of consciousness – and explaining consciousness is the biggest challenge for contemporary natural science.
>
> My Belief Barometer, with no pressure from David, reads 60–90%.

PREREGISTERED, PROSPECTIVE META-ANALYSIS

To this author, the level of subjective choice in meta-analysis about which evidence to include and which to exclude does not seem a sensible way to do science. I agree with Caroline Watt and James Kennedy (2017) that retrospective meta-analysis is as open to researcher bias as any other scientific method because it is based on the selective use of particular studies, analysed in particular ways, all decided in the full knowledge of the outcomes of those studies. Meta-analyses of random number generator (RNG) studies have found that the effect size does not increase with sample size, contrary to statistical theory. Watt and Kennedy (2017) discuss a possible solution to the impasse in suggesting a new form of prospective meta-analysis, which is registered in advance.

The extensive, unresolved debates about meta-analyses in parapsychology suggest the need for a more solid and reliable basis for making decisions about the meaning of research findings. Watt and Kennedy (2017) have suggested an enlightened way forward. They argue that: 'To provide confirmatory evidence, the methodological decisions in a meta-analysis must be made prospectively, before the results of the included studies are known and ideally before the studies have been conducted.' The decision to include or exclude any individual study in a meta-analysis should be made after the study has been registered but before data collection begins. The registration of individual studies should prevent any form of selective bias in the individual study and in subsequent meta-analysis. The steps for a registration-based prospective meta-analysis are: (a) the meta-analysis plan, power analysis, sample size, statistical methods, and criteria for including and excluding studies are all publicly preregistered; (b) a list of included studies is published together with the registration; (c) each study registration is reviewed and an advance decision is made whether to include the study in the meta-analysis; and (d) when the pre-specified criteria for concluding the meta-analysis are reached, the meta-analysis is completed.

Watt and Kennedy give an example in the form of '*A Prospective Meta-Analysis for Ganzfeld Studies*'. I base this description on the registration document.[10]

---

[10] A prospective meta-analysis of pre-registered Ganzfeld ESP studies; KPU Registry ID Number: 1024. Date revised: 22 November 2017: https://koestlerunit.wordpress.com/study-registry/

Helped to minimise avoidable controversy and enabling improvements, Caroline Watt circulated draft versions of the meta-analysis registration comments by ESP proponents and skeptics. The registration specifies the statistical methods for testing the overall ESP effect, stating that this is a confirmatory analysis. Any well-designed confirmatory analysis should provide evidence either for or against an experimental hypothesis and analysis decisions that could affect the results must be made before any data collection. A non-significant result for a high-powered study is evidence that the hypothesis is false for the predicted effect size. In the GF prospective meta-analysis, two analyses are planned for evaluating the evidence for ESP along with a correction for multiple analyses. The registration specifies the overall sample size for a computed power of 0.95 and the sample size is set at a minimum of 921 trials. A second confirmatory analysis is a subset of telepathy studies with Ps having artistic ability with at least 234 trials.

Typically, experimenters should know that a prospective meta-analysis is being conducted and they will be able to track the outcomes of the studies included in the meta-analysis. If the initial studies are favourable, the experimenters may not conduct additional studies if they know that the meta-analysis will be completed on a certain date with whatever data are available. Therefore, it was decided that a fixed sample size is the fairest method for obtaining unbiased results.

Caroline Watt and James Kennedy's initiative to preregister prospective meta-analyses appears to be the most significant methodological development in the history of parapsychology. They have created a rational, even-handed procedure for the adjudication of ESP studies that should be acceptable to believers and skeptics alike. The prospective meta-analysis of GF studies promises to be a watershed moment for anomalistic psychology. Will it or won't it find support for ESP?

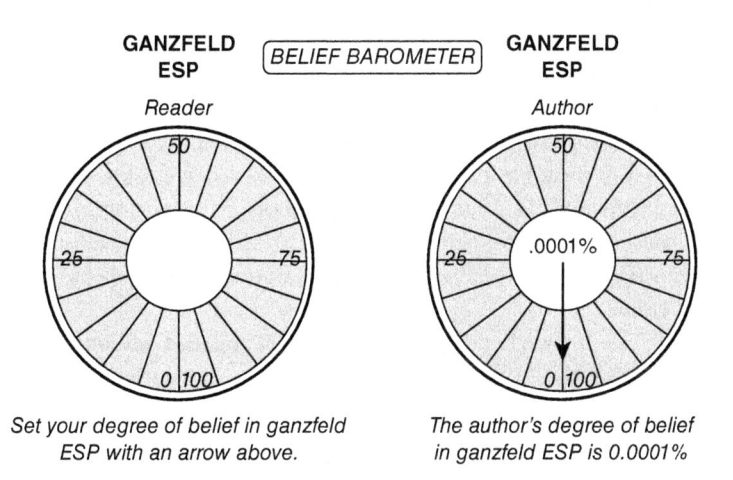

Figure 6.3 Belief barometer readings

A MAGNETO-SENSORY THEORY OF THE SIXTH SENSE

A new magneto-sensory theory (MST) explains the operation of psi quite literally as the 'sixth sense'. The MST is supported by some research in the GF, which is why the theory is here in this chapter. If true, the theory has the potential to shed light on how psi works quite generally. Therefore it deserves serious consideration even at this early stage of development, often raising more questions than answers. It is impossible to say at this stage whether the theory is 'right or wrong'. However, as one of the first to learn about this theory, perhaps you will be inspired to carry out further studies to determine in more detail how well the theory explains the characteristics of ESP. In doing this further research, it will be necessary to avoid findings from discredited studies such as many RV and GF studies that are known to have been flawed and thus have given a misleading description of psi and its operation. The MST is drawn from the writings of Taylor and Blavanosky (1978, 1979), Alan McDonnell (2014) and Abraham Liboff (2017), together with a few recent supportive findings in neuroscience.[11]

The first discovery supportive of the MST was the finding that magnetic nanoparticles in the brain are capable of responding to magneto-sensory information (Kirschvink, Kobayashi-Kirschvink, & Woodford, 1992). The second discovery was finding cryptochrome receptors of magnetic energy in the human retina (Foley, Gegear, & Reppert, 2011). The essential principles of the MST are consistent with studies in contemporary biology, physics and neuroscience and so require no special metaphysical assumptions. It is a 'brass tacks' theory that, in principle, could apply to every living creature.

Energy exists in many different forms, as light, heat, mechanical energy, gravitational energy, electricity, sound, chemical energy, atomic energy and magnetic energy. All forms of physical energy are, in principle, interchangeable without energy loss. Electrical energy is provided by electrons moving along an electric conductor, one of the most common and useful forms of energy. Large power plants convert magnetic energy stored in fuels like coal into electricity through various changes in its form. In spite of more than a century of research, the nature of the energy responsible for psi has remained a complete mystery. For good reason, this most basic of questions about psi receives almost zero attention from psi investigators. It is a taboo topic, off limits, in para-parapsychology, so to speak. Professional parapsychologists will wish to 'bite my head off' purely for going here. Bring it on. A debate about the nature of so-called 'psychic energy' is well overdue.

The MST is founded on the possibility that the one billion-plus magnetic nanoparticles that exist directly adjacent to billions of neurons in the neocortex

---

[11] An earlier version of the magneto-sensory theory was tested by Taylor and Balanovski (1978, 1979). They actually rejected the psi hypothesis *because predictions from the theory were not supported.*

(Kirschvink et al., 1992) provide the energy for so-called 'psychic information transfer'. I say 'so-called' and put the p-word inside quotes because, if the MST is correct, 'psychic information transfer' will not be considered 'psychic' after all. A new 'sixth sense' of *electromagnetoreception* would make psi, and the majority of parapsychology, 'fish and chips paper'.

The most strongly established case for a magneto-sense comes from studies of navigation and orientation in fish, birds, bees and bacteria. There is nothing really new here. Four billion years of evolution have created the sixth sense of magnetoreception, allowing billions of organisms to detect the Earth's magnetic field for sensing direction, altitude or location. Orientation, navigation and homing abilities exist within a multitude of organisms ranging from bacteria to higher vertebrates. Many living organisms are sensitive to constant or extremely low-frequency magnetic fields. Magnetoreception is evident in molluscs, insects, bony fish, amphibians, bats, rodents, artiodactylans, cetaceans, carnivorans and avian species (Walker, Diebel, Haugh, Pankhurst, Mongomery, & Green, 1997). Migratory birds (Wiltschko & Wiltschko, 1996) use the Earth's magnetic field to navigate direction, as do salmon (Putman et al., 2014), turtles (Luschi et al., 2007), honey bees (Collett & Baron, 1994; Gould, Kirschvink, & Deffeyes, 1978) and bacteria (Bharde et al., 2005). Electric fields induce a range of behaviours in ants, cockroaches, mosquitoes, fruit flies and bees (Jackson, Hunt, Sharkh, & Newland, 2011), and many species of fish. Across many species, the sixth sense is embodied in two different mechanisms: (1) tiny crystals of single-domain[12] magnetite (iron oxide; Fe_3O_4) (Kirschvink, Walker, & Diebel, 2001) and (2) magnetically sensitive chemicals formed by proteins in the retina. It has been suggested that these two separate magnetic sensory systems perform the functions of both a magnetic compass and a magnetic map (Kobayashi & Kirschvink, 1995). Magnetically sensitive chemicals involving cryptochrome seem to provide the basis of the magnetic compass sense, while magnetite particles provide a magnetic map sense (Hore & Mouritsen, 2016).

Magnetoreception in humans is much less studied and more controversial. However, a recent discovery of magnetite in the human brain raises a significant possibility:

> Humans make magnetite in many tissues and have an ophthalmic nerve in their trigeminal system. However, most humans do not claim to perceive consciously the Earth's magnetic field, and magnetoreception is not listed among the five major senses (vision, hearing, smell, taste, and touch). Therefore, if magnetoreception exists in humans, it must either be buried deeply in our subconscious or masked in some other fashion. (Kobayashi & Kirschvink, 1995: 374)

---

[12] Single domain means that the magnetisation does not vary across the magnet.

More recently, Alan McDonnell (2014) reviewed a variety of observations indicating that people seem to 'radiate magnetic fields'. In discussing what he refers to as the 'sixth sense-emotional contagion' in rioting crowds, McDonnell speculates as follows:

> the human body has retained structures in the body and brain originating from more primitive ancestors, and possibly in stressful situations these structures are inferred to be capable of being used by the unconscious to sporadically absorb data via biomagnetic emissions. These metabolic energy emissions are inferred to carry patterns reflecting the emotional state of the body and are radiated away from the body, when detected above a certain level, may be inducing a tipping point in cognitive salience for emotion related data. Part of this spectrum of data radiation is electromagnetic; magnetic signals are used in MRI scanners due to their ability to go through tissue with minimum distortion. Due to this characteristic of electromagnetic waves and a phenomenon known as Stochastic Resonance, low power signals are proposed to be detectable by others. This may be through an unconscious cognition process feeding into fight or flight related centres of the brain ... to activate unconscious reflexive mental states appropriate for responses to crisis situations. (McDonnell, 2014: 344–345)

In another statement of the hypothesis of magnetosensitivity, Abraham Liboff goes further by suggesting that:

> some fraction of an individual's central nervous system activity can be magnetically detected by nearby individuals. Even if we restrict the information content of such processes to merely simple magnetic cues that are unconsciously received by individuals undergoing close-knit continuing exposure to these cues it is likely that they will tend to associate these cues with the transmitting individual, no less than would occur if such signals were visual or auditory. (2017: 177)

Like any sensory channel, it is necessary to have two sides to magneto-sensory capability: the sensory/reception side and the emission/encoding side. Liboff hypothesises that *human beings have (1) the capability to sense the magnetic fields, which includes the magnetic fields emanating from other human beings; (2) the capability to emit and encode magnetic fields based on states of the brain associated with emotion, thought and intentionality.* If empirically supported, the McDonnell–Liboff Theory would have wide applicability to many anomalous experiences, and especially those involving psi.

Magnetoreception is established in birds, bees, fish and bacteria, so why would it not exist in humans? Recent neurobiological studies have indicated that human magnetoreception depends on light-sensitive chemical reactions involving the flavoprotein[13] cryptochrome (CRY2) which functions as a light-sensitive magnetosensor (Foley et al., 2011). However, the mechanisms are complex and not fully understood. Yung-Jong Shiah (2012) suggested that cryptochromes, present in all tissues, make ideal candidates for ESP transduction at the initial perceptual stage. He suggested that ESP information triggers chemical reactions in the cryptochromes, influencing the spin states of paired radical ions. This process spreads the summed signal of cryptochromes throughout the brain, creating a meaningful and conscious synthesis. Similarly, James Close (2012) hypothesised that human stress responses to geomagnetic storms are mediated by a cryptochrome compass system.[14]

In order to determine the spatial distribution of magnetite in the human brain, Gilder et al. (2018) made remanent magnetisation[15] measurements on 822 specimens from seven dissected human brains and mapped the concentrations of magnetic remanence across the whole brain. Remanent magnetisation from the cerebellum was approximately double the level from the cerebral cortex in all seven cases. Brain stems were more than two times higher in magnetisation on average than the cerebral cortex. Also the ventral (lower-most) horizontal layer of the cerebral cortex was consistently more magnetic than the average cerebral cortex in each of the seven studied cases.

These magnetisation patterns led Gilder et al. to conclude that magnetite is preferentially located in the human brain in the cerebellum and brain stem. The cerebellum is the key brain structure for the coordination of movement and orientation in space, and the ventral cortex in the frontal lobe, at the bottom of the cerebral hemispheres, is involved in the processing of risk and fear. It also plays a role in the inhibition of emotional responses and decision making. The role of trauma, fear and safety in the genesis of anomalous cognition is included in our earlier theory of anomalous experience (Chapter 2). Gilder et al. concluded that: 'While birds are thought to have integrated magnetic sensors to aid orientation for humans, magnetite's purpose is unclear.' Then the final sentence says: 'This has to be established in future studies. You want to be there when this happens? No reason why not.'

One significant property of an electromagnetic field (EMF) is that it influences – and is influenced by – neighbouring EMFs.[16] As noted, there are two sides to the

---

[13]Flavoproteins are proteins that contain a nucleic acid derivative of riboflavin.
[14]Cryptochromes are a class of flavoproteins that are sensitive to blue light, found in plants and animals. Cryptochromes are involved in the circadian rhythms of plants and animals, as well as the sensing of magnetic fields.
[15]Remanent magnetisation is the magnetisation left behind in a ferromagnetic material (such as iron) after an external magnetic field is removed.
[16]Consciousness could be a direct emergent property of the brain's electromagnetic field (EMF) produced by the activity of billions of neurons scattered throughout the central nervous system (e.g. Pockett, 2017).

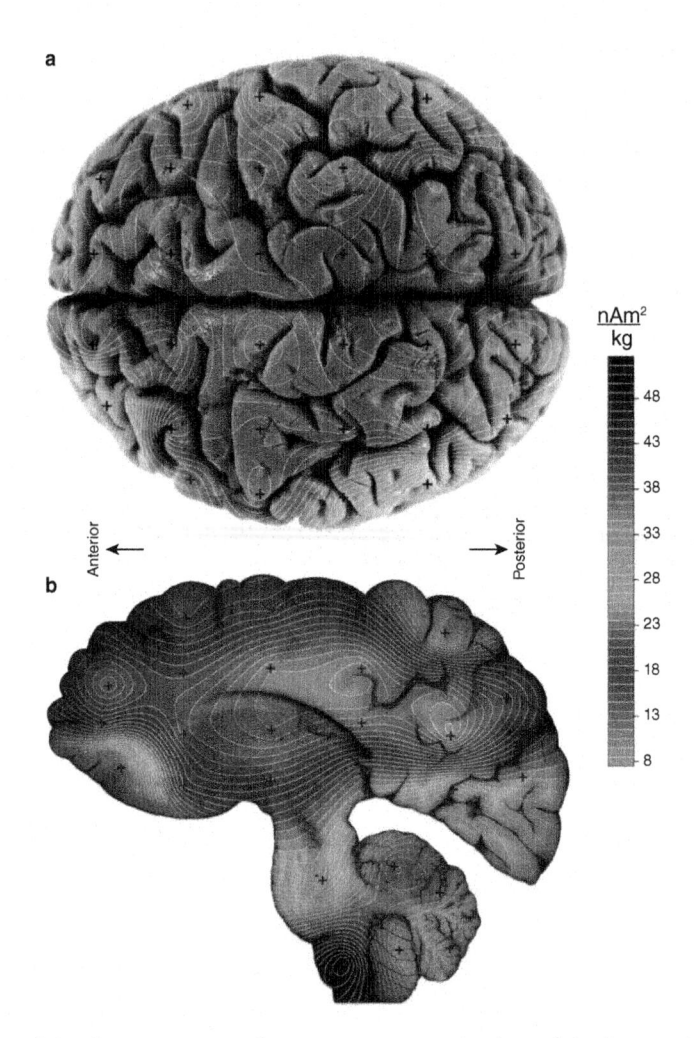

Figure 6.4 Contour maps of remanent magnetisation of the human brain: (a) horizontal view from dorsal (above) of the cerebral cortex only; (b) mid-sagittal view of the entire brain including cerebral cortex, cerebellum and brain stem. The linear scale is the same for both images.

Reproduced from Gilder et al. (2018) under a Creative Commons Attribution 4.0 International licence (https://creativecommons.org/licenses/by/4.0/). No changes made.

magnetosense: reception and emission. Neither is yet established in any detail. The emission side is based on a neurone firing to generate a disturbance to the surrounding electromagnetic energy (EME). The information is encoded in the patterns of billions of neurones in the brain's electromagnetic field. The key issue can be stated as follows. Imagine that you ask me a simple question requiring a Yes/No answer. I am blindfolded to prevent any tell-tale sensory cues. Without speaking a word, is it possible that when I think 'Yes', you receive a different signal from when I think 'No'?

Under normal circumstances, human beings are not conscious of magnetosensitivity. However, that need not be an obstacle because, if a person is looking out for any kind of signal, they will be open to any ambient stimulation coming in their direction regardless of the specific modality. The high concentrations of magnetite found in the cerebellum and brain stem indicate the involvement of the arousal, affective and action systems, and so the signal is likely to be strongly emotive. Let's examine the evidence.

STUDIES SUPPORTIVE OF A HUMAN MAGNETO-SENSE

In the light of the high levels of magnetite in the brain and cryptochromes in the retina, is there any hard evidence that human beings are actually receptive to EME like many other animals? The answer is 'Yes'. It has been suggested since 1995 or even earlier that there is a human sense of magnetoreception, but the concept remains controversial (Kobayashi & Kirschvink, 1995). Although humans make magnetite in many tissues and have an ophthalmic nerve in their trigeminal system, as noted, humans do not consciously perceive the Earth's magnetic field, and magnetoreception is not listed among the five major senses (vision, hearing, smell, taste, and touch). If human magnetoreception exists, it must be either subconscious or masked in some other fashion, perhaps by more vivid perceptions in the traditional five senses. Using surface-based electroencephalogram recordings, Bell, Marino and Chesson (1992) found that environmental magnetic stimuli can influence neurological activity in the human brain. Dobson, Fuller, Wiester, and Moser (1993) and Fuller, Dobson, Wieser, and Moser (1995) observed that a static magnetic field applied through the head of epileptic patients could elicit epilepsy-like activity, as recorded by electrodes implanted directly in the hippocampus. Fortunately, no cases exist of epileptic seizures triggered by strong (1.5-T) magnetic fields of clinical magnetic resonance imaging (MRI) machines. However, all of these observations are consistent with the MST, which suggests that external magnetic fields are being transduced into human neurological activity. If so, some form of sensory transduction must be operating, as all known inputs to the nervous system arise ultimately in cells specialised to convert external stimuli into coded bursts of action potentials.

A small set of earlier studies are also consistent with the hypothesis of human magneto-sensitivity. It has been known for many years that human beings seem to be susceptible to natural magnetic fluctuations which influence mood (Watanabe, Cornélissen, Halberg, Otsuka, & Ohkawa, 2000). Kay (1999) reported an association between geomagnetic storms and the incidence of depression as indexed by hospital admissions. Also, there may be a generalised sensitivity to ambient magnetic fields in cases of suicide (Nishimura, Tada, Nakatani, Matsuda, Teramukai, & Fukushima, 2014), and increases in the incidence of suicides correlate with perturbations in the geomagnetic field due to the 11-year solar storm cycle (Berk, Dodd, & Henry, 2006).

Lustenberger et al. (2013) explored radio frequency (RF) EMF effects on cortical activity during sleep and tested whether such effects during sleep interact with sleep-dependent performance changes. Sixteen male subjects underwent two experimental nights, one of them with all-night 0.25 e0.8 Hz-pulsed RF EMF exposure. All-night EEG was recorded. In order to investigate RF-EMF induced changes in overnight performance improvement, subjects were trained for both nights on a motor task in the evening and the morning. They obtained good sleep quality in all subjects under both conditions. After pulsed RF EMF, they found increased SWA during exposure to pulse-modulated RF EMF compared to sham exposure towards the end of the sleep period. During exposure, sleep-dependent performance improvement in a motor sequence task was reduced compared to the sham condition.

Weak, extremely low frequency (ELF) magnetic fields, both natural and human-made, are known to affect living organisms, including their behaviour. Biomagnetic emissions occur as a side-effect of the body's normal metabolic processes (Nummenmaa, Glerean, Hari, & Hietanen, 2014). The fields are far weaker than those emitted by MRI scanners, but they may contain 'uniquely organic signatures' to which the body is sensitive, even to these low power levels (Otsuka et al., 2001). Biomagnetic emissions from other humans must be considered as one possible input to the ambient field. Sources of EMF shared in social interactions possibly include muscle movements, which generate electricity and the low-frequency electric fields induced by natural body movements (Glover & Bowtell, 2008). Human biomagnetic emissions reflect the emotional state of the individual due to the emotions speeding up of the heart rate, so, when we are angry, our metabolism speeds up as we get ready to fight or run (Rainville, Bechara, Naqvi, & Damasio, 2006). McDonnell notes that the magnetic part of the spectrum has a frequency range that operates at the same frequencies as brainwaves function in thinking. Biomagnetic fields are known to radiate some distance from the body, so if a person is angry or fearful, their biomagnetic fields 'tend to resonate away from the body and carry patterns containing this information as the body produces a bio-magnetic field with patterns corresponding to its metabolic condition' (McDonnell, 2014: 342). Is this the process a person can sense when sensing 'vibes' through the process of neuroception?

For magnetoreception to be possible, as well as the ability to detect signals, the body must have an emission mechanism to project emotional content. As well as the heart appearing to be sensitive to external EME, it also produces the strongest electromagnetic field of any organ. Three possible mechanisms for magnetoreception, a biological structure that can transduce the strength and/or orientation of the local magnetic field to an animal's nervous system, have been suggested by Johnsen and Lohmann (2005).

McCarty, Carrubba, Chesson, Frilot, Gonzalez-Toledo, and Marino (2011) observed that exposure to environmental-strength EME could induce somatic reactions, or 'EMF hypersensitivity'. A female physician self-diagnosed with EMF hypersensitivity was exposed to an average (over the head) 60-Hz electric field of 300 V/m (comparable with typical environmental-strength EMFs) during controlled studies. The P felt temporal pain, headache, muscle twitching and skipped heartbeats within 100 s after initiation of the EMF exposure. The symptoms were caused by field transitions (off–on, on–off) rather than the presence of the field itself. The woman herself was not conscious of the EMF.

Carrubba, Frilot, Chesson, and Marino (2007) found evidence that human females and males respond to low-intensity electric and magnetic fields with evoked potentials, as is the case with other sensory stimuli. They observed evoked potentials caused by the onset and by the offset of a 60 Hz 2 G pulse having a field strength comparable to that in the general environment. Magneto-sensory evoked potentials in the signals from the occipital cortex were found in 16 of 17 Ps. The Ps were not consciously aware of having magnetosensitivity.

Dangling food in front of hungry Ps is almost always guaranteed to produce positive results. Using a rotatory chair, like those found in offices but more elaborate, Chae, Oh, Lee, and Kim (2019) showed that humans can sense the geomagnetic field (GMF) to orient their direction towards food. Hungry men, but – for some unknown reason, not women – significantly oriented towards the magnetic north or east directions, which had been previously food-associated, without any other helpful cues, including sight and sound. The orientation was reproduced under blue light, but was abolished under a blindfold or a longer wavelength light (> 500 nm), indicating that blue light is necessary for magnetic orientation. Inversion of the vertical component of the GMF resulted in orientation towards the magnetic south and blood glucose levels resulting from food that appeared to act as a motivator for sensing a magnetic field direction. The results demonstrate that male humans sense GMF in a blue light-dependent manner and suggest that the geomagnetic orientations are mediated by an inclination compass. Further research is necessary to determine whether the magnetic compass extends to the female component of the species.

Consistent with Carrubba et al.'s observations, Connie X. Wang et al. (2019) observed a 'strong, specific human brain response to ecologically-relevant rotations of Earth-strength magnetic fields' in both males and females. Following geomagnetic stimulation, a drop in amplitude of EEG alpha oscillations (8–13 Hz) occurred in a repeatable manner. Termed 'alpha event-related desynchronisation' (alpha-ERD), such a response has been associated previously with sensory and cognitive processing of external stimuli, including vision, auditory and somatosensory cues. Alpha-ERD in response to the geomagnetic field was triggered only by horizontal rotations when the static vertical magnetic field was directed downwards, as it is in the Northern Hemisphere; no brain responses were elicited by the same horizontal rotations when the static vertical component was directed upwards. This finding suggests a biological response tuned to the ecology of the local human population, rather than a generic physical effect. The authors suggest that ferromagnetism remains a 'viable biophysical mechanism for sensory transduction and provides a basis to start the behavioural exploration of human magnetoreception'.

Human magnetoreception is an area in much need of further investigation, and such research may shed light on putative instances of paranormal information transfer and other anomalistic experiences. Calling ESP the 'sixth sense' might have been the correct description all along.

HYPOTHESES

Three MST hypotheses[17] are available as follows:

H1: Test scores of psi ability will be affected by the Earth's geomagnetic activity

Geomagnetic activity, local sidereal time (LST) and General ESP (GESP) effects are statistically associated (Ryan, 2008; Spottiswoode, 1997). Local sidereal time is a timekeeping system used by astronomers to locate celestial objects based on the Earth's rate of rotation relative to the fixed stars. GESP performance has been observed to be less effective when geomagnetic activity is high (Dalton & Stevens, 1996; Spottiswoode, 1990). GESP tends to occur on days when global geomagnetic activity is quieter compared to the days immediately before or after the experience (e.g. Churchill, Persinger, & Thomas, 1994; Persinger, 1987; Persinger & Schaut, 1988; Schaut & Persinger, 1985). Although the effect sizes are weak, they are claimed to be persistent with correlation coefficients between 0.35 and 0.45. Several investigators have suggested that there is a positive association between ESP success and low geomagnetic activity (Berger & Krippner, 1989; Berger & Persinger, 1991) and quiet geomagnetic activity (Persinger, 1985, 1989). Ryan (2008) created a database of 343 free-response ESP trials conducted in the UK to test the hypothesis that the relatively fast varying components of geomagnetic activity, geomagnetic pulsations, drive the associations between ESP, geomagnetic activity and local sidereal time. Two patterns were observed: ESP was found to succeed only during periods of enhanced pulsation activity within the 0.2–0.5 Hz band, but not during the most disturbed periods of activity in the 0.025–0.1 Hz band. The pattern of ESP effect by LST was similar to that found by Spottiswoode (1997), and this shape was found to be attributable to the pattern of ESP results by pulsation activity in the 0.2–0.5 Hz band. An optimal time for successful ESP performance is around 'LST lunchtime', 13:00–14:00 LST.

---

[17] A fourth hypothesis following McDonnell's paper would be that intensely emotive stimuli should be more effective in ESP than non-emotive stimuli. However, curiously, little systematic research has been carried out on the association between emotion and ESP, so it cannot be considered any further here.

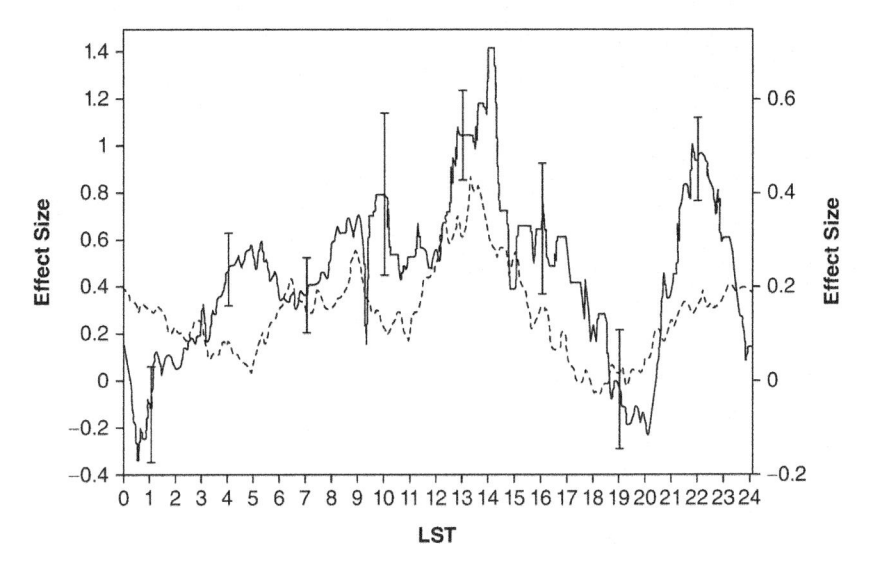

Figure 6.5 ESP effect size as a function of LST, for 204 trials in the present study (solid line, left axis) and trials in Spottiswoode's dataset (dashed line, right axis), with one standard error bars.

Reproduced from Ryan (2008) under a CC-BY-NC open access license.

Braud and Dennis (1989) conducted retrospective analyses of the associations between GMF activity and (a) electrodermal activity (as an index of sympathetic autonomic activity), (b) rate of hemolysis of human red blood cells in vitro, (c) attempted distant psychokinetic influence of electrodermal activity, and (d) attempted psychokinetic influence of the rate of hemolysis. For each measure, high activity was associated with high GMF values, while low activity was associated with low GMF values.[18] A partial replication of the ESP/GMF association was reported by Radin, McAlpine, and Cunningham (1994). The investigators placed a receiver in a shielded room, and, curiously, no evidence of GF ESP occurred (hit rate = 25%) in the unselected, 'normal' Ps, only in a creative sample who obtained a hit rate of 41%. (If this latter group was in a shielded room, then the 25% finding confirms, but the 41% finding disconfirms H3; see below.)

Eva Lobach and Dick Bierman (2004) replicated the earlier anomalous cognition studies that have shown that ESP effect sizes are highest around 13.30 LST (Spottiswoode, 1997). A post-hoc analysis of telephone telepathy data of Sheldrake (2003) also showed a peak at that time. In a new study, six women who reported frequent telephone telepathy chose four close friends or relatives

---

[18]Palmer (2007) suggested a possible artefact in Braud and Dennis's hemolysis study.

to act as callers. All completed a total of 36 trials: six sessions of six trials each, three sessions at 'peak time' (between 8.00 and 9.00 local time) and three at 'non-peak time' (between 17.30 and 18.30 local time). One of the experimenters was at the participant's home during the sessions to ensure that no 'irregular communication' was going on and logged times of the calls and responses of the P. Another experimenter used a dice to select a caller, about five minutes before the scheduled trial. The experimenter then contacted the caller who was asked to call the P five minutes later and to 'concentrate their thoughts on the participant for the last two minutes before the call was made'. When the phone rang at the participant's home, the P guessed who she thought was calling before picking up. Analyses show a significant over all scoring rate of 29.4% ($p = .05$). Almost all of this effect originated from the peak time with a scoring rate of 34.6%. A stronger emotional bond between P and the caller was associated with a higher hit rate. Lobach and Bierman (2004) concluded that the study provided tentative support for the hypothesis that local sidereal time is associated with telephone telepathy, although other explanations of the anomalous effect cannot be ruled out (e.g. precognition, retro PK by the experimenter, or clairvoyance of the dice throws).

In a study on dream ESP, Stanley Krippner and Michael Persinger (1996) hypothesised as follows:

> understanding of a process is most successful when the experimental conditions closely simulate the natural context. Because classic, spontaneous GESP experiences often occur at night and at least one half of these reported experiences are associated with dreams (e.g. Rhine, 1977), it can be conjectured that the pursuit of psi during dream periods should have the highest probability of success.

They tested two hypotheses: **H1 – nights on which the strongest experimental GESP occurred would also be nights that displayed the quietest geomagnetic activity compared to the days before and after; H2 – nights that demonstrated weak or questionable GESP would not demonstrate this effect.** These hypotheses are consistent with studies finding that GESP tends to improve when the global geomagnetic activity is significantly quieter than the days immediately before or the days after the experience (e.g. Churchill et al., 1994; Persinger, 1987; Persinger & Schaut, 1988; Schaut & Persinger, 1985).

Krippner and Persinger (1996) assessed the accuracy of the concordance (matching) between dream content and target pictures over 20 non-consecutive nights (1964–1967) for a single percipient called 'William E.' and how this matching correlated with global geomagnetic activity. They found that Spearman p correlations demonstrated 'a significant association between geomagnetic activity and accuracy (greater accuracy/less geomagnetic activity) for the 24-hour periods that corresponded with the dream nights' (p. 487).

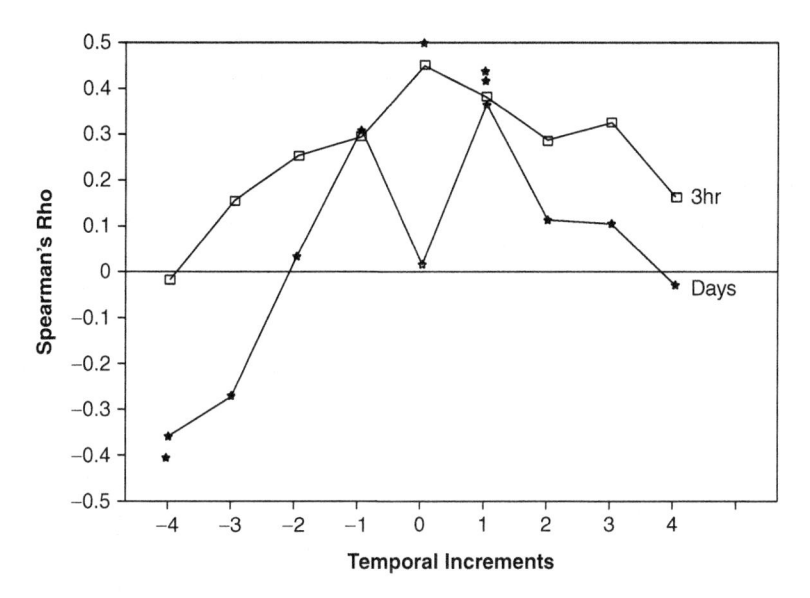

Figure 6.6 Spearman p correlation coefficients between (absence of) concordance scores between target and content for daily (pluses) and three-hour (squares) intervals of geomagnetic activity for 20 sessions with 'William E.' [*p < .05]

Reproduced from Krippner and Persinger (1996), with permission.

H2: The ability to transfer ESP information follows an inverse-square-law, falling off with distance between the sender and the receiver

William Braud (2010) cites three studies that suggest that the inverse square law may hold for ESP:

1. M. Kogan (1969: 22) reported a distance decline in psi functioning. Kogan observed a decline of psi with distance over a range from 5 meters to 107 meters, and suggested that the actual transmission rate for telepathic information was between 0.005 and 0.1 bit per second.
2. Karlis Osis and his coworkers reported a series of distance-related psi experiments, which indicated distance-related psi performance declines. Osis, Turner and Carlson (1971) observed an attenuation of between 0.7 and 1.7 units of the psi quotient measure for each 1,000 miles, over the 0 to 10,000-mile distances explored in the study.
3. Dean Radin (2006) described a study in which Ps attempted to influence cell cultures in the laboratory, through intention alone. The researchers determined the degree of intentional influence on the targeted cells and also on random number generators (RNGs) at various distances (from 0 to 10,000

miles) from the cells. The effects of intention upon the RNGs stationed at various distances from the mentally targeted cells declined with increasing distance.

It is clear from the cited studies that ESP effects are attenuated with distance. There is evidence that the attenuation follows the inverse square law. On this basis, one might be justified in questioning the reliability of any ESP study that fails to show a distance-related decrement in performance. The RV studies in particular are in this category.

H3: Electrical shielding with a Faraday cage tends to block or attenuate general ESP performance

Charles Tart (1988a) cites A. Puharich (unpublished), who suggested that general ESP performance in psychically talented percipients could be enhanced by having the percipients work inside a solid-wall-shielded enclosure (Faraday cage) if the cage was electrically connected to the ground. However, Tart states that an ungrounded, electrically floating cage, inhibited general ESP performance. Tart tested these effects in a double-blind design. Thirteen undergraduates alternated roles as percipients and experimenter/agents. A circular matching abacus test (matching 10 cards without replacement) was used for testing GESP performance. A significant above-chance hitting occurred in the grounded Faraday cage condition. However, scoring was at chance in the floating condition, as predicted. The difference between conditions was significant.

In a second paper, Tart (1988b) claims to have found a GMF/GESP relationship when the shielding structure – an intact, solid-wall Faraday cage – was in an electrically floating (with respect to ground) condition, but not when it was electrically grounded. Hypothesis H3 about the shielding of ESP is therefore open to further study. If H3 is confirmed in controlled studies, then the huge numbers of positive ESP studies where Ps were inside shielded compartments will be thrown into question.

ARGUMENTS AGAINST THE NEW THEORY

For obvious reasons, arguments against the MST tend to come from psi advocates. One can perfectly understand why: if the theory is correct, they will all have to go down to the Job Centre seeking employment. How many vacancies are there for ex-parapsychologists, one might wonder – the CIA, FBI, MI5 or MI6, perhaps? The idea that ESP is a type of 'mental radio' has been argued for some considerable time (e.g. Sinclair, 1930/1962), but it did not take hold among parapsychologists. Bryan Williams (2015) states the main counterargument against the theory thus:

> Arguably, if psi really did involve some sort of signal transmission, then we might expect to observe some degree of attenuation in the quality of psi with increased spatial distance, or whenever the supposed psi signal is met

by physical barriers such as EME shielding. But as ... a number of experiments demonstrate (Schlitz & Gruber, 1980; Schlitz & Haight, 1984; Targ, Puthoff & May, 1979/2002; Bisaha & Dunne, 1979/2002; Dunne & Jahn, 1992), spatial distance does not seem to significantly affect psi functioning very much at all. And successful psi performance has even been obtained when Ps were enclosed in Faraday cages or were placed in a deep-dive submersible several hundred feet down in the ocean (depths which effectively block out most electromagnetic signals in the extremely low-frequency spectrum) (Puthoff & Targ, 1976; Puthoff, Targ, & May, 1981). One might reasonably figure that these findings shouldn't have been obtainable if psi was being mediated by a propagating signal.

Williams's point is perfectly true, but his argument could well backfire very badly. If the theory is wrong, the findings may be right. If the theory is right, the findings must be wrong. It's one or the other. In fact, on the basis of the MST, Taylor and Balanovski argued that ESP does not exist (Taylor & Balanovski, 1979: 631).

Another argument against the MST is that the signals sent and the signals received do not perfectly match. For example, a sender sees a picture of two fire-eaters, yet the 'receiver' sees an image of volcanoes or lips, so they do not exactly match the target image but only show a general correspondence in a symbolic or associative way. Descriptions given by 'receivers' in GF experiments support this observation (Honorton & Harper, 1974). However, this argument creates no problem for the MST because it is a 'straw man'. The MST does not specify that the received image must be identical to the visual image viewed by the sender. The successful transfer of a symbol would be a perfectly useful form of communication as in any natural language, semaphore or sign language. If I send a signal that is an image of a red nose and you see an image of a red face or even just the colour red, these would be perfectly OK.

In line with the MST, Taylor and Balanovski (1979) suggested that the only scientifically feasible explanation of ESP would have to be EME involving suitably strong EM fields. The argument goes like this: ESP is produced by EME; if no EME is observed, then no ESP took place. Taylor and Balanovski (1978) searched high and low for unusual EME radiation being emitted by people while attempting to produce paranormal phenomena. However, they could find no abnormal EME signals during the occurrence of what they supposed were genuine ESP phenomena. They observed that the EME levels were 'many orders of magnitude lower than the ones we calculate here as needed to achieve paranormal effects'. On this basis, Taylor and Balanovski argued that ESP does not exist (Taylor & Balanovski, 1979: 631). The only flaw in their argument is that there are good reasons to doubt that any ESP took place in the crucial experiments.

The human brain shows variable levels of EME. Some brains show almost no EME activity, while others are highly responsive. The ambient EM field around the human body waxes and wanes in accordance with the brain's activity level and a person's emotional state. Extreme arousal, emotion and action are expected to produce the most intense EME fields. Emitted EME is a signal that would need to act as a carrier wave for specific ESP messages. The EME must be assumed to act as an 'envelope' for the specific content of ESP which is carried along with it. At this point, we have absolutely no idea how the message content is conveyed, and further studies are needed to examine this.

SUMMARY

The GF is claimed to be a 'psi-conducive' procedure that has produced some astonishing findings. However, multiple GF studies and five meta-analyses remain inconclusive. SV has been shown to be responsible for some remarkable correspondences in the GF, but there have been reports of multiple methodological shortcomings, including the alleged errors and accusations of fraud in Sargent's studies at Cambridge, studies that were subsequently used in one of Honorton and Bem's meta-analyses. In spite of the positivity and hype, some GF investigators have failed to address the familiar methodological issues. Complacent attitudes among 'old-school' investigators must wither at the vine if there is to be genuine progress. A new approach is needed, with new investigators and new theories.

A magneto-sensitivity theory (MST) has been independently proposed by Taylor and Blavanosky (1978, 1979), McDonnell (2014) and Liboff (2017). The MST is founded on the evolutionary evidence that many organisms have magneto-receptivity capability. The vestige of a hidden sensory channel of human magneto-sensitivity is supported by a small number of laboratory studies. However, the evidence is inconsistent and drawn from a few methodologically flawed studies. The formulation of the MST is at the very earliest of stages. The MST holds that the brain emits and receives electromagnetic energy (EME) outside of conscious awareness. The theory may be proved wrong, but it is a testable and more falsifiable theory than the main alternative which hypothesises the nebulous and slippery concept of 'psychic energy'.

QUESTIONS

1. Why is the GF thought to be psi-conducive?
2. What steps are necessary to prevent cheating in GF research?
3. What are the benefits of preregistered prospective meta-analysis?
4. What conclusions do you draw about the accusations of cheating in GF research?
5. What is the evidence for magnetoreception in humans?
6. What objections to the MST can you think of?
7. What degree of belief do you give to the magneto-sensitivity theory? Place an arrow on the Belief Barometer below.

The Ganzfeld, Subjective Validation and the Sixth Sense

MST
Reader

BELIEF BAROMETER

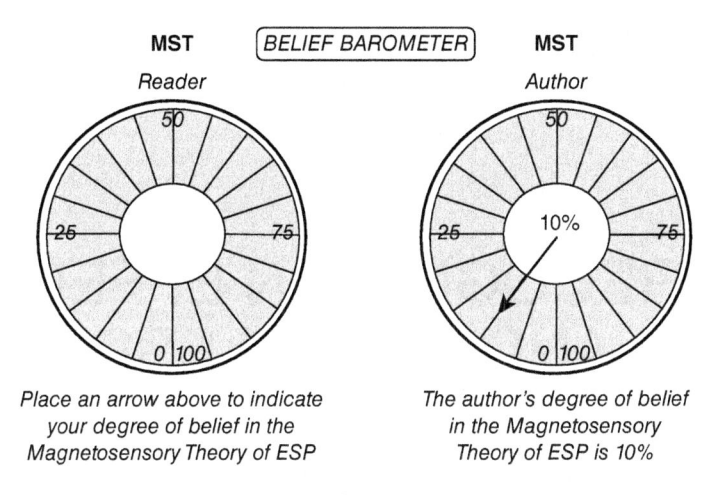

MST
Author

Place an arrow above to indicate your degree of belief in the Magnetosensory Theory of ESP

The author's degree of belief in the Magnetosensory Theory of ESP is 10%

Figure 6.7 Belief barometer readings

7

PRECOGNITION EFFECT AND DREAM-ESP

Methodological Lessons in The Search for Deep truth: Arrival of the Super-powers

With contributions from Daryl Bem, PhD and Stanley Krippner, PhD

At the heart of science is an essential tension between two seemingly contradictory attitudes – an openness to new ideas, no matter how bizarre or counterintuitive they may be, and the most ruthless skeptical scrutiny of all ideas, old and new. This is how deep truths are winnowed from deep nonsense. (Sagan & Druyan, 1995)

Flash precognition: The ability to see things seconds or minutes before they happen. (This quote comes from the 'Flash Precognition' article on the Superpower wiki at FANDOM and is licensed under the Creative Commons Attribution-Share Alike License.) (https://powerlisting.fandom.com/wiki/Flash_Precognition, 2019)

The motivating idea was to take well-established psychological effects and 'time-reverse' their standard cause-and-effect sequences by postponing the presumed causal event until after the P has already made his or her response. (Bem, 2019)

> **Outline:** Welcome to the world of super-powers. Two of the most ancient and enthralling of all paranormal claims are that human beings can (1) foretell the future using precognition, and (2) summon ESP abilities during dreaming with telepathy, clairvoyance or precognition. Precognition is the ability to access information about future events that cannot be known by normal sensory means. Dream-ESP is a form of ESP in which a dreamer appears to gain information about an event or a randomly selected target without using normal sensory modalities or logical inference. I review here the best of the scientific evidence for these two paranormal claims of precognition and dream ESP.

Among the ancients, dreams were viewed as the liberation of the 'soul', freeing it to wander in time, backwards and forwards to examine past or future actions. This concept was discussed skeptically by Aristotle, for whom dream prophecy could be no more veridical than the everyday prophecy of the waking hours:

> It is not inconsistent with reason that the images which appear in dreams should be the cause of certain definite acts. Just as those who ought to do, who are wont to do, or who have frequently done, some certain thing, think of it day and night in dream-fashion, as it were, (for the occupations of the day prepare the way in a measure for such a movement of the thought), so, conversely, the majority of the movements which are executed in sleep become the determining principle of our actions during the day ; for our train of thought has been checked at this point and has by the representations of the night prepared the way for the execution of the act. It is thus that certain dreams are causes or signs. But in the majority of cases the coincidences are fortuitous only, this being especially so in the case of those extra ordinary dreams which exceed the bounds of human credibility; and all those which thus take place in us have for their subject matter some such object as a naval battle, for example, or some other event which is not in any wise connected with our life. (Aristotle, in Waddington, 1848: 607)

The Roman philosopher Lucretius assumed a similar attitude to Aristotle. For him, dreams are the reappearance during sleep of the images that have occupied our thoughts during the day:

> The occupations which have principally held our attention during the day, those to which we have devoted ourselves with the greatest zeal, those to which the soul has applied itself with the greatest ardour, reappear in our sleep, and we abandon ourselves to them again, in that state. (Cited by Vaschide & Piéron, 1901: 192)

Not everyone has been as skeptical as Aristotle and Lucretius. That well-known Hobbit, Bilbo Baggins, son of Bungo Baggins, in *The Lord of the Rings* definitely had it, as did Irene Adler, aka Destiny, in *Marvel Comics*. Dream precognition was given a lot of impetus by J. W. Dunne, a British soldier, aeronautical engineer and philosopher. With the publication in 1927 of *The Experiment in Time*, Dunne proposes that

> the idea of a soul must have first arisen in the mind of primitive man as the result of observation of his dreams. Ignorant as he was, he could have come to no other conclusion but that, in dreams, he left his sleeping body in one universe and went wandering off into another.

The first of Dunne's recorded dreams was that his watch had stopped. On waking, Dunne discovering that his watch on the chest of drawers had stopped *at precisely the same time, to the minute, as the watch in his dream*. After many strange and compelling, precognitive dreams, Dunne was moved to conclude that dreams are 'images of past experience and images of future experience blended together in approximately equal proportions' (Dunne, 1927).

Vladimir Nabokov, the author, is said to have experimented on his dreams, from October 1964 until 3 January 1965. Every morning he would write down what he could recall of his dreams. In the following one or two days, using a prescription by Dunne, he looked out for anything that corresponded to the dream. Following Dunne, Nabokov hypothesised that time is bidirectional and reversible (Barabtarlo, 2018). Others followed suit.

Dream prophecy became trendy. Many informal studies were based on J. W. Dunne's formulae. By this point, you are well versed in the pitfalls and traps that lie in wait for the enthusiastic searcher for psi. You can imagine what can go wrong. As in all areas of psi research, views are strongly divided. A zetetic approach can help to resolve the issue about the reality of precognitive and dream psi by answering these four simple questions:

1. Are the claims for precognition supported by empirical evidence?
2. Do positive precognition studies have sound methodology?
3. Are the claims for dream-ESP supported by empirical evidence?
4. Do positive dream-ESP studies have sound methodology?

If only the answers would be as simple as the questions! The aim here is to provide those answers. The first section focuses on the series of precognition studies by Daryl Bem (2011). More than any others, Bem's studies led to the astonishing conclusion that precognition is real. To retain balance, I summarise a critique by Etienne P. LeBel and Kurt R. Peters (2011). I also draw upon the evidence of a decline effect reported by Ulrich Schimmack (2012, 2015). Blackmore's observations on Bem's use of data that are allegedly fraudulent in a meta-analysis are also discussed. The final remarks about Dr Bem's research are by Dr Bem himself. Thus, I believe this chapter offers an even-handed review of the evidence on Daryl Bem's influential research.

In the second half of the chapter, I review the landmark research of the Maimonides centre on dream-ESP and more recent studies on dream-ESP, which has been extensively studied since the early 1960s. The section ends with

Dr Krippner's personal answers to questions about his Maimonides project. Storm et al. (2017) and the reanalysis by Howard (2018) have created doubts about dream-ESP, as we shall see. First, however, a review of precognition.

PRECOGNITION

In addition to being an academic, Daryl Bem is a professional magician specialising in 'fake' mentalism. After the embarrassment suffered by parapsychologists when Randi sent a couple of young magicians to a parapsychology lab to pretend they had psi ability, Bem was asked to give his own performance at the annual meeting of the Parapsychological Association in Boston in 1985 to warn them about what to watch out for. Chuck Honorton was at the meeting and asked Daryl Bem to come to his newly established laboratory in Princeton, New Jersey, to evaluate whether a clever magician could cheat under his ganzfeld protocol. At that point, Bem decided that he needed to try running his own experiments and his first publication was with Honorton on the ganzfeld in the *Psychological Bulletin* in 1994. Because Bem has a BA in physics, he was particularly intrigued by the possible phenomenon of precognition, so his second major publication appeared in the *Journal of Personality and Social Psychology* in 2011 (Daryl Bem, 20 July 2019, personal communication).

Daryl Bem's (2011) paper described nine experiments that support the existence of precognitive ability. The location of the paper within a high-profile journal, combined with his astonishing findings, resulted in widespread media and academic interest. Bem was even on the *Colbert Report*. Justifiably, his 2011 paper made Daryl Bem the most famous psychologist alive and one of the most famous of all time.

Naturally, Bem's 2011 paper has been the focus of intense scrutiny. Some researchers claim that they have been unable to replicate Bem's experiments (Ritchie, Wiseman, & French, 2012). Galak et al. (2012) ran a set of seven studies with a total of N = 3,289 Ps to produce an average effect size of d = 0.04, which was not significantly different from zero. Others have questioned the methodology of Bem's studies (Alcock, 2011; Francis, 2012; Schimmack, 2012; Wagenmakers, Wetzels, Boorsboom, & van der Maas, 2011). As already noted in the previous chapter, others have questioned Bem's integrity (Blackmore, 2017; Vyse, 2017). Of course, the critiques will never receive the same publicity as the astonishing, original findings, including the critique here. Unless, of course, Daryl Bem says that he agrees with the criticisms, then we will be seeking a retraction of his precognition papers.

Among the leading critics have been Wagenmakers et al. (2011), who claimed that Bem's data analysis was partly exploratory and that one-sided p values may overstate the statistical evidence against the null hypothesis. When they reanalysed Bem's data, they found that the evidence for psi was 'weak to non-existent'. They concluded that Bem's p values do not indicate evidence in favour of precognition, and that psychologists need to change the way they conduct research and analyse data (see a fuller discussion of this point below).

To his credit, Daryl Bem has made all of his research materials available to independent researchers who have been able to attempt replication of his original findings. The fruits of these labours were meta-analysed by Bem, Tressoldi, Rabeyron, and Duggan (2015), 90 experiments from 33 laboratories in 14 countries.

This analysis yielded an overall effect greater than 6 sigma ($z = 6.40$, $p = 1.2 \times 10^{-0}$ with an effect size (Hedges's g) of 0.09). A Bayesian analysis yielded a Bayes factor (BF) of 5.1×10^9, thus exceeding the criterion value of 100 for 'decisive evidence' in support of the experimental hypothesis. When Bem's original experiments were excluded, the combined effect size for replications by independent investigators was 0.06 ($z = 4.16$, $p = 1.1 \times 10^{-5}$) and the BF value was a massive 3,853, greatly exceeding the 100:1 criterion for 'decisive evidence'.

The number of potentially unretrieved experiments in the 'file drawer' to reduce the overall effect size to a value of only 0.01 was 544, which means that there would need to be 544 unpublished experiments with zero effect to cancel out the obtained result. Bem et al. (2015) also reported that seven out of eight additional statistical tests supported the conclusion that the database is not compromised by selection bias or by intense 'p-hacking' – the selective suppression of findings or analyses that failed to yield statistical significance. Yet we have learned from the previous chapter that all is not well with retrospective meta-analysis and the results must be treated with caution.

One duo of critics argues that Daryl Bem's psi research should be viewed as a watershed moment in which the entire edifice of empirical psychology is brought into question. I explain this point in the next section.

FEARING FOR THE FUTURE OF EMPIRICAL PSYCHOLOGY

Two critics, Etienne P. LeBel and Kurt R. Peters (2011), wrote a paper entitled 'Fearing the Future of Empirical Psychology: Bem's (2011) Evidence of Psi as a Case Study of Deficiencies in Modal Research Practice'. Like Wagenmakers et al., they felt that there is an endemic problem in psychology in *the way research is carried out*, what they call the 'modal research practice' (MRP) of empirical psychology. 'Modal research practice' refers to the accepted methodology empirical psychologists most commonly use in their research. LeBel and Peters focus on:

a. an overemphasis on conceptual rather than close replication,
b. insufficient attention being given to verifying the soundness of measurement and experimental procedures, and
c. flawed implementation of null hypothesis significance testing.

LeBel and Peters argued that these deficiencies 'contribute to weak method-relevant beliefs that, in conjunction with overly strong theory-relevant beliefs, lead to **a systemic and pernicious bias in the interpretation of data that favours a researcher's theory**. Ultimately, this interpretation bias increases the risk of drawing incorrect conclusions about human psychology'.

In Bem's (2011) article, he claims to have 'reversed the causal direction' of four well-established psychological effects (i.e. priming, habituation, recall and approach–avoidance) so that, in a memory recall study, Bem found that participants were better able to recall rehearsed versus non-rehearsed words, although the words were rehearsed *after* the memory test had been completed. LeBel and Peters suggest that deficiencies in MRP provide an alternative explanation for the publication of Bem's article. It is not Bem who is at fault, they assume, but the MRP itself.

LeBel and Peters suggest that empirical data underdetermine theory choice (Duhem, 1954; Quine, 1953), so that alternative explanations of data are always possible, regardless of whether or not the data statistically support the researcher's hypothesis. Deficiencies in MRP lead to *interpretation bias*: a bias towards interpretations of data that favour a researcher's theory – both when the null hypothesis is statistically rejected and when it is not.[1] LeBel and Peters (2011) claim,

> As realized in MRP, this bias entails that, regardless of how data turn out, the theory whose predictions are being tested is artificially buffered from falsification (see Fanelli, 2010). The ultimate consequence is an increased risk of reporting false positives and disregarding true negatives, and so drawing incorrect conclusions about human psychology.

Their 'diagnosis' of interpretation bias is consistent with the known difficulties with scientific replication and the 'decline effect' whereby well-established effects subsequently shrink in size and become difficult to replicate (e.g. Fanelli, 2010; Lehrer, 2010; Zimmer, 2011; see section on dream-ESP). This aspect of MRP is the well-known 'file-drawer problem' (Rosenthal, 1979). According to LeBel and Peters, the file-drawer problem and interpretation bias do not operate from unscrupulous motives, but stem from the weakness of the knowledge system in empirical psychology (Meehl, 1978). The MRP leads well-intentioned researchers unwittingly down the path to biased interpretations of their data, a form of subjective validation. MRP itself seems to be the problem, not the motives of individual researchers.

LeBel and Peters pinpoint the issue of theory choice in science. They suggest that the knowledge system in psychology can be roughly divided into two types of belief: theory-relevant beliefs, which concern the theoretical mechanisms that produce behaviour, and method-relevant beliefs, which concern the procedures through which data are produced, measured and analysed. LeBel and Peters (2011) state:

> In any empirical test of a hypothesis, interpretation of the resulting data depends on both theory-relevant and method-relevant beliefs, as both types of belief are required to bring the hypothesis to empirical test. Consequently, the resulting data can always be interpreted as theory relevant (telling us something about the theoretical mechanisms underlying behaviour) or as method relevant (telling us something about the procedures used to test the theoretical hypothesis). (p. 372)

Philosophy of science provides guidance, but the human scientist can still be misled by her/his strong wish to confirm and verify a theory of his/her liking (Duhem, 1954; Quine, 1953). We visited this issue in Chapter 3.

---

[1] 'Interpretation bias' is 'confirmation bias' under a new name.

Belief centrality is one criterion for theory choice by being *conservative* in choosing the theoretical explanation that is both consistent with the data and that requires the least amount of restructuring of the existing knowledge system (Quine & Ullian, 1978). However, a theory's strength is its degree of falsifiability (Popper, 1963) but, as we noted earlier, there is a counter-tendency in science to use a box-ticking Polyfilla approach, exacerbating the file-drawer problem by running large numbers of studies generated to fill gaps.

LeBel and Peters (2011) suggest that Bem's studies were enabled to support precognition as a consequence of the faulty MRP of empirical psychology – a systemic bias towards interpretations of data that favour the researcher's theory. This is equivalent to curing the disease, not treating the symptoms. Yet in spite of everything, Bem's data remain among the strongest ever obtained in favour of psi. If the data are wrong, how are we to explain this? LeBel and Peters are gentle in their approach, rejecting the idea of foul play. Other critics, however, are less kind by suggesting wilful data selection and a lack of ethics. Susan Blackmore's (2018) comments on Daryl Bem were outlined in Chapter 6. In essence, Blackmore suggests that Bem has been guilty of 'an unethical manipulation of data in search of statistical significance' to support claims of the paranormal. Blackmore points out that such manipulation is especially serious in this field for three reasons:

1. If evidence for the paranormal were found, the implications for the rest of science would be profound.
2. There is very little evidence for the paranormal and Bem's claims are frequently cited as providing it.
3. Many people believe in the paranormal and look for evidence to back up their belief. If such a respected researcher as Bem claims there is reliable evidence, many people will be convinced with serious consequences for the public understanding of science.

Another critic, Dr Ulrich Schimmack, discovered a new questionable research practice (QRP) that is endemic in Daryl Bem's research. Schimmack's account of Bem's QPR is presented in the next section.

THE DECLINE EFFECT AND A NEW QUESTIONABLE RESEARCH PRACTICE[2]

When Dr Ulrich Schimmack examined Bem's original data, he discovered an interesting pattern. Most studies seemed to produce strong effect sizes at the beginning

---

[2]This section reproduced by kind permission of the author, Dr Ulrich Schimmack, an extract from 'Why the *Journal of Personality and Social Psychology* Should Retract Article DOI: 10.1037/a0021524 "Feeling the Future: Experimental evidence for anomalous retroactive influences on cognition and affect" by Daryl J. Bem', published on 5 January 2018 at: https://replicationindex.com/2018/01/05/why-the-journal-of-personality-and-social-psychology-should-retract-article-doi-10-1037-a0021524-feeling-the-future-experimental-evidence-for-anomalous-retroactive-influences-on-cognition-a/

of a study, but then lower effect sizes as the study continued. This 'high–low' pattern is similar to the decline effect observed across replication studies of other paranormal phenomena (Schooler, 2011; Figure 7.1 below).

The selection effect is so strong that Bem could have stopped 9 of the 10 studies after collecting a maximum of 15 Ps with a significant result. The average sample size for these 9 studies would have been only 7.75 Ps.

Table 7.1 shows the one-sided p-values for Bem's datasets separately for the first 50 Ps and for Ps 51 to 100. For the first 50 Ps, 8 out of 10 tests are statistically significant. For the following 50 Ps none of the 10 tests are statistically significant. A meta-analysis across the 10 studies does show a significant effect for Ps 51 to 100, but the Test of Insufficient Variance also shows insufficient

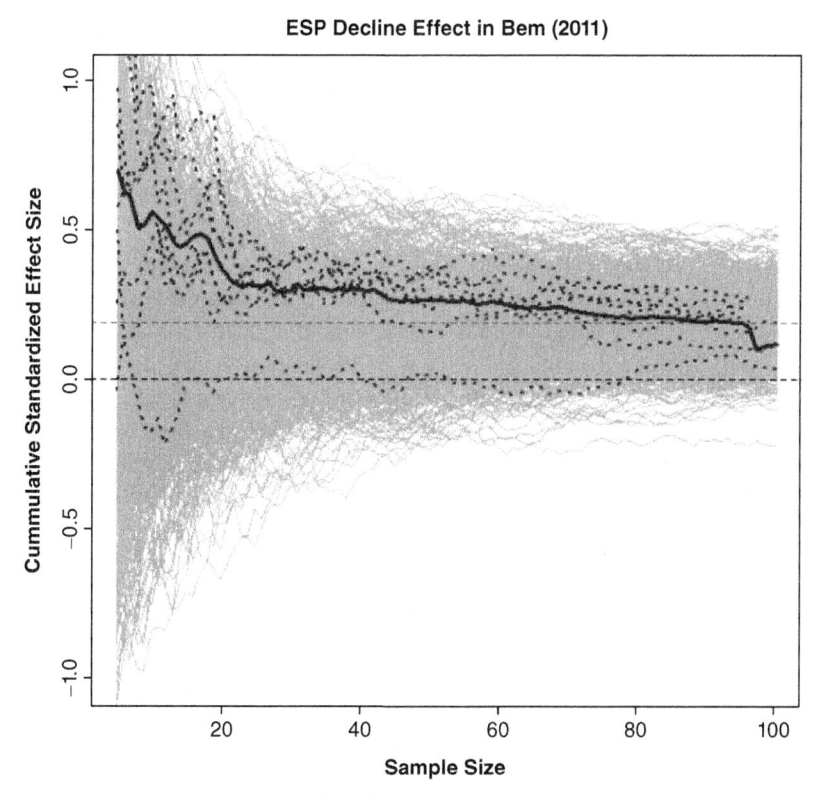

Figure 7.1 This provides a visual representation of the decline effect in Bem's studies. The x-axis is the sample size and the y-axis is the cumulative effect size. As sample sizes increase, the cumulative effect size approaches the population effect size. The grey area represents the results of simulation studies with a population effect size of d = .20. As sampling error is random, the grey area is a symmetrical funnel around the population effect size. The dotted lines show the cumulative effect sizes for Bem's studies. The solid line shows the average cumulative effect size. The figure shows how the cumulative effect size decreases by more than 50% from the first 5 Ps to a sample size of 100 Ps.

Table 7.1 P-values for Bem's 10 datasets based on analyses of the first group of 50 participants and the second group of 50 participants

EXPERIMENT	S 1-50	S 51-100
EXP1	p = .004	p = .194
EXP2	p = .096	p = .170
EXP3	p = .039	p = .100
EXP4	p = .033	p = .067
EXP5	p = .013	p = .069
EXP6a	p = .412	p = .126
EXP5b	p = .023	p = .410
EXP7	p = .020	p = .338
EXP8	p = .010	p = .318
EXP9	p = .003	NA

variance, Var(z) = 0.22, p = .013, suggesting that even these trials are biased by selection for significance (Schimmack, 2015).

Two interpretations of the decrease in effect sizes over the course of an experiment are available. The first explanation, which has been offered by one well-known psi investigator, who does not wish to be named, is that the decline effect in Bem's replications (or any set of replication studies for that matter) does not disprove the existence of psi, because of 'the corrosive psychological effects of demotivation, boredom, fatigue, etc.'. Essentially, then, any decline is an ambiguous observation, unless we have a candid account by the investigator that they did, in fact, take a peek, try and discard. It is highly unlikely that this type of confession would ever see the light of day. It is difficult to imagine why such strong and obvious decline effects should occur so prominently in psi research but not be so evident in any of the other boring tasks that experimental psychologists present to research participants.

The second explanation is that we are seeing a subset of attempts that showed promising results after peeking at the data. Unlike optional stopping, however, a researcher continues to collect more data to see whether the effect is real. Although the effect size decreases, the strong effect during the initial trials that motivated a researcher to collect more data is sufficient to maintain statistical significance because sampling error also decreases as more Ps are added. These results cannot be replicated because they capitalised on chance during the first trials, but this remains unnoticed because the next study does not replicate the first study exactly. Instead, the researcher makes a small change to the experimental procedure, and when he or she peeks at the data of the next study, the study is abandoned and the failure is attributed to the change in the experimental procedure (without checking that the successful finding can be replicated).

In this scenario, researchers are deceiving themselves that slight experimental manipulations apparently have huge effects on their dependent variable because sampling error in small samples is very large. Observed effect sizes in small samples can range from 1 to −1 (see grey area in Figure 7.1), giving the illusion that each experiment is different, but a random number generator would produce the same stunning differences in effect sizes. Bem (2011), and reviewers of his article, seem to share the belief that 'the success of replications in psychological research often depends on subtle and unknown factors' (p. 422). How could Bem reconcile this belief with the reporting of 9 out of 10 successes? The most plausible explanation is that successes are a selected set of findings out of many attempts that were not reported.

Others hint that Bem peeked at the data to decide whether to collect more data or terminate data collection. In his 2011 article, he addressed concerns about a file drawer stuffed with failed studies.

> Like most social–psychological experiments, the experiments reported here required extensive pilot testing. As all research psychologists know, many procedures are tried and discarded during this process. This raises the question of how much of this pilot exploration should be reported to avoid the file-drawer problem, the selective suppression of negative or null results.

Bem does not answer his own question, but the correct answer is clear: all of the so-called pilot studies need to be included if promising pilot studies were included in the actual studies. If Bem had clearly distinguished between promising pilot studies and actual studies, actual studies would be unbiased. However, it appears that he continued collecting data after peeking at the results after a few trials and that the significant results are largely driven by inflated effect sizes in promising pilot studies. This biased the results and can explain how Bem obtained evidence for time-reversed causality that others could not replicate when they did not peek at the data and terminated studies when the results were not promising.

Additional hints come from an interview with Engber (2017):

> 'I would start one [experiment], and if it just wasn't going anywhere, I would abandon it and restart it with changes,' Bem told me recently. Some of these changes were reported in the article; others weren't. 'I didn't keep very close track of which ones I had discarded and which ones I hadn't,' he said. Given that the studies spanned a decade, Bem can't remember all the details of the early work. 'I was probably very sloppy at the beginning,' he said.

Bem's statements about studies as rhetorical devices, sloppiness, trying and discarding, data selection, his knowing use of allegedly fraudulent data in meta-analysis, all lead to one conclusion: Bem's claim to have found evidence of psi is simply unbelievable.

In the interest of balance, however, the final word in this section is from Dr Daryl Bem himself.

I decided to see if I could design and test a set of related experiments that sought to demonstrate what seemed to me to be the most exotic and least understood psi phenomenon: precognition. My initial target audience was fellow academic psychologists, and my strategy was to develop simple but well-controlled demonstrations of precognition that they could replicate in their own laboratories. The motivating idea was to take well-established psychological effects and 'time-reverse' their standard cause-and-effect sequences by postponing the presumed causal event until after the P has already made his or her response.

These experiments are the direct descendants of 'presentiment' experiments pioneered by Dean Radin (1997) in which physiological indices of participants' emotional arousal are monitored as they view a series of pictures on a computer screen. Most of the pictures are emotionally neutral, but a highly arousing negative or erotic image is displayed on randomly selected trials. As expected, strong emotional arousal occurs when these images appear, but the remarkable finding is that the increased arousal is observed to occur a few seconds before the picture actually appears, before the computer has even selected the picture to be displayed. The presentiment effect has also been demonstrated in an fMRI (functional magnetic resonance imaging) experiment that monitored brain activity (Bierman & Scholte, 2002) and in experiments using bursts of noise rather than visual images as the arousing stimuli (Spottiswoode & May, 2003).

My project took approximately a decade to complete and the results were published in 2011 in the APA's *Journal of Personality and Social Psychology*, a journal that rejects more than 80% of manuscripts submitted to it. What follows is a brief commentary on some of the criticisms of my studies that author David Marks summarises in this chapter.

At the beginning of the chapter, Marks cites a critique by Wagenmakers et al. (2011) who claimed that my evidence for psi in those studies was 'weak to non-existent'. Moreover, they maintained that psychologists generally should abandon their current statistical practices and replace them with what are called 'Bayesian' analyses. Marks, however, fails to cite a rejoinder to Wagenmakers et al. by myself, Jessica Utts and Wesley O. Johnson which appeared in the same journal. Utts and Johnson are professors in the Department of Statistics at UC Irvine, and both are acknowledged experts in Bayesian analysis (Utts has also served as president of the American Statistical Association). Our rejoinder criticised the Wagenmakers et al. analysis and demonstrated that a correct application of Bayesian statistics supports the original conclusions of my article (Bem, Utts, & Johnson, 2011).

Marks also summarises what he judges to be a negative review of my studies by LeBel and Peters (2011). But as even his summary makes clear, they are primarily criticising what they call the Modal Research Practices (MRP) of theory testing in science generally, including psychology. They conclude: 'It is precisely because Bem's report is of objectively high quality that it is diagnostic of potential problems with MRP …. Bem has put empirical psychologists in a difficult position: forced to consider either revising beliefs about the fundamental nature of time and causality or revising beliefs about the soundness of MRP' (p. 371).

'A critique by Francis makes a similar point: 'Perhaps the most striking characteristic of [Bem's] study is that [it meets] the current standards of experimental psychology'. The implication is that it is the standards and practices of the field that are not operating properly (2012: 155).

Marks also discusses Shimmack's discovery of a 'Decline Effect' in my studies ... across sessions *within* a single experiment: Those who participate early in the study show a stronger effect than those who participate later.

I suggest that this effect has a mundane explanation, one that is likely to occur in experiments linked to the academic calendar. In many colleges and universities (including my own, Cornell), participants in experiments are recruited through an online list of experiments being offered within the psychology department. Students can sign up to participate in a listed experiment for money or for extra credit in those psychology courses that encourage or require students to participate in experiments. Students who are enthusiastic about this opportunity sign up early in the semester. As final exams loom at the end of the course, however, fewer students have the time or the motivation to participate. So the less enthusiastic students who are required to participate but haven't done so yet, postpone coming in until the end of the semester. Moreover, many students who have been doing badly in a course rush in at the last moment to participate for extra credit in the hope of boosting their course grade.

A similar dynamic affects our student experimenters, whose enthusiasm for running the same experiment over and over each day diminishes over time – despite the 'pep' sessions I hold for them. And, like our participants, the experimenters' enthusiasm declines as their own final examinations loom.

The 'File Drawer' and the Role of 'Pilot Studies'

In this chapter, Marks quotes the comment from my 2011 article in which I say that the experiments required extensive pilot testing, '... [which] raises the question of how much of this pilot exploration should be reported to avoid the file-drawer problem, the selective suppression of negative or null results.' Marks then says, 'Bem does not answer his own question, but the correct answer is clear: all of the so-called pilot studies need to be included if promising pilot studies were included in the actual studies.'

But I do answer my own question in the section on the file-drawer, where I spell out the one instance in which I went astray (which I also reported at length at a meeting of the Parapsychological Association, so they are on the written record). It is also the case that most of my work in psychology has been theory development, which is why I have published so many articles in the theory-based APA journal *Psychological Review*. In my theory-based articles I include brief simple empirical demonstrations to illustrate the conceptual arguments being made. They are meant only to act as instructive illustrations for clarifying my conceptual points.

(Continued)

More fundamentally, I believe Marks' prescription to document every minor change is virtually impossible to implement by noting and remembering minor changes made in an experiment as it is developed. For example, in developing the priming experiment, where the dependent variable is the participant's response times, measuring it milliseconds was too granular and I needed to shift to microseconds. Using a 12-point font was insufficiently legible for some participants, so I shifted to a 14-point font, etc. In yet other cases, I switched from having a P use the mouse to record a binary choice to pressing one of two keys on the keyboard so that the measure of response time would be more accurate. No journal would ever accept – and few readers would ever read – an article bloated by data deriving from such changes made along the way.

So what is the solution? As it happens, there are two unique features of my research program that made the problem much easier. First, all my 9 experiments are identical to each other in that they use the same sequence of screens throughout with the exception of the one screen that contains the specific task.

I spent a very long time writing the code for these common elements. I didn't 'peek' at the data, as Marks speculates, because there were no data to peek at, only my own judgments of how clear the instructions were. Several of my experiments used photographs drawn from the International Affective Picture System (IAPS), a set of 820 digitized photographs that have been rated for valence and arousal by both male and female raters. When I used them in my first formal experiment, only the women showed a significant psi effect. When I checked the IAPS ratings, I discovered that male raters rated virtually all the pictures as less arousing than did female raters. So in all the subsequent experiments involving arousing pictures, I used different pictures for men and women participants, replacing some of the IAPS photographs for male participants with harsher negative images and more explicit erotic images obtained from Internet sites. I also provided two additional sets of erotic pictures, so that men could choose the option of seeing male–male erotic images and women could choose the option of seeing female–female erotic images.

This one change required me to go beyond my own judgments: I didn't trust myself to select erotic pictures for participants whose age, sex, and sexual orientation might be different from my own, so my undergraduate experimenters (and my son) helped me to select the new non-IAPS erotic photographs. This change, like all potentially important changes to my procedures is fully documented in my article.

Critics of my experiments seem never to notice that while there are five precognitive phenomena explored in my article there are nine experiments. With one exception (discussed below), every experiment reported was followed by a replication of that same protocol, accompanied by a detailed description and rationale for any changes I made. So, yes, here I 'peeked' at the data from the first experiment to see if I could think of ways of strengthening the predicted effect. In my article, I present both the original experiments and their replications in full detail. I do not consider the original experiments to be merely 'pilot' experiments. I believe it was B. F. Skinner who said that there is no such thing as a pilot experiment until after it is conducted. Why conduct an ill-planned sloppy experiment to judge whether a well-planned, carefully executed experiment would succeed?

The only experiment I didn't attempt to replicate (Precognitive Detection of Erotic Stimuli) was the simplest and produced the strongest effect of my experiments in the series: On each trial, the P was shown a picture of two curtains on the screen and was told that there would be a picture behind one of the curtains and a blank wall behind the other. The P was instructed to click on the curtain he or she thought would have the picture behind it. After the P clicked on one of the curtains, it opened to reveal an erotic picture, a neutral picture, or a blank wall. Erotic pictures were correctly detected significantly more frequently than chance and significantly more frequently than neutral pictures. This simple experiment also turned out to be the strongest and most replicable experiment in the meta-analysis.

In all the experiments reported, the number of sessions to be run was declared ahead of time and was determined by using what are called 'power' calculations. I calculated that 100 was the minimum number of participants/sessions required to detect a statistically significant effect.

The second feature of my experiments that makes them easy to design and implement is that they are all purposely based on psychological phenomena that have been tested and reaffirmed repeatedly over many years. Indeed, that was the primary rationale for selecting them: Psychologists already believe that the target phenomenon exists. All I had to do was find a published version of each phenomenon that most easily lent itself to time-reversing its stimulus-response sequence.

The Meta-analysis

In this chapter, I believe that Marks has adequately summarized the results of our meta-analysis, and I welcome his approval of my attempts to make all of the research materials available to any researchers who expressed an interest in replicating of my findings.

There were four co-authors on our meta-analysis article, and it is important to note that, by design, I played no role in the meta-analysis itself. That was left to co-author Patrizio Tressoldi at the University of Padova in Italy, an acknowledged expert in performing such analyses. Similarly, I played no role in finding, collecting and independently analyzing the replications done by other researchers, in judging whether those replications were exact or modified versions of my protocols, and summarizing the results with a common set of statistical indices. Those arduous tasks were assigned to co-authors Thomas Rabeyron, and Michael Duggan. My only task was to write the article itself, reporting the results as accurately as possible, and to submit it only when all four of us agreed with my account.

Blackmore Redux

In Chapter 6, I noted that Susan Blackmore accused Charles Honorton and me of ignoring or overlooking her accusations that one of the contributors to the ganzfeld experiments had cheated. She failed to mention (or, perhaps, to even notice) that we demonstrated

(Continued)

that the meta-analysis showed a statistically significant result even if the suspected cheater's experiments were omitted. She simply ignored this and stated erroneously that there was no evidence for psi in the database.

I have not read her comments on our meta-analysis of the precognition experiments, but apparently she is accusing me of deliberate fraud in including my own experiments in our meta-analysis. At least she is being consistent in failing to acknowledge that we *did* report the results of the meta-analysis with my own experiments omitted and still found strong significant effects. (Marks also notes this in this chapter.) Blackmore didn't even have to read the article itself to discover this because it was highlighted in our abstract. Here is the relevant sentence:

'When DJB's original experiments are excluded, the combined effect size for replications by independent investigators is 0.06, $z = 4.16$, $p = 1.1 \times 10^{-5}$, and the BF value is 3,853, again exceeding the criterion for 'decisive evidence.'

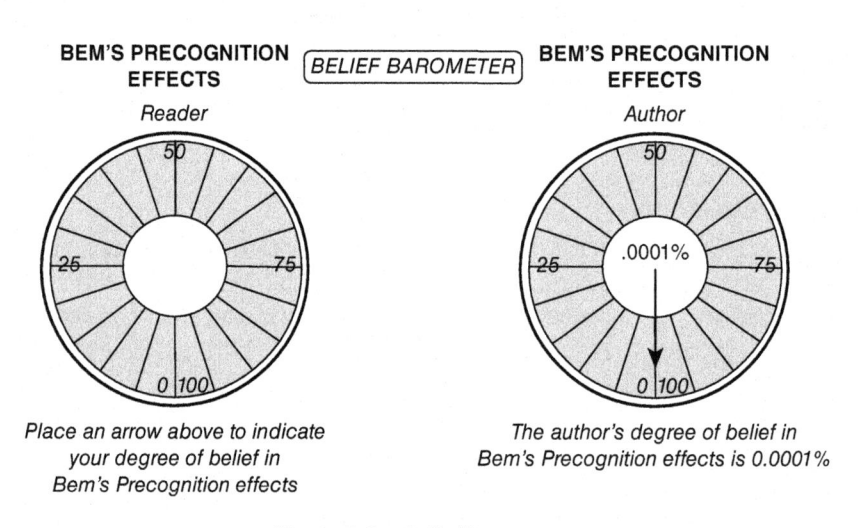

Figure 7.2 Belief barometer

DREAM ESP

Research on dream ESP began in earnest with Montague Ullman (1916–2008), a psychiatrist and psychoanalyst, who studied dream-ESP with Mrs Eileen Garrett, a medium and founder of the Parapsychology Foundation. A picture from *Life* magazine showing the chariot race in the film *Ben Hur*[3] was sent telepathically

---

[3] Often shown on television around Christmas time.

to Mrs Garrett, who later described the picture (Ullman, 1969). According to the abstract of this paper, 'It is in the nature of dreaming to combine states of high activation and dissociation and it is precisely this combination which empirically seems to facilitate telepathic transfer' (p. 19).

Dream-ESP is a form of ESP in which a dreamer is claimed to gain information about a randomly selected target without using the normal sensory modalities or logical inference. One investigator referred to the 'veridical dream' as 'an apparently paranormal dream, inasmuch as some of the dream details give information about events normally unknowable to the experient' (Thalbourne, 2003: 33). Of course, while one is asleep, access to information via the senses is shut off. But once one awakens, there is always the possibility that one could be cued in with target information, so the procedures need to be absolutely 'water tight'.

Montague Ullman established a dream laboratory at the Maimonides Medical Centre in New York in 1962 (Krippner, 1991). Between 1962 and 1978 the Maimonides team conducted thirteen formal dream-ESP studies and three pilot sessions (Krippner, 1991, 1993; Ullman, Krippner, & Vaughan, 1973). Of the 13 formal studies, 11 investigated telepathy and 2 investigated precognition. The Maimonides procedure developed over time and different procedural variations were explored. The basic procedure is described as follows:

> The percipient was attached to EEG–EOG monitoring equipment and slept in a sound-attenuated room in the laboratory. Once he or she was asleep, a target was randomly selected from among a pool of targets (typically art prints), compiled on the basis of the images' emotional intensity, vividness, colour, and simplicity. The target, in a sealed envelope, was given to the sender, who was then locked inside another sound-attenuated room in the building (or, in some studies, a different building). The experimenter monitored the percipient's EEG-EOG throughout the night and, once this indicated that the percipient had entered REM sleep, signaled the agent (via a buzzer) to open the target envelope and begin 'sending' the target. At, or towards, the end of the REM period, the experimenter awakened the percipient via an intercom and asked them to describe any dream(s) they could recall. Responses throughout the night and in the morning were tape-recorded and later transcribed. The agent heard the percipient's dream report via a loudspeaker, which may have reinforced his or her subsequent sending strategy. The percipient then went back to sleep. The above process was repeated for each REM period with the same target being sent each time. In the morning, the percipient reported any associations to the dream mentation and guessed what the target might be. Percipients typically viewed between eight and twelve pictures, one of which was the target, gave a confidence rating for each picture and also placed them in rank order according to the correspondence with their dream mentation, associations, and/or guesses. Complete dream transcripts and target sets were also sent to two or three independent judges who made similar judgments. The ratings/rankings from

the blind judges were combined. A trial was a 'binary hit' if the target picture had been ranked in the top half of the target set and a 'binary miss' if ranked in the bottom half. Performance was then evaluated to determine whether it was significantly higher or lower than mean chance expectation (MCE). (Storm et al., 2017)

During most of the telepathy studies, dreams were monitored and recorded throughout the night and the same target was sent during each REM period (Child, 1985). In the 'Sensory bombardment' and 'Grateful Dead' studies, the sending periods did not occur regularly throughout the night and did not necessarily coincide with the receivers' REM[4] periods. In a study with A. Vaughan, I. Vaughan, Harris and Parise, some trials involved sending a different target during each REM period. Studies using the same receiver across trials often used the same sender also, but not always. Successful sender and receiver pairings from two screening studies were used in later studies. Some studies used more than one sender, across a series of trials with either the same receiver or different receivers. There was not always a single sender for each receiver; for some sensory bombardment trials, a single sender was used for two receivers; for the Grateful Dead trials, a concert audience of about 2,000 people acted as senders. During precognition and clairvoyance trials, no sender was used. The distance between the sender and receiver varied across the studies. There were many other variations to the procedure of an unsystematic kind. In the early studies, confidence ratings for the rankings were given on a 5-point scale but, from the fourth study on, a 100-point scale was used.

As with all anomalous experience research, opinions about the Maimonides research are strongly divided. On the one hand, Irvin Child concluded:

> What is clear is that the tendency toward hits rather than misses cannot reasonably be ascribed to chance. There is some systematic – that is, nonrandom – source of anomalous resemblance of dreams to targets. (Child, 1985: 1220)

Child (1985) concluded that: 'The outcome is clear. Several segments of the data, considered separately, yield significant evidence that dreams (and associations to them) tended to resemble the picture chosen randomly as target more than they resembled other pictures in the pool' (p. 1220).

On the other hand, James Alcock (2003) declared that 'lack of replication is rampant'. Also, Edward Belvedere and David Foulkes (1971) found no evidence that

---

[4] Dreams occur in both rapid eye movement (REM) and non-rapid eye movement (NREM) sleep (Nielsen et al., 2000). REM dreams are relatively long, primarily visual, emotional and usually not connected to the immediate events. Non-REM dreams are shorter, less visual, less emotional, more conceptual and usually related to the current life of the dreamer. Conceptual, 'thought-like' mentation can occupy up to 50% of non-REM sleep (Kandel, 2013).

the subject or the judges could match the targets with dreams above chance level (Foulkes et al., 1972). Irvin Child (1985) encountered two difficulties evaluating the Maimonides research findings: (1) the raw data were no longer available; (2) in at least some of the studies, the 'blind' judgements may not have been independent, so judges might have obtained clues to the target identity from other transcripts (Clemmer, 1986). Alcock (1981) criticised the studies for lacking a proper control condition, but the controls in such studies are the other non-target stimuli against which the transcript is also compared. Fraud has also been suggested (e.g. Clemmer, 1986) but no method for producing the fraud has ever been proposed.

I leave the final word on the Maimonides studies to Dr Stanley Krippner, who kindly answered five direct questions as follows:[5]

1. **Which experiment in particular do you consider to be the most convincing evidence of dream-psi, and for what reason(s)?** Storm et al. found the Second Precognitive Dream Study to meet most of their standards for high quality research.

2. **How important is the qualitative judgment of accuracy in the dream report?** One never knows what aspect of a study is the most important, but qualitative judgment certainly played a key role.

3. **Why were the Maimonides studies terminated? One assumes this was because of lack of funding, but if the results were deemed successful, should the sponsors not have continued their support in order to garner a scientific revolution?** First of all, I would not use the term 'scientific revolution'. It is simply too early to make such a grandiose claim. As to your comment that the sponsors should have continued their support, I think they were less guided by lofty ideals than by their own budgetary constraints. Also remember that Montague Ullman had retired from Maimonides and had turned his attention to teaching dreamworkers his innovative dream interpretation method. I was preoccupied with finding funding for my two stepchildren's college fees. Charles Honorton was more interested in furthering his Ganzfeld research. So there were many circumstances at play.

4. **How important is the REM state to dream-ESP?** We never made a formal evaluation of REM vs. non-REM dreams. When a non-REM dream was reported, we simply added it to the data collection. Non-REM dreams are generally shorter than REM dreams and less dramatic. If you know of one of our studies that compared the two types of dreams, let me know. I do not recall any.

5. **On a scale of 0–100%, what is your current degree of belief in the reality of dream-ESP?** I would estimate it at 80%. This is a controversial topic, and I for one try to remain modest as well as cautious in over-interpreting the results.

(Krippner, 2019, personal communication)

---

[5]Dr Krippner's responses are quoted verbatim, with no editing or paraphrasing.

META-ANALYSIS OF DREAM-ESP STUDIES

One meta-analysis of experimental dream-ESP studies between 1966 and 2016 has been reported – that of Storm et al. (2017). They divided studies into the Maimonides Dream Lab (MDL) studies (n = 14) and independent (non-MDL) studies (n = 36). The MDL dataset yielded a mean effect size (ES) of .33 (SD = 0.37), while the non-MDL studies yielded a mean ES of .14 (SD = 0.27), which were not significantly different. A homogeneous dataset (N = 50) yielded a moderate mean z of 0.75 (ES = .20, SD = 0.31), giving a p value of 5.19×10^{-8}, suggesting that dream content is identifying target materials more often than would be expected by chance. No significant differences were found between telepathy (r = .22), clairvoyance (r = .18) and precognition (r = .17) in laboratory dream-ESP studies. Also, perhaps more importantly, *no differences were obtained between REM versus non-REM monitoring*. The 'REM-monitoring' studies yielded a mean z score of 0.64 (SD = 0.92). The 'no-REM-monitoring' studies yielded a mean z score of 0.84 (SD = 1.26). The difference between the two conditions was not significant (p = .271, one-tailed). The 'REM-monitoring' studies yielded a mean ES of 0.24 (SD = 0.33), while the 'no-REM-monitoring' studies yielded a mean ES of 0.16 (SD = 0.29). The difference between the two conditions was not significant (p = .180, one-tailed). Therefore, the hypothesis that dream-ESP studies using REM monitoring would produce a higher mean z score and a higher mean ES value than dream-ESP studies that do not use REM monitoring was not supported. Storm et al. (2017) conclude: 'we would argue that the mean ES is encouragingly high for studies with REM-monitoring and researchers may wish to take that finding into consideration' (p. 132). However finding that REM monitoring has no influence on the dream-ESP effect size is very odd because dreaming is meant to be responsible for the ESP effect in sleeping senders.[6]

Two other interesting findings were that the quality of the studies was unrelated to ES (curious – see later comments), but there was a significant and steady ES decline over the 51-year period (Figure 7.3). The authors state: 'Although [Figure 7.3] suggests that the accumulation of effects over time may be attributable to older ES values, we emphasize that our other analysis ... does not allow us to attribute this decline to improved study quality' (p. 130). It seems odd that they did not comment on the implications of the hugely significant decline effect any further than this. My first personal conclusion is that James Alcock's (2003) statement that 'lack of replication is rampant' is evidently untrue. The sequence of results, albeit diminishing in size, clearly shows an effect that is

---

[6]Dreams are reported on about 80% of awakenings from REM sleep (Goodenough, 1991). However, some dreaming occurs in non-REM sleep, although to a lesser degree (Nielsen, Laberge, Paquet, Tremblay, Vitaro, & Montplaisir, 2000). For example, Siclari, Larocque, Postle, and Tononi (2013) found that recall with content was reported in 34% of non-REM and in 77% of REM sleep awakenings.

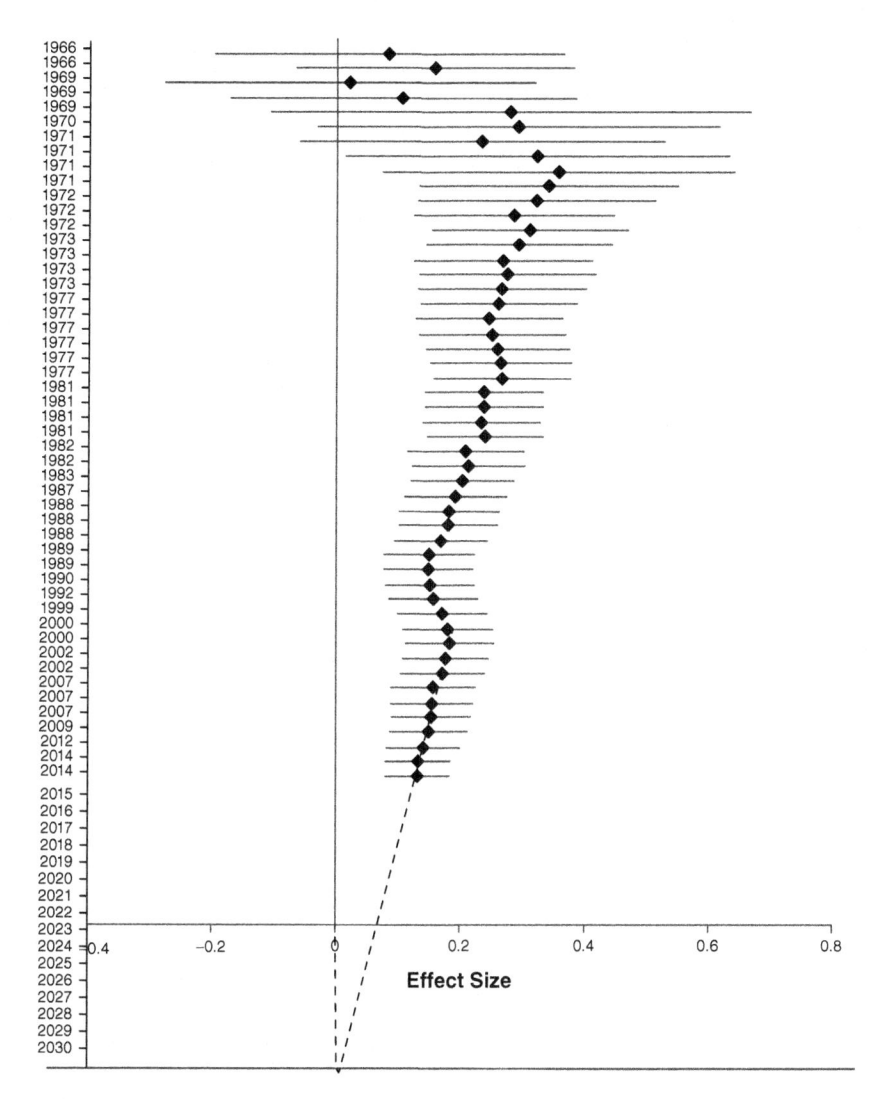

Figure 7.3 Forest plot showing that effect sizes have been in decline from 1966 to 2014 (Storm et al., 2017). Continuing the linear trend in the effect sizes into the future by extrapolation (dotted line) indicates that the effect size may well reach zero by the early 2030s.

Adapted from Storm et al. (2017).

replicable. My second conclusion is that, if the observed trend continues, *the dream-ESP effect size will reach zero by the early 2030s*. We must wait another 10 years to see whether this decline effect materialises. If so, no more dream-ESP studies.

Following best practice, Storm et al. (2017) provided sample sizes, effect sizes and partial coding decisions for each of their included studies.[7] Using the data provided by Storm et al., Matthew Howard was able to correct the funnel effect using the 'trim and fill' method.[8] To avoid any possibility of bias, one way or the other, I quote Howard verbatim. Commenting on the Storm et al. (2017) meta-analysis, Howard (2018)[9] writes:

> Certain statistical decisions, such as primarily reporting unweighted effects, may have inflated these observations. In the current article, I perform an inverse-variance weighted meta-analysis[10] using the database provided by Storm et al., finding a much smaller overall effect (r = .07). I also find evidence that a significant relationship exists between effect size and sample size, suggesting that the prior results may have been primarily driven by large effects found in small-n studies. I suggest that future researchers of ESP in dreams should produce more large-n studies, which could alleviate many notable criticisms of the current psi literature …
>
> By modern standards the overall effect of laboratory dream ESP studies was small (.07); the effect of telepathy studies was small (.07); the effect of clairvoyance studies was moderate (.19); and the effect of precognition studies was very small (.04). The overall effect as well as the effect of clairvoyance studies were statistically significant, whereas the effect of telepathy and precognition studies were not statistically significant. Thus, these results do not definitively support or not support the existence of psi in laboratory studies of ESP in dreams. (Howard, 2018: 228)

As is so often the case with meta-analyses, the Storm et al. (2017) meta-analysis of dream-ESP and Howard's (2018) reanalysis have produced more questions than answers. The results on dream-ESP to date remain *inconclusive*. Furthermore, these analyses have yielded some counterintuitive findings that raise doubts about the nature of the dream-ESP studies:

---

[7] As suggested by the Meta-Analytic Reporting Standards (MARS) and Preferred Reporting Items for Systematic Reviews and Meta-Analyses (PRISMA).

[8] The 'trim and fill' method identifies and corrects for funnel plot asymmetry arising from publication bias by 'trimming' (removing) the smaller studies causing funnel plot asymmetry, using the trimmed funnel plot to estimate the true 'centre' of the funnel, then replacing the omitted studies and their missing 'counterparts' around the centre (filling).

[9] Howard made one change to the dataset of Storm et al., who had included Watt (2014) in their analyses. Additional observations were added by Watt to 'bring them out of the file drawer' (2014: 106). Howard included these additional observations and recalculated the effect size of Watt (2014).

[10] Meta-analytic effects were calculated using a random-effects model with inverse-variance weights, and Howard reported effects sizes as correlation coefficients (r).

1. *The lack of any measurable difference between the ESP effect obtained during REM and non-REM dream state.* Since the 1950s, it has been established that the REM stage of sleep is strongly associated with dreaming (Aserinsky & Kleitman, 1953). That the REM state was found to be *un*associated with the effect size in the dream-ESP studies suggests that dreaming is *irrelevant* to 'dream-ESP'. If true, the theoretical basis for dream-ESP is thrown into question and whether ESP is actually involved is now a moot point.
2. Improvements in study *quality was also unrelated to the dream-ESP effect size.* This finding raises questions about the phenomenon the studies are producing. In light of this finding and the lack of any REM–dream-ESP association, it seems likely that the observed effects are one large artefactual experimenter effect operating independently of dreaming or anomalous cognition.
3. The dream-ESP effect is showing a near-perfect linear trend towards a gradual disappearance over time.[11] This decline is one of the most reliable, robust and replicable effects ever observed in the history of psi research. It is a genuine instance of replication, albeit with an effect in gradual decline. The linear decline in the dream-ESP effect size over time indicates that the dream-ESP effect is destined to reach zero by the early 2030s. Whether the extinction of dream-ESP actually happens is a matter for conjecture. Perhaps 'ESP-conservationists' will find ways to protect this nearly extinct 'species' of ESP?

SUMMARY

Precognition research by Dr Daryl Bem (2011) put the paranormal cat among the psychological pigeons, causing havoc and no small amount of panic throughout the psychology establishment. The search for the truth involved laborious, in-depth analysis of methodology, which serious explorers can only shirk at their peril. However, there is no convincing evidence of psi in Bem's papers, only a handful of well-recognised questionable research practices, and a lot of tiny p values.[12] From a zetetic viewpoint, the case for psi in Bem's research is unconfirmed but neither is it disconfirmed.

Dream-ESP has been studied extensively since the early 1960s. Storm et al. (2017)[13] and the reanalysis by Howard (2018) cast a shadow of doubt over dream-ESP. That the REM state has been found to be irrelevant to dream-ESP, that study quality is unrelated to effect size, and that a significant decline effect is occurring over time, are all serious problems for the dream-ESP hypothesis. The best of the

---

[11]A small 'hump' occurs in the period 2000–2003, but the annual, linear decrease in effect size is evident both before and after this hump.

[12]The tinier the p, the greater the chance of publication.

[13]In the interest of fairness, the final word on dream-ESP meta-analyses was invited from two leading investigators, Dr Patrizio Tressoldi, University of Padua, and Dr Lance Storm, University of Adelaide. Dr Storm sent a few off-the-record comments, but neither Dr Storm nor Dr Tressoldi wished to write a commentary for publication.

findings are neither evidence of the paranormal nor have any direct association to REM-state dreaming. 'Dream-ESP' could have an entirely different explanation as 'error some place' caused by questionable research practices. What other explanation could there possibly be for psi in one's sleep?

QUESTIONS

1. What was J. W. Dunne's contribution to research on anomalous cognition?
2. How do critics explain Daryl Bem's positive findings?
3. What is a conceptual replication?
4. Are Daryl Bem's findings trustworthy? Give your reasons for your answer.
5. How do you interpret the finding in a dream-ESP meta-analysis that there is no correlation between study quality and effect size?
6. To what extent is dream-ESP replicable?
7. After reading the Appendix by Arina K. Bones, is dream-ESP another form of psychological precognition?

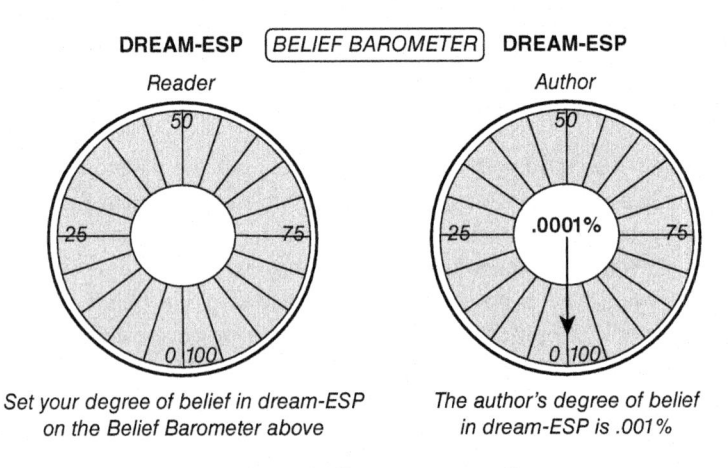

DREAM-ESP [BELIEF BAROMETER] **DREAM-ESP**
Reader   *Author*

Set your degree of belief in dream-ESP on the Belief Barometer above

The author's degree of belief in dream-ESP is .001%

Figure 7.4 Belief barometer readings

TIME TO SMILE: APPENDIX TO CHAPTER 7 BY ARINA K. BONES[14]

'WE KNEW THE FUTURE ALL ALONG: SCIENTIFIC HYPOTHESIZING IS MUCH MORE ACCURATE THAN OTHER FORMS OF PRECOGNITION – A SATIRE IN ONE PART'

Daryl Bem's 2011 article 'Feeling the Future: Experimental Evidence for Anomalous Retroactive Influences on Cognition and Affect' in the *Journal of Personality and Social Psychology (JPSP)* reported evidence of precognition. Publication of this article illustrates the lack of adherence to journal standards, and anticipates the decline of psychological science. In this article, I will inspire a course correction to assert and affirm the field's treasured practices.

A prominent prior critique focuses on supposed errors in data analysis by Bem and everyone else (Wagenmakers, Wetzels, Borsboom, & van der Maas, 2011). These Bayesians completely miss the boat (but see Kievit, 2011). They take priors so seriously. All my priors are a bunch of deadbeats, losers, and ne'er do wells. I don't want anything to do with them, so I certainly won't be accounting for them in my new pursuits. The real failure in publication of Bem (2011) is that journal editors and reviewers did not follow the core evaluation standards for scientific review – the advancement of novel theory and evidence. What is new in the Bem article? Nothing. Bem's precognition article is a weak replication of a well-established phenomenon.

Review of Evidence

The evidence for precognition is psychological science itself. Just open a random issue of any psychology journal. In it, you will find dozens of *a priori* hypotheses anticipating

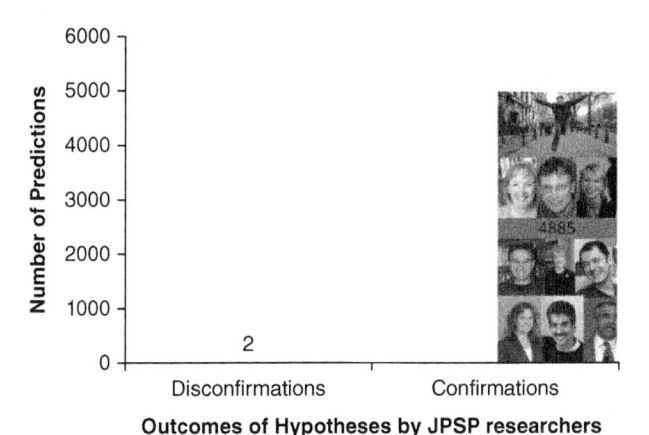

Figure 1 Evidence for JPSP researcher precognition. Although the data for this figure were not actually collected, the evidence it presents clearly demonstrates that such data collection is unnecessary.

(Continued)

---

[14]Reproduced from Bones (2012) by permission of the publisher.

findings that eventually occurred. For example, consider the very journal that published Bem (2011). Figure 1 presents the number of hypotheses by the authors of *JPSP* articles that were confirmed or disconfirmed. All hypotheses except for two were confirmed. In one of the exceptional cases, Denes-Raj and Epstein (1994) had a secondary hypothesis that their primary hypothesis would be incorrect. In the other, Zajonc, Heingartner, and Herman (1969) anticipated that by 1974 cockroaches would control most of the eastern United States because 'it would be so easy and they inspire each other so damn well' (p. 87).[15]

Further, consider the successful predictions. Correctly anticipating that people walk slower after reading the word *Florida*? That people are obsessed with thinking about white bears? That people have don't have have don't have have personalities? It is obvious that one could not have possibly anticipated the results of most of the published studies without some form of precognition. In comparison with the paltry accuracy rates by Bem's precognition subjects (less than 60%?!), the conclusion is clear: Bem's effects are startlingly weak compared to the already published evidence for precognition in psychological science.

Skeptics may think that I have simply cherry-picked a single journal that has supportive evidence for my claim. Not so – consider the sheer magnitude of hypothesis confirmation. Sterling (1959) first documented psychologists' remarkable precognitive capacities. He showed that 97% of articles across a random selection of psychology journals reported positive results. Further, Fanelli (2012) showed that psychologists have kept up this impressive prediction rate through the present. Moreover, his evidence suggests that psychologists have more positive results than virtually every other scientific discipline. For example, biologists have excellent precognition but still not as good as psychologists (Fanelli, in press), political scientists appear to be guessing randomly (Tetlock, 2005), and economists are wrong about virtually everything (see Economics, all of it).[16] Psychology is number one!

Supposed Limitations

First, some might argue that high-profile examples of prediction failures by psychologists are counterevidence to the above (see Table 1). However, the occasional misprediction only serves as confirmation of the overall result. Second, it is true that psychologists are a biased sample. But I am not generalizing to all people. Such generalization is left to those that later cite this work, as is standard practice. Third, one might claim an alternative account

---

[15] Zajonc, of course, was himself an alien with domination aspirations (Bones, 1996), as are all psychologists with last names beginning with Z (e.g. Zeigarnik; cf. Bones & Johnson, 2007).

[16] It is curious that economists have not applied the Costanza transformation to their hypotheses to reverse their persistent misprediction (David, Seinfeld, & Cowan, 1994). The most likely reason for this oversight is that they are economists.

Table 1 Notable prediction errors in psychology.

Year	Event
1961	Albert Bandura predicts that getting some kids at work to destroy his family's Bobo doll is an effective way to get rid of it without getting in trouble. Seriously misjudges his children's revenge efficacy.
1974	B.F. Skinner predicts that people could be conditioned to adopt his hairdo, abruptly ends the age of behaviorism.
1976	Langer and Rodin predict that plants would live longer if cared for by older adults. Sheepishly publish the inverse result.
1994	Spelke predicts that babies know chemical engineering too. Finds little evidence beyond methane production. Publishes it anyway in *Science* (Spelke, 1997).
1999	The *American Psychological Association* and the *National Institutes of Health* issue a joint prediction that the increasingly popular neuroscience methods will contribute new knowledge to psychology "worth their weight in grant dollars."[a]
2011	Jonathan Haidt predicts that there will someday be conservatives in social psychology.[b]

[a] Perhaps a stretch to include on this list. In 2007, researchers using *fMRI* did convincingly demonstrate that psychology occurs in the brain.
[b] Too soon to declare prediction failure? Come on. Like this is ever going to happen. (Editor's Note: I predict that data consistent with Haidt's prediction will appear in an upcoming issue of *Perspectives on Psychological Science*.)

in which psychologists are not predicting the future – they are controlling it. However, I did not predict that. And, if you do not understand this as a refutation, then you need to look at Figure 1 again.

Finally, an audacious skeptic might counter that the authors of empirical psychology articles could have conducted the studies, found results, dismissed inconsistent data, and then written the paper as if the presented results were what they had anticipated all along.[17] However, orchestrating such a large-scale hoax would require the coordination and involvement of thousands of researchers, reviewers, and editors. Researchers would have to selectively report those studies that 'worked' or reengineer those that did not for other purposes. Reviewers and editors would have to selectively accept positive, confirmatory results and reject any norm-violating negative result reports. The possibility that an entire field could be perpetrating such a scam is so counterintuitive that only a psychologist could predict it if it were actually true.

(Continued)

---

[17] It is ironic that Bem himself (Bem, 2003) predicted this practice by prefuting his own position on precognition.

Conclusion and Next Steps

With a near 100% accuracy rate, psychological scientists have clearly demonstrated that psychological scientists already know what is going to occur. This makes the subsequent empirical confirmation superfluous. Once predicted, there is no logical justification for expending the resources to actually conduct the data collection and analysis.

There are some positive signs that the revolution away from empirical confirmation is underway. *JPSP*, for one, has adopted a policy of not publishing replications to clarify their meager importance in comparison with novel findings. Indeed, if the result was known before the first empirical test, then what possible value would there be in conducting a second empirical test? Psychological science is at the vanguard for redefining reproducibility, known as the *sine qua non* of old-fashioned science (Aristotle, 1848; Popper, 1959), as the *sine qua none* of revolutionary science.[18] Also, revolutionaries in the *Skip Testing Actual Participants in Experiments League* have advanced methods for empirical reporting without being encumbered by real data. Without replication, these practices are easily implemented and highly effective. Impressively, a soon-to-be-published journal, *Bite-Size Psychology*, is pursuing a new reporting format to facilitate these practices: the 15-word-limit 'all-headline' article format. Easy-to-read. Flashy. No data or methods. Perfect for fostering real impact – media mentions. Finally, Simmons, Nelson, and Simonsohn (2011) have provided a useful step-by-step guide for ensuring that actual data (for those who choose to bear this burden) is certain to demonstrate the preknown effects. Their simulations illustrate the importance of maximizing researcher power by enhancing their freedom. Affording the researcher her fundamental right to freedom in sampling, exclusion criteria, measures, and analysis strategy, 'allows presenting anything as significant.' In psychology, the word 'significant' is the technical term for *true* which, of course, we already knew.

Correspondence concerning this article can be sent anywhere except arina.bones@gmail.com

The author declared that he [arina.bones@gmail.com] had no conflicts of interest with respect to his authorship or the publication of this article.

---

[18] But why did they fail to adhere to this policy in the case of Bem (2011)?

8
PSYCHOKINESIS, DICE AND RANDOM NUMBER GENERATORS

'Mind Over Matter' En Route to Neverland?

With a contribution by
Dean Radin, PhD

The probability that the observed effect was actually zero (i.e., no psi) was less than one part in a trillion, verifying that human consciousness can indeed affect the behaviour of a random physical system. (The Parapsychological Association, 2020)

There are three kinds of lies: lies, damned lies, and statistics. (True saying. Source unknown.)

Outline: If we accept the view of the Parapsychological Association, there can be no disputing that psychokinesis (PK) is absolutely proven:

A meta-analysis of the database, published in 1989, examined 800 experiments by more than 60 researchers over the preceding 30 years. The effect size was found to be very small, but remarkably consistent, resulting in an overall statistical

(Continued)

> deviation of approximately 15 standard errors from a chance effect. The probability that the observed effect was actually zero (i.e., no psi) was less than one part in a trillion, verifying that human consciousness can indeed affect the behaviour of a random physical system. Furthermore, while experimental quality had significantly increased over time, this was uncorrelated with the effect size, in contradiction to a frequent, but unfounded skeptical criticism. Some parapsychologists believe that these results can be accounted for by ESP if the experimenter (or their participants) intuitively know the right moment to start their studies to get significant results. This is known as Decision Augmentation Theory. However, the apparent effect of focused mass consciousness on a worldwide network of RNGs (see the Global Consciousness Project) suggest that at least some of the time, there is an element of mind-matter interaction. (The Parapsychological Association, 2020).

In a search for the truth, I review here the best evidence from 2000 to 2019.[1] My review is focused on a large meta-analysis. 'Psychokinesis' (from Greek ψυχή 'mind' and κίνησις 'movement'), or 'PK', is a lazy person's dream. With PK, one could move objects without lifting a finger. One definition of PK is: 'The alleged capability to influence a physical system without any physical interaction.' By the standards of everyday physics, that definition is oxymoronic (i.e. senseless). However, if one is to explore PK in a zetetic manner, one must set aside the rules of everyday physics. Be ready for a 'Neverland'[2] world where impossible things happen and are published by a professional organisation of scientists as factually proven.

Dice for divination and games of chance – gambling essentially – have been used for thousands of years. In 1627, one of the founders of scientific empiricism, Francis Bacon, proposed that the 'force of imagination' could be studied with objects that 'have the lightest and easiest motions', including 'the casting of dice' (Radin, Nelson, Dobyns, & Houtkooper, 2006). Over several thousand years of playing dice games of chance, one wonders why not a single individual has consistently produced above-chance results. Beyond-chance PK capability would be, de facto, every dice gambler's dream. Better than everyone else, the dice gambler knows that psi is only a dream that never comes true in reality.

Consider the game of craps.[3] The aim of craps is to influence the way that two dice fall to give a 7 or 11, and then, after that, to keep throwing two dice against the back wall to avoid a 7. If any consistently successful dice control should actually

---

[1] This chapter is the most challenging from a statistical point of view. It introduces the statistical complexities of psi research using meta-analysis.
[2] The fictional island featured in the works of J. M. Barrie.
[3] A gambling game in which two dice are thrown. In casinos, a roll totalling 2, 3 or 12 is called 'craps', or 'crapping out'. 'Dice control' is the trained ability to influence the score.

occur, the player will feel a firm hand on their shoulder and be given a stern invitation to move on.[4] No casino is in the business to lose money.

In spite of the harsh realities of games of chance, words about luck, chance and fate are interesting. Luck is said to be the spontaneous occurrence of certain events having either a positive or negative influence. People may view themselves as 'lucky' or 'unlucky', and carry charms to bring them better luck (Wiseman & Watt, 2004). In English, the word 'luck' expresses a fortunate and, at least partially, unanticipated occurrence. The word may come from the fifteenth-century Middle High German *gelücke*, which means both happiness and luck (Wit, 1997). The word is still popular today. When the Dutch women's football team lost 2:0 to the US in Lyon on 7 July 2019, then if you're Dutch, the US team didn't win because they played more skilfully, the US team simply 'lucked out' (*geluk gehad*).

Both 'chance' and 'coincidence' have roots in the Latin verb *cadere*, to fall, and its conjunction, *cadens*, falling. Chance is something that 'falls down from the heavens onto the people', authored by God(s) in heaven, just like a lucky fall of the dice (Wit, 1997).

Figure 8.1 Roman lead dice. A cube measuring 12 × 12 × 12mm, with one to six impressed dots on each face; found in Leicestershire, England, dated between AD1 and 410. Creative Commons: The Portable Antiquities Scheme/ The Trustees of the British Museum.

The pertinent question to ask here is: can dice be rolled at above-chance levels using psi-PK? To answer this question, one returns to the laboratory. Experimental PK research uses one of two laboratory tasks to determine whether humans can

---

[4]The connection between gambling and theories of probability and statistics is far from coincidental. A 'card sharp' might well end up as professor of statistics in an Ivy League university – e.g. Persi Diaconis, Mary V. Sunseri, Professor of Statistics and Mathematics at Stanford University (Diaconis & Mosteller, 1989). Diaconis began his career playing poker on ships between New York and South America (Wikipedia: https://en.wikipedia.org/wiki/Persi_Diaconis).

use psi to intentionally influence (i) the fall of manually thrown dice, and (ii) the output of random number generators (RNGs). As for most things to do with psi, the earliest laboratory research on PK was carried out by Rhine (Rhine, 1943). Later, Helmut Schmidt, a physicist who had previously worked at Boeing, took over from Rhine (Schmidt, 1974). Recent research has followed Schmidt in using electronic RNGs instead of dice. RNGs have the considerable advantage of being programmable and automatically controlled by the investigator, and also the source can be made truly random. However, anything can go wrong in even the best designed RNG research (or aeroplane!).

Owing to increased automation, scientific papers on PK have increased exponentially over time. The number of documents mentioning 'psychokinesis' in Google Scholar increased from 6 in the 20-year-period 1900 to 1919, to 4,400 during 2000 to 2019. Many reports are secondary (reports of reports) or tertiary (reports of reports of reports). In this author's opinion, only one PK paper of any genuine merit has been published in the 21st century: the meta-analysis of 380 studies by Holger Bösch, Fiona Steinkamp and Emil Boller ('BSB', 2006a). These authors concluded that RNG output does correlate with human intention but with a minuscule effect size. BSB also reported that study effect sizes were strongly and inversely related to sample size and extremely heterogeneous. A Monte Carlo simulation[5] revealed that the small effect size, the relation between sample size and effect size, and the extreme effect size heterogeneity[6] could, in principle, be the result of a publication bias.

As night follows day, the BSB (2006a) paper ('Round 1') was immediately followed by a critical response (Radin et al., 2006) ('Round 2') and a counter response (Bösch, Steinkamp, & Boller, 2006b) ('Round 3'). One could easily imagine 'the ball' (or were they 'punches'?) going back and forth several more times if the journal editor hadn't 'stopped play' at Round 3. Because of the 'ping-pong' nature of the debate, progress in the PK field is disappointing.

In 1962, Edward Girden (1962a) concluded a review of PK research as follows:

> Few of the PK reports fulfil the basic requirement of a psychological experiment. To have psychological justification, there must be a controlled comparison such as wish for versus wish against, or wish for versus no wishing, or Believers versus Disbelievers .... Evidence of PK

---

[5]A Monte Carlo simulation is named after the Monaco town renowned for its casinos (appropriate!). A Monte Carlo simulation provides a range of possible outcomes and the probabilities that will occur for any choice of action.

[6]Effect size heterogeneity occurs when studies have a differing population of Ps, instructions, procedures, choice of analysis or experimental design that can cause problems in attempts to summarise the meaning of the studies using meta-analysis. Extreme effect-size heterogeneity radically reduces the observed overall effect size.

as a psychological phenomenon is therefore totally lacking. And this deficiency will persist until the effect is produced in the presence of a specified psychological variable, and the effect does not appear in its absence.

In response to a critic, Gardner Murphy (1962), Girden (1962b) states: 'Many of the criticisms leveled by Murphy ... on an earlier paper by Girden (1962a) are considered. It is concluded that *the existence of PK has not been proven.*'

According to BSB, Girden's 44-year-old conclusion still remained correct in 2019. BSB concluded their enormous review as follows: 'Girden's (1962b) verdict of "not proven" (p. 530), which he mooted more than 40 years ago in the same journal with respect to dice experiments, also holds for human intentionality on RNGs.' Thus, in spite of all of the 'blood, sweat and tears' of 44 years' research, BSB reached the same 'unproven' verdict as Girden. For anybody seeking progress, this conclusion is disappointing, if not downright depressing.

In order to explore the truth of BSB's claim, it is necessary to dig deeply into BSB's review to see why they reached their pessimistic conclusion. This foray into BSB's meta-analysis seems a far cry from the simple question that we started with – can dice be rolled at above-chance levels using psi-PK? Unfortunately, the search for psi regresses into an ever deeper exposure of 'lies, damned lies and statistics'. For any would-be connoisseur of the paranormal, there is no other option but to enter the regress. You, dear reader, are the lucky one – you can read this summary of 50 years of PK research without lifting a finger. I examine the BSB debate in three rounds.

Round 1 (Bösch et al., 2006a)

BSB combined the effect sizes of individual studies into composite weighted effect size measures[7] using an intuitive measure suggested by Rosenthal and Rubin (1989).[8] Think of each study as a single P contributing one score (its effect size) to a set of results that are being analysed in an 'experiment' (a meta-analysis). First, we want to know the overall mean effect size from all 380 studies. Then, second, we want to know the results when the 380 studies are broken down into groups using various 'moderator variables' such as sample size, nature of Ps, when the study was done, etc.

First, the overall results were reported as follows:

> When combined, the overall result of the 380 intentional studies depended on the statistical model applied. The overall effect size of the FEM (fixed

---

[7] A weighted effect size takes into account the sample size so that a larger sample counts proportionately more to the overall effect size than a smaller sample.
[8] Owing to their complexity, it is not possible or even necessary here to provide a detailed description of the statistical procedures that BSB employed. Interested readers should consult the original paper.

effects model)[9] indicated an effect opposite to intention, whereas the effect size of the REM (random effects model) indicated an effect in the intended direction [see Table 8.1]. The considerable difference between the two models was due to the three by far largest studies in the meta-analysis (see Figure 2), published in a single experimental report (Dobyns, Dunne, & Nelson, 2004). The effect sizes of these three studies, ranging from $\pi = .499989$ to $\pi = .499997$, indicated a result opposite to intention. Without these three studies, both models showed a statistically highly significant effect in the intended direction. (BSB, 2006a: 506)

Figure 8.2 shows a funnel plot, the conventional way of determining whether there is publication bias.[10] Using the FEM, and starting with the smallest study ($n = 20$, $\pi = .75$), then consecutively adding the next largest study to the sample, BSB (2006a) report that the overall effect size of the FEM became progressively closer to the theoretical mean value of $\pi = .50$:

The cumulative analysis became opposite to the direction of intention ($\pi < 0.50$) at the very point at which the first of the three largest studies was added to the cumulative sample. However, even as each of the final three studies was added, the overall effect size approached closer and closer to the theoretical mean value. The studies in the meta-analysis had an extremely heterogeneous effect size distribution, $Q(380) = 1,508.56$, $p = 2.07 \times 10^{-141}$, and remained extremely heterogeneous even when the three largest studies were removed from the sample, $Q(377) = 1,489.99$, $p = 2.50 \ 10^{-138}$. This heterogeneity may be the reason for the large difference in effect size between the FEM and REM. Even when the three largest studies were removed, the difference between the two models was highly significant (delta $z = 3.34$, $p = .0008$). (BSB, 2006a: 507)

The reasons for the extreme heterogeneity between studies remains somewhat mysterious. This fact suggests that extreme caution is necessary in interpreting BSB's findings one way or the other because the FEM and the REM results are so different. There is no objective way of determining which set of results is the most reliable, but the extreme level of heterogeneity across the 380 studies suggests that the REM should, perhaps, be considered the superior approach.

The results of a moderator analysis are shown in Table 8.2. Please take some time to study this table and the description written below it. It is a little complex, but I will try to unpick it bit by bit in the following text. For simplicity's sake, I have divided the table into seven boxes, A–G. Let's consider each box in turn.

---

[9] The results of the meta-analysis are obtained using two different models: a fixed-effect model (FEM) and a random effects model (REM). Please see the Appendix for a definition of these two models.

[10] Publication bias is the tendency for academic journals to not publish studies with statistically non-significant findings even when a study is of high quality.

Table 8.1 Overall sample summary statistics

		Fixed-effects model			Random effects model						
Sample	n	$\bar{\pi}$	SE	z	$\bar{\pi}$	SE	z	M bit	Mdn bit	M py	Q
Overall	380	.499997	.000001	−3.67***	.500035	.000014	2.47*	787,888,669	8,596	1981	1,508.56***
Overall-3 largest	377	.500048	.000013	3.59***	.500286	.000070	4.08***	3,707,412	8,039	1981	1,489.99***

Note. py = publication year.
*p < .05. ***p < .001.
Reproduced from Bösch et al. (2006a), with permission.

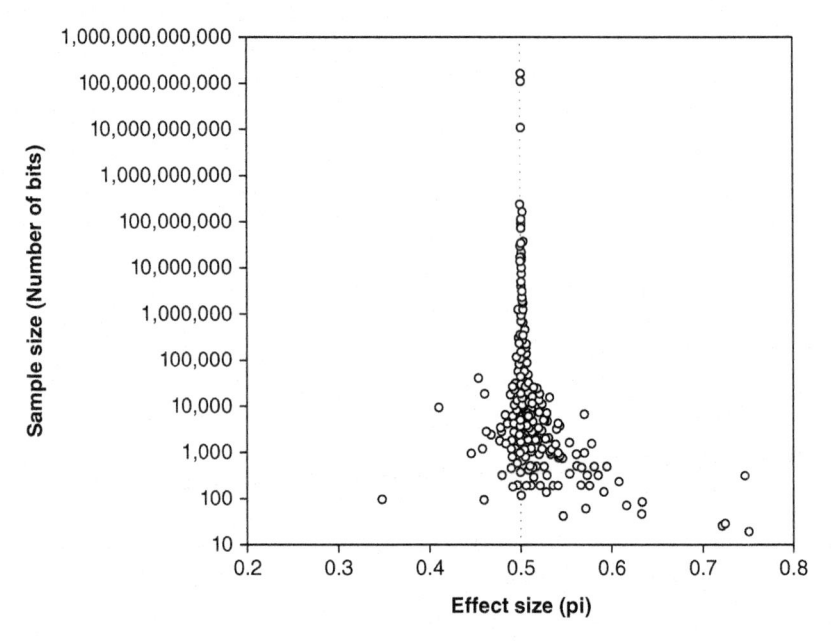

Figure 8.2 Funnel plot intentional studies with respect to number of bits. The effect size of PK diminishes towards the chance level of 0.500000 as the sample size increases.

Reproduced from Bösch, Steinkamp, and Boller (2006), with permission.

Box A: Sample size

The results show that the studies with the smallest sample sizes produce the largest effect sizes. Curiously, Q4, the quartile containing the largest quartile of 94 studies, produced a negative effect of intention (−.499997; $z = -3.70$, $p < .001$). One wonders what kind of process would swing from a positive to a negative effect simply by increasing the sample size? Weird – very weird! For both models, a perfect inverse relationship occurs between sample size and effect size. This scenario looks familiar. Is this another case of peek and run – i.e. run a small sample, take a peek at the results, and then, depending upon the initial results, either place the unfinished study in the file drawer or run more participants? If so, then the first half of the results should be more significant than the second half à la Daryl Bem.

Box B: Year of publication

Older studies, in general, obtained a larger effect size. Weirdly again, the newest quartile of 82 studies produced a negative effect of intention (−.499997; $z = -3.73$, $p < .001$). One wonders why on earth the results should swing from a positive effect to a negative effect over time? Is God playing dice with the universe? (see Hawking: http://hawking.org.uk/does-god-play-dice.html)

Table 8.2 Moderator variables' summary statistics

		Fixed-effects model				Random effects model					
Variable and class	n	$\bar{\pi}$	SE	z	$\bar{\pi}$	SE	z	M bit	Mdn bit	M py	Q
Sample size (bit) **A**											
Smallest (Q1)	95	.519908	.002070	961***	.525523	.004616	5.23***	641	490	1978	393.31***
Small(Q2)	95	.506320	.000788	8.02***	.505900	.001541	3.83***	4,726	4,900	1979	333.86***
Large(Q3)	96	.502087	.000362	5.76***	.502335	.000703	3.35***	21,833	20,034	1980	331.69***
Largest(Q4)	94	.499997[a]	.000001	−3.70***	.500009[a]	.000008	1.19	3,185,054,132	727,620	1989	259.46***
Year of Publication **B**											
Oldest (Q1)	99	.505342	.000393	13.60***	.511509	.001505	7.65***	17,578	3,000	1972	719.66***
Old(Q2)	96	.500194	000148	1.31	.500811	.000369	2.20*	119,912	6,800	1979	185.03***
New(Q3)	103	.500382	.000115	3.33***	.500702	.000307	2.28*	187,156	12,288	1983	230.00***
Newest(Q4)	82	.499997[a]	.000001	−3.73***	.500003	.000006	0.47	3,650,794,697	380,000	1996	175.69***
Number of participants **C**											
One: 1 (Q1)	96	.500499	.000130	3.84***	.503208	.000610	5.26***	171,288	7,640	1981	644.17***
Few: 2-10 (Q2)	107	.499995[a]	.000001	−353***	.500025[a]	.000030	0.83	1,216,285,332	5,000	1980	339.94***
Several: 11-20 (Q3)	61	.499997[b]	.000001	−207*	.500190	.000164	1.16	2,755,175,923	12,288	1981	169.39***
Many: 21-299 (Q4)	80	.500033	.000015	2.14*	.500001	.000043	0.03	13,026,064	22,446	1984	140.90***
Unknown	36	.500123	.000044	2.80**	.500453	.000180	2.51*	3,636,208	17,875	1984	183.66***

(Continued)

Table 8.2 (Continued)

			Fixed-effects model			Random-effects model					
Variable and class	n	$\bar{\pi}$	SE	z	$\bar{\pi}$	SE	z	M bit	Mdn bit	M py	Q
Participants											
Selected	59	.500603	.000151	3.99***	.506450	.000939	687***	187,290	8,000	1977	578.98***
Unselected	261	.499997[a]	.000001	−369***	.500020[a]	.000011	1.84	1,147,069,802	15,057	1982	720.20***
Other	60	.500408	.000422	0.97	.504691	.001308	3.59***	23,761	1,280	1981	183.34***
Study status											
Formal	209	.499997[a]	.000001	−3.31***	.500024	.000013	1.84	1,374,014,360	12,000	1982	668.85***
Pilot	160	.499990[b]	.000005	−2.17*	.500493	.000141	3.50***	76,366,304	7,350	1980	813.15**
Other	11	.500325	.000157	2.07*	.500505	.000481	1.05	916,957	7,926	1979	23.09*
Feedback											
Visual	227	.500030	.000016	1.81	.500228	.000092	2.48*	4,149,925	6,400	1980	845.78***
Auditory	34	.502377	.000382	6.22***	.505422	.001392	3.90***	51,695	18,100	1976	253.38***
Other	119	.499997[a]	.000001	−3.79***	.500009	.000011	0.83	2,508,015,996	20,000	1986	366.54***
Random sources											
Noise	228	.499997[a]	.000001	−3.68***	.500026	.000012	2.13*	1,313,136,638	18,375	1985	913.03***
Radioactive	93	.503354	.000601	5.58***	.509804	.001778	5.51***	8,339	2,000	1974	467.69***
Other	59	.500945	.000382	2.48*	.501562	.000633	2.47*	29,920	13,600	1979	93.41**

Note. py = publication year; Q = quartile.
[a] With the three largest studies removed from the sample, the effect size is significantly larger ($p < .05$, $z > 1.96$) than the mean chance expectation (MCE). [b] With the three largest studies removed from the sample, the effect size is larger than .50 (MCE) but not significantly so.
*$p < .05$. **$p < .01$. ***$p < .001$.
Reproduced, in amended form, from BSB with permission.

Box C: Number of participants
There is a reduction in the effect size as the number of Ps increases from 1 to many (21–299). One reason could be that if any procedural issues such as sensory cueing, poor randomisation or cheating existed, they would tend to be more difficult to detect when only one, or a few, P(s) is/are tested. Or something else? Who knows what.

Box D: Selected versus unselected participants
In the fixed effects model, the effect of intention changes from a positive effect in 59 studies with selected Ps to a negative effect in 261 studies with unselected Ps. In the random-effects model, the intention effect is positive in both cases, but it changes from being statistically significant to non-significant. Another of God's dice games?

Box E: Pilot versus formal study status
In the fixed-effects model, the effect of intention is negative in both formal and pilot study categories. In the random-effects model, the effect is positive in both cases, but reached statistical significance only for the pilot studies. This box illustrates what we have seen elsewhere, that the results one obtains by meta-analysis depends entirely on the nature of the model one uses. The overall directions of the effect of intention for the random-effects model (significantly positive effect of intention) and the fixed-effects model (significantly negative effect of intention) are completely the opposite to one another. Box E appears to be a proper 'Pandora's box' with all kinds of problems inside.

Time to move on to Round 2.

Round 2 (Radin et al., 2006)
In Round 2, Radin et al. (2006; RNDH) disagrees with BSB by maintaining that selective reporting is 'an implausible explanation for the observed data and hence that these studies provide evidence for a genuine psychokinetic effect' (p. 529). No surprise here. They discuss the issue of what they call 'Experimenters' Regress' and, implicitly, accuse BSB of entering it:

> different predilections lead to different assessments of the same evidence. Those scientists who fret over Type I errors[11] insist on proof positive before taking the evidence seriously, whereas those who worry more about Type II errors prefer to take a more affirmative stance to counteract the prejudices invariably faced by anomalies research. Type I preference appears to have led to Bösch et al.'s comment that 'this unique experimental approach will gain scientific recognition only when we know with certainty what an unbiased funnel plot ... looks like' (p. 517). This

---
[11] Please see the Appendix for a definition of Type I and Type II errors.

sounds reasonable until it is unpacked, and then it is found to hide an irresolvable paradox. Collins (1992) called this problem the experimenters' regress, a catch-22 that arises when the correct outcome of an experiment is unknown. To settle the question under normal circumstances, in which results are predicted by a well-accepted theory, one can simply compare an experimental outcome to the prediction. If they match, then the experiment was conducted in a proper fashion, and the outcome is regarded as correct. If not, the experiment was flawed. Unfortunately, when it comes to a pretheoretical concept like PK, to judge whether an experiment was performed well, one first needs to know whether PK exists. But to know whether PK exists, one needs to conduct the correct experiment. But to conduct that experiment, one needs a well-accepted theory. And so on, ad infinitum. For Type I scientists, this loop will continue indefinitely and remain unresolved in spite of the application of the most rigorous scientific methods. The stalemate can be broken only by Type II scientists who are willing to entertain the possibility that Nature consists of many curious phenomena, some of which are not yet described by adequate theories. (RNDH, 2006: 531).

[Using my hidden precognitive ability, I am guessing that by this point you have fallen deeply asleep and may be entering the REM state, an allegedly optimal time for dream-ESP. I am therefore sending you an ESP signal that says: 'PLEASE WAKE UP NOW!']

To continue: RNDH (2006) appear to be arguing that accepting the risk of a Type II error is a progressive move in science when compared to having a Type I error-avoidance mentality. A zetetic position would possibly be to accept neither type of error – to seek a happy medium that lies in between. RNDH propose that 'a more satisfactory explanation for the observed heterogeneity is that effect size (per bit) is not independent of sample size. In summary, we believe that the cumulative data are now sufficiently persuasive to advance beyond the timid conclusion of 'not proven' and that it is more fruitful to focus on understanding the nature of PK rather than to concentrate solely on the question of existence' (p. 532).

The title of a paper by two other critics in Round 2 begins: 'On Blowing Trumpets to the Tulips'[12] (Wilson & Shadish, 2006). Apart from raising a very welcome smile, I could find little here to alter the complete sense of ambiguity that surrounds the BSB meta-analysis. Sometimes, apparently, an editor accepts a paper purely because it has a funny, attention-grabbing title, as long as the paper itself isn't completely rubbish (early researchers: please remember that).

---

[12]This is a reference to a statement attributed to Sir George Darwin, the fifth child of Emma and Charles Darwin, who apparently said: 'Every once and while one should do a completely crazy experiment, like blowing the trumpet to the tulips every morning for a month. Probably nothing would happen, but what if it did?'

Round 3 (BSB, 2006b)

In Round 3, BSB (2006b) repeat their claim that their meta-analysis demonstrated (i) a small, but highly significant overall effect, (ii) a small study effect, and (iii) extreme study heterogeneity. They reaffirm that 'publication bias is the most parsimonious model to account for all three findings'. They go on to suggest an idea that has appeared elsewhere in this book: compulsory preregistration of studies:

> The effect of human intention on random number generators (RNGs) is either genuine or it is not. The widely differing responses from Wilson & Shadish (2006) (WS) and Radin, Nelson, Dobyns, & Houtkooper (2006) (RNDH) suggest that currently any conclusion about the evidence lies in the eye of the beholder. This situation is unlikely to change any time soon. It would be desirable in the future for parapsychology experimenters to submit to trial registries prespecified protocols detailing (i) their proposed primary and secondary analyses and (ii) the defining characteristics of their forthcoming RNG trials. However, the answer to the question will still remain ambiguous if the data remain poorly replicable. Indeed, we ourselves remain undecided about the precise conclusions to be drawn from the existing data.

Yet again, our search for psi arrives at an impasse, an impasse that is steadfast and unyielding. This rock-solid impasse is as good as it gets. Nothing in the literature[13] between 2006 and 2020 gives this author any indication that this situation will ever change. The 'stale-mate' between psi-believers and psi-skeptics is more definitive now than ever before. The only way out would be a prospective meta-analysis with pre-registered studies. In a footnote, BSB (2006b) noted the necessity of registering not only primary research but also meta-analyses themselves: 'for meta-analysts too could analyze different samples until a few significant ones are found, or they could apply different inclusion criteria until the result is as desired, or a meta-analysis could be discontinued after the initial data have been analyzed if the results look to be unfavourable to the hypothesis' (p. 11). There is every reason to agree with this conclusion.

To provide a balanced picture of PK/RNG research, I sent this chapter and the Preface to a world-leading investigator, Dr Dean Radin, a world-leading investigator. Dean Radin is Chief Scientist, Institute of Noetic Sciences, Associated Distinguished Professor, California Institute of Integral Studies, and Past President of the Parapsychological Association. Dr Radin agreed to provide the following remarks:[14]

---

[13] I am excluding books because they are not normally peer reviewed and so authors have free rein to express their personal opinions independently of the evidence. This book is the exception because large sections have been peer reviewed.

[14] 23 September 2019.

ON THE EXISTENCE OF PSYCHOKINESIS

The American Psychological Association (APA) is one of the principal organizations for academic and clinical psychologists in the USA. In the May 2018 issue of *American Psychologist*, the APA's flagship journal, the lead article was entitled, 'The experimental evidence for parapsychological phenomena: A review,' by Etzel Cardeña from Lund University in Sweden (Cardeña, 2018). The article analyzed 10 classes of experiments, comprising over a thousand studies published in peer-reviewed journals. Cardeña's conclusion was unequivocal: 'The evidence for psi is comparable to that for established phenomena in psychology and other disciplines.'

A response to Cardeña's paper was published the following year, also in *American Psychologist*, by psychologists Arthur Reber from the University of British Columbia and James Alcock of York University (Reber & Alcock, 2019). The title of their paper stated their position: 'Searching for the impossible: Parapsychology's elusive quest'. The abstract confirmed their skeptical stance, saying in part:

> Claims made by parapsychologists cannot be true. The effects reported can have no ontological status; the data have no existential value. We examine a variety of reasons for this conclusion based on well understood scientific principles. In the classic English adynaton, 'pigs cannot fly.' Hence, data that suggest that they can are necessarily flawed and result from weak methodology or improper data analyses or are Type I errors (p. 1).

How can a reader begin to understand these two diametrically opposed positions without having to study a thousand original research articles, understand research methods and statistics, and also have some familiarity with modern physics?

One approach is to examine the opinions of professionals who specialize in the evaluation of empirical data. We turn to Jessica Utts, emerita chair and professor of statistics at the University of California at Irvine. Utts is also a past-president of the American Statistical Association and author of several popular college textbooks on statistics. As a recognized authority in her field, Utts was asked to evaluate evidence for various forms of psychic phenomena investigated under controlled conditions by a formerly classified US government research program (May & Marwaha, 2018). In a portion of her 2016 Presidential Address to the American Statistical Association, Utts briefly talked about that work:

> The data in support of precognition and possibly other related phenomena are quite strong statistically and would be widely accepted if they pertained to something more mundane. Yet, most scientists reject the possible reality of these abilities without ever looking at data! (Utts, 2016, p. 1379).

In other words, based on a wealth of scientific evidence evaluated by an expert in the discipline that specializes in the evaluation of research methods and data analysis, the conclusion is clear: Psychic phenomena exist. This is not a surprise to the majority of the world's population who have had one or more psychic experiences (Wahbeh et al., 2018), but it may raise an eyebrow among those who are chronically skeptical.

Evidence

The chapter on PK in this book begins with a comment that questions its definition: '[PK is] "[t]he alleged psychic capability to influence a physical system without any physical interaction." By the standards of everyday physics, that definition is oxymoronic.' Fortunately, David Marks (DM) acknowledges that it is a mistake to decide what is real based on yesterday's physics, but he does warn the reader to be prepared to accept 'impossible' things. That said, it is worth keeping in mind that many well-accepted aspects of physics today (e.g. nonlocality, black holes, gravitational waves) were considered impossible a century ago, so it is wise to remain flexible about what the physical world supposedly can or cannot allow.

DM begins his evaluation of the evidence by stating that his opinion was shaped by a single article: 'Only one PK paper of any genuine merit has been published in the 21st century: a meta-analysis of 380 studies by Holger Bösch, Fiona Steinkamp and Emil Boller' (Bosch, Steinkamp, & Boller, 2006, henceforth 'BSB'). For readers who may not be familiar with the relevant literature, DM' selection of that article might seem reasonable. But given that the relevant literature is enormous – over a thousand published PK experiments – is it realistic to gain a comprehensive understanding of a complex, controversial topic from one paper? I don't think so, especially because the BSB paper only reviews a small subset of the literature, and also because it glosses over a number of problems which we'll discuss later.

DM continues by priming the reader with a shibboleth often attributed to 19th century British prime minister, Benjamin Disraeli:[15] 'The search for psi becomes an ever deeper examination of "lies, damned lies and statistics."' Given this quip, we wonder why DM placed any faith at all in BSB's analysis given the implication that statistical arguments, which is the basis of BSB's article, are merely lies and damned lies.

But DM forges ahead by briefly mentioning PK studies involving the tossing of dice. Rather than discussing any of the source literature, which reports an increasingly sophisticated series of 148 published experiments, instead he only cites the opinions of critics. Because DM concentrates on the best evidence after 2000, he does not mention that a colleague and I published a comprehensive meta-analysis of dice-tossing studies in 1991 (Radin & Ferrari, 1991).

Our meta-analysis retrieved all known dice experiments as of 1991 (very few were reported after that date) and coded them according to 14 quality criteria, including all of the methodological issues raised in an earlier critical review (Girden, 1962). After a thorough search of the relevant literature, we found that 2,569 subjects had attempted to mentally influence 2.6 million dice-casts in 148 studies reported by a total of 52 investigators; we also

(Continued)

---

[15] www.york.ac.uk/depts/maths/histstat/lies.htm

found 153,288 dice-casts reported in 31 control studies. The overall result for the control experiments was consistent with chance. But the quality-weighted outcome for the experimental studies produced an effect size of $e = 0.00723 \pm 0.00071$, which is associated with a probability of $p < 10^{-9}$, i.e. odds against chance of a billion to one. We also addressed the effects of selective reporting, homogeneity of effect sizes, and all of the other factors that are standard methods in meta-analyses (at least as of 1991, when our article was published).

After sifting through every known or suspected flaw, we concluded that 'this database provides weak cumulative evidence for a genuine relationship between mental intention and the fall of dice' (p. 61). This real but fragile relationship helps explain, as DM asked, 'Why there has never appeared a single individual who could consistently produce above-chance results attributable to "mind over matter."' The answer is simple: It's difficult to beat casino games because the odds are always in favor of the house. To overcome that bias would require the player to achieve robust, systematically above-chance results, which is not easy given that casinos are designed to distract the player with free alcohol, disorienting colors, flashing lights, and loud music. Our dice meta-analysis indicates that the effect is real, but it is not strong enough to challenge the profits of casinos.

We should also keep in mind that the question of whether dice can be intentionally influenced is ultimately an existential issue (i.e., does PK *exist*?), and the size of an effect is irrelevant when it comes to the question of existence. Tiny effects that cannot be seen without specialized methods and equipment can nevertheless be exceptionally powerful, as anyone who has ever picked up a bad bacterium or virus can readily attest.

Then DM turns to the BSB paper, which reviewed a subset of PK studies using electronic truly random number generators (RNG). In parapsychology, these studies are often referred to as RNG-PK studies. DM describes BSB's summary statistics, effect sizes, issues of heterogeneity, moderator variables, and so on. After reviewing those results, he ends by restating BSB's principal conclusion: There is a small but highly significant overall effect, but it's probably not real because it might be due to a selective reporting bias.

What is left out of the latter part of that conclusion is a big problem. The problem is that the model that BSB used to describe their selective reporting bias could not account for the actual distribution of results. It wasn't even close. And this means that BSB's confidence that the PK effect that they observed but ultimately dismissed was unjustified.

DM then briefly reviews a portion of our response to BSB (Radin, Nelson, Dobyns, & Houtkooper, 2006), but he leaves out the main reason why we felt BSB's conclusion was wrong. As we put it,

> In terms of [random] bits measured for the PK hypothesis … the four largest studies contain more than 320 times as much data as all other experiments in the [BSB] meta-analysis combined. [BSB's] selection of just three of those four [experiments] contains over 210 times as much data as the remaining 377 studies in their meta-analysis.

> These four large studies also have an aggregate z equal to –4.03. Thus, if one takes seriously [BSB's] hypothesis that PK effects manifest as shifts in the probabilities of individual random bits ..., then the overwhelming preponderance of data in these large experiments *should be taken as definitive* (emphasis added, p. 530).

A more recent critique of BSB was published by Varvoglis & Bancel (2015). After reviewing all of the issues already discussed, they concluded:

> It is clear that correctly treating the asymmetric heterogeneity is key to resolving the debate, and that the heterogeneity limits [the meta-analytical] effectiveness in providing evidential support for micro-PK .... A substantial source of heterogeneity, we suggest, lies in those studies that cannot be reasonably accounted for by publication bias – namely the studies with high z scores. About 40 of the total dataset have zs between 2.6 and 5; these contribute nearly half of the total heterogeneity. To generate these studies of artifactual selection would require an extremely large file-drawer. The BSB simulation ignores them, which is why the residual heterogeneity of their model is so large (in fact, the first file-drawer calculation by [Radin & Nelson (1989)] included these studies and produced a correspondingly large file drawer of over 50,000). (p. 274)
>
> Given the relatively large proportion of these [large z] studies in the database, and the difficulty of explaining them by artifacts, *we feel that the meta-analytical evidence for micro-PK is in fact quite strong* (we would expect 2 studies in the BSB database to have a z score of 2.6 or more; instead, we note that there were over 40). (emphasis added, p. 275)

Beyond the meta-analytic evidence, which requires some statistical sophistication to fully appreciate, some individual RNG–PK studies provide independently strong evidence for PK. One such example is a large-scale, long-term experiment reported by the Princeton (University) Engineering Anomalies Research (PEAR) Laboratory (Jahn, Dunne, Nelson, Dobyns, & Bradish, 2007). Data in that study were contributed by many participants over 12 years, their database explicitly excluded selective reporting, they included systematic control and calibration tests which demonstrated that their results were not contaminated by subtle artifacts, and overall their results provided crystal clear evidence in favor of genuine PK.

By the end of the chapter, DM agrees that there seems to be an anomaly in the RNG–PK database, but because it is so small in magnitude, he deems it has no practical importance. As we noted earlier, the magnitude of an effect is irrelevant when it comes to the question of *existence*. For example, when Benjamin Franklin was criticized for flying kites in electrical storms so he could study sparks, little did anyone at the time imagine that one day the world would run on gigawatt electrical grids (MacLaren, 1945). Franklin's interest in sparks was not driven by his desire to create an electrical grid, but rather by simple curiosity, the prime motivator in science. With dedicated effort, sometimes curiosity develops

(Continued)

into confident knowledge, and then with any luck it might advance into a technology. Similarly, exploring PK is motivated today by curiosity. If enough knowledge could be gained to better understand that phenomenon, then someday it might turn into the basis of a technology. Just as Franklin would have been hard-pressed to say how an improved understanding of sparks would one day lead to a method of powering the entire globe, it is difficult today to imagine how PK might turn into a technology. But if it does, could it have an equally profound impact on civilization?

Conclusion

Analyses of experiments exploring PK indicate that an anomaly associated with human intention has been observed in many physical targets, from tossed dice and electronic circuits to a wide variety of living and non-living systems. The anomaly is small in magnitude, which raises legitimate doubts about claims of large-scale PK effects. But based on the preponderance of empirical data, if the evidence were about a more conventional phenomenon there would be little controversy about its existence.

There are two ways to respond to anomalies. One is to assume that it's probably nothing after all. Sometimes anomalies turn out to be mistakes, and even if it is real there's no reliable technology based on it, and so why bother? The other approach is to assume that we had better figure out what is causing that anomaly, because if it's a genuine effect it would have profound consequences for the scientific understanding of reality.

How one chooses to respond to the evidence is, of course, each individual's choice. When making that choice it's worth bearing in mind that the history of science shows that scientific breakthroughs often come from noticing and then carefully studying anomalies that challenge prevailing theories (Kuhn, 1962).

Breakthroughs do not happen by ignoring anomalies because they're 'not proven.'

SUMMARY

Systematic research on PK was started by J. B. Rhine in the 1940s and continues to the present day. Authors of early meta-analyses claimed that PK was a proven capability. The Parapsychological Association states that 'the probability of the observed PK effect occurring by chance was less than one part in a trillion' (Parapsychological Association, 2019). A large meta-analysis by Holger Bösch, Fiona Steinkamp, and Emil Boller (2006) suggests that the issue of PK is complicated. Although RNG output is associated with human intention, the effect size is miniscule: an average of .000035 above the chance level of 0.500000. Worryingly, study effect sizes are strongly inversely related to sample size. The larger sample sizes, capable of producing the most reliable results, show the smallest effects, exactly what one expects if the true result is zero.

Monte Carlo simulation led the BSB authors to conclude that the small effect size, the inverse relation between sample size and effect size, and the extreme heterogeneity could all, in principle, be caused by publication bias. This author sees no reason to disagree. In this light, the Parapsychological Association's (2019) statements about PK, quoted at the start of this chapter, are, at best, a half-truth, and need to be brought into line with the most recent findings. The evidence reviewed here suggests that the PK effect is vanishing towards zero, becoming ever more elusive over time. Technically, the PK effect may be statistically significant but, for any practical purpose, it is beyond trivial. Casino bosses can rest easily at night, secure in the knowledge that their in-built advantage is forever immune to the powers of psi. Like dream-ESP, PK is another form of psi that is en route to Neverland, a one-stop journey for any dreamer.

QUESTIONS

1. Give three reasons why the BSB meta-analysis suggests PK is unconfirmed (yet not disconfirmed).
2. What interpretation(s) do you put on BSB's funnel plot?
3. What is the main difference between a FEM and an REM?
4. Which do you prefer, the REM or the FEM, and why?
5. Why should a PK investigator prefer Type II to Type I error, according to RNDH?
6. To what extent has Dean Radin's response influenced your personal belief in PK as a genuine form of psi?
7. After reading this chapter, how valid is the Parapsychological Association's statement that 'human consciousness can indeed affect the behaviour of a random physical system'?

Before moving on, please mark your degree of belief in the scientific case for PK on the Belief Barometer below.

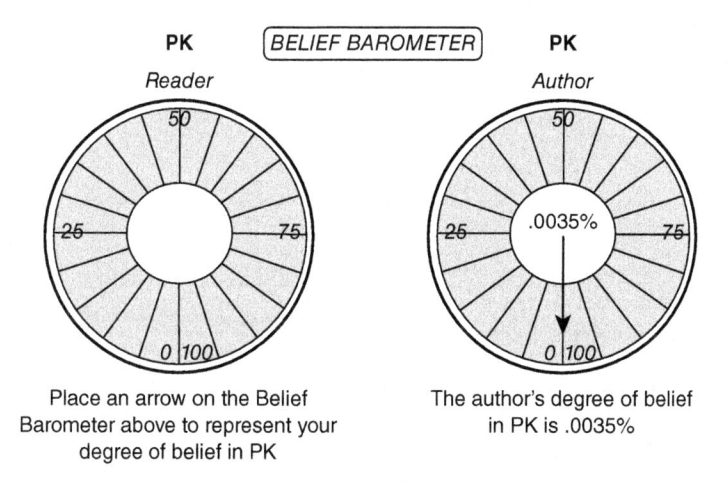

Figure 8.3 Belief barometer readings

PART III
SUBJECTIVE ANOMALOUS EXPERIENCE USUALLY NOT – BUT OCCASIONALLY – CLAIMED TO BE PARANORMAL

9
THE HYPNOTIC TRANCE AS AN ALTERED STATE OF CONSCIOUSNESS

A good example [of trance logic] is the reaction of many Ss in hypnosis who see a hallucination of a person sitting in a chair and describe it as 'This is very peculiar, I can see Joe sitting in the chair and I can see the chair through him.' This type of reaction, when made spontaneously, was absolutely diagnostic of the 'real' [hypnotic] S. (Orne, 1959: 295)

Outline: Hypnosis is a subject that attracts intense public curiosity, and more than its fair share of mythology. Exactly like ESP, beliefs about hypnosis fall into the usual two main camps, skeptics and believers. And guess what, this author is a believer! My aim in this chapter is to demonstrate why. Contrary to the impressions given by personable but deeply pseudo-scientific scallywags on TV, people cannot, do not and will not commit murder or rob banks under hypnosis. Entertaining though it may be, people do not fall into deep trance states at a click of the fingers and the command to 'Sleep'. That hypnotic induction is capable of inducing a special state of consciousness – the 'hypnotic trance' – is particularly tantalising. Experts are evenly divided between those who consider hypnosis an extension of ordinary fantasy and imagination produced by suggestion and the view that hypnosis involves an anomalous, special state of consciousness that may include 'trance logic'. I describe here a unique Trance Logic Study which compared a group of highly hypnotisable Ps who were hynotised with a matched group of highly hypnotisable Ps who role-played the hypnotic state as simulators. These striking findings are supported by brain imaging studies using fMRI and positron emission tomography (PET), which indicate that the hypnotic trance state is associated with reduced contextual vigilance, *a disconnection from the default mode of resting activity and enhanced coordination of networks engaged in executive control*. The involvement of the lingual gyrus, a cortical structure

(Continued)

that 'lights up' with vivid visual imagery, suggests that the hypnosis trance state is a sensorial process involving a remarkable kind of logical inconsistency. A striking confirmation that trance logic is a genuine phenomenon has been overlooked in a real-life scientific example of confirmation bias. The proponents of the approved theory of the day, the Social-Cognitive Formulation, are 100% skeptical about the hypnotic trance state. The evidence suggests that the capability to experience a special trance state containing tolerance of logical inconsistency is genuine. The trance phenomenon is fully consistent with the finding of activation of the lingual gyrus in hypnosis as observed in several independent neuro scientific studies.

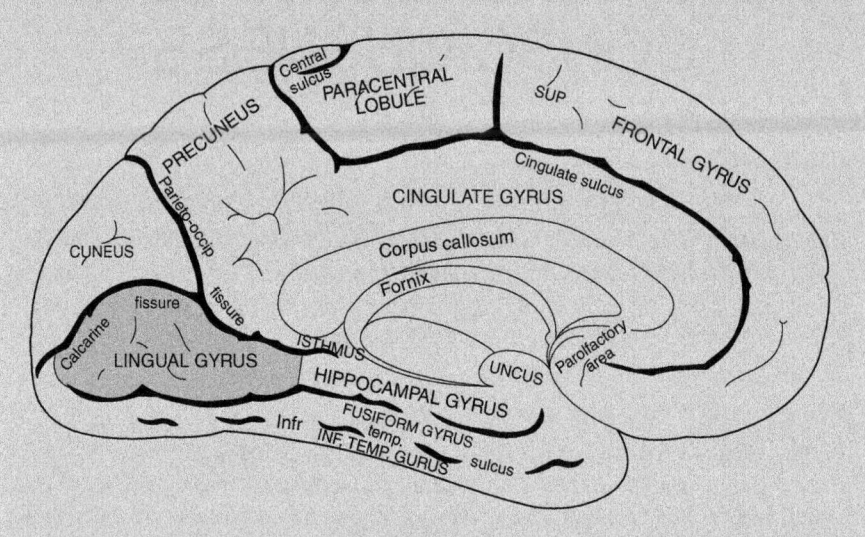

Figure 9.1 The lingual gyrus, named for its tongue-shaped appearance, is the 'visual imagery vividness' centre of the brain. The structure has been implicated in several studies as the principal neural centre involved in hypnosis and vivid visual imagery. (Image in the public domain under a Creative Commons CC0 License.)

THE NATURE OF HYPNOSIS

In 2015, the American Psychological Association's Society of Psychological Hypnosis adopted a definition of hypnosis as 'a state of consciousness involving focused attention and reduced peripheral awareness characterized by an enhanced capacity for response to suggestion' (Elkins, Barabasz, Council, & Spiegel, 2015). Hypnosis is a procedure in which one person – the hypnotist – offers suggestions to another person – the participant (P) – to imagine alterations in perception, memory and action. These experiences may be associated with a feeling of involuntariness in the context of a social interaction (Kihlstrom, 2008). Contrary to the impression given by stage hypnotists, who simply click their fingers and say 'sleep', *the hypnotic state is nothing like the state of sleep and has none of the characteristics of sleep*, with the exception that the eyes may be closed, although this is unnecessary. It is possible to even manage without a hypnotist because techniques of 'self-hypnosis' using relaxation and guided imagination can be reliably produced, enabling both psychological and physiological changes that can bring effective results in the treatment of illnesses (e.g. habit cough: Anbar & Hall, 2004; recurrent abdominal pain: Ball, Shapiro, Monheim, & Weyert, 2003; irritable bowel syndrome: Vlieger, Menkko-Frankenhuis, Wolfkamp, Tromp, & Benninga, 2007; chronic and procedure-related pain: Tomé-Pires & Miró, 2012). Hypnosis research has been influential in theories of mental illness and psychotherapy and is one of the topics that promoted the 'consciousness revolution' (Hilgard, 1977, 1987) and a revival of interest in the unconscious (Kihlstom, 2007).

There are wide individual differences in the degree to which people respond to hypnotic procedures and in their level of 'hypnotisability'. Hypnosis researchers need to select people who show high susceptibility to hypnotic procedures if they wish to verify the condition's more dramatic features. Special scales are used for screening potential research Ps such as the group-administered Harvard Group Scale of Hypnotic Susceptibility and the individually administered Stanford Hypnotic Susceptibility Scale, Form C (Woody & Barnier, 2008). In a typical experiment, Ps are screened and classified using standardised scales as low, medium or high in hypnotisability and then randomly allocated to a standard hypnotic induction or a control procedure. The responses of highly hypnotisable Ps in the hypnosis condition are compared to a control condition. One control condition is the 'simulator' control – asking Ps to behave as they imagine a hypnotised person would behave. The simulator condition controls for the expectancy and placebo effects that may be obtained in hypnosis and provides a way of unravelling such effects from genuine hypnotic effects.

Three hypnotic phenomena have been intensively studied: suggested amnesia, suggested analgesia and 'trance logic'. Few authorities doubt the existence of these phenomena but opinions vary concerning the ontological status of the hypnotic trance. Some authorities – the skeptics – yes, here they are again – have suggested that a social–psychological interpretation best explains hypnotic phenomena as role-playing behaviour. Nick Spanos (1986) hypothesised that hypnotic behaviours and experiences are acted out in accordance with the social context and hypnotist's expectations by the person undergoing hypnosis even though they may sometimes experience their behaviour as involuntary – i.e. not controlled by them. This is the so-called 'Social–Cognitive Formulation' of hypnosis. From this perspective, there is no hypnotic trance state, only a form of voluntary behaviour and an illusion of loss of control. Spanos suggested that hypnotic amnesics 'pretend not to remember' by accommodating their lack of recall to the social demands of the test situation. Similarly, hypnotic suggestions of analgesia do not produce a dissociation of pain from phenomenal awareness, Spanos conjectures. When appropriately motivated, even Ps with low in hypnotic suggestibility are alleged to report pain reductions as large as those reported by highly suggestible hypnotically analgesic Ps.

According to Spanos (1968), trance logic simply reflects the attempts by 'good subjects' to meet the experimenter's demands to report accurately what they experience. A similar view was espoused by Irving Kirsch (1985), who viewed hypnotic responses as response expectancy. Other well-known theorists such as Jack Hilgard, Martin Orne and John Kihlstrom have persistently argued that hypnosis is a special state of consciousness, advocating the Special State Theory. The debate about the nature of hypnosis can only be settled by empirical studies designed specifically to examine hypotheses drawn from the special state theory. One particular study with great relevance to the Special State Theory was conducted by the author and his colleagues at the University of Otago in New Zealand (Marks, Baird, & McKellar, 1989).

This experiment is unique in the history of hypnosis research. Highly hypnotisable Ps were placed in both of two experimental groups, one a genuine hypnotic group and the other a simulator control group who were instructed to pretend they were hypnotised. All other trance logic studies put high hypnotisable Ps in the hypnosis condition and low hypnotisable Ps in the control condition, a wholly unconvincing design. In the latter, the independent variable, the hypnotic versus non-hypnotic state, is confounded with the level of hynotisability of the Ps, thus producing inconclusive results. Not only is it unique, the Trance Logic Study is one of the hypnosis field's best kept 'secrets',[1] yet it produced one of the most definitive confirmations of the Special State Theory there has ever been.[2]

THE TRANCE LOGIC STUDY[3]

Here we examine a study of a hypnotic phenomenon in some depth: an investigation of the anomalous experience of 'trance logic'. This phenomenon occurs when a hypnotised P accepts logically impossible situations as something that is really happening. The specific case that we are dealing with involves *seeing a particular uniquely identifiable individual person in two different places at the same moment of time* – that's right, the same person in two places at the same time! This is called the 'doubled-person hallucination', or DPH that can be associated with a spontaneous reporting of 'transparency' (the hallucinated image lacks 'solidity'). Orne (1959) observed that these two criteria of trance logic tend to be

---

[1] The author's study with an improved experimental design (Marks et al., 1989) has received only 7 citations compared to 1,362 citations of Orne's (1959) original, uncontrolled study (20 March 2020).

[2] There are two main types of hallucination – positive or negative. A negative hallucination is not seeing something that is really there. A positive hallucination is seeing something that isn't really there. The Trance Logic Study used the 'doubled-person hallucination', seeing a person in one location when that person is in another location nearby.

[3] This section is based on Marks et al. (1989), with permission.

passed by hypnotised Ps, but not by Ps who are simulating the hypnotic state, thus providing evidence of a special, qualitatively different state of consciousness. This investigation is a replication study, an attempt to reproduce a surprising anomalous phenomenon that had been previously reported by Martin Orne (1959).[4] The results confirmed the existence of a special trance state, thus having high relevance to the exploration of anomalistic experience. The 'Trance Logic Study' used a variety of procedures to bring under experimental control a phenomenon that had been elusive over numerous previous studies. The elusive nature of the phenomenon is reminiscent of psi covered in Chapters 5–8. The specific feature under review is not easily investigated and has been observed in only one or two laboratories. Many of the familiar controls used in psi research are necessary in hypnosis research: avoidance of sensory cues, operating single 'blind',[5] matching Ps' hypnotic ability across conditions, controlling for the Ps' expectancies and, finally, controlling the environment to ensure that the investigation offers a true test of the experimental hypothesis in the absence of known artefacts.

The hypothesis of interest concerns the hypnotic trance state, one of the defining features claimed for hypnosis as a special state of consciousness. The study design included the comparison of hypnotised Ps with Ps who are instructed to simulate hypnosis, which provides a control for role-playing or acting ability. Owing to the sensitive nature of hypnotic effects, and the risk of possible harm to the Ps, this study went through a robust ethical review by the institution in consultation with two outside experts.[6] This study is certainly not something that anybody should 'try at home'. It requires many safeguards and should only be attempted in a laboratory under the supervision of experts in experimental and clinical hypnosis.

In the double-hallucination test,[7] or 'doubled-person hallucination' (DPH), P is given a suggestion to hallucinate the target person (T),[8] and if P reports this hallucination, P is then asked to identify the actual target person who is behind P. According to Orne's original report (1959), almost invariably the hypnotic P who acknowledges the hallucination also reports the real person behind, whereas the simulating P who reports the hallucination seldom reports the real person behind.

---

[4]This was a conceptual replication that corrected a design error in Orne's (1959) study.
[5]Double 'blind' control is impossible because the P is aware of having a hypnotic induction.
[6]Professors Peter Sheehan and Ernest Hilgard, two world leaders in hypnosis research at that time, were consulted by Otago University to obtain ethical approval of this study.
[7]While the term 'double-hallucination' is employed throughout the previous literature, the term is technically awkward as only one image in the experimental situation can potentially be a hallucination, the other being a veridical perception. The term 'doubled-person hallucination' is preferred on technical grounds because a perceived person is confused with a double in the hallucination.
[8]The target person was Professor Peter McKellar, whose image is shown in Figure 9.2.

Since hypnotised Ps can tolerate the incongruity of two physically separate but simultaneous images of the same person, they are said to display 'trance logic'. The second criterion of trance logic, spontaneous transparency, is recorded when P spontaneously reports that the hallucination is transparent or lacks solidity. Orne claims that spontaneous reports of transparency are diagnostic of hypnotised Ps, and this observation has been confirmed by several investigators (Blum & Graef, 1971; Johnson, Maher, & Barber, 1972; McDonald & Smith, 1975; Peters, 1973; Sheehan, Obstoj, & McConkey, 1976; Spanos, de Groot, Tiller, Weekes, & Bertrand, 1985). The transparency effect, therefore, is highly robust and has been observed across a wide variety of procedures and settings.

On the other hand, many investigations attempting to replicate Orne's first criterion of trance logic, DPH, have failed to receive DPH reports from their Ps (Blum & Graef, 1971; Johnson et al., 1972; McDonald & Smith, 1975; Peters, 1973; Sheehan et al., 1976; Spanos et al., 1985). With the exception of the Johnson et al. (1972) study, all studies followed Orne's (1959) original quasi-control design by using highly hypnotisable Ps in the hypnotic group and low hypnotisables in the simulator group. The quasi-control procedure is designed to evaluate effects due to the active thinking processes of Ps. To the extent that an individual is able to produce behaviour identical to that of the hypnotised individual, it is necessary to consider role-playing as a theoretical explanation (Orne, 1962, 1969, 1973).

There is a problem with this quasi-control procedure in that the two experimental conditions differ in two confounded respects, hypnotisability (high vs. low) and treatment (hypnosis vs. simulation). There is a good reason for placing low hypnotisables in the simulator condition because under Orne's procedures all Ps are given a hypnotic induction and, even though simulators are told to fake hypnotic behaviour, they could become hypnotised if they were high hypnotisables. In the traditional real-simulator design, however, a difference between high hypnotisable hypnotised Ps and low hypnotisable simulating Ps cannot be attributed unequivocally to hypnosis because it could be caused by differences in the trait of hypnotisability as this interacts with the experimental conditions (Orne, 1977). Hypnotised Ps may, therefore, satisfy both DPH and transparency criteria, not because they are hypnotised, but because they are more highly responsive to imaginative suggestions in the normal waking state. Thus, in Orne's original real-simulator design, hypnosis and hypnotisability were confounded. In the present investigation, high hypnotisable Ps were employed for both simulator and hypnotic conditions, using a design originally employed by Austin, Perry, Sutcliffe, and Yeomans (1963). The experimental manipulation was, therefore, the presentation of a hypnotic induction as compared to simulator instructions, all other factors being held constant.

Why is there such a discrepancy in results between Orne's original work and subsequent studies in regard to the DPH test? The answer may lie in a close examination of the investigators' methodology. Orne's original report lacked the kind of detail that would assist precise replication, and subsequent studies have varied considerably in methodology. Unfortunately, in many cases further methodological problems have been created, especially in terms of the criteria for recording DPH responses. For instance, in the McDonald and Smith (1975) study, Ps were required to give an immediate report of the real target person in order to be credited with DPH response. Presumably, this procedure was used to reduce the risk of cuing, but such a procedure could have decreased the rate of recorded responses among DPH hypnotised Ps since they may have been given insufficient time to report the real target person.

In their more tightly controlled 'Easter Tree' studies, Sheehan et al. (1976) and Obstoj and Sheehan (1977) found that hypnotic Ps seldom hallucinated the intricate and complex target object. The Es had to repeat the suggestion that the model tree was present in its original position a number of times before Ps would report the hallucination of the target object. By repeating this suggestion, the investigators may have created strong demands to comply, which could well have relegated the responses of 'hypnotised' Ps to those of simulators. Spanos and colleagues (1985) and Peters (1973) also used artificial objects rather than a real human target figure for the DPH test, a procedure that would not be optimal for the induction of vivid, eidetic-like images. A further disadvantage in the use of artificial objects is that they can easily be duplicated, and DPH is therefore much less significant ontologically than in the case of a distinctive, unique person.

Johnson et al. (1972) did not use very highly hypnotisable Ps, thus reducing the possibility of a high rate of hallucinatory responses among the hypnotised group. Furthermore, Johnson et al. failed to conduct a post-experimental enquiry. Such an enquiry could have provided confirmation as to whether the hypnotised Ps actually hallucinated T, whether simulators succumbed to the induction, whether Ps actually saw two-person images and whether the hallucination had a transparent appearance. A third problem with this study was that of the incorrect statistical analyses performed on the data (see Hilgard, 1972).

The present experiment avoided all of these various methodological problems. The suggestion to hallucinate T was given only after P had been given adequate opportunity to report the actual target person, the target was a readily memorable, high-status person rather than a toy or a model, and a post-experimental enquiry was conducted.

Five major changes were made to Orne's original experiment. First, instead of having high hypnotisable hypnotic Ps and low hypnotisable simulators, high hypnotisable Ps were used for both the simulator and hypnotic conditions. Second, because high hypnotisable simulating Ps were used, it could not be expected that the simulators could resist any hypnotic induction and thus special simulating instructions were given to this group of Ps. Third, one experimenter administered either a hypnotic induction or the simulator instructions and a second, independent ('blind') experimenter conducted the various tests. Fourth, auditory cues, which are potentially created by T as they move around P, were eliminated by using a sound-attenuated experimental room with one-way windows through which

P could clearly see T. This modification was made after rehearsing this part of Orne's procedure. An experimenter playing the part of P could readily detect the position of someone moving past him when this was done in the same room. A fifth innovation was the use of a combination of two hypnotisability measures, one of imagination ability and the other a more conventional behavioural criterion of suggestibility. This was felt to be desirable in the light of the essentially imagistic nature of DPH experience.

The view of this author that the use of highly hypnotisable Ps in both conditions provides an interesting variation on the traditional real-simulator paradigm. This is because hypnotisability can be eliminated as a causal factor of any differences that are found between hypnotic and simulator Ps. Of course, this alternative design implies a different logical rationale than that originally intended by Orne's (1959) design. The possibility of differences in hypnotisability being responsible for possible differences between the experimental Ps and the quasi-controls is thus prevented. While this strategy carries the advantage of separately investigating hypnotic effects and hypnotisability effects, it carries the disadvantage that so-called simulators may actually become hypnotised. If this remains undiscovered by the investigators, then it will militate against finding differences between the hypnotic and non-hypnotic conditions when in fact such differences may well be occurring. From this point of view, the design has substituted one kind of ambiguity for another. It should be possible, however, to identify any cases of spontaneous hypnosis within the control group by the careful administration of a post-experimental enquiry during which Ps are placed at ease and encouraged to provide honest reports on their experiences during the experiment. This new variant of the original design may, therefore, help to clarify our understanding of trance-logic and related hypnotic trance state experience.

METHOD
Participants

The Ps were 36 highly hypnotisable university students, aged 18 to 23 years. They were selected by screening approximately 1,500 students from lecture classes by administering three brief behavioural measures: hand levitation, hand heaviness and hand grip. Those who scored positively on two or three of the items were invited to participate in a more intensive screening session. The three sessions were attended by 150 students. Individuals were selected as Ps for the experiment only if they obtained a high score on a combination of two scales employed in the intensive screening session. The first of these was the Barber Suggestibility Scale (BSS) of Barber (1965) and the second was the Creative Imagination Scale (CIS) of Wilson and Barber (1983) and Barber and Wilson (1978). Both scales were presented by means of a tape recording. Since BSS has a maximum score of 8 and CIS a maximum score of 40, BSS score was multiplied by 5 so that both tests had equal weighting when summed. A score of 55 out of 80 was used as the criterion for P selection. Of the 150 preselected individuals, only 36 reached the criterion score of 55 – 26 females and 10 males. This arbitrary cut-off point produced group sizes that were reasonably close to the target figure of 20 per group.[9] A total of 5 male and 13 female Ps were allocated to each of the two hypnotic and simulator groups. The hypnotic (N = 18) simulator (N = 18) groups had mean BSS scores of 6.97 and 6.69, mean CIS scores of 30.28 and 27.72, and mean total scores of 65.14 (SD = 6.48) and 61.19 (SD = 4.52). The laboratory setting for the experiment is shown in Figure 9.2.

Procedure

Because the procedure is rather elaborate and technical, it is necessary to provide quite a lot of detail. However, if the reader is not much interested in this aspect, please head straight to the results. Ps were given either simulator instructions or a hypnotic induction by experimenter (E)1 (DM) and were tested by E2 (JB). When each P arrived at the experimental location, she[10] was met by E2 who informed her that there were two experimental groups, a hypnotic and a simulator group, and that he was unaware of which group P was going to be allocated to. E2 emphasised that he, E2, would still be blind to P's experimental condition when he returned later to test P. After signing a consent form, P was introduced to E1, who also, at this stage, did not know which experimental condition she was going to be allocated to, thus avoiding any possibility of cuing E2. E1 then took P into Target Room 1 where he introduced her to the target person (E3). E3 (PM) was a distinct figure, well known to many Ps as he was a senior professor in the Psychology Department. E3 and P talked for approximately two minutes about P's university work, then E3 located himself in Target Position 1 and E1 took P through to the central experimental room closing both doors. As shown in Figure 9.2A, P sat in a seat facing towards the one-way mirror and T, clearly visible through the one-way mirror. E1 sat alongside P and pointed out the location of E3. At this point, P's experimental condition was determined by using a randomly ordered pile of envelopes, each containing a card, half labelled 'H' (hypnosis) and half 'S' (simulator). E1 opened the top envelope and informed P of her condition.

If a 'hypnosis' card was drawn, E1 told P to sit back and relax and look at a small piece of chalk situated beneath the window through which S could see T. Standardised hypnotic instructions were then introduced, repeatedly suggesting

---

[9]The choice of hypnotisability measures in trance logic studies has pragmatic rather than theoretical significance. Trance logic can only be assessed following a positive response to a difficult test item (positive hallucination of a recently seen person) and which scale predicts such 'virtuosos' with most reliability is still an open question (cf. Spanos et al., 1985, footnote 1). The results of this investigation suggest that a combination of the BBS and CIS scales could be a useful, diagnostic measure of 'virtuoso' hypnotisability.

[10]As the majority of Ps were female and all the Es were male, I shall refer to these persons as 'she' and 'he' respectively throughout this section.

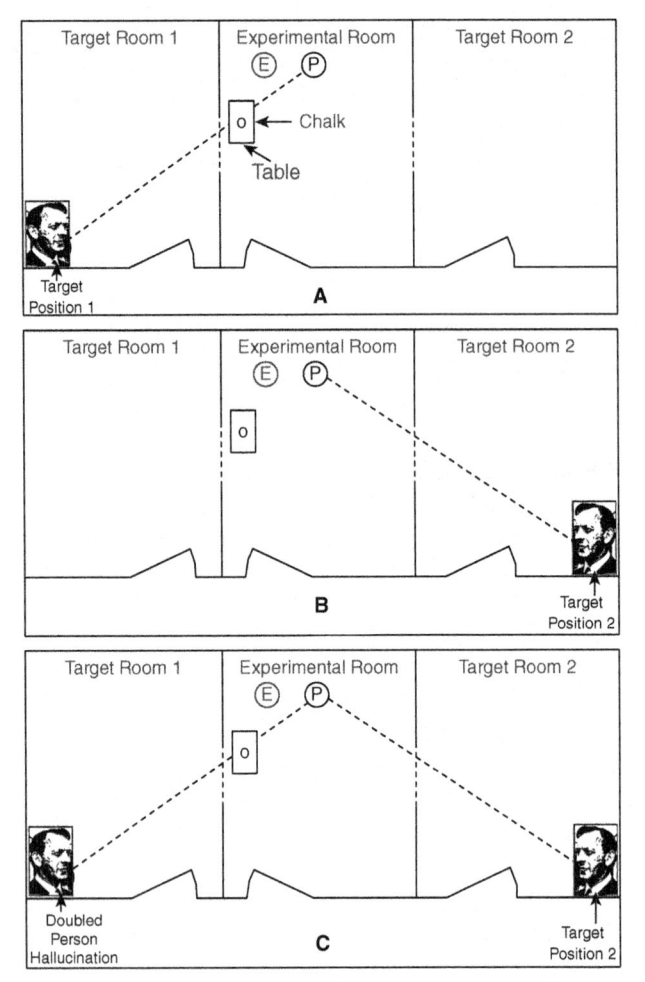

Figure 9.2 The experimental setting showing the position of P, E and T in the two target positions. The central room housed P and E, while the outer rooms housed T. The central room was dimly lit by a 25-watt bulb and dark shade. From P's chair, the lighting level and physical appearance of the target person in the two target rooms were identical. A tape recorder on the bookshelf beside E was used to record P's verbal responses during the experiment. The three phases of the experiment are shown with the positions of the P, experimenter (E) and each position of T. A piece of chalk was located on the table under the one-way mirror in direct line of sight between P and T in Target Room 1. Likewise, the one-way mirror on P's left side was in direct line of sight between P's chair and the T's chair in Target Room 2. Panel A: before a hypnotic induction or simulator instructions, T is in the room on P's right-hand side. Panel B: during the induction or simulator instructions, T has moved to the room on P's left-hand side. Panel C: after the induction, T has remained in position on P's left-hand side, but P has been given the suggestion that, when she opened her eyes, she will see T through the mirror in the original position in Target Room 1. If P positively identifies T in Target Position 1, she is told 'to turn around and look behind you and tell me what you see'. If P reports T, the real person behind, and as a hallucinated person in front, a doubled-person hallucination (DPH) is recorded.

deeper relaxation, comfort and drowsiness. This induction took approximately 15 minutes. If a 'simulator' card was drawn, E1 instructed P to behave to the best of her ability in a manner similar to that of a genuinely hypnotised person. Motivation to perform this role was established by informing P that detection of simulation by E2, who would be administering a series of tests, would bring about termination of the experiment and make analysis of the data impossible. To quell any anxiety, E1 informed P that it is difficult to differentiate between hypnotic and simulator Ps with any certainty, although E2 would try his best to do so. The P was challenged to try to 'fool' E2 to the best of her ability. The simulating Ps were told they would have to close their eyes and wait for 15 minutes as this was the time required to present a standard hypnotic induction. This 15-minute waiting period eliminated any cuing of E2 to each P's condition. No further instructions were given to simulator Ps.

Once the induction or the 15-minute period had been completed, E1 informed both simulator and hypnotic Ps that he was now leaving and that E2 would soon arrive to give P some 'hypnotic tests'. P was told to keep both eyes closed, until E2 arrived and gave the instruction to open them. E1 then left P and, by knocking on the door of a nearby room, signalled E2 to begin testing. No verbal or visual communication between E1 and E2 occurred, merely an acoustic, non-verbal signal (two taps on the door).

E2 entered the central room and asked P to keep her eyes closed. At this point, E3 quietly left Target Room 1 and moved to Target Room 2 using the connecting corridor (see Figure 9.2B).[11] E2 asked P to remember T, whom she had met earlier and whom she had seen sitting in the other room through the window. P was told that when she opened her eyes she would see T through the window. E2 then instructed P to open her eyes and describe what she could see. If P failed to report T through the window, no further suggestion to see T was given. The experiment was terminated for these Ps.

If, upon opening her eyes, P positively identified T, she was told: 'Now I would like you to turn around and look behind you and tell me what you see.' If P failed to report T behind, E2 then asked: 'Can you see anything through the window?' If P still did not acknowledge the real target person behind, a non-DPH response was recorded. If P reported the real target person behind and continued to accept

Table 9.1 Number of Ps reporting DPH in hypnotised and simulator groups

Group	Ps reporting hallucinations	Ps reporting real person	Ps failing to report real person
Hypnotied Ps (N=18)	8	8	0
Simulator Ps (N=18)*	12 (11)	7 (6)	5

*This group contained one P who actually experienced DPH, and eliminating her from the results would give the totals shown in parentheses.

---

[11]Tests had confirmed that this simple manoeuvre by E3 could be carried out without any sound that was audible to P in the central room.

the hallucinated target person in front, however, a DPH response was recorded. P was told to compare the images and was then asked: 'Can you see any difference between the two?' This provided P with the opportunity to spontaneously report transparency. If P stated that she could not detect any difference, E2 suggested a cognitive strategy, described originally by Hilgard (1981), in which P gives each figure a mental instruction to stand up. The P was told that whichever figure obeyed the command was the imagined figure.

Once testing was completed, E2 informed P that he was now leaving and that E1 would return shortly. E2 then left the room and signalled E1, who was located in a nearby room, by using the same acoustic signal previously used by E1. E2, at this point recorded his judgement as to whether P was in the 'hypnotic' or 'simulator' condition. When E1 returned to the experimental room, he 'awakened' P if hypnotised, and told all Ps that the experiment was over.

A detailed 16-item post-experimental questionnaire was then given to all Ps to obtain reports on the depth of hypnosis, the vividness of hallucination, the transparency of hallucination, the truth of responses, the perceived success of her performance and several other points considered important to the trance logic hypothesis. On completion of the enquiry, P was debriefed and told that it was of the utmost importance not to talk to anyone about the experiment so that the naivety of Ps yet to take part could be protected.

RESULTS
Doubled-person hallucination

A total of 8 of the 18 hypnotised Ps reported the initially suggested hallucination of T, while 12 of the 18 simulators did so. It is a common result for simulators to react beyond the hypnotised when the demands are clear.[12] When asked to report the perceived target person, however, all 8 of the hypnotic hallucinators reported the perceived target person, while only 7 of the 12 simulating hallucinators reported seeing the actual (perceptual) person. Fisher's exact

---

[12]It should be noted that the simulation instructions provided in the present investigation differed from those given by Orne (1971). In the latter experiment, simulators were told that 'The experimenter will stop the experiment if he catches on to the fact that you are faking'. This helped to prevent Ps who thought that they may have made an error from stopping the simulation, providing reassurance to S that he/she has not failed in the required task. A further difference was that in Orne's (1971) study, simulators were probably more highly motivated to simulate because they were told that 'intelligent subjects are able to do this ... I can't tell you how to behave or what to do, you have to use whatever you know about hypnosis' (p. 195). The degree of over-acting in the simulator group would quite possibly have been higher had Orne's (1971) instructions been utilised. Future investigators using highly hypnotisable simulators may wish to consider very carefully how best to motivate simulators, while at the same time providing the necessary reassurance.

probability test (Siegel, 1956) indicated that there was a 1-in-20 probability of this distribution occurring by chance (p = .051).[13]

Spontaneous transparency

Spontaneous transparency responses occurred at a lower frequency than hallucination responses. In the hypnosis group, 6 of the 8 hallucinators spontaneously reported that the hallucination was transparent, and none among the 12 'hallucinators' in the simulator group. Fisher's exact probability test indicated that the probability of this result occurring by chance was 7×10^{-4}. The six hypnotic Ps' spontaneous descriptions of transparency were as follows: 'an outline, not as distinct'; 'a shadow, cloudy, hazy, transparent'; 'a shadowy figure'; 'faint outline'; 'I see bits of him'; 'an outline of Professor McKellar'. Although only one P actually used the word 'transparent', the other verbal responses all made reference to the lack of solidity of the imaged figure.[14]

Post-experimental enquiry

In the post-experimental enquiry, we were interested in distinguishing between those Ps who were actually hypnotised and who hallucinated successfully from those who were not hypnotised but who merely tried to mimic what hypnotised Ps were supposed to do. Detailed information was also obtained on Ps' hypnotic and simulator experiences. In the post-experimental enquiry, transparency was reported by three additional Ps. These were the remaining two hypnotic Ps who reported seeing the hallucination, and a simulator who revealed that she had also actually seen the T before her. This P stated that she had self-induced a 'sort of meditational state' during the 15-minute waiting period. She was one of the simulators who had reported the double-hallucination. The remaining members of the simulator group all confirmed that they definitely had not hallucinated T in Target Room 1 following the 15-minute waiting period. All eight members of the hypnotic group who had originally reported the hallucination during the test confirmed that they had seen T in both positions. This distribution was statistically significant (chi-squared = 7.26, p < .01).

Six Ps in the hypnotic group reported that they had not been properly hypnotised, in four cases because of noise outside in the street. If these six Ps are removed from the hypnotised group and the self-hypnotised P is added, the data can be

---

[13] We conducted t-tests on the hypnotisability scores of the 8 Ps who reported DPH and the 10 Ps who did not. These two groups showed a significant difference in average BSS scores, the DPH group giving the higher mean score. A similar analysis was conducted for the 7 simulators who reported DPH and the 11 who did not, but there were no significant differences on any of the hypnotisability measures utilised in the present study.

[14] Comparisons were made between the imagery, hypnotisability and absorption scores of the two Ps reporting solid hallucinations and those of the six Ps reporting transparency. There were no significant differences.

corrected to characterise more accurately Ps' experiences. These adjusted data show that 9 out of 13 hypnotic Ps experienced DPH (69%), while 11 out of 17 simulators reported DPH without actually experiencing it (65%).[15] Six DPH experiencers saw DPH as transparent from the beginning of their DPH experience, while the remaining three experienced DPH initially as solid and later as transparent when the image faded.

In answer to the question 'Do you think you made any mistakes?', four of the simulators reported that they thought they should have reported seeing DPH, and the remaining two were not sure. One reported that she did not think a P who is hypnotised by one person would be expected to respond to suggestions given by a second person.

In answer to the question 'When you looked round and saw the second figure, were you surprised?', only one of the nine DPH experiencers stated that she was not surprised. The remaining eight Ps all stated that they were surprised and gave the following reasons:

Hl: Didn't expect to see him there. Thought he could run fast. H2: Person can't be in two different places at the same time. H3: Suppose I expected him to be gone. His first image suggested he was there in front of me. H4: What's going on? A twin brother sitting behind. Knew one couldn't be him. Felt confused. H5: Because I'd already seen the figure. H6: Only a little surprised because I did not expect to see him there. Immediate reaction was that there weren't two. He'd just moved. H7: Even though the first figure was faint. I still thought it was there so I was surprised to see one behind. S1: Didn't seem as though he should be in two places. … Felt funny.

E2's judgements of Ps' conditions

The judgements made by E2 indicated that he could not predict experimental conditions above chance level. He correctly identified only 11 of the 18 hypnotic Ps and 9 of the 18 simulators.

DISCUSSION

The results indicate that the distribution of hypnotised and simulator Ps reporting DPH has a 1-in-20 probability of occurring by chance. These results confirm Orne's (1959) original claim that hypnotised Ps who report the hallucination will tend to acknowledge the real target person. In contrast with most of the previous research, the present study replicated Orne's finding that 100% of reals who acknowledge

---

[15]One of the six non-hypnotised Ps experienced anxiety during the early stages of the induction procedure and reported that she had deliberately 'held back from being hypnotised'. She was intrigued by hypnosis and the investigation being conducted, and requested to be allowed to be retested after the formal investigation had been completed. On this and other later occasions, she experienced both DPH and transparency effects.

the hallucination also report DPH. Orne also claimed that simulators who report the hallucination will seldom report DPH. In the present experiment, 58% of the simulators produced DPH responses, a greater number than would be expected on the basis of Orne's (1959) original data. In the 25-year period between the two studies, however, the sophistication of the university student population with regard to hypnotic effects could well have increased, and therefore a better level of hypnotic simulation might well be expected. Additionally, and perhaps more importantly, highly hypnotisable simulators can be expected to be more successful at accurately playing the role of hypnotised Ps, because they are more likely to have had direct access to relevant fantasy-oriented experiences than are low hypnotisables.

Although DPH response was not as diagnostic of true hypnosis as in Orne's original report, it is important to note, nevertheless, that all hypnotised Ps who reported seeing the hallucination went on to acknowledge the real target person behind. This is contrary to the findings of other studies, which found that hypnotised Ps frequently responded as Orne claimed only simulators would (Johnson et al., 1972; McDonald & Smith, 1975; Obstoj & Sheehan, 1977; Sheehan et al., 1976). Certain problems in the methodology of these experiments, as outlined earlier, may account for their failure to replicate Orne's findings: a possible lack of very highly hypnotisable Ps who could hallucinate; the possibility of auditory cues during T's movement; failure to provide an adequate opportunity to report the real target person; the use of complex or artificial target objects instead of a readily memorable target person; or some interaction of these factors. The fact that all the hallucinating hypnotised Ps in the present study went on to report DPH provides strong confirmation of Orne's original findings – i.e. that highly hypnotisable people have the ability to experience the doubled-person hallucination and the associated trance logic.

In addition, six Ps gave spontaneous reports of transparency, and all six Ps were from the subgroup of eight hypnotised Ps who reported DPH.[16] Results indicated that the probability of this distribution occurring by chance was 7×10^{-4}. The claim by Orne (1959) that a spontaneous transparency response is 'absolutely diagnostic' of the hypnotised P therefore appears to be correct, and this observation has now been independently replicated at least seven times. The two hypnotised Ps who reported solid rather than transparent hallucinations were ranked fifth and eighth out of 36 on the Vividness of Visual Imagery Questionnaire (Marks, 1973), but they were no higher in hypnotisability than other Ps who experienced DPH.

These two cases, and also the self-induced hypnotic, reported that DPH eventually faded and became transparent. The observation of differences in the rate of transparency reports between groups of Ps who are matched for hypnotisability is of particular significance for Orne's original trance logic hypothesis. Spanos and Radtke (1981) suggested that differences between reals and simulators in transparency reports simply reflect different implicit demands, such that reals interpret the hallucination suggestion as an instruction to form a visual image with their eyes

---

[16]See footnote 13.

open, while simulators assume that the investigator is calling for a report of a solid object. This account seems implausible in the present case, because the highly hypnotisable simulators had the same knowledge and beliefs about the nature of images and fantasised events as the real hypnotic Ps. Yet none reported transparency. Therefore, we seem to have observed a genuine hypnotic effect which cannot be an artefact of differing task demands. A further observation that hallucinated Ps reported surprise at seeing the real Professor McKellar was never obtained in the case of simulators. This finding suggests that DPH is definitely more than an ordinary mental image and that it is indeed a hallucination.

An additional finding was that one of the simulating Ps who reported DPH also reported in the post-experimental inquiry that she had actually hallucinated T. This is a very revealing observation. Even without any formal hypnotic induction, this highly hypnotisable P hallucinated T. This finding supports the view that hypnotic induction is not necessary for producing hypnotic-like altered states of consciousness in which hallucinatory experiences may occur (Braffman & Kirsch, 1999; McGeown et al., 2012). In the post-experimental enquiry, this P reported that she had been mildly traumatised and confused because she knew she was not in the hypnotic group and therefore had not expected such an anomalous experience. When questioned further, she revealed that such hallucinatory experiences were quite common to her in other contexts, although normally these were not threatening. This particular S was of Maori descent and she reported that within Maori culture it is not uncommon for one's ancestors to share in family and tribal life. She had frequently encountered her deceased grandparents and uncles around the family home but was reluctant to go into any detail, apparently because the ancestral spirits may have been offended by her confiding in strangers. In the period while she waited with her eyes closed prior to testing, she practised a meditation procedure that she had learned, although this had not been suggested to her by the Es.

It is apparent that although hallucinations of people may not have been foreign to her waking experience, she did not expect such a vivid and logically inconsistent experience as that embodied in a double-hallucination. On ethical grounds, further investigation of 'trance logic' with high hypnotisables in simulator or other control conditions should proceed with some degree of caution. Instructions prior to the experiment should indicate the possibility of bizarre or inconsistent experiences that may be confusing and difficult to accept. A formal induction procedure carries with it the implication that something 'weird and wonderful' may be about to happen, and outside of this procedure such experiences may not be so easily handled. Similar considerations apply to experimentation with hallucinogenic drugs; only if hallucinations and other bizarre experiences are actually expected can they be coped with, and therefore research normally proceeds only following full informed consent, even if a placebo is actually administered.

The proportion of simulators (falsely) reporting DPH (11 of 17) was lower in the present study than is typically the case. Four of the six non-reporters, however, thought that not reporting DPH could have been a mistake in their performance. Another simulator made the significant comment that she assumed suggestions given by a person other than the hypnotist would not be followed by a hypnotised P. Perhaps others thought similarly, including members of the hypnotic group, thus lowering the DPH response rate in both groups. In previous research, Ps received their hypnotic induction and DPH suggestion from a single hypnotist investigator and so this factor would have been absent. This provides yet another illustration of the importance of understanding the experiment from P's perspective (Orne, 1973).

Hypnosis brings about alterations in imagery, memory, mood, motor control or perception. These alterations are subjectively real, and while the circumstances under which these alterations occur most reliably entail co-operative, highly hypnotisable Ps following hypnotic induction, highly hypnotisable Ps may also experience hypnotic kinds of phenomena quite spontaneously in their everyday life (Shor, 1959; Shor, Orne, & O'Connell, 1962). The results of the present investigation correspond well to the description of 'trance logic' given originally by Orne (1959). Ps were selected from the high end of a continuum which has variously been characterised as 'tranceability' or suspension of usual 'generalised reality-orientation' (Shor et al., 1962), 'absorption' (Tellegen & Atkinson, 1974), 'fantasy-proneness' (Wilson & Barber, 1983), and in the general literature, 'hypnotisability' or 'hypnotic susceptibility'. Ps who experienced DPH would likely have been characterised by high scores on other measures of hypnotisability, and they were found to have significantly higher scores on the measure of hypnotisability used in the present study (CIS plus BSS).

The present results suggest that tolerance of the logically inconsistent DPH was higher among Ps who were deliberately hypnotised than in the individual in the 'simulator' condition who had not received a formal induction procedure. This was indicated by the degree of confusion experienced by the latter. It must be stated, however, that even the hypnotic Ps who experienced DPH reported being 'surprised' in the majority of cases and they produced various 'logical' explanations of how the experience might have been brought about. It was only surprise, however, not shock, and perhaps this relative acceptance does represent the essence of the hypnotic state as originally suggested by Orne. Also, it should be noted that Ps' explanations were produced retrospectively in the non-hypnotic state, and they could well have resulted from normal cognitive rationalisations. Perhaps future studies should try to investigate the characteristics of trance logic using experiential reports during hypnosis itself, rather than those obtained post-experimentally.

Some evidence regarding the capacity for logical thinking in hypnotic Ps arises from their ability to use rational cognitive strategies for differentiating between the hallucinatory and perceptual images during DPH experience itself. All Ps were able to use the strategy described originally by Hilgard (1981) in which a silent (mental) command is delivered to each of the two images. In this study, Ps mentally instructed each 'person' to stand and the one who did so was inferred correctly to be the hallucination. One P was 'thrown' by the imaged person who subsequently refused to sit down again when asked to do so! This suggests that hypnotic hallucinations, like other kinds of vivid imagery (e.g. hypnagogic imagery, dreams), are not always fully controllable by P (McKellar, 1977).

Knowing that one is undergoing a formal induction carries with it an implicit 'contract' or 'meta-suggestion' to expect alterations in one's experience. This meta-suggestion conveys to P that ordinary logic as it applies to perception, memory or mood can be expected to go into temporary suspension and that new rules of behaviour and experience will take over for a while. When this meta-suggestion is absent, logically inconsistent experiences will not be so easily tolerated, and therefore trance logic will not occur. Instead, P experiences cognitive confusion and some emotional shock as the perceptual world is invaded by unexpected fantasies and hallucinations generated by thoughts, ideas or suggestions.

CONCLUSIONS FROM THE TRANCE LOGIC STUDY

All of the hallucinating hypnotised Ps in the Trance Logic Study reported a DPH. In addition, six Ps made spontaneous reports of transparency or lack of solidity of the doubled-person ($p = 7 \times 10^{-4}$). This finding confirms the hypothesis that highly hypnotisable individuals have the ability to experience a doubled-person hallucination, one index of trance logic. The Trance Logic Study confirms that the special state hypothesis of hypnosis suggesting that, in highly hypnotisable people, the hypnotic trance state involves anomalies in perception, imagery and action that are above and beyond the role-playing behaviour of a matched group of highly hypnotisable people who are merely simulating hypnosis. The findings from this well-controlled and rigorously peer-reviewed study support the Special State Theory of hypnosis.

Next, I examine recent neuroscientific studies of brain activity associated with hypnosis. From these studies it is possible to examine the evidence for and against the Special State Theory and to pinpoint the neural structures that are activated in the hypnotic trance state.

BRAIN CHANGES INDICATIVE OF A HYPNOTIC TRANCE STATE

Hypnosis uses attention, suggestion and imagery to alter states of consciousness in hypnotisable people across a wide range of experiences and behaviours. Hypnosis provides a laboratory technique for exploring brain mechanisms involved in attention, motor control, pain perception, beliefs and volition. Hypnotic procedures can be objectively investigated using imaging technologies such as as fMRI and PET (Oakley & Halligan, 2013).[17] Kosslyn, Thompson, Constantini-Ferrando, Alpert,

---

[17]In this section, the reader will be confronted by numerous acronyms. Unfortunately, there is no easy way of avoiding them because they come with the territory of brain research. fMRI, (functional magnetic resonance imaging) measures brain activity by detecting changes associated with blood flow, which increases when an area of the brain is in use. PET (positron emission tomography) is a way of imaging brain function by using radio tracers that emit positrons. Gamma rays, produced when a positron meets an electron inside the patient's body, are used to generate images.

and Spiegel (2000) reported changes in colour-processing areas of the visual cortex after hypnotic suggestions that are consistent with the particular colours suggested. Hofbauer, Rainville, Duncan, and Bushnell (2001) explored how hypnotic suggestions targeting either the affective or the sensory components of a physically induced pain experience result in activation in selective and different areas of the brain. Derbyshire, Whalley, Stenger, and Oakley (2004) used hypnotic suggestion and neuroimaging (fMRI) to demonstrate the neural correlates of functional pain in 'normal' Ps. Lifshitz, Aubert-Bonn, Fischer, Kashem, and Raz (2013) reviewed 'top-down' influences of hypnotic suggestion on cognitive processes traditionally considered involuntary and 'automatic'. Cardeña, Jönsson, Terhune, and Marcusson-Clavertz (2013) showed that variations in EEG band wave activity were dependent on phenomenology and hypnotic suggestibility when Ps are engaged in a hypnotic state in which targeted suggestions were excluded. Dienes and Hutton (2013) used repetitive transcranial magnetic stimulation to show that responsiveness to hypnotic suggestion could be increased by disrupting activity in frontal cortical areas.

Hypnosis is related to cortical activation in structures known as the 'central executive network' (CEN), which is active when the brain is engaged in a task requiring attention, the 'default network' (DN), which is active when the brain is not engaged in a specific task (see also pp. 42–3) and the 'salience network' (SN), which responds to the degree of subjective salience of a stimulus. All three brain systems are associated with higher order cognition. It is believed that the SN is responsible for switching between the DN and the CEN (Goulden et al., 2014). Highly suggestible individuals have been found to produce greater reductions in frontal cortical regions following hypnotic induction compared to low suggestible controls (Jiang, White, Greicius, Waelde, & Spiegel, 2017). Two frontal regions that are activated in hypnosis are the anterior cingulate cortex (ACC) and anterior insula – two frontal nodes of the SN – and the dorsolateral prefrontal cortex (DLFPC), the main frontal component of the CEN (Oakley & Halligan, 2013). One model of hypnosis suggests a 'top-down' system of involving systems of attention and executive top-down control (Landry, Lifshitz, & Raz, 2017). A second model focuses on the association between hypnosis and deactivation in the medial prefrontal cortex (MPFC) (Deeley et al., 2012; McGeown, Mazzoni, Venneri, & Kirsch, 2009). The MPFC is the frontal node of the 'default network' (DN; Buckner et al., 2008; Raichle, 2015), a brain network associated with internal attention, autobiographical thought, social cognition and mind-wandering (Christoff, Gordon, Smallwood, Smith, & Schooler, 2009; Mason, Norton, Van Horn, Wegner, Grafton, & Macrae, 2007). Thus, two distinct neurocognitive hypotheses about hypnosis are available:

H1: Hypnosis engages the frontal regions of the central executive and salience networks, which are associated with attention, executive control and cognitive monitoring.

H2: Hypnosis deactivates the anterior part of the default network, which is associated with social cognition, internal attention, and self-related thought (Figure 9.3).

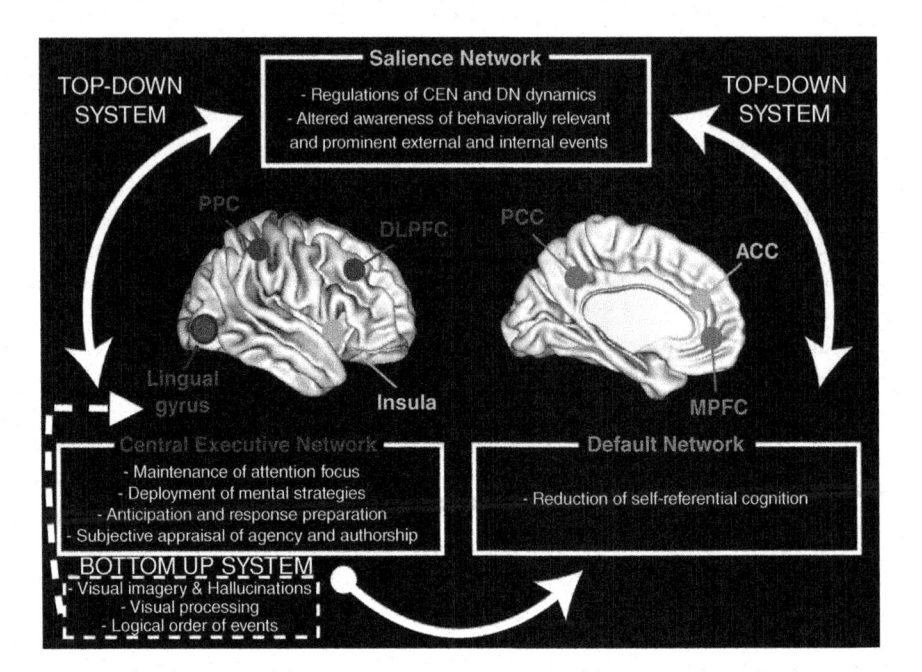

Figure 9.3 A general framework for integrating the neural correlates of hypnosis in highly hypnotisable people. Some loss of clarity compared to the original illustration is due to the inability to print in colour. There are top-down and bottom-up systems of control. The top-down system has central hubs for a 'Central Executive Network' (CEN), which plays a role in maintaining attentional focus on relevant information, deploying mental strategies to produce a reliable hypnotic response, anticipating and preparing the hypnotic response and appraising the subjective feelings of agency/self-control. Moreover, the CEN likely exerts a causal influence over the 'default network' (DN) (Chen et al., 2013). The 'Salience Network' (SN) regulates CEN and DN dynamics as a function of behaviourally prominent events. Modulations of this network alter awareness of external and internal signals. Finally, hypnosis relates to reduced DN activity. This neural pattern likely reflects decreased self-referential thoughts during hypnosis. A bottom-up system (indicated by the white dotted lines and arrow) is also evident in fMRI studies of hypnotic experience. This system includes vivid mental imagery, hallucinations and changes of logical inference and is indexed by activation of the lingual gyrus (bottom right-hand side). See also Figures 9.4 and 9.5. ACC = Anterior Cingulate Cortex. DLPFC = Dorsolateral Prefrontal Cortex. MPFC = Medial Prefrontal Cortex. PCC = Posterior Cingulate Cortex. PPC = Posterior Parietal Cortex.

Adapted from Landry, Lifshitz, and Raz (2017), with permission.

Jiang et al. (2017) investigated cortical activity and functional connectivity among the DN, CEN and SN networks in hypnosis using fMRI. They selected 57 of 545 healthy Ps with very high or low hypnotisability scores on two hypnotisability scales. All Ps were tested in four conditions: rest, memory retrieval and two hypnosis experiences ('happy' and 'vacation') guided by pre-recorded instructions in a counterbalanced order. They utilised the 'fALFF' of the fMRI signal to measure the amplitude of regional spontaneous activity throughout the brain. The fALFF is a ratio of the power spectrum of low frequency (0.01–0.08 Hz)

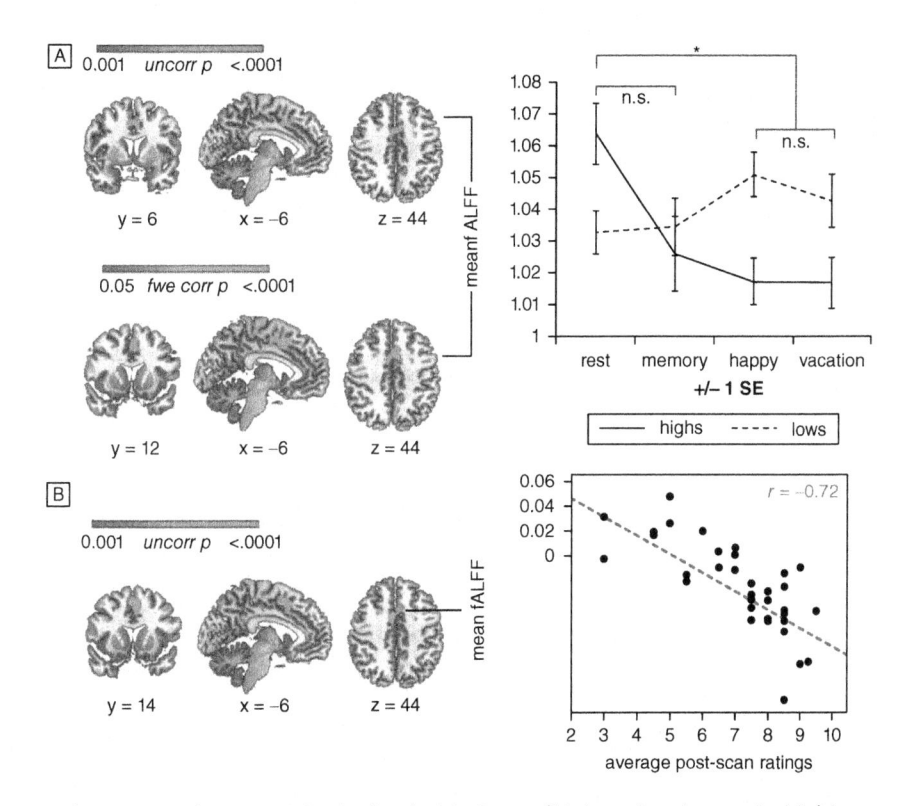

Figure 9.4 fALFF activity in the dACC. Group (high vs. low hypnotisable) by condition (rest/memory vs. hypnosis in random order) differences in dACC activity. Some loss of clarity compared to the original illustrations is due to the inability to print in colour. The left side of the image corresponds to the right side of the brain. (A) Group by condition interaction (upper panel): blue regions show an interaction between group (high vs. low) and condition (hypnosis vs. rest). The interaction is not significant for memory relative to rest at the same threshold. The two hypnosis conditions do not show significantly different fALFF. Mean z scores extracted from significant dACC cluster are plotted across group and condition (right panel). Hypnosis versus rest within highs (lower panel): dark grey regions confirm significantly decreased fractional amplitude during hypnosis relative to rest only for highs. The effect is not significant for memory relative to rest at the same threshold. (B) Hypnotic response scores correlate with fALFF: dark grey regions show decreasing fractional amplitude during hypnosis relative to rest as post-scan intensity of hypnosis ratings increases, among all 36 highs. Scatterplot shows individual mean z scores extracted from the significant dACC region against individual mean intensity of hypnosis ratings.

Reproduced from Jiang et al. (2017), with permission.

to that of the entire frequency range, which controls for overall physiological noise and indexes the intensity of regional spontaneous brain activity. Jiang et al. found that hypnosis reduced the activity in the dorsal anterior cingulate cortex (dACC), increased functional connectivity between the dorsolateral prefrontal cortex (DLPFC; CEN) and the insula in the SN, and reduced connectivity between the CEN (DLPFC) and the DN (PCC). A few of the complex set of findings are illustrated in Figure 9.4.

In a nutshell, the fMRI findings of Jiang et al. (2017) provide support to the theory that hypnosis provides increased top-down control of cognitive functions of perception, thinking and self-control.

META-ANALYSIS

To explore the two hypotheses about the top-down operation of hypnosis described above (Figure 9.3), Mathieu Landry, Michael Lifshitz, and Amir Razin (2017) carried out a meta-analysis on functional imaging studies that had used fMRI or PET during hypnosis. Landry et al. adopted the following criteria to select studies:

1. Publications must be in peer-reviewed journals.
2. Reports had to include stereotaxic coordinates[18] for group results.
3. To ensure compatibility with activation likelihood estimation meta-analysis (ALE)[19] and minimise bias, neuroimaging results had to report peak coordinate foci from whole-brain analysis (Fox, Lancaster, Laird, & Eickhoff, 2014).
4. Studies had to have a 'reasonable sample size'; case studies or single-subject data were excluded.
5. To ensure quality control, studies had to provide sufficient detail regarding the hypnotic induction procedure.
6. To isolate the neural correlates of hypnosis, they only included imaging studies that contrasted task-related or resting-state brain activity during hypnosis with comparable brain activity in a matched control condition outside of hypnosis, and studies that correlated hypnotic depth with brain activity.
7. They excluded investigations that measured the effects of post-hypnotic suggestions, limiting their analyses to findings under hypnosis. Of the initial 56 published papers, a total of 16 studies satisfied the criteria: 15 for the first analysis (i.e. hypnosis minus control) and 10 for the second (i.e. control minus hypnosis).

---

[18] Based on the Talairach and Tournoux (1988) or Montreal Neurological Institute (MNI) systems.
[19] ALE is a method for assessing the overlap between brain foci based on modelling them as probability distributions centred at the respective coordinates (Eickhoff, Laird, Grefkes, Wang, & Fox, 2009). A little bit too 'geeky' to discuss in full detail here, trust me!

The hypnosis-minus-control analysis produced a single activation cluster located in the medial lingual gyrus (Figure 9.1). The lingual gyrus, also known as the medial occipitotemporal gyrus, is a brain structure that is linked to processing vision, especially letters, and also plays a role in analysis of logical conditions (i.e. logical order of events) and encoding visual memories. This visual area appeared as the sole reliable neural pattern for hypnosis.

The medial lingual gyrus is an occipital region mainly involved in higher order visual processing (Machielsen, Rombouts, Barkhof, Scheltens, & Witter, 2000; Mechelli, Humphreys, Mayall, Olson, & Price, 2000). Its role in colour vision has been mapped using PET since 1991 when the V1 area and the cuneate gyrus above V2 and the fusiform and lingual gyri below V2 were found to be activated by coloured stimulation (Zeki, Watson, Lueck, Friston, Kennard, & Frackowiak, 1991). The right lingual gyrus (BA 18) has also been associated with inductive, but not deductive, reasoning, when compared to baseline (Goel & Dolan, 2004). Examples of these two reasoning types are: *inductive* – house cats have 32 teeth; lions have 32 teeth; all felines have 32 teeth; *deductive* – all animals with 32 teeth are cats; no cats are dogs; no dogs have 32 teeth. This finding fits well with the observation that the DPH is possible in trance logic because a 'doubled person' is only possible inductively, but not deductively. This is indicated by the fact that deductive inference is apparent only in non-hypnotised

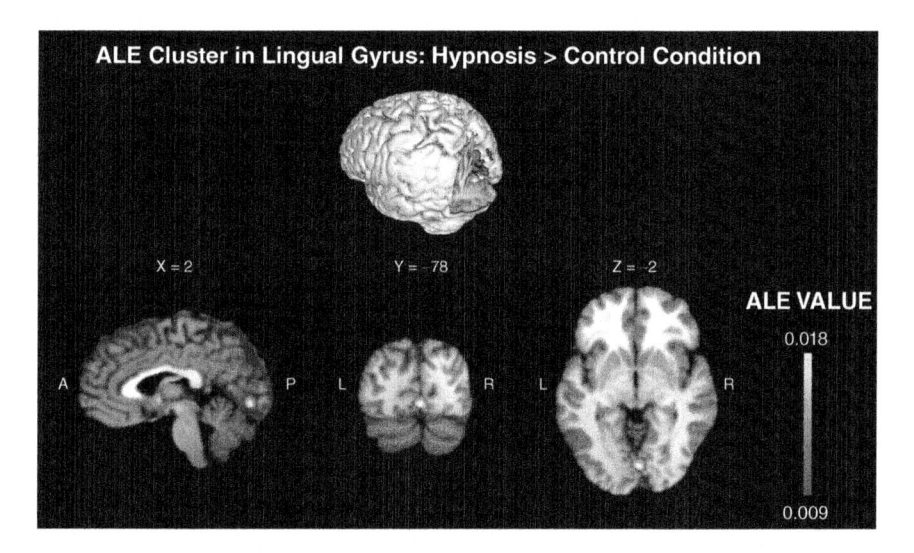

Figure 9.5 The meta-analytic activation pattern related to hypnosis (Hypnosis > Control Condition) across the entire brain. Some loss of clarity compared to the original illustration is due to the inability to print in colour. The vertical bar indicates ALE values. Stereotaxic coordinates according to Talairach and Tournaux Atlas.

Reproduced from Landry, Lifshitz, and Raz (2017), by permission.

simulators because, once they have (falsely) declared that they see the person hallucination, they always deny seeing the real person because it is a logical impossibility. The entranced hypnotic Ps, on the other hand, show no qualms about reporting T in two places at once.

Against the hypothesis that hypnosis operates as a top-down cognitive control, this meta-analysis did not reveal any consistent changes in the CEN, SN or DN. However, the finding of the significant role of the lingual gyrus is consistent with the trance logic hypothesis. The meta-analytic results highlight that hypnosis is *not only a top-down process of executive control* but a *sensory-based process of the imagination.*[20]

SUMMARY

1. Hypnosis is associated with a state of reduced contextual vigilance (indicated by dACC activity), consistent with a special state of consciousness, the hypnotic trance.
2. Hypnosis involves a disconnection from the default mode of resting activity and an enhanced coordination of networks engaged in top-down executive control.
3. The significant involvement of the lingual gyrus suggests that hypnosis additionally involves a sensorily-based, bottom-up process of the imagination alongside a top-down process of executive control.
4. That hypnosis is associated with activation of the lingual gyrus, a neural centre for vivid visual imagery and logical induction, makes a perfect fit with the findings from the Trance Logic Study findings. The capability to hallucinate a doubled-person that is transparent or lacking in solidity is consistent with hypnotic activation of the lingual gyrus found by Landry et al.'s meta-analysis.[21]
5. The findings support the Special State Theory that, when hypnotised, some highly hypnotisable people, can experience a special trance state of consciousness involving altered attention, vivid visual imagery, hallucinations and tolerance of logical inconsistency.

---

[20]Certain limitations of the meta-analysis need to be taken into account: the modest number of included papers; the absence of a standardised experimental approach in the selected studies; the exclusion of many studies; and what this author would term the 'wash-out' effect, caused by combining diverse types of experimental designs and outcome variables into a single analysis.

[21]To date, the Landry et al. study is the *only* meta-analysis of studies of brain activity associated with hypnosis. Landry et al.'s association between hypnosis and activation of the lingual gyrus provided striking convergence with the Trance Logic Study findings.

QUESTIONS

1. Describe two criteria of trance logic.
2. What is the design feature that makes the Trance Logic Study unique?
3. How did one of the simulator Ps help to confirm the trance logic hypothesis?
4. Which ethical principles must be considered in carrying out hypnosis research?
5. Name three cortical networks that are thought to play a role in hypnosis.
6. Name three tasks that involve the lingual gyrus.
7. On the Belief Barometer below (Figure 9.6), considering everything you have learned about hypnosis to date, indicate your degree of belief that highly hypnotisable people can experience trance logic.

Set your degree of belief that highly hypnotisable people can experience trance logic

The author's degree of belief that highly hypnotisable people can experience trance logic

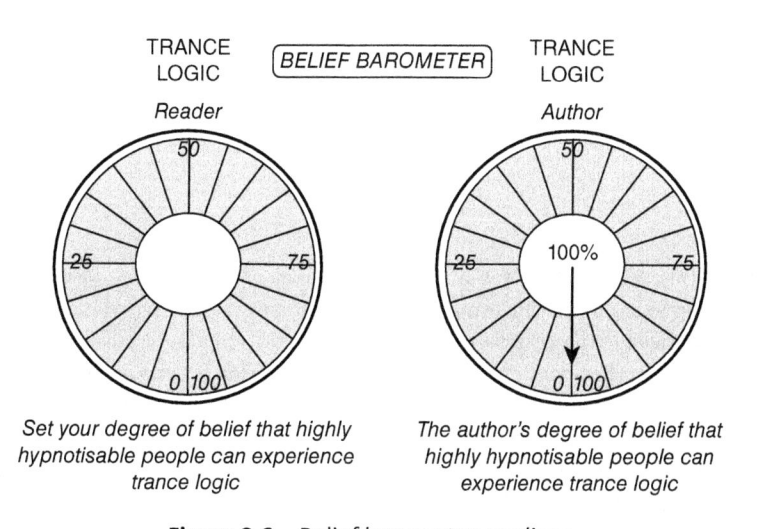

Figure 9.6 Belief barometer readings

10

OUT-OF-BODY AND NEAR-DEATH EXPERIENCES

[Consciousness] provides the person with the sense of owning or being the subject of his/her conscious experience ... 'the sense of self'. (Marchetti, 2012: 57)

Outline: This chapter provides a scientific account of two of the most tantalising, magical-like experiences: the out-of-body and the near-death experiences (OBE and NDE respectively). Their subjectivity and relative rarity make systematic study difficult under controlled conditions. For the OBE, *one needs great clarity about what it is that is alleged to go out of body.* For the NDE, to make any research do-able, *one needs great clarity about what 'near-death' and 'death' mean in operational terms.* In neither case are these issues simple and rarely are they adequately defined. What exactly do OBErs themselves and investigators expect to observe when an OBE occurs? Similarly, we need to be clear about the parameters of the NDE – for example, the criteria for death and 'near-death'. Subject to these criteria, the phenomena can be investigated using (a) first-person methodologies (introspective and phenomenological investigations) and/or (b) third-person methodologies (psychological and neuroscientific investigations). Both (a) and (b) are feasible for the OBE, but only (a) is feasible for the NDE. Here I review the most recent evidence concerning OBE and NDE, and discuss what these experiences mean for science.

SELF

Let's start from first principles. Without any defining criteria and a concrete way of measuring an OBE, there can be no scientific understanding of it. You wouldn't necessarily guess that surfing the Internet. It is almost a cast-iron guarantee that any webpage on OBE or NDE leads one into a dark lonely place *or* promises of heaven. Before discussing the OBE, it is necessary to clarify what 'out of the body' actually means? One strong candidate for the out-going entity is the *self*, one's sense of *agency* or *ipseity*.[1] If, indeed, it is the self that goes out of the body, what actually is the 'self' to start off with? This is not an easy question. Fortunately, in philosophy there is no shortage of answers: there are dozens. Galen Strawson lists 25:

> the cognitive self, the conceptual self, the contextualized self, the core self, the dialogic self, the ecological self, the embodied self, the emergent self, the empirical self, the existential self, the extended self, the fictional self, the full-grown self, the interpersonal self, the material self, the narrative self, the philosophical self, the physical self, the private self, the representational self, the rock bottom essential self, the semiotic self, the social self, the transparent self, and the verbal self (Strawson, 2000: 39; cited by Legrand & Ruby, 2009).

Please breathe a great sigh of relief because here we consider only three.[2]

1 The skeptical theory of self

Skeptics doubt even the existence of themselves. They claim that the self does not exist. Period. Metzinger claims: 'nobody ever was or had a self' (Metzinger, 2003: 1). People have an experience of self but it would be a fallacy to infer the existence of an internal non-physical object of self. The self is an illusion created in the brain: 'Our self-experience, our feeling of being a conscious self, is never truthful; it merely testifies to the fact that we tend to confuse a representational construct with a really existing entity' (p. 390).

William James stated: 'The "Self" ... when carefully examined, is found to consist mainly of ... peculiar motions in the head or between the head and throat' (James, 1890).[3] For James, physiological changes cause emotions and each specific emotion has a unique pattern of physiological arousal. The Self as the central author of the emotions should, then, be a nuclear collection of physiological changes principally in the head, neck and glottis in the throat.

Daniel Dennett (2014) suggests the self is a story we tell ourselves about an imaginary entity 'inside' each of our physical bodies. Following Gilbert Ryle, his thesis adviser, the self is a fictive ghost inside the machine. The evidence suggests that the 'lay person' has a sense of self more in line with James than with Dennett. Surveys find that the self is placed inside the head, just behind

---

[1] Ipseity is the quality of being oneself; the essential element of individuality.
[2] For a philosophical discussion of the self, see Zahavi (2014).
[3] Between the head and the throat? The mouth perhaps?

the eyes, in or around the brain.[4] Imagination, folklore and speech habits conspire to make the self substantially 'real', so the skeptics argue, but the self remains a complete delusion. Thus, skeptics, the OBE and NDE are delusions – end of story.

2 The phenomenological theory of self

A more nuanced notion of self holds that the self is a subjective, phenomenological experiencing of the world from a unique first-person point of view. Zahavi (2014) describes this concept as follows:

> phenomenal consciousness involves self-consciousness .... Experiences necessarily involve an experiential perspective or point of view, they come with perspectival ownership, and rather than speaking simply of phenomenal what-it-is-likeness, it is more accurate to speak of what-it-is-like-for-me-ness. Importantly, this for-me-ness of experience doesn't denote some special kind of I-qualia; rather, it refers to the first-personal character or presence of experience, to the fact that we have a different pre-reflective acquaintance with our own ongoing experiential life than we have with the experiential life of others and vice versa. My central claim was then that this feature of experience amounts to and can be identified with experiential selfhood. (Zahavi, 2014: 88)

The experiential self can be considered on two levels:

> (2A) The 'minimal' self, also referred to as the 'basic' self, 'core' self or 'ipseity', is a pre-reflective, tacit level of selfhood referring to the first-person quality of consciousness, being aware that all experience is '*my*' experience and that all conscious acts have intrinsic self-consciousness.

> (2B) The 'social' self is one's social identity or self-concept, which includes one's habits, history and personal attributes. This level presupposes the minimal self and involves reflective, metacognitive processes, in which one's own self is an object of awareness (Nelson, Parnas, & Sass, 2014). An essential feature of self is *agency*, the belief that one controls one's actions and, through them, events in the world. Agency carries the status of a legal person, the legal and moral responsibility for one's voluntary action, and the belief that we understand the nature and meaning of those actions.[5] (Haggard, 2017; House of Lords, M'Naghten Rules, 1843).

---

[4]Bertossa, Besa, Ferrari, and Ferri (2008) reported that the majority of people locate themselves midway behind the eyes. Limanowski and Hecht (2011) found two locations, within the head, and within the chest. Starmans and Bloom (2012) reported that people believe the self is in the eyes.

[5]Agency to change the world is also a homeostatic striving for equilibrium (Marks, 2018).

3 The objective theory of self

The objective theory of self is that the self is one's physical body. The living physical body is the ultimate proof of one's existence, the habeas corpus. The body and the brain provide the 'shell' where our thoughts, feelings and actions have their 'centre of gravity'. Being able to recognise one's own image in the mirror and having an awareness of authoring one's own actions with agency bridges the gap between the psychological self and the physical self. Normally, these selves are wedded together in lifelong union except when an OBE or other autoscopic phenomenon occurs. Before exploring the OBE in some depth, it is helpful to understand how the self is represented by the brain.

THE BRAIN'S 'SIGNATURE' OF SELF[6]

The physical self is represented in the brain as homunculi, two representations of human sensory and motor proclivities. Wilder Penfield and Theodore Rasmussen (1950) used cortical stimulation to map the sensory and motor systems of the body. These two homunculi require significant cortical and subcortical networks to produce meaningful images and actions.

The principal cortical regions of the motor system are the primary motor cortex (M1) that lies along the precentral gyrus, the posterior parietal cortex, the premotor cortex and the supplementary motor area (SMA). The cerebellum coordinates voluntary movements, posture, balance, coordination and speech, resulting in smooth and balanced muscular activity. The prefrontal cortex is a 'hotspot' for the sense of agency in choosing between actions (e.g. Khalighinejad, Di Costa, & Haggard, 2016). Paul Downing et al. (2001) found distinct cortical regions that respond to images of the human body in the lateral occipitotemporal cortex, quite near to the lingual gyrus. This 'body recognition area' is also nearby, but distinctly does not overlap the 'face recognition area' (Kanwisher, McDermott, & Chun, 1997).

To pinpoint the neural 'signature' of the self, we need to employ a clear definition of the concept of self, which has three essential features: *the subjective self provides a first-person perspective (I), agency (me) and ownership of actions (mine)*. This multi-stranded concept enables neuroscientific studies to operationalise the self in brain activity. Skeptics, of course, argue that this is a futile task. Daniel Dennett suggests that 'it is a category mistake to start looking around for the self in the brain', which is why he couldn't imagine finding 'that cell there, right in the middle of the hippocampus (or wherever) – that's the self!' (Dennett, 1992). Here Dennett employs a 'straw man' fallacy, which does him no credit. Neuroscience is concerned with the organisation and networking of the brain's 100 billion cells, not the discovery of a single 'self cell'. It would be foolish to bet

---

[6]Lest there be any doubt, I am using the word 'signature' metaphorically. There can be no single physical mark of the self in the brain.

one's shirt that brain networks associated with the self will not be found, because one would certainly lose it. 'Your shirt, please, Professor Dennett!'

Enough distractions – let's get down to business. One needs to proceed by asking a sensible question. On this score, one can learn from a false start by Seth Gillihan and Martha Farah (2005), who asked 'Is self special?' – i.e. 'does [self] emerge from systems that are physically and functionally distinct from those used for more general purpose cognitive processing?'. This question turns the clock back to the nineteenth century when phrenology was all the vogue. Franz Joseph Gall's system (Figure 10.1) claimed that the brain is divided into a set of distinct physical and functional systems and people had their personalities 'read' by readers feeling the lumps and bumps on their heads. Now we have personality theory, à la Eysenck (3 factors), Jung (4 factors), Costa and McCrae (5 factors), Cattell (16 factors) or SAPA (27 factors). All we are looking for here is a humble, singular self.

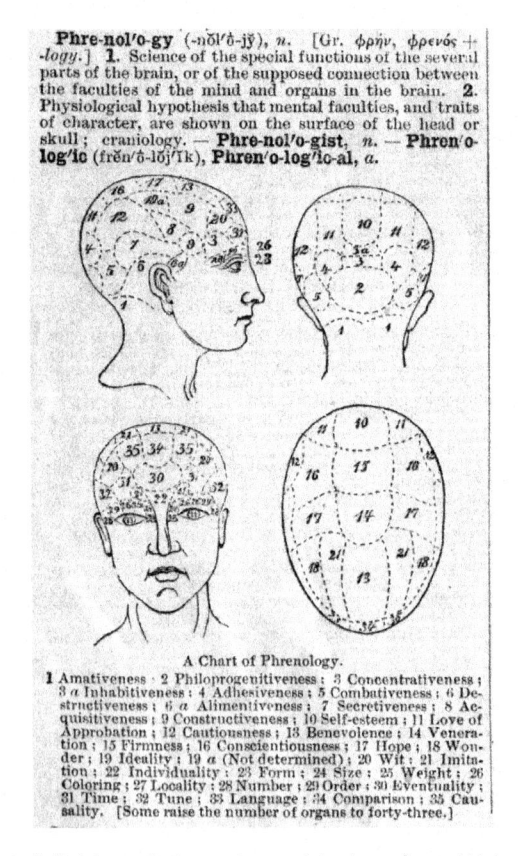

Figure 10.1 A definition of phrenology with chart from *Webster's Academic Dictionary, c.* 1895. Area 22 for 'Individuality' in the centre, right behind the eyes, corresponds most closely to the self. Public domain.

The brain is the most complex living structure known to science. It deserves respect. It won't give out its secrets to the armchair philosopher any more than to the lumps-and-bumps phrenologist. Each brain region is complexly networked to many others and serves multiple different psychological functions. There are no real surprises that Gillihan and Farah failed to identify a special brain region for the self. Their final paragraph quotes Steven Pinker: 'The "I" is not a combination of body parts or brain states or bits of information, but a unity of selfness over time, a single locus that is nowhere in particular' (Pinker, 1997: 564). Momentarily, Daniel Dennett and fellow skeptics could celebrate. They knew they were right and here was the proof. But wait – a few years later, a more nuanced study arrived on the airwaves with a much more successful attempt to identify the brain's 'self-signature'. Dennett and Pinker needed to rethink their positions.

Dorothée Legrand and Perrine Ruby (2009) asked a more astute question: 'What is self-specific?' Legrande and Ruby focused on *self-relatedness*, which involves a wide cerebral network they called the 'E-network': the medial prefrontal cortex, precuneus, temporoparietal junction and temporal poles. Legrande and Ruby showed that the E-network is also recruited in the resting state, in reading others' minds, memory recall and reasoning.

Another strong candidate for the 'self-signature' has been studied for at least 20 years: the 'default mode network' (DMN), which has already made an appearance in the previous chapter. The DMN 'switches off' into inactivity at the default setting as soon as the brain is not busy dealing with the pressing demands of active tasks (Raichle, MacLeod, Snyder, Powers, Gusnard, & Shulman, 2001). The DMN is the default setting for self-reflection and introspection. The DMN consists of three main structures: the medial prefrontal cortex (MPFC) and posterior cingulate cortex (PCC), both situated along the brain's midline, together with a structure in the inferior parietal and medial temporal regions (Figure 10.2). The DMN was first reported when it was found to become less active during goal-directed tasks (Shulman et al., 1997). The DMN story became interesting when it was found to be closely involved with self-referential mental activity.

Christopher Davey, Jesus Pujol and Ben Harrison used functional magnetic resonance imaging (fMRI) to examine self-referential and resting-state processes in the DMN (Davey, Pujol, & Harrison, 2016). Davey et al. wanted to identify brain areas that are activated by both self-reference *and* rest, but also show increased activity in self-reference versus rest. They examined three 'core-self' DMN regions: the medial prefrontal cortex (MPFC), posterior cingulate cortex (PCC) and inferior parietal lobule (IPL). A total of 88 Ps completed three experimental conditions: self-reference, non-self-referential external attention and rest-fixation. For self-reference, Ps received a trait adjective (e.g. 'skeptical', 'perfectionistic' or 'lucky') and were asked 'Does this word describe you?'. The Ps indicated their choice by pressing the left or right button on a button-box. In the external attention condition, Ps also viewed words and responded to the question 'Does this word have four or more vowels?'. This condition required a high level of attention to minimise the likelihood of task-independent thoughts during its performance. Each trial block (2-s instruction followed by 6 words presented for 5 s each) was interspersed with a 10-s rest block in which Ps fixated a centrally presented cross. The fMRI analyses yielded three neural centres involved in the tasks: MPFC, ventral PCC and left IPL (Figure 10.2).

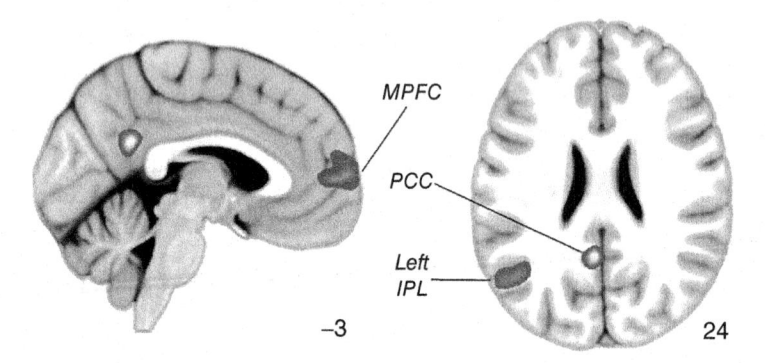

Figure 10.2 Conjunction analysis of the rest-fixation and self-reference minus rest-fixation contrasts. The conjunction test identified regions that were not only active in rest-fixation (compared to the external attention task), but also showed greater activation to self-reference relative to rest-fixation. Such activity was demonstrated in MPFC, ventral PCC and left IPL. Some loss of clarity compared to the original illustration is due to the inability to print in colour.

Reproduced in slightly adapted form from Davey et al. (2016), with permission.

The investigators used a Bayesian technique to imply effective connectivity between brain regions to determine the optimal model from a set of 32 candidate models. Model 27 was found to outperform the other models (Figure 10.3). This model contains a 'broad self' (self-referential and rest-fixation) as a driving influence on PCC, with self-reference modulating.

Davey et al. successfully identified a special neural network associated with self-reference consisting of a set of three regions – the PCC, MPFC and left IPL. They concluded that this core-self system is driven primarily by the activity of the PCC, which has a positive influence on the MPFC and the IPL. The MPFC has a moderating influence on the PCC, acting to regulate its activity in resting and self-referential conditions, but to a greater extent during self-reference.

The self's neural network 'overlaps' with the DMN, making a 'rest-self overlap', which suggests that neural encoding of the self is also involved in resting state activity, an association that is called 'rest-self-containment' (Northoff, 2016). Annemarie Wolff, Daniel Giovanni and colleagues (2019) investigated temporal measures of resting state EEG as related to self-consciousness. They used the Self-Consciousness Scale to measure the Private, Public and Social dimensions of self with 50 Ps. Wolff, Giovanni et al. found significant positive correlations between Private self-consciousness and three measures of resting activity, which supported

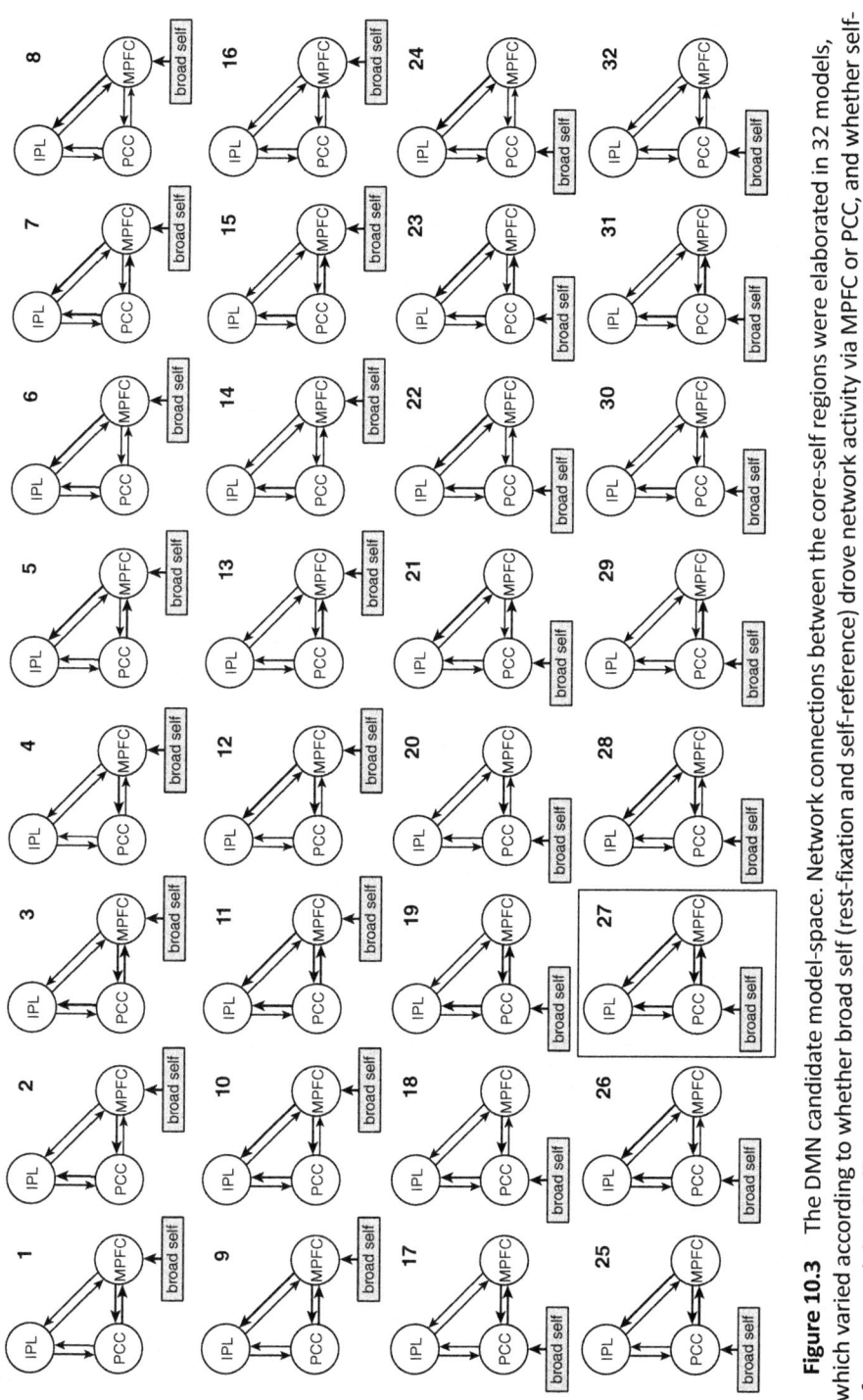

Figure 10.3 The DMN candidate model-space. Network connections between the core-self regions were elaborated in 32 models, which varied according to whether broad self (rest-fixation and self-reference) drove network activity via MPFC or PCC, and whether self-reference modulated efferent connections from MPFC to PCC, IPL, both or neither, and connections from PCC to MPFC, IPL, both or neither (i.e. a 2 × 4 × 4 = 32 candidate model-space). Bayesian model selection favoured model 27 (see Figure 10.5). Reproduced from Davey et al. (2016), with permission.

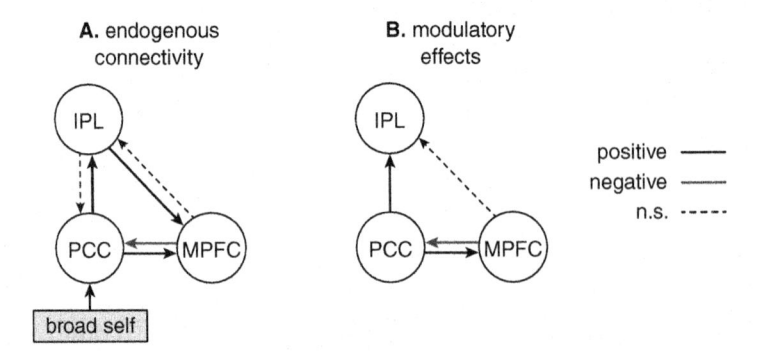

Figure 10.4 (A) The broad self is driving PCC with PCC having a positive influence on MPFC – both directly and indirectly via its influence on IPL – and MPFC having negative influence on PCC; (B) These effects are enhanced by the modulatory effects of self-reference: PCC has a greater positive influence on MPFC and IPL, and MPFC has a greater negative influence on PCC.

Reproduced from Davey et al. (2016), with permission.

the hypothesis that self-related information is temporally contained within the brain's resting state. 'Rest-self-containment' is one candidate for the 'signature' of self of the conscious brain.

The right temporoparietal junction (TPJ) has particular relevance to the OBE. Decety and Lamm's (2007) meta-analysis of 70 fMRI studies demonstrated that the TPJ is engaged in lower-level computational processes associated with the sense of agency and reorienting attention to salient stimuli. Their meta-analyses indicated that the TPJ is associated with four functions: reorienting, empathy, agency and theory of mind (Figure 10.5).

In a related study, Mars, Neubert, Noonan, Sallet, Toni, and Rushworth (2012) explored links between the right TPJ and the DMN. They separated the right TPJ into three components: a dorsal area and two ventral regions. The dorsal area overlapped with the IPL regions of the DMN. Ventrally, they identified two areas: one anterior (TPJa) and one posterior (TPJp), which they believe shows that the posterior TPJ region overlaps with the foci traditionally associated with social cognition and theory of mind. Thus, the cortical encoding network of 'self' within the DMN is linked to the key processes of agency, empathy, theory of mind and reorienting via the TPJ.

It is time to turn to examine the OBE phenomenon itself: the nature of the OBE and its indicators and explanation.

OBE: ANECDOTE VERSUS CONTROLLED INVESTIGATIONS

Blackmore (1982) defined the OBE as 'an experience in which a person seems to perceive the world from a location outside his physical body' (p. 1).

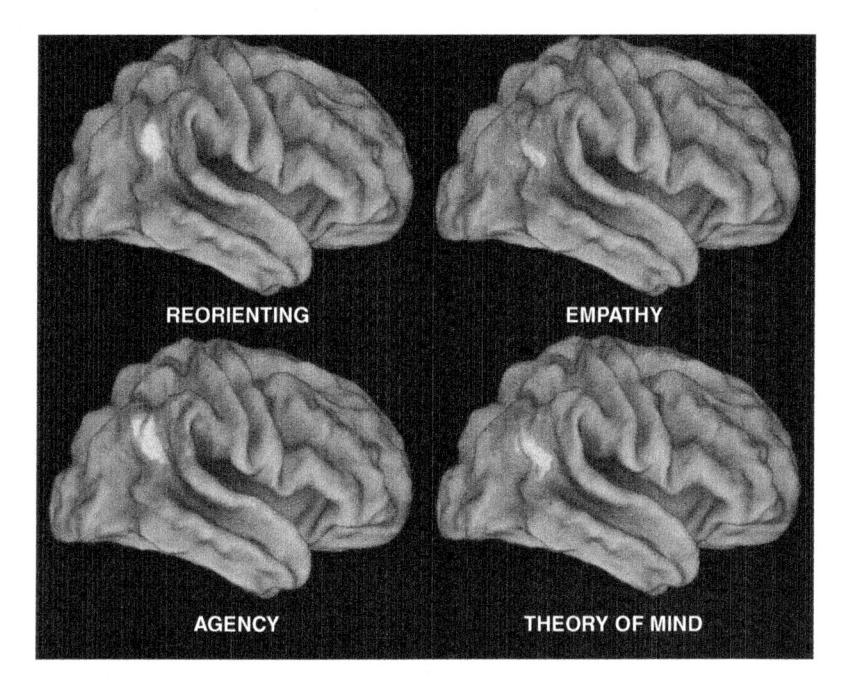

Figure 10.5 Activation maps in the right temporoparietal junction (TPJ) for four psychological functions. The lighter areas indicate higher activation probability.

Reproduced from Decety and Lamm (2007), with permission.

During an OBE,[7] which usually occurs when lying supine (flat on one's back). A person typically feels as if s/he is spatially separated from the physical body. An OBE often includes a sensation of floating, a fantasy of being connected by a silver cord, seeing one's own physical body from the outside, usually from above, possibly with the experience of travel to a place remote from one's actual physical location, or possibly even flying (Alvarado, 1992). The OBE could be related to the hypnagogic state that occurs when one is drifting off to sleep. OBErs report more frequent hypnagogic imagery than non-OBErs. Blackmore's personal OBE, so central to her theories, occurred when she was 'stoned on weed' (cannabis sativa; Blackmore, 2017). She mentions:

> … the awkward question of whether spontaneous OBEs and drug-induced OBEs are the same thing or not. When I told people about my experience all those years ago, many derided it as a 'drug induced fantasy' or a 'stoned

---

[7] I consider here spontaneous OBEs arising naturally or in neurosurgical procedures, but not laboratory-induced body illusions such as the rubber hand illusion (Botvinick & Cohen, 1998), because the latter does not involve the entirety of the body or self.

hallucination' and not 'the real thing'.[8] So we have to ask, as we did with dream-induced OBEs, and will with near-death experiences (NDEs), whether drugs can induce a 'genuine' OBE or not. (Blackmore, 2017)

There can be little doubt that cannabis can trigger OBEs (Tart, 1971). People who use cannabis report more OBEs and more multiple OBEs. A cannabis-induced OBE – let's call it a 'COBE' – is likely to be different from a spontaneous OBE – a 'SOBE' – in the absence of cannabis. Cannabis effects are strongly influenced by the 'set', the participant's mental state and expectations, and the setting. While at the University of Otago in New Zealand in the 1970s I held a MRC research grant and a New Zealand Government licence to administer cannabis to humans to study the drug's psychological effects. The principal aim was to determine the impact of cannabis and alcohol on tasks related to driving. We were able to use natural, pure plant material seized by customs from large shipments of South African 'Durban Poison'. This material is described on one website in the following terms: 'This pure sativa ... has gained popularity worldwide for its sweet smell and energetic, uplifting effects. Durban Poison is the perfect strain to help you stay productive through a busy day, when exploring the outdoors, or to lend a spark of creativity' (https://www.leafly.com/strains/durban-poison). Our laboratory administrations were uncontaminated with tobacco or other substances. We observed that cannabis produces perceptual confusion and temporal disintegration, effects that are synergised (increased) by alcohol (Casswell & Marks, 1973a, b; MacAvoy & Marks, 1975; Marks & MacAvoy, 1989).

On a few, rare occasions Ps experienced adverse reactions. These experiences could be extremely unpleasant and disturbing. One female P, on her first occasion taking cannabis, had arrived at the laboratory wearing a cool-looking but overly tightly tied bandana-style headscarf. After smoking the cannabis, she hallucinated that *the top half of her head had detached from the rest of her head and floated in mid-air above her body*. This autoscopic sensation was extremely weird and very scary. Fortunately, except for her future avoidance of cannabis, psychiatric follow-up revealed no long-lasting effects.

It was always necessary to ask Ps to abstain from drug and alcohol use for 24 hours prior to each lab visit. For perfectly 'human' reasons, this request was not always followed. One study used nine sessions with three doses of alcohol combined with three doses of cannabis plus one practice session. One P's responses appeared highly erratic, and we stopped the session to find out what was going on. With a wide smile on his face, the P said that he had tried 'to help' the investigation along by 'dropping a tab of acid' (LSD) half an hour before the session. We deleted his data and replaced him with a less 'helpful' P. For this kind of reason it is never possible

---

[8]These objections are valid: nobody would choose to investigate non-drug-induced subjective experiences with Ps who had taken a drug, unless the drug itself was a part of the investigation.

to assume that every OBE is from the same fixed category of experience, because it can so easily be altered by an array of physical, chemical and psychological variables. Blackmore reports multiple factors that may have affected the content, quality and duration of her OBE: sleep deprivation, REM intrusion, confused bodily sense, closed eyes, memories of cycling through leaves, hyperactivity of the auditory cortex and the cannabis of unknown strength and purity (Blackmore, 2017). In the UK of the 1970s hashish from Afghanistan or Pakistan was used in 'joints' mixed with tobacco.[9] The cannabis could also have been bulked with flour and 'spiced' with chemicals. As Blackmore points out, her OBE will forever remain mysterious.

Blackmore (2017)[10] describes her personal OBE thus:

> I was just nineteen when everything I thought I knew was overthrown and my life changed direction. If I had imagined a future in some sensible university job, that was now impossible for I was determined to understand what had happened to me. For just a couple of hours I was no longer confined to a slow, heavy, physical body but escaped through a tunnel into a world of flying, exploring the world from outside my body and finally entering the mystical experience of oneness, of unity with the universe. (Blackmore, 2017, location 91)

Another OBE example is from Celia Green, about to take her driving test:

> [A]s I settled myself, switched on the engine, let in the gear, I seemed to fill with horror because I simply wasn't in the car at all, I was settled firmly on the roof watching myself and despite a fearsome mental struggle to get back into myself. I was unable to do so and carried out the whole test, (30 mins?) watching the body part of me making every sort of fool of myself that one could possibly manage in a limited time. (Green, 1968: 64)

This OBE account is from Charles Tart, also driving a vehicle:

> I was riding my motorcycle home from school (with girl passenger). While I was operating all the controls (of the motorcycle), I was watching my motorcycle with the girl and me from a distance of about six to eight feet

---

[9]The chemistry of cannabis is complex, with several dozen constituents in any given sample. Cannabidiol, Δ-1 tetrahydrocannabinol (THC) and cannabinol are three of the cannabinoids, of which THC is the most psychotropically active. Samples of hash and marihuana from Asia in the early 1970s were found to contain propyl cannabinoids, such as Δ^1- tetrahydrocannabinolic acid, which is also psychoactive (de Zeeuw, Wijsbeek, Breimer, Vree, van Genneken, & van Rossum, 1972).

[10]Blackmore's *Seeing Myself: The New Science of Out-of-Body Experiences* (2017) includes many candid revelations which become solipsistic in places. The word 'I' appearing 500 times, 'me', 248 times and 'myself' 96 times.

above our physical existence. I had no noticeable physical sensations such as feeling while operating the motorcycle, though I seemed to be functioning fairly well. Physical sound didn't register either. I thought I was hearing wonderful, powerful, colorful, emotional, free music. The whole experience was remarkably enjoyable. (Tart, 1971: 103–4)[11]

How common is the OBE? Blackmore states:

You might have the impression that OBEs happen only to special people – whether you think that means they are spiritually developed or mentally unhinged. Yet tales of leaving the body seem to come from perfectly ordinary people who have OBEs in all sorts of circumstances .... As a rough estimate, somewhere between 8 and 25 per cent of the population claim to have had at least one OBE. (Blackmore, 2017: loc. 1699)

In a sample of 1,000 non-patients, Pechey and Halligan (2012) found that 10% had experienced an OBE at least occasionally, with around 2% reporting OBEs sometimes and 1% often experiencing them. Interpretations of OBEs range from the esoteric (e.g. astral travelling) to the prosaic (e.g. dreaming).

The main defining feature of the OBE is the subjective self taking off towards the ceiling. 'Dislocating' from the physical self, moving to an illusory position above the physical body, but beneath the ceiling, so that the person sees herself lying below (Figure 10.7C). The OBE may occasionally occur in combination with the near-death experience (NDE), a double-whammy. The OBE as a type of 'autoscopy'[12] does not always include perception of the physical body, however.

Figure 10.6 illustrates three 'autoscopic' phenomena. OBEs differ from 'autoscopic hallucinations' and 'heautoscopy' (Blanke, Faivre, & Dieguez, 2016). No 'disembodiment' is reported in autoscopic hallucinations, but there is always 'disembodiment' in an OBE or it couldn't be called that. In heautoscopy there is a doubling, a classic 'doppelganger' in which the experiencer is unable to localize her/his self. The self's perceived location alternates between in-the-body and out-of-body, or can even be at both locations at the same time, an extremely weird and freakish experience. One patient gave the following account:

---

[11] Tart's (1968) OBE laboratory protocol placed a target on a shelf above eye level to determine whether the P could read a number on a sheet of paper. Unfortunately, he left the P unmonitored and uncontrolled.

[12] Autoscopic phenomena are experiences of perceiving one's body or face within space either from an internal point of view, as in a mirror, or from an external point of view. Peter Brugger, Marianne Regard, and Theodor Landis (1997) proposed six autoscopic phenomena: the feeling of a presence, the negative heautoscopy, the inner heautoscopy, the autoscopic hallucination, the out-of-body experience and the heautoscopy, also defined as heautoscopic proper.

On the respective morning he got up with a dizzy feeling. Turning around, he saw himself still lying in bed. He became angry about 'this guy who I knew was myself and who would not get up and thus risked being late at work'. He tried to wake the body in the bed first by shouting at it; then by trying to shake it and then repeatedly jumping on his alter ego in the bed. The lying body showed no reaction. Only then did the patient begin to be puzzled about his double existence and become more and more scared by the fact that he could no longer tell which of the two he really was. Several times his bodily awareness switched from the one standing upright to the one still lying in bed; when in the lying in bed mode he felt quite awake but completely paralysed and scared by the figure of himself bending over and beating him. His only intention was to become one person again and, looking out of the window (from where he could still see his body lying in bed), he suddenly decided to jump out 'in order to stop the intolerable feeling of being divided in two'. At the same time, he hoped that 'this really desperate action would frighten the one in bed and thus urge him to merge with me again'. The next thing he remembered was waking up in pain in the hospital (Brugger et al., 1994). No surprise here but suicide is a fairly common outcome of the doppelganger. Or a movie.

Only a small minority of people experience more than one or two OBEs in a lifetime and the OBEs are of short duration, so the OBE is not easy to study. Blanke and Mohr (2005) suggest that OBEs are related to activation of the right TPJ, while heautoscopy (HAS) may correspond to activity of the left TPJ.

A game-changing discovery was the report of Olaf Blanke, a Swiss neurosurgeon that 'The part of the brain that can induce out-of-body experiences has been located' (Blanke, Ortigue, Landis, & Seeck, 2002; Figure 10.6). Blanke and his team were operating on a 43-year-old epileptic woman who had suffered frequent fits for 11 years and drugs had proved ineffective. The neurosurgeons were using brain stimulation to pinpoint the epileptic focus and to remove it. Unexpectedly, the team triggered some weird experiences when stimulating a small area on the right side of her brain .... At first, the woman reported 'falling from a height' or 'sinking into the bed' or that her legs were moving or being shortened. With an increased current she said that she could: 'see myself lying in bed, from above, but I only see my legs and lower trunk'. Then, at last, she reported a full-blown OBE, the sensation of floating close to the ceiling above the bed.[13]

---

[13]Consistent with a feeling of flying or floating in space, OBErs may report a sense of exhilaration, but also a fear of being unable to return to the body. The connection to their bodies by an imaginary 'silver cord' tends to lesson this fear.

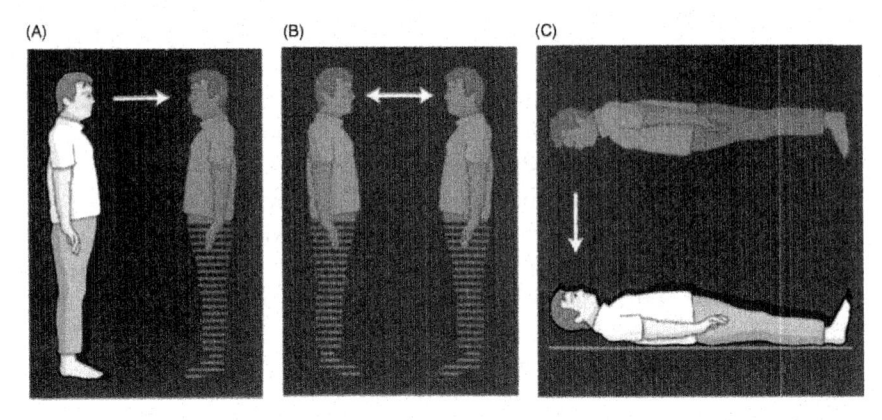

Figure 10.6 Illustration of three types of autoscopic phenomena. In this figure the phenomenology of (A): autoscopic hallucination (AH), (B) heautoscopy (HAS) and (C) out-of-body experience (OBE) is represented schematically. The experienced position and posture of the physical body for each autoscopic phenomenon is indicated by full lines, and the experienced position and posture of the disembodied body (OBE) or autoscopic body (AH, HAS) in blurred lines. The finding that AH and HAS were mainly reported from a sitting/standing position and OBE in a supine position is integrated into the figure. The experienced visuo-spatial perspective during the autoscopic phenomenon is indicated by the arrow pointing away from the location in space from which the patient has the impression to see (AH: from the physical body; OBE: from a disembodied body or location; HAS: alternating or simultaneously from either the fashion between physical and/or the autoscopic body).

Reproduced from Blanke, Faivre, and Dieguez (2016), with permission.

This OBE 'hotspot' was located in the right angular gyrus, a small area at the TPJ, which has since been seen in many other studies. Bos, Spoor, Smits, Schouten, and Vincent (2016) observed a case of an OBE during awake craniotomy. Stimulation of the left TPJ repetitively induced OBEs, in which the patient felt as if she was floating above the operating table looking down on herself. Nakul and Lopez (2017) comment on the Bos et al. report: 'During resection of the tumour, electrical stimulation of the peritumoral subcortical tissue at the left TPJ first evoked the feeling that the patient's right leg was "drawn toward the opposite wall of the operating theatre", suggesting that TPJ stimulation distorted the patient's body schema. During subsequent stimulations of the same area, she reported three full-blown OBEs.' De Ridder, Van Laere, Dupont, Menovsky, and Van de Heyning, P. (2007) also observed that OBEs could be repeatedly elicited by stimulating the right TPJ.[14]

---

[14] A persistent and uncontrollable sensation of noise such as rapping or ringing 'in the ears'.

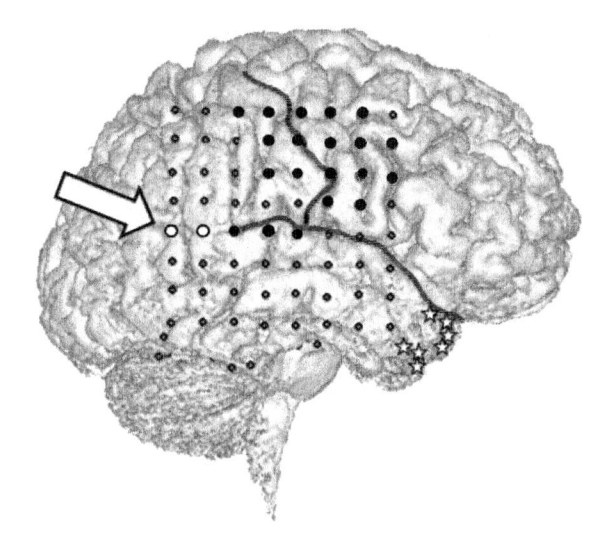

Figure 10.7 Three-dimensional surface reconstruction of the right hemisphere of the brain from magnetic-resonance imaging. Subdural electrodes were implanted in the brain of an epileptic patient undergoing presurgical evaluation; the locations at which focal electrical stimulation (ES) evoked behavioural responses are shown. The white circles show points at which OBE, body part illusions and vestibular responses were induced (arrow). Stars indicate the epileptic focus in the medial temporal lobe. Since undergoing a right anterior temporal lobectomy in 2000, the patient was reported as being free of complex partial seizures.

Reproduced from Blanke, Ortigue, Landis, and Seeck (2002), by permission.

What are the personality characteristics of people who experience OBEs (OBErs)? Epileptic patients and 'schizotypes' tend to show disruptions in 'multi-sensory integration processes' that are thought to predispose people to report OBEs (Blanke, Landis, Spinelli, & Seeck, 2004; Braithwaite, Samson, Apperley, Broglia, & Hulleman, 2011). Such disruptions could cause a breakdown in 'own-body' processes and embodiment. Braithwaite et al. (2011) investigated people's predisposition to OBEs in the non-patient population using the Cardiff Anomalous Perception Scale (CAPS; Bell, Halligan, & Ellis, 2006). The Launaye Slade Hallucination scale (LSHS) provided a measure of general hallucination proneness. In Study 1, OBEers reported significantly more perceptual anomalies on the CAPS. Study 2 demonstrated that OBEers and those scoring high on temporal-lobe instability and body distortion were significantly impaired making mental own-body transformations. The Braithwaite team's results are consistent with the hypothesis that there is a disruption in temporal lobe and body-based processing underlying OBEs.

OBES AND PSYCHEDELIC DRUGS

In a formative review, David Luke (2012) from the University of Greenwich, writes:

> Ever since the beginning of the 20th century when Western scientists and academics began earnestly turning their attention to psychedelics there has been a clear association between the use of these substances and the transpersonal or paranormal experience. Indeed, those people most readily associated with the discovery and popularization of psychedelics also witnessed and explored both the transpersonal and the parapsychological dimensions that these substances induced, such as Albert Hofmann, Humphrey Osmond, John Smythies, Aldous Huxley, Gordon Wasson, Timothy Leary, Ken Kesey, Duncan Blewett, Walter Pahnke, James Fadiman, and Stanislav Grof, to name but a few. (Luke, 2006; Stevens, 1988).

Luke's review focuses on psychoactive substances that induce visionary and trance-like experiences, drugs and sacramentals such as mescaline, lysergic acid diethylamide (LSD), psilocybin, ayahuasca, N, N-dimethyltryptamine (DMT), marijuana (treated as a psychedelic) and ketamine, but not opiates or cocaine. Following Osmond, the term 'psychedelic' is a category descriptor, which means 'mind manifesting' (Osmond, 1961: 76). As Luke points out: 'given that an altered state of consciousness (ASC) is assumed to be a common feature in the occurrence of subjective paranormal experiences ... and has often been incorporated into experimental attempts to induce ESP ... then visionary drugs are, potentially, a reliable means of accessing such a state.'

The relevant features of psychedelics have been categorised as follows:[15]

1. Increase in mental imagery, in both vividness and quality, and the dreamlike state.
2. Altered perception of self-identity, such as unity consciousness: the mystical experience of becoming one with everything in the universe.
3. Altered body perceptions and dissociation – this is of particular interest and relevance to the OBE.
4. Distorted sensory input.
5. Increased absorption and focused attention.
6. Increased empathy.
7. Emotional flexibility, which may also assist in negotiating the fear of psi.
8. Increased alertness and awareness.
9. Increased inwardly focused attention and awareness, and decreased external and bodily awareness.

---

[15] For full details and citations, see Luke (2012).

10. Increased spontaneity.
11. Sensitivity to subtle changes and intensity of feeling.
12. Physical relaxation (although this has been questioned).
13. Increased suggestibility.
14. Increase in intuitive thought processes.
15. Reduced critical conscious faculty and increased optimism towards impossible realities
16. Increased openness and extroversion.
17. Release of repressed and unconscious material into the conscious mind-brain.
18. Complex distortions, and transcendence, of space and time.

To Luke's list, I would add the following specific effects:

19. Easily distracted.
20. Tendency not to notice clear signals, especially in the periphery.
21. Temporal disintegration.
22. State-dependent memories.
23. Strong effects of set and setting.
24. Synaesthesia.
25. Noetic joy.
26. Closeness to nature.
27. Creativity.
28. Ineffability.
29. 'Bad trip'.
30. Loss of mental and physical control.

Luke has contributed personal accounts of ketamine-induced OBE ('K-OBE'). In discussing the links between anaesthetic states and the K-OBE, Luke states:

> [I]n repeated ketamine experiences I observed that the initial stages of anaesthesia and out-of-body-ness are accompanied by increasing difficulty in controlling one's body and a growing sense of body dysmorphia, in a non-clinical sense, in that part of one's body may appear longer (macrosomatognosia) or shorter (microsomatognosia), as described by Frederiks (1963). For example, on one occasion I recall being unable to successfully maneuver out of the door because my legs appeared to be the approximate distance of an entire football pitch away. It is observed that the relatively changing gradation in increased anaesthesia, body dysmorphia and motor control continues, with a sufficient dosage, as the trip intensifies towards a full-blown out-of-body experience, total anaesthesia, and ultimately no motor control. Indeed, while some K-OBEs are accompanied by autoscopy, even awareness of one's body can disappear at the peak of a high dose ketamine experience, even to the point of not realizing one actually has a body but instead just experiencing the present as a single point of consciousness

and nothing more. On one such occasion I was seemingly privileged to a view of earth from space and yet I did not even know who or what I was, let alone that I was human and apparently had a body. This relatively changing relationship between anaesthesia, motor control, out-of-body-ness, and even body-ownership-awareness is apparent on both entering and exiting the ketamine experience, although seemingly more so in exiting (although in reverse), as the entrance to a ketamine experience can often be abrupt, with a swift and intense onset, whereas the departure is more gradual. ... Observing the ketamine experience from the recipient's perspective, it appears that the anaesthesia occurs because one's consciousness is no longer connected to one's body, and certainly the OBE and anaesthesia are intimately connected, but why and how deserve further investigation and may shed light on the neurobiological factors of OBEs and NDEs. (Luke, 2012: 108)

The higher incidence of OBEs among regular users of psychedelics, including cannabis, is well established (Luke & Kittenis, 2005). Survey research investigating OBEs finds strong relationships between OBE reports and the use of psychoactive drugs, such as LSD and cannabis, with 18–37% of OBEs occurring through such drug usage (Blackmore, 1982, 1984; Blackmore & Harris, 1983). Tart's (1993) survey of Californian marijuana users, many of whom had also tried LSD, found reports of psi experiences, telepathy (69–83%), precognition (32%) and even PK (13%); 44% reported having OBEs.

Kjellgren and Norlander (2000) surveyed psychedelic drug users who reported OBEs, telepathy, empathy with other organisms, psychogeographic travelling and contact with entities, with heavier users reporting more experiences overall.

White (1997) found many reports of psi among dextromethorphan (DXM) users. DXM is a dissociative drug commonly found in cough remedies. DXM users report OBEs, NDEs, loss of the sense of causality, as well as a sense of presence, encounters with entities, and the occasional experience of ESP but not PK (cited in Luke & Kittenis, 2005).

David Luke and Marios Kittenis (2005) carried out an online survey with 139 Ps recruited through parapsychology or psychedelic interest groups. They completed a questionnaire detailing psychoactive drug-use behaviour and the frequency of occurrence of a number of paranormal, shamanic and mystical-type experiences. Luke and Kittenis replicated the patterns of drug-induced transpersonal experiences reported elsewhere, particularly the tendency to have telepathic experiences with cannabis, OBEs with ketamine, entity encounter experiences with N,N-dimethyltryptamine (DMT), and plant-spirit encounters with psychedelic plants. Except for precognition, they observed a clear trend for a greater proportion of drug users to report OBEs, telepathy, encounters with 'beings' and mystical experiences.

Systematic research on psychedelics, OBEs and psi is still in its infancy. The majority of research is unsystematic and uncontrolled, using survey data on retrospective self-reports collected online. More laboratory-controlled studies are needed to explore which drugs with which people with which levels of arousal and wakefulness tend to precipitate OBEs. Without these kinds of data, it is impossible to delineate the causal predetermining and precipitating processes from significant amounts of 'noise in the system'. With these reservations in mind, it is time to turn to explanations of the OBE.

EXPLANATIONS OF THE OBE

Susan Blackmore suggests three theories:

A. Something leaves the body (dualist theories in which we all have a soul, spirit or astral body). 1. The brain always releases the soul after death and if stimulated in the right way during life, it can do the same. 2. The brain is a container or conduit for the soul and prevents it leaving until death but in some circumstances the soul can be accidentally released during life.
B. Nothing leaves the body (dualism is false; mind and brain are not separate and there is no soul, spirit or astral body). 1. The brain can sometimes create the sensation, or hallucination, of leaving the body and when stimulated in the right way it does so. 2. The brain constructs our normal sense of being inside the body and when it malfunctions we have the illusion of leaving the body.
C. There are two different kinds of OBE: 'real' OBEs in which something leaves the body, and 'fake' ones which are illusions or hallucinations. (Blackmore, 2017: loc. 2000–17)

Blackmore rejects Type A and Type C theories in favour of Type B – *that nothing leaves the body in an OBE* – a view with which I concur. Theories B1 and B2 are consistent with everything we know about vivid mental imagery. The vivid hallucinations induced by hypnotic trance indicated the prominence of the lingual gyrus (Chapter 9). In the intense vivid imagery that occurs with a shamanistic brew used in the Amazon, ayahuasca, the lingual gyrus has also been observed to be active (de Araujo et al., 2012). Multisensory mental imagery is a 'foundation stone' of altered states of consciousness and anomalous experience. A breakdown in the integration of the bodily self and the subjective self may cause the OBE.

Olaf Blanke's 'Proprioceptive Breakdown Theory' suggests that the OBE and other autoscopic phenomena are caused by a breakdown of multisensory integration of the proprioceptive, tactile, visual and vestibular information of one's body due to 'discrepant central own body representations' (Blanke et al., 2016). Thus, OBEs could be the result of (1) a failure to integrate multisensory bodily information due to conflicting tactile, proprioceptive, kinaesthetic and visual signals; or (2) a disintegration between personal and extrapersonal space due to conflicting visual and vestibular signals caused by vestibular dysfunction. The vestibular system enables human beings to know 'Which way is up' and 'Where I am going'.

Two sets of vestibular organs – the three semicircular canals sense head rotation, and the otolith organs (the utricle and saccule) detect linear acceleration. Signals from the semicircular canals and otolith organs are carried in the vestibular nerve to the vestibular nuclei. Rapid projections from the vestibular nuclei to the oculomotor system allow eye muscles to compensate for head movement by moving to hold the image of the external world motionless on the retina (Kandel, 2013).

Blanke's Proprioceptive Breakdown Theory receives support from other investigators (Cheyne & Girard, 2009; Lopez, 2013). Lopez and Elzière (2018) found a significantly higher occurrence of OBE in patients with dizziness (14%) than in healthy Ps (5%). Most patients experienced OBE only after they started having dizziness for the first time, which was mainly related to peripheral vestibular disorders. They also found depersonalisation–derealisation, depression and anxiety as predictors of OBE in patients with dizziness, as well as migraine. Depersonalisation/derealisation was also a significant predictor of OBE in healthy controls. The authors concluded that OBE in patients with dizziness may arise from a combination of perceptual incoherence evoked by the vestibular dysfunction with psychological factors (depersonalisation–derealisation, depression and anxiety) and neurological factors (migraine).

In conclusion, following her nearly 50 years of research, Blackmore states:

> Like so many others who have OBEs I jumped to the obvious conclusion that my soul or astral body had left its physical shell and could think and feel and travel without it. It has taken a lot of thinking, experiencing, meditating and science for me to travel from that dualism to its utter rejection – to seeing the duality of body and mind, or physical and mental, as a feature of the way we model the world, not of the world itself. I no longer think that my soul left my body; that my astral body separated from its physical shell to travel on the astral planes or that my deep and unforgettable experience has anything to do with life after death. Thanks to decades of science and philosophy I have a far better idea of what happened to me during those special few hours back in 1970. I am alive here and now in a vivid and colourful world …. It is not this human being that is conscious. There is nothing it is like to be a bat, cat, dog or human being. There is only something it is like to be the stories we tell, or the models we construct, about what it's like to be me now. And that's enough. (Blackmore, 2017: loc. 6762)

Human beings each have our own particular, personal values and beliefs. As a person who has never experienced an OBE, I may have missed something profound, ineffable and noetic. I respect Blackmore's knowledge, spiritual awareness and interpretations of the OBE. However, for me, stories, models and 'being me now', enchanting though that may be, are not enough.

Here's why: you, me, everyone, depend on others and the world around us for security, safety and equilibrium. Agency, empathy and consciousness took aeons to evolve, and all of this, and more besides, would be wasted if we simply remain satisfied with 'being me now'. We have an in-built imperative to look out for each other and the planet. It is within the capability of the conscious brain to desire, envision and implement more sustainable ways of living on this planet. We neglect this imperative at our peril, for ultimately we may have no planet to call our home.

CONCLUSIONS ON OBE

1. Self is the experience of agency with a first-person perspective. The self's 'signature' is written in the brain's default resting state and its connections with the right TPJ where multisensory bodily information is integrated.
2. Proprioceptive breakdown in the TPJ's ability to integrate conflicting visual and vestibular signals may provide one explanation for the OBE.
3. Subjective experiences similar to the OBE may occur with drugs and other clinically significant circumstances, which suggests the need for a broad, generic explanation of OBE.
4. There are connections between the OBE and NDE, to be discussed next. As research on the OBE and NDE continues, we can expect to learn more about the self and the conscious brain.

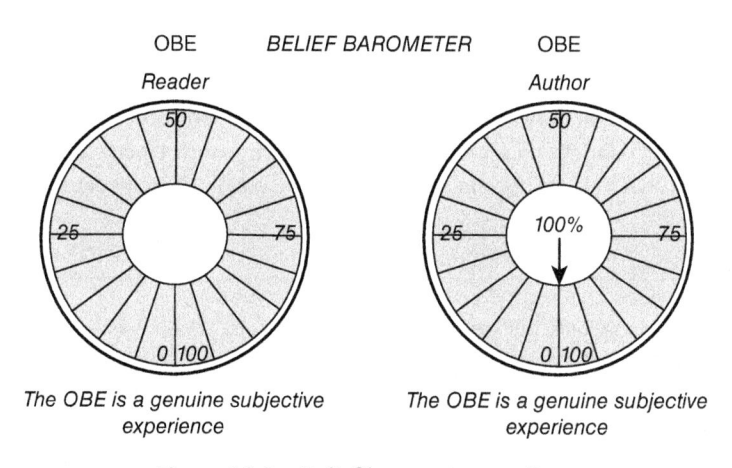

Figure 10.8 Belief barometer readings

NEAR-DEATH EXPERIENCES

When the time comes, and one never knows when that will be, then unless one 'passes' quickly, the end of life can be a fearful, uncertain affair with much angst for self, family and friends. Unexplained sudden death is frequently recorded as death from 'natural causes'. Many such deaths are due to sudden cardiac arrest, the largest cause of natural death. 'Old age' is not a scientifically recognised cause of death; a more direct cause is sought, although it may not be established in certain cases. Deaths caused by active intervention or 'unnatural' causes are usually from accidents, misadventure (accident following a wilful and dangerous risk), suicide or murder. A person's death is recorded on their death certificate completed by a doctor. In the vast majority of cases, the cause of a person's death is known and can be recorded with adequate certainty (Marks, Murray, & Estacio, 2018).

Brain death is irreversible brain damage causing the end of independent respiration and is regarded as indicative of death. When a person is 'brain dead', the brain can no longer function. The three essential features in brain death are coma, absence of brainstem reflexes and apnoea. The brain will not recover function and the person is considered dead. Clinicians can support the heart with medication and also provide oxygen through a ventilator or breathing machine. The person's body can be supported for days and, sometimes, even weeks. However, without a functioning brain, the person can no longer be considered as living. A brain death diagnosis is final and cannot be reversed. Prior to the time of death, in addition to any pain or anxiety, there can sometimes exist altered mental states that transform the near-death experience into an episode of meaning, peace and joy.

Near-death experiences (NDEs) have been defined as 'unusual, often vivid and realistic, and sometimes profoundly life-changing experiences occurring to people who have been physiologically close to death, as in cardiac arrest or other life-threatening conditions, or psychologically close to death, as in accidents or illnesses in which they feared they would die' (Greyson, Kelly, & Kelly, 2009). NDEs are reported by 10% to 20% of people who have come close to death (Greyson, 2014). Most individuals react to a life-threatening trauma with intense fear and anxiety that may last long after the threat has subsided.

I can vouch for the qualities of the NDE from a direct personal encounter. While on a visit to Cuba, I went swimming in the sea at a beach near Havana.

> On entering the sea, one could tell the ocean floor felt quite steep. Swimming only 15–20 meters from the shore, I was already well out of my depth. The sea was choppy and, without realising, I was caught by a riptide and was being pulled away from the shore. I attempted to swim back towards shore but it was proving impossible and I was struggling against the current. Before very long, I had already swallowed two or three large gulps of sea water. Very quickly things were getting out of hand and the uncontrolled swallowing of water became life threatening. This was not swimming as I had ever known it and things were rapidly getting out of control. Quite suddenly I had the feeling that things were becoming hopeless, that I was being dragged down, and that the next gulp or two of sea water could be my last. I floated on my back to conserve energy. It was hard not to swallow more water as the waves lapped over my floating body. I looked back to the shore. I could see a few people but they seemed a long distance away, relaxing in the midday sun. Nobody else was swimming. Nobody realized what was happening. The distance to the shore had stretched out and people on the beach seemed a mile away and quite oblivious that this crazy swimmer was on the brink of drowning. Weirdly, it all seemed

> inevitable, uncontrollable, as if there was nothing anybody could do. I 'belonged' to the ocean – it was swallowing me up and this was 'it', the end of 'me'.
>
> Somewhere inside, an automatic survival force sprang into gear, which pushed my right arm upwards to wave frantically and my voice began shouting for help.
>
> By this point, time had almost stopped still, with what could only have been a few precious final seconds stretching into an indefinitely long time. There was an uncanny silence, no sound from the wind, no sound from the waves, nothing at all, just one vast sky, and lapping water all around. I felt strongly connected with Nature, a sublime, noetic state, impossible to translate into words. I took what I thought would be my last look at the sky as if to say 'Goodbye'. It was gloriously beautiful. I was in a kind of dream, in unity with Nature. My fear had gone. I was saying 'Goodbye' without a single pang of fear.[16]
>
> Then, out of nowhere, the silence was broken by the sudden arrival of a swimmer to save me. He used the rescue technique I had learned at swimming club and took me swiftly back to the shore. This total stranger saved my life. I never discovered who he was nor even his name. In a flash, he had disappeared as quickly as he had arrived. It was as if nothing of moment had happened.
>
> Half an hour later, back at my hotel, I came across a family having lunch on the balcony of the fourth floor with a view of the beach. From there, the very spot where I had almost drowned was in clear sight.
>
> 'What did you do this morning?' they inquired. 'I went swimming,' I said.
>
> 'Did you hear what happened at the beach?' they inquired. 'No ... ', I replied, hesitatingly.
>
> 'Someone drowned.'
>
> 'No, they didn't drown', I said, 'they were rescued. That someone was me.'

To date, this incident is my only NDE. It was a small miracle. A total stranger out of the blue saved my life and, a few moments later, disappeared. *Who were you? Where are you? Are you still alive?*

Post-traumatic stress disorder (PTSD) with flashbacks, nightmares, significant distress and dissociative phenomena often follow traumas such as near-drowning. However, PTSD did not occur in my case, perhaps because the trauma was replaced so quickly by a deep sense of relief. NDE is said to be peaceful, joyful, otherworldly. I understand these feelings. I experienced a quietness, not peace or joy exactly, but a timeless silence, a feeling of inevitability, a 'This is it' feeling. The NDE is sometimes claimed to bring long-term positive changes, decreases in fear and anxiety and increased positive affect (Greyson & Stevenson, 1980; Groth-Marnat & Summers, 1998). Unsurprisingly, in my case, it felt great to be alive.

---

[16] At no point did I experience an OBE, not then, or on any other occasion.

A gift. Long term, I am unaware of any major changes; subtle changes may be happening but, if so, beyond conscious awareness. Typically, NDEs include a transcendence of space, time and self; feelings of peace and euphoria; an encounter with a bright light, religious figures or deceased relatives (Greyson & Stevenson, 1980). I can acknowledge a sense of transcendence, a stretching of space and time standing still. The positive after-effects of NDE contrast with those seen in PTSD, but they have received relatively little scientific attention (Britton & Bootzin, 2004). More research could be done on these.

The Greyson NDE Scale

Bruce Greyson (1998) suggested an incidence of NDE in the range 9–18%. In 1983, he constructed a 16-item scale from a pool of 80 'manifestations' characteristic of NDEs (Greyson, 1983). The scale successfully differentiated those claiming NDEs from those with qualified or questionable claims. Answers to items are on a 3-point scale – e.g. the answers to question 1 state: 2 = Everything seemed to be happening all at once; 1 = Time seemed to go faster than usual; 0 = Neither. A score of 7 is considered an NDE.[17]

The items are as follows:

1. Did you have the impression that everything happened faster or slower than usual?
2. Were your thoughts speeded up?
3. Did scenes from your past come back to you?
4. Did you suddenly seem to understand everything?
5. Did you have a feeling of peace or pleasantness?
6. Did you have a feeling of joy?
7. Did you feel a sense of harmony or unity with the universe?
8. Did you see, or feel surrounded by, a brilliant light?
9. Were your senses more vivid than usual?
10. Did you seem to be aware of things going on that normally should have been out of sight from your actual point of view as if by extrasensory perception?
11. Did scenes from the future come to you?
12. Did you feel separated from your body?
13. Did you seem to enter some other, unearthly world?
14. Did you seem to encounter a mystical being or presence, or hear an unidentifiable voice?
15. Did you see deceased or religious spirits?
16. Did you come to a border or point of no return?

NDE received wide attention in 2001 when an article in one of the world's most respected medical journals, *The Lancet*, implied that the self is not simply what

---

[17]My NDE scored 7.

the brain does, but may exist independently of it. A Dutch cardiologist, Pim Van Lommel, and his team aimed to establish the cause of the NDE and 'assess factors that affected its frequency, depth, and content' (Van Lommel, Van Wees, Meyers, & Elffich, 2001). The prospective study included 344 consecutive cardiac patients[18] who had been successfully resuscitated after cardiac arrest in 10 hospitals. Van Lommel's team compared demographic, medical, pharmacological and psychological data between patients with and without NDE after resuscitation. They followed up the groups two and eight years later. A total of 62 patients (18%) had reported NDE, of whom 41 (12%) described a core experience. NDE was not associated with duration of cardiac arrest or unconsciousness, medication or fear of death. Significantly, more patients with an NDE died within 30 days of CPR, validating the NDE reports.

Van Lommel's team found that any transformation after NDE took several years and differed from those of patients who survived cardiac arrest without NDE. The investigators' conclusion was, 'We do not know why so few cardiac patients report NDE after CPR, although age plays a part. With a purely physiological explanation such as cerebral anoxia for the experience, most patients who have been clinically dead should report one'. From this statement, one might infer that the investigators had favoured a non-physiological explanation. Personally, I would not rule out vivid imagery.

Pim Van Lommel's *Lancet* study was roundly criticised. To quote one critic, Jason Braithwaite (2008):

> Based on their findings, van Lommel et al. (2001) concluded that we now require a new approach to consciousness – one that gives provision for non-irreducibility of the mind to the brain. In other words, the mind is not what the brain does and may indeed be independent of it. This neo-dualism is worrying. It is worrying as it appears to be primarily based on a potent combination of both factual and logical errors concerning the role of the brain in mental experience. The present paper will argue that the conclusions van Lommel et al. propose are at least premature and are at most unfounded. As such, the van Lommel study poses no serious challenge at all to current neuroscientific accounts of the NDE.

Van Lommel's study was followed by a book where he gave free rein to his imagination with speculation and phantasmagoria (Van Lommel, 2010). Van Lommel advocated the Survival Hypothesis in which the mind can become 'unhinged' from the brain: following tradition in NDE research, the self – aka the 'soul 'or 'spirit' – humans survive bodily death (Moody and Hill, 1976; Siegel, 1980). Ancient cultural and religious traditions implant survival as a deep conviction, as the tombstone epigraphs in any graveyard readily confirm. Even Blackmore

---

[18]Obtaining a series of 344 consecutive cardiac patients was no mean feat.

(1996) states that 'it is probably a matter of personal preference whether to interpret the NDE as a glimpse of the life beyond or the product of the dying brain' (p. 75). The unfalsifiable nature of the Survival Hypothesis provides sustenance to believers everywhere. When a survival advocate says they have proof after clinical death, the provenance of the memories is impossible to determine.[19] In terminal illness, living with belief of survival brings higher well-being than non-belief (Reed, 1987). Spiritual beliefs have positive associations with well-being (Nelson, Rosenfeld, Breitbart, & Galietta, 2002).

Lacking the means to test the Survival Hypothesis, it is important to search for empirical evidence about the veridicality of OBE/NDE. Interestingly, in certain cases the NDE also includes an OBE. This fact opens the door to a testable hypothesis that, while out of the body, the subject may perceive objects that would be invisible from the in-body vantage point. Based on Charles Tart's 'Shelf Test' (Tart, 1968), the ability to see from a higher level would provide a 'bird's-eye view'.

THE 'BIRD'S-EYE VIEW'

The 'Bird's-Eye View', or 'BEV', hypothesis was tested in a large four-year study called 'AWAreness during REsuscitation' (AWARE). This study of cardiac arrest included a test of the veridicality of perceptions during the OBE part of the NDE (Parnia et al., 2014). To assess the accuracy of the BEV claim, 50 to 100 shelves were installed near the ceiling in the resuscitation areas in a number of hospitals where cardiac arrest resuscitation was likely to occur. Each shelf displayed an image that was only visible from a viewpoint above the shelf. The BEV hypothesis predicts that the images on the shelves would be veridical (accurate) if and only if the patient has any visual awareness from a BEV vantage point high enough to see the image. The results tell a disappointing story for survivalists.

Of 2,060 cardiac arrests that occurred during the study, 140 patients survived. Of these, 101 patients gave detailed interviews, of whom nine reported an NDE. Some 46% of the cardiac arrest survivors reported memories within seven themes: fear, animals/plants, bright light, violence/persecution, déjà vu, family, recalling events post-cardiac arrest, 9% had NDEs; while 2% described awareness with explicit recall of 'seeing' and 'hearing' actual events related to their resuscitation. Only 22% of cardiac arrest events took place in the critical and acute medical wards where the BEV shelves had been installed. Disappointingly for the BEV hypothesis, only two survivors recalled any detailed BEV memories of the physical environment. One is alleged to report an accurate BEV, while the other was reputedly too ill to be interviewed in-depth. The unique BEV patient claimed to have 'risen' to near the ceiling where he 'looked down' on his physical body and 'saw' a nurse and another man, who he described as 'bald and quite a chunky

---

[19]Patients might perceive something before entering or on the way out of an NDE and, subsequently, create a visual recall about it (Agrillo, 2011).

fella', wearing blue 'scrubs' and a blue hat (hmmm – fascinating; nothing actually 'seen' on any shelves, apparently). The next day, the patient claimed to recognise the same man working on the ward. The medical records confirmed the use of a defibrillator (no surprises here) and the role that the 'bald, chunky' man had played during the resuscitation. This solitary report of a defibrillator and a bald, chunky man in a blue uniform[20] is the best piece of BEV evidence this huge four-year study could discover. Unfortunately, this cannot be accepted as definitive evidence because the description is far too vague and non-specific. Anybody in any hospital anywhere in the world could easily produce a similar report and it would never cause waves. To the best of this author's knowledge, no well-controlled study has ever produced evidence supportive of the BEV hypothesis in any peer-reviewed journal. Thus, the paranormal hypothesis of OBE/NDE remains unconfirmed, yet not disconfirmed. *There is no scientific evidence of survival, BEV or any other 'miracle' associated with the OBE or NDE.*

If not here, where else should one look?

A BRAIN PREDISPOSED TO NDE BY EARLY TRAUMA

According to AWARE, around 90% of cardiac arrest survivors do not experience NDE. Greyson (1998) indicated an incidence of 9–18%. How is the small minority of NDE cases to be explained? Exploring life histories of NDErs and their brains makes two sensible starting points. Michael Marsh (2016) explored both. Marsh suggests NDE experiencers' brains may be predisposed to NDE/OBE by different kinds of crisis or trauma:

> An analogous occurrence is post-traumatic stress disorder (PTSD), for whom following the endurance of a severe, life-threatening crisis, there is a marked later change in phenotypic behaviour as well as manifest epigenetic changes to the genome (Mehta et al., 2013). For many PTSD candidates, there is a clear history of childhood abuse – verbal, physical, even sexual. And with other forms of fearful, threatening assault, including facing a gun or knife, or undergoing rape, the residual horrifying trauma of such encounters can be persistent and hence life-destroying. These early influences have profound, long-lasting influences on subjects' subsequent mental profiles – however that profile may be realised in later years ... And if severely stressful occasions interfere with later life behaviours, might not lesser impacts likewise lead to other forms of deviant or unexpected behavioural responsiveness?
>
> Previous demographic observations on ND/OBE subjects have not elicited general factors (ethnicity, gender, age, profession, social class) of

---

[20]In hospitals, bald, chunky men wearing blue are not all that unusual. Not all of them are doctors.

apparent relevance. Thus, other deeper factors need to be considered, and appropriate methods employed in the exposure of their contributory role(s). The interdependence of gene and environment is not well explored in terms of ND/OBE ... (Marsh, 2016: 18)

That the brains of NDE/OBE experiencers are predisposed to SPE by early trauma fits the 'Trauma + Dissociation' Theory proposed in Chapter 2. Evidence supportive of the theory comes from Britton and Bootzin (2004), who compared NDErs with controls. Admission to the NDE group required life-threatening physical distress as the result of an accident or other injury and a minimum score of 7 on the Near Death Experience Scale (Greyson, 1983). Life-threatening events included accidents (43.5%), medical complications (17.4%), heart attacks (17.5%), allergic reactions (8.7%) and suicide attempts (8.7%). Head trauma was sustained in 21.7% of the accidents. However, life-threatening situations before the age of 5 were *not* included. Also, the high rate of head trauma should have biased the sample towards having higher rates of brain damage symptoms. Britton and Bootzin (2004) compared the personality profiles, sleep and EEG activity of 23 NDE experiencers with a group of 20 controls. As predicted, they found that some NDE/OBE Ps showed signs of subclinical structural damage in the temporal lobes. Dissociative Experiences Scale scores were significantly higher in the NDE group than in the controls ($p < .05$, one tailed test). The NDE group also exhibited different sleep patterns than the controls.

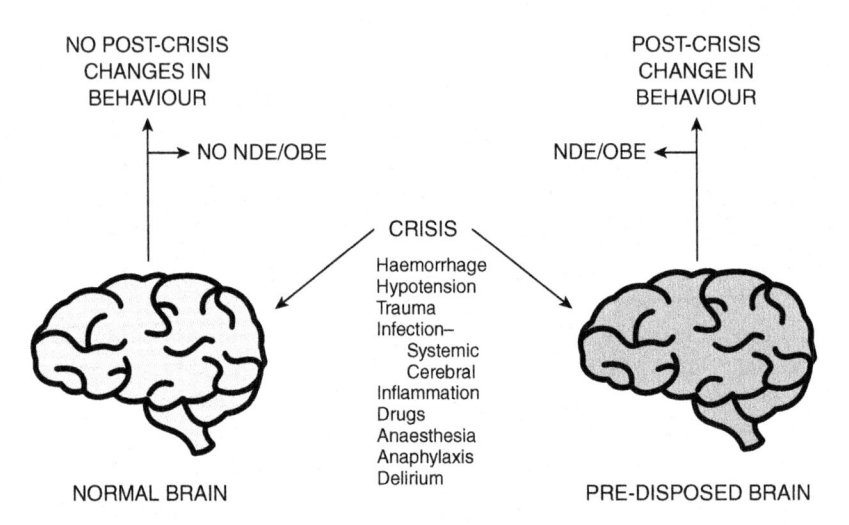

Figure 10.9 The theory that NDE arises following brain changes post-crisis or post-trauma. This theory is another version of the Homeostasis Theory.

Reproduced from Marsh (2016).

They slept about an hour less, had longer REM sleep latency and had fewer REM sleep periods than the controls.

Based on the findings of Britton and Bootzin and others, Marsh suggests that 'Some analogous form of cerebral pre-disposition could be the initiating trigger (Figure 10.9) which exposes these subjects to an altered behavioural phenotype following exposure to acute psychological or physiological crisis (infection: inflammation: dissociating drug usage: haemorrhage: child-birth ... '

DISSOCIATION AND OBE/NDE

Following trauma or crisis, the self may become compartmentalised and detached from bodily sensations, which signifies *dissociation*. Ring and Rosing (1990) surveyed 74 NDErs and 54 persons interested in NDEs with a questionnaire to assess psychological factors influencing susceptibility to NDEs and to measure after-effects. NDErs were not found to be more fantasy-prone than control Ps, but they reported having had greater sensitivity to 'non-ordinary realities' as children and a higher incidence of child abuse and trauma. NDErs reported a greater incidence of childhood abuse and trauma for all five components: physical mistreatment, psychological abuse, sexual abuse, neglect and a negative home atmosphere. NDErs also gave higher scores on a measure of psychological dissociation. In addition to substantial shifts in values and beliefs, NDErs reported psychophysical changes following their NDEs.

Irwin's (1993b) study with a postal survey of 121 Australian university students provided data relevant to the 'Trauma + Dissociation' Theory. It offered only partial support. The study failed to identify a dissociative response style in the NDErs. However, the NDErs reported a distinctive history of traumatic childhood events.

In another questionnaire study, Greyson (2000) invited 96 individuals who had self-reported NDEs, and 38 individuals who had come close to death but had not reported NDEs to complete the NDE scale and a measure of dissociative symptoms (the Dissociative Experiences Scale). NDE experiencers reported significantly more dissociative symptoms than the comparison group. NDE depth was positively correlated (.26) with dissociative symptoms, although the level of dissociative symptoms was substantially lower than that of patients with dissociative disorders. The pattern of dissociative symptoms reported by people with NDEs was consistent with a non-pathological dissociative response to stress, but not with psychiatric disorder.

Evidence of dissociative tendencies in OBErs was found by Murray and Fox (2005) in a questionnaire study with 243 respondents, 62 of whom reported at least one OBE. Respondents reporting a previous OBE scored significantly higher on measures of somatoform dissociation, self-consciousness and body dissatisfaction, but lower in confidence in their physical self-presentation than non-OBE respondents.

Overall, the evidence gives strong support to the Homeostasis Theory. The OBE and NDE are both commonly associated with a history of childhood trauma and abuse and adults' dissociative tendencies at subclinical or clinical levels. There is no shame here. An abused child or young adolescent can do little or nothing to stop the overpowering abuse against them. The homeostatic defence of dissociative freezing is usually the only response available, while older and stronger victims might be able to take flight or even fight. All of the guilt and all of the shame should be owned by the abusers. Innocent victims require help, support and understanding if they are ever to vanquish the pain and after-effects of their traumas.

From a scientific viewpoint, any convincing attempt to investigate the Homeostasis Theory must include a built-in ability to falsify it, which requires prospective investigations with large cohorts of people. This can best be achieved by identifying people who are and who are not victimised by trauma in childhood, people who enter and do not enter dissociation, and those who have and do not have SPEs, OBEs or NDEs. Until such evidence is available, the Trauma + Dissociation Theory appears a promising avenue to pursue but more robust evidence is clearly necessary. We turn next to consider explanations of the NDE.

EXPLANATIONS OF NDE AND KINDRED ANOMALOUS EXPERIENCE

NDEs are subjectively compelling. They often contain noetic feelings of peace, joy, white light, encounters with – or images of – significant figures, and there can be transcendence in space and time. It has been suggested that these experiences stem from brain changes and/or psychological responses to the perception of danger or threat. A summary of theories of NDE is shown in Table 10.1.

In spite of all of these available explanations, Enrico Facco and Christian Agrillo (2012) reported a case with many of the NDE features *but entirely in the absence of any life-threatening fear or trauma.* This evidence is theoretically incompatible with any of the hypotheses listed in Table 10.1, suggesting that a broader interpretation of the phenomenon is required.

The P was an electro-technician who came under observation because he had sought advice regarding a strange experience a few years earlier, when going through a divorce. He gave the following account:

> I was spending my summer holidays in the mountains with my four-year-old child. I had recently separated from my wife; it was a difficult time. One evening, while I was in the room where we were staying, I suddenly saw a great white light. It was not dazzling, but its whiteness was unnatural, I mean it did not seem to be like the white light from natural or artificial sources we know, nor did it come in from outside. Then, some balls of light appeared; I did not count them, but there

Table 10.1 Neurobiological and psychological explanations of NDE

Neurobiological hypotheses	Psychological hypotheses
Altered blood gas level	Expectation
• Hypoxia	
• Anoxia	
• Hypercapnia	
Periphery-to-fovea retinal ischemia	Depersonalisation
Neurological factors	Derealisation
• Epilepsy	
• Excitotoxic damage (glutamate)	
• Neurotransmitter imbalance	
• REM-sleep intrusion	
• Temporal lobe disorders	
• Multisensory breakdown – right angular gyrus dysfunction	
Pharmacological factors	Dissocation
• Opioids	
• Steroids	
• Ketamine	
• Hallucinogens	
	Personality
	Birth model
	False memories

Reproduced from Facco and Agrillo (2012) under a Creative Commons Attribution Licence.

were perhaps five or six, and they could have been about 1.5 meters in diameter. These balls were translucent with the same colour as the light, but less transparent and thicker, though I noticed that they did not cast any shadow. At the time, I had a profound feeling as if all the beings of the world were within me and, at the same, I felt as if I were within them. The source of light was ellipsoid. It was Love and Joy, and I felt a sort of stream through me. I use the term 'stream', but it was not so clearly definable. I cannot use the term 'wind', because wind comes from outside, while I felt this stream inside me. I was so enraptured that I had stopped breathing. I was fully lucid, however, and realized that I was not breathing, so I started breathing again, but my breathing disturbed the vision and, after a few breaths, it vanished. (Facco & Agrillo, 2012: 490)

The man had rejected any form of religion as a reaction to a Catholic college he had attended during his adolescence. The experience was powerful and had greatly surprised him with a profound transformation. As a consequence, he had overcome any fear of death, which he saw as 'an intrinsic, inseparable part of life, and of an ineffable divine beyond any conventional concept'. He was continuing to search for the meaning of the experience and of life itself. His score on the Greyson (1983) scale was 16 by affirming the following items: (a) vision of a supernatural light; (b) complete loss of the sense of time; (c) peacefulness; (d) deep joy; (e) empathic fusion with the whole world; (f) clear perception of a reality beyond the ordinary world; (g) understanding everything about the universe; and (h) encounter with entities.

After his experience, he felt the need to write his thoughts down in a poem, symbolising the 'immanence of an impersonal divine in the world and its loss with the exclusive use of logic, reasoning and erudition'. Facco and Agrillo (2012) reported that this putative 'NDEr' remained unable to explain his profoundly noetic experience, causing him disappointment.

Facco and Angrillo (2012) concluded that:

> NDEs cannot be explained solely by the closeness to death or by the etiology of the precipitating factor. The question whether the NDEs' extraordinary features can be fully explained by cerebral activity is still a matter of debate and a challenge awaiting the neuroscientific analysis of this phenomenon is to identify the neural correlates of such a physiologically real yet unexplained cognitive experience … NDE research might benefit from the introduction of a new terminology to account for 'NDE-like' experiences. In addition to the use of closed NDE questionnaires, which only leave restricted choices for describing the experience, future studies should employ statistical examination of freely expressed NDEs narratives using automated user-independent qualitative analyses of their content.

CONCLUSIONS ON NDE

1. The NDE is a profound, subjectively 'real' noetic experience involving vividly experienced imagery and an altered state of consciousness, which may include bright white light, imagery of deceased relatives or religious figures, and transcendence of space and time.
2. Subjective experiences similar to the NDE may occur in the absence of near death, cardiac arrest or other clinically significant circumstances, suggesting the need for a more generic explanation than those offered in the literature.
3. As with subjective anomalous experiences more generally, and in support of the Homeostasis Theory, there is a statistical association between the NDE, early childhood trauma and dissociation.
4. The scientifically untestable Survival Hypothesis provides solace to patients and families when death is drawing ever closer. For obvious reasons, it remains unconfirmed but not disconfirmed, and will ever remain so.

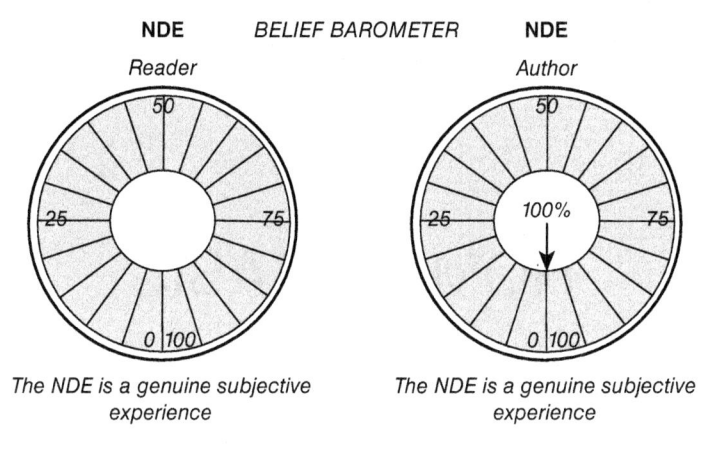

Figure 10.10 Belief barometer readings

QUESTIONS

1. Describe three features of the self.
2. Describe three theories of the self.
3. The OBE is one type of autoscopy. What are two other types?
4. What is the 'Proprioceptive Breakdown Theory' of OBE?
5. What is the 'Trauma + Dissociation Theory' of NDE?
6. What is the main problem with the latter theory?
7. What factors allow the Survival Hypothesis to survive?

11

HOMEOSTASIS

Letting the Genie Out of the Bottle

I believe in everything until it's disproved. So I believe in fairies, the myths, dragons. It all exists, even if it's in your mind. Who's to say that dreams and nightmares aren't as real as the here and now? (John Lennon)

Perceived reality: a person's subjective experience of reality, in contrast to objective, external reality.

Reality: in philosophy, that which genuinely exists, usually in contrast to that which only seems to exist. (APA Dictionary of Psychology, 2020)

> **Outline:** The hypnotic trance, the OBE and NDE are created out of who knows what by the conscious brain. There is something we cannot know directly, a powerful motivational force, the principle of homeostasis. Over four billion years, the architect of this grand design evolved parallel systems of homeostasis to regulate living organisms at all levels, cellular, physiological and mental. Homeostasis freely endowed every human being who has ever lived with a sense of self and three pillars of selfhood: purpose, agency and intention. A 'Reset Equilibrium Function', or 'REF' system of meta-control, keeps the continuous flow of mental and physical activity in order. The REF system delivers images, feelings and actions with a unifying sense of ipseity – the 'I am' centre for integrating and regulating (my) thoughts, (my) feelings, and (my) actions. The subjective anomalies reviewed in this book provide valuable clues to the nature of living systems or, in the vernacular, to what makes us 'tick'.

A scientific account of subjective anomalous experience ideally requires a General Theory. Without a General Theory, one is reduced to the endless gap-filling of a Polyfilla vision of science. The 'breaking news' – as far as this book is concerned – is the revolutionary concept of psychological homeostasis. After four billion years of evolution, homeostasis itself is far from new. Psychological homeostasis, however, as a theory of behaviour, is very new. There is nothing quite like it in behavioural science.[1] The story begins with evolution itself.

Conscious organisms adapt to each other and the environment because there is an inbuilt striving towards stability – a behavioural form of homeostasis. The theory flows out of recent concepts within evolutionary biology. One key part of behavioural homeostasis is called 'niche construction'. Niche construction is influenced by, and influences in return, evolutionary processes by generating less variation in selection than there would be without it (Marks, 2018).[2] The individual extends their ability to thrive by creating zones of safety and security in occupation and control of the environment (Laland, Odling-Smee, & Feldman, 2000). There are many examples: tools for hunting and 'defense',[3] fire for cooking, domestication of animals for food and/or friendship, language, money, goods, trade, agriculture, science, technology, engineering, medicine, culture, music and social media are all niches of safety, well-being and control. These are all forms of niche construction.

On an individual scale, here's a mundane example. Take a look around your personal workspace, study or bedroom. What do you notice? Do you see any posters, photos, DVDs, CDs, knick-knacks or trinkets? These all serve to make the place personal to you, to make it 'special', all yours and yours alone. Family, friends, social media, affiliations, associations, food preferences, habits, addictions, hobbies, sports, and many other things are all niches, as are your beliefs and values.[4] Any and all of the 'you-extensions' that you put into the world are parts of your constructed niche.

The underlying motivation for all of this outreaching, niche-building activity is a striving for safety, security equilibrium and control – in other words, homeostasis. Each and every individual has an in-built desire to create, project and preserve an identity of who they are now and wish to become in the future (Marks, 2018, 2019b). This theory has five characteristics that are rare in psychology: the theory of psychological homeostasis is: general, necessary, novel, evidence-based, and

---

[1] The General Theory explains: entrainment, rhythm and synchrony, approaching, avoiding and learning, consciousness, imagery, action, mood, emotion and its regulation, stress, coping, calming, smoking, drinking, gambling, eating, overeating, obesity, waking, sleeping, dreaming, and subjective well-being. See Marks (2018) for full details.
[2] Unfortunately, owing to laziness and greed, human niche construction is as destructive of the planet as it can be constructive and beneficial.
[3] The PC word for outright aggression.
[4] The sports teams you support, your musical tastes, interests, chosen mode(s) of transport, whatever you choose to do or wear, your hairstyle, hair colour, bodily accoutrements, piercings, tattoos, surgical alterations, where you hang out, and anything else that puts a piece of you into the world is niche construction.

continuous with a well-established principle in physiology. But we are not quite finished just yet. The General Theory also encompasses consciousness.

Enter mental images, feelings, and actions, the foundation stones of the conscious self. Every action is made with desire, intentionality and purpose. The specific means by which one achieves one's goals are controlled without awareness of exactly what one is doing. I know that I am writing these sentences and I am aware of the ideas that I want to express. But which specific keys I must press to produce these words is not the focus of my conscious attention. One can observe what one is doing if one wants to and change one's key tapping if the need arises – change one word here, another one there, and so on, ad infinitum – and the right amount of attention is there to steer one's actions and it always seems to be just enough. The less capacity one uses to control the specifics of action, the more capacity is left over for executive functions. One lets things happen automatically as far as possible without conscious direction from any higher executive level. These meta-level processes dictate the actions that are necessary to achieve one's goals and get things done. Each action is a means to an end, to take one from A to B with the least effort, the most satisfaction and the minimum of hassle and stress. The vast majority of actions contain highly practiced elements that run off automatically. If an action is performed more than once, it is never the same action; the second action is always different from the first, and the third always different from the second, and so on because the immediate prior context is always different, indefinitely so, way into the future. Goals are designed by the self, the agent of action, intentionally to create and optimise stability, safety and equilibrium.

In waking and sleep, the flow of images is the 'blood in the veins' of consciousness, the will to act, the incessant striving for stability, security and equilibrium. As long as we are alive, conscious and awake, the flow of awareness never stops protecting, harmonising and calming. When wide-awake, there is a continuous production of goal-directed behaviour. In lower wakefulness, goal-directedness gives way to vivid, fantasy-prone imagery and feelings are more autistic (McKellar, 1957b). When our circadian processes shift towards rest, thought slows down and self-control over mental activity becomes more passive. Ordered, logical thinking become unnecessary, and transitional states of free association, daydreaming or hypnagogic imagery take centre stage. As sleep beckons, action is unnecessary and the flow of rational thought almost ceases. In slow-wave sleep, images are memory spill-overs and dreams recount episodes from the recent day. With an absence of realistic thinking, the REM state gives fantasy and emotion free rein, and the ability to exert conscious control over the flow of imagery is absent.[5] Imagery goes haywire, following a structure and system all of its own and there is no ability to predict what will happen next.

---

[5] With the exception of partially lucid dreams (Barrett, 1992).

The goal of the flow of experience is to maintain equilibrium – it can only be described in this way – in cycles of activity with a goal, the means to reach it, and the consequences for the organism and objective world. The control system is organised hierarchically with a 'meta level', 'schema level' and 'automatised level'. The meta level sets the goals. The schema level controls the flow, making momentary adjustments. The automatised level delivers robotic routines that require no attention higher up. When one hammers a nail into a piece of wood, one checks whether the nail straight, whether it is going in properly, whether it has hit an obstacle, and so on. In cooking a soup, one tastes and seasons it with salt and pepper – not too much and not too little. The REF system, to be described later, has much in common with the 'TOTE' system of test/operate/test/exit, described by Miller, Galanter and Pribram (1960). The TOTE model assumes that one's actions are continuously guided by images of the environment, plans for attaining specific goals in the environment and the outcomes of one's behaviour. TOTE units are feedback loops through which particular plans are enacted, tested and terminated upon completion. Behaviour patterns comprise hierarchically arranged TOTE units that occur in a cyclical fashion. In driving along the highway, one keeps to one's lane, attends to the road, monitors the other vehicles, keeps an eye on one's speed, looks out for signs and warning signals, adjusting, adapting, correcting. The REF is a descendant of the TOTE, the process that gives purpose to every action, striving for equilibrium with desire and intentionality at every twist and turn of the road.

The behavioural control system uses feedback, modifying outputs, according to 'set-points'. The thermostat regulating a central heating system is one everyday example. When the temperature reaches the set temperature, the system switches off. It comes back on when the temperature drops below the threshold setting. Behaviours also operate using a system of 'switches', graded by degrees according to set points. Following billions of years of evolution, completely parallel systems of homeostasis operate in the body, mind and brain. Why need it be otherwise?

BRAIN HOMEOSTASIS

Homeostasis maintains equilibrium of body and brain in a continuously changing flow of environmental stimulation. Brain homeostasis is linked to plasticity, the brain's ability to change structure and function in light of experience (Kolb & Whishaw, 1998). The serotonin system is one of the brain's many systems of homeostasis. Serotonin (5-HT) is found in plants and predates the formation of neural tissue (Kang, Kang, Lee, & Back, 2007). Operating as a 'neurotransmitter', serotonin regulates feelings, moods, cognition, reward, learning, memory and numerous physiological processes. The source of serotonin is the raphe nuclei in the brain stem. The raphe nuclei send serotonin to many brain regions, integrating sensory and motor systems with endocrine, glial and vascular signals.

A large number of biological systems, behaviours and diseases are associated with serotonergic neurones (Azmitia, 1999)[6] (Figures 11.1 and 11.2). The homeostatic role of serotonin in the brain is shown in Figure 11.2. This suggests a model that incorporates globally projecting neurones divided into three orders of control.

Studies of the brain's 'connectome' show that the CNS is at once more complex and more simple than previously assumed. Regions of interest produce fluctuations in neural activity and patterns of activation. Networks occur at different organisational levels, from cell-specific regulatory pathways inside neurones to interactions between systems of cortical areas and subcortical nuclei. Architecture that supports cognition, feeling and action is found at the highest level of the cortical system. One study takes a huge leap forward because it places the physiological (Type I) and behavioural (Type II) forms of homeostasis within a single cortical system of control. That jolly old Franciscan friar, William of Occam, can smile again. ☺

Edlow, McNab, Witzel, and Kinney (2016) investigated the structures forming a 'central homeostatic network' (CHN) responsible for autonomic, respiratory, neuroendocrine, emotional, immune and cognitive adaptations to stress. These structures include the limbic system and frontal lobe.

Brian Edlow's research on the central homeostatic system explored the forebrain nodes that receive sensory information concerning external threats and internal metabolic derangements from the brainstem, resulting in arousal from

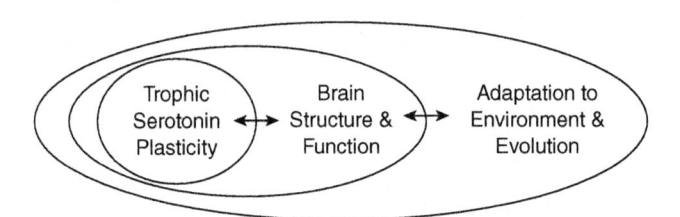

Figure 11.1 Brain homeostasis operating in three spheres. The inner sphere comprises brain homeostasis where serotonin (5-HT) neurones influence target-cell neuronal morphology. In the outer sphere, the interactions between the environment and the brain are shown. An ability to adapt to the environment has direct implications on evolution. Our model predicts that serotonin dysfunction results in maladjustment of the organism to the environment because of deficits in brain morphology.

Reproduced from Azmitia (1999), with permission.

---

[6]Azmitia states: 'If 5-HT [serotonin] is a regulator of homeostasis, then a dysfunction of serotonin should have major consequences. One consequence of lowered serotonin is depression. Suicide is the ultimate rejection of the evolutionary drive to survive.' In brains of suiciders, 5-HT neurones are found to be smaller and less numerous.

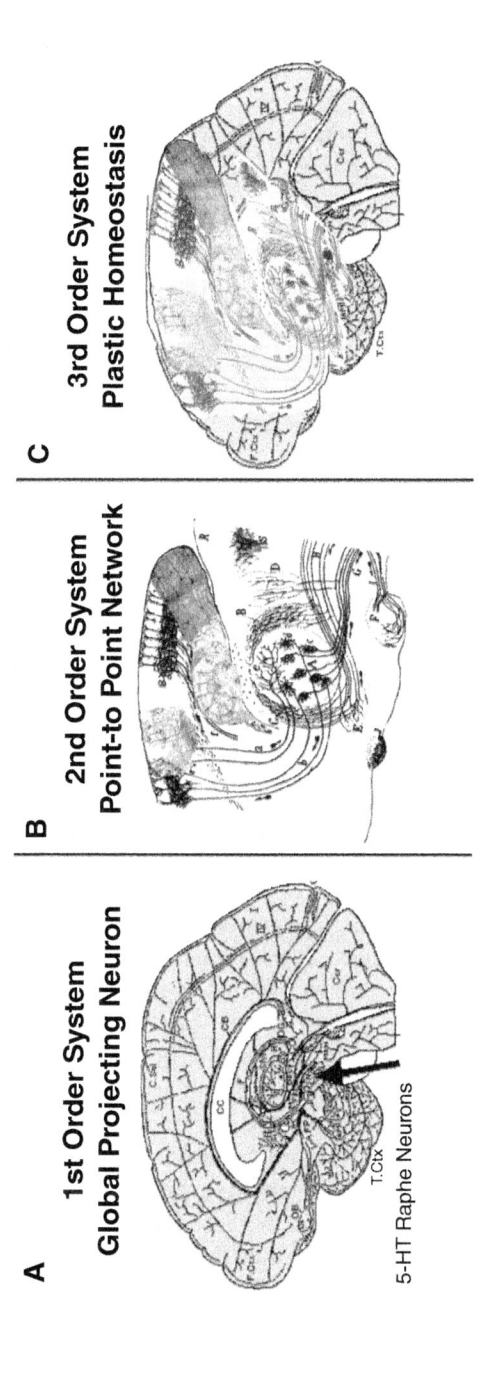

Figure 11.2 A model of the mind that incorporates globally projecting neurones and homeostasis. According to the model, brain regulation is divided into three orders of control:

A) 1st Order System — Global Projecting Neuron
B) 2nd Order System — Point-to Point Network
C) 3rd Order System — Plastic Homeostasis

A) The globally projecting neurones of 5-HT principally provide the unity, harmony and essence of mental expression, a first-order system. Globally projecting neurones are principally the monoamines (i.e. serotonin, norepinephrine and dopamine). These are all ancient molecules that served basic anti-oxidant and differentiating functions in unicellular organism. In the human brain these chemicals function as neurotransmitters (largely working by 'mass action' rather than acting exclusively through a specific synapse). In addition, these chemicals regulate cell differentiation (mitosis, migration and maturation) and are especially important in stimulating neuroplasticity of their target cells. These neurones have fine, highly branched axons that innervate the entire brain. The importance of this system to the mind is illustrated by the actions of 'mind-expanding drugs' that target these monoamines. These neurones can be considered first order.

B) The point-to point neurones underlie the quality, depth and speed of mind expression, a second order system .... The networks propagate through specific synapses and convey precise and rapid information. The point-to-point connections have increased in complexity as the brain has evolved, and the principal neurones (pyramidal and Purkinje) are large, multipolar cells with long, myelinated axons. These neurones can be considered the second-order system.

C) Both systems working together create a unique, complex and personable third-order system. Here lies the full expression of the mind based on a plastic neurone, which provides for the fluidity and changing states of consciousness. Homeostasis keeps two or more systems in balance. In the neuroplasticity mind model, the process is in constant flux and dependent on the inherent plasticity of the neuron. The two systems in balance are the globally projecting neurones and the point-to-point neurones. Both sets of neurones change their morphology in response to the actions of the other set.

Reproduced from Azmitia (2007), with permission.

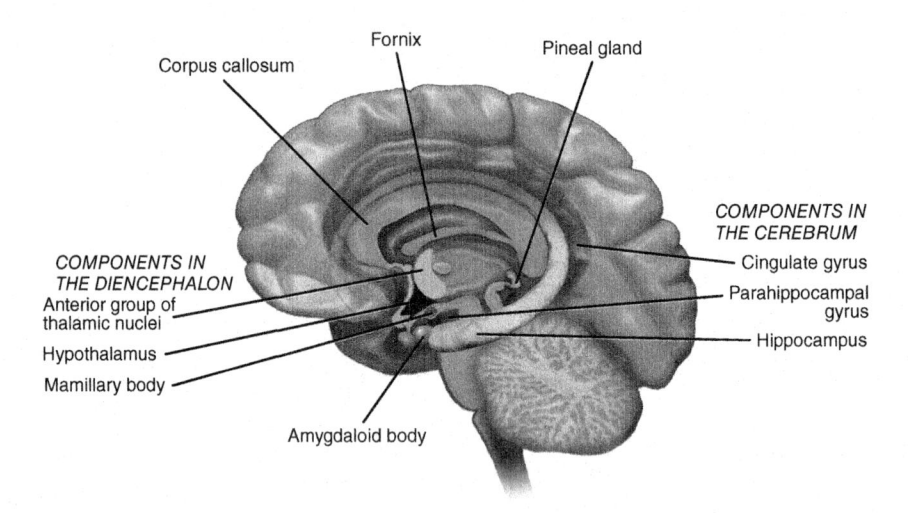

Figure 11.3 The limbic system is a set of brain structures located on both sides of the thalamus, immediately beneath the medial temporal lobe. The limbic system is activated in emotion, motivation, long-term memory and olfaction. It is central to the homeostatic stress responses of fight, flight or freeze.

Reproduced from the Medical Gallery of Blausen Medical (2014) under a Creative Commons Attribution 3.0 License.

sleep, heightened attention, vigilance during waking, and visceral and somatic motor defences. These findings suggest that homeostasis is mediated by ascending and descending interconnections between the brainstem and frontal cortex, which together regulate autonomic, respiratory and arousal responses to stress. The role of the limbic system in homeostasis complements the central autonomic network to produce 'flight, fight, or freeze'. Edlow's findings demonstrate that homeostasis of both types I and II are controlled by a single executive controller in the forebrain. The limbic system is located on both sides of the thalamus which, recent studies indicate, has a special role to play in consciousness (Redinbaugh et al., 2019).

That the homeostasis in the mind, brain and body share a single central homeostasis system is a beautiful example of how complexity reduces to simplicity in the central nervous system. If a single system is regulating homeostasis in body, brain and mind, then the REF system exists in the same brain networks available to the common ancestors of reptiles and mammals (the amniotes), which all have a well-developed limbic system (Bruce & Neary, 1995). In all vertebrates, behavioural states are controlled by common brainstem neuro-modulatory circuits, such as the serotoneric system. The cerebral cortex is not a mammalian invention either, but an ancient dorsal structure that predates the split between sauropsids and therapsids, the precursors of mammals (Laurent et al., 2016). Thus, a precursor of the REF system has existed for at least a third of a billion years.

PSYCHOLOGICAL HOMEOSTASIS IN PLAIN LANGUAGE

We switch now to look at behaviour using a principle from physiology. The nineteenth-century French physiologist, playwright and wine maker, Professor Claude Bernard, described how the *milieu intérieur* (bodily organs and fluids) requires stability:

'The stability of the internal environment is the condition for a free and independent life.'

Claude Bernard put away his wine making for an excellent cause: to discover the physiological control processes that exist in every living system. The process of homeostasis that Bernard described can be extended way beyond Physiology into the science of mind and behaviour. Bernard's basic postulate is the basis for a far-reaching new principle for the science of psychology:

'The stability of the external environment is the condition for a free and independent life.'

With this adaption of homeostasis from physiology into psychology, a whole new vista opens. One envisions a completely new way of thinking about mind and behaviour, motivation, thinking and emotion, all energised by a process of homeostasis. The quest for stability, security and equilibrium – so I believe – is the guiding force for all human thought, feeling and action. I have called this psychological form of homeostasis 'type II homeostasis' or the 'Reset Equilibrium Function' (REF).[7] We can even now imagine that the legendary genie has escaped from the bottle – a 'Theory of Everything' for psychological science. This idea is exciting and huge.

Every conscious living organism is automatically regulated by a system of corrective behaviours, thoughts and feelings: eating, drinking, sleeping and so on. Physiological homeostasis – 'type I homeostasis' – is a familiar concept since Claude Bernard sat in humble vintner's cottage in the 1860s to write his *Introduction to the Study of Experimental Medicine*.[8] In *A General Theory of Behaviour* (Marks, 2018), the same principle of homeostasis is proposed to undergird all human thinking, feeling, and behaviour.

The REF is always present; whatever one thinks, feels or does, the REF is jogging along with one every step of the way. The REF is not something one focuses attention on. There is no need to. The REF doesn't need that, because the 'boot is on the other foot': the REF is watching over every single thing that we think, feel or do. For the vast majority of the time the REF is operating outside of one's

---

[7]For a more detailed description of the REF theory, see Marks (2018, 2019).
[8]Bernard (1865/1957).

conscious experience, automatically taking care of everything, 100% of the time. Usually we are only conscious of the outcome, not the process. For a majority of time, almost everybody wants a calm and 'quiet life', minimising disturbances rather than make them worse. Through homeostasis, the waking brain triggers imagery, feeling and action in a continuous flow which, together with learned social norms and etiquette, minimise disruption to produce as tranquil life as is humanly possible. Unless they are being selfish or deliberately perverse, people can successfully achieve many of their goals without hurting or upsetting others along the way. Tooth-and-claw competition is avoided, especially in communities where the thriving of all is in the private interest of every individual. The battle for calmness and civility cannot be won indefinitely, however, because there is a finite risk that an unintended consequence such as an accident, or a calamity, or something worse might happen.

As long as we are in a healthful state, one's body, mind and 'spirit' efficiently adapt to changing circumstances by frequent resets and adjustments. From cradle to grave, the internal REF guarantees optimum levels of equilibrium, keeping everybody jogging along safely within their 'comfort zones'. The REF is wise, learns from experience, knows when to 'blow a whistle', or 'wave a flag' or 'wave play on'. The REF is fair, reasonable and cautious, checking all relevant circumstances before producing the penalty cards: 'yellow' for a minor infringement (making one feel guilty) or a 'red' for a major infringement (ignominy and humiliation). Whenever one strays beyond the permitted set range, the REF issues a corrective. The REF is fast, fair and flawless. Without the REF, human beings would be lost, surrounded by chaos with all hell breaking loose.

At every level, from the cell to the organism, from the individual to the population, and from the local ecosystem to the entire planet, homeostasis is the driving force towards stability, security and equilibrium. Homeostasis occurs in an infinite variety of forms throughout evolution, an inbuilt function with the sole purpose of producing equilibrium, both inside and outside the body. Conscious organisms are genetically endowed with both kinds of homeostasis, psychological (type I) and physiological (type II). Non-conscious organisms only have physiological homeostasis (type I).

Any set of processes is a subset of multiple networked processes coding, transferring and feeding back information inside the body and brain (Figure 11.4). Every process is connected with hundreds or thousands of other processes, any one of which can push a particular network out of equilibrium, which consequentially, requires resetting. As any particular process resets, there is a 'domino effect' among interconnected processes, which may themselves require a reset in a chain reaction. Thus, any individual reset can involve a reset of large parts of the entire system. Psychological and physiological processes operate in tandem to maximise the equilibrium for each particular set of functions.

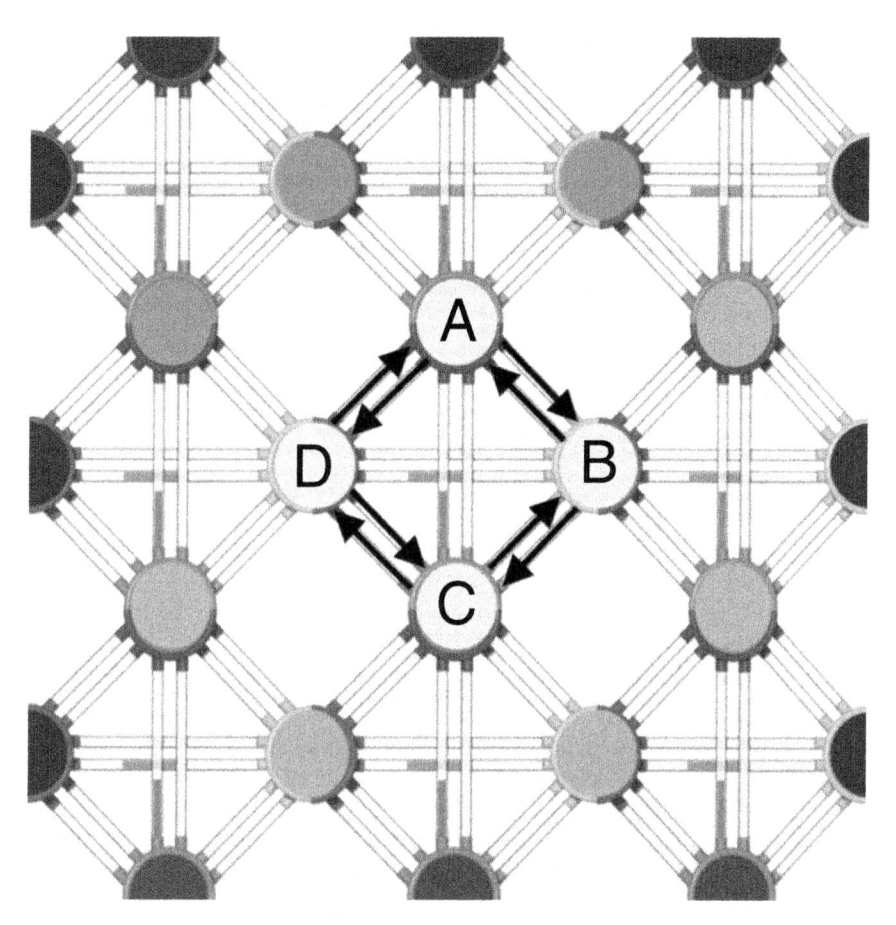

Figure 11.4 A network of interconnected processes (A–D) within a larger matrix of processes. Whenever equilibrium is disturbed, the Reset Equilibrium Function (REF) returns each process into its set range. An adjustment in one process may necessitate a compensatory adjustment in one or more of the other interacting processes until equilibrium is restored. Thus, when A stimulates B to lower its activity level, the reduced level in B stimulates C, D and A, in a chain reaction.

The General Theory explains the relevance of the REF to numerous psychological functions, including those where reset is a condition for change – e.g. feeling, excessive behaviours, smoking, drinking, gambling, overeating, pain, sleep loss and low well-being.[9] In all of these situations, the subject's

---

[9] The theory was originally developed to explain the rising incidence of obesity (Marks, 2015, 2016a, b), then extended into a general theory of behaviour (Marks, 2018) and consciousness (Marks, 2019b).

conscious acknowledgement that there is behaviour in need of change is of primary importance.

The central executive system enables organisms to mentally map the environment, observe events, image different scenarios to make predictions, test those predictions and act. The main purpose of the entire behavioural system is to retain equilibrium with the environment. Equilibrium can only be retained by predicting what is going to happen next. The enabler for modelling, predicting and acting is mental imagery. Mental imagery can, in principle, provide preparatory images in any sensory modality; for the majority, however, mental imagery is predominantly visual. On the other hand, imagining the smell and taste of a delicious meal, 'hearing' the sound of some enchanting music, and imagining scenes and feelings of relaxation from a recent holiday, or 'tasting' a delicious wine are all possible (Croijmans, Speed, Arshamian, & Majid, 2019). As noted previously, subjective paranormal experiences such as auras, remote healing and apparitions, are reported at significantly higher rates among people with vivid VVIQ (Vividness of Visual Imagery Questionnaire) scores in the open-eyes condition (Parra, 2015). A balance must be struck between successfully predicting future events with one's imagery and using it recreationally for daydreaming and fantasy. Reality and fantasy can easily clash.

The imagery system does not produce action by itself. It is complemented by the *schemata system*. Frederic Bartlett (1932) proposed that schemata are much more than elementary reactions ready for use: 'they are also arrangements of material, sensory at a low level, affective at a higher level, imaginal at a higher level yet, even ideational and conceptual'. Action is inextricably linked to perception, so that perceiving generally leads to acting in covert or overt form using schemata. Imagined simulation consists of covert performances in which specific intentions, purposes and actions are fulfilled (Marks, 1990). Mentally simulating an experience serves as a substitute for the corresponding experience (Kappes & Morewedge, 2016). A Mental Imagery Principle (MIP) can be stated as follows: 'A mental image is a quasi-perceptual experience that includes action schemata, affect, and a goal.' A system based on this principle is shown in Figure 11.5.

A huge variety of processes participate in the MIP. Involuntary images, persistent, unpleasant memories and repetitive habits may signify the development of difficult-to-control disorders – e.g., post-traumatic stress disorder, anxiety disorders, depression, eating disorders and psychosis. All are associated with repetitive visual intrusions concerning real or imaginary events that can be extremely vivid and detailed with highly distressing content (Brewin et al., 2010). Hallucinations are reported by people with a diagnosis of psychosis with a significant overlapping phenomenology with subjective paranormal experiences of precognition and out-of-the-body experience. One definition of hallucination states it to be 'any percept-like experience which (a) occurs in the absence of an appropriate stimulus, (b) has the full force of impact of the corresponding actual (real) perception, and (c) is not amenable to the direct or voluntary control of the experiencer (Slade & Bentall, 1988: 23). In the first two parts, hallucination is a form of mental imagery.

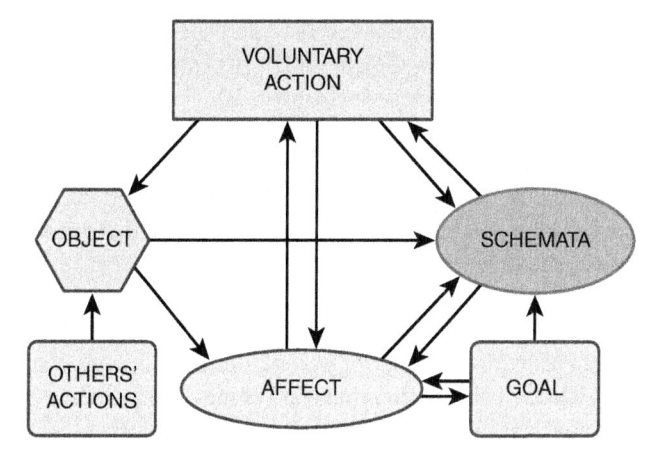

Figure 11.5 A model of action with six modules. Schemata control voluntary actions to operate on salient objects in the pursuit of a goal. Affect influences and is influenced by the goal, the schemata and the voluntary action (Marks, 2018, 2019b).

The third part provides the distinguishing feature because, in order to be beneficial, mental images need to be voluntary and controllable by the experiencer. The full spectrum of conscious experience includes subjective paranormal experience, dissociative states, voices, hallucinations, pseudo-hallucinations, OBEs and NDEs, all with varying degrees of voluntary control. The control system has different levels, including an executive level and a schema level. This duality of levels enables moment-by-moment adjustments to goal-seeking behaviour at the schema level.

In competent performers, speech, decisions, routines and many complex behaviours normally do not require any deliberate conscious control (Bargh & Ferguson, 2000). Afferents from the muscles and the activity of the cerebellum, where movement is organised, operate entirely preconsciously and produce no conscious images (Guell, Gabrieli, & Schmahmann, 2018; Schmahmann & Sherman, 2001).

Conscious imagery is an essential enabler in the planning and organisation of behaviour. Imagery enables simulation of action sequences at the object level without wasting energy or taking any risk. The object level interfaces with the social level in the public domain of shared activities and object levels. The possible likely outcomes of alternative actions is appraised prior to any course of action. In this way, conscious mental imagery is a 'mental toolbox', to enable the user to plan, predict and optimise future physical and social activity.

THE NATURE AND FUNCTION OF IMAGERY

Mental imagery, such as 'pictures in the mind's eye', is an equivalent process but not identical to perception. Mental images can stand for perceptions of real objects, or they can be purely made-up fantasies. Similar, but not identical, anatomical patterning of neural activity for imagery and perception occurs in the cerebral cortex (Dijkstra, Bosch, & van Gerven, 2019; Kosslyn, Alpert, & Thompson, 1997; Pearson, Naselaris, Holmes, & Kosslyn, 2015). Similar neural representations of imagined and perceived stimuli are observed in the visual, parietal and frontal cortex for perception and imagery which seem to rely on similar top-down connectivity. Dijkstra et al. (2019) suggest bottom-up processing may be absent during imagery. Others believe exactly the opposite. A brain coordinate-based meta-analysis of 40 studies found 11 activated cortical areas in imagery, the majority in the left hemisphere (Winlove et al., 2018). This large study found that imagery is associated with activated regions predominantly in the left hemisphere, with the superior parietal lobule showing consistent activation, suggesting the role of attentional processes. This finding confirms an EEG study discovering activation of the left posterior cortex in vivid visual imagery (Marks & Isaac, 1995). When Ps have their eyes closed, activation of area V1, which includes the lingual gyrus, occurs in visual mental imagery. Thorudottir, Sigurdardottir, Rice, Kerry, Robotham, Leff, et al. (2020) investigated the brain of an architect who had lost the ability to imagine. The only area of selective lesion was a small patch in the left fusiform gyrus and part of the right lingual gyrus. This corroborates the findings of Landry et al. regarding hypnosis (Chapter 9).

Incipient action – the readiness to act with a corresponding degree of anticipation – is part of conscious imagery experience. One doesn't simply '*see*' a sunset in one's mind's eye, one *feels something* along with the vision, and an associated action springs into mind. All imagery is laden with expectancy and feeling – e.g. attraction, calm, tranquillity, fear, anger or anticipation. For these reasons reflections about key life events provide essential material for analysis in psychotherapy (e.g. Holmes & Mathews, 2005). The anticipation – or what could be termed the 'action potential' – and feeling attributes of mental imagery explain why stories and literary works move readers to experience fiction, film and fantasy as if they are 'real'. Research with poetry suggests vividness itself, rather than arousal, that is most closely associated with aesthetic appreciation (Belfi, Vessel, & Starr, 2018). The extensive literature on mental 'practice' demonstrates that imagery is routinely and systematically deployed in preparation and rehearsal of sports activity and produces enhanced performance across a huge range of skill sets (Brown & Fletcher, 2017; Feltz & Landers, 1983; Harwick, Caspers, Eickhoff, & Swinnen, 2018; Jeannerod, 2003; Lebon, Ruffino, Greenhouse, Labruna, Ivry, & Papaxanthis, 2018; Markman, Klein, & Suhr, 2009; Richardson, 1967). Olympic athletes and virtuoso performers' activity cycles are more effectively rehearsed when the imagery is vivid (Isaac & Marks, 1994; Marks & Isaac, 1995). Rehabilitation after stroke and total hip arthroplasty follow similar principles (Butler & Page, 2006; Marusic, Grosprêtre, Paravlic, Kovač, Pišot, & Taube, 2018).

Research reviewed below shows that reported vividness is associated with early visual cortex activity relative to the whole-brain activity measured by fMRI in the performance of a novel psychophysical task. Vividness correlates with fMRI activity in the visual cortex, demonstrating that higher visual cortex activity indexes more vivid imagery. Variations in imagery vividness depend on a large network of brain areas, including frontal, parietal and visual areas. The more similar the neural response for imagery to the neural response for perception, the more vivid (i.e. perception-like) the imagery experience will be. Upon reflection on the alternative actions available, it is possible to inhibit certain actions, put them 'on hold' for the future and implement others. Thus, type II homeostasis facilitates successful striving towards goals, new niche construction and interactions with the external environment, all providing a huge evolutionary advantage over organisms that lack such functions (Marks, 2018).

META-ANALYSIS OF VIVIDNESS STUDIES

The intimate connections between image vividness, behavioural–cognitive measures and brain activation have been demonstrated in a meta-analysis which reported significant effect sizes for vividness measures and produced larger effect sizes for neuroscientific than behavioural–cognitive measures (Runge et al., 2017). Two key studies were as follows:

STUDY 1: Vividness of mental imagery: individual variability can be measured objectively (Cui, Jeter, Yang, Montague, & Eagleman, 2007):

> When asked to imagine a visual scene, such as an ant crawling on a checkered table cloth toward a jar of jelly, individuals subjectively report different vividness in their mental visualization. We show that reported vividness can be correlated with two objective measures: the early visual cortex activity relative to the whole-brain activity measured by fMRI and the performance on a novel psychophysical task. These results show that individual differences in the vividness of mental imagery are quantifiable even in the absence of subjective report. (Cui et al., 2007: 474)

> Results 3.1. Vividness of visual imagery correlates with fMRI activity in early visual cortex scores. We found a strong correlation ($r = -0.73$, $p = 0.04$), demonstrating that higher relative visual cortex activity indexes more vivid imagery (a lower VVIQ score). This result suggests that one can measure visual cortex activity to probe the vividness of a subject's imagery, thus obtaining a more objective measure of a previously subjective rating. (Cui et al., 2007: 476)

STUDY 2: Vividness of visual imagery depends on the neural overlap with perception in visual areas (Dijkstra et al., 2017). The authors state:

Research into the neural correlates of individual differences in imagery vividness point to an important role of the early visual cortex. However, there is also great fluctuation of vividness within individuals, such that only looking at differences between people necessarily obscures the picture. In this study, we show that variation in moment-to-moment experienced vividness of visual imagery, within human subjects, depends on the activity of a large network of brain areas, including frontal, parietal, and visual areas. Furthermore, using a novel multivariate analysis technique, we show that the neural overlap between imagery and perception in the entire visual system correlates with experienced imagery vividness. This shows that the neural basis of imagery vividness is much more complicated than studies of individual differences seemed to suggest ... we show that the more the neural response during imagery is similar to the neural response during perception, the more vivid or perception-like the imagery experience is. (Dijkstra et al., 2017: 1327)

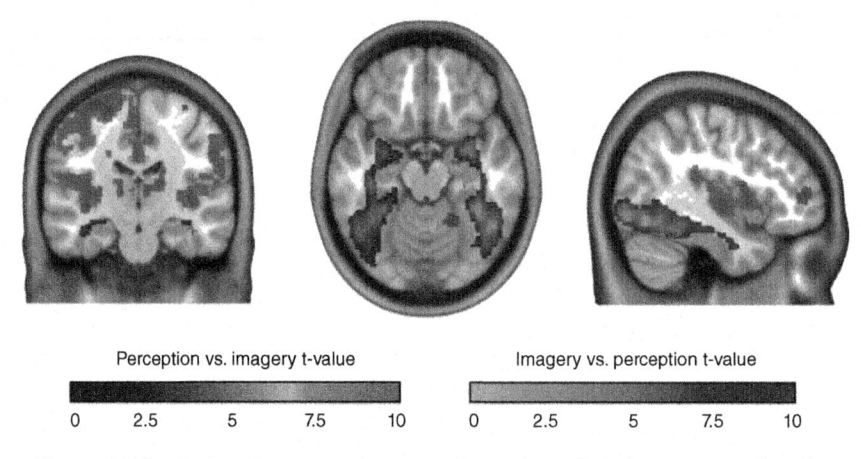

Figure 11.6 Perception versus imagery. Some loss of clarity compared to the original illustration is due to the inability to print colour. Dark areas show *t*-values for perception versus imagery and light areas show *t*-values for imagery versus perception. Shown *t*-values were significant at the group level. Even though both conditions activated the visual cortex with respect to baseline, stronger activity occurred during perception than imagery throughout the whole ventral visual stream. In contrast, imagery led to stronger activity in more anterior areas, including insula, left dorsal lateral prefrontal cortex, and medial frontal cortex.

Reproduced from Dijkstra et al. (2017), with permission.

Results: To directly compare activity between perception and imagery, we contrasted the two conditions (see Figure 11.6). Even though both conditions activated the visual cortex with respect to baseline, we observed stronger activity during perception than imagery throughout the whole ventral visual stream. In contrast, imagery led to stronger activity in more anterior areas, including insula, left dorsal lateral prefrontal cortex, and medial frontal cortex .... We modeled the imagery response for each vividness level separately.

In Figure 11.7 the investigators plotted the difference between the main effect of perception and the main effect of imagery in the early visual cortex for each vividness level.

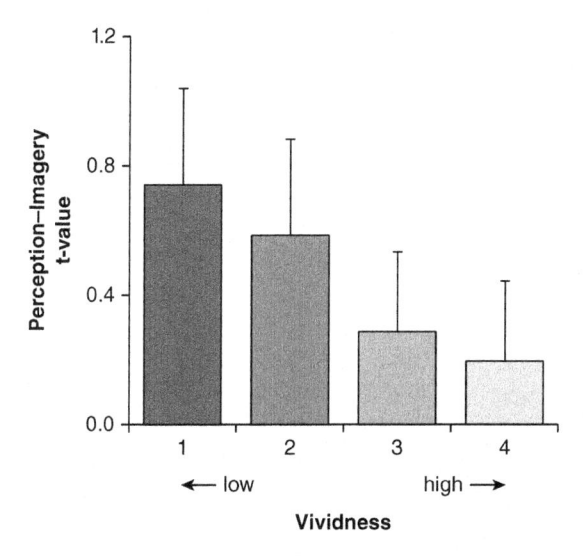

Figure 11.7 Difference between the effect of perception and the effect of imagery, separately for the four vividness levels. The higher the vividness is, the lower the difference between imagery and perception will be. In each trial, Ps were shown two objects successively, followed by a cue indicating which of the two they subsequently should imagine. During imagery, a frame was presented within which Ps were asked to imagine the cued stimulus as vividly as possible. After this, they indicated their experienced vividness on a scale from one to four, where one was low vividness and four was high vividness. The results are shown for a voxel in the early visual cortex that showed the highest overlap between the main effect of perception and the main effect of imagery. More vivid imagery was associated with a smaller difference between perception and imagery.

Reproduced from Dijkstra et al. (2017), with permission.

ACTION

I always like to picture the game the night before: I'll ask the kitman what kit we're wearing, so I can visualize it. It's something I've always done, from when I was a young boy. It helps to train your mind to situations that might happen the following day. I think about it as I'm lying in bed. What will I do if the ball gets crossed in the box this way? What movement will I have to make to get on the end of it? Just different things that might make you one percent sharper. (Wayne Rooney, 2019)

The imagery system is intimately involved with the action system, so that perceiving something often leads to corresponding activity whether covert or overt. Activity also has an emotive component within the 'activity cycle'. Activity Cycle Theory (ACT) has been supported by an extensive literature (Marks, 1990, 1999, 2019b).[10]

Proving that there is nothing new under the sun, Frederic Bartlett (1925) theorised about images arising when there is a conflict of tendencies to action (i.e., when a reaction is held up) as a way of helping the person to choose between alternatives (Wagoner, 2013). Bartlett theorised about the whole organism actively dealing with its environment.[11] For Bartlett, remembering and imaging are 'situated' activities, bringing multiple different processes together, to act in the world and to make environmental adaptations. His suggestions that schemas are situated actions and that images arise in a conflict of action tendencies chime in synchrony with the theory presented here. The ACT proposes that the primary functions of consciousness are simulation and prediction, both made possible by mental rehearsal of adaptive, goal-directed action through mental imagery (Marks, 1999). This viewpoint is strongly supported by two meta-analyses conducted 32 years apart which demonstrate that the greater the level of image vividness, the more closely its neural activation resembles that of real physical activity (McKelvie, 1995; Runge et al., 2017).

Evidence for a feeling component of mental imagery is strong. The primary motivational system is certainly affective because biological drives only have impact when amplified by emotion (Tomkins, 1962). As we all learn from a young age, people's emotions are written all over their faces. This knowledge transfers to one's mental images. If we imagine happy, sad or angry scenes, then correspondingly different patterns of facial muscle activity can be measured using electromyography (Franzen, Brinkmann, Gendolla, & Sentissi, 2019; Schwartz, Fair, Salt, Mandel, & Klerman, 1976). We perceive objects with feeling. The fruit in the bowl looks tempting: one feels hungry looking at it, forbidden though it may be. Ditto the

---

[10]Jeannerod (1999, 2003) postulated that 'covert actions like motor images are actions on their own right, except for the fact that they are not executed'. Exactly in line with the action cycle theory (ACT), Jeannerod sees covert and overt stages on a continuum, in which every overtly executed action implies the existence of a covert stage, whereas a covert action does not necessarily turn out into an overt action.

[11]A direct line concerning the schema theory can be traced back to the theories of Sir Frederic C. Bartlett. I note that Marc Jeannerod's (1999) quite similar theory (see previous footnote) was presented as the 25th Bartlett Lecture: 'To act or not to act: Perspectives on the representation of actions.'

chocolate cake in the cake shop window. Affective representations ('yum, that looks good') of visual sensations ('large, rich chocolate cake') are translated into the brain's predictions about what those sensations stand for ('tasty food, eat it') and how to act on them in the future ('eat more chocolate cake') (Barrett & Bar, 2009; Caplette, Gosselin, Mermillod & Wicker, 2018). Affective responses when one mentally images can be equally seductive, not only faces, fruit or cakes, but complex scenes and activities. However, the physiological responses are generally less intense with mental images than with perceptions of actual objects (Davis, Ollendick & Öst, 2019; Lang, 1979), which is very wise of Mother Nature.

Agency is the bedrock of ipseity throughout the sleep–wake cycle. Rarely does our human predilection for making images, affect and action break down in normal physiological and psychological states of consciousness (SOCs), even in the REM state. However, systems of action control can break down cases that become labeled as 'psychosis'. Patients diagnosed with 'schizophrenia' often report anomalous experiences that are attributed to their own actions. They may feel that their actions and/or thoughts are being controlled by external forces, or that they are controlling events that have no real connection to their actions. Some theories link these disturbances of agency to deficits in motor prediction, resulting in a mismatch between predicted and actual sensory feedback at a central comparator mechanism (Voss, Moore, Hauser, Gallinat, Heinz, & Haggard, 2010). The full story is yet to be told.

CONSCIOUSNESS

After millennia of deep thinking, one question continues to baffle philosophers more than almost any other: Why on earth do we need consciousness? I believe that all of the hard-earned knowledge about vividness helps one to answer this question. It is one tenet of the current theory that *sensory–affective mental images are basic building blocks of consciousness in perception, memory, and imagination* (Marks, 1999, 2019b). Thus, to answer the question 'Why do we need consciousness?' it is sensible to consider what we think we mean when we conceptualise consciousness and work from there. This set of five propositions provides a starting position:

1. Consciousness is the central, meta-level, executive process of the brain.
2. It builds images of the world.
3. It makes predictions about future events.
4. It tests those predictions by carrying out covert simulations.
5. It selects goals for future actions.

The inputs to consciousness are exteroceptive, sensory stimuli – sight, sound, taste, smell, touch, temperature, vibration, proprioception and pain – and interoceptive stimuli, which form a cortical image of homeostatic afferent activity from the body's tissues. This system provides experiences and visceral feelings such as pain, temperature, itch, sensual touch, muscular and visceral sensations, vasomotor activity, hunger, thirst and 'air hunger'. Interoceptive activity is represented in the right anterior insula, providing subjective imagery of the material self as a feeling (sentient) entity of emotional awareness (Craig, 2003).

According to the third criterion in the list above, consciousness makes predictions, which is something that we, and any other species, could not possibly do without. Predictions are rehearsals involving 'what if?' or 'if then' relationships of the type: 'If one does X, will Y or Z happen?'

Anything that happens between stimulus (S) and response (R) – let's call it O – is based on 'if then' operations and simulations geared towards testing for stability and safety. If one sees a dog in the park and wants to approach it to give it a pat, one studies its face and body language closely before doing so. This caution is wise because it helps to prevent upsetting the dog along with the incumbent risks. Private fantasy and daydreaming are alleged to take up about 50% of our waking time (Singer, 1975/2014) and a proportion of this activity is predicting. The controlled processing of complex activity is serial, attention-demanding, methodical, and slow – e.g. preparing a meal using a cookery book or reading a manual on how to operate a DVD player or coffee-making machine (Norman & Shallice, 1986). Automatic processing, on the other hand, is efficient and economical – e.g. reading, writing, walking, riding a bicycle, driving a car or piloting a plane. Of course, doing something 'on automatic' can go wrong, especially if alertness fails and an operator takes a mini-sleep while at the controls of a fast-moving vehicle (Brown et al., 2008). This is where the meta-level is so essential to planning, e.g., when to take a sleep before or after a long journey.

Brain science suggests that the frontal lobe of the cerebral cortex is the site of the central control system, the meta-level of consciousness (Wheeler, Stuss, & Tulving, 1997). The forebrain itself is involved in regulation of both autonomic and non-autonomic human responses in stress and feeling. Conveniently the forebrain is also the seat of both types of homeostasis (Edlow et al., 2016). As noted, a significant part of the content of conscious experience consists of mental imagery, the process that carries us from one point in our mental model of the world to the next. Two other significant modular systems required for the executive control of behaviour are the CLOCK system and the approach avoidance inhibition (AAI) system. The CLOCK and AAI are described in detail elsewhere (Marks, 2018).

IMITATION AND PERSPECTIVE-TAKING

Imagery is intimately linked with imitation. Most likely, either one is impossible without the other. Three observations suggest why this is the case. Human newborns imitate, suggesting a common representation mediating the observation and execution of human action. Second, the discovery of mirror neurones in monkeys provides a physiological model for this perception–action coupling, which is involved in imitation and action understanding (Rizzolatti and Craighero, 2004). Mirror neurones in the ventral premotor cortex (area F5) and parietal area (PF) fire when a monkey carries out a goal-directed action and when it observes the same action performed by another individual. It is apparent that mirror neurones represent goals and consequences rather than elementary movement properties of the movements (i.e. schemas). Third, neurophysiological studies with humans demonstrate that a 'motor resonance mechanism' exists in the premotor and posterior parietal cortices when people observe goal-directed actions being executed by other people or even when only the goal of these action is visible (Jackson, Meltzoff & Decety, 2006). This motor resonance mechanism also is activated by action imitation so that interference occurs between action observation and action execution, which suggests a direct link between perception and action, as we have proposed, with mental imagery, action schemata, affect and a goal all included in one coherent system of control (Figure 11.4).

Jackson et al. (2006) measured the cerebral changes in Ps who watched video-clips depicting simple hand or foot actions. I quote from the abstract as follows:

> The participants either watched passively or imitated these actions. Half the video-clips depicted actions filmed from the perspective of the participant (1st-person perspective) and half from a frontal view as if watching someone else (3rd-person perspective). Behavioural results showed that latency to imitate was significantly shorter for the 1st-person perspective than the 3rd-person perspective. Functional imaging results demonstrate that the observation of intransitive actions engaged primary visual and extrastriate visual areas, but not the premotor cortex. Imitation vs. observation of actions yielded enhanced signal in the contralateral somatosensory and motor cortices, cerebellum, left inferior parietal lobule and superior parietal cortex, and left ventral premotor cortex. Activity in the lateral occipital cortex around the extrastriate body area was significantly enhanced during imitation, as compared to observation of actions confirming that this region involvement reaches beyond the perception of body parts. Moreover, comparisons of the two visual perspectives showed more activity in the left sensory-motor cortex for 1st-person, even during observation alone, and in the lingual gyrus for 3rd-person perspective. These findings suggest that the 1st-person perspective is more tightly coupled to the sensory-motor system than the 3rd-person perspective, which requires additional visuospatial transformation. (Jackson et al., 2006: 429)

These findings support the view that imagery, observation and imitation of movement share the same neural control system. Why would it be any other way? The left sensory-motor cortex for the first-person perspective, even during observation alone, and the lingual gyrus for the third-person perspective are of special relevance to the ACT system. Finally, we must return to that nagging question that won't go away — why do we have consciousness?

THE SPECTRUM OF CONSCIOUSNESS

There can be no escaping it – it is necessary to answer this question: Why do we have consciousness? One general answer concerns evolution, the survival of the fittest and all of that. It seems difficult to deny the evolutionary advantage to possessing the purposeful and protective process of homeostasis. As noted previously, the case for consciousness as an emergent property was made by the neuropsychologist Roger Sperry in 1969:[12]

> consciousness, interpreted to be a direct emergent property of cerebral activity, is conceived to be an integral component of the brain process that functions as an essential constituent of the action and exerts a directive holistic form of control over the flow pattern of cerebral excitation. (p. 532)

There is also a more specific and detailed answer that I will attempt to offer here. First, in order to avoid linguistic and conceptual confusion, it is essential to tease apart two dimensions of consciousness: *awareness*, providing the content, and *wakefulness*, governing the level (Laureys, 2005; Figure 11.8). These are different and separate, but they show a correlated variability. In normal physiological states, level and content are positively correlated (with the exception of dream activity during REM-sleep). Patients in pathological or pharmacological coma (general anaesthesia) are unconscious because they cannot be awakened. Dissociated states of consciousness – i.e. patients seemingly awake but lacking 'voluntary' or 'willed' behaviour – such as the vegetative state, absence, or complex partial seizures and sleepwalking, provide an opportunity to study the neural correlates of awareness.

The conscious spectrum can be understood by considering the intimate connections between the self, intentionality and purposive goal-seeking. These connections enable the pre-eminent quality of *ipseity*. Without ipseity, the conscious brain would be little more than a chaotic picture box, like a TV constantly switching channels all on its own. Most likely, only a conscious being with a large forebrain can experience selfhood, the first-person quality that provides the unity of perspective as 'my' experience (Nelson et al., 2014). Dolphins, whales, frogs, crows and beaver-rats may also possess it but, as yet, we have no definitive proof, only a few small indications. With present levels of technology, we cannot know for certain, and we should never rule out the possibility and so mustn't opine too grandly about our tendentious superiority within the animal kingdom. One thing is absolutely certain, all creatures possess homeostasis type I and those that are conscious, also possess type II.

---

[12]That date, 1969, again.

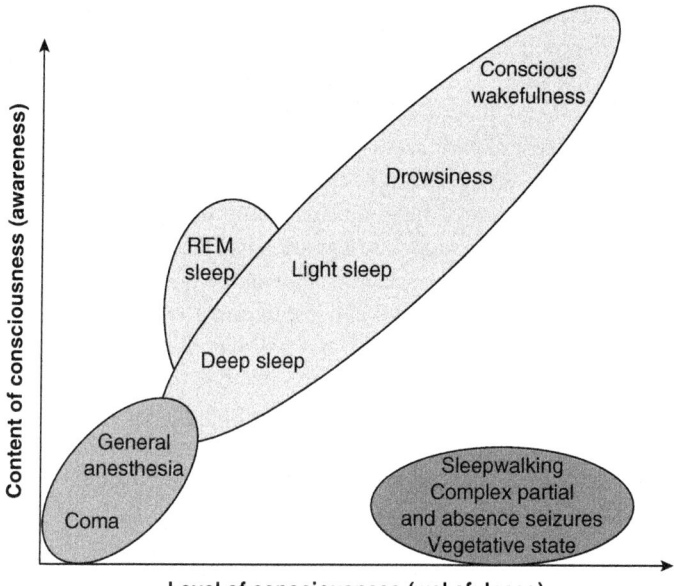

Figure 11.8 An illustration of the two major components of consciousness: level of wakefulness (or arousal) and content of consciousness (i.e. awareness or experience). This system places different SOCs in an ordered array.

Reproduced from Laureys (2005), with permission.

Figure 11.9 presents a 'Spectrum of Consciousness'. The diagram shows a 'spectrum' of 17[13] states with two determinants, 'predisposition' (upper panel) and 'precipitation' (lower panel). Predisposing elements consist of genetics, epigenetics and early childhood experience. Of special significance are trauma and dissociation, which are liable to influence behaviour and experience throughout the lifetime. Three overlapping trajectories consisting of 'Trauma and Dissociation', 'Trauma Alone' or 'Trauma Free' create life-long consequences for the trait of selfhood/ipseity. The ipseity trait develops early and influences individual behaviour for life.

In the lower panel, two orthogonal axes represent control and ipseity, which independently influence the content of consciousness. Control closely follows the sleep–wake cycle and reaches a maximum in the wide-awake state. Control exists at moderate levels in intermediate wakefulness, and at a minimal level during the REM state. Independently of control, ipseity moderates the content of conscious

---

[13]This figure is schematic for purposes of illustration. A full-scale scheme would need to be much larger than this page. Many more SOCs are available, perhaps 50–100, but space isn't available to include them. Readers may choose to make a large-scale poster version of the diagram, enabling many more SOCs to be included.

states. The four corners of the lower panel indicate where ipseity and control are at maximal or minimal levels. A spectrum 'wavelengths' gradually orders transitions between brain states and SOCs. The brain states on the right-hand side are assumed to be universal; those on the left of the central position, meditation, are associated with lower levels of ipseity and less commonly reported.

Cutting across the entire spectrum is the circadian sleep–wake cycle. This cycle is controlled by a homeostatic mechanism in the brain stem together with the hypothalamus, pons and medulla (Kandel, 2013). Similar endogenous circadian rhythms of around 24 hours occur throughout the plant and animal kingdoms. Human arousal has a 24-hour circadian cycle of sleep and waking, with an ultradian rhythm during sleep of non-REM and REM periods. Although the precise function of sleep is the subject of speculation, the one thing that is known is that human beings cannot survive without it. Upsetting disturbances of sleep and dreams are difficult to control, including chronic insomnia itself, and a range of sleep-related phenomena such as sleepwalking. The distribution of sleep disturbances is uneven, with a greater frequency in people with higher levels of anxiety and depression (Alvaro, Roberts, & Harris, 2013) and/or higher levels of dissociation, especially in traumatised children as young as 3–6 years of age (Hébert, Langevin, Guidi, Bernard-Bonnin, & Allard-Dansereau, 2017).

Sleepwalking and other unusual sleep experiences result from predisposing, priming and precipitating factors (Pressman, 2007). In the absence of one or more factors, sleepwalking is unlikely to occur. Priming factors, not included in the diagram, include conditions that increase slow-wave sleep (SWS) or make arousal from sleep more difficult – e.g. sleep deprivation, alcohol, medications, situational stress and fever. The patient with a genetic predisposition to sleepwalking and who is exposed to priming factors still requires a precipitating trigger to set sleepwalking in motion – e.g. extreme anxiety (Petit, Touchette, Tremblay, Boivin, & Montplaisir, 2007).

Nightmares involve minimal control in combination with low ipseity (upper left-hand corner), enabling by a wild level of chaotic dream content, which is mirrored in daytime passivity and lack of aggressiveness (Godin, Montplaisir, & Nielsen, 2015). Minimal control combined with high ipseity (upper right-hand corner) enables dreaming within the REM state. Upon awakening, REM dreams are accepted to be normal fantasy products of self ('my' dreams) whereas nightmares are associated with insomnia, unusual sleep experiences and indications of psychopathology (Ohayon, Morselli, & Guilleminault, 1997).

Ipseity is both a trait and a state. To give one example, trait ipseity is weaker in people experiencing repeated nightmares than for people who never have nightmares. This ipseity difference is related to the higher rate of childhood traumatic experiences, which is known to exist among nightmare sufferers. People who have undergone physical and sexual abuse also usually suffer from more dream anxiety. The dissociation scores of people reporting frequent nightmares are significantly higher than those who never report nightmares (Agargun, Kara, Özer, Selvi, Kiran, & Kiran, 2003).

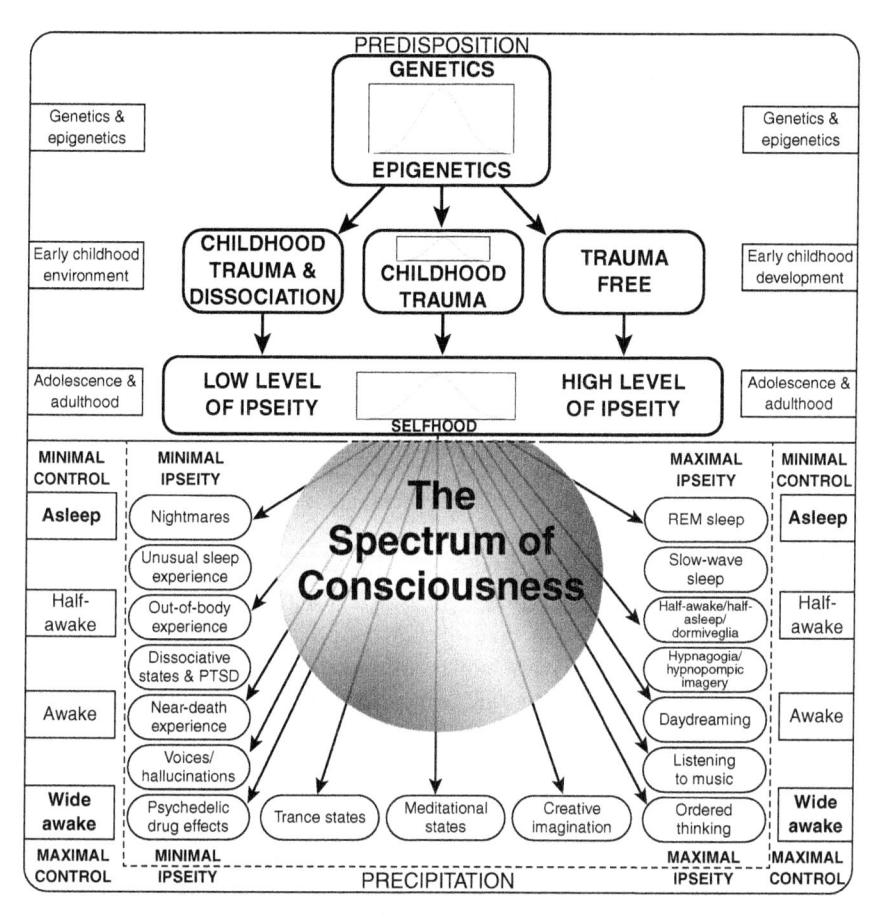

Figure 11.9 The Spectrum of Consciousness showing 17 states. Coma and general anaesthesia are excluded.

In sum, the conscious spectrum is one of Nature's most glorious productions, feeding back into evolution to moderate the direction and flow of change. With magnificent fluidity and power, the waking brain triggers thought, feeling and action in one continuous, uninterrupted flow, the so-called 'stream' (James, 1890) or 'river' of consciousness (Sacks, 2017). This remarkable 'live streaming' should never be taken for granted. Possibly it isn't present in exactly the same form in other animals – we simply do not know – but it could be, and it is known that animals and birds do consciously control their behaviour and indicate altered SOCs (e.g. Brecht, Hage, Gavrilov, & Nieder, 2019). In humans, the altered awareness of action that occurs in psychosis is suggestive of a deficit in agency, especially in the ability to understand the consequences and causes of one's actions (Voss et al., 2010).

The flow of conscious experience is at its fastest, with most content and highest ipseity while we are wide awake. As stated in Chapter 10, in susceptible people, hypnosis enables a full trance-like SOC. As wakefulness slides towards resting, the brain switches into default mode, the flow becomes sluggish, and ipseity and self less clear-cut so OBEs are enabled to take place in a minority of people. Relaxed, reflective spells and playful hypnogogic displays ready the conscious self for the world of dreams.

With the arrival of dreams anything is possible, and, to repeat John Lennon, 'Who's to say that dreams and nightmares aren't as real as the here and now'.

SUMMARY

1. The conscious brain is an open system with many relations to the surroundings. Changes in the surroundings produce alterations in equilibrium that require continual adjustment, adaptation and reset.
2. Throughout the wake–sleep cycle, in response to the environment, homeostasis produces a continuous flow of imagery for goal-directed behaviour, thought and feeling.
3. In states of reduced wakefulness, goal-directedness gives way to thinking of a more autistic nature. At its epitome in the REM state, loss of realistic thinking gives way to fantasy and feelings of an autistic nature.
4. No control system is 100% fool-proof and there are always going to be 'blips'. Subjective anomalies are restabilised by adjustments by the control system's REF.
5. These 'blips' contain valuable messages about the operating system, if only we are willing to pay attention.
6. The new 'spectral theory of consciousness' holds that discrete states of consciousness are identifiable by their levels of ipseity and control, with the latter being mediated by the circadian wake–sleep cycle.

Set your degree of belief in the spectral theory of consciousness

The author's degree of belief in the spectral theory of consciousness

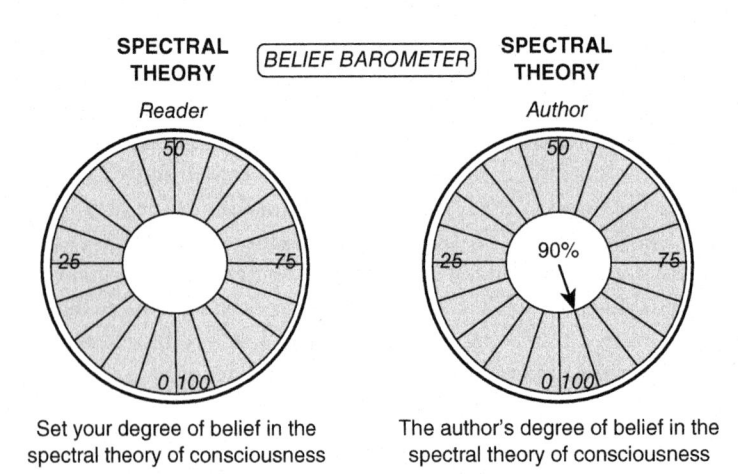

Figure 11.10 Belief barometer readings

QUESTIONS

1. Brain homeostasis is said to operate in three spheres using serotonin (5-HT) neurones. What are these three spheres and how do they interact? Answer from memory using a diagram.
2. According to 'Action Cycle Theory', mental imagery involves four modules. What are those four modules and how are they related? Answer from memory using a diagram.
3. A more advanced model of action contains six modules that show schemata controlling voluntary actions to operate on salient objects in the pursuit of a goal. From memory, draw this system of six modules.
4. The REF operates in networks of interconnected processes within a larger matrix of processes. What does the REF do? Answer from memory using a diagram.
5. List five propositions that describe consciousness.
6. The limbic system is a set of brain structures located on both sides of the thalamus, immediately beneath the medial temporal lobe. The limbic system is activated in emotion, motivation, long-term memory and olfaction. Draw a diagram of the limbic system showing at least six interconnected structures.
7. According to the Spectral Theory, states of consciousness are represented as a graded series of identifiable categories. Name five predisposing and three precipitating determinants of SOCs suggested by the theory.

PART IV
CONCLUSIONS

12

TAKE-HOME MESSAGE

Psi is a Spontaneous Process that Cannot be Summoned at Will in a Laboratory Experiment

For nearly half a century parapsychologists of the statistical school have been hankering after the ideal experiment which would satisfy the strictest criteria of repeatability and predictability. This might turn out to be a will-o'-the-wisp until psychologists discover a technique to induce extra-sensory perceptions at will. (Koestler, 1972: 29)

A wild goose chase (noun): a foolish and hopeless search for or pursuit of something unattainable: 'physicists searching for the hypothetical particle may be on a wild goose chase.' (Online dictionary, *Lexico*, 2019: www.lexico.com/en/definition/wild_goose_chase)

Outline: It is almost half a century since Arthur Koestler wrote that the ideal experiment for the demonstration of psi 'might turn out to be a will-o'-the-wisp'. Koestler thought that psi is governed by unconscious processes of an involuntary nature. If laboratory psi is, after all, a will-of-the-wisp, Parapsychology has been a wild goose chase since the very start. Over a century of laboratory research, the brutal truth is that psi has not been reliably demonstrated. The controlled scientific experiment, so it would seem, is an alien environment for psi. The same is true of other subjective processes that are subtle, spontaneous and partly unconscious, such as creativity, moods and sexual arousal. One is forced to consider that it may not be feasible to measure these processes by objective methods in the laboratory. At the same time, one can never assert that *the processes do not exist*. Psi is in this very situation. Psi is not 'on tap' to be turned on or off. ESP cannot be induced at

(Continued)

will anywhere, not in scientific laboratories, military spying missions, predicting stocks and shares, or in casinos. Psi has not been confirmed nor disconfirmed by scientific studies. Like all other categories of anomalous experience, psi lies within a 'spectrum' of consciousness. Parapsychology needs to change direction by investigating the hypothesis that *psi is a spontaneous process that cannot be summoned at will*.

PSI CANNOT BE INDUCED AT WILL

Before reading further, please indicate your degree of belief in laboratory psi on the Belief Barometer below. (To avoid biasing, I am keeping my own belief covered.)

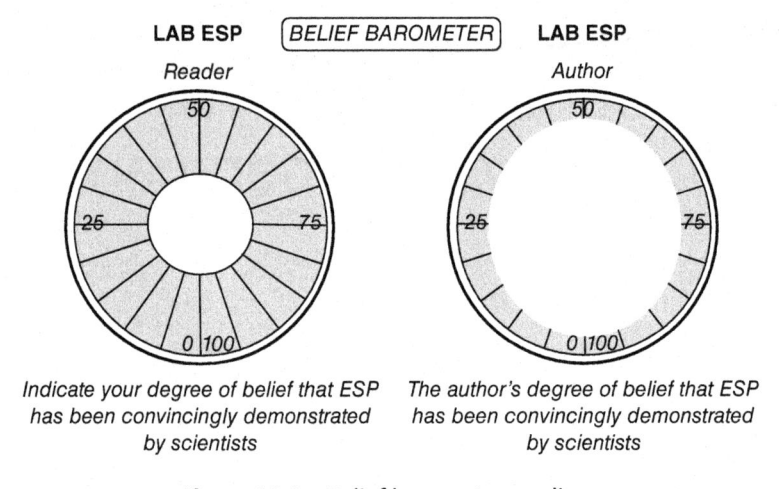

Figure 12.1 Belief barometer readings

In this book, I have provided a critical examination of the best scientific evidence for psi from laboratory investigations over the last half-century. Every corner of the scientific literature has been combed for evidence of psi. Yet consistent, robust and replicable evidence has not come to light. Five of the world's leading psi advocates have made the best case they can muster in support of the psi hypothesis. In spite of everything, disappointingly, the overall weight of the evidence points to a null effect. Why?

My answer is simple: *ESP cannot be induced at will*. Psi cannot be summoned in the controlled laboratory environment. How then does one explain why there are some statistically significant findings? Psi advocates have strong convictions, with ingenuity and diligence by the bucket-load. With subjective validation, some statistical wizardry and no small amount of confirmation bias, the null effect of psi has been transformed into the illusion of a vanishingly tiny but statistically significant effect. I do not doubt for one moment that the statistical effects are there, but they are illusory. My disagreement lies not with the numbers on the page, but with the interpretations given to those numbers.

In the final analysis, the author's belief in laboratory ESP plummeted to the rock-bottom figure of .00000000001 (10^{-11}). The author's barometer readings for different ESP settings can be reviewed in a single diagram (Figure 12.2). The author's zetetic view started at 50%, shot up to 75%, took a nose-dive downwards for remote viewing and psychic staring, and stayed down low for all five of the remaining lab ESP domains. The picture could not be any plainer. In spite of almost a century of 'blood, sweat and tears', laboratory ESP is nothing more than a myth.

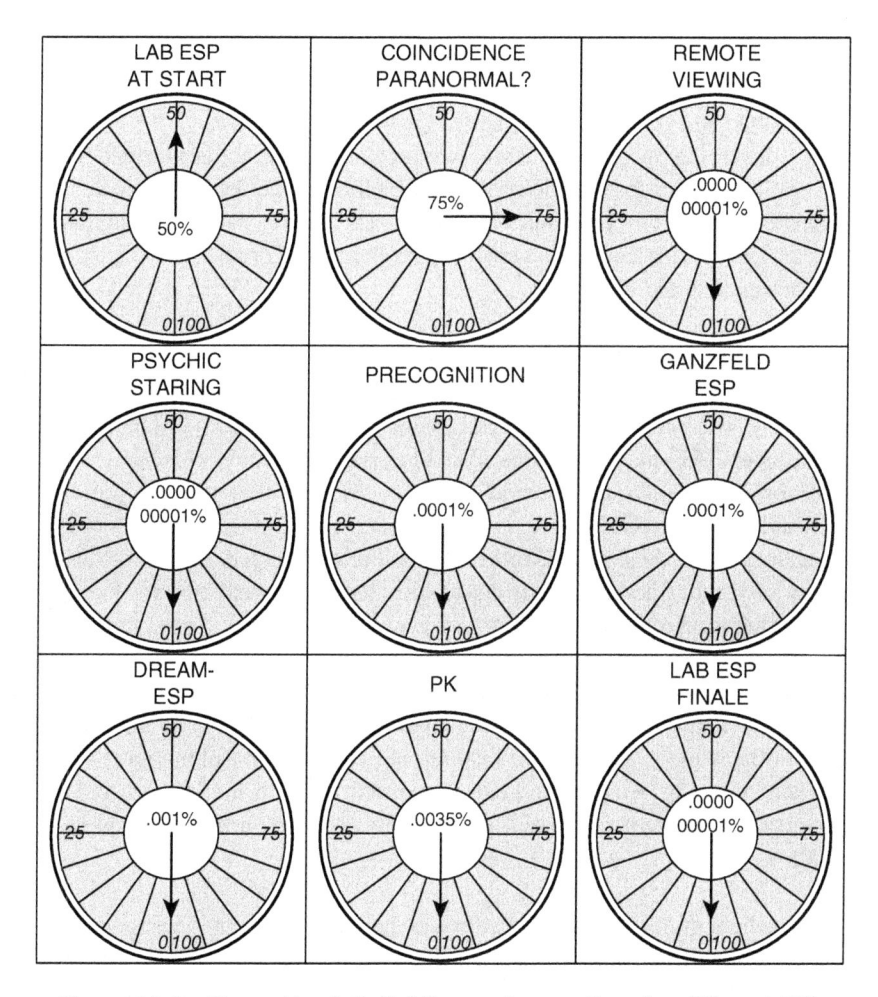

Figure 12.2 The author's Belief Barometer readings for different ESP phenomena examined in this book. This 3 × 3 matrix began with a deliberately even-handed value of 50%. Then the non-laboratory 'Chiswick Coincidence' produced a score of 75%. However, for none of the lab ESP domains did the author's belief exceed .001% (10^{-5}). After evaluating every peer-reviewed publication in this book, the author's final reading for laboratory ESP settled at 10^{-11} (one in one hundred thousand million).

CONTRIBUTORS' COMMENTARIES

The contributors provide a set of authoritative, independent perspectives on psi. The world's leading investigators offer insightful reflections on the psi hypothesis as a counterpoise to the discussion. The first of the commentors, Professor Adrian Parker (AP), begins by expressing points of agreement:

> David Marks and I share the same starting point. Science should function as "a candle in the dark" but skeptics are not always the good guys and not always holding the candle. Nor are scientific laws written in stone ... we deplore the hostility in this field in making it more like religious confrontations than an expression of curiosity.
>
> Concerning my ganzfeld work, we agree on the precautions needed ...
>
> What remains to be made crystal clear is that it is perfectly legitimate to analyse subjective experiences in experiments that are statistically significant. These experiences can generate hypotheses and predictions, which in turn can be tested.

Based on his several decades of in-depth investigation, AP's astute observation that *sudden unpredictable changes of content are associated with psi-hitting* warrants further investigation, especially in spontaneous ESP occurrences. AP also indicates the importance of the *closeness of the relationship between sender and receiver*, an idea that was supported by Wickramasekera (1991).

Psi-skeptic, Dr Susan Blackmore (SB) is the only expert to discuss the possibility of fraud. She was unwilling to give barometer readings for her belief in psi at the time of her visit to Carl Sargent at Cambridge. This is fair – retrospective judgements would likely be invalid. However, SB writes: 'My beliefs were in turmoil throughout this period. I certainly had a phase of significant belief after I saw how well-designed his studies appeared to be and before I spent further time in his lab. But I cannot put any meaningful numbers to this.' SB states that she believes Sargent committed fraud in his lab at Cambridge University on at least one specific trial. She expands on her personal beliefs as follows:

> In the light of my decades of research on psi, and especially because of my experiences with the GF, I now believe that the possibility of psi existing is vanishingly small, though not zero. I am glad other people continue to study the subject because it would be so important to science if psi did exist. But for myself, I think doing any further psi research would be a complete waste of time. I would not expect to find any phenomena to study, let alone any that could lead us to an explanatory theory. I may yet be proved wrong of course.

Psi-advocate Dr Daryl Bem (DB) writes with the expertise of a professional magician and long-term psi investigator. DB explains what he meant when he told SB that 'it did not matter whether Sargent cheated or not'. The database showed a significant effect *even if Sargent's studies are omitted* so, contrary to SB's opinion, DB concludes that there *is* reputable scientific evidence for psi in Honorton's meta-analysis. Furthermore, DB believes that his own independent ganzfeld experiments yielded strong and significant positive results.

One surprising aspect of DB's account of GF-ESP research is that *he believes subjective validation is impossible in the GF protocol*. Yet a huge body of evidence indicates that SV is a universal process that every magician – and every other person – can be fooled by. DB is certain that he prevented the SV illusion in his own GF study: 'Where is there room for any "illusion of subjective validation"?' (DB, 2 October 2019, personal communication). There is ample room. Let me explain how. The experimenter has to interact with the receiver when they are shown four video clips and asked to rate each video on a 100-point scale to rate how similar it is to their earlier free association. The investigator is able to prompt the receiver to choose a specific video as the target. Also, the receiver is prone to select the first or the last video clip as the target influenced by their own SV bias.

This bias was previously confirmed in data analysed by none other than Daryl Bem (2004) himself in 'Study 302'. Imagine that a receiver is biased to choose video clips 1 and 4 30% of the time, and clips 2 and 3 only 20% of the time. Only if the probability that the target appears in each position is exactly 25% will the position bias not effect the expected hit rate. However, if the target clip happens to be placed more frequently in positions 1 or 4 by inadequate randomisation, then the hit rate exceeds 25% artifactually. Thus a combination of position bias caused by the receiver's SV together with inadequate randomisation can produce artifactually high hit rates in the autoganzfeld protocol. DB is hoist with his own petard.

In DB's comments in Chapter 7, he does not deny that there is a strong decline effect in his precognition experiments. However, DB speculates that the decline is linked to changes in student motivation across the semester. According to DB's Semester Decline hypothesis, enthusiastic students sign up early in the semester, while less enthusiastic students postpone joining the experiment until the end of the semester: 'Many students who have been doing badly in a course rush in at the last moment to participate for extra credit in the hope of boosting their course grade.' A similar decline in enthusiasm, DB suggests, also occurs in the experimenters. DB offers only anecdotal evidence to support this post hoc Semester Decline. Also, the hypothesis is unsupported by empirical research which finds no evidence for semester decline across a large array of experimental or correlational studies (Ebersole et al., 2016). In my experience, more highly motivated students postpone their involvement in their professors' studies, which are regarded as a necessary drudgery.

DB's response to the issue of pilot studies appears confusing and contradictory in equal measure. Engber (2017) quotes DB as saying: 'I would start one [experiment], and if it just wasn't going anywhere, I would abandon it and restart it with changes.' DB does not deny saying this. However, at the same time he denies that any 'peeking' at the data ever took place: 'because there were no data to peek at, only my own judgments of how clear the instructions were'. No offence to DB but I suggest that it is a natural part of human curiosity to take a peek at one's data. *DB would have us believe that he waited an entire semester, while data from 100 Ps was being collected without taking a single sneaky peek?* Is DB not human?

In offering this defence DB boxes himself into a corner from which there is no escape. There is no sense in claiming that (A) 'there were no data to peek at' and (B) that he would abandon an experiment if it wasn't going anywhere. The two statements are self-contradictory. The bottom line is this: which of the following two sets of propositions is more plausible?

1. DB has a 'Super-Power'. Together with his student Ps and assistants, DB has reliably produced 'Flash Precognition' which 'time-reverses' cause-and-effect. DB's time-reversal means that *the causes of the observed effects occur AFTER the effects themselves.* This ability to produce time-reversal weakens across the semester due to a decline in motivation and ability of the students involved. The whole of physics and science as we know it are in need of revolutionary correction [A P-Theory explanation].

Or:

2. Lacking any Super-Power, but wishing to demonstrate its existence – for he is a magician after all – DB and his student co-investigators and Ps are prone to the normal human errors of confirmation bias and subjective validation. Motivated by the desire to please DB as he is their professor who will grade their papers at the end of the semester, the students do their utmost to provide confirmation of DB's cause-and-effect time-reversal hypothesis (even if they privately think its a little crazy). Impatient to check how each semester-long experiment is going, DB takes a sneaky peek at his data about half-way through. If the early results look 'good', DB continues with the data collection. If the early results look 'bad', DB ceases the data collection because to carry on would be a waste of time. The already-collected data are discarded or filed away. Although DB does not always keep a record or remember all of the specific details, he changes the conditions of the experiment to see whether the effect he is looking for appears. None of the different experiments, even the unfinished ones, are viewed as pilot studies; they are all regarded by DB as true experiments. [An N-Theory explanation.]

The reader is invited to judge which set of propositions is more likely to be true.

Another leading psi advocate, Dr Hal Puthoff (HP), shows his awareness of the primary role of subjective validation when he writes:

> Recognition of this factor has in the field led to an analysis protocol wherein judges are asked to blind-match the RV-generated materials to the target materials on a blind basis wherein the judge does not know during judging

which RV-generated response goes with which target. Unfortunately, even this attempt at objective analysis can introduce subjective factors of its own, e.g., have transcript materials presented to a blind judge been sufficiently scrubbed to remove tell-tale clues that provide information about, say, other targets in a series and thereby eliminate the possibility of completely unbiased matches.

Contrary to his practice in past exchanges, HP offers no defence of the 'classic' RV studies (Targ & Puthoff, 1974) or challenges any of my criticisms regarding sensory cueing and SV (Marks, 1986; Marks & Kammann, 1978; Marks & Scott, 1986). This change in stance hopefully signals a degree of convergence between critic and advocate, a sign of progress in the science of psi.

Unlike most other psi advocates, HP's research is based in real-life settings and applications, military and monetary. HP states that he believes that RV provides a hit rate that would be sufficient to determine a simulated missile location with high accuracy. He points out that: '*confirmation bias* is a two-edged sword that can show up for both advocates and skeptics'. Nobody is immune from confirmation bias. On this point we are in 100% agreement. Progress.

Another psi advocate, Dr Rupert Sheldrake, writes in his commentary:

> The great majority of studies on the detection of unseen stares have shown positive, statistically significant effects. In my review in the *Journal of Consciousness Studies*, I summarise data from tens of thousands of trials, including 21 experiments of my own (excluding online tests), in 20 of which the outcome was positive, and also from 37 independent investigations in universities, colleges and schools of which 36 showed a positive effect.

I did not include Sheldrake's (2005) article in the *Journal of Consciousness Studies* because I have been informed that this paper was not peer reviewed. I could not trace any peer-reviewed papers reporting psychic staring over the last 15–20 years. Like many other psi phenomena – remote viewing, ganzfeld ESP, dream-ESP, precognition and PK – 'scopaesthesia' appears to be withering on the vine.

In discussing the 'classic' Maimonides dream-ESP studies, Dr Stanley Krippner (SK) writes that he 'would not use the term "scientific revolution." It is simply too early to make such a grandiose claim.' About his research sponsors, he writes: 'I think they were less guided by lofty ideals than by their own budgetary constraints.' SK estimates his degree of belief in dream-ESP at 80%. He writes: 'This is a controversial topic, and I for one try to remain modest as well as cautious in over-interpreting the results.' For somebody so universally respected in Parapsychology, SK writes with humility and decorum, admirable traits in any scientist.

Finally, at the time when he was the 2018–2019 President of the Parapsychology Association, Dr Dean Radin (DR) vigorously defends the evidence supporting the PK hypothesis. DR asserts that PK does not work in the casino because:

It's difficult to beat the house in any casino game because the odds are always in favour of the house. To overcome that bias would require the player to achieve systematic, robust, above-chance results, which is not easy given that casinos are designed to distract the player with free alcohol, disorienting colors, flashing lights, and continuous loud music. The dice meta-analysis indicates that the effect is real, but it is not strong enough to challenge the profits of casinos.

So PK is real but weak.

An effect that is too weak for the casino is also claimed to be as strong as a bacterium or a virus: 'Small effects can be quite powerful, as anyone who has ever picked up a bad bacterium or virus can readily attest.' One cannot be sure which particular 'bad bacterium or virus' Radin has in mind. Could it perhaps be tetanus, typhoid or tuberculosis (bacteria) or chickenpox, HIV or Ebola (virus)?[1]

So PK is real but strong.

Turning to DR's reference to Benjamin Franklin, it is informative to make a few comparisons with psi research, as follows.

BENJAMIN FRANKLIN'S KITE EXPERIMENT

DR states:

> ... when Benjamin Franklin was criticized for flying kites in electrical storms so he could study sparks, little did anyone at the time imagine that one day the world would run on gigawatt electrical grids (MacLaren, 1945). Franklin's interest in sparks was not driven by his desire to create an electrical grid, but rather by simple curiosity, the prime motivator in science. With dedicated effort, sometimes curiosity develops into confident knowledge, and then with any luck it might advance into a technology. Similarly, exploring PK is motivated today by curiosity. If enough knowledge could be gained to better understand that phenomenon, then someday it might turn into the basis of a technology. Just as Franklin would have been hard-pressed to say how an improved understanding of sparks would one day lead to a method of powering the entire globe, it is difficult today to imagine how PK might turn into a technology. But if it does, could it have an equally profound impact on civilization?

DR is right to suggest that 'simple curiosity' is a prime motivator in science. Yet often, scientific curiosity involves a 'hunch' in the form of a particular theoretical point of view about the nature of a phenomenon. Benjamin Franklin's curiosity about sparks was motivated by a lifelong drive to exploit ideas that made life easier and safer. One example is the frequent, uncontrolled house fires in Franklin's home city of Philadelphia, which were often caused by lightning. On the principle that

---

[1] The COVID-19 virus was not yet known at this time.

'An ounce of prevention is worth a pound of cure', in 1736 Franklin already had helped to establish the Union Fire Company, 'Benjamin Franklin's Bucket Brigade', as a volunteer fire department. There is little, if any, evidence that Franklin was criticized for his 1752 Kite Experiment. Franklin's motivation for his Kite Experiment was 'to demonstrate the electrical nature of lightning, and to do so, he needed a thunderstorm. He had his materials at the ready: a simple kite made with a large silk handkerchief, a hemp string, and a silk string. ... Franklin's experiment demonstrated the connection between lightning and electricity' (Franklin Institute, 2019). It is thought likely that by 7 November 1749, about three years after he had first seen a Leyden jar, Franklin had reached the conclusion that lightning was a manifestation of electricity. In 1750, Franklin wrote:

> Estimating what an electrical cloud of 10,000 acres would do he is led to the conception of a lightning rod. 'I say, if these things are so, may not the knowledge of this power of points be of use to mankind, in preserving houses, churches, ships, etc. from the stroke of lightning, by directing us to fix on the highest part of those edifices upright rods of iron, made sharp as a needle and gilt to prevent rusting. ... Would not these pointed rods probably draw the electrical fire silently out of a cloud before it came nigh enough to strike and thereby secure us from that most sudden and terrible mischief?' This precedes the letter about the kite, two years. (McAdie, 1925)

This letter reveals Franklin's motivation for carrying out his courageous experiment with lighning, for, let us not forget, if it had gone wrong, Franklin could easily have been killed. The historical record shows the following. 1) The first experiments on electricity and lightning were carried out in France in the early 1750s. Franklin knew about these and found his own unique way to demonstrate what the lightning sparks meant. 2) Far from being criticised for his Kite Experiment, Franklin had a very serious purpose in mind, and won a prestigious medal for the invention of the lightning rod, which, for ever more, prevents fires by the million. 3) Apart from its obvious connection with electricity, however, Franklin's Kite Experiment had nothing whatsoever to do with 'gigawatt electrical grids', which were developed some 30 years later by Edison and Tesla.

Franklin's Kite Experiment illustrates some key differences in comparison to psi research. The Kite Experiment was based on Franklin's theory that lightning was a form of electricity. First, by comparison, there is no established theory that psi is a specific form of any established kind of energy. Second, Franklin's finding could be put to immediate practical use with the installation of lightning rods on major houses, buildings, bridges and ships, a technology that saves huge numbers of lives and buildings from destruction up to the present day. Psi does not pass the 'so what' test. Nobody can find it, see it, hear it, use it. The suggestion that psi could have an 'equally profound impact on civilisation' may keep hope alive, but that hope hangs by a thin thread of pure conjecture.

Looking for the common threads between the five psi-advocates, one can identify an extreme poverty of theory with some substantial gaps:

1. All five strongly believe in the reality of psi in spite of the weak evidence.
2. Nobody offers a single explanatory theory about how psi is developed or produced.
3. Bem's post hoc attempt to explain the within-experiment decline effect as a loss of 'enthusiasm' is unsupported by a long tradition of empirical research in experimental psychology.
4. Nobody offers any theory about why psi evolved in the first place.
5. Nobody offers any scientific explanation for the well-established sheep–goat effect.
6. Nobody attempted to explain how psi is related to states of consciousness more generally.

ALTERED STATES OF CONSCIOUSNESS

Turning to altered states of consciousness, we have discussed four in some depth: trance logic, OBE, NDE and spontaneous psi. The author's Belief Barometer was 100% for the first three and 75% for spontaneous ESP. The author's zetetic stance is vindicated by these high scores – a skeptic would be unlikely to ever assign values in the 75–100% range to these four categories of conscious experience.

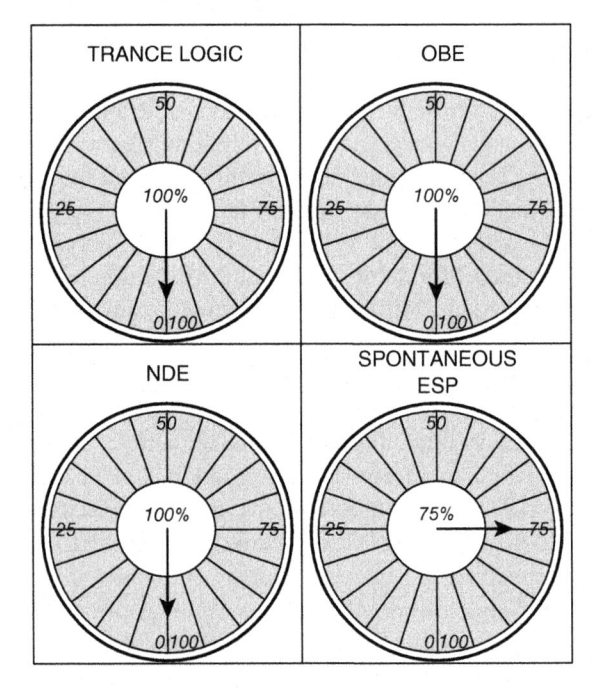

Figure 12.3 The author's Belief Barometer readings for four altered states of consciousness

THEORIES OF ANOMALOUS EXPERIENCE

Over the course of this book, five theories have been presented. They are listed below with the author's barometer readings:

T1: The 'theory' that psychological processes influence anomalous experience – 100%.

T2: The theory of subjective paranormal experience – 50%.

T3: The Magneto-Sensory Theory of psi – 10%.

T4: The Theory of Homeostasis – 100%.

T5: The Spectral Theory of altered states of consciousness – 90%.

The author's barometer readings show a large variation across the five theories (Figure 12.4) and remain contingent on any new evidence that becomes available.

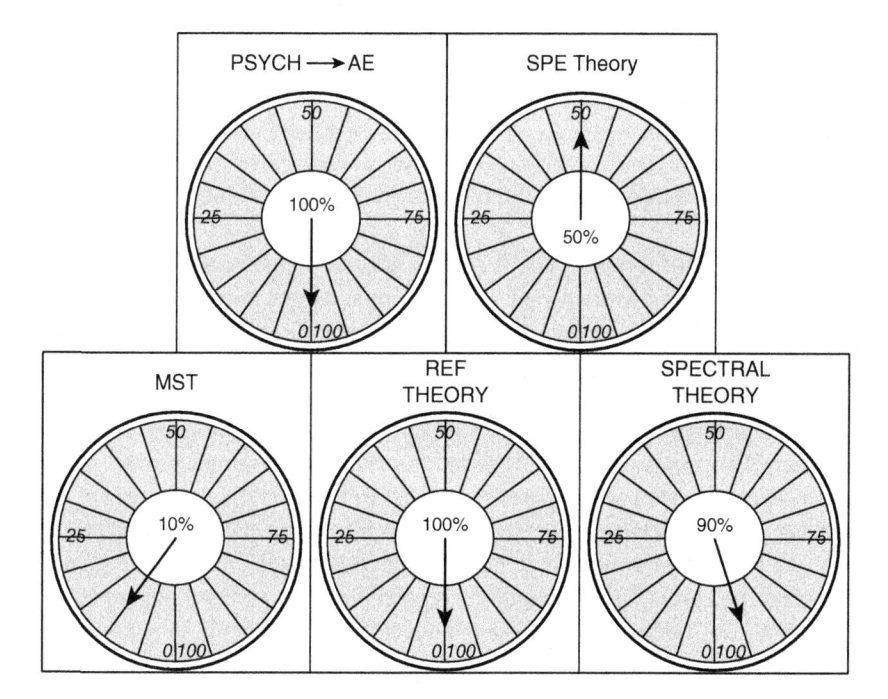

Figure 12.4 The Belief Barometer swings from 10% for Magneto-sensory Theory (bottom left), to 50% for the SPE Theory (top right), to 90% for the Spectral Theory (bottom right), and all the way to 100% for the Psychological Theory of Anomalous Experience (top left) and Homeostasis Theory (bottom centre).

SPONTANEITY AS A FACTOR IN ESP

Wallace Brown Scherer (1913–2006) completed a masters degree in J. B. Rhine's Parapsychology Laboratory at Duke University. His masters research was published as 'Spontaneity as a factor in ESP' (see Figure 12.5).

SPONTANEITY AS A FACTOR IN ESP

By Wallace B. Scherer

ABSTRACT: In an experiment designed to study the effect of spontaneity in ESP tests, subjects made trials, one at a time at widely spaced intervals, only when they had a definite impulse or hunch as to the correct response. The results of these "spontaneous" trials were compared with three types of "control" series: those in which the trials were made one at a time at widely spaced intervals but with conscious deliberation on the part of the subject before he made his response; those made with the trials grouped into runs and with conscious deliberation before each trial; and those made in runs with no directions as to method of response. Two self-testing devices were used (the Marble Machine and the Hunch Box) in both of which the subject was required to identify, by ESP, one of five colors.

The combined "spontaneous" data proved to be highly significant. None of the control series, either singly or in combination, yielded extrachance data. The results therefore support the hypothesis that conditions favoring spontaneity are more likely to produce good ESP scoring than conditions like those of the control series in which spontaneity was presumably at a minimum.

Mr. Scherer is Research Assistant in the Parapsychology Laboratory.—Ed.

Figure 12.5 Abstract from 'Spontaneity as a factor in ESP' by Wallace B. Scherer (1948). After completing his masters, Wallace Scherer worked as a professor and became director of a psychological instruments company

Scherer's (1948) article begins: 'There is wide agreement among parapsychologists upon the importance of subtle personal factors in tests of extrasensory perception.' In his innovative experiments, Scherer discovered that one crucial 'subtle personal factor' was spontaneity. He found that ESP worked much more effectively when the P had a definite impulse or hunch as to the correct response. In three control series of trials, in accordance with the standard expectations of a laboratory ESP experiment, the P needed to use conscious deliberation to predict the target colour. However, in none of the control trials did Scherer observe any evidence of above-chance scores. On the other hand, in the spontaneous trials, when the P could freely wait for a 'definite impulse or hunch' while spontaneously choosing when to respond, the results exceeded the chance level. Scherer made the deduction that conditions favouring spontaneity are more likely to produce good ESP scoring than conditions like those of the control series in which spontaneity was presumably at a minimum.

Wallace B. Scherer's (1948) contribution to ESP research deserves wider recognition. If his boss, J. B. Rhine, had only listened to Scherer (and to Louisa E. Rhine) concerning the *spontaneous nature of ESP*, the history of parapsychology could have been radically different.

Experimental studies require 'subjects' to respond on cue to the instructions from the investigator to produce psi at their command. The randomised sequences of targets and experimental conditions remove all possibility of subtle personal factors such as spontaneity, the element that, according to Scherer, is the *sine qua non* for successful ESP. Psi 'evades' capture in the scientific laboratory due to

Figure 12.6 Louisa E. Rhine (public domain)

this vital missing element of spontaneity. The inability to capture subtle personal factors is not unique to psi, however. Other significant psychological processes are equally difficult to capture in the laboratory for a similar reason – e.g. creativity, sexual arousal and moods. None of these can be easily induced at will inside the experimental laboratory.

One illustrative example from the field of creativity research is a meta-analysis of imagery and creativity studies (LeBoutillier & Marks, 2003). Multiple reports from creative individuals suggest that mental imagery is crucial to scientific and artistic production and so the theoretical rationale for predicting an association between mental imagery and creativity scores is strong (Table 12.1).

Table 12.1 Creative individuals who reported the use of mental imagery

Area	Creative individual
Science and philosophy	Bohr, Cannon, Maxwell, Crick, Descartes, Edison, Einstein, Freud, Faraday, Galton, Hadamard, Helmholtz, Herschel, Kant, Kekulé, Leibniz, Loewi, Nietszche, Poincaré, Snyder, Tesla, Watson, Watt
Art, film and sculpture	Breton, Cocteau, Dali, Ernst, Hitchcock, Hockney, Kandinsky, Moore, Surls
Literature	Asimov, Baudelaire, Borges, Castanada, Coleridge, Dickens, Didion, Fitzgerald
	Goethe, Keats, Lessing, Nabokov, Poe, Rimbaud, Schiller, Shelley, Tennyson, Wordsworth
Music	Beethoven, Berlioz, Brahms, Debussy, Mozart, Puccini, Scriabin, Wagner

Reproduced from LeBoutillier and Marks (2003), with permission.

Figure 12.7 Imaginary response by Leonardo da Vinci to the 'Uses' creativity test

A huge variety of lab protocols have been used to investigate the reported association between mental imagery and creativity. To put it bluntly some of them are just plain bonkers. Creativity measures are universally shallow renderings of real-life forms of creativity. One typical example was the test developed by J. P. Guilford in 1967, the Alternative Uses Test evaluates one's creativity by allowing two minutes to think of as many uses as possible for an everyday object such as a chair, coffee mug, or brick (Figure 12.7).

People with high creativity scores are predicted to have correspondingly high imagery vividness scores. Nick LeBoutillier assessed the existing findings through meta-analysis. Searches revealed 18 papers that had used the individual differences approach and these were subjected to conservative selection criteria leaving nine studies (1,494 Ps). A marginal, but statistically significant, Fisher's Z-transformed correlation coefficient was revealed. A dismal 3% of the variance in the data sets was found between mental imagery ability and creativity scores. Yet we know from the accounts of highly creative individuals that the ability to conjure up vivid images is crucial to the creative process. The laboratory fails to measure up to the task of demonstrating the role of imagery in the creative process.

Laboratory creativity measures are woefully inadequate for multiple reasons: test administration, reliability, content, criterion validity, construct validity and the scoring rules used for the tasks. Laboratory studies do not enable true creativity to occur. Creativity measures are not amenable to mental imagery in the spontaneous manner that is described by so many objectively creative individuals. One basic problem is the time limitation imposed in their administration – from 10 to 30 minutes. Laboratory creativity tests are mostly tests of speed (Jankowska & Karwowski, 2015), as are many lab tests of psi. It is not surprising that meta-analyses show small effect sizes if the creativity tests themselves have such low validity.

Meta-analyses of the association between creativity and theoretically relevant constructs such as mood, schizotypy, psychoticism and academic achievement also produce only tiny effects. The results show the correlation between creativity scores and mood, r = .15 (Baas, De Dreu, & Nijstad, 2008); schizotypy, r = .14; negative disorganized schizotypy, r = .09 (Acar & Sen, 2013); mental illness, < 3% variance (Silvia & Kimbrel, 2010); psychoticism, r = .16 (Acar & Runco, 2012); and academic achievement, r = .22 (Gajda, Karwowski, & Beghetto, 2017). Thus, creativity scores typically account for 1–4% of the variance in these relevant psychological variables. The problem lies not with the theoretical rationale, but with laboratory testing procedures that are non-conducive to genuine creativity which cannot be induced at will.

Laboratory methods are inadequate or plainly inappropriate for several other 'subtle personal processes', e.g. deception (Sip, Roepstorff, McGregor, & Frith, 2008), sexual arousal (Marshall & Fernandez, 2000) and mood (Polivy, 1981). Experimental role-play or simulation of any of these processes is always possible in the lab if one is prepared to accept play-acting as a proxy for the real thing, but simulation is never an authentic process, only a faked copy.

One wonders why psi is widely considered to be such a versatile and robust process that it can be put 'on tap' for laboratory investigators. If one accepts the existence of psi, then it is as a hypothetical process closely allied to other noetic experiences with conscious and unconscious elements (Figure 12.8). It is implausible to expect that psi could be produced automatically like so many key-presses, verbal responses or recalls from memory.

A mixture of tradition, naivety and scientific arrogance made psi a candidate for controlled laboratory study. Rarely can states of consciousness be switched on and off at will like so many light bulbs. Wakefulness and sleep are everyday examples of states involving a strong element of spontaneity combined with appropriate set and setting together with homeostatic and circadian regulation. The sleep–wake cycle is subject to significant disrupting effects from negative emotion. Insomnia is produced by negative emotionality and sleep quality is linked with positive emotionality (Baglioni, Spiegelhalder, Lombardo, & Riemann, 2010). Moods, feelings and motives, both conscious and unconscious, surely influence psi to make it even more unpredictable and unreliable than the ability to control sleeping and waking. In the case of psi there are also subtle social factors. Ian Wickramasekera (1991) suggested that psi is dependent upon the existence of an 'ideal' interpersonal relationship between the sender and receiver, so that psi might only occur when the couple are closely related, such as parent–child or husband–wife. Laboratory investigators of psi have not made a habit of testing psi among loving family couples or parent–child dyads, yet these interpersonal relationships between senders and receivers must surely be crucial for psi to occur.

Louisa E. Rhine was well aware of the difficulties with ESP laboratory studies: 'The general impression one would get from this record of low, even if significant, scoring is that ESP, at least under laboratory conditions, is exercised with difficulty; that it is somehow restricted, able to function only imperfectly and sporadically' (1962: 88). Perhaps there was pillow talk about this with husband Joseph.

States of consciousness, which are not available at the will of Ps or investigators, can only be studied in the laboratory using special procedures. For example, special states of consciousness can only be made fully operational in the laboratory after the administration of psychedelic substances (Luke, 2012; McKellar, 1961). Regular users of psychoactive drugs commonly report psi and related anomalous experiences (Luke & Kittenis, 2005). Psychedelic states of consciousness are conducive to psi and these psychic states can readily flow into other noetic experiences (Luke, 2015). Writing about mescaline, Peter McKellar observed:

> Thus mescaline may well provide insight into two kinds of human thinking: those we call mystical, and those we call psychotic. There is a third possibility which may also be kept in mind. Mescaline and other hallucinogenic drugs may alert people to notice things that are going on all the time in normal mental life. Typical human thinking is less characterized either by realistic assessment of evidence, or by sustained acts of logical inference than is often supposed. Mescaline provides a useful technique for amplifying and caricaturing deviations from realism. These deviations are by no means uncommon in everyday thought. (1961: 12)

Peter McKellar did not discuss psi in his publications, but his early research with Lorna Simpson and J. Amor Ardis explored the increased capability to induce subtle states of consciousness such as hypnagogic imagery following ingestion of mescaline (Ardis & McKeller, 1956; McKellar & Simpson, 1954). In his path-breaking book, *Imagination and Thinking*, McKellar (1957a) also focused on mescaline-induced 'model psychosis'. In the same period, *Doors of Perception: And Heaven and Hell*, by Aldous Huxley (1954/2010) also described the psychedelic world of mescaline.

Pharmaceutical companies today are giving new, synthetic psychedelic drugs active attention. Use of synthetic psychedelic drugs is increasing (Orsolini et al., 2015). Psychedelics are serotonergic hallucinogens of three chemical types: tryptamines, ergolines and phenethylamines. In the brain, the serotonin 5-HT2A receptor, which plays a key role in regulation of cortical function and cognition, also appears to be the principal target for hallucinogenic/psychedelic drugs such as LSD (Nichols, 2017). All things considered, without the possibility to give participants psychedelic drugs, the parapsychology laboratory is perhaps one of the last places on Earth where one would expect to observe genuinely produced spontaneous psi.

Parapsychologists themselves have often expressed doubts about their access to psi in the laboratory, but usually not in print. However, there are a few exceptions. Louisa E. Rhine's (1962) opinion that ESP is 'somehow restricted, able to function only imperfectly and sporadically' has already been noted above. Another querier J. E. Kennedy (2003) describes psi as 'capricious, actively evasive, unsustainable' for good reason. Kennedy suggests the primary function of psi is to induce a sense of mystery and wonder, and he speculates: 'Some type of higher consciousness may influence or control psi effects.'

In an earlier publication, I concluded that 'Parascience has so far failed to produce a single repeatable finding and, until it does, will continue to be viewed as an incoherent collection of belief systems steeped in fantasy, illusion and error' (Marks, 1986a). Has this book revealed any persuasive reason to change this conclusion? Disappointingly, the answer is a resounding 'No'.

CONCLUSION

The psi hypothesis remains unconfirmed but neither is it disconfirmed. If psi exists at all, it is an intuitive, subtle and intrinsically subjective human capability that cannot be summoned at will. Searching for psi in the laboratory is a wild goose chase and psi will never be found there using traditional experimental methods. This is for the fundamental reason that *it is impossible for a research participant to produce psi at will.*

If psi exists, it happens in a spontaneous, unpredictable and uncontrollable manner – e.g. as a remarkable coincidence or other anomalous experience. In spite of a prodigious effort over a century of endeavour, no scientist has yet demonstrated psi in a replicable, reliable and robust manner. Psi does not appear to demand whether in the laboratory, casino, stock exchange, military setting or in the search for missing persons or criminals. Any self-proclaimed psychic – claiming the ability to produce psi at will – is announcing to the world that they are a charlatan.[2] Owing to the essential principle that psi cannot be summoned at will, the deliberate, willful demonstration of psi has never happened in the past, will not happen in the present, nor will it ever happen in the future. Psi is a spontaneous, uncontrollable process having both conscious and unconscious elements (Figure 12.8).

TAKE-HOME MESSAGE: SKEPTICS

Skeptics, you are right to be critical of the exaggerated claims of parapsychologists. However, as unbending skeptics you are guilty of an unfortunate piece of flawed reasoning that I call the 'Skeptic's Fallacy':

1. If psi exists, then evidence of psi will be found in laboratory experiments.
2. Evidence of psi has not been found in laboratory experiments.
3. Therefore, psi does not exist.[3]

---

[2] Self-proclaimed psychics (e.g. Kreskin, Geller) were debunked in earlier books (Marks, 2000; Marks & Kammann, 1980).
[3] Similar arguments can be applied to the evidence from casinos, stocks and shares, and alleged military use of psi.

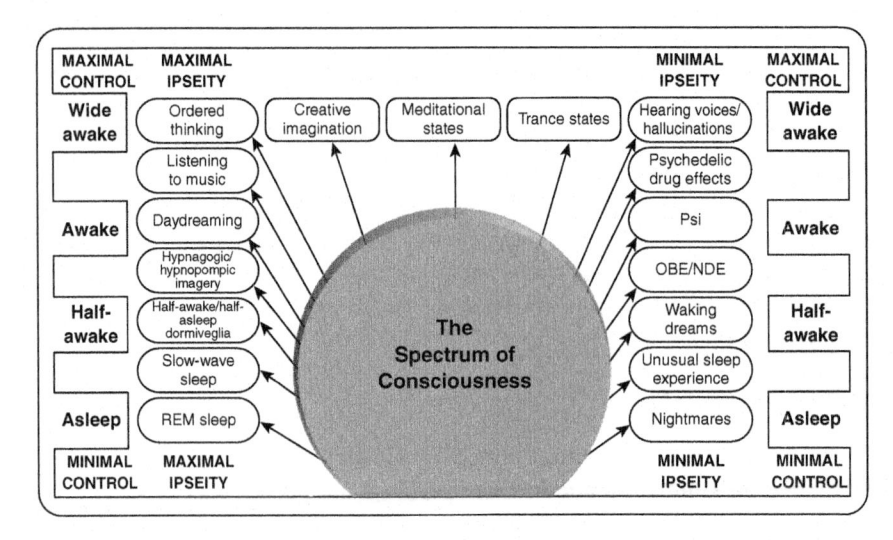

Figure 12.8 The spectral theory of consciousness. States of consciousness (SOCs) lie on a continuum and coalesce with their immediate neighbours so that daydreaming merges with the hypnagogic state on one side and with music listening on the other. According to the theory, psi is positioned between psychedelic drug states and the OBE/NDE. A symmetry between the left- and right-hand sides suggests the hypothesis of mirror-image correspondence between REM sleep and nightmares, slow-wave sleep and unusual sleep experiences, daydreaming and psi, and so on. Further investigation of these ideas could prove fruitful in future studies.

The 'Skeptic's Premise' (Premise 1) is false. Advocates claim that 2) is false also. However, the conclusion 3) is false. To avoid the Skeptic's Fallacy, a different premise, 1B), the 'Zetetic's Premise', is necessary:

1B. If psi exists, evidence of psi will be found either in laboratory experiments or spontaneous reports.
2. Evidence of psi has not been found in laboratory experiments.
3. Therefore, psi does not exist in laboratory experiments, but it may exist in spontaneous reports.

To avoid an easy take-down, skeptics must avoid the Skeptic's Fallacy. They also need to moderate the tone and quality of their argumentation. They need to avoid 'straw man' arguments and *ad hominem* attacks. They need to display more humility and respect for others' opinions, especially opinions with which they do not agree. The 'old ways' of attacking and belittling parapsychologists have been and always will be counterproductive. In spite of all of the skeptics' strenuous efforts, psi remains an intriguing, if yet unconfirmed, scientific hypothesis.

TAKE-HOME MESSAGE: PARAPSYCHOLOGISTS

There has been a collective failure in parapsychology to find any convincing, replicable evidence of psi in laboratory investigations. The main reason for this failure – so I wish to maintain – lies beyond the control of investigators and research participants. *Psi is not a process that is available at will.* The assumption that psi is automatically turned on or off for the convenience of the investigator is an error, a myth. In the programme of laboratory research started by Joseph Banks Rhine, a trained botanist, parapsychologists have all been operating on the false premise that research participants can induce psi at will. All of the evidence suggests that such spontaneous evocation of psi is an impossibility.

Many leading parapsychologists and psi-advocates are not trained in psychology; they are biologists, physicists, engineers, psychiatrists or doctors of medicine. The assumption that psi can be investigated using the same methodological framework as plants, particles or proteins is intuitively appealing, but, in my opinion, seriously mistaken. The murky pool of parapsychology may provide a smaller pond to work in than physics, biology or engineering but, in operational terms, it is much more complex. Understanding a psychological process requires an in-depth appreciation of psychological theory, research and practice, which many of the leading parapsychologists do not possess. The superficial simplicity of the 'stimulus-response' approach to conducting laboratory experiments on psi is purely illusory. There is a complex interplay of social and psychological processes in any laboratory experiment with human Ps that is underestimated by the vast majority of investigators. Many of the greatest minds in the field have fallen prey to methodological traps and pitfalls without even realising it. Thinking one is immune to being fooled is foolishness itself and a sure way of being fooled.

For the J. B. Rhine school of parapsychologists, a psi experiment is akin to a tray of seedlings. Take compost, add seeds, light and water, and you produce thriving plants. Take a P, stick halved-ping-pong balls on their eyes, switch on the red light and white noise, tell them their instructions, and you produce above-chance ESP. In moving from a plant to a person, the seed tray makes an inappropriate analogy. The 'seed-tray' approach to parapsychology does not succeed because *psi does not respond to the 'cultivation' of the investigator*. Wallace B. Scherer knew this but his was a lone voice in the wilderness.

One of the many troubles with parapsychology is that it revolves around the constant struggle for scientific respectability. The laboratory experiment and the white laboratory coat have totemic significance. The scientific models are physics, botany and chemistry. Yet none is an appropriate model for a 'science of the soul'. Dean Radin (2019) suggests that 'psychophysics' would have made a more appropriate title for the discipline, but this label also privileges the laboratory. Perhaps parapsychology should look to geography, archaeology or geology for an approach to the discovery of hidden and elusive psychological processes within the 'substrata' of the human mind. Inevitably, at the end of what we can now see has been a wild goose chase. The century-long obsession with the laboratory experiment is being superseded by alternative approaches with greater potential.

The few investigators like the late Dr John Beloff, who have had the courage to publicly speak out about their inability to produce psi in the laboratory, are not the abject 'failures' they viewed themselves to be. These null-effect finders are the stars, the beacons of excellence, the champions of well-controlled experimentation, the discoverers of the well-manicured null effect. If the null effect is the true effect, then all of Parapsychology's positive findings are 'Error Some Place' (ESP): subjective validation, incomplete randomisation, lapses in experimental control, questionable research practices (QRPs) and occasional investigator fraud. I encourage Drs. Dean Radin, Daryl Bem and Rupert Sheldrake to give this conclusion some serious thought: *the Null Effect is the True Effect.*

Parapsychologists often complain about their lack of research funding. Yet not unreasonably, sponsors require concrete results in the form of discoveries, patents and inventions. Putting research funds into a stagnant field is to pour 'good money after bad'. There is not one single non-frivolous invention based on parapsychology. Patents in the psychic realm are only playthings, toys and games – e.g. a 1891 patent for 'Fortune-telling games', a 1920 'Ouija Board Print' patent, a 1934 application for 'Fortune telling cards' and a 2016 'Device for fanciful detection of ghosts'.

Beyond any doubt, the most lucrative fields of exploitation have been in literature (e.g. J. K. Rowling/*Harry Potter* book series sales exceeding 500 million copies and having its own mini-town in Hollywood's Universal City), films (e.g. *Ghostbusters, The Blair Witch Project, Paranormal Activity*, and many others), fantasy games (e.g. *Carl Sargent/Keith Martin*), and the so-called 'precog economy' (Julia Mossbridge, cited by Tait, 2019). These works make fine profits as entertainment, but they also promote pseudo-science.

In mental health settings, increasing acceptance of psychedelic drugs as a health intervention is opening new doors to treatment and research. Psilocybin with psychological support has been found to be safe and helpful for people with depression (Carhart-Harris et al., 2016) and LSD has been found safe and efficacious in people suffering with anxiety and life-threatening diseases (Gasser et al., 2014). Following approval of psychedelic administration in psychotherapy, opportunities for many more scientific studies of psychedelic-induced psi and other anomalous experiences are becoming more widely available.

Newer research methods are extending the scope of the field away from quantitative towards qualitative studies. In addition to the traditional survey method using instruments such as the Survey of Anomalous Experiences (Irwin et al., 2013), innovative methods for studying spontaneous paranormal experiences are available, including qualitative research approaches such as thematic analysis (e.g. Drinkwater, Dagnall, Grogan, & Riley, 2017) and narrative approaches (e.g. Hill et al., 2018). Innovative non-laboratory methods of exploration such as 'para-design' (paranormal design – thinking beyond or outside 'normal' design scenarios) can be considered. Reconceptualisation and measurements of core experiences commonly attributed to anomalous experiences need to be created. For example, in the context of haunts and poltergeists, Houran, Laythe, O'Keeffe, Dagnall, Drinkwater, and Lange (2019) identified 28 base experiences that include subjective experiences, typical of haunts, and objective manifestations, more common to poltergeist-like disturbances. Their qualitatively vetted list is proposed as 'the foundation for new measurement approaches, research designs and analytical methods aimed to advance model-building and theory-formation'. Rasch scaling methods need to be employed to make psychometric improvements to the most frequently used scales (e.g. Lange, 2017; Lange, Ross, Dagnall, Irwin, Houran, & Drinkwater, 2019).

Recent innovative studies have explored noetic experience (Yaden et al., 2017), theorised about the connections between emotions and higher order states instantiated in cortical circuits (LeDoux & Brown, 2017), the feeling of personal ownership of one's mental states (Klein 2015), weak and visionary fantasy (Horváth, Szummer, & Szabo, 2018), and have theorised about selfhood and ipseity within a General Theory of Consciousness (Marks, 2019b). None of these studies has taken place in a parapsychological framework, yet they are highly relevant and applicable to psi as one form of anomalous experience.

New generations of parapsychologists (who most likely will not use the term) will reflect on how best to carve out their research careers in the field of subjective anomalous experience. New scholars of anomalous experience will likely consider anomalistic psychology, neuroscience, clinical psychology, psychopharmacology or psychiatry equally compelling career routes. These fields offer alternative theories and methods for the exploration of subjective anomalous experiences as processes of the conscious brain. They will be the future, make no mistake about it.

TAKE-HOME MESSAGE: THE PARAPSYCHOLOGICAL ASSOCIATION

In George Orwell's *Nineteen Eighty-Four* 'doublethink' is a technique for exploiting contradiction especially as a form of indoctrination. The Parapsychological Association's (PA) method of dealing with the evidence on psi is the perfect example of doublethink. In spite of the continuing claims of advocates, the facts show that reliable, replicable laboratory evidence of psi has not been demonstrated. Yet the PA claims that ESP is proven. Period. The PA's statements about psi are nothing more than propaganda, more fitting to a religious cult than to science. To cite one example, the association claims that the 'cumulative database strongly indicates that information about remote photos, actual scenes, and events can be perceived'. This statement is contradicted by all of the evidence if viewed critically from a methodological perspective. It is shameful that in purporting to be the scientific voice of parapsychology, the PA is so manifestly unwilling to be the objective purveyor of truth. There is not a single replicated finding to support the

PA's above-quoted claim. Surely I cannot be the only one of the 400 PA members who thinks that the grossly exaggerated information put out by the PA is okay.

Parapsychologists' fixation with the laboratory experiment must change. As the 2018–19 President of the PA, Dean Radin (2019), stated:

> My professional interest in these anomalies has focused on psychic phenomena, because now we are dealing with anomalies that can be studied under laboratory conditions. Rather than relying on spontaneous events or extremely rare people, we can study ordinary people performing simple tasks. I believe that makes our topic of study far more tractable than trying to figure out what made Leonardo da Vinci tick.

The latter strikes on as a self-deceiving remark. Being 'tractable' but misguided is a strategy for looking where the light is. Dean Radin confesses his personal conviction that laboratory ESP is real is partly based on an external authority, Jessica Utts, Professor of Statistics at the University of California, Irvine, to bolster his beliefs:

> Because the empirical database is so strong, I now have an easy way to respond to skeptics who argue that there is no scientific evidence for psi. I ask them, rhetorically, what discipline is the best arbiter of the proper interpretation of data? The answer, when we think about it for a while, is statistics. Then I show them what Jessica Utts said about psi as part of her 2016 presidential address to the American Statistical Association (Utts, 2016): 'The data in support of precognition and possibly other related phenomena are quite strong statistically, and would be widely accepted if they pertained to something more mundane'. (p. 1379)

Radin does the very same thing in Chapter 8 of this book. There are many statisticians opposition to the views expressed by Jessica Utts – e.g. Persi Diaconis, Professor of Statistics and Mathematics at Stanford University (Diaconis, 1978). Resorting to a single statistician as an authority in support of the psi hypothesis does not resolve the existential question. A statistician is an expert on the analysis of data, not in the methodology of carrying out laboratory experiments.

There can be no substitute for building a consensus across science. When there is no consensus, perhaps there is nothing there.

The Orwellian Parapsychological Association must stop propagandising what it calls a 'strong indication' of ESP in the cumulative database, stop ignoring the methodological problems that pervade parapsychology, must start being truthful. The following honest message needs to be published at the top of each and every PA publication:

'The psi hypothesis is neither confirmed nor disconfirmed.'

Publishing this statement would bring the PA and lay public into honest alignment with the best current evidence. To give any other impression is to play fast and loose with the facts and an indulgence in double-think.

TAKE-HOME MESSAGE: STUDENTS OF ANOMALISTIC PSYCHOLOGY

Anomalistic psychology is a wonderful field that is wide open to new explorations, new theories and new discoveries. There is no conceivable limit to the expansion of knowledge about the human mind, the conscious brain and the world of anomalous experience. Ceasing the wild goose chase for laboratory psi would help to clear the way to replicable scientific research without the endless controversies about statistics, meta-analyses and ever-shrinking decline effects.

Finally, I return to the idea mentioned in the Preface – the streetlight effect – searching for a missing 'key' where it is easiest to look. If no 'key' is found under that streetlight, one risks the false conclusion that there is no key. If the elusive psi cannot be found where it is easiest to look – the laboratory – investigators should redouble their search in the world outside. This change in approach is both a challenge and an opportunity.

Psi is an anomaly of ceaseless wonder and mystery. The psi hypothesis remains neither confirmed nor disconfirmed but it connects us to our fellow beings, to nature and the cosmos at large. In passing the baton to a new generation of explorers, the search for psi and other anomalous experiences continues with redoubled efforts. You know the many pitfalls and you will strive to avoid them. You may not find what you are looking for, but there will be many discoveries along the way. If psi is one day finally discovered, you will have solved an enigma like no other.

APPENDIX

Concepts, Measures and Methods

> Any field of science should properly be judged on the basis of its methods of investigation. (Rhine & Pratt, 1962: 17)

Outline: This Appendix provides an A–Z of concepts, measures and methods relevant to investigations of anomalistic and paranormal phenomena.[1] Key concepts are defined. Experimental procedures, commonly used measures and statistical techniques necessary for research in anomalistic psychology are introduced. Possible reasons for the poor replication in research and scientific fields more generally are discussed. The use of meta-analysis is explained and critiqued. For more depth and detail, the reader should consult a specialist textbook.

A priori   an opinion or belief that is fixed in advance producing a strong likelihood of confirmation bias.

Ad hoc hypothesis   a hypothesis created after the fact to explain evidence that appears inconvenient to a theory.

Ad hominem   a strategy used in a debate, discussion or argument that involves attacking the character, motive or attributes of the person making the argument, rather than the substance of the argument itself. The term *ad feminam* is an equivalent term applied to females. Both are always best avoided.

---

[1] More in-depth treatment can be found in research methods texts such as Marks and Yardley (2004), *Research Methods for Clinical and Health Psychology*.

Anomalous cognition a term for phenomena such as clairvoyance, precognition, remote viewing and telepathy, collectively known as 'psi'.

Anomalous Experiences Inventory (AEI) a 70-item true–false questionnaire to investigate anomalous and paranormal experiences, beliefs and abilities, drug and alcohol use, and fear of the paranormal – e.g. 'I have had a psychic experience'; 'I am able to communicate with the dead'. The AEI is claimed to have adequate reliability and validity (Gallagher, Kumar, & Pekala, 1994).

Anomaly an event or experience that deviates from an accepted norm, theory or principle established in science.

Artefact (UK) or artifact (US) a misleading result in a study caused by a hidden or uncontrolled factor such as incomplete randomisation, sensory cues, subject selection or demand characteristics.

Australian Sheep–Goat Scale (ASGS) a measure of belief in and alleged experience of the paranormal. The scale contains 18 items about three core concepts of parapsychology: ESP (extrasensory perception), PK (psychokinesis) and life after death (Thalbourne, 1995). The term 'sheep' is used for a 'believer' in psychic phenomena, while 'goat' is used for a 'disbeliever' or 'skeptic'. The ASGS also has an improved 26-item measure (Thalbourne, 2010).

Autocorrelation also called 'serial correlation', this is a method for investigating whether there is a correlation between different sectors within the series.

Bayes factor a way of directly comparing one theory against another – for example, P Theory against N Theory.[2] Once new data have been collected, we can calculate the likelihood of the data for each theory. As noted, the Bayes factor (B) is the ratio of the likelihoods:

$$B = P(HN/D)/P(HP/D)$$

From the axioms of probability theory:

$$\text{Posterior Odds} = \text{Prior Odds} \times \text{Bayes factor (B)}$$

If B is greater than 1, then the data support the experimental hypothesis over the null hypothesis. If B is less than 1, then the data support the null hypothesis over the experimental one. B scores above 3 or below one-third are said to be 'substantial'. B scores above 100 or below .01 represent a notable finding. However, if the prior odds are at an extremely low level, then the posterior odds will remain low even if the Bayes factor of the data is extremely high.

Bayes's rule a rational method for revising one's degree of belief about the plausibility of a hypothesis after new evidence. One's degree of belief concerning the hypothesis can be compared to an opposing hypothesis such as a null hypothesis. If two hypotheses exist, HN and HP, before we collect new data (D), one assigns one's initial beliefs or 'prior odds' as the ratio of the strength of belief in the two hypotheses, p(HN)/P(HP). Imagine a person, X, believes that HN is 10 times more plausible than HP. In this case the prior odds for this person, p(HN)/P(HP), is 10. New data are collected. Suppose the new data are 100 times more likely on the basis of HP

---

[2] For a user-friendly introduction to the Bayesian approach, see the papers by Zoltan Dienes (2011, 2016).

being true than on the basis of HN being true. In this case, the likelihood ratio or Bayes factor is 1/100. Using Bayes's rule, then, the posterior odds are calculated by the formula:

$$\text{Posterior Odds} = \text{Prior Odds} \times P(HN/D)/P(HP/D) = 10 \times 1/100 = 1/10$$

Thus, in the light of the new data, X must revise their beliefs in the plausibility of HN and HP. For X, P(HP) is 10 times more probable than P(HN) after the new data – a complete reversal of opinion brought about the new data being so strongly favourable to HP. Research shows that people tend not to change their opinions as much as the new data require. Hence, it is preferable to use a formal Bayesian procedure to adjust one's beliefs in response to new data.

Bonferroni correction a method for controlling the risk of type I error when making multiple statistical tests, multiple comparisons or statistical tests. If one makes m multiple comparisons, and wishes to have an overall confidence level of alpha (e.g. $p < .05$), then each individual test or multiple comparison can be adjusted to the level of alpha/m. Thus, with 10 tests or multiple comparisons and the significance level or alpha set at .05, then the Bonferroni correction would be set to a new alpha level of $.05/10 = .005$. This lowers the risk of a type I error. It is a common procedure in research to make multiple statistical comparisons. If these comparisons are unplanned, then this strategy is referred to as a 'fishing expedition'. When a study is published, the extent of the 'fishing' may not be obvious to readers. Hence, this fishing strategy is one example of a Questionable Research Practice (or QRP). At the .05 or 5% significance level known as the 'alpha' (α) level, with 20 tests there is a 64% chance of observing at least one significant result, even if none is actually significant (a type I error). In a research project, numerous simultaneous tests may be required and the probability of obtaining a significant result purely by chance can be very high. Hence, the Bonferroni correction reduces the required α level so that the probability of observing at least one significant result due to chance remains below the desired significance level.

However, the Bonferroni adjustment procedure does not distinguish between exploratory and data-driven testing versus hypothesis-driven testing. Instead, procedures derived from limiting false discovery rates may be a more appealing method to control error rates in multiple tests. An alternative to the Bonferroni correction is the *false discovery rate correction* (Glickman, Rickman, & Schultz, 2014).

Cardiff Beliefs Questionnaire consists of three scales: 1) a measure of 'delusion-like beliefs' – i.e. beliefs that constitute the delusional ideation as specified by the DSM-IV-TR (*American Australian Journal of Parapsychology & Psychiatric Association*, 2000) – e.g. the convictions that 'people say or do things that contain special messages for you', and 'there is another person who looks and acts like you'; 2) a measure of paranormal and religious beliefs with items drawn from earlier questionnaires and instruments; 3) a set of scientific, political and social beliefs that are widely viewed in society as having a rational grounding (Pechey & Halligan, 2012).

Case-study methodology begins with reports of spontaneous occurrences of anomalous experiences (aka 'spontaneous cases'). There is always a need to authenticate such cases by carefully checking the circumstances and the reliability of reporting together with any evidence that may be available from other sources. However, even elaborate efforts made towards substantiating spontaneous experiences may fail to reveal definite evidence that can be relied upon to draw definite conclusions. The case study is an exploratory method that is difficult, if not impossible, to convert into reliable scientific data. However, the case method is an important source of ideas concerning the properties of psi as it functions spontaneously even if it is impossible to reach any definite conclusions.

Causation   a special connection between one process or state – the cause – with another process or state – the effect – in which the cause is wholly or partially responsible for the effect; the first process or state is said to cause the second process or state.

Cherry-picking   a misleading and self-delusory QRP involving the selection of research findings that fit one's prior beliefs, retaining confirming findings and dispatching unfitting findings into the file drawer. Cherry-picking is a form of bad science. There are several well-known examples of cherry-picking on both sides of the paranormal divide. It is a procedure guaranteed to produce confirmation bias.

Cold reading   a set of techniques for performing as a mind-reader, techniques used to convince strangers that you know all about them (Hyman, 1977). Hyman states: 'To be popular with your fellow [man or woman], tell [them] what s/he wants to hear.' It is possible to achieve success as a character reader using a 'stock spiel' that is given to every client. Sundberg (1955) found that the following character sketch will usually be accepted as a reasonably accurate description:

> You are a person who is very normal in his attitudes, behavior and relationships with people. You get along well without effort. People naturally like you, and you are not overly critical of them or yourself. You are neither overly conventional nor overly individualistic. Your prevailing mood is one of optimism and constructive effort, and you are not troubled by periods of depression, psychosomatic illness or nervous symptoms.

Sundberg conducted his research over 60 years ago, yet the standard sketches still work well today. The statements were first used in 1943 by Bertram Forer (1949) in a classroom demonstration of personal validation. Forer obtained most of the statements from a newsstand astrology book.

Committee for Skeptical Inquiry (CSI)   formerly known as the Committee for the Scientific Investigation of Claims of the Paranormal (CSICOP), this is an organisation that claims to 'promote scientific inquiry, critical investigation, and the use of reason in examining controversial and extraordinary claims'. Paul Kurtz, Martin Gardner, Ray Hyman and the conjuror James Randi established CSICOP in 1976 to counter what they regarded as an uncritical acceptance of paranormal claims in the media and society in general. The organisation has a magazine called *Skeptical Inquirer*. The author was appointed a Fellow of the committee in the early 1980s after the publication of his skeptical book with Richard Kammann, *The Psychology of the Psychic* (1980). Kammann left the organisation after an embarrassing controversy about astrology. While working on this book, this author also resigned. With some validity, critics claim that CSI is biased and non-scientific, seeking only to block and ridicule scientific inquiry and investigation into parapsychological and other anomalous claims (e.g. Truzzi, 1987). Available online at: https://centerforinquiry.org/

Conceptual replication   an attempt to test a hypothesis proposed in an earlier study to determine whether the results will generalise to different samples, times or situations.

Confederate   aka as a 'stooge', an actor working in cahoots with an investigator to deceive unsuspecting research Ps.

Confidence Interval (CI) the interval around the mean of a sample that has a known probability of containing the mean of the population. A population parameter is normally estimated using a sample. The reliability of the estimate varies according to sample size. A confidence interval specifies a range of values in which a parameter is estimated to lie. The narrower the interval, the more reliable the estimate. Typically the 95% or the 99% CI is stated in the results of a study that has obtained a representative sample of values – e.g. the mean heart rate for a sample might be 75.0 with a 95% CI of 72.6 to 77.4. Confidence intervals are reported in tables or graphs along with point estimates of the parameters to indicate the reliability of the estimates.

Confirmation bias the pervasive tendency to notice elements of data or experience that are consistent with one's hypotheses or expectations and to ignore the elements that are inconsistent with, or in opposition to, one's point of view.

Conflicts of interest (or 'competing interests') exist when an investigator is affected by personal, financial or institutional bias towards a conclusion that is favourable to a hypothesis, theory or finding. Authors are expected to declare any conflicts of interest, whether actual or perceived, at the point of peer review prior to publication. Undeclared conflicts of interest can result in an expression of concern or retraction of a paper by the editor.

Controlled experimental design a design that allows one or more experimental conditions to be compared with a control condition. The Ps are randomised to each experimental condition. If possible, the investigator and the Ps do not know which condition the P has been allocated to, so-called 'double blinding', until the data are analysed. This type of design is used for testing the efficacy of therapies and treatments in clinical trials aka randomised controlled trials (RCTs). However, in many studies where there is an obvious type of intervention – e.g. a special therapy or procedure – double blinding is impossible and the results are open to controversy.

Correlation an association between two or more processes or states that is not necessarily causal in nature.

Correlation coefficient a measure of the strength of the relationship between two variables. The Pearson correlation coefficient, or Pearson's r, one of the most commonly used statistical measures of association, is a measure of the linear correlation between two normally distributed variables X and Y. It is also known as the Pearson product-moment correlation coefficient. Non-normally distributed variables require a non-parametric rank correlation such as Kendall's tau or Spearman's (rho) rank correlation coefficient.

Creative Experiences Questionnaire (CEQ) a brief self-report measure of fantasy proneness (Merckelbach, Horselenberg, & Muris, 2001).

Cross-sectional designs used in investigations that obtain scores from one or more samples of Ps on a single occasion. The average scores can be compared between groups and the scores can also be correlated to determine the degree of association between those scores. The procedure is popular especially in student projects because they are relatively inexpensive in time and resources. However, there are major problems of interpretation. Cause and effect can never be implied between one variable and another, and it is impossible to say whether the observed associations are caused by a third background variable not measured in the study. Many studies are done with students as Ps and we can never be sure that the use of a non-random, non-representative sample of students is methodologically rigorous. The ecological validity of the findings is contentious in the sense that they are unlikely to be replicated in a random sample from the general population. Any study with a non-random student sample ideally should be repeated with a representative sample from a known population. Cross-sectional designs are unsuited to studies of behaviour change and they also provide weak evidence in the testing of theories.

Data   the plural of the noun 'datum'; it refers to items of information or observations collected, collated and analysed in a research investigation. 'Data are' and not 'data is' is correct grammar.

Data-sharing   the idea that all the data and derived data from a scientific study should be available for sharing with other investigators, including the mean, median, mode, standard deviation, effect size, confidence intervals and Bayes factor. These data should be included as supplementary tables or made available as raw data on an archive. It is essential to report all of the tests performed (all t, F, chi-squared and p values) because of the increase in Type I error rate due to selective reporting of multiple comparisons. The shared availability of such information allows other independent researchers to compare their results in quantitative terms, to compute power in future studies and aggregate results for meta-analyses.

Decline effect   the reduction in significant experimental effects that is claimed to occur over a sequence of trials or studies of psi.

Demand characteristics   a biasing of study findings produced by inadvertent influences that have not been adequately eliminated or controlled (Orne, 1962). One example is the sheep–goat experimenter effect that plagues studies in parapsychology (Thalbourne & Delin, 1993).

Diaries, blogs and vlogs   diaries (Schredl, 2002) and diary techniques such as 'blogging' (Evrard, 2016) and 'vlogging' (Snelson, 2015) are literary products that can also be used as sources of information, data and opinions. Blogs and vlogs are produced by a multitude of diverse Ps and also by some investigators. They include details that are quantitative, e.g. dates, times, durations, and qualitative, e.g. detailed descriptions of what happened, who did what, who said what – followed by reflections on meaning and interpretations. Investigators in anomalistic psychology find it helpful to keep separate diaries for different categories of experience such as Dreams, Anomalies and Coincidences. However, there are ethical issues about the use of public comments posted in blogs or social media without permission from the posters. It is usual to obtain approval from the blog authors or forum moderators.

Direct observation   occurs in the simplest kind of study by directly observing behaviour in a relevant setting – e.g. people attending a séance with spirit mediums, or other kinds of session where 'psychic readings' or performances are offered. Direct observation may be accompanied by recordings in written, oral, auditory or visual form. Several investigators may observe the same events and reliability checks conducted. Direct observation includes casual observation, formal observation and participant observation. Ethical issues are raised by planned formal observational study of people who have not given informed consent to such observations.

Direct replication   an attempt to reproduce the methods used in an earlier study to determine whether the same or similar results can be obtained to indicate that the previous results are reliable.

Dissociative Experiences Scale (DES)   a 28-item self-report questionnaire in which respondents indicate the percentage of the time the described phenomenon happens to them, ranging from 0% to 100% at 10% intervals. One typical example is: 'Some people have the experience of finding themselves in a place and having no idea how they got there.' (Bernstein & Putnam, 1986).

Double-masked or double-'blind' controls   a systematic method for preventing biasing of study findings. Neither the person collecting the data nor the P knows, in advance, the sequences, hypotheses or, in the case of clinical trials, the treatments being presented. Computers, assistants or intermediaries present the stimuli according to a previously agreed principle of randomisation or other systematic method to prevent sensory leakage or communications between the investigator(s) and the Ps concerning the sequence of presentation and the investigator's hypotheses to eliminate or minimise demand characteristics.

Effect size   a calculation that quantifies the difference between groups or conditions in light of the variability of the scores. An estimate of the effect size is needed before starting a piece of research in order to calculate the number of Ps that are required to avoid a type II error. It is prudent to determine the number of Ps that will be necessary to ensure, with a known degree of confidence – e.g. 80%, that the study has sufficient power to support the null hypothesis; i.e. if no difference is found between the groups, then it is good to be confident to a known extent (e.g. 80%) that the finding can be relied on.

Confidence intervals are more informative than statistical significance. Having a p value that is smaller than the chosen alpha level (e.g. $p < .05$) is always possible if the sample is sufficiently large. With a sufficiently sized sample, a significant difference may be obtained even with a very small difference, which can be quite meaningless. The *importance* of a finding is more important and significant than *statistical significance*. P values are confounded with sample size while effect size is independent of sample size.

One example is the Physicians' Health Study of aspirin to prevent myocardial infarction (MI), which contained more than 22,000 Ps over an average of five years, reported that aspirin was associated with a reduction in MI that was statistically significant at $p < .00001$ (Steering Committee of the Physicians' Health Study Research Group, 1989). Aspirin was recommended for general prevention of MI. However, the effect size was very small: a risk difference of 0.77% with an r^2 value of .001 – an extremely small effect size.

Ideally, effect size should be reported in the results section of a study report accompanied by confidence, likelihood or credible intervals. This is because the variability of a set of results is as important as the mean value and one cannot evaluate any quantity without an account of the surrounding variability.

Ethnographic methods   seek to build a systematic understanding of a culture from the viewpoint of the insider. Ethnographic methods are multiple attempts to describe the shared beliefs, practices, artefacts, knowledge and behaviours of an intact cultural group. They attempt to represent the totality of a phenomenon in its complete, naturalistic setting. Detailed observation is an important part of ethnographic fieldwork. Ethnography can provide greater ecological validity. The processes of transformation can be observed and documented, including how the culture becomes embodied in Ps, alongside the recording of their narratives. It is labour-intensive, but combining ethnography with narrative interviews produces 'richer' information than interviews alone. A subcategory of ethnographic methods called 'autoethnography' involves research by an individual about their own experiences, values and beliefs.

Experimental control   of the utmost importance in any laboratory investigation of any scientific hypothesis. There can be no room for any laxity with regard to experimental controls. Rhine and Pratt (1962) were well aware of the need for such control: 'The conclusions, of course, depend upon the adequacy of the weakest feature, not upon an elaborate display of many precautions' (p. 25). Many useful features of experimental control are described throughout this Appendix.

Experimenter effects   effects obtained from different experimenters with differing beliefs – e.g. sheep versus goats – who obtain different results in highly similar or identical conditions. Experimenter effects in Psychology were comprehensively reviewed by Robert Rosenthal (1976, 1994). Experimenter effects are a particularly notable feature of parapsychological research. John Palmer (1986) stated: ' the experimenter effect is the most important challenge facing modern parapsychology. It may be that we will not be able to make too much progress in other areas of the field until the puzzle of the experimenter effect is solved' (pp. 220–221).

An example is a study by Richard Wiseman (RW) and Marilyn Schlitz (MS) (1997) with the 'psychical staring' effect. RW had previously found no significant effects, while the MS study had obtained positive findings. Their study involved MS and RW carrying out separate experiments in the same location with the same equipment, procedures and Ps chosen from the same pool. The Ps' electrodermal activity (EDA) was continuously recorded. The EDA of RW's Ps was not significantly different between the 'stare' and 'non-stare' trials, while the EDA for three of MS's Ps was significantly higher in 'stare' than 'non-stare' trials. No rational explanation has been suggested for this difference.

Factor analysis   a statistical method to describe variability among observed, correlated variables in terms of a potentially lower number of unobserved variables called factors. For example, variations in 10 observed variables may be mainly determined by the variations in two unobserved variables. This method is seldom used in research on psi.

Faked or falsified data   made up or fabricated data by researchers intentionally trying to pass off research findings that are inaccurate.

Fallacies   errors in reasoning. The *Internet Encyclopedia of Philosophy* (www.iep.utm.edu/fallacy/#H6) lists 224 common fallacies, and provides brief explanations and examples of each of them. The vast majority of fallacies involve arguments, although some involve explanations, or definitions. Sometimes the term 'fallacy' is used more broadly to indicate any false belief or cause of a false belief (see Chapters 3 and 4 for further details).

False discovery rate correction   recommended as an alternative to Bonferroni-type adjustment due to its ability to localise the error-rate control to individual tests without the loss of power to detect real effects (Glickman, Rao, & Schultz, 2014). The use of false discovery rate control with multiple testing can provide a more solid basis for drawing conclusions about statistical significance.

Fantasy-proneness (FP)   an enduring personality trait of individuals who are thought to spend a large part of their life daydreaming in fantasy. High FP individuals experience vivid memories, the ability to voluntarily hallucinate and superior hypnotic abilities. FP is often indexed with the 'Inventory of Childhood Memories and Imaginings' (ICMI; Wilson & Barber, 1983) and the 'Creative Experiences Questionnaires' (CEQ; Merckelbach, Horselenberg, & Muris, 2001).

File-drawer effect   the phenomenon that the published studies in journals are most likely a biased sample of the totality of studies carried out (Rosenthal, 1979). It is difficult to know how many studies have been conducted but not reported. The extreme view of the 'file drawer problem' was stated by Robert Rosenthal, 'that journals are filled with the 5% of the studies that show type I errors, while the file drawers are filled with the 95% of the studies that show nonsignificant results' (1979: 638). Rosenthal presents formulae for computing the tolerance for filed and future null results. It is a serious issue for the field of anomalistic psychology because the majority of studies concern effects that are relatively rare.

Fixed-effects model (FEM) or random-effects model (REM) in any study, data can be grouped according to various observed factors (sample size, type of task, type of Ps, etc.). The group means can be modelled as a fixed or a random effect for each grouping. In an FEM, each group mean is assumed to be a group-specific fixed quantity so that the individual specific effect is correlated with the independent variables. In meta-analysis the FEM assumes that there is one fixed effect size that underlies all the studies and each individual study is showing a chance or random variation from that fixed value. However, heterogeneity (unequal effect sizes) makes an FEM seem implausible and the REM is therefore more appealing. In an REM, one assumes two sources of variance, within-study variance and between-study variance. The type of model one adopts makes a difference to the way the weights of studies are counted. The FEM weight is calculated as:

$$W_i = 1/V_i$$

The REM weighting of studies is calculated as:

$$W_i^* = 1/V_i + V^*$$

where: V_i = within study variance

V^* = between study variance

There is no definitive way of deciding whether an FEM or an REM is most appropriate in any particular case. However, this decision can make a major difference to the findings of a meta-analysis. For this reason, many people running a meta-analysis hedge their bets and run the analysis using both the FEM and the REM. This places much of the onus on the reader of the meta-analysis report to interpret the findings in the most appropriate manner. A subjective decision may be involved.

Functional magnetic resonance imaging (fMRI) functional magnetic resonance imaging, or functional MRI (fMRI), measures brain activity by detecting changes associated with blood flow. This technique relies on the fact that cerebral blood flow and neuronal activation are coupled. When an area of the brain is in use, blood flow to that region also increases (Figure 13.1).

Funnel plot a graph designed to check for the existence of publication bias commonly used in systematic reviews and meta-analyses. In the absence of publication bias, studies with high precision (large samples) are expected to be near the average, and studies with low precision (small samples) are expected to be evenly spread on both sides of the average, creating a funnel-shaped distribution. Any deviation from this shape can indicate publication bias. However, investigators can be misled by the shape of funnel plots and they cannot be assumed to be fool-proof. The trim-and-fill method provides a summary effect adjusted

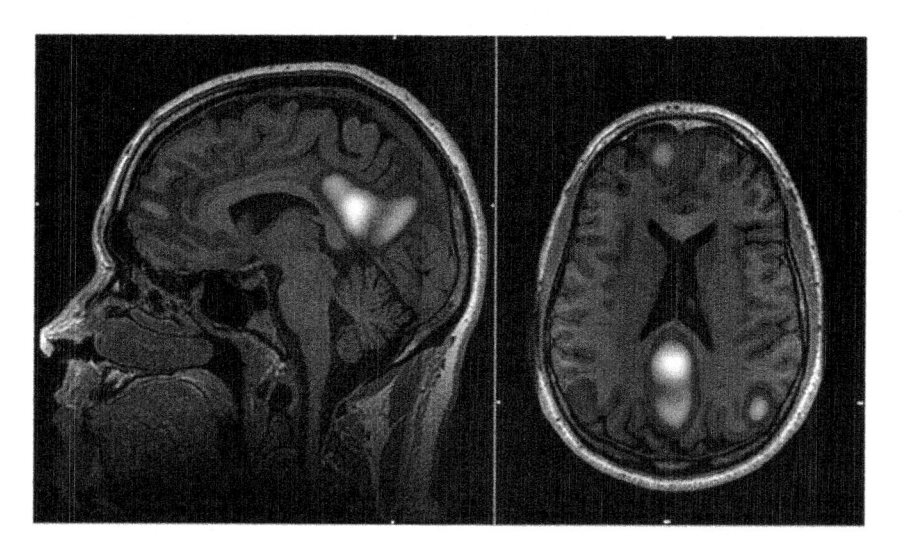

Figure 13.1 The default mode network (DMN) includes regions in the medial pre-frontal cortex, precuneus and bilateral parietal cortex. Some loss of clarity compared to the original illustration is due to the inability to print in colour. (Reproduced from Graner, Oakes, French, & Riedy (2013) under a Creative Commons Attribution licence.) See Chapters 9, 10 and 11 for further details.

for publication bias by estimating the number of unpublished studies (Duval & Tweedie, 2000). However, the trim-and-fill method assumes that publication bias is the only reason for funnel plot asymmetry, which is probably untrue.

HARKing a QRP involving '(H)ypothesising (A)fter the (R)esults are (K)nown', as discussed by Norbert Kerr (1998). HARKing is also referred to as 'researcher degrees of freedom' (Simmons, Nelson, & Simonsohn, 2011). HARKing has been advocated by Daniel Bem (2002), who stated: 'Which Article Should You Write? There are two possible articles you can write: (1) the article you planned to write when you designed your study or (2) the article that makes the most sense now that you have seen the results. They are rarely the same, and the correct answer is 2' (p. 2). The main contributing factor to HARKing is the routine expectation that any study should have a set of hypotheses. On this point, Bem states: 'Psychology is more exciting than that, and the best journal articles are informed by the actual empirical findings from the opening sentence. Before writing your article, then, you need to Analyze Your Data.' Opportunistic investigators, following Bem's advice, can HARK to give the impression of telling a convincing story about their studies: Hypotheses, Results, Hypotheses Confirmed. However, the assumptions of null hypothesis significance testing are broken when an investigator employs HARKing. The practice must be discouraged. This author suspects that everybody does it to some extent.

Heuristic an approach to problem solving, learning or discovery that is practical but not guaranteed to be optimal or perfect, although sufficient for the immediate goals.

Individual screening methods widely employed to screen individuals prior to their participation in laboratory research. Traditionally, standard methods of testing are used such as Tobacyk's (2004) Revised Paranormal Belief Scale.

Informed consent required in all research with human Ps to fulfil the ethical requirements of research. If deception is involved in the investigation, the Ps should be thoroughly debriefed immediately after the data have been collected.

Interpretative phenomenological analysis a qualitative procedure for analysing text which emphasises its meaning. For example, the meaning of out-of-the body-experiences has been studied using this method (see Wilde, 2012) and also the impact of encounters with paranormal experience (Drinkwater, Dagnall, & Bate, 2013).

Junk science (JS) a derogatory term referring to badly done or discredited scientific studies.

Magneto-Sensitivity Theory (MST) has been independently proposed by Alan McDonnell (2014) and Abraham Liboff (2017) as a sixth sensory modality. The McDonnell–Liboff Theory is supported by the evidence from evolution that many organisms have magneto-receptivity capability for use both as a compass and a map. In addition, the vestige of a hidden sensory channel of human magneto-sensitivity is supported by a small number of laboratory studies. The evidence that geomagnetic activity blocks ESP scoring rates is consistent with the theory, and other evidence includes distance and shielding effects, although there is contrary evidence also (see Chapter 6 for full details).

Meta-analysis the use of statistical techniques to combine the results of primary studies addressing the same question into a single pooled measure of effect size, with a confidence interval. To date, the majority of meta-analyses have been retrospective using pre-existing studies. The analysis is often based on the calculation of a weighted mean effect size in which each primary study is weighted according to the number of Ps. A meta-analysis follows a series of steps as follows: (1) develop a research question; (2) identify all relevant studies; (3) select studies on the basis of the issue being addressed and methodological criteria; (4) decide which dependent variables or summary measures are allowed; (5) calculate a summary effect; and (6) reach a conclusion in answer to the original research question.

In a pessimistic paper, Kennedy (2013) stated that, in the past 25 years:

> meta-analyses have not and cannot provide convincing evidence for psi. The meta-analyses inevitably get bogged down in debates and controversy about the many decisions that affect the outcome of the analyses. Such controversy is intrinsic to post hoc analyses, and particularly to meta-analyses. These problems with meta-analyses are not unique to parapsychology. My experience working in medical research over the past two decades is that medical researchers increasingly do not consider meta-analyses as a means for resolving controversial issues. (p. 21)

Furthermore, Kennedy argues that retrospective meta-analyses are post hoc analyses that have not been effective at resolving scientific controversies, particularly when based on underpowered experiments. Evaluations of moderating factors, including study flaws, small-study effects, and other sources of heterogeneity, are not able to neutralise confounding and cannot fully compensate for weaknesses in the original experiments. Watt and Kennedy (2017) suggested that one solution to many of these problems with retrospective meta-analyses could be solved by using 'registration-based prospective meta-analysis'.

Narrative analysis (NA) begins with a repeated reading of the text to identify the story or stories within it. The primary focus is on maintaining the narrative integrity of the account. The researcher may develop a summary of the narrative account that will help identify the structure of the narrative, its tone and the central characters. It may be useful to engage in a certain amount of thematic analysis to identify some underlying themes, but this does not equate with narrative analysis. NA involves trying to see the interconnections between events rather than separating them. Having analysed one case, the researcher can then proceed to the next, identifying similarities and differences in the structure and content of the narratives.

Narrative approaches seek insight and meaning through the acquisition of data in the form of stories concerning personal experiences. The narrative approach assumes that human beings are natural storytellers and that the principal task of the psychologist is to explore the different stories being told (Murray, 2015). The most popular source of material for the narrative researcher is the interview. The focus of the narrative interview is the elicitation of storied accounts from the interviewee. This can take various forms. The life-story interview is the most extended form of interview. As its name implies, the life-story interview seeks to obtain an extended account of the person's life. The primary aim is to put the P at ease and encourage him/her to tell their story at length.

A particular version of the narrative interview is the episodic interview in which the researcher encourages the P to speak on a variety of particular experiences. This approach assumes that experiences are often stored in memory in narrative episodes and that the challenge is to reveal these without integrating them into a larger narrative. The role of the interviewer is to encourage sustained narrative accounting. This is achieved by a variety of supportive but non-leading remarks. The researcher can deliberately encourage the P to expand upon remarks about particular issues.

A variety of software is available to expedite rapid power analyses, including G* Power 3 (Faul, Erdfelder, Lang, & Buchner, 2007) and free online software online such as OpenEpi (Dean, Sullivan, & Soe, 2014).

Normal distribution a bell-shaped distribution that defines the values of any naturally occurring process (Figure 13.2).

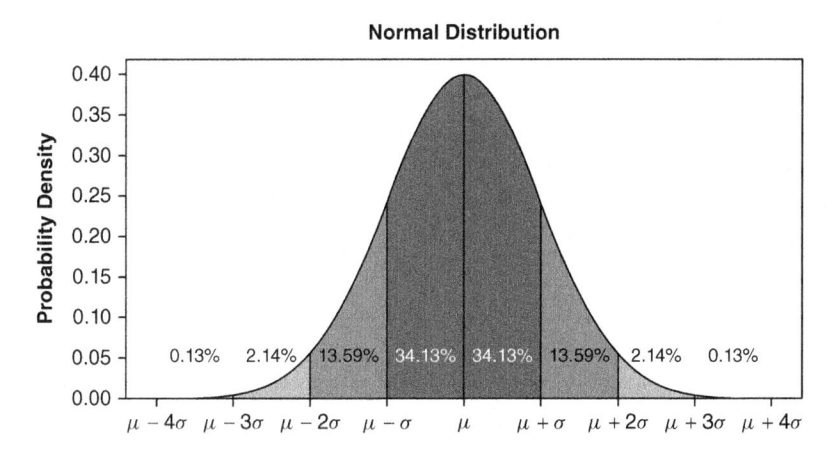

Figure 13.2 The normal distribution with a mean value of μ (Greek letter 'mu', M) and a standard deviation of σ (Greek letter sigma, s). The percentages show the proportion of values within segments of the distribution that are defined by standard deviations above and below the mean.

N-Theory and P-Theory   categories of theory with particular a priori assumptions to generate explanations of a putative paranormal event. 'N-Theory' employs traditional scientific principles to explain an observation. 'P-Theory' employs explanations based on principles or ideas about the paranormal. The two types of theory are not symmetrical because P Theory can be applied only after N Theory has been ruled out. Thus, the attribution of P Theory is contingent upon the failure to find a suitable N Theory attribution. This means that an event cannot be described as 'paranormal' unless all rational or 'normal' explanations have been eliminated. As our knowledge and understanding of Nature and the ways of the world expand, the necessity for paranormal explanations decreases and, in theory, the less often we should find it necessary to invoke P Theory. However, for some anomalous experiences, and also for some meta-analyses, there is no objective way of knowing which theory is correct – e.g. coincidences.

This asymmetrical situation of N Theory hypothesis followed by confirmation or disconfirmation requires scrutiny at each stage when there are opportunities for disagreement between N Theorists (skeptics) and P Theorists (believers).

The necessary condition to exhaustively disconfirm any and every N Theory interpretation that is offered puts paranormal theory at a disadvantage. Whenever a P Theory case is put forward it is vulnerable to criticism by N theorists, who almost never run out of N Theory explanations. Thus science is structurally loaded in favour of N Theory, which has a seemingly 'bottomless bucket' of scientific explanations, however implausible. If no other hypothesis can be verified, the ultimate fall-back position for N Theory is scientific fraud. Many skeptics privately believe the fraud theory applies much more frequently than they are able to publicly state owing to laws of libel.

Null hypothesis significance testing (NHST)   a method for estimating statistical inference in which data are tested against a hypothesis of a null (no) effect or null (no) relationship. Statistical tests are used to allow the computation of the probability of observing a result at least as extreme as a test statistic (such as a t-value), assuming that the null hypothesis is true. This p-value reflects the conditional probability of achieving the observed outcome or larger, the area under the null probability distribution curve – e.g. $(-\infty, -t)$ and $(+t, +\infty)$ for a two-tailed t-test. The smaller the p-value, the greater the likelihood that the null hypothesis is false.

The p-value is a probability value estimated using a standard statistical test – e.g. a t-test or analysis of variance, and is no indication of the magnitude of an effect. A small p value means that the results were unlikely to have been the consequence of chance. It indicates the likelihood of obtaining the same results if the study is repeated. If there is a null (non-significant) effect, we should be able to replicate the null effect with a probability equal to $1 - p$. The significance level or alpha (α) level is the maximum probability that a test statistic falls into the rejection region when the null hypothesis is true. By failing to reject the null hypothesis, we continue to assume that H0 is true.

However, one never accepts a null hypothesis on the basis that a p value is non-significant. One can only fail to disconfirm the null hypothesis. *One should never say, on the basis of NHST, that one accepts the null hypothesis.* To accept or reject a null hypothesis, a Bayesian approach or confidence intervals must be used.

One-tailed test   used when the hypothesis of a difference also contains a direction – e.g. condition A will have a higher mean than condition B. In this case, if the mean for A is found to be higher than the mean for B, an alpha level of $p < .10$ can be used instead of $p < .05$.

Ontological the existence or not of a process or condition such as the four categories of psi.

Open data refers to data that are freely available to analyse, publish and synthesise without restriction by patents, publishers or copyrights. Traditionally, a lot of time and stress has been wasted by individual investigators applying for access to original data-sets of key publications. Access has often been refused and not always for the most honourable of reasons. The open access movement encourages open access to original scientific findings and promotes a culture of transparency and sharing of research data among research communities. The UK Government is committed to ensuring that publicly funded research findings should be made freely accessible. There are many benefits of open data and open access.

Psi Open Data (https://open-data.spr.ac.uk/) is an open data repository for storage of parapsychological and psychical research data undertaken by the Society for Psychical Research. The repository is an open source data platform with a full suite of cataloguing, publishing and visualisation features. Users are able to freely upload datasets and visitors can search for and download datasets.

The initiative to bring open data to parapsychology will be an evolving process. The first step is bringing the open data repository into existence. Gradually, the community can consider how to incorporate data publication within research and publication practices, and how to encourage researchers to make full use of the facility (Ryan, 2018).

p level an arbitrary cut-off level of probability used in null hypothesis testing which sets the threshold for rejection of the null hypothesis, e.g. $p < .05$ or $p < .01$. However, if the probability falls above the cut-off p level, it can still have value as a finding unless the effect obtained is exactly zero.

Paranormal belief an opinion about something that holds that the thing, capability or experience is beyond known scientific principles.

Paranormal Beliefs Scale (PBS) a 26-item scale that assesses beliefs about five areas of paranormal beliefs: Psychic Beliefs, Superstitions, Traditional Religious Belief, Witchcraft and Anomalous Natural Phenomena – e.g. the Loch Ness monster (Lange, Thalbourne, Houran, & Storm, 2000).

Paranormal experience (or subjective paranormal experience) is an experience that defies known scientific or rational explanations.

Parapsychological Association (PA) established in 1957 by J. B. Rhine, the PA is an international organisation of scientists and scholars engaged in the study of 'psi' (or 'psychic') experiences, such as telepathy, clairvoyance, remote viewing, psychokinesis, psychic healing and precognition. Such experiences seem to challenge contemporary conceptions of human nature and of the physical world, appearing to involve the transfer of information and the influence of physical systems independently of time and space, via mechanisms we cannot currently explain. The stated objective of the Parapsychological Association (2020) is to achieve a scientific understanding of these experiences. In this author's opinion, the PA presents a highly exaggerated and contestable perspective on psi as a scientifically established process. Available online at: www.parapsych.org/base/about.aspx

Participant (P) a person who serves as a 'subject' in a scientific investigation. The role is taken either in a voluntary capacity or for compensation by payment, credit points or in some other form.

Peer-review a system used by scholarly journals in which two or more independent experts are invited to review manuscripts to check for errors, which must be corrected before the papers are accepted for publication.

P-hacking a QRP in which an investigator trawls though a set of data using basic significance tests to pick out the statistically significant findings. After identifying the statistically significant results, the investigator then writes out a set of hypotheses to 'predict' the very findings that they found to be significant. Allegedly, QRP is increasingly common (Simonsohn, Nelson, & Simmons, 2014).

Placebo a control procedure or substance to control for expectancy in studies of interventions including therapies, interventions or drugs. The typical placebo consists of an inert procedure such as reading a book or administering an inert substance as a control in a drug trial. An active placebo is one that mimics certain side-effects of a drug to provide a more convincing control for the effect of the drug.

Placebo effect the measurable improvement in a condition or performance that quite often occurs following the administration of a placebo.

Polyfilla approach a systematic filling of the 'holes' or gaps in empirical research by identifying areas that have not been investigated without any particular theory. Typically, this approach adopts a cross-sectional, correlational design to fill as many holes as possible in a single study.

Population stereotypes common biases in the selection of numbers, letters or other symbols. For example, if you ask a group of people to choose a number between zero and 50, with two digits, both different, so that 33 would not be acceptable, then the most popular choices will tend to be 37 and 35 (Marks & Kammann, 1980).

Post hoc multiple comparisons when a researcher tests multiple averages of groups or conditions looking for statistical significance. If this practice is unplanned and opportunistic, it is considered to be a QRP.

Power an index of the ability of a study to find a statistically significant effect when a genuine effect exists. The recommended standard for experimental research is adequate power to obtain significant results on at least 80% of confirmatory experiments. The power increases as the probability of a false negative (β), or type II error, decreases. The power is defined as $(1 - \beta)$. Statistical power relies on three parameters: (1) the significance level – i.e. the type I error probability or α level; (2) the size of the sample; (3) an effect size parameter defining H_1 and thus indicating the degree of deviation from H_0 in the underlying population.

There are several different types of power analysis, some being more robust than others. In a priori power analyses (Cohen, 1988), sample size N is computed as a function of the required power level $(1 - \beta)$, the pre-specified significance level α, and the population effect size to be detected with probability $1 - \beta$. Cohen's definitions of small, medium and large effects can be helpful in giving effect size specifications in reports.

Typically, investigations in Psychology are low-powered. Cohen (1962) found that psychology studies typically have only a 50% chance of finding a genuine effect. The situation has changed little over the last four or five decades. The endemic lack of power is caused by study samples being too small. By tradition, if an investigator asked how large their sample should be, the figure of 30 was recommended. This is an arbitrary and scientifically meaningless practice on a large scale in many academic psychology departments. Given the easy availability of free software online, there is little excuse for not doing a power analysis before starting a study. Funding agencies, institutional ethics boards, research review panels and journal editorial policies may require evidence of a power analysis as a condition of funding, approval and publication.

Pseudoskeptic a person who denies a claim of psi while showing the desire to discredit the claim, or even the investigator personally, by suggesting that the claim and/or the investigator should be dismissed (Truzzi, 1987).

Psi a term proposed by Thouless and Wiesner (1948) for the processes of telepathy, clairvoyance and precognition.

Psychic energy a non-scientifically vague, nebulous and loosely applied term that nobody seems to understand. If you see this term in a book or website being used in any serious way, move quickly on.

Putative paranormal phenomenon a phenomenon that is considered or reputed to be paranormal, such as ESP, clairvoyance, precognition or PK.

Qualitative research methods aim to understand the meaning, purpose or intention of behaviour or experience, not its quantitative characteristics. A huge variety of qualitative methods is available and a few are described in this Appendix under the following headings: diaries and blogs; interviews, especially semi-structured; interpretative phenomenological analysis, and narrative approaches. A wide variety of software is available to support qualitative and mixed methods research analyses, such as NVivo, MAXQDA and QDA Miner Lite.

Questionable research practices (QRP) methods used to exploit research and statistical procedures to misrepresent findings, such as excluding data points using post hoc criteria to spuriously increase the support of data to a hypothesis. A high percentage of researchers admit to having engaged in questionable practices, with approximately one-third of psychology researchers indicating doubts about the integrity of their own research on at least one occasion (John, Loewenstein, & Prelec, 2012). QRPs are a general problem throughout scientific work and are not only an issue for anomalistic psychology.

Questionnaires research instruments consisting of a standard set of questions with accompanying instructions concerning attitudes, beliefs, perceptions or values. A questionnaire needs to be a reliable and valid measure of the construct(s) it purports to measure. Questionnaires vary in objectives and content, especially in their generic versus specific content, question format, the number of items, and sensitivity or responsiveness to change. Questionnaires may be employed in cross-sectional and longitudinal studies. When looking for changes over time, the responsiveness of a questionnaire to clinical and subjective changes is a crucial feature. A questionnaire's content, sensitivity and extent, together with its reliability and validity, influence a questionnaire's selection. The investigator must ask: What is it that I want to know? The answer will dictate the selection of the most relevant and useful questionnaire. The most important aspect of questionnaire selection is therefore to match the objective of the study with the objective of the questionnaire. For example, are you interested in a specific or broad-ranging research question? When this question is settled, one needs to decide whether there is anything else that one's research objective will require one to know. Usually the researcher needs to develop a specific block of questions that will seek vital information concerning the respondents' socio-demographic characteristics that can be placed at the beginning or the end of the main questionnaire. Questionnaires such as the Revised Paranormal Belief Scale (Tobacyk, 1988) are frequently used to measure what are taken to be descriptions of Ps' paranormal beliefs. Some investigators have questioned the scientific value of such questionnaires (e.g. Lawrence, 1995; Lawrence, Roe, & Williams, 1998) and two leading researchers (Wiseman and Watt, 2006) explicitly called for a new measure of paranormal belief.

Whether a questionnaire actually 'measures' any such thing as a 'belief' is itself contentious. Discursive psychologists interested in the nature of discourse have been critical of the approach. An expressed belief is viewed as a phenomenon that has social consequences (Billig, 1987; Edwards, 1997). Cromby (2012) has argued that

> beliefs are enduring, yet variable and flexible; they have largely predictable content, yet are contingent upon the actions and talk of others; they are social, yet can be endowed with deep personal significance. Believing is not merely information-processing activity, and belief is not an individual cognitive entity. Belief is the somewhat contingent, socially co-constituted outcome of repeated articulations between activities, discourses, narratives and socialized structures of feeling.

Wooffitt and Allistone (2005) advocate a discursive approach for parapsychology which analyses the interactions and discourses within parapsychological experiments and documents. One example is Lamont's (2007) exploration of 'avowals of attitude'. Avowals of belief are not considered as straightforward representations of actual beliefs, and it is their functional properties rather than their descriptive nature within discursive approaches.

Randomisation a formalised system used 1) to allocate Ps to conditions to minimise selection bias, or 2) to organise stimuli into a sequence to minimise bias stemming from the risk that one's research Ps can correctly predict the identity of the next stimulus based on patterning in the sequence. If a sequence contains predictable patterns, then any task that involves predicting the stimuli, especially if there is feedback, will likely show above-chance results. Such pseudo-randomisation does not properly control for experimental effects (see Chapters 5 and 6 for examples).

Rational-Experiential Inventory (REI) contains scales for measuring analytical and intuitive thinking, both consisting of 20 items with five-point rating scales: 1 = strongly disagree; 5 = strongly agree. Examples of items measuring analytical and intuitive thinking, respectively, are 'I enjoy intellectual challenges' and 'I like to rely on my intuitive impressions' (Pacini & Epstein, 1999).

Registered (or preregistered) reports the preregistration of a research study with an official registration body prior to data collection. The need for preregistered, well-powered confirmatory studies is recognised by many investigators working today. Preregistration helps to prevent selective publication and selective reporting of research outcomes, to prevent duplication of research effort, to help people to know what trials are planned or ongoing into which they might want to enrol, and to give ethics review boards a view of similar work and data relevant to the research they are considering. Registration can be made at the Koestler Parapsychology Unit here: https://koestlerunit.wordpress.com/study-registry/

Journal editors consider whether any failure to appropriately register a clinical trial is likely to have been intended to or resulted in biased reporting. Registration was initiated in the mid-1970s in the *European Journal of Parapsychology* (*EJP*). A retrospective comparison of Registered and non-Registered Reports published in the *EJP* suggested that the approach may have reduced QRPs (Wiseman, Watt, & Kornbrot, 2019). The principles of preregistered, well-powered confirmatory research also apply to meta-analyses as well as individual studies (Watt & Kennedy, 2017).

Regression analysis a set of statistical processes for estimating the relationships among variables. It includes many techniques for modelling and analysing several variables, when the focus is on the relationship between a dependent variable and one or more independent variables.

Replication/lack of replication a bone of contention in many areas of psychology and parapsychology. Traditionally, a low priority has been given to replication of other researchers' results. Perhaps researchers believe that they will not be perceived as sufficiently creative if they replicate somebody else's research. In a similar vein, journal editors do not give replications of research, especially failed replications, the same priority as novel findings. This bias towards new positive results and away from failed replications produces a major distortion in the academic literature. Lack of replication before publication is the main reason for the so-called 'repeatability crisis' in psychology and other disciplines.

Replication is one of the most important research methods. Yet it is hardly used or mentioned in textbooks about research methods. Replication refers to the attempt by an investigator to repeat a study purely to determine whether the original findings can be repeated. Essentially, the researcher wants to know whether the original findings are reliable or whether they have been produced by some combination of chance or spurious factors. If study findings can be replicated, then they can be accepted as reliable and valuable to knowledge and understanding. However, if the findings of a study cannot be replicated, then the findings cannot be accepted as a genuine contribution to knowledge.

The reluctance of parapsychologists to repeat and replicate a particular effect, before moving on to study another effect, led Chris Roe (2012) to refer to Parapsychology as 'a butterfly science'. Another commentator, Stephen E. Braude (2012) has expressed his embarrassment that

> psi researchers have clung desperately to their most prominent members in order to tout their endorsements or support. To take just one example: how often are we reminded that Brian Josephson – who does no psi research but who actively and effectively defends it – is a Nobel winning physicist supporting the field of parapsychology? ... personally, I'm embarrassed by parapsychologists' frequent and dialectically shabby appeals to his authority and prestige.

The ability to replicate and reproduce studies and findings is one of the criteria for progress in science. If a study is repeated under similar conditions, then it should be possible to obtain the same findings. However, journal reviewers and editors may not accept a replication or failed replication for publication on the grounds that it is not as 'newsworthy' as an original study. In one landmark study, fewer than half of 100 studies published in 2008 in three 'top' psychology journals could be successfully replicated (Open Science Collaboration (OSC), 2015). Lack of replication indicates that: 1) Study A's result may be false, or 2) Study B's results may be false, or 3) both may be false, or 4) there may be some subtle differences in the way the two studies were conducted – in other words, there were differences in the context. The OSC analysis showed that a low p value was predictive of which studies could be replicated. Of the 32 original studies with a p < 0.001, only 20 could be replicated, while only 2 of the 11 papers with a value greater than 0.04 were successfully replicated. The reproducibility of parapsychology studies is yet to be fully evaluated. Leading parapsychologists remain optimistic in believing that it is only a matter of time before a replicable experiment is developed (e.g. see Bierman & Spottiswoode, 2012).[3] It hasn't yet happened.

Revised Paranormal Belief Scale (RPBS) a 26-item scale designed to measure paranormal beliefs with items in seven subscales: traditional religious beliefs, spiritualism, extraordinary life forms, psi, witchcraft, precognition and superstition (Tobacyk, 2004).

Revised Transliminality Scale (RTS) the 17-item Revised Transliminality Scale includes magical ideation, mystical experience, absorption, hyperaesthesia, manic experience, dream interpretation and fantasy proneness. Low scores on transliminality are correlated with 'tough-mindedness' on a Cattell 16PF test, as well as 'self-control' and 'rule consciousness', whereas high scores are associated with 'abstractedness' and an 'openness to change' (Lange et al., 2000).

Safeguarding a method reputedly used to prevent confusing the operation of one aspect of psi with another. For example, a telepathy test needs to be safeguarded against the possibility of precognitive clairvoyance by avoiding having any objective target recorded or existing anywhere, either at the time of the test or later on (Rhine & Pratt, 1962: 40). This condition is almost impossible to meet because there is always the possibility that the target stimuli will be present somewhere at some future time. The term also applies to the attempt to avoid sensory cues unwittingly introduced which might interfere with the experimental protocols. Any necessary signalling should in all cases come from automated equipment or from the P or receiver who indicates when (s)he is ready for the next trial. No signalling or communication from the sender is allowable after a run of trials has begun.

(A) Sample a set of Ps that are selected to represent the study population as closely as possible. In some cases, the sample can consist of the entire study population – e.g. every pupil in a school; every student at a university; every patient in a hospital. More usually, however, the sample is a random selection of a proportion of the members of a population – e.g. every tenth person in a community or every fourth patient admitted into a hospital. This method is called simple random sampling (SRS). A variation on SRS is systematic sampling. In this case, the first person in the sampling frame is chosen at random and then every nth person on the list from there on, where n is the sample fraction being used.

All such sampling methods are like to be biased; there is no perfect method of sampling because there will always be a category of people that any sampling method underrepresents. In any survey it is necessary to maximise the proportion of selected people who are recruited. If a large proportion of people refuse to participate, the sample cannot be assumed to represent the population, but is likely to be biased in unknown ways. As a general principle, surveys that recruit at least 70% of those invited to participate are considered representative, but this figure is arbitrary. The sample size is a key issue. The variability of scores obtained from the sample diminishes as the sample size increases, so the larger the

---

[3] Putting on my skeptic's hat, this belief has been aired for at least 50 years since I first became interested in parapsychology.

sample, the more precise will be the estimates of the population scores, but the more the survey will cost.

As in any research, it is essential to have a clear idea about the objective: Why is one doing the study (the theory behind the research), what is one looking for (the research question), what is the setting or domain, who will be in the study sample and which 'tools' will one use? The investigator is cautious not to generate self-fulfilling prophecies with confirmation bias and subjective validation. Any lack of clarity about purposes and objectives is one of the main stumbling blocks for the novice investigator. This is particularly the case when carrying out a survey, especially in a team of investigators who, before the survey can begin, may have varying agendas regarding why, what, where and how particular kinds of questions must be put and answered.

Secondary analysis the analysis of previously existing data that have been shared by the owners of the data. Authors must always reference the source of the data using a unique, persistent identifier to provide appropriate credit to those who generated it and to allow searching for studies it has supported and that support it. Authors of secondary analyses need to explain how their analyses differ from previous analyses. In addition, those who generate and then share clinical trial data sets deserve credit for their efforts. Those using data collected by others need to seek collaboration with those who collected the data.

Selective exposure a tendency for people to favour information that reinforces the pre-existing (a priori) views while avoiding contradictory information. Associated with subjective validation and confirmation bias.

Self-fulfilling prophecies predictions in the form of hypotheses, expectations or experimenter effects in which the investigator's beliefs in their correctness wittingly or unwittingly translate into the concrete findings to confirm those beliefs.

Sensory cues (aka sensory leakage) are information about an experimental hypothesis, condition or sequence of stimuli that is intended to be hidden but which, nevertheless, can be obtained by the Ps. Sensory cueing is likely to interfere with and bias the data that are collected. Unwitting sensory cueing can always be a concern in any investigation involving perception, learning or cognition. For example, software that has many lines of code could produce a differential delay for different categories of stimuli, this providing a cue. The unwitting presentation of sounds that are specific to each stimulus class could be another possible cue. It is always good practice to run pilot studies to test the equipment and procedures before collecting one's data.

Single case experimental designs investigations of a series of experimental observations with a single research P.

Skeptic a person who questions, doubts or disbelieves the evidence of psi. The term has been adopted by a priori disbelievers in psi who are antagonistic towards any evidence that is supportive of paranormal claims.[4] Extreme skepticism is intransigent and insensitive to new

---

[4]That I once held an entrenched skeptical stance is evidenced by my earlier books and articles – e.g. see Marks & Kammann (1980), Marks (1986, 2000). I believe now that I had been inducted into a 'cult of disbelief' where the will to disbelieve (as is the will to believe in many psi advocates) acted as a pseudo-scientific credo. I discuss the reasons for changing this position in the Preface and in Chapter 3.

evidence, contrary to the principles of Science. According to Marcello Truzzi (1987), most skeptics are 'pseudoskeptics', a term he coined to describe those who assume that an occult or paranormal claim is false without bothering to investigate it. Parapsychologists are dismissive of the more extreme forms of skeptical intransigence. Chris Roe (2016) stated that he thought parapsychologists 'spent too much time and energy engaging with skeptics whose reputations are too strongly associated with the counter-advocate position for there to be any prospect of realistic movement from it change to "any realistic prospect of a shift in their public pronouncements", whatever the quality of methods or data we present'. Roe points out that the substantive arguments offered by Ray Hyman (2010) and James Alcock (2010) are essentially the same as those they offered 20 years earlier (Alcock, 1990; Hyman, 1989).

Spontaneous cases are putative paranormal phenomena recorded on single occasions outside of any formal research project, experiment or laboratory. A thousand cases were collected and analysed by Louisa E. Rhine (1953). Rhine observed four main types of spontaneous cases: intuitive, hallucinatory, unrealistic dreaming and realistic dreaming. Rhine suggested that the information transmitted in such cases must have become accessible at an unconscious level: 'From the unconscious level the information, it appears, is then transferred to consciousness by various psychological processes. They are distinguishable mainly by the presence or absence of imagery or, if imagery is present, by its specific form' (Rhine, 1978: 20).

Statistical power the level of probability that a study will find a statistically significant difference between conditions when an actual difference exists. When statistical power is high, the likelihood of deciding there is an effect, when one exists, is high. Power is $1 - \beta$, where β is the probability of wrongly concluding that there is no effect when one actually exists (type II error). Statistical power depends upon the effect size and the sample size. If the effect size is large, it is possible to detect an effect in a smaller sample. However, a smaller effect size requires a larger sample size. The power of a study can be increased by: 1) including larger effects, 2) increasing sample size, or 3) reducing measurement error by using highly valid outcome measures.

Stratified sampling used to divide a population into groups or 'strata'. The groups are randomly sampled, but in different proportions so that the overall sample sizes of the groups can be made equal, even though they are not equal in the population (e.g. the 40–59, 60–79 and 80–99 age groups in a community sample, or men and women). These groups will be equally represented in the data. Other methods include non-probability sampling of six kinds: convenience samples, most similar/dissimilar samples, typical case samples, critical case samples, snowball samples and quota samples.

Subjective Paranormal Experience Scale (SPES) an 18-item measure designed by Dagnall et al. (2016) to assess the incidence of subjective paranormal experiences. Respondents use 'yes' or 'no' to indicate whether they believe they have had a 'genuine' paranormal experience. If they respond 'yes', they indicate the type of experience and its frequency of occurrence. Listed experiences include ESP (extrasensory perception), PK (psychokinesis), witchcraft, OBE/NDE, haunting, contact/communication with the dead, UFO visitation, UFO sighting, astrological prediction, or other.

Subjective validation (SV) occurs when a person considers that an item of data is supportive evidence or proof of a belief when there is no objective support. Subjective validation occurs most frequently when a description has personal meaning or significance. Subjective validation is an important element in cold reading, astrology, ESP studies and other performance in which a script contains ambiguous information that may or may not be true. It is relevant to claims of the paranormal phenomena, especially by untrained explorers. The term 'subjective validation' was coined by Marks and Kammann (1980). In the context of a personality description of oneself, SV is called the personal validation effect or Forer Effect (Forer, 1949).

Survey of Anomalous Experiences   a questionnaire that separates reports of anomalous or inexplicable events and the interpretation of the event as paranormal (Irwin et al., 2013). The P is asked to click on the option that most closely represents their own position; if they have had the experience more than once, they choose the option that is most often the case – e.g.

> 'Q1. I have had a dream about something of which I was previously unaware, and subsequently the dream turned out to be accurate.'

Response options:

> 'Yes, and it must have been an instance of telepathy or ESP.'
>
> 'Yes, but it was probably just a coincidence or unwitting insight.'
>
> 'No.'

Surveys   systematic methods for determining how a sample of Ps representative of a population respond to a set of standard questions attempting to assess their attitudes, beliefs or knowledge – e.g. we may want to know the incidence and intensity of beliefs in various paranormal claims among a population across different age groups and genders. Modes of administration include face-to-face interview, telephone interview, social media, group self-completion and postal self-completion. Next, you need to decide who will comprise the sample for the survey and also where it will be carried out. Which population is relevant to the research question? The survey method, whether using interviews, questionnaires or some combination of the two, is versatile and can be applied equally well to research with individuals, groups, organisations, communities or populations to inform understanding of a host of very different types of research issues and questions. Normally, a survey is conducted on a sample of the study population of interest – e.g. people aged 18–80; students aged 11–18; members of a special interest organisation, etc. Issues of key importance in conducting a survey are the objective(s), the mode of administration, the method of sampling, the sample size, and the preparation of the data for analysis.

Systematic review (SR)   a method of integrating the evidence about an effect or intervention from all known relevant and usable primary sources, whether published or unpublished. What counts as relevant and usable is a matter for debate and judgement. Rules and criteria concerning the necessary quality standards for studies and data are agreed in advance by those carrying out the review. Publishing these rules and criteria along with the review enables such reviews to be replicable and transparent. Proponents of the SR view it as a way of integrating research that limits bias. Traditionally, the method has been applied to quantitative data. Researchers have begun to investigate ways and means to synthesise qualitative studies also. The main stages of a systematic review are:

1. Defining a question and agreeing an objective method.
2. Searching for relevant data from research that is of acceptable quality and answers the defined question.

3. 'Extracting' relevant data from research publications. This can include the method or 'intervention', nature and number of Ps, funding sources and the findings/outcomes.
4. Assessing the quality of the data using the agreed criteria.
5. Analysing and combining the data using statistical methods which provide a summary score for the overall result obtained from integrating all of the data. This combination of data can be visualised using a blobbogram, or forest plot. The diamond in the blobbogram represents the combined results of all the data included and is considered more reliable and better evidence, the more data there is.
6. Publishing, disseminating and translating into practice.

Systematic reviews act like a filter, selecting some evidence but rejecting other evidence. To retain the metaphor, what the reviewers see and report depends on how the selection process is operated. Whenever there is ambiguity, the process may well tend to operate in confirmatory mode, seeking positive support for a position, model or theory rather than disconfirmation. It is essential to be critical and cautious in interpreting and analysing SRs of biomedical and related topics. If we want to implement new practice as a direct consequence of such reviews, we had better make certain that the findings are solid and not a mirage. This is why the study of the method itself is so important.

Systematic reviews of the same topic can produce significantly different results, indicating that bias is difficult to control. Like all forms of knowledge, the results of an SR are the consequences of a process of negotiation about rules and criteria, and cannot be accepted without criticism and debate. There are many examples of controversies created by SRs – e.g. Law, Frost, and Wald (1991), Swales (2000), Millett (2011), Roseman et al. (2011), and Coyne & Kok (2014). SRs about different aspects of psi are reviewed in this book – e.g. see Chapters 6, 7 and 8.

Type I error   falsely rejecting an H_0, leading to the false conclusion that there is a statistically significant effect, a false positive. A type I error is detecting an effect that is not present. At the .05 significance level, the probability of a Type I error is .05.

Type II error   falsely retaining an incorrect null hypothesis, H_0, a false negative; failure to detect a real effect that is present. The lower the power of a test, the higher the probability of making a type II error.

Uncontrolled variables   variables that operate within the research environment to affect the outcome in a haphazard, unpredictable manner. As a consequence, the study contains the risk of producing false findings sometimes referred to artefacts.

Variables   quantities or measures of behaviour in a scientific investigation. Variables are divided into two main types: independent – under the control of the investigator; dependent – produced by the P.

Veridical   coinciding with actual events.

Vividness of Visual Imagery Questionnaire (VVIQ)   a 16-item instrument used in studies of individual differences in the capacity to form vivid visual images with eyes open or eyes closed (Marks, 1972, 1973).

Yoga   a group of physical, mental – and spiritual practices that facilitate altered states of consciousness that may be psi-conducive (e.g. Sidorov, 2001).

Zetetic   a person who suspends judgement and explores scientific questions by using discussion or dialogue to enquire into a topic.

EXERCISE

Carry out a Parapsychological Research Project in the following stages:

1. Literature review.
2. Develop one or more hypotheses.
3. Design a study with a procedure, Ps and a series of trials or questionnaires.
4. Collect the data – either task performance and one or more self-report measures.
5. Data analysis – choose a statistical approach that fits the data collected.
6. Write a report.
7. Present the findings.

BIBLIOGRAPHY

Abelson, R. P. (1986). Beliefs are like possessions. *Journal for the Theory of Social Behaviour, 16*(3), 223–250.

Acar, S., & Runco, M. A. (2012). Psychoticism and creativity: a meta-analytic review. *Psychology of Aesthetics, Creativity, and the Arts, 6*(4), 341–350.

Acar, S., & Sen, S. (2013). A multilevel meta-analysis of the relationship between creativity and schizotypy. *Psychology of Aesthetics, Creativity, and the Arts, 7*(3), 214–228.

Agargun, M. Y., Kara, H., Özer, Ö. A., Selvi, Y., Kiran, Ü., & Kiran, S. (2003). Nightmares and dissociative experiences: the key role of childhood traumatic events. *Psychiatry and Clinical Neurosciences, 57*(2), 139–145.

Agrillo, C. (2011). Near-death experience: out-of-body and out-of-brain? *Review of General Psychology, 15*(1), 1–10.

Alcock, J. (2003). Give the null hypothesis a chance: reasons to remain doubtful about the existence of psi. *Journal of Consciousness Studies, 10*, 29–50.

Alcock, J. (2010). In S. Krippner & H. Friedman (Eds.), *Debating psychic experiences: human potential or human illusion?* Santa Barbara, CA: Praeger.

Alcock, J. E. (1981). *Parapsychology: science or magic?* Oxford: Pergamon.

Alcock, J. E. (1990). *Science and supernature: a critical appraisal of parapsychology.* New York: Prometheus Books.

Alvarado, C. S. (1992). The psychological approach to out-of-body-experiences: a review of early and modern developments. *The Journal of Psychology, 12*, 237–250.

Alvarez López, E., Teixeira do Carmo, J., & Pueyo, A. A. (2000). Creencias y experiencias paranormales en esquizotipia. *Revista de Psicologia Universitas Tarraconensis.*

Alvaro, P. K., Roberts, R. M., & Harris, J. K. (2013). A systematic review assessing bidirectionality between sleep disturbances, anxiety, and depression. *Sleep, 36*(7), 1059–1068.

American Psychiatric Association (2013). *Diagnostic and statistical manual of mental disorders* (5th ed.). Washington, DC: American Psychiatric Association.

Amir, Y. & Sharon, I. (1991). Replication research: a 'must' for the scientific advancement of psychology. In J. W. Neuliep (Ed.), *Replication research in the social sciences* (pp. 51–69). Newbury Park, CA: Sage.

Anbar, R. D., & Hall, H. R. (2004). Childhood habit cough treated with self-hypnosis. *The Journal of Pediatrics, 144*(2), 213–217.

Anda, R. F., Felitti, V. J., Bremner, J. D., Walker, J. D., Whitfield, C. H., Perry, B. D., ... & Giles, W. H. (2006). The enduring effects of abuse and related adverse experiences in childhood. *European Archives of Psychiatry & Clinical Neuroscience, 256*, 174–186.

Ardis, J. A., & McKellar, P. (1956). Hypnagogic imagery and mescaline. *Journal of Mental Science, 102*(426), 22–29.

Aristotle (1848). On divination by dreams. In C. T. Waddington (Ed.), *La psychologie d'Aristotle* (p. 607). Paris: Joubert.

Aserinsky, E., & Kleitman, N. (1953). Regularly occurring periods of eye motility, and concomitant phenomena, during sleep. *Science, 118*(3062), 273–274.

Astafiev, S. V., Stanley, C. M., Shulman, G. L., & Corbetta, M. (2004). Extrastriate body area in human occipital cortex responds to the performance of motor actions. *Nature Neuroscience, 7*(5), 542.

Austin, M., Perry, C. W., Sutcliffe, J. P., & Yeomans. N. (1963). Can somnambulists successfully simulate hypnotic behavior without becoming entranced? *International Journal of Clinical and Experimental Hypnosis, 11*, 175–186.

Ayton, P., & Fischer, I. (2004). The hot hand fallacy and the gambler's fallacy: two faces of subjective randomness? *Memory & Cognition, 32*(8), 1369–1378.

Azmitia, E. C. (1999). Serotonin neurons, neuroplasticity, and homeostasis of neural tissue. *Neuropsychopharmacology, 21*(S1), 33S.

Azmitia, E. C. (2007). Cajal and brain plasticity: insights relevant to emerging concepts of mind. *Brain Research Reviews, 55*(2), 395–405.

Baas, M., De Dreu, C. K., & Nijstad, B. A. (2008). A meta-analysis of 25 years of mood-creativity research: hedonic tone, activation, or regulatory focus? *Psychological Bulletin, 134*(6), 779.

Bacon, F. (1620/1900). Novum organum. *A history of western philosophy, 3*.

Baglioni, C., Spiegelhalder, K., Lombardo, C., & Riemann, D. (2010). Sleep and emotions: a focus on insomnia. *Sleep Medicine Reviews, 14*(4), 227–238.

Bagri, G., & Jones, G. V. (2018). The role of first person perspective and vivid imagery in memory for written narratives. *Educational Psychology in Practice, 34*, 229–244.

Bailey, T. D., & Brand, B. L. (2017). Traumatic dissociation: theory, research, and treatment. *Clinical Psychology: Science & Practice, 24*, 170–185.

Bailey, T. D., Alvarez-Jimenez, M., Garcia-Sanchez, A. M., Hulbert, C., Barlow, E., & Bendall, S. (2018). Childhood trauma is associated with severity of hallucinations and delusions in psychotic disorders: a systematic review and meta-analysis. *Schizophrenia bulletin, 44*(5), 1111–1122.

Bainbridge, W. S. (1978). *Satan's power: a deviant psychotherapy cult*. Berkeley, CA: University of California Press.

Bakan, D. (1966). The test of significance in psychological research. *Psychological Bulletin, 66*, 1–29.

Baker, R. A. (2000). Can we tell when someone is staring at us from behind? *Skeptical Inquirer, 24*(2), 34–40.

Baker, R. R., Mather, J. G., & Kennaugh, J. H. (1983). Magnetic bones in human sinuses. *Nature, 301*(5895), 78.

Ball, T. M., Shapiro, D. E., Monheim, C. J., & Weydert, J. A. (2003). A pilot study of the use of guided imagery for the treatment of recurrent abdominal pain in children. *Clinical Pediatrics, 42*(6), 527–532.

Bandura, A. (1989). Human agency in social cognitive theory. *American Psychologist, 44*, 1175–1184.

Barabtarlo, G. (2018). *Nabokov, Vladimir. Insomniac Dreams*. Princeton, NJ: Princeton University Press. Kindle edition.

Barber, T. X. (1965). Measuring 'hypnotic-like' suggestibility with and without 'hypnotic induction'; psychometric properties, norms, and variables influencing response to the Barber Suggestibility Scale (BSS). *Psychological Reports*, *16*(3), 809–844.

Barber, T. X., & Wilson, S. C. (1978). The Barber suggestibility scale and the creative imagination scale: experimental and clinical applications. *American Journal of Clinical Hypnosis*, *21*(2–3), 84–108.

Bargh, J. A., & Ferguson, M. J. (2000). Beyond behaviourism: on the automaticity of higher mental processes. *Psychological Bulletin*, *126*, 925–945.

Barnard, J. P., Bennett, C., Voss, L. J. & Sleigh, J.W. (2007). Can anaesthetists be taught to interpret the effects of general anaesthesia on the electroencephalogram? Comparison of performance with the BIS and spectral entropy. *British Journal of Anaesthesia*, *99*, 532–537.

Barrett, D. (1992). Just how lucid are lucid dreams? *Dreaming*, *2*(4), 221.

Barrett, L. & Bar, M. (2009). See it with feeling: affective predictions during object perception. *Philosophical Transactions of the Royal Society B: Biological Sciences*, *364*, 1325–1334.

Bartholomew, R. E., Basterfield, K., & Howard, G. S. (1991). UFO abductees and contactees: psychopathology or fantasy proneness? *Professional Psychology: Research and Practice*, *22*(3), 215.

Bartlett, F. C. (1925). Feeling, imaging and thinking. *British Journal of Psychology*, *16*(1), 16.

Bartlett, F. C. (1932). *Remembering*. Cambridge: Cambridge University Press.

Beitman, B., Coleman, S., & Celebi, E. (2010). Synchronicity and healing. In D. Monti & B. D. Beitman (Eds.), *Integrative psychiatry* (pp. 445–484). New York: Oxford University Press.

Belfi, A. M., Vessel, E. A., & Starr, G. G. (2018). Individual ratings of vividness predict aesthetic appeal in poetry. *Psychology of Aesthetics, Creativity, and the Arts*, *12*, 341–350.

Belk, R. W. (1988). Possessions and the extended self. *Journal of Consumer Research*, *15*(2), 139–168.

Bell, G. B., Marino, A. A., & Chesson, A. L. (1992). Alterations in brain electrical activity caused by magnetic fields: detecting the detection process. *Electroencephalography and Clinical Neurophysiology*, *83*(6), 389–397.

Bell, V., Halligan, P. W., & Ellis, H. D. (2006). The Cardiff Anomalous Perceptions Scale (CAPS): a new validated measure of anomalous perceptual experience. *Schizophrenia Bulletin*, *32*(2), 366–377.

Belli, R. F., & Loftus, E. F. (1994). Recovered memories of childhood abuse: a source monitoring perspective. In S. J. Lynn & J. W. Rhue (Eds.), *Dissociation: clinical and theoretical perspectives* (pp. 415–433). New York: Guilford Press.

Beloff, J. (1974). *New directions in parapsychology*. London: Elek Science.

Beloff, J. (1993). *Parapsychology: a concise history*. London: Athlone Press.

Belvedere, E., & Foulkes, D. (1971). Telepathy and dreams: a failure to replicate. *Perceptual and Motor Skills*, *33*, 783–789.

Bem, D., Tressoldi, P., Rabeyron, T., & Duggan, M. (2015). Feeling the future: a meta-analysis of 90 experiments on the anomalous anticipation of random future events. *F1000Research*, *4*, 1188.

Bem, D. J. (2002). Writing the empirical journal article. In J. M. Darley, M. P. Zanna, & H. L. Roediger III (Eds.), *The compleat academic: a career guide*. Washington, DC: American Psychological Association.

Bem, D. J. (2003). Writing the empirical journal article. In J. M. Darley, M. P. Zanna, & H. L. Roediger III (Eds.), *The compleat academic: a career guide* (2nd ed.) (pp. 171–201). Washington, DC: American Psychological Association.

Bem, D. J. (2004). Precognitive avoidance and precognitive déjà vu. In *Proceedings of Presented Papers: The Parapsychological Association 47th Annual Convention* (pp. 431–432).

Bem, D. J. (2011). Feeling the future: experimental evidence for anomalous retroactive influences on cognition and affect. *Journal of Personality and Social Psychology, 100*, 407–425.

Bem, D. J., & Honorton, C. (1994) Does psi exist? Replicable evidence for an anomalous process of information transfer. *Psychological Bulletin, 115*(1), 4–18.

Bem, D. J., Utts, J., & Johnson, W.O. (2011) Must psychologists change the way they analyze their data? *Journal of Personality and Social Psychology, 101*(4): 716–719.

Berger, R. E., & Persinger, M. A. (1991). Geophysical variables and behavior: LXVII. Quieter annual geomagnetic activity and larger effect size for experimental psi (ESP) studies over six decades. *Perceptual and Motor Skills, 73*(3, suppl.), 1219–1223.

Berk, M., Dodd, S., & Henry, M. (2006). Do ambient magnetic fields affect behavior? A demonstration of the relationship between geomagnetic storm activity and suicide. *Bioelectromagnetics, 27*, 151–155.

Berkowski, M., & MacDonald, D. A. (2014). Childhood trauma and the development of paranormal beliefs. *The Journal of Nervous and Mental Disease, 202*(4), 305–312.

Bernard, C. (1865/1957). *An introduction to the study of experimental medicine* (Dover ed., 1957; originally published in 1865; first English translation by Henry Copley Greene, published by Macmillan & Co., 1927).

Bernard, C. (1975). Lectures on the phenomena of life common to animals and plants (trans. H. Hoff, R. Guillemin, & L. Guillemin) (review). *Perspectives in Biology and Medicine, 19*, 151–152.

Bernstein, E. M., & Putnam, F. W. (1986). Development, reliability and validity of a dissociation scale. *Journal of Nervous and Mental Diseases, 74*, 727–735.

Bertossa, F., Besa, M., Ferrari, R., & Ferri, F. (2008). Point zero: a phenomenological inquiry into the subjective physical location of consciousness. *Perceptual and Motor Skills, 107*, 323–335.

Bharde, A., Wani, A., Shouche, Y., Joy, P. A., Prasad, B. L., & Sastry, M. (2005). Bacterial aerobic synthesis of nanocrystalline magnetite. *Journal of the American Chemical Society, 127*(26), 9326–9327.

Bierman, D. (2010). Consciousness-induced restoration of time symmetry (CIRTS). A psychophysical theoretical perspective. *Journal of Parapsychology, 24*, 273–300.

Bierman, D., & Spottiswoode, J. (2012). The final breakthrough. *Journal of Parapsychology. 76*, 13–14.

Bierman, D. J., & Scholte, H. S. (2002, August). *Anomalous anticipatory brain activation preceding exposure of emotional and neutral pictures*. Paper presented at the meeting of the Parapsychological Association, Paris, France.

Bierman, D. J., Spottiswoode, J. P., & Bijl, A. (2016). Testing for questionable research practices in a meta-analysis: an example from experimental parapsychology. *PloS ONE, 11*(5), e0153049.

Billig, M. (1987). *Arguing and thinking: a rhetorical approach to social psychology.* Cambridge: Cambridge University Press.

Billows, H., & Storm, L. (2015). Believe it or not: a confirmatory study on predictors of paranormal belief, and a psi test. *Australian Journal of Parapsychology*, *15*(1), 7.

Billows, H., & Storm, L. (2016). Believe it or not: III. Further analyses on predictors of paranormal belief. *Australian Journal of Parapsychology*, *16*(1), 41.

Birchwood, M., Meaden, A., Trower, P., Gilbert, P., & Plaistow, J. (2000). The power and omnipotence of voices: subordination and entrapment by voices and significant others. *Psychological Medicine*, *30*(2), 337–344.

Bisaha, J. P., & Dunne, B. J. (1979/2002). Multiple subject and long-distance precognitive remote viewing of geographical locations. In C. T. Tart, H. E. Puthoff, & R. Targ (Eds.), *Mind at large: IEEE symposia on the nature of extrasensory perception* (pp. 98–111). Charlottesville, VA: Hampton Roads Publishing Company.

Blackmore, S. J. (1982). *Beyond the body: an investigation of out-of-the-body experiences*. London: Heinemann.

Blackmore, S. J. (1983). Birth and the OBE: an unhelpful analogy. *Journal of the American Society for Psychical Research*, *77*, 229–238.

Blackmore, S. J. (1984). A postal survey of OBEs and other experiences. *Journal of the Society for Psychical Research*, *52*, 225–244.

Blackmore, S. J. (1987). A report of a visit to Carl Sargent's laboratory. *Journal of the Society for Psychical Research*, *54*, 186–198.

Blackmore, S. J. (1996). *In search of the light: the adventures of a parapsychologist*. Amherst, NY: Prometheus Books.

Blackmore, S. J. (2017). *Seeing myself: the new science of out-of-body experiences*. London: Little, Brown. Kindle edition.

Blackmore, S. J. (2018). Daryl Bem and psi in the ganzfeld. *Skeptical Inquirer*, *42*(1), 44–45.

Blackmore, S. J., & Harris, B. (1983). OBEs and perceptual distortions in schizophrenic patients and students. In W. G. Roll, J. Beloff, & R. A. White (Eds.), *Research in parapsychology*, 1989 (pp. 232–234). Metuchen, NJ: Scarecrow Press.

Blanco, F., Barberia, I., & Matute, H. (2015). Individuals who believe in the paranormal expose themselves to biased information and develop more causal illusions than nonbelievers in the laboratory. *PloS one*, *10*(7), e0131378.

Blanke, O., & Mohr, C. (2005). Out-of-body experience, heautoscopy, and autoscopic hallucination of neurological origin: implications for neurocognitive mechanisms of corporeal awareness and self-consciousness. *Brain Research Reviews*, *50*(1), 184–199.

Blanke, O., Faivre, N., & Dieguez, S. (2016). Leaving body and life behind: out-of-body and near-death experience. In S. Laureys, O. Gosseries, & G. Tononi (Eds.), *The neurology of consciousness* (pp. 323–347). Cambridge, MA: Academic Press.

Blanke, O., Landis, T., Spinelli, L., & Seeck, M. (2004). Out-of-body experience and autoscopy of neurological origin. *Brain*, *127*(2), 243–258.

Blanke, O., Ortigue, S., Landis, T., & Seeck, M. (2002). Neuropsychology: stimulating illusory own-body perceptions. *Nature*, *419*(6904), 269.

Blum, G. S., & Graef, J. R. (1971). The detection over time of subjects simulating hypnosis. *The International Journal of Clinical and Experimental Hypnosis*, *19*(4), 211–224.

Bolles, R. C. (1970). Species-specific defense reactions and avoidance learning. *Psychological Review*, *77*(1), 32.

Bones, A. K. (1996). Invaders need no facilitators: merely exposing the alien 'Zajonc'. *American Psychologist*, *51*, 1231–1238.

Bones, A. K., & Johnson, N. R. (2007). Measuring the immeasurable: or 'could Abraham Lincoln take the implicit association test?', *Perspectives on Psychological Science*, 2, 406–411.

Borsboom, D., Mellenbergh, G. J., & van Heerden, J. (2004). The concept of validity. *Psychological Review*, *111*, 1061–1071.

Bos, E. M., Spoor, J. K., Smits, M., Schouten, J. W., & Vincent, A. J. (2016). Out-of-body experience during awake craniotomy. *World Neurosurgery*, *92*, 586-e9.

Bösch, H., Steinkamp, F., & Boller, E. (2006a). Examining psychokinesis: the interaction of human intention with random number generators – a meta-analysis. *Psychological Bulletin*, *132*(4), 497.

Bösch, H., Steinkamp, F., & Boller, E. (2006b). In the eye of the beholder: reply to Wilson and Shadish (2006) and Radin, Nelson, Dobyns, and Houtkooper (2006). *Psychological Bulletin*, *132*(4), 533–537.

Botvinick, M., & Cohen, J. (1998). Rubber hands 'feel' touch that eyes see. *Nature*, *391*(6669), 756.

Bougie, M. (2017). *Bigfoot, the Loch Ness monster, and unexplained creatures*. New York: Cavendish Square Publishing.

Bouvet, R., & Bonnefon, J. F. (2015). Non-reflective thinkers are predisposed to attribute supernatural causation to uncanny experiences. *Personality and Social Psychology Bulletin*, *41*(7), 955–961.

Braffman, W., & Kirsch, I. (1999). Imaginative suggestibility and hypnotizability: an empirical analysis. *Journal of Personality and Social Psychology*, *77*, 578–587.

Brainard, G. C., Hanifin, J. P., Greeson, J. M., Byrne, B., Glickman, G., Gerner, E., & Rollag, M. D. (2001). Action spectrum for melatonin regulation in humans: evidence for a novel circadian photoreceptor. *Journal of Neuroscience*, *21*(16), 6405–6412.

Braithwaite, J. J., Samson, D., Apperly, I., Broglia, E., & Hulleman, J. (2011). Cognitive correlates of the spontaneous out-of-body experience (OBE) in the psychologically normal population: evidence for an increased role of temporal-lobe instability, body-distortion processing, and impairments in own-body transformations. *Cortex*, *47*(7), 839–853.

Brand, B. L., Dalenberg, C. J., Frewen, P. A., Loewenstein, R. J., Schielke, H. J., Brams, J. S., & Spiegel, D. (2018). Trauma-related dissociation is no fantasy: addressing the errors of omission and commission in Merckelbach and Patihis (2018). *Psychological Injury and Law*, *11*(4), 377–393.

Braud, W. G. (2010). Psi and distance: is a conclusion of distance independence premature? Available online at: https://pdfs.semanticscholar.org/f3fd/03ce8974530b378a754387344606aa16a896.pdf

Braud, W. G., & Dennis, S. P. (1989). Geophysical variables and behavior: LVIII. Autonomic activity, hemolysis, and biological psychokinesis: possible relationships with geomagnetic field activity. *Perceptual and Motor Skills*, *68*(3, suppl.), 1243–1254.

Braud, W. G., Shafer, D., & Andrews, S. (1993a). Reactions to an unseen gaze (remote attention): a review, with new data on autonomic staring detection. *Journal of Parapsychology*, *57*, 372–390.

Braud, W. G., Shafer, D., & Andrews, S. (1993b). Further studies of autonomic detection of remote staring: replication, new control procedures, and personality correlates. *Journal of Parapsychology*, *57*, 391–409.

Braud, W. G., Wood, R., & Braud, L. W. (1975). Free-response GESP performance during an experimental hypnagogic state induced by visual and acoustic ganzfeld techniques: a replication and extension. *Journal of American Society for Psychic Research*, *69*, 105–113.

Braude, S. E. (2012). Parapsychology's future: a curmudgeonly perspective. *The Journal of Parapsychology*, *76*, 15.

Brecht, K. F., Hage, S. R., Gavrilov, N., & Nieder, A. (2019). Volitional control of vocalizations in corvid songbirds. *PLoS Biology*, *17*(8), e3000375.

Bressan, P. (2002). The connection between random sequences, everyday coincidences, and belief in the paranormal. *Applied Cognitive Psychology*, *16*, 17–34.

Brewin, C. R., & Andrews, B. (2017). Creating memories for false autobiographical events in childhood: a systematic review. *Applied Cognitive Psychology*, *31*(1), 2–23.

Brewin, C. R., Andrews, B., & Valentine, J. D. (2000). Meta-analysis of risk factors for posttraumatic stress disorder in trauma-exposed adults. *Journal of Consulting and Clinical Psychology*, *68*(5), 748.

Brewin, C. R., Dalgleish, T., & Joseph, S. (1996). A dual representation theory of posttraumatic stress disorder. *Psychological Review*, *103*(4), 670.

Brewin, C. R., Gregory, J. D., Lipton, M., & Burgess, N. (2010). Intrusive images in psychological disorders: characteristics, neural mechanisms, and treatment implications. *Psychological Review*, *117*(1), 210.

Briere, J. (2006). Dissociative symptoms and trauma exposure: specificity, affect dysregulation, and posttraumatic stress. *Journal of Nervous and Mental Disorders*, *194*(2), 78–82.

Britton, W. B., & Bootzin, R. R. (2004). Near-death experiences and the temporal lobe. *Psychological Science*, *15*(4), 254–258.

Broad, C. D. (1953). The relevance of psychical research to philosophy. In J. Ludwig (Ed.), *Philosophy and parapsychology* (pp. 43–63). Buffalo, NY: Prometheus.

Brosky, B. A., & Lally, S. J. (2004). Prevalence of trauma, PTSD, and dissociation in court-referred adolescents. *Journal of Interpersonal Violence*, *19*(7), 801–814.

Brotherton, R., & French, C. C. (2014). Belief in conspiracy theories and susceptibility to the conjunction fallacy. *Applied Cognitive Psychology*, *28*, 238–248.

Brown, C., Hofer, T., Johal, A., Thomson, R., Nicholl, J., Franklin, B. D., & Lilford, R. J. (2008). An epistemology of patient safety research: a framework for study design and interpretation. Part 4: One size does not fit all. *BMJ Quality & Safety*, *17*(3), 178–181.

Brown, D. J., & Fletcher, D. (2017). Effects of psychological and psychosocial interventions on sport performance: a meta-analysis. *Sports Medicine*, *47*(1), 77–99.

Brown, R. J. (2006). Different types of 'dissociation' have different psychological mechanisms. *Journal of Trauma & Dissociation*, *7*(4), 7–28.

Brown, R. J., & Donderi, D. C. (1986). Dream content and self-reported well-being among recurrent dreamers, past-recurrent dreamers, and nonrecurrent dreamers. *Journal of Personality and Social Psychology*, *50*(3), 612.

Browne, L. (2017). *The many faces of coincidence*. Exeter: Imprint Academic. Kindle edition.

Bruce, L. L., & Neary, T. J. (1995). The limbic system of tetrapods: a comparative analysis of cortical and amygdalar populations. *Brain, Behavior and Evolution*, *46*(4–5), 224–234.

Brugger, P., Agosti, R., Regard, M., Wieser, H. G., & Landis, T. (1994). Heautoscopy, epilepsy, and suicide. *Journal of Neurology, Neurosurgery & Psychiatry*, *57*(7), 838–839.

Brugger, P., Landis, T., & Regard, M. (1990). A 'sheep-goat effect' in repetition and avoidance: extra-sensory perception as an effect of subjective probability? *British Journal of Psychology*, *81*, 455–468.

Brugger, P., Regard, M., & Landis, T. (1997). Illusory reduplication of one's own body: phenomenology and classification of autoscopic phenomena. *Cognitive Neuropsychiatry*, *2*(1), 19–38.

Brugger, P., Regard, M. A., Landis, T., & Graves, R. E. (1995). The roots of meaningful coincidence. *The Lancet, 345*, 1306–1307.

Buckner, R. L., Andrews-Hanna, J. R., & Schacter, D. L. (2008). The brain's default network. *Annals of the New York Academy of Sciences, 1124*(1), 1–38.

Bullock, T. H., & Szabo, T. (1986). Introduction. In T. H. Bullock & W. Heiligenberg (Eds.), *Electroreception* (pp. 1–12). New York: Wiley.

Butler, A. J., & Page, S. J. (2006). Mental practice with motor imagery: evidence for motor recovery and cortical reorganization after stroke. *Archives of Physical Medicine and Rehabilitation, 87*(12), 2–11.

Byrom, G. (2009). Differential relationships between experiential and interpretive dimensions of mysticism and schizotypal magical ideation in a university sample. *Archive for the Psychology of Religion, 31*(2), 127–150.

Callow, N., Edwards, M. G., Jones, A. L., Hardy, L., & Connell, S. (2018). Action dual tasks reveal differential effects of visual imagery perspectives on motor performance. *Quarterly Journal of Experimental Psychology, 72*, 1401–1411.

Calne, D. B. (2000). *Within reason: rationality and human behaviour*. New York: Vintage.

Cambray, J. (2004). Synchronicity as emergence. In J. Cambray & L. Carter (Eds.), *Analytical psychology: contemporary perspectives in Jungian analysis* (pp. 235–260). Abingdon: Routledge.

Cannon, W. B. (1929). Organization for physiological homeostasis. *Physiological Review, 9*, 399–431.

Caplette, L., Gosselin, F., Mermillod, M., & Wicker, B. (2018). Real-world expectations and their affective value modulate object processing. *bioRxiv*, 408542.

Cardeña, E. (1994). The domain of dissociation. In S. J. Lynn & J. W. Rhue (Eds.), *Dissociation: clinical and theoretical perspectives* (pp. 15–31). New York: Guilford Press.

Cardeña, E. (2012). Psi is here to stay. *Journal of Parapsychology, 76*, 17–19.

Cardeña, E. (2018). The experimental evidence for parapsychological phenomena: a review. *American Psychologist, 73*(5), 663–677. https://doi.org/10.1037/amp0000236

Cardeña, E., & Carlson, E. (2011). Acute stress disorder revisited. *Annual Review of Clinical Psychology, 7*, 245–267.

Cardeña, E., Jönsson, P., Terhune, D. B., & Marcusson-Clavertz, D. (2013). The neurophenomenology of neutral hypnosis. *Cortex, 49*, 375–385.

Cardeña, E., Lynn, S. J., & Krippner, S. (2000). Introduction: anomalous experiences in perspective. In E. Cardeña, S. J. Lynn, & S. Krippner (Eds), *Varieties of anomalous experience. examining the scientific evidence* (pp. 3–20). Washington, DC: American Psychological Association.

Carhart-Harris, R. L., Bolstridge, M., Rucker, J., Day, C. M., Erritzoe, D., Kaelen, M., … & Taylor, D. (2016). Psilocybin with psychological support for treatment-resistant depression: an open-label feasibility study. *The Lancet Psychiatry, 3*(7), 619–627.

Carr, B. (2008). Can psychical research bridge the gulf between matter and mind? *Proceedings of the Society for Psychical Research, 59*(221), 1–96.

Carrubba, S., Frilot II, C., Chesson Jr, A. L., & Marino, A. A. (2007). Evidence of a non-linear human magnetic sense. *Neuroscience, 144*(1), 356–367.

Carter, C. (2010). 'Heads I lose, tails you win', or, how Richard Wiseman nullifies positive results, and what to do about it: a response to Wiseman's (2010) critique of parapsychology. *Journal of the Society for Psychical Research, 74*, 156–167.

Casswell, S., & Marks, D. (1973a). Cannabis induced impairment of performance of a divided attention task. *Nature*, *241*(5384), 60–61.

Casswell, S., & Marks, D. F. (1973b). Cannabis and temporal disintegration in experienced and naive subjects. *Science*, *179*(4075), 803–805.

Castanho, S. B., Vegetti, F., & Littvay, L. (2017). The elite is up to something: exploring the relation between populism and belief in conspiracy theories. *Swiss Political Science Review*, *23*(4), 423–443.

Castro, M., Burrows, R., & Wooffitt, R. (2014). The paranormal is (still) normal: the sociological implications of a survey of paranormal experiences in Great Britain. *Sociological Research Online*, *19*(3), 1–15.

Cattaneo, L., & Pavesi, G. (2014). The facial motor system. *Neuroscience & Biobehavioral Reviews*, *38*, 135–159.

Chae, K. S., Oh, I. T., Lee, S. H., & Kim, S. C. (2019). Blue light-dependent human magnetoreception in geomagnetic food orientation. *PloS ONE*, *14*(2), e0211826.

Chapman University (2018). The Chapman University survey of American fears, Wave 5. Orange, CA: Earl Babbie Research Center (producer).

Chayko, M. (2018). In sync, but apart: temporal symmetry, social synchronicity, and digital connectedness. In B. Wellman, L. Robinson, C. Brienza, W. Chen, & S. Cotten (Eds.), *Networks, Hacking, and Media – CITAMS@30: Now and Then and Tomorrow* (pp. 63–72). Bingley: Emerald Publishing.

Chesterton, G. K. (1908 [2004]). *The man who was Thursday: a nightmare*. San Francisco, CA: Ignatius Press.

Cheyne, J. A., & Girard, T. A. (2009). The body unbound: vestibular–motor hallucinations and out-of-body experiences. *Cortex*, *45*(2), 201–215.

Child, I. L. (1985). Psychology and anomalous observation: the question of ESP in dreams. *American Psychologist*, *40*, 1219–1220.

Children's Bureau, US Department of Health and Human Services, Administration for Children and Families, Children's Bureau. (2010). Child maltreatment 2009. Available online at: http://archive.acf.hhs.gov/programs/cb/pubs/cm09/cm09.pdf

Christoff, K., Gordon, A. M., Smallwood, J., Smith, R., & Schooler, J. W. (2009). Experience sampling during fMRI reveals default network and executive system contributions to mind wandering. *Proceedings of the National Academy of Sciences*, *106*(21), 8719–8724.

Chu, J. A., & Dill, D. L. (1990). Dissociative symptoms in relation to childhood physical and sexual abuse. *The American Journal of Psychiatry*, *147*(7), 887.

Churchill, D. R., Persinger, M. A., & Thomas, A. W. (1994). Geophysical variables and behavior: LXXVII. Increased geomagnetic activity and decreased pleasantness of spontaneous narratives for percipients but not for agents. *Perceptual and Motor Skills*, *79*, 387.

Clancy, S. A., McNally, R. J., Schacter, D. L., Lenzenweger, M. F., & Pitman, R. K. (2002). Memory distortion in people reporting abduction by aliens. *Journal of Abnormal Psychology*, *111*(3), 455.

Claridge, G., & Beech, T. (1995). Fully and quasi-dimensional constructions of schizotypy. *Schizotypal Personality*, *29*, 192–216.

Clements-Croome, D., & Cabanac, M. (1999). Pleasure and joy, and their role in human life. In D. Clements-Croome (Ed.), *Creating the Productive Workplace* (pp. 40–50). Boca Raton, FL: CRC Press.

Clemmer, E. J. (1986). Not so anomalous observations question ESP in dreams. *American Psychologist*, *41*, 1173–1174.

Close, J. (2012). Are stress responses to geomagnetic storms mediated by the cryptochrome compass system? *Proceedings of the Royal Society B: Biological Sciences, 279*(1736), 2081–2090.

Cocchiarella, F., & Drinkwater, K. (2019). Para-design: engaging the anomalous, a design research workshop to investigate paranormal phenomena through a series of location based studies. Available online at: https://iasdr2019.org/uploads/files/Proceedings/op-f-1371-Coc-F.pdf

Cohen, J. (1962). The statistical power of abnormal-social psychological research: a review. *Journal of Abnormal and Social Psychology, 65*, 145–153.

Cohen, J. (1988). *Statistical power analysis for the behavioral sciences* (2nd ed.). Hillsdale, NJ: Erlbaum.

Cohen, J. (1994). The earth is round (p < .05). *American Psychologist, 49*, 997–1003.

Cohen, J. A., Deblinger, E., Mannarino, A. P., & Steer, R. A. (2004). A multisite, randomized controlled trial for children with sexual abuse–related PTSD symptoms. *Journal of the American Academy of Child & Adolescent Psychiatry, 43*(4), 393–402.

Cole, C. L., Newman-Taylor, K., & Kennedy, F. (2016). Dissociation mediates the relationship between childhood maltreatment and subclinical psychosis. *Journal of Trauma & Dissociation, 17*(5), 577–592.

Collett, T. S., & Baron, J. (1994). Biological compasses and the coordinate frame of landmark memories in honeybees. *Nature, 368*, 137–140.

Collins, H. M. (1984). Discussion: when do scientists prefer to vary their experiments? *Studies in the History and Philosophy of Science, 15*, 169–174.

Colwell, J., Schröder, S., & Sladen, D. (2000). The ability to detect unseen staring: a literature review and empirical tests. *British Journal of Psychology, 91*, 71–85.

Cook, A., Spinazzola, J., Ford, J., Lanktree, C., Blaustein, M., Cloitre, M., ... & Mallah, K. (2017). Complex trauma in children and adolescents. *Psychiatric Annals, 35*(5), 390–398.

Cook, T. D., & Groom, C. (2004). The methodological assumptions of social psychology: the mutual dependence of substantive theory and method choice. In C. Sansone, C. C. Morf, & A. T. Panter (Eds.), *The SAGE handbook of methods in social psychology* (pp. 19–44). Thousand Oaks, CA: Sage.

Coover, J. E. (1913). The feeling of being stared at. *American Journal of Psychology, 24*, 570–575.

Costello, E. J., Erkanli, A., Fairbank, J. A., & Angold, A. (2002). The prevalence of potentially traumatic events in childhood and adolescence. *Journal of Traumatic Stress: Official Publication of The International Society for Traumatic Stress Studies, 15*(2), 99–112.

Council, J. R., & Huff, K. (1990) Hypnosis, fantasy activity and reports of paranormal experiences in high, medium and low fantasizers. *British Journal of Experimental and Clinical Hypnosis, 7*, 9–15.

Coutinho, S. A., & Woolery, L. M. (2004). The need for cognition and life satisfaction among college students. *College Student Journal, 38*(2), 203–207.

Coyne, J. C., & Kok, R. N. (2014). Salvaging psychotherapy research: a manifesto. *Journal of Evidence-Based Psychotherapies, 14*(2).

Craig, A. (2003). Interoception: the sense of the physiological condition of the body. *Current Opinion in Neurobiology, 13*, 500–505.

Craig, W. M., & Harel, Y. (2001). Bullying, physical fighting and victimization. *Young People's Health in Context: International Report from the HBSC, 2*, 133–144.

Crawford, H. J., & Allen, S. N. (1983). Enhanced visual memory during hypnosis as mediated by hypnotic responsiveness and cognitive strategies. *Journal of Experimental Psychology: General, 112*(4), 662–685.

Croijmans, I., Speed, L. J., Arshamian, A., & Majid, A. (2019). Measuring multisensory imagery of wine: the vividness of wine imagery questionnaire. *Multisensory Research, 1*, 1–17.

Cromby, J. (2012). Beyond belief. *Journal of Health Psychology, 17*(7), 943–957.

Cui, X., Jeter, C. B., Yang, D., Montague, P. R., & Eagleman, D. M. (2007). Vividness of mental imagery: individual variability can be measured objectively. *Vision Research, 47*, 474–478.

Cumming, G. (2008). Replication and p intervals: p values predict the future only vaguely, but confidence intervals do much better. *Perspectives on Psychological Science, 3*, 286–300.

D'Argembeau, A., & Van der Linden, M. (2006). Individual differences in the phenomenology of mental time travel: the effect of vivid visual imagery and emotion regulation strategies. *Consciousness and Cognition, 15*(2), 342–350.

Dagnall, N., Denovan, A., Drinkwater, K., Parker, A., & Clough, P. J. (2017). Urban legends and paranormal beliefs: the role of reality testing and schizotypy. *Frontiers in Psychology, 8*, 942.

Dagnall, N., Drinkwater, K., Parker, A., Denovan, A., & Parton, M. (2015). Conspiracy theory and cognitive style: a worldview. *Frontiers in Psychology, 6*, 206.

Dagnall, N., Drinkwater, K., Parker, A., & Rowley, K. (2014). Misperception of chance, conjunction, belief in the paranormal and reality testing: a reappraisal. *Applied Cognitive Psychology, 28*(5), 711–719.

Dagnall, N., Parker, A., & Munley, G. (2007). Paranormal belief and reasoning. *Personality and Individual Differences, 43*(6), 1406–1415.

Dagnall, N. A., & Drinkwater, K. (2019). The science of why so many people believe in psychic powers. *The Conversation*, 4 February.

Dagnall, N. A., Drinkwater, K., Parker, A., & Clough, P. (2016). Paranormal experience, belief in the paranormal and anomalous beliefs. *Paranthropology: Journal of Anthropological Approaches to the Paranormal, 7*(1), 4–15.

Dagnall, N. A., Irwin, H., & Drinkwater, K. (2017). Tweedledum and Tweedledee: are paranormal disbelievers a mirror image of believers? *Journal of the Society for Psychical Research, 81*(3), 161–180.

Dainton, B. (2008). *The phenomenal self*. Oxford: Oxford University Press.

Dalenberg, C. J., Brand, B. L., Gleaves, D. H., Dorahy, M. J., Loewenstein, R. J., Cardena, E., ... & Spiegel, D. (2012). Evaluation of the evidence for the trauma and fantasy models of dissociation. *Psychological Bulletin, 138*(3), 550.

Dalenberg, C. J., Brand, B. L., Loewenstein, R. J., Gleaves, D. H., Dorahy, M. J., Cardeña, E., ... & Spiegel, D. (2014). Reality versus fantasy: reply to Lynn et al. (2014). *Psychological Bulletin, 140*(3), 911–920.

Dalkvist, J. A. N., Mossbridge, J., & Westerlund, J. (2014). How to remove the influence of expectation bias in presentiment and similar experiments: a recommended strategy. *Journal of Parapsychology, 78*(1), 5–18.

Dallam, S. J. (2001). Crisis or creation? a systematic examination of 'false memory syndrome'. *Journal of Child Sexual Abuse, 9*(3/4), 9–36.

Dalton, K., & Stevens, P. (1996). Geomagnetism and the Edinburgh automated ganzfeld. *European Journal of Parapsychology, 12*, 23–34.

Damasio, A. (2018). *The strange order of things: life, feeling, and the making of cultures.* New York: Vintage.

Davey, C. G., & Harrison, B. J. (2018). The brain's center of gravity: how the default mode network helps us to understand the self. *World Psychiatry, 17*(3), 278.

Davey, C. G., Pujol, J., & Harrison, B. J. (2016). Mapping the self in the brain's default mode network. *NeuroImage, 132*, 390–397.

David, L., Seinfeld, J., Cowan, A. (writers) Cherones, T. (Director) (1994). The opposite (television series episode). In L. David (Executive Producer), *Seinfeld.* New York: NBC Broadcasting.

Davis, J. L., & Petretic-Jackson, P. A. (2000). The impact of child sexual abuse on adult interpersonal functioning: a review and synthesis of the empirical literature. *Aggression and Violent Behavior, 5*, 291–328.

Davis III, T. E., Ollendick, T. H., & Öst, L. G. (2019). One-session treatment of specific phobias in children: recent developments and a systematic review. *Annual Review of Clinical Psychology, 15*, 233–256.

Dawes, R. M. (1988). *Rational choice in an uncertain world.* San Diego, CA: Harcourt Brace Jovanovich.

de Araujo, D. B., Ribeiro, S., Cecchi, G. A., Carvalho, F. M., Sanchez, T. A., Pinto, J. P., ... & Santos, A. C. (2012). Seeing with the eyes shut: neural basis of enhanced imagery following ayahuasca ingestion. *Human Brain Mapping, 33*(11), 2550–2560.

De Ridder, D., Van Laere, K., Dupont, P., Menovsky, T., & Van de Heyning, P. (2007). Visualizing out-of-body experience in the brain. *New England Journal of Medicine, 357*(18), 1829–1833.

de Zeeuw, R. A., Wijsbeek, J., Breimer, D. D., Vree, T. B., van Genneken, C. A., & van Rossum, J. M. (1972). Cannabinoids with a propyl side chain in cannabis: occurrence and chromatographic behavior. *Science, 175*(4023), 778–779.

Dean, A. G., Sullivan, K. M., Soe, M. M. (2014). OpenEpi: Open Source Epidemiologic Statistics for Public Health, Version. www.OpenEpi.com (updated 6 June 2013, accessed 14 February).

Decety, J., & Lamm, C. (2007). The role of the right temporoparietal junction in social interaction: how low-level computational processes contribute to meta-cognition. *The Neuroscientist, 13*(6), 580–593.

Deco, G., Rolls, E. T., & Romo, R. (2009). Stochastic dynamics as a principle of brain function. *Progress in Neurobiology, 88*(1), 1–16.

Deeley, Q., Oakley, D. A., Toone, B., Giampietro, V., Brammer, M. J., Williams, S. C., & Halligan, P. W. (2012). Modulating the default mode network using hypnosis. *International Journal of Clinical and Experimental Hypnosis, 60*(2), 206–228.

Dement, W., & Kleitman, N. (1957). The relation of eye movements during sleep to dream activity: an objective method for the study of dreaming. *Journal of Experimental Psychology, 53*(5), 339.

Denes-Raj, V., & Epstein, S. (1994). Conflict between intuitive and rational processing: when people behave against their better judgment. *Journal of Personality and Social Psychology, 66*, 819–829.

Dennett, D. (1992). The self as the center of narrative gravity. In F. S. Kessel, P. M. Cole, & D. L. Johnson (Eds.), *Self and consciousness* (pp. 106–115). Hillsdale, NJ: Erlbaum.

Dennett, D. C. (2014). The self as the center of narrative gravity. In F. S. Kessel, P. M. Cole, D. L. Johnson & M. D. Hakel (Eds.), *Self and consciousness* (pp. 111–123). New York: Psychology Press. Kindle edition.

Derbyshire, S. W. G., Whalley, M. G., Stenger, V. A., & Oakley, D. A. (2004). Cerebral activation during hypnotically induced and imagined pain. *NeuroImage, 23*, 392–401.

DeShon, R. P. (2004). Measures are not invariant across groups without error variance homogeneity. *Psychology Science, 46*, 137–149.

Diaconis, P. (1978). Statistical problems in ESP research. *Science, 201*(4351), 131–136.

Diaconis, P., & Mosteller, F. (1989). Methods for studying coincidences. *Journal of the American Statistical Association, 84*(408), 853–861.

Dienes, Z. (2011). Bayesian versus orthodox statistics: which side are you on? *Perspectives on Psychological Science, 6*(3), 274–290.

Dienes, Z. (2016). How Bayes factors change scientific practice. *Journal of Mathematical Psychology, 72*, 78–89.

Dienes, Z. & Hutton, S. (2013). Understanding hypnosis metacognitively: rTMS applied to DLPFC increases hypnotic suggestibility. *Cortex, 49*, 386–392.

Dijkstra, N., Bosch, S. E., & van Gerven, M. A. (2017). Vividness of visual imagery depends on the neural overlap with perception in visual areas. *Journal of Neuroscience, 37*, 1367–1373.

Dijkstra, N., Bosch, S. E., & van Gerven, M. A. (2019). Shared neural mechanisms of visual perception and imagery. *Trends in Cognitive Sciences, 23*(5), 423–434.

Dixon, N. F. (1981). *Preconscious processing*. Chichester: Wiley.

Dobson, J. P., Fuller, M., Wieser, H. G., & Moser, S. (1993). *Transactions American Geophysical Union, 74*(16), *117*(60).

Dobyns, Y. (2009). Physics with an open mind. In C. A. Roe, L. Coly, & W. Kramer (Eds.), *Utrecht II: charting the future of parapsychology* (pp. 490–521). New York: Parapsychology Foundation, Inc. & Het Johan Borgmanfonds Foundation.

Doherty, R. (2019). Uri Geller says he will use 'telepathic powers' to stop Jeremy Corbyn becoming PM. *Jewish Chronicle*, 31 January.

Dorahy, M. J., Brand, B. L., Şar, V., Krüger, C., Stavropoulos, P., Martínez-Taboas, A., ... Middleton, W. (2014). Dissociative identity disorder: an empirical overview. *Australian & New Zealand Journal of Psychiatry, 48*(5), 402–417.

Downing, P. E., Jiang, Y., Shuman, M., & Kanwisher, N. (2001). A cortical area selective for visual processing of the human body. *Science, 293*(5539), 2470–2473.

Drinkwater, K., Dagnall, N., & Bate, L. (2013). Into the unknown: using interpretative phenomenological analysis to explore personal accounts of paranormal experiences. *The Journal of Parapsychology, 77*(2), 281–294.

Drinkwater, K., Dagnall, N., Grogan, S., & Riley, V. (2017). Understanding the unknown: a thematic analysis of subjective paranormal experiences. *Australian Journal of Parapsychology, 17*, 23–46.

Drinkwater, K., Dagnall, N., & Parker, A. (2012). Reality testing, conspiracy theories, and paranormal beliefs. *Journal of Parapsychology, 76*, 57–78.

Driskell, J. E., Copper, C., & Moran, A. (1994). Does mental practice enhance performance? *Journal of Applied Psychology, 79*, 481–492.

Duhem, P. (1954). *The aim and structure of physical theory* (trans. P. P. Wiener). Princeton, NJ: Princeton University Press.

Dullin, E., & Jamet, D. (2018). A methodology proposal for conducting a macro-PK test on light spinning objects, in a non-confined environment. *Journal of Scientific Exploration, 32*(3).

Dunlap, K. (1926). The experimental methods of psychology. In C. Murchison (Ed.), *Psychologies of 1925* (pp. 331–351). Worcester, MA: Clark University Press.

Dunn, D. S., & Chew, S. L. (Eds.) (2006). *Best practices for teaching introduction to psychology*. Hove: Psychology Press.

Dunne, B. J., & Jahn, R. G. (1992). Experiments in remote human/machine interaction. *Journal of Scientific Exploration, 6*, 311–332.

Dunne, J. W. (1927). *An experiment with time*. New York: Macmillan.

Duval, S. J., & Tweedie, R. L. (2000). A nonparametric 'trim and fill' method of accounting for publication bias in meta-analysis. *Journal of the American Statistical Association, 95*, 89–98.

Dyer, K. D., & Hall, R. E. (2018). Effect of critical thinking education on epistemically unwarranted beliefs in college students. *Research in Higher Education*, 1–22.

Ebersole, C. R., Atherton, O. E., Belanger, A. L., Skulborstad, H. M., Allen, J. M., Banks, J. B., ... & Brown, E. R. (2016). Many Labs 3: Evaluating participant pool quality across the academic semester via replication. *Journal of Experimental Social Psychology, 67*, 68–82.

Economics. (1776–2008). Rest in peace.

Edlow, B. L., McNab, J. A., Witzel, T., & Kinney, H. C. (2016). The structural connectome of the human central homeostatic network. *Brain Connect, 6*, 187–200.

Edwards, D. (1997). *Discourse and cognition*. London: Sage.

Eickhoff, S. B., Laird, A. R., Grefkes, C., Wang, L. E., Zilles, K., & Fox, P. T. (2009). Coordinate-based activation likelihood estimation meta-analysis of neuroimaging data: a random-effects approach based on empirical estimates of spatial uncertainty. *Human Brain Mapping, 30*(9), 2907–2926.

Eisen, M. L., Qin, J., Goodman, G. S., & Davis, S. L. (2002). Memory and suggestibility in maltreated children: age, stress arousal, dissociation, and psychopathology. *Journal of Experimental Child Psychology, 83*(3), 167–212.

Elkins, G. R., Barabasz, A. F., Council, J. R., & Spiegel, D. (2015). Advancing research and practice: the revised APA Division 30 definition of hypnosis. *International Journal of Clinical and Experimental Hypnosis, 63*(1), 1–9.

Ellason, J. W., & Ross, C. A. (1997). Childhood trauma and psychiatric symptoms. *Psychological Reports, 80*(2), 447–450.

Ellenberger, H. F. (1970). *The discovery of the unconscious: the history and evolution of dynamic psychiatry* (Vol. 1). New York: Basic Books.

Elliot, A. J. (1999). Approach and avoidance motivation and achievement goals. *Journal of Educational Psychology, 34*, 169–189.

Emmons, C. F. (2017). *Chinese ghosts revisited: a study of paranormal beliefs and experiences*. Hong Kong: Blacksmith Books.

Emmons, C. F., & Sobal, J. (1981). Paranormal beliefs: testing the marginality hypothesis. *Sociological Focus, 14*(1), 49–56.

Engber, D. (2017). Daryl Bem proved ESP is real: which means science is broken. Available online at: https://slate.com/health-and-science/2017/06/daryl-bem-proved-esp-is-real-showed-science-is-broken.html

Etkin, A., Büchel, C., & Gross, J. J. (2015). The neural bases of emotion regulation. *Nature Reviews Neuroscience, 16*, 693–700.

Evrard, R. (2016). Illuminations: the UFO experience as a parapsychological event. *The Journal of Parapsychology, 80*(1), 115.

Evrard, R., Massicotte, C., & Rabeyron, T. (2017). Freud as a psychical researcher: the impossible Freudian legacy. *IMÁGÓ BUDAPEST, 6*(4), 9–32.

Eysenck, H. J., & Sargent, C. (1982). *Explaining the unexplained: mysteries of the paranormal*. London: Weidenfeld & Nicolson.

Eysenck, H. J., & Sargent, C. (1984). *Know your own PSI-Q*. London: Michael Joseph.

Eysenck, H. J., & Sargent, C. (1993). *Explaining the unexplained: mysteries of the paranormal*. London: Multimedia Books.

Facco, E., & Agrillo, C. (2012). Near-death-like experiences without life-threatening conditions or brain disorders: a hypothesis from a case report. *Frontiers in Psychology, 3*, 490.

Falk, R. (1989) Judgment of coincidences: mine versus yours. *American Journal of Psychology, 102*(4), 477–493.

Falk, R. (1998). Replication – a step in the right direction. *Theory & Psychology, 8*, 313–321.

Falk, R., & Greenbaum, C. W. (1995). Significance tests die hard: the amazing persistence of a probabilistic misconception. *Theory & Psychology, 5*, 75–98.

Fanelli, D. (2010). 'Positive' results increase down the hierarchy of the sciences. *PLoS ONE 5*, e10068.

Fanelli, D. (2012). Negative results are disappearing from most disciplines and countries. *Scientometrics, 90*, 891–904.

Farias, M., Claridge, G., & Lalljee, M. (2005). Personality and cognitive predictors of New Age practices and beliefs. *Personality and Individual Differences, 39*(5), 979–989.

Faul, F., Erdfelder, E., Lang, A. G., & Buchner, A. (2007). G* Power 3: A flexible statistical power analysis program for the social, behavioral, and biomedical sciences. *Behavior Research Methods, 39*(2), 175–191.

Feinberg, G. (1975). Precognition: a memory of things future. In L. Oteri (Ed.), *Quantum physics and parapsychology* (pp. 54–64). New York: Parapsychology Foundation.

Feltz, D., & Landers, D. (1983). The effects of mental practice on motor skill learning and performance: a meta-analysis. *Journal of Sport Psychology, 5*, 25–57.

Ferris, L. J., & Rock, A. J. (2009). Mental boundaries, staring detection and phenomenology: a synthesised ganzfeld and remote staring study (online). *Australian Journal of Parapsychology, 9*, 193–213.

Finkelhor, D. (1987). The trauma of child sexual abuse: two models. *Journal of Interpersonal Violence, 2*(4), 348–366.

Finkelhor, D. (1994). The international epidemiology of child sexual abuse. *Child Abuse & Nglect, 18*(5), 409–417.

Finkelhor, D. (2008). *Childhood victimization: violence, crime, and abuse in the lives of young people*. Oxford: Oxford University Press.

Finkelhor, D., Shattuck, A., Turner, H. A., & Hamby, S. L. (2014). The lifetime prevalence of child sexual abuse and sexual assault assessed in late adolescence. *Journal of Adolescent Health, 55*(3), 329–333.

Finucane, R. C. (1985). *Appearances of the dead*. Buffalo, NY: Prometheus.

Fisher, R. A. (1934). *Statistical methods for research workers* (5th ed.). London: Oliver & Boyd.

Fisher, R. J. (1993). Social desirability bias and the validity of indirect questioning. *Journal of Consumer Research, 20*(2), 303–315.

Flaxman, S., Goel, S., & Rao, J. M. (2016). Filter bubbles, echo chambers, and online news consumption. *Public Opinion Quarterly, 80*(S1), 298–320.

Fleck, J. I., Green, D. L., Stevenson, J. L., Payne, L., Bowden, E. M., Jung-Beeman, M., & Kounios, J. (2008). The transliminal brain at rest: baseline EEG, unusual experiences, and access to unconscious mental activity. *Cortex, 44*(10), 1353–1363.

Flynn, D. J., Nyhan, B., & Reifler, J. (2017). The nature and origins of misperceptions: understanding false and unsupported beliefs about politics. *Political Psychology, 38*, 127–150.

Foley, L. E., Gegear, R. J., & Reppert, S. M. (2011). Human cryptochrome exhibits light-dependent magnetosensitivity. *Nature Communications*, *2*, 356.

Forer, B. R. (1949). The fallacy of personal validation: a classroom demonstration of gullibility. *The Journal of Abnormal and Social Psychology*, *44*(1), 118.

Foulkes, D., Belvedere, E., Masters, R. E. L., Houston, J., Krippner, S., Honorton, C., & Ullman, M. (1972). Long-distance, 'sensory-bombardment' ESP in dreams: a failure to replicate. *Perceptual and Motor Skills*, *35*(3), 731–734.

Fox, P. T., Lancaster, J. L., Laird, A. R., & Eickhoff, S. B. (2014). Meta-analysis in human neuroimaging: computational modeling of large-scale databases. *Annual Review of Neuroscience*, *37*, 409–434.

Francis, G. (2012). Too good to be true: publication bias in two prominent studies from experimental psychology. *Psychonomic Bulletin & Review*, *19*(2), 151–156.

Francis, L. J., Williams, E., & Robbins, M. (2016). Personality, conventional Christian belief and unconventional paranormal belief. In M. Robbins, & L. J. Francis (Eds.), *The empirical science of religious education: a study among teenagers* (pp. 237–245). Abingdon: Routledge.

Franklin Institute (2019). Benjamin Franklin and the kite experiment. Available online at: www.fi.edu/benjamin-franklin/kite-key-experiment

Franklin, M. S., Baumgart, S. L., & Schooler, J. W. (2014). Future directions in precognition research: more research can bridge the gap between skeptics and proponents. *Frontiers in Psychology*, *5*, 907.

Fransella, F., & Bannister, D. A. (1977). *Manual for repertory grid technique*. London: Academic.

Franzen, J., Brinkmann, K., Gendolla, G. H., & Sentissi, O. (2019). Major depression impairs incentive processing: evidence from the heart and the face. *Psychological Medicine*, *49*(6), 922–930.

Frederick, S. (2005). Cognitive reflection and decision making. *Journal of Economic Perspectives*, *19*(4), 25–42.

Frederiks, J. A. M. (1963). Macrosomatognosia and microsomatognosia. *Psychiatria, Neurologia, Neurochirurgia*, *66*, 531–536.

French, C. (2009). Families are still living the nightmare of false memories of sexual abuse. *The Guardian*. Available online at: www.theguardian.com/science/2009/apr/07/sexual-abuse-false-memory-syndrome

French, C. C. (2005). Near-death experiences in cardiac arrest survivors. *Progress in Brain Research*, *150*, 351–367.

French, C. C., Santomauro, J., Hamilton, V., Fox, R., & Thalbourne, M. A. (2008). Psychological aspects of the alien contact experience. *Cortex*, *44*(10), 1387–1395.

Freud, S. (1925). The occult significance of dreams. In G. Devereux (Ed.), *Psychoanalysis and the occult* (pp. 87–90.). London: International University Press.

Freud, S., & Strachey, J. (1916). *The interpretation of dreams*. London: Macmillan.

Fuller, M., Dobson, J., Wieser, H. G., & Moser, S. (1995). On the sensitivity of the human brain to magnetic fields: evocation of epileptiform activity. *Brain Research Bulletin*, *36*(2), 155–159.

Furnham, A. (1986). Response bias, social desirability and dissimulation. *Personality and Individual Differences*, *7*(3), 385–400.

Gajda, A., Karwowski, M., & Beghetto, R. A. (2017). Creativity and academic achievement: A meta-analysis. *Journal of Educational Psychology*, *109*(2), 269.

Galak, J., Leboeuf, R. A., Nelson, L. D., & Simmons, J. P. (2012). Correcting the past: failures to replicate psi. *Journal of Personality and Social Psychology, 103*, 933–948.

Gallagher, C., Kumar, V. K., & Pekala, R. J. (1994). The anomalous experiences inventory: reliability and validity. *The Journal of Parapsychology, 58*(4), 402–429.

Gamble, K. L., Berry, R., Frank, S. J., & Young, M. E. (2014). Circadian clock control of endocrine factors. *Nature Reviews Endocrinology, 10*, 466–475.

Ganis, G., Thompson, W. L., & Kosslyn, S. M. (2004). Brain areas underlying visual mental imagery and visual perception: an fMRI study. *Brain and Cognition, 20*, 226–241.

Gardner, M. (1956). *Math, magic and mystery*. New York: Dover.

Gardner, M. (1957). *Fads and fallacies in the name of science*. New York: Dover.

Gardner, M. (1999) *The man who was Thursday: the annotated Thursday*. San Francisco, CA: Ignatius.

Gardner, M. (2000). *The annotated Alice: the definitive edition. Lewis Carroll*. New York, London: W. W. Norton & Co.

Gardner, M. (2013). *Undiluted hocus-pocus*. Princeton, NJ: Princeton University Press. Kindle edition.

Gasser, P., Holstein, D., Michel, Y., Doblin, R., Yazar-Klosinski, B., Passie, T., & Brenneisen, R. (2014). Safety and efficacy of lysergic acid diethylamide-assisted psychotherapy for anxiety associated with life-threatening diseases. *The Journal of Nervous and Mental Disease, 202*(7), 513.

Gatlin, L. L. (1977). Meaningful information creation: an alternative interpretation of the psi phenomenon. *Journal of the American Society for Psychical Research, 73*, 1–18.

Gawronski, B., Deutsch, R., & Banse, R. (2011). Response interference tasks as indirect measures of automatic associations. In K. C. Klauer, C. Stahl, & A. Voss (Eds.), *Cognitive methods in social psychology* (pp. 78–123). New York: Guilford Press.

Geppert, A. C. (Ed.). (2018). *Imagining outer space: European astroculture in the twentieth century*. New York: Springer.

Geraerts, E., Merckelbach, H., Jelicic, M., Smeets, E., & van Heerden, J. (2006). Dissociative symptoms and how they relate to fantasy proneness in women reporting repressed or recovered memories. *Personality and Individual Differences, 40*(6), 1143–1151.

Gergen, K. J. (1982). *Toward transformation in social knowledge*. New York: Springer-Verlag.

Giambra, L. M. (2000). The temporal setting, emotions, and imagery of daydreams: age changes and age differences from late adolescent to the old-old. *Imagination, Cognition and Personality, 19*(4), 367–413.

Giesbrecht, T., & Merckelbach, H. (2006). Dreaming to reduce fantasy? Fantasy proneness, dissociation, and subjective sleep experiences. *Personality and Individual Differences, 41*(4), 697–706.

Giesbrecht, T., Lynn, S. J., Lilienfeld, S. O., & Merckelbach, H. (2008). Cognitive processes in dissociation: an analysis of core theoretical assumptions. *Psychological Bulletin, 134*(5), 617–647.

Gilder, S. A., Wack, M., Kaub, L., Roud, S. C., Petersen, N., Heinsen, H., ... & Schmitz, C. (2018). Distribution of magnetic remanence carriers in the human brain. *Scientific Reports, 8*(1), 11363.

Gillihan, S. J., & Farah, M. J. (2005). Is self special? A critical review of evidence from experimental psychology and cognitive neuroscience. *Psychological Bulletin, 131*, 76–97.

Girden, E. (1962a). A review of psychokinesis (PK). *Psychological Bulletin, 59*(5), 353.

Girden, E. (1962b). A postscript to 'A Review of Psychokinesis (PK)'. *Psychological Bulletin, 59*(6), 529–531.

Glasser, M. F., Coalson, T. S., Robinson, E. C., Hacker, C. D., Harwell, J., Yacoub, E., ... & Van Essen, D. C. (2016). A multi-modal parcellation of human cerebral cortex. *Nature, 536*(7615), 171–178.

Glickman, M. E., Rao, S. R., & Schultz, M. R. (2014). False discovery rate control is a recommended alternative to Bonferroni-type adjustments in health studies. *Journal of Clinical Epidemiology, 67*(8), 850–857.

Glicksohn, J. (1990). Belief in the paranormal and subjective paranormal experience. *Personality and Individual Differences, 11*(7), 675–683.

Glicksohn, J., & Barrett, T. R. (2003). Absorption and hallucinatory experience. *Applied Cognitive Psychology: The Official Journal of the Society for Applied Research in Memory & Cognition, 17*(7), 833–849.

Glover, P. M., & Bowtell, R. (2008). Measurement of electric fields induced in a human subject due to natural movements in static magnetic fields or exposure to alternating magnetic field gradients. *Physics in Medicine and Biology, 53*, 361.

Godin, I., Montplaisir, J., & Nielsen, T. (2015). Dreaming and nightmares in REM sleep behavior disorder. *Dreaming, 25*(4), 257.

Goel, V., & Dolan, R. J. (2004). Differential involvement of left prefrontal cortex in inductive and deductive reasoning. *Cognition, 93*(3), B109–B121.

Goertzel, T. (1994). Belief in conspiracy theories. *Political Psychology, 15*, 731–742.

Goertzen, J.R. (2008). On the possibility of unification: the reality and nature of the crisis in psychology. *Theory and Psychology, 18*(6), 829–852.

Gómez, J. M., Kaehler, L. A., & Freyd, J. J. (2014). Are hallucinations related to betrayal trauma exposure? A three-study exploration. *Psychological Trauma: Theory, Research, Practice, and Policy, 6*(6), 675.

Goodenough, D. R. (1991). Dream recall: history and current status of the field. In S. J. Ellman & J. S. Antrobus (Eds.), *The mind in sleep: psychology and psychophysiology* (2nd ed.) (pp. 143–171). New York: John Wiley.

Gould, J. L., Kirschvink, J. L., & Deffeyes, K. S. (1978). Bees have magnetic remanence. *Science, 201*(4360), 1026–1028.

Goulden, N., Khusnulina, A., Davis, N. J., Bracewell, R. M., Bokde, A. L., McNulty, J. P., & Mullins, P. G. (2014). The salience network is responsible for switching between the default mode network and the central executive network: replication from DCM. *NeuroImage, 99*, 180–190.

Goulding, A. (2004). Schizotypy models in relation to subjective health and paranormal beliefs and experiences. *Personality and Individual Differences, 37*, 157–167.

Goulding, A., Westerlund, J., Parker, A., & Wackermann, J. (2004). The first digital autoganzfeld study using a real-time judging procedure. *European Journal of Parapsychology, 19*, 66.

Gow, K. M., Hutchinson, L., & Chant, D. (2009). Correlations between fantasy proneness, dissociation, personality factors and paranormal beliefs in experiencers of paranormal and anomalous phenomena. *Australian Journal of Clinical & Experimental Hypnosis, 37*(2), 169–191.

Gow, K., Lang, T., & Chant, D. (2004). Fantasy proneness, paranormal beliefs and personality features in out-of-body experiences. *Contemporary Hypnosis, 21*, 107–125.

Graner, J. L., Oakes, T. R., French, L. M., & Riedy, G. (2013). Functional MRI in the investigation of blast-related traumatic brain injury. *Frontiers in Neurology, 4*, 16.

Gray, S. J., & Gallo, D. A. (2016). Paranormal psychic believers and skeptics: a large-scale test of the cognitive differences hypothesis. *Memory & Cognition, 44*(2), 242–261.

Greeley, A. M. (1975). *The sociology of the paranormal: a reconnaissance.* Beverly Hills, CA: Sage.

Greeley, A. M. (1987). Mysticism goes mainstream. *American Health, 6,* 47–49.

Greeley, A. M. (1991). The paranormal is normal: a sociologist looks at parapsychology. *Journal of the American Society for Psychical Research, 85,* 367–374.

Green, C. E. (1968). *Out-of-the-body experiences.* London: Hamish Hamilton.

Green, J. P., & Lynn, S. J. (2008). Fantasy proneness and hypnotizability: another look. *Contemporary Hypnosis, 25*(3–4), 156–164.

Green, J. P., & Lynn, S. J. (2010). Hypnotic responsiveness: expectancy, attitudes, fantasy proneness, absorption, and gender. *International Journal of Clinical and Experimental Hypnosis, 59*(1), 103–121.

Greenwald, A. G., Gonzalez, R., Harris, R. J., & Guthrie, D. (1996). Effect size and p values: what should be reported and what should be replicated? *Psychophysiology, 33,* 175–183.

Greyson, B. (1983). Near-death experiences and personal values. *American Journal of Psychiatry, 140*(5), 618–620.

Greyson, B. (1998). The incidence of near-death experiences. *Medicine & Psychiatry, 1,* 92–99.

Greyson, B. (2000). Dissociation in people who have near-death experiences: out of their bodies or out of their minds? *The Lancet, 355*(9202), 460–463.

Greyson, B. (2014). Congruence between near-death and mystical experience. *The International Journal for the Psychology of Religion, 24*(4), 298–310.

Greyson, B., Kelly, E. W., & Kelly, E. F. (2009). Explanatory models for near-death experiences. In J. M. Holden, B. Greyson, & D. James (Eds.), *The handbook of near-death experiences: thirty years of investigation* (pp. 213–234). Santa Barbara, CA: Praeger/ABC-CLIO.

Griffiths, T. L., & Tenenbaum, J. B. (2007). From mere coincidences to meaningful discoveries. *Cognition, 103*(2), 180–226.

Groth-Marnat, G., & Summers, R. (1998). Altered beliefs, attitudes, and behaviors following near-death experiences. *Journal of Humanistic Psychology, 38*(3), 110–125.

Guell, X., Gabrieli, J. D., & Schmahmann, J. D. (2018). Triple representation of language, working memory, social and emotion processing in the cerebellum: convergent evidence from task and seed-based resting-state fMRI analyses in a single large cohort. *NeuroImage, 172,* 437–449.

Gurney, E. & Myers. F. W. H. (1889). On apparitions occuring soon after death. *Proceedings of the Society for Psychical Research, 5,* 403–485.

Guttman, L. (1997). What is not what in statistics. *The Statistician, 26,* 81–107.

Haggard, P. (2017). Sense of agency in the human brain. *Nature Reviews Neuroscience, 18*(4), 196.

Hall, J. M. (2003). Dissociative experiences of women child abuse survivors: a selective constructivist review. *Trauma, Violence, & Abuse, 4*(4), 283–308.

Halpern, D. F. (1993). Assessing the effectiveness of critical-thinking instruction. *Journal of General Education, 42*(4), 239–254.

Hand, D. J. (2014). *The improbability principle: why coincidences, miracles, and rare events happen every day.* New York: Scientific American/Farrar, Straus and Giroux.

Hanegraaff, W. J. (2018). *New Age religion and Western culture: esotericism in the mirror of secular thought.* Leiden: Brill.

Hansel, C. E. M. (1989). *The search for psychic power: ESP and parapsychology revisited.* New York: Prometheus Books.

Haraldsson, E., & Houtkooper, J. M. (1991). Psychic experiences in the multinational human values study: who reports them? *Journal of the American Society for Psychical Research*, *85*(2), 145–165.

Hardell, L., & Sage, C. (2008). Biological effects from electromagnetic field exposure and public exposure standards. *Biomedicine & Pharmacotherapy*, *62*(2), 104–109.

Hardwick, R. M., Caspers, S., Eickhoff, S. B., & Swinnen, S. P. (2018). Neural correlates of action: comparing meta-analyses of imagery, observation, and execution. *Neuroscience & Biobehavioral Reviews*, *94*, 31–44.

Hardy, A. C., Harvie, R., & Koestler, A. (1974). *The challenge of chance: a mass experiment in telepathy and its unexpected outcome*. New York: Random House.

Harley, T., & Matthews, G. (1987) Cheating, psi, and the appliance of science: a reply to Blackmore. *Journal of the Society for Psychical Research*, *54*, 199–207.

Hart, W., Albarracín, D., Eagly, A. H., Brechan, I., Lindberg, M. J., & Merrill, L. (2009). Feeling validated versus being correct: a meta-analysis of selective exposure to information. *Psychological Bulletin*, *135*(4), 555.

Hastorf, A. H., & Cantril, H. (1954). They saw a game: a case study. *The Journal of Abnormal and Social Psychology*, *49*(1), 129.

Hayden, B. Y., Heilbronner, S. R., Pearson, J. M., & Platt, M. L. (2011). Surprise signals in anterior cingulate cortex: neuronal encoding of unsigned reward prediction errors driving adjustment in behavior. *Journal of Neuroscience*, *31*(11), 4178–4418.

Hebb, D. (1968). Concerning imagery. *Psychological Review*, *75*, 466–477.

Hébert, M., Langevin, R., Guidi, E., Bernard-Bonnin, A. C., & Allard-Dansereau, C. (2017). Sleep problems and dissociation in preschool victims of sexual abuse. *Journal of Trauma & Dissociation*, *18*(4), 507–521.

Hegarty, M. (2004). Mechanical reasoning by mental simulation. *Trends in Cognitive Science*, *8*, 280–285.

Hendrick, C. (1991). Replications, strict replications, and conceptual replications: are they important? In J. W. Neuliep (Ed.), *Replication research in the social sciences* (pp. 41–49). Newbury Park, CA: Sage.

Hilgard, E. R. (1972). A critique of Johnson, Maher, and Barber's 'Artifact in the "essence of hypnosis": an evaluation of trance logic': with a recomputation of their findings. *Journal of Abnormal Psychology*, *79*(2), 221.

Hilgard, E. R. (1977). *Divided consciousness: multiple controls in human thought and action*. Hoboken, NJ: Wiley.

Hilgard, E. R. (1981). Imagery and imagination in American psychology. *Journal of Mental Imagery*, *5*, 5–19.

Hilgard, E. R. (1987). *Psychology in America: a historical survey*. New York: Harcourt Brace Jovanovich.

Hill, A. (2010). *Paranormal media: audiences, spirits and magic in popular culture*. Abingdon: Routledge.

Hill, C. E., Diemer, R. A., & Heaton, K. J. (1997). Dream interpretation sessions: who volunteers, who benefits, and what volunteer clients view as most and least helpful. *Journal of Counseling Psychology*, *44*(1), 53.

Hill, S. A., O'Keeffe, C., Laythe, B., Dagnall, N. Drinkwater, K., Ventola, A., & Houran, J. (2018). 'Meme-spirited': I. The VAPUS model for understanding the prevalence and potency of ghost narratives. *Australian Journal of Parapsychology*, *18*, 117–152.

Hochberg, J. E., Triebel, W., & Seaman, G. (1951). Color adaptation under conditions of homogeneous visual stimulation (Ganzfeld). *Journal of Experimental Psychology, 41*, 153–159.

Hoebens. P. H. (1982). The modern revival of 'Nostradamitis': testing a phenomenal book's interpretations. *Skeptical Inquirer, 7*(1), 38–45.

Hofbauer, R. K., Rainville, P., Duncan, G. H., & Bushnell, M. C. (2001). Cortical representation of the sensory dimension of pain. *Journal of Neurophysiology, 86*, 402–411.

Hofmann, A., & Ott, J. (1980). *LSD, my problem child* (Vol. 5). New York: McGraw-Hill.

Holmes, E. A., & Mathews, A. (2005). Mental imagery and emotion: a special relationship? *Emotion, 5*, 489–497.

Holmes, E. A., Arntz, A., & Smucker, M. R. (2007). Imagery rescripting in cognitive behaviour therapy: images, treatment techniques and outcomes. *Journal of Behavior Therapy and Experimental Psychiatry, 38*(4), 297–305.

Holmes, E. A., Brown, R. J., Mansell, W., Fearon, R. P., Hunter, E. C., Frasquilho, F., & Oakley, D. A. (2005). Are there two qualitatively distinct forms of dissociation? A review and some clinical implications. *Clinical Psychology Review, 25*, 1–23.

Holt, N. J. (2007). *Creativity, altered states of consciousness and anomalous cognition: the role of epistemological flexibility in the creative process*. Doctoral dissertation, The University of Northampton.

Holt, N. J., & Roe, C. A. (2006). The sender as a PK agent in ESP studies: the effects of agent and target system lability upon performance at a novel PK task. *The Journal of Parapsychology, 70*(1), 49.

Holton, G. J. (1988). *Thematic origins of scientific thought: Kepler to Einstein*. Cambridge, MA: Harvard University Press.

Honorton, C. (1977). Psi and internal attention states. In B. B. Wolman (Ed.), *Handbook of Parapsychology* (pp. 435–472). New York/London: Van Nostrand Reinhold.

Honorton, C. (1985). Meta-analysis of psi ganzfeld research: a response to Hyman. *Journal of Parapsychology, 49*(1), 51.

Honorton, C. (1995). Impact of the sender in ganzfeld communication: meta-analysis and power estimates. In *Proceedings of Presented Papers: The Parapsychological Association 38th Annual Convention* (pp. 132–140).

Honorton, C., & Harper, S. (1974). Psi-mediated imagery and ideation in an experimental procedure for regulating perceptual input. *Journal of the American Society for Psychical Research, 68*, 156–168.

Honorton, C., Berger, R. E., Varvoglis, M. P., Quant, M., Derr, P., Schechter, E. I., & Ferrari, D. C. (1990). Psi communication in the ganzfeld: experiments with an automated testing system and a comparison with a meta-analysis of earlier studies. *Journal of Parapsychology, 54*(2), 99.

Hore, P. J., & Mouritsen, H. (2016). The radical-pair mechanism of magnetoreception. *Annual Review of Biophysics, 45*, 299–344.

Horváth, L., Szummer, C., & Szabo, A. (2018). Weak phantasy and visionary phantasy: the phenomenological significance of altered states of consciousness. *Phenomenology and the Cognitive Sciences, 17*(1), 117–129.

Hough, P., & Rogers, P. (2007). Individuals who report being abducted by aliens: investigating the differences in fantasy proneness, emotional intelligence and the big five personality factors. *Imagination, Cognition and Personality, 27*(2), 139–161.

Houran, J., & Lange, R. (2004). Redefining delusion based on studies of subjective paranormal ideation. *Psychological Reports, 94*(2), 501–513.

Houran, J., Laythe, B., O'Keeffe, C., Dagnall, N., Drinkwater, K., & Lange, R. (2019). Quantifying the phenomenology of ghostly episodes: Part I – need for a standard operationalization 5. *The Journal of Parapsychology*, *83*(1), 25–46.

House of Lords, M'Naghten Rules (1843). United Kingdom House of Lords Decisions. Daniel M'Naghten's Case. May 26, June 19, 1843. British and Irish Legal Information Institute. Retrieved 15 February 2020.

Howard, M. C. (2018). A meta-reanalysis of dream-ESP studies: comment on Storm et al. (2017). *International Journal of Dream Research*, *11*(2), 224–229.

Hughes, K., Bellis, M. A., Hardcastle, K. A., Sethi, D., Butchart, A., Mikton, C., ... & Dunne, M. P. (2017). The effect of multiple adverse childhood experiences on health: a systematic review and meta-analysis. *The Lancet Public Health*, *2*(8), e356–e366.

Hume, D. (1902). *An Enquiry Concerning Human Understanding*, Ed. L. A. Selby Bigge. Oxford: Clarendon Press.

Hundman, K., Constantinou, V., Laporte, C., Colwell, I., & Soderstrom, T. (2018). Detecting spacecraft anomalies using LSTMs and nonparametric dynamic thresholding. *arXiv preprint* arXiv:1802.04431.

Huxley, A. (1954/2010). *The doors of perception: and heaven and hell*. New York: Random House.

Hyman, R. (1977). Cold reading: how to convince strangers that you know all about them. *Skeptical Inquirer*, 79–96.

Hyman, R. (1985). The ganzfeld psi experiment: a critical appraisal. *Journal of Parapsychology*, *49*, 3–49.

Hyman, R. (1986). Maimonides dream-telepathy experiments. *Skeptical Inquirer*, *11*, 91–92.

Hyman, R. (1989). The psychology of deception. *Annual Review of Psychology*, *40*(1), 133–154.

Hyman, R. (1994). Anomaly or artifact? Comments on Bem and Honorton. *Psychological Bulletin*, *115*(1), 19–24.

Hyman, R. (2010). Meta-analysis that conceals more than it reveals: comment on Storm et al. (2010). *Psychological Bulletin*, *136*, 486–490.

Hyman, R., & Honorton, C. (1986). A joint communiqué: the psi ganzfeld controversy. *The Journal of Parapsychology*, *50*(4), 351.

Hyman, R., & Honorton, C. (2018). A joint communiqué: the psi ganzfeld controversy 1. *The Journal of Parapsychology*, *82*, 106–117.

Iachini, T., Maffei, L., Masullo, M., Senese, V. P., Rapuano, M., Pascale, A., Sorrentino, F., & Ruggiero, G. (2018). The experience of virtual reality: are individual differences in mental imagery associated with sense of presence? *Cognitive Processing*, *20*(3), 1–8.

Imhoff, R., & Bruder, M. (2014). Speaking (un-)truth to power: conspiracy mentality as a generalised political attitude. *European Journal of Personality*, *28*, 25–43.

Inglis, B. (1977). *Natural and supernatural: a history of the paranormal from earliest times to 1914*. London: Hodder & Stoughton.

Irwin, H. J. (1990). Fantasy proneness and paranormal beliefs. *Psychological Reports*, *66*(2), 655–658.

Irwin, H. J. (1991). A study of paranormal belief, psychological adjustment, and fantasy proneness. *Journal of the American Society for Psychical Research*, *85*(4), 317–331.

Irwin, H. J. (1993a). Belief in the paranormal: a review of the empirical literature. *Journal of the American Society for Psychical Research*, *87*(1), 1–39.

Irwin, H. J. (1993b). The near-death experience as a dissociative phenomenon: an empirical assessment. *Journal of Near Death Studies*, *12*(2), 95–103.

Irwin, H. J. (2009) *The psychology of paranormal belief: a researcher's handbook*. Hatfield: University of Hertfordshire Press. Kindle edition.

Irwin, H. J., Dagnall, N., & Drinkwater, K. (2012). Paranormal belief and biases in reasoning underlying the formation of delusions. *Australian Journal of Parapsychology*, *12*(1), 7.

Irwin, H. J., Dagnall, N., & Drinkwater, K. (2013). Parapsychological experience as anomalous experience plus paranormal attribution: a questionnaire based on a new approach to measurement. *Journal of Parapsychology*, *77*(1), 39–53.

Irwin, H. J., Dagnall, N., & Drinkwater, K. (2016). Dispositional skepticism, attitudes to science, and belief in the paranormal. *Australian Journal of Parapsychology*, *16*(2), 117.

Isaac, A., Marks, D. F., & Russell, D. G. (1986). An instrument for assessing imagery of movement: the Vividness of Movement Imagery Questionnaire (VMIQ). *Journal of Mental Imagery*, *10*, 23–30.

Isaac, A. R., & Marks, D. F. (1994). Individual differences in mental imagery experience: developmental changes and specialization. *British Journal of Psychology*, *85*, 479–500.

Itti, L., & Baldi, P. F. (2006). Bayesian surprise attracts human attention. *Advances in Neural Information Processing Systems*, *19*, 547–554.

Jackson, C. W., Hunt, E., Sharkh, S., & Newland, P. L. (2011). Static electric fields modify the locomotory behaviour of cockroaches. *Journal of Experimental Biology*, *214*, 2020–2026.

Jackson, P. L., Meltzoff, A. N., & Decety, J. (2006). Neural circuits involved in imitation and perspective-taking. *Neuroimage*, *31*(1), 429–439.

Jacobs, C., Schwarzkopf, D.S., & Silvanto, J. (2018). Visual working memory performance in aphantasia. *Cortex*, *105*, 61–73.

Jahn, R. G., Dunne, B. J., Nelson, R. G., Dobyns, Y. H., & Bradish, G. J. (2007). Correlations of random binary sequences with pre-stated operator intention: a review of a 12-year program. *Explore*, *3*(3), 244–253, 341–343. https://doi.org/10.1016/j.explore.2007.03.009

Jahoda, G. (2018). Social aspirations, magic and witchcraft in Ghana: a social psychological interpretation. In P. Lloyd (Ed.), *The new elites of tropical Africa* (pp. 199–215). Abingdon: Routledge.

James, W. (1890). *The principles of psychology*. New York: Holt & Company.

Janet, P. (1889/1973). *L'automatisme psychologique*. Paris: Felix Alcan.

Janet, P. (1907). *The major symptoms of hysteria* New York: Hafner.

Jankowska, D. M., & Karwowski, M. (2015). Measuring creative imagery abilities. *Frontiers in Psychology*, *6*, 1591.

Jastrzębski, J., & Chuderski, A. (2017). Reasoning ability predicts irrational worldview but not conspiracy belief. Available online at: https://mindmodeling.org/cogsci2017/papers/0436/paper0436.pdf (last accessed 21 February 2019).

Jeannerod, M. (1999). The 25th Bartlett Lecture: to act or not to act: perspectives on the representation of actions. *Quarterly Journal of Experimental Psychology A*, *52*, 1–29.

Jeannerod, M. (2003). The mechanism of self-recognition in humans. *Behavioural Brain Research*, *142*(1–2), 1–15.

Jiang, H., White, M. P., Greicius, M. D., Waelde, L. C., & Spiegel, D. (2017). Brain activity and functional connectivity associated with hypnosis. *Cerebral Cortex*, *27*(8), 4083–4093.

Johansen, M. K., & Osman, M. (2015). Coincidences: A fundamental consequence of rational cognition. *New Ideas in Psychology*, *39*, 34–44.

John, L. K., Loewenstein, G., & Prelec, D. (2012). Measuring the prevalence of questionable research practices with incentives for truth telling. *Psychological Science*, *23*(5), 524–532.

Johnsen, S., & Lohmann, K. J. (2005). The physics and neurobiology of magnetoreception. *Nature Reviews Neuroscience, 6,* 703–712.

Johnson, R. F., Maher, B. A., & Barber, T. X. (1972). Artifact in the 'essence of hypnosis': an evaluation of trance logic. *Journal of Abnormal Psychology, 79,* 212–220.

Johnston, M. J. S., & Stacey, F. D. (1969). Transient magnetic anomalies accompanying volcanic eruptions in New Zealand. *Nature, 224*(5226), 1289.

Jung, C. G. (1960). *Synchronicity: an acausal connecting principle.* Princeton, NJ: Princeton University Press.

Jung, C. G. (1967). *Memories, dreams, reflections.* London: Fontana Library of Theology and Philosophy.

Kahneman, D., & Egan, P. (2011). *Thinking, fast and slow* (Vol. 1). New York: Farrar, Straus and Giroux.

Kahneman, D., & Frederick, S. (2002). Representativeness revisited: attribute substitution in intuitive judgment. *Heuristics and biases: the psychology of intuitive judgment, 49,* 81.

Kahneman, D., & Tversky, A. (1996). On the reality of cognitive illusions. *Psychological Review, 103,* 582–591.

Kandel, E. R. (2013). *Principles of neural science* (5th ed.). New York: McGraw-Hill Education. Kindle edition.

Kane, M. J., Brown, L. H., McVay, J. C., Silvia, P. J., Myin-Germeys, I., & Kwapil, T. R. (2007). For whom the mind wanders, and when: an experience-sampling study of working memory and executive control in daily life. *Psychological Science, 18,* 614–621.

Kang, S., Kang, K., Lee, K., & Back, K. (2007). Characterization of tryptamine 5-hydroxylase and serotonin synthesis in rice plants. *Plant Cell Reports, 26*(11), 2009–2015.

Kanwisher, N., McDermott, J., & Chun, M. M. (1997). The fusiform face area: a module in human extrastriate cortex specialized for face perception. *Journal of Neuroscience, 17*(11), 4302–4311.

Kaplan, A. (1964). *The conduct of inquiry.* San Francisco, CA: Chandler.

Kappes, H. B., & Morewedge, C. K. (2016). Mental simulation as substitute for experience. *Social and Personality Psychology Compass, 10,* 405–420.

Kashy, D. A., Donnellan, M. B., Ackerman, R. A., & Russell, D. W. (2009). Reporting and interpreting research in PSPB: practices, principles, and pragmatics. *Personality and Social Psychology Bulletin, 35,* 1131–1142.

Katz, D. L., Grgić, I., & Fendley, T. W. (2018). An ethnographical assessment of project firefly: a yearlong endeavor to create wealth by predicting FOREX currency moves with associative remote viewing. *Journal of Scientific Exploration, 32*(1), 21–54.

Kay, R. W. (1999). Geomagnetic storms: association with incidence of depression as measured by hospital admissions. *British Journal of Psychiatry, 164,* 403–409.

Kennedy, J. E. (2003). The capricious, actively evasive, unsustainable nature of psi: a summary and hypotheses. *Journal of Parapsychology, 67*(1), 53–74.

Kennedy, J. E. (2013). Can parapsychology move beyond the controversies of retrospective meta-analyses? *Journal of Parapsychology, 77*(2), 239–250.

Kerr, N. L. (1998). HARKing: hypothesizing after the results are known. *Personality and Social Psychology Review, 2*(3), 196–217.

Khalighinejad, N., Di Costa, S., & Haggard, P. (2016). Endogenous action selection processes in dorsolateral prefrontal cortex contribute to sense of agency: a meta-analysis of tDCS studies of 'intentional binding'. *Brain Stimulation, 9*(3), 372–379.

Khoddam, M., Sheidafar, Z., Niry, M. D., & Khajehpour, M. R. H. (2018). Criticality in collective behavior of biogenic single-domain nanomagnetites. *Physical Review E*, *98*(3), 032133.

Kievit, R. A. (2011). Bayesians caught smuggling priors into Rotterdam harbor. *Perspectives on Psychological Science*, *6*, 313.

Kihlstrom, J. F. (1992). Dissociation and dissociations: a comment on consciousness and cognition. *Consciousness and Cognition: An International Journal*, *1*(1), 47–53.

Kihlstrom, J. F. (2007). Consciousness in hypnosis. In P. D. Zelazo, M. Moscovitch, & E. Thompson (Eds.), *Cambridge handbook of consciousness* (pp. 445–479). Cambridge: Cambridge University Press.

Kihlstrom, J. F. (2008). The domain of hypnosis, revisited. In M. R. Nash & A. J. Barnier (Eds.), *The Oxford handbook of hypnosis: theory, research and practice* (pp. 21–52). Oxford: Oxford University Press.

Kinzel, V., & Kubler, D. (1971). Facial muscle patterning to affective imagery in depressed and nondepressed subjects. *Proceedings of the National Academy of Sciences of the United States of America*, *68*, 2153.

Kirk, R. E. (1996). Practical significance: a concept whose time has come. *Educational and Psychological Measurement*, *56*, 746–759.

Kirsch, I. (1985). Response expectancy as a determinant of experience and behavior. *American Psychologist*, *40*(11), 1189.

Kirsch, I., & Council, J. R. (1992). Situational and personality correlates of hypnotic responsiveness. In E. Fromm & M. R. Nash (Eds.), *Contemporary hypnosis research* (pp. 267–291). New York: Guilford Press.

Kirschvink, J. L., Kobayashi-Kirschvink, A., & Woodford, B. J. (1992). Magnetite biomineralization in the human brain. *Proceedings of the National Academy of Sciences*, *89*(16), 7683–7687.

Kirschvink, J. L., Walker, M. M., & Diebel, C. E. (2001). Magnetite-based magnetoreception. *Current Opinion in Neurobiology*, *11*(4), 462–467.

Kjellgren, A., & Norlander, T. (2000). Psychedelic drugs: a study of drug-induced experiences obtained by illegal drug users in relation to Stanislav Grof's model of altered states of consciousness. *Imagination, Cognition and Personality*, *20*(1), 41–57.

Klein, S. B. (2015). The feeling of personal ownership of one's mental states: a conceptual argument and empirical evidence for an essential, but underappreciated, mechanism of mind. *Psychology of Consciousness: Theory, Research, and Practice*, *2*(4), 355.

Kline, R. B. (2004). *Beyond significance testing*. Washington, DC: American Psychological Association.

Klinger, E. (1990). *Daydreaming*. Los Angeles, CA: Jeremy Tarcher.

Kobayashi, A., & Kirschvink, J. L. (1995). Magnetoreception and electromagnetic field effects: sensory perception of the geomagnetic field in animals and humans. *ACS Advances in Chemistry Series*, *250*, 367–394.

Koch, C. (2005). Email to Anthony Freeman, 10 February, 2005. Quoted in A. Freeman, *The sense of being glared at. What is it like to be a heretic? Journal of Consciousness Studies*, *12*(6), 4.

Koestler, A. (1972). *The roots of coincidence*. London: Hutchinson.

Koffel, E., & Watson, D. (2009). Unusual sleep experiences, dissociation, and schizotypy: evidence for a common domain. *Clinical Psychology Review*, *29*(6), 548–559.

Kogan, I. M. (1969). The information theory aspect of telepathy. Paper presented at the symposium 'A New Look at Extrasensory Perception', UCLA, 7 June. Available online at: www.rand.org/pubs/papers/P4145/

Kolb, B., & Whishaw, I. Q. (1998). Brain plasticity and behavior. *Annual Review of Psychology, 49*(1), 43–64.

Koopman, C., Classen, C., & Spiegel, D. (1994). Predictors of posttraumatic stress symptoms among survivors of the Oakland/Berkeley, Calif., firestorm. *The American Journal of Psychiatry, 151*(6), 888.

Kosslyn, S. M., Alpert, N. M., & Thompson, W. L. (1997). Neural systems that underlie visual imagery and visual perception: a PET study. *Journal of Nuclear Medicine, 38*(5), 1205e1205.

Kosslyn, S. M., Thompson, W. L., Costantini-Ferrando, M., Alpert, N. M., & Spiegel, D. (2000). Hypnotic visual illusion alters color processing in the brain. *American Journal of Psychiatry, 157*, 1279–1284.

Kreitler, H., & Kreitler, S. (1973). Subliminal perception and extrasensory perception. *The Journal of Parapsychology, 37*(3), 163.

Krippner, S. (1991). An experimental approach to the anomalous dream. In J. Gackenbach & A. A. Sheikh (Eds.), *Dream images: a call to mental arms* (pp. 31–54). Amityville, NY: Baywood.

Krippner, S. (1993). The Maimonides ESP-dream studies. *The Journal of Parapsychology, 57*(1), 39–55.

Krippner, S., & Persinger, M. (1996). Evidence for enhanced congruence between dreams and distant target material during periods of decreased geomagnetic activity. *Journal of Scientific Exploration, 10*(4), 487–493.

Krueger, J. I., & Funder, D. C. (2004). Towards a balanced social psychology: causes, consequences, and cures for the problem-seeking approach to social behavior and cognition. *Behavioral and Brain Sciences, 27*(3), 313–327.

Krumrei-Mancuso, E. J., & Rouse, S. V. (2016). The development and validation of the comprehensive intellectual humility scale. *Journal of Personality Assessment, 98*(2), 209–221.

Kruschke, J. K. (2010). Bayesian data analysis. *Cognitive Science, 1*, 658–676.

Kuhn, T. S. (1962/2012). *The structure of scientific revolutions* (4th ed.). Chicago, IL: University of Chicago Press.

Kumar, V. K., & Pekala, R. J. (1992). The mental experience inventory. Unpublished psychological test. West Chester, PA: West Chester University.

Kunzendorf, R. G., Hulihan, D. M., Simpson, W., Pritykina, N., & Williams, K. (1997–1998). Is absorption a diathesis for dissociation in sexually and physically abused patients? *Imagination, Cognition, & Personality, 17*, 277–291.

Laland, K. N., Odling-Smee, J., & Feldman, M. W. (2000). Niche construction, biological evolution, and cultural change. *Behavioral and Brain Sciences, 23*(1), 131–146.

Lamont, P. (2007). Paranormal belief and the avowal of prior scepticism. *Theory & Psychology, 17*(5), 681–696.

Landry, M., Lifshitz, M., & Raz, A. (2017). Brain correlates of hypnosis: a systematic review and meta-analytic exploration. *Neuroscience & Biobehavioral Reviews, 81*, 75–98.

Lang, P. J. (1979). A bio-informational theory of emotional imagery. *Psychophysiology, 16*, 495–512.

Lang, P. J. & Bradley, M. M. (2010). Emotion and the motivational brain. *Biological Psychology, 84*(3), 437–450.

Lange, R. (2017). Rasch scaling and cumulative theory-building in consciousness research. *Psychology of Consciousness: Theory, Research, and Practice, 4*(1), 135.

Lange, R., Ross, R. M., Dagnall, N., Irwin, H. J., Houran, J., & Drinkwater, K. (2019). Anomalous experiences and paranormal attributions: psychometric challenges in studying their measurement and relationship. *Psychology of Consciousness: Theory, Research, and Practice*, 10.1037/cns0000187.

Lange, R., Thalbourne, M. A., Houran, J., & Storm, L. (2000). The revised transliminality scale: reliability and validity data from a Rasch top-down purification procedure. *Consciousness and Cognition*, *9*(4), 591–617.

Larøi, F., DeFruyt, F., van Os, J., Aleman, A., & Van der Linden, M. (2005). Associations between hallucinations and personality structure in a non-clinical sample: comparison between young and elderly samples. *Personality and Individual Differences*, *39*(1), 189–200.

Laurent, G., Fournier, J., Hemberger, M., Müller, C., Naumann, R., Ondracek, J. M., ... & Yamawaki, T. (2016). Cortical evolution: introduction to the reptilian cortex. In G. Buzsáki & Y. Christen (Eds.), *Micro-, Meso-and Macro-Dynamics of the Brain* (pp. 23–34). Cham: Springer.

Laureys, S. (2005). The neural correlate of (un)awareness: lessons from the vegetative state. *Trends in Cognitive Sciences*, *9*(12), 556–559.

Lavín, C., San Martín, R., & Rosales Jubal, E. (2014). Pupil dilation signals uncertainty and surprise in a learning gambling task. *Frontiers in Behavioral Neuroscience*, *7*, 218.

Law, M. R., Frost, C. D., & Wald, N. J. (1991). By how much does dietary salt reduction lower blood pressure? III – Analysis of data from trials of salt reduction. *BMJ*, *302*(6780), 819–824.

Lawrence, T., Edwards, C., Barraclough, N., Church, S., & Hetherington, F. (1995). Modelling childhood causes of paranormal belief and experience: childhood trauma and childhood fantasy. *Personality and Individual Differences*, *19*(2), 209–215.

Lawrence, T. R. (1995). How many factors of paranormal belief are there? A critique of the paranormal belief scale. *Journal of Parapsychology*, *59*, 3–25.

Lawrence, T. R., Roe, C. A., & Williams, C. (1998). On obliquity and the PBS: thoughts on Tobacyk and Thomas (1997). *Journal of Parapsychology*, *62*, 147–151.

LeBel, E. P., & Paunonen, S. V. (2011). Sexy but often unreliable: impact of unreliability on the replicability of experimental findings involving implicit measures. *Personality and Social Psychology Bulletin*, *37*, 570–583.

LeBel, E. P., & Peters, K. R. (2011). Fearing the future of empirical psychology: Bem's (2011) evidence of psi as a case study of deficiencies in modal research practice. *Review of General Psychology*, *15*(4), 371–379.

Lebon, F., Ruffino, C., Greenhouse, I., Labruna, L., Ivry, R. B., & Papaxanthis, C. (2018). The neural specificity of movement preparation during actual and imagined movements. *Cerebral Cortex*, *29*(2), 689–700.

LeBoutillier, N., & Marks, D. F. (2003). Mental imagery and creativity: a meta-analytic review study. *British Journal of Psychology*, *94*(1), 29–44.

LeDoux, J. E., & Brown, R. (2017). A higher-order theory of emotional consciousness. *Proceedings of the National Academy of Sciences*, *114*(10), E2016–E2025.

Legrand, D., & Ruby, P. (2009). What is self-specific? Theoretical investigation and critical review of neuroimaging results. *Psychological Review*, *116*(1), 252.

Lehrer, J. (2010). The truth wears off: is there something wrong with the scientific method? *The New Yorker*, 13 December, p. 52. Retrieved from: www.newyorker.com/reporting/2010/12/13/101213fa_fact_lehrer Google Scholar

Leknes, S., & Tracey, I. (2008). A common neurobiology for pain and pleasure. *Nature Reviews Neuroscience*, *9*(4), 314.

Lemche, E., Surguladze, S. A., Brammer, M. J., Phillips, M. L., Sierra, M., David, A. S., ... & Giampietro, V. P. (2016). Dissociable brain correlates for depression, anxiety, dissociation, and somatization in depersonalization-derealization disorder. *CNS Spectrums*, *21*(1), 35–42.

Levin, R., & Young, H. (2002). The relation of waking fantasy to dreaming. *Imagination, Cognition and Personality*, *21*(3), 201–219.

Lewandowsky, S., Gignac, G. E., & Oberauer, K. (2013). The role of conspiracist ideation and worldviews in predicting rejection of science. *PloS ONE*, *8*(10), e75637.

Li, Q., Wang, S., Milot, E., Bergeron, P., Ferrucci, L., Fried, L. P., & Cohen, A. A. (2015). Homeostatic dysregulation proceeds in parallel in multiple physiological systems. *Aging Cell*, *14*, 1103–1112.

Libby, L. K., Shaeffer, E. M., & Eibach, R. P. (2009). Seeing meaning in action: a bidirectional link between visual perspective and action identification level. *Journal of Experimental Psychology: General*, *138*(4), 503.

Liboff, A. R. (2017). The electromagnetic basis of social interactions. *Electromagnetic Biology and Medicine*, *36*(2), 177–181.

Lifshitz, M., Aubert-Bonn, N., Fischer, A., Kashem, I. F. & Raz, A. (2013). Using suggestion to modulate automatic processes: from Stroop to McGurk and beyond. *Cortex*, *49*, 463–473.

Lilienfeld, S. O., Ammirati, R., & Landfield, K. (2009). Giving debiasing away: can psychological research on correcting cognitive errors promote human welfare? *Perspectives on Psychological Science*, *4*(4), 390–398.

Limanowski, J., & Hecht, H. (2011). Where do we stand on locating the Self? *Psychology*, *2*, 312–317.

Lindeman, M. (2017). Paranormal beliefs. In V. Zeigler-Hill & T. K. Shackelford (Eds.), *Encyclopedia of personality and individual differences* (pp. 1–4). Cham: Springer.

Lindeman, M., & Aarnio, K. (2006). Paranormal beliefs: their dimensionality and correlates. *European Journal of Personality: Published for the European Association of Personality Psychology*, *20*(7), 585–602.

Lindeman, M., & Svedholm, A. M. (2012). What's in a term? Paranormal, superstitious, magical and supernatural beliefs by any other name would mean the same. *Review of General Psychology*, *16*(3), 241–255.

Lindquist, K. A., Satpute, A. B., Wager, T. D., Weber, J., & Barrett, L. F. (2015). The brain basis of positive and negative affect: evidence from a meta-analysis of the human neuroimaging literature. *Cerebral Cortex*, *26*, 1910–1922.

Lindsay, R. M., & Ehrenberg, A. S. C. (1993). The design of replicated studies. *The American Statistician*, *47*, 217–228.

Lobach, E., & Bierman, D. J. (2004, August). Who's calling at this hour? Local sidereal time and telephone telepathy. In *Proceedings of the 47th Parapsychology Association Annual Convention*, Vienna. pp. 91–97.

Lobato, E., Mendoza, J., Sims, V., & Chin, M. (2014). Examining the relationship between conspiracy theories, paranormal beliefs, and pseudoscience acceptance among a university population. *Applied Cognitive Psychology*, *28*(5), 617–625.

Lopez, C. (2013). A neuroscientific account of how vestibular disorders impair bodily self-consciousness. *Frontiers in Integrative Neuroscience*, *7*, 91.

Lopez, C., & Elzière, M. (2018). Out-of-body experience in vestibular disorders: a prospective study of 210 patients with dizziness. *Cortex*, *104*, 193–206.

Loudon, A. S. (2012). Circadian biology: a 2.5 billion year old clock. *Current Biology*, *22*, R570–R571.

Lovelock, J. (1987). *Gaia: a new look at life on earth*. New York: Oxford University Press.

Ludwig, A. M. (1983). The psychobiological functions of dissociation. *American Journal of Clinical Hypnosis*, *26*(2), 93–99.

Luke, D. (2011). Experiential reclamation and first person parapsychology. *Journal of Parapsychology*, *75*(2), 185–200.

Luke, D. (2012). Psychoactive substances and paranormal phenomena: a comprehensive review. *International Journal of Transpersonal Studies*, *31*(1), 12.

Luke, D. (2015). Drugs and psi phenomena. In E. Cardeña, J. Palmer, & D. Marcusson-Clavertz (Eds.), *Parapsychology: a handbook for the 21st century* (pp. 149–164). Jefferson, NC: McFarland & Co.

Luke, D. P., & Kittenis, M. (2005). A preliminary survey of paranormal experiences with psychoactive drugs. *Journal of Parapsychology*, *69*(2), 305.

Luschi, P., Benhamou, S., Girard, C., Ciccione, S., Roos, D., Sudre, J., & Benvenuti, S. (2007). Marine turtles use geomagnetic cues during open-sea homing. *Current Biology*, *17*(2), 126–133.

Lustenberger, C., Murbach, M., Dürr, R., Schmid, M. R., Kuster, N., Achermann, P., & Huber, R. (2013). Stimulation of the brain with radiofrequency electromagnetic field pulses affects sleep-dependent performance improvement. *Brain Stimulation*, *6*(5), 805–811.

Lykken, D. T. (1968). Statistical significance in psychological research. *Psychological Bulletin*, *70*, 151–159.

Lynn, S. J., & Rhue, J. W. (1988). Fantasy proneness: hypnosis, developmental antecedents, and psychopathology. *American Psychologist*, *43*(1), 35.

Lynn, S. J., & Rhue, J. W. (Eds.) (1994). *Dissociation: clinical and theoretical perspectives*. New York: Guilford Press.

Lynn, S. J., Lilienfeld, S. O., Merckelbach, H., Giesbrecht, T., McNally, R. J., Loftus, E. F., … & Malaktaris, A. (2014). The trauma model of dissociation: inconvenient truths and stubborn fictions. Comment on Dalenberg et al. (2012). *Psychology Bulletin*, *140*(3), 896–910.

Lynn, S. J., Neufeld, V., & Matyi, C. L. (1987). Inductions versus suggestions: effects of direct and indirect wording on hypnotic responding and experience. *Journal of Abnormal Psychology*, *96*(1), 76.

Lyssenko, L., Schmahl, C., Bockhacker, L., Vonderlin, R., Bohus, M., & Kleindienst, N. (2017). Dissociation in psychiatric disorders: a meta-analysis of studies using the dissociative experiences scale. *American Journal of Psychiatry*, *175*(1), 37–46.

Maaranen, P., Tanskanen, A., Honkalampi, K., Haatainen, K., Hintikka, J., & Viinamäki, H. (2005). Factors associated with pathological dissociation in the general population. *Australian & New Zealand Journal of Psychiatry*, *39*(5), 387–394.

MacAvoy, M. G., & Marks, D. F. (1975). Divided attention performance of cannabis users and non-users following cannabis and alcohol. *Psychopharmacologia*, *44*(2), 147–152.

Machielsen, W. C., Rombouts, S. A., Barkhof, F., Scheltens, P., & Witter, M. P. (2000). FMRI of visual encoding: reproducibility of activation. *Human Brain Mapping*, *9*(3), 156–164.

MacLaren, M. (1945). Early electrical discoveries by Benjamin Franklin and his contemporaries. *Journal of the Franklin Institute, 240*(1), 1–14.

Maddox, J. (1981). A book for burning? *Nature, 293*(5830), 245–246.

Maltby, J., & Day, L. (2002). Religious experience, religious orientation and schizotypy. *Mental Health, Religion & Culture, 5*(2), 163–174.

Maquet, P., Péters, J. M., Aerts, J., Delfiore, G., Degueldre, C., Luxen, A., & Franck, G. (1996). Functional neuroanatomy of human rapid-eye-movement sleep and dreaming. *Nature, 383*(6596), 163.

Marchetti, G. (2012). How consciousness builds the subject through relating. In R. J. Jenkins & W. E. Sullivam (Eds.), *Philosophy of mind* (pp. 37–69). New York: Nova Science.

Markman, K., Klein, W., & Suhr, E. (2009). *Handbook of mental simulation and human imagination*. Hove: Psychology Press.

Marks, D. F. (1972). Individual differences in the vividness of visual imagery and their effect on function. In P. W. Sheehan (Ed.), *The function and nature of imagery* (pp. 83–108). New York: Academic Press.

Marks, D. F. (1973). Visual imagery differences in the recall of pictures. *British Journal of Psychology, 64*(1), 17–24.

Marks, D. F. (1986a). Investigating the paranormal. *Nature, 320*(6058), 119–124.

Marks, D. F. (1986b). The neuropsychology of imagery. In D. F. Marks (Ed.), *Theories of image formation* (pp. 225–242). New York: Brandon House.

Marks, D. F. (1988). The psychology of paranormal beliefs. *Experientia, 44*, 332–337.

Marks, D. F. (1990). On the relationship between imagery, body and mind. In P. J. Hampson, D. F. Marks, & J. T. E. Richardson (Eds.), *Imagery: current development* (pp. 1–38). New York: Routledge.

Marks, D. F. (1995). New directions for mental imagery research. *Journal of Mental Imagery, 19*(3–4), 153–167.

Marks, D. F. (1999). Consciousness, mental imagery and action. *British Journal of Psychology, 90*, 567–585.

Marks, D. F. (2000). *The psychology of the psychic* (2nd ed.). New York: Prometheus Books.

Marks, D. F. (2003). What are we to make of exceptional experience? Part 3: unseen staring detection and ESP in pets. *The Skeptic, 16*, 8–12.

Marks, D. F. (2006). Biased beliefs and the subjective. In P. Halligan & M. Aylward (Eds.), *The power of belief: psychosocial influences on illness, disability and medicine*. Oxford: Oxford University Press.

Marks D. F. (2015) Homeostasis theory of obesity. *Health Psychology Open*. Epub ahead of print, 29 June. Doi 10.1177/2055102915590692.

Marks, D. F. (2016a). *Obesity: comfort vs discontent*. Scotts Valley, CA: CreateSpace.

Marks, D. F. (2016b). Dyshomeostasis, obesity, addiction and chronic stress. *Health Psychology Open, 3*(1), 2055102916636907.

Marks, D. F. (2018). *A general theory of behaviour*. London: Sage. Kindle edition.

Marks, D. F. (2019a). The Hans Eysenck affair: time to correct the scientific record. *Journal of Health Psychology, 24*(4), 409–420.

Marks, D. F. (2019b). I am conscious, therefore, I am: imagery, affect, action, and a General Theory of Behavior. *Brain Sciences, 9*(5), 107.

Marks, D. F. (2019c). 'God spoke to me': subjective paranormal experience and the brain's homeostatic response to early trauma. *Preprints*, 2019060269 (doi: 10.20944/preprints 201906.0269.v1).

Marks, D. F. (2020). 'God spoke to me': subjective paranormal experience and the brain's homeostatic response to early trauma. *Imagination, Cognition and Personality* (in press).

Marks, D. F., & Colwell, J. (2000). The psychic staring effect: an artifact of pseudo randomization. *Skeptical Inquirer* (September/October), pp. 41–49.

Marks, D. F., & Colwell, J. (2001). Fooling and falling into the sense of being stared at. *Skeptical Inquirer* (March/April), pp. 62–63.

Marks, D. F., & Isaac, A. R. (1995). Topographical distribution of EEG activity accompanying visual and motor imagery in vivid and non-vivid imagers. *British Journal of Psychology*, *86*(2), 271–282.

Marks, D. F., & Kammann, R. (1978). Information transmission in remote viewing experiments. *Nature*, *274*(5672), 680.

Marks, D. F., & Kammann, R. (1980). *The psychology of the psychic*. New York: Prometheus Books.

Marks, D. F., & MacAvoy, M. G. (1989). Divided attention performance in cannabis users and non-users following alcohol and cannabis separately and in combination. *Psychopharmacology*, *99*(3), 397–401.

Marks, D. F., & McKellar. P. J. (1982). The nature and function of eidetic imagery. *Journal of Mental Imagery*, *6*, 1–124.

Marks, D. F., & Scott, C. (1986). Remote viewing exposed. *Nature*, *319*(6053), 444.

Marks, D. F., & Yardley, L. (Eds.) (2004). *Research methods for clinical and health psychology*. London: Sage.

Marks, D. F., Baird, J. McR., & McKellar, P. (1989). Replication of trance logic using a modified experimental design: highly hypnotizable subjects in both real and simulator groups. *International Journal of Clinical and Experimental Hypnosis*, *37*(3), 232–248.

Marks, D. F., Murray, M., & Estacio, E. V. (2018). *Health psychology: theory, research & practice* (5th ed.). London: Sage.

Marmar, C. R., Weiss, D. S., & Metzler, T. J. (1997). The peritraumatic dissociative experiences questionnaire. *Assessing Psychological Trauma and PTSD*, *2*, 144–168.

Mars, R. B., Neubert, F. X., Noonan, M. P., Sallet, J., Toni, I., & Rushworth, M. F. (2012). On the relationship between the 'default mode network' and the 'social brain'. *Frontiers in Human Neuroscience*, *6*, 189.

Marsh, M. (2016). The near-death experience: a reality check? *Humanities*, *5*(2), 18.

Marshall, W. L., & Fernandez, Y. M. (2000). Phallometric testing with sexual offenders: limits to its value. *Clinical Psychology Review*, *20*(7), 807–822.

Marshall, W. L., Marshall, L. E., Serran, G. A., & O'Brien, M. D. (2009). Self-esteem, shame, cognitive distortions and empathy in sexual offenders: their integration and treatment implications. *Psychology, Crime & Law*, *15*(2–3), 217–234.

Marusic, U., Grosprêtre, S., Paravlic, A., Kovač, S., Pišot, R., & Taube, W. (2018). Motor imagery during action observation of locomotor tasks improves rehabilitation outcome in older adults after total hip arthroplasty. *Neural Plasticity, 2018*.

Mason, M. F., Norton, M. I., Van Horn, J. D., Wegner, D. M., Grafton, S. T., & Macrae, C. N. (2007). Wandering minds: the default network and stimulus-independent thought. *Science*, *315*(5810), 393–395.

Mason, O., & Claridge, G. (1999). Individual differences in schizotypy and reduced asymmetry using the chimeric faces task. *Cognitive Neuropsychiatry*, *4*(4), 289–301.

Mason, O., Claridge, G., & Jackson, M. (1995). New scales for the assessment of schizotypy. *Personality and Individual Differences*, *18*(1), 7–13.

Mathijsen, F. (2011). *Young people and paranormal experiences: cognitive and emotional outcomes*. Doctoral dissertation, UCL – Université Catholique de Louvain.

Matthews, R. (1997). *The Sunday Telegraph*. 2 November, p. 6.

Matute, H., Yarritu, I., & Vadillo, M. A. (2011). Illusions of causality at the heart of pseudoscience. *British Journal of Psychology*, *102*(3), 392–405.

Mauritz, M. W., Goossens, P. J., Draijer, N., & Van Achterberg, T. (2013). Prevalence of interpersonal trauma exposure and trauma-related disorders in severe mental illness. *European Journal of Psychotraumatology*, *4*(1), 19985.

Maxwell, S. E. (2004). The persistence of underpowered studies in psychological research: causes, consequences, and remedies. *Psychological Methods*, *9*, 147–163.

May, E. C. (2010). Technical challenges for the way forward. *The Journal of Parapsychology*, *74*(2), 211.

May, E. C., & Marwaha, S. B (2018). *The Star Gate Archives, Volume 1: Remote Viewing, 1972–1984. Reports of the United States Government Sponsored Psi Research Project, 1972–1995.* Jefferson, NC: McFarland & Co.

McAdie, A. (1925). The date of Franklin's kite experiment. *American Antiquarian Society*, 188.

McCarty, D. E., Carrubba, S., Chesson Jr, A. L., Frilot, C., Gonzalez-Toledo, E., & Marino, A. A. (2011). Electromagnetic hypersensitivity: evidence for a novel neurological syndrome. *International Journal of Neuroscience*, *121*(12), 670–676.

McClenon, J. (1994a). *Wondrous events: foundations of religious belief*. Philadelphia, PA: University of Pennsylvania Press.

McClenon, J. (1994b). Surveys of anomalous experience: a cross-cultural analysis. *Journal of the American Society for Psychical Research*, *88*, 117–135.

McClenon, J. (2000). Content analysis of an anomalous memorate collection: testing hypotheses regarding universal features. *Sociology of Religion*, *61*(2), 155–169.

McConkey, K. M., Bryant, R. A., Bibb, B. C., & Kihlstrom, J. F. (1991). Trance logic in hypnosis and imagination. *Journal of Abnormal Psychology*, *100*(4), 464.

McCreery, C., & Claridge, G. (2002). Healthy schizotypy: The case of out-of-the-body experiences. *Personality and Individual Differences*, *32*(1), 141–154.

McDonald, R. C., & Smith, J. R. (1975). Trance logic in tranceable and simulating subjects. *International Journal of Clinical and Experimental Hypnosis*, *23*, 80–89.

McDonnell, A. (2014). The sixth sense-emotional contagion: review of biophysical mechanisms influencing information transfer in groups. *Journal of Behavioral and Brain Science*, *4*(7), 342.

McGeown, W. J., Mazzoni, G., Venneri, A., & Kirsch, I. (2009). Hypnotic induction decreases anterior default mode activity. *Consciousness and Cognition*, *18*(4), 848–855.

McGeown, W. J., Venneri, A., Kirsch, I., Nocetti, L., Roberts, K., Foan, L., & Mazzoni, G. (2012). Suggested visual hallucination without hypnosis enhances activity in visual areas of the brain. *Consciousness and Cognition*, *21*(1), 100–116.

McGrath, J. J., McLaughlin, K. A., Saha, S., Aguilar-Gaxiola, S., Al-Hamzawi, A., Alonso, J., ... & Florescu, S. (2017). The association between childhood adversities and subsequent first onset of psychotic experiences: a cross-national analysis of 23 998 respondents from 17 countries. *Psychological Medicine*, *47*(7), 1230–1245.

McGuire, W. J. (1973). The yin and yang of progress in social psychology: seven koan. *Journal of Personality and Social Psychology*, *26*, 446–456.

McHugh, P. R. (2008). *Try to remember: psychiatry's clash over meaning, memory and mind*. New York: Dana Press.

McKellar, P. (1957a). *Imagination and thinking*. London: Cohen & West.

McKellar, P. (1957b). Scientific theory and psychosis: The 'model psychosis' experiment and its significance. *International Journal of Social Psychiatry, 3*(3), 170–182.

McKellar, P. M. (1961). Mescaline and human thinking. *Hallucinogenic Drugs, 12*.

McKellar, P. (1977). Autonomy, imagery, and dissociation. *Journal of Mental Imagery, 1*, 93–108.

McKellar, P., & Simpson, L. (1954). Between wakefulness and sleep: hypnagogic imagery. *British Journal of Psychology, 45*(4), 266.

McKelvie, S. J. (1995). The VVIQ as a psychometric test of individual differences in visual imagery vividness: a critical quantitative review and plea for direction. *Journal of Mental Imagery, 19*, 1–106.

McLaughlin, K. A., Koenen, K. C., Hill, E. D., Petukhova, M., Sampson, N. A., Zaslavsky, A. M., & Kessler, R. C. (2013). Trauma exposure and posttraumatic stress disorder in a national sample of adolescents. *Journal of the American Academy of Child & Adolescent Psychiatry, 52*(8), 815–830.

Mechelli, A., Humphreys, G. W., Mayall, K., Olson, A., & Price, C. J. (2000). Differential effects of word length and visual contrast in the fusiform and lingual gyri during. *Proceedings of the Royal Society of London. Series B: Biological Sciences, 267*(1455), 1909–1913.

Meehl, P. E. (1967). Theory testing in psychology and physics: a methodological paradox. *Philosophy of Science, 34*, 103–115.

Meehl, P. E. (1978). Theoretical risks and tabular asterisks: Sir Karl, Sir Ronald, and the slow progress of soft psychology. *Journal of Consulting and Clinical Psychology, 46*, 806–834.

Meehl, P. E. (1990). Why summaries of research on psychological theories are often uninterpretable. *Psychological Reports, 66*, 195–244.

Mehta, D., Klengel, T., Conneely, K. N., Smith, A. K., Altmann, A., Pace, T. W., ... & Bradley, B. (2013). Childhood maltreatment is associated with distinct genomic and epigenetic profiles in posttraumatic stress disorder. *Proceedings of the National Academy of Sciences, 110*(20), 8302–8307.

Melzack, R. (1975). The McGill Pain Questionnaire: major properties and scoring methods. *PAIN, 1*, 277–299.

Merckelbach, H., & Patihis, L. (2018). Why 'trauma-related dissociation' is a misnomer in courts: a critical analysis of Brand et al. (2017a, b). *Psychological Injury and Law, 11*(4), 370–376.

Merckelbach, H., Horselenberg, R., & Muris, P. (2001). The Creative Experiences Questionnaire (CEQ): a brief self-report measure of fantasy proneness. *Personality and Individual Differences, 31*(6), 987–995.

Messick, S. (1989). Validity. In R. L. Linn (Ed.), *Educational measurement* (3rd ed.) (pp. 13–103). Washington, DC: American Council on Education.

Metzinger, T. (2003). *Being no one: the self-model theory of subjectivity*. Cambridge, MA: MIT Press.

Michell, J. (1997). Quantitative science and the definition of measurement in psychology. *British Journal of Psychology, 88*, 355–383.

Miller, G. A. (1956). The magical number seven, plus or minus two: some limits on our capacity for processing information. *Psychological Review, 63*(2), 81.

Miller, G. A., Galanter, E., & Pribram, K. H. (1960). *Plans and the structure of behavior*. New York: Henry Holt.

Miller, J. (2009). What is the probability of replicating a statistically significant effect? *Psychonomic Bulletin & Review, 16*, 617–640.

Milton, J. (1999). Should ganzfeld research continue to be crucial in the search for a replicable psi effect? Part, I. Discussion paper and introduction to an electronic-mail discussion. *Journal of Parapsychology, 63*, 309–333.

Milton, J., & Wiseman, R. (1999). Does psi exist? Lack of replication of an anomalous process of information transfer. *Psychological Bulletin, 125*, 387–391.

Minakowska-Gruda, I. (2006). Relations and differences among three kinds of imagery related traits: visual cognitive style, imagery vividness and imagination immersion. *Imagination, Cognition and Personality, 26*(1), 43–63.

Mistlberger, R. E., & Rechtschaffen, A. (1984). Recovery of anticipatory activity to restricted feeding in rats with ventromedial hypothalamic lesions. *Physiology & Behavior, 33*, 227–235.

Monti, M. M., Vanhaudenhuyse, A., Coleman, M. R., et al. (2010). Willful modulation of brain activity in disorders of consciousness. *New England Journal of Medicine, 362*, 579–589.

Moody, R. A., & Hill, D. (1976). *Life after life: the investigation of a phenomenon–survival of bodily death. 100080*(7). New York: Bantam Books.

Moonesinghe, R., Khoury, M. J., & Janssens, C. J. W. (2007). Most published research findings are false – but a little replication goes a long way. *PLoS Medicine, 4*, 218–221.

Moore, L. E., & Greyson, B. (2017). Characteristics of memories for near-death experiences. *Consciousness and Cognition, 51*, 116–124.

Morris, R. L. (1972). An exact method for evaluating preferentially matched free response material. *Journal of the American Society for Pychical Research, 66*, 401.

Morris, R. L. (1986). What psi is not: the necessity for experiments. In H. L. Edge, R. L. Morris, J. Palmer & J. H. Rush (Eds.), *Foundations of parapsychology: exploring the boundaries of human capability* (pp. 70–110). Abingdon: Routledge & Kegan Paul.

Mossbridge, J. A., & Radin, D. (2018). Precognition as a form of prospection: a review of the evidence. *Psychology of Consciousness: Theory, Research, and Practice, 5*(1), 78.

Muenzenmaier, K. H., Seixas, A. A., Schneeberger, A. R., Castille, D. M., Battaglia, J., & Link, B. G. (2015). Cumulative effects of stressful childhood experiences on delusions and hallucinations. *Journal of Trauma & Dissociation, 16*(4), 442–462.

Mulaik, S. A., Raju, N. S., & Harshman, R. A. (1997). There is a time and a place for significance testing. In L. L. Harlow, S. A. Mulaik, & J. H. Steiger (Eds.), *What if there were no significance tests?* (pp. 65–115). Mahwah, NJ: Erlbaum.

Mulcahy, C. (2014). Martin Gardner, puzzle master extraordinaire. *BBC News*. Available online at: www.bbc.com/news/magazine-29688355

Mulkay, M., & Gilbert, G. N. (1986). Replication and mere replication. *Philosophy of the Social Sciences, 16*, 21–37.

Münzer, A., Fegert, J. M., & Goldbeck, L. (2016). Psychological symptoms of sexually victimized children and adolescents compared with other maltreatment subtypes. *Journal of Child Sexual Abuse, 25*(3), 326–346.

Murphy, G. (1962). Report on paper by Edward Girden on psychokinesis. *Psychological Bulletin, 59*(6), 520–528. https://doi.org/10.1037/h0044213

Murray, C. D., & Fox, J. (2005). Dissociational body experiences: differences between respondents with and without prior out-of-body-experiences. *British Journal of Psychology, 96*, 441e456.

Musch, J., & Ehrenberg, K. (2002) Probability misjudgment, cognitive ability, and belief in the paranormal. *British Journal of Psychology, 93*, 169–177.

Myers, S. A. (1983) The Wilson–Barber inventory of childhood memories and imaginings: children's form and norms for 1337 children and adolescents. *Journal of Mental Imagery, 7*, 83–94.

Nagel, T. (1974). What is it like to be a bat? *The Philosophical Review, 83*(4), 435–450.

Nagel, T. (2012). *Mind and cosmos: why the materialist neo-Darwinian conception of nature is almost certainly false*. Oxford: Oxford University Press.

Nakul, E., & Lopez, C. (2017). Commentary: out-of-body experience during awake craniotomy. *Frontiers in Human Neuroscience, 11*, 417.

National Institute of Justice (2003). Annual report. Washington, DC. Available online at: www.ncjrs.gov/pdffiles1/nij/205944.pdf

Neher, A. (2011). *Paranormal and transcendental experience: a psychological examination*. New York: Dover Publications.

Neisser, U. (1967). *Cognitive psychology*. New York: Appleton-Century-Crofts.

Nelson, B., Parnas, J., & Sass, L. A. (2014). Disturbance of minimal self (ipseity) in schizophrenia: clarification and current status. *Schizophrenia Bulletin, 40*, 479–482.

Nelson, C. J., Rosenfeld, B., Breitbart, W., & Galietta, M. (2002). Spirituality, religion, and depression in the terminally ill. *Psychosomatics, 43*(3), 213–220.

Nelson, K. R., Mattingly, M., Lee, S. A., & Schmitt, F. A. (2006). Does the arousal system contribute to near death experience? *Neurology, 66*(7), 1003–1009.

Nemeroff, C. B. (2016). Paradise lost: the neurobiological and clinical consequences of child abuse and neglect. *Neuron, 89*(5), 892–909.

Neuliep, J. W., & Crandall, R. (1993). Reviewer bias against replication research. *Journal of Social Behavior and Personality, 8*(6), 21.

Newport, F., & Strausberg, M. (2001). Americans' belief in psychic and paranormal phenomena is up over last decade. *Gallup Poll News Service*, 8 June.

Nichols, D. E. (2017). Chemistry and structure–activity relationships of psychedelics. In A. L. Halberstadt, F. X. Vollenweider, & D. E. Nichols (Eds.), *Behavioral neurobiology of psychedelic drugs* (pp. 1–43). Berlin: Springer.

Nickerson, R. S. (1998). Confirmation bias: a ubiquitous phenomenon in many guises. *Review of General Psychology, 2*(2), 175–220.

Nielsen, T. A., Laberge, L., Paquet, J., Tremblay, R. E., Vitaro, F., & Montplaisir, J. (2000). Development of disturbing dreams during adolescence and their relation to anxiety symptoms. *Sleep, 23*(6), 1–10.

Nisbett, R., & Ross. L. (1980). *Human inference: strategies and shortcomings of social judgment*. Englewood Cliffs, NJ: Prentice-Hall.

Nishimura, T., Tada, H., Nakatani, E., Matsuda, K., Teramukai, S., & Fukushima, M. (2014). Stronger geomagnetic fields may be a risk factor of male suicides. *Psychiatry and Clinical Neurosciences, 68*, 404–409.

Norman, D. A., & Shallice, T. (1986). Attention to action. In R. J. Davidson, G. E. Schwartz, & D. Shapiro (Eds.), *Consciousness and self-regulation* (pp. 1–18). Boston, MA: Springer.

Northoff, G. (2016). Is the self a higher-order or fundamental function of the brain? The 'basis model of self-specificity' and its encoding by the brain's spontaneous activity. *Cognitive Neuroscience, 7*, 203–222.

Nummenmaa, L., Glerean, E., Hari, R., & Hietanen, J.K. (2014). Bodily maps of emotions. *Proceedings of the National Academy of Sciences of the United States of America, 111,* 646–651.

O'Keefe, D. (1982). *Stolen lightning: the sociological theory of magic.* Oxford: Robertson.

Oakley, D. A. (1999). Hypnosis and conversion hysteria: a unifying model. *Cognitive Neuropsychiatry, 4*(3), 243–265.

Oakley, D. A., & Halligan, P. W. (2013). Hypnotic suggestion: opportunities for cognitive neuroscience. *Nature Reviews Neuroscience, 14*(8), 565.

Oakley, D. A., & Halligan, P. W. (2017). Chasing the rainbow: the non-conscious nature of being. *Frontiers in Psychology, 8,* 1924.

Obstoj, I., & Sheehan, P. W. (1977). Aptitude for trance, task generalizability, and incongruity response in hypnosis. *Journal of Abnormal Psychology, 86*(5), 543.

Ohayon, M. M., Morselli, P. L., & Guilleminault, C. (1997). Prevalence of nightmares and their relationship to psychopathology and daytime functioning in insomnia subjects. *Sleep, 20*(5), 340–348.

Olff, M. (2017). Sex and gender differences in post-traumatic stress disorder: an update. *European Journal of Psychotraumatology, 8*(suppl. 4), 1351204.

Oliver, J. E., & Wood, T. (2014). Medical conspiracy theories and health behaviors in the United States. *JAMA Internal Medicine, 174*(5), 817–818.

Open Science Collaboration. (2015). Estimating the reproducibility of psychological science. *Science, 349*(6251), aac4716.

Oppenheimer, D. M., Meyvis, T., & Davidenko, N. (2009). Instructional manipulation checks: detecting satisficing to increase statistical power. *Journal of Experimental Social Psychology, 45,* 867–872.

Orne, M. T. (1959). The nature of hypnosis: artifact and essence. *Journal of Abnormal Social Psychology, 58,* 277–299.

Orne, M. T. (1962). On the social psychology of the psychological experiment: with particular reference to demand characteristics and their implications. *American Psychologist, 17*(11), 776.

Orne M. T. (1969). Demand characteristics and the concept of quasi-controls. In R. Rosenthal & R. Rosnow (Eds.), *Artifact in behavioral research* (pp. 143–179). New York: Academic Press.

Orne, M. T. (1970). Hypnosis, motivation and the ecological validity of the psychological experiment. In W. J. Arnold & M. Page (Eds.), *Nebraska Symposium on Motivation* (pp. 187–265). Lincoln, NE: University of Nebraska Press.

Orne, M. T. (1971). The simulation of hypnosis: why, how, and what it means. *The International Journal of Clinical and Experimental Hypnosis, 19*(4), 183–210.

Orne, M. T. (1973). Communication by the total experimental situation: why it is important, how it is evaluated, and its significance for the ecological validity of findings. In P. Pliner, L. Krames, & T. Alloway (Eds.), *Communication and affect* (pp. 157–191). New York: Academic Press.

Orne, M. T. (1977). The construct of hypnosis: implication of the definition for research and practice. *Annals of the New York Academy of Sciences, 296,* 14–33.

Orsolini, L., Papanti, G. D., Francesconi, G., & Schifano, F. (2015). Mind navigators of chemicals' experimenters? A web-based description of e-psychonauts. *Cyberpsychology, Behavior, and Social Networking, 18*(5), 296–230.

Osis, K., Turner, M., & Carlson, M. L. (1971). ESP over distance: research on the ESP channel. *Journal of the American Society for Psychical Research, 65*, 245–288.

Osmond, H. (1961). Peyote night. *Tomorrow Magazine, IX*(2), 105–125.

Otis, K. (1961). *Deathbed observations by physicians and nurses.* New York: Parapsychology Foundation.

Otsuka, K., Oinuma, S., Cornélissen, G., Weydahl, A., Ichimaru, Y., Kobayashi, M., . . . & Halberg, F. (2001). Alternating light-darkness-influenced human electrocardiographic magnetoreception in association with geomagnetic pulsations. *Biomedicine & Pharmacotherapy, 55*, 63s–75s.

Pacini, R., & Epstein, S. (1999). The relation of rational and experiential information processing styles to personality, basic beliefs and the ratio-bias phenomenon. *Journal of Personality and Social Psychology, 76*, 972–987.

Paivio, A. (2013). *Imagery and verbal processes.* New York: Psychology Press.

Palmer, J. (1986). ESP research findings: the process approach. In H. L. Edge, R. L. Morris, J. Palmer & J. H. Rush (Eds.), *Foundations of parapsychology* (pp. 184–222). London: Routledge & Kegan Paul.

Palmer, J. (2007). A statistical artifact in William Braud's (1990) experiment on remote mental influence of hemolysis. *The Journal of Parapsychology, 71*, 151–158.

Paolucci, E. O., Genuis, M. L., & Violato, C. (2001). A meta-analysis of the published research on the effects of child sexual abuse. *The Journal of Psychology, 135*(1), 17–36.

Parapsychological Association (2020). Website: www.parapsych.org/base/about.aspx

Parker, A. (2000). A review of the ganzfeld work at Gothenburg University. *Journal of the Society for Psychical Research, 64*, 1–15.

Parker, A., & Brusewitz, G. (2003). A compendium of the evidence for psi. *European Journal of Parapsychology, 18*, 29–48.

Parker, A., & Millar, B. (2014). Revealing psi secrets: successful experimenters seem to succeed by using their own psi. *Journal of Parapsychology, 78*(1), 39–55.

Parker, A., & Sjödén, B. (2010). Do some of us habituate to future emotional events? *The Journal of Parapsychology, 74*(1), 99.

Parker, A., Frederiksen, A., & Johansson, H. (1997). Towards specifying the recipe for success with the ganzfeld: replication of the ganzfeld findings using a manual ganzfeld with subjects reporting paranormal experiences. *European Journal of Parapsychology, 13*, 15–27.

Parker, A., Grams, D., & Pettersson, C. (1998). Further variables relating to psi in the ganzfeld. *The Journal of Parapsychology, 62*(4), 319.

Parker, A., Persson, A., & Haller, A. (2000) Using qualitative Ganzfeld research for theory development: top down processes in psi-mediation. *Journal of the Society for Psychical Research, 64*, 65–81.

Parnia, S., Spearpoint, K., de Vos, G., Fenwick, P., Goldberg, D., Yang, J., ... & Wood, M. (2014). AWARE – AWAreness during REsuscitation – a prospective study. *Resuscitation, 85*(12), 1799–1805.

Parra, A. (2006). 'Seeing and feeling ghosts': absorption, fantasy proneness, and healthy schizotypy as predictors of crisis apparition experiences. *Journal of Parapsychology, 70*(2), 357.

Parra, A. (2015). Seeing rare things with the mind's eye: visual imagery vividness and paranormal/anomalous experiences. *Australian Journal of Parapsychology, 15*(1), 37.

Parra, A. (2018). Perceptual-personality variables associated with entity encounter experiences. *Australian Journal of Parapsychology*, *18*(1), 23.

Parra, A. (2019). Negative experiences in childhood, parental style, and resilience among people reporting paranormal experiences. *The Journal of Nervous and Mental Disease*, *207*(4), 264–270.

Parra, A., & Argibay, J. C. (2012). Dissociation, absorption, fantasy proneness and sensation-seeking in psychic claimants. *Journal of the Society for Psychical Research*, *76*(909), 193–203.

Parra, A., & Villanueva, J. (2006). ESP under the ganzfeld, in contrast with the induction of relaxation as a psi-conducive state. *Australian Journal of Parapsychology*, *6*(2), 167.

Paxton, B. (2017). Speaking to and theorizing about the dead in a postmodern world: an autoethnographic possibility? *Qualitative Research Journal*, *17*(1), 20–31.

Pearson, J., Naselaris, T., Holmes, E. A., & Kosslyn, S. M. (2015). Mental imagery: functional mechanisms and clinical applications. *Trends in Cognitive Sciences*, *19*(10), 590e602. https://doi.org/10.1016/j.tics.2015.08.003

Peat, F. D. (1987). *Synchronicity: the bridge between matter and mind*. New York: Bantam.

Pechey, R., & Halligan, P. (2012). Prevalence and correlates of anomalous experiences in a large non-clinical sample. *Psychology and Psychotherapy: Theory, Research and Practice*, *85*(2), 150–162.

Pekala, R. J., Kumar, V. K., Ainslie, G., Elliott, N. C., Mullen, K. J., Salinger, M. M., & Masten, E. (1999). Dissociation as a function of child abuse and fantasy proneness in a substance abuse population. *Imagination, Cognition and Personality*, *19*(2), 105–129.

Pelosi, A. J. (2019). Personality and fatal diseases: revisiting a scientific scandal. *Journal of Health Psychology*, *24*(4), 421–439.

Penfield, W., & Rasmussen, T. (1950). *The cerebral cortex of man: a clinical study of localization of function*. New York: Macmillan.

Perkins, S. L. (2001). *Paranormal beliefs: developmental antecedents, perceived control, and defensive coping*. Doctoral dissertation, Long Island University.

Perkins, S. L., & Allen, R. (2006). Childhood physical abuse and differential development of paranormal belief systems. *The Journal of Nervous and Mental Disease*, *194*(5), 349–355.

Perona-Garcelán, S., Carrascoso-López, F., García-Montes, J. M., Ductor-Recuerda, M. J., López Jiménez, A. M., Vallina-Fernández, O., ... & Gómez-Gómez, M. T. (2012). Dissociative experiences as mediators between childhood trauma and auditory hallucinations. *Journal of Traumatic Stress*, *25*(3), 323–329.

Perry, B. D. (2001). The neurodevelopmental impact of violence in childhood. In D. Schetky & E. P. Benedek (Eds.), *Textbook of child and adolescent forensic psychiatry* (pp. 221–238). Washington, DC: American Psychiatric Press.

Perry, B. D., Pollard, R. A., Blakley, T. L., Baker, W. L., & Vigilante, D. (1995). Childhood trauma, the neurobiology of adaptation, and 'use-dependent' development of the brain: how 'states' become 'traits'. *Infant Mental Health Journal*, *16*(4), 271–291.

Persinger, M. A. (1985). Geophysical variables and behavior: XXX. Intense paranormal experiences occur during days of quiet, global, geomagnetic activity. *Perceptual and Motor Skills*, *61*(1), 320–322.

Persinger, M. A. (1987). Spontaneous telepathic experiences from phantasms of the living and low global geomagnetic activity. *Journal of the American Society for Psychical Research*, *81*, 23–36.

Persinger, M. A. (1989). Geophysical variables and behavior: LV. Predicting the details of visitor experiences and the personality of experients: the temporal lobe factor. *Perceptual and Motor Skills, 68*(1), 55–65.

Persinger, M. A., & Krippner, S. (1989). Dream ESP experiments and geomagnetic activity. *Journal of the American Society for Psychical Research, 83*, 101–116.

Persinger, M. A., & Schaut, G. B. (1988). Geomagnetic factors in subjective telepathic, precognitive, and postmortem experiences. *Journal of the American Society for Psychical Research, 82*, 217.

Peters, J. E. (1973). *Trance logic: artifact or essence of hypnosis?* Unpublished doctoral dissertation, Pennsylvania State University.

Peters, K. R. (2011). Cronbach's challenge: putting psychological explanation in context. Unpublished manuscript, The University of Western Ontario.

Petersen, S.E., & Sporns, O. (2015). Brain networks and cognitive architectures. *Neuron, 88*, 207–219.

Peterson, J. B. (2018). *12 Rules for Life*. London: Penguin. Kindle edition.

Petit, D., Touchette, E., Tremblay, R. E., Boivin, M., & Montplaisir, J. (2007). Dyssomnias and parasomnias in early childhood. *Pediatrics*, 119, e1016–25.

Pichiorri, F., Morone, G., Petti, M., Toppi, J., Pisotta, I., Molinari, M., . . . & Mattia, D. (2015). Brain-computer interface boosts motor imagery practice during stroke recovery. *Annals of Neurology, 77*, 851–865.

Pilton, M., Varese, F., Berry, K., & Bucci, S. (2015). The relationship between dissociation and voices: a systematic literature review and meta-analysis. *Clinical Psychology Review, 40*, 138–155.

Pinker, S. (2009). *How the mind works* (1997/2009). New York: WW Norton.

Pockett, S. (2017). Consciousness is a thing, not a process. *Applied Sciences, 7*(12), 1248.

Polivy, J. (1981). On the induction of emotion in the laboratory: discrete moods or multiple affect states? *Journal of Personality and Social Psychology, 41*(4), 803–817.

Popper, K. R. (1959). *The logic of scientific discovery*. New York: Basic Books.

Popper, K. R. (1963). *Conjectures and refutations*. Abingdon: Routledge & Kegan Paul.

Porges, S. W. (2007). The polyvagal perspective. *Biological Psychology, 74*(2), 116–143.

Porges, S.W. (2012). The origins of compassion: A phylogenetic perspective. https://issuu.com/ccare/docs/porges_pdf

Porges, S. W. (2017). *The pocket guide to the polyvagal theory: the transformative power of feeling safe*. New York: W. W. Norton & Company. Kindle edition.

Porter, S., Yuille, J. C., & Lehman, D. R. (1999). The nature of real, implanted, and fabricated memories for emotional childhood events: implications for the recovered memory debate. *Law and Human Behavior, 23*(5), 517–537.

Pressman, M. R. (2007). Factors that predispose, prime and precipitate NREM parasomnias in adults: clinical and forensic implications. *Sleep Medicine Reviews, 11*(1), 5–30.

Preuschoff, K., 't Hart, B. M., & Einhauser, W. (2011). Pupil dilation signals surprise: evidence for noradrenaline's role in decision making. *Frontiers in Neuroscience, 5*, 115.

Prilleltensky, I., Nelson, G., & Peirson, L. (2001). The role of power and control in children's lives: an ecological analysis of pathways toward wellness, resilience and problems. *Journal of Community & Applied Social Psychology, 11*(2), 143–158.

Pulliam, J. (2007). The zombie. In S. T. Joshi (Ed.), *Icons of horror and the supernatural: an encyclopedia of our worst nightmares* (Vol. 2) (pp. 723–727). London: Greenwood Icons.

Puthoff, H. E. (1984). ARV (Associational Remote Viewing) applications. In R. White & J Solfvin (Eds.), *Research in parapsychology* (pp. 121–122). Metuchen, NJ: Scarecrow Press.

Puthoff, H. E. (1996). CIA-initiated remote viewing program at Stanford Research Institute. *Journal of Scientific Exploration, 10*(1), 63–76.

Puthoff, H. E. (2019). CIA-initiated remote viewing at Stanford Research Institute. *The Intelligencer: Journal of US Intelligence Studies, 12*.

Puthoff, H. E., & Targ, R. (1976). A perceptual channel for information transfer over kilometer distances: historical perspective and recent research. *Proceedings of the IEEE, 64*(3), 329–354.

Puthoff, H. E., Targ, R., & May, E. C. (1981). Experimental psi research: implications for physics. In R. G. Jahn (Ed.), *The role of consciousness in the physical world*. AAAS Selected Symposium 57 (pp. 37–86). Boulder, CO: Westview Press.

Putman, N. F., Scanlan, M. M., Billman, E. J., O'Neil, J. P., Couture, R. B., Quinn, T. P., ... & Noakes, D. L. (2014). An inherited magnetic map guides ocean navigation in juvenile Pacific salmon. *Current Biology, 24*(4), 446–450.

Putnam, F. W. (1985). Dissociation as a response to extreme trauma. In R. P. Kluft (Ed.), *Childhood antecedents of multiple personality* (pp. 63–97). Washington, DC: American Psychiatric Press.

Putnam, F. W. (1991). Dissociative disorders in children and adolescents: a developmental perspective. *Psychiatric Clinics, 14*(3), 519–531.

Putnam, F. W. (1997). *Dissociation in children and adolescents: a developmental perspective*. New York: Guilford Press.

Putnam, F. W., & Trickett, P. K. (1993). Child sexual abuse: a model of chronic trauma. *Psychiatry, 56*(1), 82–95.

Putnam, F. W., Carlson, E. B., Ross, C. A., Anderson, G., Clark, P., Torem, M., . . . & Braun, E. G. (1996). Patterns of dissociation in clinical and nonclinical samples. *Journal of Nervous and Mental Disorders, 184*(11), 673–679.

Quine, W. V. O. (1953). Two dogmas of empiricism. In W. V. O. Quine, *From a Logical Point of View* (2nd ed.) (pp. 20–46). Cambridge, MA: Harvard University Press.

Quine, W. V. O., & Ullian, J. S. (1978). *The web of belief* (2nd ed.). New York: Random House.

Rabeyron, T., & Watt, C. (2010). Paranormal experiences, mental health and mental boundaries, and psi. *Personality and Individual Differences, 48*(4), 487–492.

Radin, D. (2006). *Entangled minds: extrasensory experiences in a quantum reality*. New York: Paraview.

Radin, D. (2018). *Real magic: ancient wisdom, modern science, and a guide to the secret power of the universe*. New York: Harmony.

Radin, D. (2019). Parapsychological Association Presidential Address, 2018. *Journal of Parapsychology, 67*(2).

Radin, D., & Nelson, R.D. (1989). Evidence for consciousness-related anomalies in random physical systems. *Foundations of Physics, 19*, 1499–1514.

Radin, D., Michel, L., Galdamez, K., Wendland, P., Rickenbach, R., & Delorme, A. (2012). Consciousness and the double-slit interference pattern: six experiments. *Physics Essays, 25*(2).

Radin, D., Nelson, R., Dobyns, Y., & Houtkooper, J. (2006). Reexamining psychokinesis: comment on Bösch, Steinkamp, and Boller (2006). *Psychological Bulletin, 132*, 529–532.

Radin, D. I. (1997). Unconscious perception of future emotions: an experiment in presentiment. *Journal of Scientific Exploration, 11*, 163–180.

Radin, D. I., & Ferrari, D. C. (1991). Effects of consciousness on the fall of dice: a meta-analysis. *Journal of Scientific Exploration, 5*(1), 61–83.

Radin, D. I., McAlpine, S., & Cunningham, S. (1994). Geomagnetism and psi in the ganzfeld. *Journal of the Society for Psychical Research, 59*, 352–352.

Raichle, M. E. (2015). The brain's default mode network. *Annual Review of Neuroscience, 38*, 433–447.

Raichle, M. E., MacLeod, A. M., Snyder, A. Z., Powers, W. J., Gusnard, D. A., & Shulman, G. L. (2001). A default mode of brain function. *Proceedings of the National Academy of Sciences, 98*(2), 676–682.

Rainville, P., Bechara, A., Naqvi, N., & Damasio, A. (2006) Basic emotions are associated with distinct patterns of cardiorespiratory activity. *International Journal of Psychophysiology, 61*, 5–18.

Rapoport, A., & Budescu, D. V. (1997). Randomization in individual choice behavior. *Psychological Review, 104*(3), 603–617.

Rattet, S. L., & Bursik, K. (2001). Investigating the personality correlates of paranormal belief and precognitive experience. *Personality and Individual Differences, 31*, 433–444.

Rauschenberger, S. L., & Lynn, S. J. (1995). Fantasy proneness, DSM-II – R Axis 1 psychopathology, and dissociation. *Journal of Abnormal Psychology, 104*(2), 373.

Reber, A. S. (1989). Implicit learning and tacit knowledge. *Journal of Experimental Psychology: General, 118*, 219–235.

Reber, A. S., & Alcock, J. E. (2019). Searching for the impossible: parapsychology's elusive quest. *American Psychologist*, https://doi.org/10.1037/amp0000486

Reddish, P., Fischer, R., & Bulbulia, J. (2013). Let's dance together: synchrony, shared intentionality and cooperation. *PLoS ONE, 8*(8), e71182.

Redinbaugh, M. J., Phillips, J. M., Kambi, N. A., Mohanta, S., Andryk, S., Dooley, G. L., ... & Saalmann, Y. (2019). Thalamus modulates consciousness via layer-specific control of cortex. *NEURON-D-19-01899*.

Reed, P. G. (1987). Spirituality and well-being in terminally ill hospitalized adults. *Research in Nursing & Health, 10*(5), 335–344.

Reppert, S. M., Schwartz, W. J., & Pearson, J. F. (1983). Maternal coordination of the fetal biological clock in utero. *International Journal of Obstetric Anesthesia, 3*, 113.

Rhine, J. B. (1934/2012). *ESP extra-sensory perception*. eBookIt.com.

Rhine, J. B. (1943). Dice thrown by cup and machine in PK tests. *The Journal of Parapsychology, 7*(3), 207.

Rhine, J. B., & Pratt, J. G. (1962). *Parapsychology, frontier science of the mind: a survey of the field, the methods, and the facts of ESP and PK research*. Springfield, IL: Charles C Thomas.

Rhine, L. E. (1953). Subjective forms of spontaneous psi experiences. *The Journal of Parapsychology, 17*(2), 77.

Rhine, L. E. (1962). Psychological processes in ESP experiences part I: Waking experiences. *The Journal of Parapsychology, 26*(2), 88.

Rhine, L. E. (1977). Research methods with spontaneous cases. In B. B. Walman (Ed.), *Handbook of parapsychology* (pp. 59–80). New York: Van Nostrand Reinhold.

Rhine, L. E. (1978). The psi process in spontaneous cases. *The Journal of Parapsychology, 42*(1), 20.

Rhue, J. W., & Lynn, S. J. (1987). Fantasy proneness: developmental antecedents. *Journal of Personality, 55*(1), 121–137.

Rhue, J. W., Lynn, S. J., Henry, S., Buhk, K., & Boyd, P. (1990). Child abuse, imagination and hypnotizability. *Imagination, Cognition & Personality, 10*, 53–63.

Rice, T. W. (2003). Believe it or not: religious and other paranormal beliefs in the United States. *Journal for the Scientific Study of Religion, 42*(1), 95–106.

Richards, D. (2017). *Dear Martin/Dear Marcello: Gardner and Truzzi on skepticism.* WSPC. Kindle edition.

Richardson, A. (1967). Mental practice: a review and discussion part II. *Research Quarterly. American Association for Health, Physical Education and Recreation, 38*(2), 263–273.

Rindermann, H., Falkenhayn, L., & Baumeister, A. E. E. (2014). Cognitive ability and epistemic rationality: a study in Nigeria and Germany. *Intelligence, 47*, 23–33.

Ring, K., & Rosing, C. J. (1990). The Omega Project: an empirical study of the NDE-prone personality. *Journal of Near-Death Studies, 8*(4), 211–239.

Risen, J. L. (2016). Believing what we do not believe: acquiescence to superstitious beliefs and other powerful intuitions. *Psychological Review, 123*, 182–207.

Ritchie, S. J., Wiseman, R., & French, C. C. (2012). Failing the future: three unsuccessful attempts to replicate Bem's 'Retroactive Facilitation of Recall Effect'. *PloS one, 7*(3), e33423.

Rizzolatti, G., & Craighero, L. (2004). The mirror-neuron system. *Annual Review of Neuroscience, 27*, 169–192.

Roe, C. A. (1999). Critical thinking and belief in the paranormal: a re-evaluation. *British Journal of Psychology, 90*(1), 85–98.

Roe, C. A. (2012). Parapsychology in the next 25 years – still a butterfly science? *Journal of Parapsychology, 76*, 46–48.

Roe, C. A. (2016). As it occurred to me: lessons learned in researching parapsychological claims. *Journal of Parapsychology, 80*(2), 144–155.

Roe, C. A., & Bell, C. (2016). Paranormal belief and perceived control over life events. *Journal of the Society for Psychical Research, 80*(2), 65–76.

Roe, C. A., & Morgan, C. L. (2002). Narcissism and belief in the paranormal. *Psychological Reports, 90*(2), 405–411.

Roe, C. A., Sherwood., S. J., Farrell, L., Savva, L., & Baker, I. S. (2007). Assessing the roles of the sender and experimenter in dream ESP research. *European Journal of Parapsychology, 22*(2), 175–192.

Rogers, P., Davis, T., & Fisk, J. (2009). Paranormal belief and susceptibility to the conjunction fallacy. *Applied Cognitive Psychology: The Official Journal of the Society for Applied Research in Memory and Cognition, 23*(4), 524–542.

Rogers, P., Fisk, J. E., & Lowrie, E. (2016). Paranormal believers' susceptibility to confirmatory versus disconfirmatory conjunctions. *Applied Cognitive Psychology, 30*(4), 628–634.

Rogers, P., Fisk, J. E., & Lowrie, E. (2017). Paranormal belief and errors of probabilistic reasoning: the role of constituent conditional relatedness in believers' susceptibility to the conjunction fallacy. *Consciousness and Cognition, 56*, 13–29.

Rogers, P., Fisk, J. E., & Wiltshire, D. (2011). Paranormal belief and the conjunction fallacy: controlling for temporal relatedness and potential surprise differentials in component events. *Applied Cognitive Psychology, 25*(5), 692–702.

Rogers, P., Qualter, P., & Phelps, G. (2007). The mediating and moderating effects of loneliness and attachment style on belief in the paranormal. *European Journal of Parapsychology, 22*(2), 138.

Rogers, P., Qualter, P., & Wood, D. (2016). The impact of event vividness, event severity, and prior paranormal belief on attributions towards a depicted remarkable coincidence experience: two studies examining the misattribution hypothesis. *British Journal of Psychology, 107*(4), 710–751.

Romano, E., & De Luca, R. V. (2001). Male sexual abuse: a review of effects, abuse characteristics, and links with later psychological functioning. *Aggression and Violent Behavior, 6*(1), 55–78.

Rominger, C., Schulter, G., Fink, A., Weiss, E. M., & Papousek, I. (2018). Meaning in meaninglessness: the propensity to perceive meaningful patterns in coincident events and randomly arranged stimuli is linked to enhanced attention in early sensory processing. *Psychiatry Research, 263,* 225–232.

Roney-Dougal, S. M., Ryan, A., & Luke, D. (2013). The relationship between local geomagnetic activity, meditation and psi. Part I: literature review and theoretical model. *Journal of the Society for Psychical Research, 77*(2), 72–88.

Roney-Dougal, S. M., Solfvin, J., & Fox, J. (2008). An exploration of degree of meditation attainment in relation to psychic awareness with Tibetan Buddhists. *Journal of Scientific Exploration, 22*(2), 161–178.

Rooney, W. (2019). FourFourTwo. Performance. Available online at: www.fourfourtwo.com/us/performance/training/wayne-rooney-big-match-preparation (accessed 9 May 2019).

Roseman, M., Milette, K., Bero, L. A., Coyne, J. C., Lexchin, J., Turner, E. H., & Thombs, B. D. (2011). Reporting of conflicts of interest in meta-analyses of trials of pharmacological treatments. *Jama, 305*(10), 1008–1017.

Rosenthal, R. (1976). *Experimenter effects in behavioral research* (enlarged ed.). Oxford: Irvington.

Rosenthal, R. (1979). The 'file drawer' problem and tolerance for null results. *Psychological Bulletin, 86,* 638–641.

Rosenthal, R. (1991). Replication in behavioral research. In J. W. Neuliep (Ed.), *Replication research in the social sciences* (pp. 1–30). Newbury Park, CA: Sage.

Rosenthal, R. (1993). Cumulating evidence. In K. Gideon & C. Lewis (Eds.), *A handbook for data analysis in the behavioral sciences: methodological issues* (pp. 519–559). Hillsdale, NJ: Erlbaum.

Rosenthal, R. (1994). Interpersonal expectancy effects: a 30-year perspective. *Psychological Science, 3,* 176–179.

Rosenthal, R., & Rubin, D. B. (1989). Effect size estimation for one-sample multiple-choice-type data: design, analysis, and meta-analysis. *Psychological Bulletin, 106*(2), 332.

Ross, C. A., & Joshi, S. (1992). Paranormal experiences in the general population. *Journal of Nervous and Mental Disease, 180*(6), 357–361.

Ross, C. A., Joshi, S., & Currie, R. (1990). Dissociative experiences in the general population. *American Journal of Psychiatry, 147*(11), 1547–1552.

Rouder, J. N., Morey, R. D., & Province, J. M. (2013). A Bayes factor meta-analysis of recent extrasensory perception experiments: comment on Storm, Tressoldi, & Di Risio (2010). *Psychological Bulletin, 139,* 241–247.

Roxburgh, E. C., Ridgway, S., & Roe, C. A. (2015). Exploring the meaning in meaningful coincidences: an interpretative phenomenological analysis of synchronicity in therapy. *European Journal of Psychotherapy and Counselling, 17*(2), 144–161.

Rozeboom, W. W. (1997). Good science is abductive, not hypothetico-deductive. In L. L. Harlow, S. A. Mulaik, & J. H. Steiger (Eds.), *What if there were no significance tests?* (pp. 335–391). Hillsdale, NJ: Erlbaum.

Runge, M. S., Cheung, M. W.-L., & D'Angiulli, A. (2017). Meta-analytic comparison of trial versus questionnaire-based vividness reportability across behavioural, cognitive and neural measurements of imagery. *Neuroscience of Consciousness*, *1*, nix006.

Runkel, P. J. (2007). *Casting nets and testing specimens: two grand methods of psychology.* Hayward, CA: Living Control Systems.

Ryan, A. (2008). New insights into the links between ESP and geomagnetic activity. *Journal of Scientific Exploration*, *22*(3), 335–358.

Ryan, A. (2018). Open data in parapsychology: introducing psi open data 1. *The Journal of Parapsychology*, *82*(1), 65–76.

Sacks, O. (2017). *The river of consciousness.* London: Picador.

Sagan, C. (1995). Wonder and skepticism. *Skeptical Inquirer*, *19*, 24–30.

Sagan, C., & Druyan, A. (1995). *The demon-haunted world: science as a candle in the dark.* New York: Ballantine Books.

Sánchez-Bernardos, M. L., & Avia, M.D. (2004). Personality correlates of fantasy proneness among adolescents. *Personality and Individual Differences*, *37*, 1069–1079.

Sanders, R. D., G. Tononi, G., Laureys, S., & Sleigh J. W. (2012). Unresponsiveness not equal unconsciousness. *Anesthesiology*, *116*(2012), 946–959.

Santoro, G., Costanzo, A., & Schimmenti, A. (2019). Playing with identities: the representation of dissociative identity disorder in the videogame 'Who am I?'. *Mediterranean Journal of Clinical Psychology*, *7*(1).

Sar, V., Alioğlu, F., & Akyüz, G. (2014). Experiences of possession and paranormal phenomena among women in the general population: are they related to traumatic stress and dissociation? *Journal of Trauma and Dissociation*, *15*(3), 303–318.

Sargent, C. L. (1981). Extraversion and performance in 'extra-sensory perception' tasks. *Personality and Individual Differences*, *2*(2), 137–143.

Sargent, C. L. (1982). A ganzfeld GESP experiment with visiting subjects. *Journal of the Society for Psychical Research*, *51*, 222–232.

Sargent, C. L. (1987). Skeptical fairytales from Bristol. *Journal of the Society for Psychical Research*, *54*, 208–218.

Sargent, C. L., & Harley, T. A. (1982). Precognition testing with free-response techniques in the ganzfeld and the dream state. *European Journal of Parapsychology*, *4*, 243–256.

Sawa, R., Winchester, I., Doetzel, N., & Meynell, H. (2018). Spirituality and healing: results of a ten year study of spiritual healers. *Medica and Clinica Press*, *2*(1): 71–82. doi: 10.28964/MedClinPress-2-113.

Schacter, D. L., & Addis, D. R. (2007). The cognitive neuroscience of constructive memory: remembering the past and imagining the future. *Philosophical Transactions of the Royal Society B: Biological Sciences*, *362*(1481), 773–786.

Schauer, M., & Elbert, T. (2010). Dissociation following traumatic stress. *Zeitschrift für Psychologie*, *218*(2): 109–127.

Schaut, G. B., & Persinger, M. A. (1985). Subjective telepathic experiences, geomagnetic activity and the ELF hypothesis. Part I: Data analysis. *Psi Research*, *4*(1), 4–20.

Scherer, W. B. (1948). Spontaneity as a factor in ESP. *The Journal of Parapsychology*, *12*(2), 126.

Schifano, F., Napoletano, F., Chiappini, S., Orsolini, L., Guirguis, A., Corkery, J. M., ... & Vento, A. (2019). New psychoactive substances (NPS), psychedelic experiences and dissociation: clinical and clinical pharmacological issues. *Current Addiction Reports*, 1–13.

Schimmack, U. (2012). The ironic effect of significant results on the credibility of multiple-study articles. *Psychological Methods*, *17*, 551–566.

Schimmack, U. (2015). The test of insufficient variance: a new tool for the detection of questionable research practices. Available online at: https://replicationindex.wordpress.com/2014/12/30/the-test-of-insufficient-variance-tiva-a-new-tool-for-the-detection-of-questionable-research-practices/

Schimmenti, A. (2017). The developmental roots of dissociation: a multiple mediation analysis. *Psychoanalytic Psychology*, *34*(1), 96–105.

Schimmenti, A. (2018). The trauma factor: examining the relationships among different types of trauma, dissociation, and psychopathology. *Journal of Trauma & Dissociation*, *19*(5), 552–571.

Schlitz, M., & Gruber, E. (1980). Transcontinental remote viewing. *Journal of Parapsychology*, *44*, 305–317.

Schlitz, M., Wiseman, R., Watt, C., & Radin, D. (2006). Of two minds: skeptic-proponent collaboration within parapsychology. *British Journal of Psychology*, *97*(3), 313–322.

Schlitz, M. J., & Haight, J. M. (1984). Remote viewing revisited: an intrasubject replication. *Journal of Parapsychology*, *48*, 39–49.

Schlitz, M. J., & Laberge, S. (1997). Covert observation increases skin conductance in subjects unaware of when they are being observed: a replication. *Journal of Parapsychology*, *61*, 185–196.

Schmahmann, J. D., & Sherman, J. C. (1998). The cerebellar cognitive affective syndrome. *Brain*, *121*, 561–579.

Schmidt, H. (1974). Comparison of PK action on two different random number generators. *The Journal of Parapsychology*, *38*(1), 47.

Schmidt, S., Schneider, R., Utts, J., & Walach, H. (2004). Distant intentionality and the feeling of being stared at: two meta-analyses. *British Journal of Psychology*, *95*(2), 235–247.

Schmied-Knittel, I., & Schetsche, M. T. (2005). Everyday miracles: results of a representative survey in Germany. *European Journal of Parapsychology*, *20*(1), 3–21.

Schooler, J. W. (2011). Unpublished results hide the decline effect: some effects diminish when tests are repeated. Jonathan Schooler says being open about findings that don't make the scientific record could reveal why. *Nature*, *470*(7335), 437–438.

Schooler, J. W., Baumgart, S., & Franklin, M. (2018). Entertaining without endorsing: the case for the scientific investigation of anomalous cognition. *Psychology of Consciousness: Theory, Research, and Practice*, *5*(1), 63.

Schredl, M. (2002). Questionnaires and diaries as research instruments in dream research: methodological issues. *Dreaming*, *12*(1), 17–26.

Schreiber, F. R. (1973). *Sybil*. Chicago, IL: Henry Regnery.

Schwartz, G. E. (2012). Consciousness, spirituality, and post-materialist science: an empirical and experiential approach. In L. J. Miller (Ed.), *The Oxford handbook of psychology and spirituality* (pp. 584–597). New York: Oxford University Press.

Schwartz, G. E., Fair, P. L., Salt, P., Mandel, M. R., & Klerman, G. L. (1976). Facial muscle patterning to affective imagery in depressed and nondepressed subjects. *Science*, *192*(4238), 489–491.

Scimeca, G., Bruno, A., Cava, L., Pandolfo, G., Muscatello, M. R. A., & Zoccali, R. (2014). The relationship between alexithymia, anxiety, depression, and internet addiction severity in a sample of Italian high school students. *The Scientific World Journal*, 1–8.

Scimeca, G., Bruno, A., Pandolfo, G., La Ciura, G., Zoccali, R. A., & Muscatello, M. R. (2015). Extrasensory perception experiences and childhood trauma: a Rorschach investigation. *The Journal of Nervous and Mental Disease*, *203*(11), 856–863.

Servan-Schreiber, E., & Anderson, J. R. (1990). Learning artificial grammars with competitive chunking. *Journal of Experimental Psychology: Learning, Memory, and Cognition, 16*, 592–608.

Sheehan, P. W., Obstoj, I., & McConkey, K. (1976). Trance logic and cue structure as supplied by the hypnotist. *Journal of Abnormal Psychology, 85*, 459–472.

Sheldrake, R. (1994). *Seven experiments that could change the world: a do-it-yourself guide to revolutionary science.* London: Fourth Estate.

Sheldrake, R. (2001). Experiments on the sense of being stared at: the elimination of possible artefacts. *Journal of the Society for Psychical Research, 65*, 122–137.

Sheldrake, R. (2003). *The sense of being stared at, and other aspects of the extended mind.* London: Hutchinson.

Sheldrake, R. (2004). The need for open-minded skepticism: a reply to David Marks. *The Skeptic, 16*, 8–13.

Sheldrake, R. (2005). The sense of being stared at – Part 1: Is it real or illusory? *Journal of Consciousness Studies, 12*(6), 10–31.

Sheldrake, R. (2013). *The sense of being stared at: and other unexplained powers of human minds.* South Paris, ME: Park Street Press.

Sheldrake, R., Overby, C., & Beeharee, A. (2008). The sense of being stared at: an automated test on the internet. *Journal of the Society for Psychical Research, 72*(891), 86.

Sherwood, S., & Roe, C. A. (2003). A review of dream ESP studies conducted since the Maimonides dream ESP programme. *Journal of Consciousness Studies, 10*(6–7), 85–109.

Shiah, Y. J. (2012). A possible mechanism for ESP at the initial perceptual stage. *Journal of Parapsychology, 76*(1), 147.

Shor, R. E. (1959). Hypnosis and the concept of the generalized reality-orientation. *American Journal of Psychotherapy, 13*(3), 582–602.

Shor, R. E., Orne, M. T., & O'Connell, D. N. (1962). Validation and cross-validation of a scale of self-reported personal experiences which predicts hypnotizability. *Journal of Psychology, 53*, 55–75.

Shoup, R. (2009). Empirical pictures of time. In C. A. Roe, L. Coly, & W. Kramer (Eds.), *Utrecht II: charting the future of parapsychology* (pp. 463–489). New York: Parapsychology Foundation, Inc. & Het Johan Borgmanfonds Foundation.

Shulman, G. L., Fiez, J. A., Corbetta, M., Buckner, R. L., Miezin, F. M., Raichle, M. E., & Petersen, S. E. (1997). Common blood flow changes across visual tasks: II. Decreases in cerebral cortex. *Journal of Cognitive Neuroscience, 9*(5), 648–663.

Siclari, F., Larocque, J. J., Postle, B. R., & Tononi, G. (2013). Assessing sleep consciousness within subjects using a serial awakening paradigm. *Frontiers in Psychology, 4*, 542.

Sidgwick, H. (1894). Report on the census of hallucinations, *Proceedings of the Society of Psychical Research, 10*, 25–422.

Sidorov, L. (2001). On the possible mechanism of intent in paranormal phenomena. *The Journal of Theoretics.*

Siegel, R. K. (1980). The psychology of life after death. *American Psychologist, 35*(10), 911.

Siegel, S. (1956). *Non-parametric statistics for the behavioural sciences.* New York: Mcraw-Hill.

Sierra, M., & Berrios, G. E. (1998). Depersonalization: neurobiological perspectives. *Biological Psychiatry, 44*(9), 898–908.

Silbersweig, D. A., Stern, E., Frith, C., Cahill, C., Holmes, A., Grootoonk, S., . . . & Frackowiak, R. S. J. (1995). A functional neuroanatomy of hallucinations in schizophrenia. *Nature, 378*, 176–179.

Silvia, P. J., & Kimbrel, N. A. (2010). A dimensional analysis of creativity and mental illness: do anxiety and depression symptoms predict creative cognition, creative accomplishments, and creative self-concepts? *Psychology of Aesthetics, Creativity, and the Arts, 4*(1), 2.

Simmonds, C. A., & Fox, J. (2004). A pilot investigation into sensory noise, schizotypy and extrasensory perception. *Journal of the Society for Psychical Research, 68*(4), 253–261.

Simmonds-Moore, C., & Holt, N. J. (2007). Trait, state, and psi: a comparison of psi performance between clusters of scorers on schizotypy in a ganzfeld and waking control condition. *Journal of the Society for Psychical Research, 71*(889), 197–215.

Simmons, J., Nelson, L., & Simonsohn, U. (2011). False-positive psychology: undisclosed flexibility in data collection and analysis allow presenting anything as significant. *Psychological Science, 22*, 1359–1366.

Simonsohn, U., Nelson, L. D., & Simmons, J. P. (2014). P-curve: a key to the file-drawer. *Journal of Experimental Psychology: General, 143*(2), 534.

Sinclair, U. (1930/1962). *Mental radio* (revised ed.). Springfield, IL: Charles C. Thomas.

Singer, J. L. (1975/2014). *The inner world of daydreaming*. London: Harper & Row.

Singer, J. L., & McCraven, V. G. (1961). Some characteristics of adult daydreaming. *Journal of Psychology, 51*, 151–164.

Sip, K. E., Roepstorff, A., McGregor, W., & Frith, C. D. (2008). Detecting deception: the scope and limits. *Trends in Cognitive Sciences, 12*(2), 48–53.

Slade, P. D., & Bentall, R. P. (1988). *Sensory deception: a scientific analysis of hallucination*. Baltimore, MD: Johns Hopkins University Press.

Slaughter, J. W. (1902). The moon in childhood and folklore. *American Journal of Psychology, XIII*, 294–318. doi:10.2307/1412741.

Slovic, P. (2016). *The perception of risk*. Abingdon: Routledge.

Smith, C. C., Laham, D., & Moddel, J. (2014). Stock market prediction using associative remote viewing by inexperienced remote viewers. *Journal of Scientific Exploration, 28*, 7–16.

Smith, J. A., Flowers, P., & Larkin, M. (2009). *Interpretative phenomenological analysis: theory, method and research*. London: Sage.

Smythies, J. R. (1967). *Science and ESP*. Abingdon: Routledge.

Snelson, C. (2015). Vlogging about school on YouTube: an exploratory study. *New Media and Society, 17*(3), 321–339.

Sohn, D. (1998). Statistical significance and replicability: why the former does not presage the latter. *Theory & Psychology, 8*, 291–311.

Somer, E., & Herscu, O. (2018). Childhood trauma, social anxiety, absorption and fantasy dependence: two potential mediated pathways to maladaptive daydreaming. *Journal of Addictive Behaviors, Therapy and Rehabilitation, 6*(4).

Spanos, N. P. (1986). Hypnotic behavior: a social-psychological interpretation of amnesia, analgesia, and 'trance logic'. *Behavioral and Brain Sciences, 9*(3), 449–467.

Spanos, N. P., & Radtke, H. L. (1981). Hypnotic visual hallucinations as imaginings: a cognitive-social psychological perspective. *Imagination, Cognition and Personality, 1*(2), 147–170.

Spanos, N. P., Cross, P. A., Dickson, K., & DuBreuil, S. C. (1993). Close encounters: an examination of UFO experiences. *Journal of Abnormal Psychology, 102*(4), 624.

Spanos, N. P., De Groot, H. P., Tiller, D. K., Weekes, J. R., & Bertrand, L. D. (1985). 'Trance logic' duality and hidden observer responding in hypnotic, imagination control, and simulating subjects: a social, psychological analysis. *Journal of Abnormal Psychology, 94*, 611–623.

Sparks, G., & Miller, W. (2001). Investigating the relationship between exposure to television programs that depict paranormal phenomena and beliefs in the paranormal. *Communication Monographs, 68*(1), 98–113.

Spelke, E. S. (1997). Babies fart. *Science, 318*, 1235–1236.
Sperry, R. W. (1969). A modified concept of consciousness. *Psychological Review, 76*, 532–536.
Spitzer, C., Klauer, T., Grabe, H. J., Lucht, M., Stieglitz, R. D., Schneider, W., & Freyberger, H. J. (2003). Gender differences in dissociation. *Psychopathology, 36*(2), 65–70.
Spottiswoode, S. J. P. (1990). Geomagnetic activity and anomalous cognition: a preliminary report of new evidence. *Subtle Energies, 1*(1), 91–102.
Spottiswoode, S. J. P. (1997). Geomagnetic fluctuations and free-response anomalous cognition: a new understanding. *Journal of Parapsychology, 61*(1), 3–12.
Spottiswoode, S. J. P., & May, E. C. (2003). Skin conductance prestimulus response: analyses, artifacts and a pilot study. *Journal of Scientific Exploration, 17*, 617–641.
Ståhl, T., & Van Prooijen, J. W. (2018). Epistemic rationality: skepticism toward unfounded beliefs requires sufficient cognitive ability and motivation to be rational. *Personality and Individual Differences, 122*, 155–163.
Stam, H. J., & Spanos, N. P. (1980). Experimental designs, expectancy effects, and hypnotic analgesia. *Journal of Abnormal Psychology, 89*(6), 751–762.
Stanford, R. G. (1977). Conceptual frameworks of contemporary psi research. In B. B. Wolman (Ed.), *Handbook of parapsychology* (pp. 823–858). New York: Van Nostrand.
Stanovich, K. E., & West, R. F. (2000). Individual differences in reasoning: implications for the rationality debate? *Behavioral and Brain Sciences, 23*(5), 645–665.
Starmans, C., & Bloom, P. (2012). Windows to the soul: children and adults see the eyes as the location of the self. *Cognition, 123*(2), 313–318.
Steering Committee of the Physicians' Health Study Research Group (1989). Final report on the aspirin component of the ongoing Physicians' Health Study. *New England Journal of Medicine, 321*(3), 129–135.
Stein, D. J., Koenen, K. C., Friedman, M. J., Hill, E., McLaughlin, K. A., Petukhova, M., ... & Bunting, B. (2013). Dissociation in posttraumatic stress disorder: evidence from the world mental health surveys. *Biological Psychiatry, 73*(4), 302–312.
Steinkamp, F., & Böhm, G. (2000). 1998 Parapsychological Association bibliography. *The Journal of Parapsychology, 64*(4), 417.
Sterling, T. D. (1959). Publication decisions and their possible effects on inferences drawn from tests of significance – or vice versa. *Journal of the American Statistical Association, 54*, 30–34.
Steuwe, C., Lanius, R. A., & Frewen, P. A. (2012). Evidence for a dissociative subtype of PTSD by latent profile and confirmatory factor analyses in a civilian sample. *Depression and Anxiety, 29*(8), 689–700.
Stevens, J. (1988). *Storming heaven: LSD and the American dream*. London: William Heinemann.
Stevenson, R. L. (1886/1924). *The strange case of Dr. Jekyll and Mr. Hyde: fables, other stories and fragments*. London: Heinemann.
Stewart-Williams, S., & Podd, J. (2004). The placebo effect: dissolving the expectancy versus conditioning debate. *Psychological Bulletin, 130*(2), 324.
Stockbridge, G., & Wooffitt, R. (2019). Coincidence by design. *Qualitative Research, 19*(4), 437–454.
Stokkan, K.-A. (2001). Entrainment of the circadian clock in the liver by feeding. *Science, 291*, 490–493.
Storm, L. (2003). Remote viewing by committee: RV using a multiple agent/multiple percipient design. *Journal of Parapsychology, 67*(2), 325–342.

Storm, L. (2006). Technical Paper No. 11: meta-analysis in parapsychology: I. The ganzfeld domain. *Australian Journal of Parapsychology*, *6*(1), 35.

Storm, L., & Ertel, S. (2001). Does psi exist? Comments on Milton and Wiseman's (1999) meta-analysis of Ganzfield research. *Psychological Bulletin*, *127*(1), 424–443.

Storm, L., Sherwood, S. J., Roe, C. A., Tressoldi, P. E., Rock, A. J., & Di Risio, L. (2017). On the correspondence between dream content and target material under laboratory conditions: a meta-analysis of dream-ESP studies, 1966–2016. *International Journal of Dream Research*, *10*(2), 120–140.

Storm, L., Tressoldi, P. E., & Di Risio, L. (2010). Meta-analysis of free-response studies, 1992–2008: assessing the noise reduction model in parapsychology. *Psychological Bulletin*, *136*(4), 471.

Storm, L., Tressoldi, P. E., & Utts, J. (2013). Testing the Storm et al. (2010) meta-analysis using Bayesian and frequentist approaches: reply to Rouder et al. (2013). *Psychological Bulletin*, *139*, 248–254.

Strawson, G. (2000). The phenomenology and ontology of the self. *Exploring the Self: Philosophical and Psychopathological Perspectives on Self-experience*, *23*, 39–54.

Strawson, G. (2006). Realistic monism: why physicalism entails panpsychism. *Journal of Consciousness Studies*, *13*(10/11), 3.

Stroud, N. J. (2010). Polarization and partisan selective exposure. *Journal of Communication*, *60*(3), 556–576.

Studerus, E., Gamma, A., & Vollenweider, F. X. (2010). Psychometric evaluation of the altered states of consciousness rating scale (OAV). *PloS ONE*, *5*(8), e12412.

Sundberg, N. D. (1955). The acceptability of 'fake' versus 'bona fide' personality test interpretations. *The Journal of Abnormal and Social Psychology*, *50*(1), 145.

Sutherland, S. (1992). *Irrationality: the enemy within*. London: Constable.

Swales, J. (2000). Population advice on salt restriction: the social issues. *American Journal of Hypertension*, *13*(1), 2–7.

Swami, V., Coles, R., Stieger, S., Pietschnig, J., Furnham, A., Rehim, S., & Voracek, M. (2011). Conspiracist ideation in Britain and Austria: evidence of a monological belief system and associations between individual psychological differences and real-world and fictitious conspiracy theories. *British Journal of Psychology*, *102*, 443–463.

Tachibana, K., Suzuki, K., Mori, E., Miura, N., Kawashima, R., Horie, K., ... & Mushiake, H. (2009). Neural activity in the human brain signals logical rule identification. *Journal of Neurophysiology*, *102*(3), 1526–1537.

Tait, A. (2019). Psychic future: what next for the 'precog economy'? *The Guardian*, 29 September. Available online at: www.theguardian.com/global/2019/sep/29/psychic-future-what-next-for-the-precognition-economy

Targ, R. (2010). Invited address: why I am absolutely convinced of the reality of psychic abilities, and why you should be, too. Outstanding Career Award, 2009. *Journal of Parapsychology*, *74*, 269–272.

Targ, R. (2012). *The reality of ESP: a physicist's proof of psychic abilities*. Wheaton, IL: Quest Books.

Targ, R., & Katra, J. E. (2000). Remote viewing in a group setting. *Journal of Scientific Exploration*, *14*(1), 107–114.

Targ, R., & Puthoff, H. (1974). Information transmission under conditions of sensory shielding. *Nature*, *251*(5476), 602.

Targ, R., Puthoff, H. E., & May, E. C. (1979/2002). Direct perception of remote geographical locations. In C. T. Tart, H. E. Puthoff, & R. Targ (Eds.), *Mind at Large: IEEE Symposia on the Nature of Extrasensory Perception* (pp. 71–95). Charlottesville, VA: Hampton Roads Publishing Company.

Tart, C. T. (1968). A psychophysiological study of out-of-the-body experiences in a gifted subject. *Journal for the American Society of Psychical Research, 62*, 3–27.

Tart, C. T. (1971). *On being stoned: a psychological study of marijuana intoxication*. Palo Alto, CA: Science and Behavior Books.

Tart, C. T. (1976). *Learning to use extrasensory perception*. Chicago, IL: University of Chicago Press.

Tart, C. T. (1988a). Effects of electrical shielding on GESP performance. *Journal of the American Society for Psychical Research, 82*(2), 129–146.

Tart, C. T. (1988b). Geomagnetic effects on GESP: two studies. *Journal of the American Society for Psychical Research, 82*(3), 193–216.

Tart, C. T. (1993). Marijuana intoxication, psi, and spiritual experiences. *Journal of the American Society for Psychical Research, 87*(2), 149–170.

Tart, C. T. (2018). Remote viewing, psychic functioning, works well enough for the CIA. Star Gate Archives review for Amazon, 23 January 2019. Accessed at: www.amazon.co.uk/gp/product/1476667527/ref=ppx_yo_dt_b_asin_title_o06_s00?ie=UTF8&psc=1

Tart, C. T., Palmer, J., & Redington, D. J. (1978). Effects of immediate feedback on ESP performance: a second study. *Journal of the American Society for Psychological Research, 73*, 151–165.

Tart, C. T., Puthoff, H. E., & Targ, R. (1980). Information transmission in remote viewing experiments. *Nature, 284*(5752), 191.

Taylor, J. G. (1980). *Science and the supernatural: an investigation of paranormal phenomena including psychic healing, clairvoyance, telepathy, and precognition by a distinguished physicist and mathematician*. London: Temple Smith.

Taylor, J. G., & Balanovski, E. (1978). Can electromagnetism explain ESP? *Nature, 275*, 64.

Taylor, J. G., & Balanovski, E. (1979). Is there any scientific explanation of the paranormal? *Nature, 279*, 631–633.

Taylor, S. E., & Armor, D. A. (1996). Positive illusions and coping with adversity. *Journal of Personality, 64*(4), 873–898.

Taylor, S. E., & Gollwitzer, P. M. (1995). Effects of mindset on positive illusions. *Journal of Personality and Social Psychology, 69*(2), 213.

Tellegen, A., & Atkinson, G. (1974). Openness to absorbing and self-altering experiences ('absorption'), a trait related to hypnotic susceptibility. *Journal of Abnormal Psychology, 83*(3), 268.

Tellegen, A., Lykken, D. T., Bouchard, T. J., Wilcox, K. J., Negal, N. L., & Rich, S. (1988). Personality similarity in twins reared apart and together. *Journal of Personality & Social Psychology, 54*, 1031–1039.

Terhune, D. B., Cardeña, E., & Lindgren, M. (2010). Disruption of synaesthesia by post-hypnotic suggestion: an ERP study. *Neuropsychologia, 48*(11), 3360–3364.

Terry, J. C., & Honorton, C. (1976). Psi information retrieval in the ganzfeld: two confirmatory studies. *Journal of the American Society for Psychical Research, 70*, 2017–2217.

Tetlock, P. E. (2005). *Expert political judgment*. Princeton, NJ: Princeton University Press.

Thalbourne, M. A. (1995). Further studies of the measurement and correlates of belief in the paranormal. *Journal of the American Society for Psychical Research*, *89*, 233–247.

Thalbourne, M. A. (1996). Belief in life after death: psychological origins and influences. *Personality and Individual Differences*, *21*(6), 1043–1045.

Thalbourne, M. A. (1998). Transliminality: further correlates and a short measure. *Journal of the American Society for Psychical Research*, *92*(4), 401–419.

Thalbourne, M. A. (2000). Transliminality: a review. *International Journal of Parapsychology*, *11*(2), 1–34.

Thalbourne, M. A. (2003). *A glossary of terms used in parapsychology*. Charlottesville, VA: Puente Publications.

Thalbourne, M. A. (2006). A brief treatise on coincidence. Unpublished manuscript. Available online at: http://parrochia.wifeo.com/documents/coincidence.pdf (accessed 6 December 2010).

Thalbourne, M. A. (2010). The Australian sheep-goat scale: development and empirical findings. *Australian Journal of Parapsychology*, *10*(1), 5.

Thalbourne, M. A., & Delin, P. S. (1993). A new instrument for measuring the sheep-goat variable: its psychometric properties and factor structure. *Journal of the Society for Psychical Research*, *59*, 172–186.

Thalbourne, M. A., & Delin, P. S. (1994). A common thread underlying belief in the paranormal, creative personality, mystical experience and psychopathology. *The Journal of Parapsychology*, *58*(1), 3–39.

Thalbourne, M. A., & Haraldsson, E. (1980). Personality characteristics of sheep and goats. *Personality and Individual Differences*, *1*(2), 180–185.

Thigpen, C. H., & Cleckley H. M. (1957). *The three faces of Eve*. New York: McGraw-Hill.

Thompson, B. (1992). Two and one-half decades of leadership in measurement and evaluation. *Journal of Counseling and Development*, *70*, 434–438.

Thompson, B. (1996). AERA editorial policies regarding statistical significance testing: three suggested reforms. *Educational Researcher*, *25*, 26–30.

Thorudottir, S., Sigurdardottir, H. M., Rice, G., Kerry, S. J., Robotham, R. J., Leff, A. P., & Starrfelt, R. (2020). The architect who lost the ability to imagine: The cerebral basis of visual imagery. *Brain Sciences*, *10*(2). https://doi.org/10.3390/brainsci10020059

Thouless, R. H., & Wiesner, B. P. (1948). The psi processes in normal and 'paranormal' psychology. *Journal of Parapsychology*, *12*, 192–212.

TIME (1964). A compendium of curious coincidences, *TIME*, 21 August, 'Archived copy'. Archived from the original on 29 January 2007.

Titchener, E. B. (1898). The feeling of being stared at. *Science* (new series), *VIII*(208), 23 December, 895–897.

Tobacyk, J. J. (2004). A revised paranormal belief scale. *International Journal of Transpersonal Studies*, *23* (1), 94–98. Available online at: http://dx.doi.org/10.24972/ijts.2004.23.1.94

Tobacyk, J. J. (2004). A revised paranormal belief scale. *The International Journal of Transpersonal Studies*, *23*(23), 94–98.

Tomé-Pires, C., & Miró, J. (2012). Hypnosis for the management of chronic and cancer procedure-related pain in children. *International Journal of Clinical and Experimental Hypnosis*, *60*(4), 432–457.

Tomkins, S. (1962). *Affect imagery consciousness, volume I: the positive affects*. New York: Springer.

Tressoldi, P. E., & Pederzoli, L. (2018). Mental technologies: distant mental influence on the behaviour, physiology, and emotions of human beings, and on biological and physical targets. *Physiology, and Emotions of Human Beings, and on Biological and Physical Targets*, 10 August.

Truzzi, M. (1987). On pseudo-skepticism. *Zetetic Scholar*, 12/13, 3–4.

Tukey, J. W. (1969). Analyzing data: sanctification or detective work? *American Psychologist*, 24, 83–91.

Tukey, J. W. (1991). The philosophy of multiple comparisons. *Statistical Science*, 6, 100–116.

Tversky, A., & Kahneman, D. (1974). Judgment under uncertainty: heuristics and biases. *Science*, 185(4157), 1124–1131.

Ullman, M. (1969). Telepathy and dreams. *Experimental Medicine & Surgery*, 27, 19–38.

Ullman, M., Krippner, S., & Vaughan, A. (1973). *Dream telepathy: experiments in nocturnal ESP*. Harmondsworth: Penguin.

US Department of Health and Human Services, Administration for Children and Families, Administration on Children, Youth and Families, Children's Bureau. (2016). Child maltreatment 2014. Retrieved from: www.acf.hhs.gov/programs/cb/research-data-technology/statistics-research/child-maltreatment

Utts, J. (1995). An assessment of the evidence for psychic functioning. *Journal of Parapsychology*, 59, 289–320.

Utts, J. (2001). An assessment of the evidence for psychic functioning. In K. Ramakrishna Rao (Ed.), *Basic research in parapsychology* (2nd ed.) (pp. 110–141). Jefferson, NC: McFarland & Co.

Utts, J. (2016). Appreciating statistics. *Journal of the American Statistical Association*, 111(516), 1373–1380.

Vacha-Haase, T., Ness, C., Nilsson, J., & Reetz, D. (1999). Practices regarding reporting of reliability coefficients: a review of three journals. *Journal of Experimental Education*, 67, 335–341.

Valenti, G., Libby, L. K., & Eibach, R. P. (2011). Looking back with regret: visual perspective in memory images differentially affects regret for actions and inactions. *Journal of Experimental Social Psychology*, 47(4), 730–737.

Van der Hart, O., & Horst, R. (1989). The dissociation theory of Pierre Janet. *Journal of Traumatic Stress*, 2(4), 397–412.

Van der Kolk, B. A., & van der Hart, O. (1989). Pierre Janet and the breakdown of adaptation in psychological trauma. *The American Journal of Psychiatry*, 146, 12.

Van der Linden, S. (2015). The conspiracy-effect: exposure to conspiracy theories (about global warming) decreases pro-social behavior and science acceptance. *Personality and Individual Differences*, 87, 171–173.

van Heugten-van der Kloet, D., Merckelbach, H., Giesbrecht, T., & Broers, N. (2014). Night-time experiences and daytime dissociation: a path analysis modeling study. *Psychiatry Research*, 216(2), 236–241.

Van Lommel, L. (2010). *Consciousness beyond life*. New York: HarperCollins.

Van Lommel, P. (2011). Near-death experiences: the experience of the self as real and not as an illusion. *Annals of the New York Academy of Sciences*, 1234(1), 19.

Van Lommel, P., Van Wees, R., Meyers, V., & Elfferich, I. (2001). Near-death experience in survivors of cardiac arrest: a prospective study in the Netherlands. *The Lancet*, 358(9298), 2039–2045.

Van Prooijen, J. W., Douglas, K. M., & De Inocencio, C. (2018). Connecting the dots: illusory pattern perception predicts belief in conspiracies and the supernatural. *European Journal of Social Psychology*, *48*(3), 320–335.

Varese, F., Barkus, E., & Bentall, R. P. (2012). Dissociation mediates the relationship between childhood trauma and hallucination-proneness. *Psychological Medicine*, *42*(5), 1025–1036.

Varvoglis, M., & Bancel, P. A. (2015). Micro-psychokinesis. In E. Cardeña, J. Palmer & D. Marcusson-Clavertz (Eds.), *Parapsychology: a handbook for the 21st century* (pp. 266–281). Jefferson, NC: McFarland & Co.

Vaschide, N., & Piéron, H. (1901). Prophetic dreams in Greek and Roman antiquity. *The Monist*, *11*(2), 161–194.

Vissia, E. M., Giesen, M. E., Chalavi, S., Nijenhuis, E. R., Draijer, N., Brand, B. L., & Reinders, A. A. (2016). Is it trauma- or fantasy-based? Comparing dissociative identity disorder, post-traumatic stress disorder, simulators, and controls. *Acta Psychiatrica Scandinavica*, *134*(2), 111–128.

Vlieger, A. M., Menko–Frankenhuis, C., Wolfkamp, S. C., Tromp, E., & Benninga, M. A. (2007). Hypnotherapy for children with functional abdominal pain or irritable bowel syndrome: a randomized controlled trial. *Gastroenterology*, *133*(5), 1430–1436.

Voltaire, V. (1764/2019). *Voltaire's philosophical dictionary*. Available online at: https://www.gutenberg.org/files/18569/18569-h/18569-h.htm

Von Stumm, S., & Scott, H. (2019). Imagination links with schizotypal beliefs, not with creativity or learning. *British Journal of Psychology*, *110*(4), 707–726.

Vonderlin, R., Kleindienst, N., Alpers, G. W., Bohus, M., Lyssenko, L., & Schmahl, C. (2018). Dissociation in victims of childhood abuse or neglect: a meta-analytic review. *Psychological Medicine*, *48*(15), 2467–2476.

Voss, M., Moore, J., Hauser, M., Gallinat, J., Heinz, A., & Haggard, P. (2010). Altered awareness of action in schizophrenia: a specific deficit in predicting action consequences. *Brain*, *133*, 3104–3112.

Vyse, S. (2017). P-hacker confessions: Daryl Bem and me. *Skeptical Inquirer*, *41*(5), 25–27.

Wackermann, J. (2002). On cumulative effects and averaging artefacts in randomised SR experimental designs. In *45th Annual Convention of the Parapsychological Association* (August) (pp. 293–305).

Wackermann, J., Pütz, P., & Allefeld, C. (2008). Ganzfeld-induced hallucinatory experience, its phenomenology and cerebral electrophysiology. *Cortex*, *44*(10), 1364–1378.

Wackermann, J., Pütz, P., Büchi, S., Strauch, I., & Lehmann, D. (2002). Brain electrical activity and subjective experience during altered states of consciousness: Ganzfeld and hypnagogic states. *International Journal of Psychophysiology*, *46*(2), 123–146.

Waddington, C. T. (Ed.) (1848). *La psychologie d'Aristotle*. Paris: Joubert.

Wagenaar, W. A. (1970). Subjective randomness and the capacity to generate information. *Acta Psychologica*, *34*, 233–242.

Wagenaar, W. A. (1972). Generation of random sequences by human subjects: a critical survey of literature. *Psychological Bulletin*, *77*(1): 65–72.

Wagenmakers, E.-J. (2007). A practical solution to the pervasive problems of p values. *Psychonomic Bulletin & Review*, *14*, 779–804.

Wagenmakers, E.-J., Wetzels, R., Borsboom, D., & van der Maas, H. L. J. (2011). Why psychologists must change the way they analyze their data: the case of psi: comment on Bem (2011). *Journal of Personality and Social Psychology*, *100*, 426–432.

Wagoner, B. (2013). Bartlett's concept of schema in reconstruction. *Theory & Psychology*, *23*(5), 553–575.

Wahbeh, H., McDermott, K., & Sagher, A. (2018). Dissociative symptoms and anomalous information reception. *Activitas Nervosa Superior*, *60*(3–4), 75–85.

Wahbeh, H., Radin, D., Mossbridge, J., Vieten, C., & Delorme, A. (2018). Exceptional experiences reported by scientists and engineers. *EXPLORE*, *14*(5), 329–341.

Wain, O., & Spinella, M. (2007). Executive functions in morality, religion, and paranormal beliefs. *International Journal of Neuroscience*, *117*(1), 135–146.

Walker, M. M., Diebel, C. E., Haugh, C. V., Pankhurst, P. M., Montgomery, J. C., & Green, C. R. (1997). Structure and function of the vertebrate magnetic sense. *Nature*, *390*, 371–376.

Wallach, L., & Wallach, M. A. (1994). Gergen versus the mainstream: are hypotheses in social psychology subject to empirical test? *Journal of Personality and Social Psychology*, *67*, 233–242.

Wang, C. X., Hilburn, I. A., Wu, D. A., Mizuhara, Y., Cousté, C. P., Abrahams, J. N., ... & Kirschvink, J. L. (2019). Transduction of the geomagnetic field as evidenced from alpha-band activity in the human brain. *eNeuro*, ENEURO-0483.

Wason, P. C. (1964). The effect of self-contradiction on fallacious reasoning. *Quarterly Journal of Experimental Psychology*, *16*(1), 30–34.

Watanabe, Y., Cornélissen, G., Halberg, F., Otsuka, K., & Ohkawa, S. I. (2000) Associations by signatures and coherences between the human circulation and helio- and geomagnetic activity. *Biomedicine & Pharmacotherapy*, *55*, s76–s83.

Watt, C. (2006). Research assistants or budding scientists? A review of 96 undergraduate student projects at the Koestler Parapsychology Unit. *The Journal of Parapsychology*, *70*, 335–356.

Watt, C. (2014). Precognitive dreaming: investigating anomalous cognition and psychological factors. *Journal of Parapsychology*, *78*(1), 115–125.

Watt, C. (2017). *Parapsychology*. Abingdon: Routledge.

Watt, C., & Wiseman, R. (2002). Experimenter differences in cognitive correlates of paranormal belief and in psi. *The Journal of Parapsychology*, *66*(4), 371.

Watt, C., & Wiseman, R. (2009). Foreword. In H. J. Irwin (Ed.), *The psychology of paranormal belief: a researcher's handbook* (p. 7). Hatfield: University of Hertfordshire Press.

Watt, C., Wiseman, R., & Schlitz, M. (2002). Tacit information in remote staring research: the Wiseman-Schlitz interviews. *The Paranormal Review*, *24*, 18–25.

Watt, C. A., & Kennedy, J. E. (2017). Options for prospective meta-analysis and introduction of registration-based prospective meta-analysis. *Frontiers in Psychology*, *7*, 2030.

Wertheimer, M. (1923). Untersuchungen zur Lehre von der Gestalt. *Psycologische Forschung*, *4*, 301–350. English translation (Laws of organization in perceptual forms) published in W. Ellis (Ed.) (1938) *A source book of Gestalt psychology* (pp. 71–88). Abingdon: Routledge & Kegan Paul.

West, J., & Bhattacharya, M. (2016). Intelligent financial fraud detection: a comprehensive review. *Computers and Security*, *57*, 47–66.

Westerlund, J., Parker, A., Dalkvist, J., & Hadlaczky, G. (2006). Remarkable correspondences between ganzfeld mentation and target content – a psychical or psychological effect? *Journal of Parapsychology*, *70*(1), 23.

Wheeler, M. A., Stuss, D. T., & Tulving, E. (1997). Toward a theory of episodic memory: the frontal lobes and autonoetic consciousness. *Psychological Bulletin*, *121*(3), 331.

White, W. E. (1997). Altered states and paranormal experiences. In W. E. White, *The Dextromethorphan FAQ: answers to frequently asked questions about DXM* (version 4). Retrieved online from: http://www.erowid.org/chemical/dxm/faq/dxm_paranormal.shtml

Whitehead, A. N. (1938). Social motives in economic activities. *Occupational Psychology*, *12*(4), 271–290.

Wichers, M., Kasanova, Z., Bakker, J., Thiery, E., Derom, C., Jacobs, N., & van Os, J. (2015). From affective experience to motivated action: tracking reward-seeking and punishment-avoidant behaviour in real-life. *PloS ONE*, *10*(6), e0129722.

Wickramasekera, I. (1991). Model of the relationship between hypnotic ability, psi, and sexuality. *The Journal of Parapsychology*, *55*(2), 159.

Wilde, D. J. (2012). *Finding meaning in out-of-body experiences: an interpretative phenomenological analysis.* Doctoral dissertation, University of Manchester.

Wilkinson, L., and the Task Force on Statistical Inference (1999). Statistical methods in psychology journals: guidelines and explanations. *American Psychologist*, *54*, 594–604.

Williams, B. J. (2015). *Psychic phenomena and the brain: exploring the neurophysiology of psi*. Gladesville, NSW: Australian Institute of Parapsychology Research Inc.

Williams, L. (1983). Minimal cue perception of the regard of others: the feeling of being stared at. *Journal of Parapsychology*, *47*, 59–60.

Wilson, D. B., & Shadish, W. R. (2006). On blowing trumpets to the tulips: to prove or not to prove the null hypothesis – comment on Bösch, Steinkamp and Boller (2006). *Psychological Bulletin*, *132*, 524–528.

Wilson, J. A. (2018). Reducing pseudoscientific and paranormal beliefs in university students through a course in science and critical thinking. *Science and Education*, *27*(1–2), 183–210.

Wilson, S. C., & Barber, T. X. (1983). The fantasy-prone personality: implications for understanding imagery, hypnosis, and parapsychological phenomena. In A. A. Sheikh (Ed.), *Imagery: current theory, research, and applications* (pp. 340–387). New York: Wiley.

Wiltschko, W., & Wiltschko, R. (1996). Magnetic orientation in birds. *Journal of Experimental Biology*, *199*(1), 29–38.

Windholz, G., & Diamant, L. (1974). Some personality traits of believers in extraordinary phenomena. *Bulletin of the Psychonomic Society*, *3*(2), 125–126.

Winlove, C. I., Milton, F., Ranson, J., Fulford, J., MacKisack, M., Macpherson, F., & Zeman, A. (2018). The neural correlates of visual imagery: a co-ordinate-based meta-analysis. *Cortex*, *105*, 4–25.

Wiseman, R. (2010). 'Heads I win, tails you lose': how parapsychologists nullify null results. *Skeptical Inquirer*, *34*, 36–39.

Wiseman, R., & Schlitz, M. (1997). Experimenter effects and the remote detection of staring. *Journal of Parapsychology*, *61*, 197–207.

Wiseman, R., & Smith, M. D. (1994). A further look at the detection of unseen gaze. In *Proceedings of Presented Papers: The 37th Annual Convention.* D. J. Bierman (Ed.), (pp. 465–478). Parapsychological Association, Fairhaven, MA.

Wiseman, R., & Watt, C. (2004). Measuring superstitious belief: why lucky charms matter. *Personality and Individual Differences*, *37*(8), 1533–1541.

Wiseman, R., & Watt, C. (2006). Belief in psychic ability and the misattribution hypothesis: a qualitative review. *British Journal of Psychology*, *97*(3), 323–338.

Wiseman, R., & Watt, C. (2010). 'Twitter' as a new research tool: a mass participation test of remote viewing. *European Journal of Parapsychology*, *25*, 89–100.

Wiseman, R., Smith, M. D., Freedman, D., Wasserman, A. T., & Hurst, C. (1995). Two further experiments concerning the remote detection of unseen gaze. *Proceedings of Presented Papers 38th Annual Convention.* D. J. Bierman (Ed.), (pp. 480–492). Parapsychological Association, Fairhaven, MA.

Wiseman, R., Smith, M., & Kornbrot, D. (1996). Exploring possible sender-to-experimenter acoustic leakage in the PRL autoganzfeld experiments. *Journal of Parapsychology*, *60*(2): 97.

Wiseman, R., Watt, C., & Kornbrot, D. (2019). Registered reports: an early example and analysis. *PeerJ*, *7*, e6232.

Wit, E. J. C. (1997). *The ethics of chance*. PhD dissertation, The Pennsylvania State University, Department of Philosophy.

Wolf, E. J., Lunney, C. A., Miller, M. W., Resick, P. A., Friedman, M. J., & Schnurr, P. P. (2012a). The dissociative subtype of PTSD: a replication and extension. *Depression and Anxiety*, *29*(8), 679–688.

Wolf, E. J., Miller, M. W., Reardon, A. F., Ryabchenko, K. A., Castillo, D., & Freund, R. (2012b). A latent class analysis of dissociation and posttraumatic stress disorder: evidence for a dissociative subtype. *Archives of General Psychiatry*, *69*(7), 698–705.

Wolff, A., Di Giovanni, D. A., Gómez-Pilar, J., Nakao, T., Huang, Z., Longtin, A., & Northoff, G. (2019). The temporal signature of self: temporal measures of resting-state EEG predict self-consciousness. *Human Brain Mapping*, *40*(3), 789–803.

Wolfradt, U. (1997). Dissociative experiences, trait anxiety and paranormal beliefs. *Personality and Individual Differences*, *23*(1), 15–19.

Wolfradt, U., Oubaid, V., Straube, E. R., Bischoff, N., & Mischo, J. (1999). Thinking styles, schizotypal traits and anomalous experiences. *Personality and Individual Differences*, *27*(5), 821–830.

Wood, M. J., Douglas, K. M., & Sutton, R. M. (2012). Dead and alive: beliefs in contradictory conspiracy theories. *Social Psychological and Personality Science*, *3*, 767–773.

Woodruff, R. J. (2018). Neutrality in science and technology. *Encyclopedia of science, technology, and ethics*. Retrieved from: www.encyclopedia.com/science/encyclopedias-almanacs-transcripts-and-maps/neutrality-science-and-technology (accessed 30 November 2018).

Woody, E. Z., & Barnier, A. J. (2008). Hypnosis scales for the 21st century: what do we need and how should we use them? In M. R. Nash, & A. J. Barnier (Eds.), *Oxford handbook of hypnosis: theory, research and practice* (pp. 255–282). Oxford: Oxford University Press.

Wooffitt, R., & Allistone, S. (2005). Towards a discursive parapsychology: language and the laboratory study of anomalous communication. *Theory and Psychology*, *15*(3), 325–355.

Wright, D. B., & Loftus, E. F. (1999). Measuring dissociation: comparison of alternative forms of the dissociative experiences scale. *American Journal of Psychology*, *112*(4), 497–519.

Wulf, G., McNevin, N., & Shea, C. H. (2001). The automaticity of complex motor skill learning as a function of attentional focus. *Quarterly Journal of Experimental Psychology*, *54*, 1143–1154.

Wundt, W. M. (1907). *Outlines of psychology*. Wilhelm Engelmann: Leipzig.

Wuthnow, R. (1976). Astrology and marginality. *Journal for the Scientific Study of Religion*, 157–168.

Yaden, D. B., Le Nguyen, K. D., Kern, M. L., Wintering, N. A., Eichstaedt, J. C., Schwartz, H. A., ... & Newberg, A. B. (2017). The noetic quality: a multimethod exploratory study. *Psychology of Consciousness: Theory, Research, and Practice*, *4*(1), 54.

Yamane, D., & Polzer, M. (1994). Ways of seeing ecstasy in modern society. Experiential-expressive and cultural–linguistic views. *Sociology of Religion*, *55*, 1–25.

Yong, E. (2012). Replication studies: bad copy. *Nature News*, *485*(7398), 298.

Zahavi, D. (2014). *Self and other*. Oxford: Oxford University Press. Kindle edition.

Zajonc, R. B., Heingartner, A., & Herman, E. M. (1969). Social enhancement and impairment of performance in the cockroach. *Journal of Personality and Social Psychology, 13*, 83–92.

Zeki, S., Watson, J. D., Lueck, C. J., Friston, K. J., Kennard, C., & Frackowiak, R. S. (1991). A direct demonstration of functional specialization in human visual cortex. *Journal of Neuroscience, 11*(3), 641–649.

Zeman, A., Dewar, M., & Della Sala, S. (2016). Reflections on aphantasia. *Cortex, 74*, 336–337.

Zimmer, C. (2011). It's science, but not necessarily right. *The New York Times*, 25 June. Retrieved from www.nytimes.com/2011/06/26/opinion/sunday/26ideas.html

Zimmermann, M. (1983). Ethical guidelines for investigations of experimental pain in conscious animals. *PAIN, 16*, 109–110.

Zusne, L., & Jones, W. H. (1981). *Anomalistic psychology*. Hillsdale, NJ: Lawrence Erlbaum Associates.

Zusne, L., & Jones, W. H. (2014). *Anomalistic psychology: a study of magical thinking*. Hove: Psychology Press.

INDEX

Aarnio, K., 11
Acausal Connecting Principle, 85
Action Schemata system, 32
Action System, 32, 33fig, 36fig
Activity Cycle Theory, 278
ad hoc hypothesis, 314
ad hominem, 314
Aether Theory, 5
agency, 18, 222, 229, 230, 231, 236, 237fig, 248, 249, 262, 279, 284
Agrillo, Christian, 258–60
Alcock, James, 194
aliens, 10fig, 11fig, 12
Allistone, S., 330
alpha event-related desynchronisation, 144, 145
Alternative Uses Test, 304
American Psychological Association, 194
American Psychologist, 194
anomalies, x, 3–6, 314
anomalistic psychology, xii, xiii, xv, 312
anomalous cognition, 6, 117, 315
anomalous experiences, 6, 60–1, 301
Anomalous Experiences Inventory, 8, 315
approach avoidance inhibition system, 31–2, 280
Ardis, J. Amor, 306
Aristotle, 155
artefacts, 315
aspirin, 320
associative remote viewing, 91, 103–6
Australian Sheep Goat Scale, 8, 41, 124, 315
autocorrelation, 315
autonomic nervous system, 29–30
autoscopy, 240, 245, 247
avowals of attitude, 330
awareness, 282, 283fig
AWAreness during Resuscitation, 254–5
ayahuasca, 244, 247
Azmitia, E.C., 265–7

Bacon, Francis, 182
Baird, J.McR., 206–20
Baker, Robert, 115
Bancel, P.A, 197
Barber Suggestibility Scale, 210, 211
Barnum Effect, 47–9
Barnum Index, 50–1
Bartlett, Frederick, 53, 272, 278
Bayes factor, 315–16
Bayes's rule, 315
beliefs
 belief barometers, xi, xiv, 135–6
 confirmation bias, 47
 conspiracy theories, 43–4, 51
 overview, 10–11
 paranormal, 11–14, 40–2, 43, 51
Beloff, John, 7, 310
Bem, Daniel, 131, 132–3, 152, 154, 156, 157–68, 175, 177, 188, 295–6, 300, 323
Bernard, Claude, 269
Bertossa, F., 230
Bird's-Eye View hypothesis, 254–5
Blackmore, Susan, 128, 129, 131, 132, 133, 135, 156, 160, 167–8, 236, 237–9, 240, 247, 248, 253–4, 294–5
Blanke, Olaf, 241, 243fig, 247, 248
blogs, 319
Bloom, P., 230
Boller, Emil, 184, 185–93, 195, 196–7, 198–9
Bones, Arina K., 176–80
Bonferroni correction, 316
Bonnefon, Jean-François, 50–1
Bootzin, R.R., 256
Bos, E. M., 242
Bösch, Holger, 184, 185–93, 195, 196–7, 198–9
Bouvet, Romain, 50–1
Boyle, Robert, 5

Index

brain, 141–3, 144, 152, 203–4, 220–4, 241–3, 249, 255–7, 280
   see also cerebral cortex; dorsal anterior cingulate cortex (dACC); limbic system; lingual gyrus; prefrontal cortex; temporal lobes; temporoparietal junction
brain death, 250
brain homeostasis, 265–8
   see also homeostasis; psychological homeostasis
Braithwaite, J.J., 243, 253
Braud, William, 122, 147, 149–50
Braude, Stephen E., 331
Britton, W.B., 256
Broad, C.D., 8
Brugger, Peter, 240
bullying, 35

Cambray, Joseph, 86
cannabis, 237–9, 246
Cardeña, Etzel, 194, 221
Cardiff Anomalous Perception Scale, 243
Cardiff Beliefs Questionnaire, 316
case-study methodology, 67–8, 316–17
Cattell 16PF test, 232, 332
causality, 63, 75–6, 296, 316–17
central executive network, 221–2, 224, 226
central executive system, 272
central homeostatic network, 266, 268
cerebral cortex, 141, 142fig, 268, 274, 280
Chapman University, 11–12
cheating, 108, 109, 113, 120, 128, 129, 131, 133, 135, 152, 160, 171, 191, 294, 295, 310
cherry picking, 317
Chesterton, G. K., 66, 68, 69, 70, 71, 72, 74, 75, 87
Cheung, M.W.-L., 274–5
Child, Irvin, 170, 171
child abuse, 16–22, 23, 26–7, 34, 255, 257, 258, 260, 284
   see also Homeostasis Theory
childhood trauma, 17–22, 27–9
Chiswick Coincidence, 66–77, 87, 293fig
circadian cycles, 284, 305
clairvoyance, 75, 76, 91, 99, 102tab, 121, 126, 148, 155, 170, 174
climate change, xx, 44
CLOCK system, 280
cognitive biases, 39
cognitive deficits, 62–3
Cognitive Reflection Test, 50
Cohen, J., 328
coincidences, 60–88
   see also synchronicity

cold reading, 48, 317
Colwell, J., 110–11, 112–13, 115, 116
Committee for Skeptical Inquiry, 317
Committee for the Scientific Investigation of Claims of the Paranormal (CSICOP), xiii
compartmentalisation, 18, 19, 20, 23
conceptual replication, 317
confederates, 317
confidence intervals, 318, 320
confirmation bias, 45–7, 60, 81, 103, 106, 129, 292, 296, 297, 318
   see also interpretation bias
conflicts of interest, 318
conjunction errors, 51, 63
consciousness, xv, 51–3, 85–7, 135–6, 264, 268, 270, 275, 278, 279–80, 282–6, 300, 301, 308fig
conspiracy theories, 43–4, 51
controlled experimental design, 318
CORE scale, 42–3
correlation coefficients, 65, 318
Creative Experiences Questionnaire, 25, 318, 321
Creative Imagination Scale, 210, 211
creativity, 303–5
critical thinking, 41
Cromby, J., 330
cross-sectional studies, 40, 65, 318
cryptochromes, 120, 138, 141, 143
CSICOP (the Committee for the Scientific Investigation of Claims of the Paranormal), xiii
Cui, X., 275
Cultural Source Theory, 16

Dagnall, Neil, 40, 44, 51
D'Angiulli, A, 274–5
data-sharing, 319
Davey, Christopher, 233, 235–6fig
De Ridder, D., 242
death, 249–50
Decety, J., 236, 237fig
Decision Augmentation Theory, 182
decline effect, 159, 160–3, 165, 173, 175, 300, 319
default mode network, 22–3, 221–2, 224, 226, 233, 234, 236
Defence Mechanism Test, 124, 125
Delin, P.S., 9
delusions, 28–9, 64
demand characteristics, 66, 319
Dennett, Daniel, 229, 231–2, 233
depersonalisation, 248
Derbyshire, S.W.G., 221
derealisation, 248

detachment, 19, 21, 32, 34
dextromethorphan (DXM), 246
Di Risio, L., 99, 101–2tab
Diaconis, Persi, 183, 312
diaries, 319
dice, 148, 182–5, 195–6, 198, 298
Dienes, Z., 221
Dijkstra, N., 274, 275–7
direct observation, 319
direct replication, 319
dissociation, 17–18, 20–2, 23, 25, 26–9, 34, 257–60, 283, 284, 285fig
  see also Homeostasis Theory
dissociative experiences, 9tab
Dissociative Experiences Scale, 19, 256, 257, 319–20
dissociative identity disorder (DID), 18, 25
Doors of Perception: And Heaven and Hell, 306
dorsal anterior cingulate cortex (dACC), 223fig, 224, 226
double-blind controls, 320
doubled-person hallucination, 206, 207–9, 213–17, 218–19, 220
doublethink, 311
Downing, Paul, 231
dream-ESP, 155–7, 168–76, 297
dreams, 148, 264
Dunne, J.W., 156

Easter Tree studies, 209
Edlow, B.L., 266
effect size, 320
effort after meaning, 47, 53
Einstein, Albert, 5
electrodermal activity, 147
electromagnetoreception, 139
Elzière, M., 248
emotion-based reasoning, 63–4
emotions, 278–9
empiricist worldview, 42, 43, 61
E-network, 233
Engber, D., 132, 163, 295
ethnographic methods, 320
European Journal of Parapsychology (EJP), 331
executive dysfunction, 65
Experiential Source Theory, 16
experimental control, 320–1
experimenter effects, 321
experimenters' regress, 191–2
extrasensory perception (ESP)
  beliefs in, 12
  Carl Jung, 86
  conjunction errors, 63
  growth in research publications, xv

Homeostasis Theory, 34
  overview, 9tab, 121
  synchronicity, 85
  see also remote viewing
extremely low frequency magnetic fields, 141, 144

Facco, Enrico, 258–60
factor analysis, 321
fake data, 321
fALFF, 223
fallacies, 39, 78, 321
false discovery rate correction, 321
false memory syndrome, 25
fantasy theory, 24–5
fantasy-proneness, 22–3, 26, 34, 257, 321
Faraday cages, 150, 151
Farah, Martha, 232, 233
Feinberg, Gerald, 76
file-drawer effect, 321–2
file-drawer problem, 159, 160, 165
fishing expedition, 316
fixed effects model, 186, 187tab, 322
Forer, Bertram, 317
Forer Effect, 47–9, 335
Fox, J., 257
Franklin, Benjamin, 197–8, 298–9
fraud *see* cheating
functional magnetic resonance imaging (fMRI), 220, 221, 222–4, 233–4, 236, 275, 322, 323fig
funnel plots, 186, 188fig, 322–3

Galanter, E., 265
Gall, Franz Joseph, 232
Gallo, David, 40–2
ganzfeld
  Adrian Parker, 294
  Daryl Bem, 295
  magneto-sensitivity theory, 138–52
  meta-analyses, 130–6
  methodological complications, 127–9
  overview, 119–23, 152
  preregistered, prospective meta-analysis, 136–7
  subjective validation, 125–7
  Swedish studies, 123–5
Gardner, Martin, xiii, 69–71, 72, 317
Garrett, Mrs Eileen, 167–8
Geller, Uri, 91, 92fig, 133
Gemmell, Professor Neil, 10
General ESP (GESP), 146
General Theory of Behaviour, 21, 52–3
geomagnetic activity, 146

geomagnetic fields, 145, 147, 150
Gillihan, Seth, 232, 233
Giovanni, Daniel, 234
Girden, Edward, 184–5
globally projecting neurones, 266, 267fig
goals, 264–5, 282
Golden Rule of Science, xii
Gray, Stephen, 40–2
Greeley, Andrew, xiv
Green, Celia, 239
Greyson, Bruce, 157, 252, 255
Greyson NDE Scale, 252, 260
Guilford, J.P., 304

Halligan, P., 64, 240
hallucinations, 28–9, 272
HARKing, 323
Harrison, Ben, 233, 235–6fig
Harvard Group Scale of Hypnotic Susceptibility, 205
haunts, 311
Hawking, Stephen, xvi
Hecht, H., 230
heuristics, 39, 51, 323
Hilgard, Ernest, 207, 214, 219
Hilgard, Jack, 206
Hofbauer, R.K., 221
homeopathy, xv, 15fig
homeostasis, 21, 27, 32, 258, 270, 282, 284, 285, 301
  see also brain homeostasis; psychological homeostasis
Homeostasis Theory 21, 27, 30–5, 36fig, 256, 257, 258
Honorton, Charles, 130, 131, 132, 133, 152, 157, 167, 171, 295
Houran, J., 311
Howard, M.C., 157, 174, 175
Hutton, S., 221
Huxley, Aldous, 306
Hyman, R., 317
hypnosis, 203–27, 284

Image System, 32, 33fig, 36fig
imagery, 272–5, 277–9, 280–1, 303–4
Imagination and Thinking, 306
imitation, 280–1
implicit learning, 112, 113, 115, 116
incipient action, 274
individual screening methods, 323
informed consent, 324
intentionality, 52, 87, 140, 185, 264, 265, 282
interpretation bias, 158, 159, 160
  see also confirmation bias

interpretative phenomenological analysis, 324
interviews, 325
Inventory of Childhood Memories and Imaginings, 321
inverse-square law, 149–50
ipseity, 87, 229, 230, 262, 279, 282, 283–4, 285fig, 311
  see also self
Irwin, H.J., 8, 43, 62, 63, 64, 65, 257

Jackson, P.L., 281
James, William, 18, 42, 229
Janet, Pierre, 18, 23, 27
Jiang, H., 222–4
Johnson, R.F., 209
Johnson, Wesley O., 164
Josephson, Brian, 331
Journal of Consciousness Studies, 115, 297
Journal of Parapsychology, 7, 131
Journal of Personality and Social Psychology, 157, 164, 177
Jung, Carl, x, 59, 66, 75, 84, 85, 86, 87, 88
junk science, 324

Kahneman, Daniel, 39
Kammann, Richard, 20, 69, 92–3, 97, 317, 328, 335
Kennedy, James, 136–7
Kennedy, J.E., 306–7, 324
ketamine, 245–6
Kihlstrom, John, 206
Kirsch, Irving, 206
kite experiment (Benjamin Franklin), 197–8, 298–9
Kittenis, Marios, 246
Kjellgren, A., 246
Koestler, Arthur, 61, 77–8, 80, 291
Kosslyn, S.M., 220–1
Krippner, Dr Stanley, 171, 297
Kuhn, Thomas, 6, 45
Kurtz, Paul, 317

Lamm, C., 236, 237fig
Lamont, P., 330
Lancet, 252–3
Landis, Theodor, 240
Landry, Mathieu, 224–6
Launaye Slade Hallucination scale, 243
Law of Parsimony, 61
LeBel, Etienne P., 156, 158–60, 164
LeBoutillier, N., 303, 304
Legrand, Dorothée, 233
Liboff, Abraham, 140, 152, 324
Lifshitz, M., 221

Lifshitz, Michael, 224–6
Limanowski, J., 230
limbic system, 266, 268fig
Lindeman, M., 6, 11, 64
lingual gyrus, 204, 225, 226, 247, 274, 281
local sidereal time, 145, 146–8
Loch Ness Monster, xii, 10tab, 327
Lopez, C., 242, 248
LSD, 25, 244, 246, 306, 310
luck, 183
Luke, David, 244–6

Magical Ideation Scale, 124–5, 332
magnetite, 120, 138, 139, 141, 143
magneto-sensitivity theory, 120, 138–52, 301, 324
Maimonides project, 156–7, 169–72, 297
Marchetti, G., 228
Marks, D.F., 97, 103, 106, 115–6, 133–4, 135, 165–7, 195, 206–20, 303, 335
Mars, R.B., 236
Marsh, Michael, 255–6
Mathijsen, F., 45
May, Edwin, 6, 8
McClenon, J., 16
McDonnell, Alan, 140, 144, 146, 152, 324
McDonnell–Liboff Theory, 324
McKellar, P., 206–20, 306
Measure of Anomalous Experiences and Beliefs, 26
memory, 40, 41
mental imagery *see* imagery
Mental Imagery Principle, 272
mescaline, 244, 306
meta-analyses, 18, 24, 28, 99, 101tab, 102tab, 109–10, 130–7, 172–5, 224–6, 275–7, 278, 324
metaphysical worldview, 42, 43, 51, 61
Metzinger, T., 229
Michelson, Albert, 5
Miller, G.A., 265
Miller, George A., 78–9
mirror neurons, 280–1
misrepresentation of randomness, 40, 51
modal research practice, 158–9, 160, 164
moderator analysis, 185, 188–91
Mohr, C., 241
monoamines, 267fig
monsters, 10fig
mood, 303, 305
Morley, Edward, 5
motor resonance mechanism, 281
multiple protective shelter series, 104
Murphy, Gardner, 185
Murray, C.D., 257

Nabokov, Vladimir, 156
Nakul, E., 242
narrative analysis, 324–5
narrative approaches, 325
Near Death Experience Scale, 256
near-death experiences
    Bird's-Eye View hypothesis, 254–5
    conclusions on, 260
    dissociation, 257–60
    early brain trauma, 255–7
    including out-body eperiences, 254
    out-of-body experiences, 254
    overview, 9tab, 228–9, 249–54
neuroception, 29, 30
neuroplasticity, 267fig
neurotransmitters, 267fig
niche construction, 263
nightmares, 251, 262, 284, 285fig, 308fig
noetic zone, 67
non-reflective thinkers, 50–1
Norlander, T., 246
normal distribution, 325
N-theory, 61, 74–5, 76, 83, 88, 326
null hypothesis significance testing, 326

Obstoj, I., 209
one-tailed tests, 326
open data, 327
Orne, Martin, 203, 206, 207–9, 210, 214, 216–17, 219
out-of-body experiences
    anecdote versus controlled investigations, 236–43
    brain, 241–3
    conclusions on, 249
    definition, 9tab
    detachment, 19
    dissociation, 257–8
    explanations of, 247–8
    versus hallucinations, 272
    and near-death experiences, 254
    overview, 228–9
    psychedelic drugs, 244–7

Palmer, John, 321
pan-psychism, xv
paradesign, 311
paradigms, 6, 45
paranormal
    beliefs, 7–8
    definition, 6, 7, 8–9
Paranormal Beliefs Scale, 50, 327
Parapsychological Association, 7, 89–90, 98, 106, 128–9, 157, 165, 181–2, 198, 199, 298, 311–13, 327

parapsychology, 309–11
Parker, Adrian, 123–7, 132, 133–6, 294
Parsimony, Law of, 61
partisan selective exposure, 46
pattern learning, 112, 113
Pearce, Hubert, 7, 7fig
Pearson correlation coefficient, 318
Pechey, R., 64, 240
Penfield, Wilder, 231
peri-traumatic dissociation, 19
perspective-taking, 281
PET (positron emission tomography), 220, 224
Peters, Kurt R., 156, 158–60, 164
p-hacking, 120, 158, 328
phrenology, 232, 233
Physicians Health Study (of aspirin), 320
Pinker, Steven, 233
placebo effect, 328
plastic neurones, 267fig
p-level, 328
point-to-point neurones, 267fig
poltergeists, 311
Polyfilla Science, xvi, xvii, 39, 41, 160, 263, 328
Polyvagal Theory, 21, 29–30
population stereotypes, 328
positron emission tomography (PET), 220, 224
post-hoc multiple comparisons, 328
post-traumatic stress disorder (PTSD), 19, 21, 24, 35, 251, 252, 255, 272
power, 328–9
Pratt, J. G., 321
precognition
    Arina Bones satire, 176–80
    cannabis, 246
    Chiswick Coincidence, 71, 75–6
    definition, 9tab, 121
    growth in research publications, xv, 15fig
    versus hallucinations, 272
    overview, 155–68, 175
    remote viewing, 90, 91
prefrontal cortex, 221, 222fig, 224, 231, 233, 276fig, 277
preregistered reports, 330–1
presentiment experiments, 164
Pribram, K.H., 265
Princeton Engineering Anomalies Research (PEAR) Laboratory, 197
Principle of Equivalent Coincidences, 81
Principle of the Long Run, 78–82, 84
Principle of the Unseen Cause, 81–2
probability learning, 112
Proprioceptive Breakdown Theory, 247, 248
pseudoskeptics, 329, 334
psi, xi, 5, 6, 7, 121, 291–313, 327, 329
psychedelic drugs, 238, 244–7, 306, 310

psychic energy, 329
psychic healing, 9tab
psychic staring, 9tab, 107–17, 321
psychokinesis
    cannabis, 246
    conjunction errors, 12, 63
    Dean Radin, 298
    definition, 9tab, 182
    evidence, 181–99
    growth in research publications, xv, 15fig
Psychological Association, 204
Psychological Bulletin, 131, 132, 157
psychological homeostasis, xx, 52, 263–5, 269–70
    see also brain homeostasis; homeostasis
Psychological Review, 165
The Psychology of the Psychic, 317
psychosis, 27–9, 64, 272, 279, 284, 305
P-theory, 61, 75–6, 78, 81, 83, 88, 326
publication bias, 186, 193, 199, 322–3
Pujol, Jesus, 233, 235–6fig
putative paranormal phenomenon, 326, 329, 334
Puthoff, Harold, 91–3, 97–8, 103–6, 296–7

qualitative research methods, 329
questionable research practices, 160–2, 329
questionnaires, 329–30

Radin, Dean, 120, 149–50, 164, 191–2, 193–8, 298–9, 310, 312
Radtke, H.L., 217–18
Randi, James, 157, 317
random number generators, 184, 193, 196, 197
random-effects model, 174, 186, 187tab, 189tab, 190tab, 191, 322
randomisation, 92, 98, 111, 113, 115, 117, 128, 131, 295, 310, 330
raphe nuclei, 265, 267fig
Rasmussen, Theodore, 231
Rational-Experiential Inventory, 330
Razin, Amir, 224–6
reality testing, 64–5
reasoning ability, 43–4
Reber, Arthur, 194
reflective thinkers, 50–1
Regard, Marianne, 240
registered reports, 330–1
regression analysis, 331
remote viewing, 9tab, 89–107, 117, 296–7
    see also extrasensory perception (ESP)
repeatability crisis, 331
replication, 110–14, 135, 331–2
Reset Equilibrium Function, 262, 265, 268, 269–73, 285, 301
rest-self-containment, 234
reversed causality, 75–6

Revised Paranormal Belief Scale, 8, 20, 51, 330, 332
Revised Transliminality Scale, 332
Rhine, J.B., 6–7, 86, 184, 198, 301, 302, 306, 309, 321, 327
Rhine, Louisa E., 302, 303fig, 305–6, 334
Ring, K., 257–8
Roe, Chris, 63, 328, 331, 334
Rooney, Wayne, 277–8
Rosenthal, Robert, 321, 322
Rosing, C.J., 257–8
Ruby, Perrine, 233
Runge, M.S., 274–5
Ryle, Gilbert, 229

safeguarding, 332
Sagan, Carl, xiv–xv
salience network, 221–2, 224, 226
sampling, 332–3
Sargent, Carl, 128–9, 131, 133, 135, 152, 294
schemata system, 272, 273fig
Scherer, Wallace B., 301–2, 309
Schimmack, Ulrich, 156, 160–2, 165
schizophrenia, 279
schizotypy, 51, 65, 305
Schlitz, Marilyn, 321
Schmidt, Helmut, 184
Schmidt, S., 110
Schröder, S., 110–11, 112–13, 116
Schwartz, Gary E., 10
science
  conspiracy theories, 44
  paranormal beliefs, 43
  progress in, xv–xvii
  scientifically unaccepted beliefs, 8
  spiral of, 4–5
secondary analysis, 333
selection bias, 158, 162
selective exposure, 333
self
  brain's signature of, 231–6
  objective theory, 231
  overview, 228–9, 249
  phenomenological theory, 229–30
  skeptical theories, 229–30
  see also ipseity
Self-Consciousness Scale, 234
self-fulfilling prophecies, 333
Semester Hypothesis, 295
sensory cues, 6, 81, 92, 97–8, 101tab, 103, 106, 109, 113, 117, 120, 127–8, 142, 191, 207, 297, 315, 332, 333
serotonin (5-HT), 265–7, 268, 306
sexual arousal, 303, 305
Sheehan, Peter, 207, 209

sheep-goat effect, 65–6, 300
  see also Australian Sheep Goat Scale
Sheldrake, Rupert, 107–8, 111–12, 113, 114–16, 147, 297
Shelf Test, 254
Short Run Illusion, 81
signal-detection model, 122
Simpson, Lorna, 306
single case experimental designs, 333
Skeptical Inquirer, 317
skeptics, xiii, 43, 333–4
Skeptic's Fallacy, 307, 308
Sladen, D., 110–11, 112–13, 116
sleep, 284
sleepwalking, 282, 283fig, 284
Smythies, J.R., x
Social Marginality Theory, 16
Social–Cognitive Theory, 205
Society of Psychical Research, 128
soul, 10
Spanos, Nick, 205–6, 209, 217–18
special relativity theory, 5
Special State Theory, 206, 220
Spectral theory, 286, 301, 308
Sperry, Roger, 86–7, 282
spirit, 10
spiritualism, 9tab
spontaneity, 301–3, 305, 309
spontaneous cases, 334
Stanford Hypnotic Susceptibility Scale, 205
Star Gate, 90, 93
Starmans, C., 230
statistical power, 334
statistical significance, 320
Steinkamp, Fiona, 184, 185–93, 195, 196–7, 198–9
stock market series, 104–6
Storm, L., 99, 100tab, 101–2tab, 103, 114, 157, 171, 174, 175
stratified sampling, 334
Strawson, Galen, 228–9
subjective anomalous experiences, 37
Subjective Paranormal Experience Scale, 8, 12, 34–5, 334
subjective paranormal experiences
  author belief in, 301
  child abuse/trauma, 19–21
  dissociation theory, 20–2
  existing theories, 15–16
  versus paranormal beliefs, 7–8
subjective validation, xviii, 46, 47, 49, 60, 81, 82, 93, 94–7, 103, 106, 117, 123, 125–7, 134, 152, 292, 295, 296–7, 310, 334–5
suggested amnesia, 205
suggested analgesia, 205
Sundberg, N.D., 317

supernatural, 6, 8, 9
surprise, 53–4
Survey of American Fears Wave 5, 11–12
Survey of Anomalous Experiences, 62, 310, 335
surveys, 335
Survival Hypothesis, 253, 260
sympathetic nervous system, 30, 113, 147
synchronicity, 59, 66, 68–73, 74, 75, 76, 79, 81, 83, 85–7, 88
  see also coincidences
systematic reviews, 335–6

Targ, Russell, 91–3, 97–8, 106, 107
Tart, Charles, 104, 150, 239–40, 246, 254
telekinesis, 9tab
telepathy, 91, 121, 169–70, 246
temporal lobes, 256
temporoparietal junction, 236, 237fig, 241, 242, 249
Thalbourne, M.A., 8, 9, 25
theory of mind, 236, 237fig
Thouless, R.H., 329
Tobacyk, J. J, 8, 20
TOTE model, 265
trance logic, 203, 205, 206, 208
trance logic experiments, 4, 203, 205, 206–20
transliminality, 26, 124
trauma, 19–21, 23–5, 255–7, 258, 283, 284, 285fig
Tressoldi, P.E., 99, 101–2tab, 167
Truzzi, Marcello, xiii, xiv, 334
Two Systems Theory, 39, 50
Type I errors, 191–2, 316, 319, 322, 336
Type I homeostasis, 266, 269, 270, 280, 282
Type II errors, 191–2, 320, 336
Type II homeostasis, 266, 269, 270, 275, 280, 282

Ullman, Montague, 167–8, 171
uncontrolled variables, 336
Union Fire Company, 299
urban legends, 51
Utts, Jessica, 120, 164, 194, 312

Van Lommel, Pim, 253
Varvoglis, M., 197
vestibular system, 247–8
vividness, 25, 169, 274–8, 279, 304
Vividness Hypothesis, 25–6
Vividness of Visual Imagery Questionnaire (VVIQ), 26, 217, 272, 274–5, 336
vlogs, 319

Wagenmakers, E.-J, 157, 158, 164
wakefulness, 282, 283fig
Wason, P.C., 37, 39
Watt, C.A., 324
Watt, Caroline, 136–7
Westerlund, J., 125, 134–5
White, W. E., 246
WHO International Report from the HBSC, 35
  see also Homeostasis Theory
Wickramasekera, Ian, 305
Wiesner, B.P., 329
Williams, Bryan, 150–1
Wiseman, Richard, 12, 25, 116, 321
Wolff, Annemarie, 234
Wooffitt, R., 330
worldviews, 42–5
Wundt, Wilhelm, 18

Zahavi, D., 230
zetetic, xi, xiii, xiv, 308, 336